THE POWER HOUSE

ROBERT KEITH GRAY AND THE SELLING OF ACCESS AND INFLUENCE IN WASHINGTON

SUSAN B. TRENTO

St. Martin's Press · New York

Design by Ann Gold

ISBN 0-312-08319-X

First Edition: July 1992

10 9 8 7 6 5 4 3 2 1

CONTENTS

INTRODUCTION

Everything came together on Kuwait. Every part of the intricate, well-oiled public relations and lobbying machine Robert Gray had assembled was in place. Gary Hymel had Capitol Hill covered. Frank Mankiewicz oversaw the massive PR machinery that dazzled the media. Gray had just made another one of his trademark reaches into the White House, hiring George Bush's former chief of staff, and friend, Craig Fuller, as President and CEO of Hill and Knowlton Worldwide. Gray had years of experience lobbying for controversial foreign clients, from "Baby Doc" Duvalier to China in the aftermath of the Tienanmen Square massacre. Most important, the client had money. Lots of it.

Fuller joined the firm on August 1, 1990. The next day, Saddam Hussein launched his massive assault against the Emirate of Kuwait. On August 6, President Bush announced that he was sending American troops to the Persian Gulf. The reason given was the Iraqi threat to Saudi Arabia. On August 10, eight days after Kuwait was overrun, Hill and Knowlton had prepared a contract to represent an organization called "Citizens for a Free Kuwait." By August 20, the contract had been signed by Robert Gray, and Hill and Knowlton had registered as a foreign agent on behalf of "Citizens for a Free Kuwait."

Gray and his elite corps of lobbyists and PR executives had run huge accounts before; Hill and Knowlton ran the first multi-million-dollar lobbying-PR blitz for the American Truckers Association antideregulation campaign in the late 1970s. They had worked for Exxon after the Exxon–Valdez oil spill, for Metropolitan Edison after Three Mile Island, for AT&T. Kuwait was bigger.

And the men and women who worked for Gray had taken on tough assignments before: trying to convince Congress and the American public that countries with abysmal human rights records—Haiti, Morocco, Turkey, China—were misunderstood. They had worked with the Scientologists, the Catholic Bishops antiabortion campaign, Marc Rich, the Teamsters—they were used to controversy. Kuwait was tougher.

Exxon, AT&T, and Metropolitan Edison paid their money to handle public relations disasters or promote a product or influence legislation on the Hill. Morocco, Turkey, and China paid Hill and Knowlton to influence public opinion and American foreign policy. But the government of Kuwait was funneling millions of dollars to Hill and Knowlton for an unprecedented reason: Hill and Knowlton was going to lobby for war.

The client was not listed as the Emirate of Kuwait; it was never done that way. Hill and Knowlton's spin doctors came up with a more patriotic moniker: "Citizens for a Free Kuwait." Very little money, of course, was going to come from either Kuwaiti or American citizens, and the adjective "free" was something of a stretch in describing a country where there was no religious freedom, women had few rights, dissidents were arrested without trial and tortured, and all the power resided in a monarchial family headed by an Emir with literally dozens of wives. But Hill and Knowlton had two tremendous advantages: Most Americans had never even heard of the tiny oil kingdom so there was no negative impression to counter, and they were pushing the White House line, reinforcing the daily press briefings and presidential speeches that carried such enormous weight with the public and the press.

Money was no object. Hill and Knowlton put seventy people on the account at once. They paid pollster Richard Wirthlin over one million dollars to produce a survey of the American public that ascertained which issues moved people towards accepting American military intervention on behalf of Kuwait. The number one answer was Iraqi atrocities against the Kuwaitis. Soon, commercials, news accounts, and congressional hearings were filled with terrifying accounts of Iraqi misbehavior. Press conferences were arranged with Kuwaiti "freedom fighters" to present an image of a strong, gallant Kuwaiti resistance (this to counter reports of young Kuwaitis partying the war away in Cairo discos). Video news releases were produced, many of which aired on the nightly news programs interspersed with objective network reports.

A "National Prayer Day" was promoted; Hill and Knowlton did not mention that a Christian or Jewish "Prayer Day" would be impossible in pre-invasion Kuwait. Student rallies were organized on college campuses, complete with perfectly lettered signs, color-coordinated balloons and tee-shirts; this in an effort to counter any press coverage of the college antiwar movement. A constant flow of radio shows were produced and distributed. Countless press conferences and interviews were arranged with the Kuwaitis to keep their side of the story uppermost in the public mind. For these services and more, "Citizens for a Free Kuwait" paid Hill and Knowlton upwards of $10 million.

The issue involved in all this activity is not whether the United States should have gone to war in the Persian Gulf. The issue is whether there is something fundamentally wrong when a foreign government can pay a powerful, well-connected lobbying and public relations firm millions of dollars to convince the American people and the American government to support a war halfway around the world. In another age this activity would have caused an explosion of outrage. But something has changed in Washington. Boundaries no longer exist.

To become one of the most powerful private persons in Washington takes extraordinary effort. Robert Gray had achieved that position by the time Ronald Reagan took office. It had taken nearly all of his energy for much of his life. Being at the center of this world can be financially rewarding. Corporations, foreign interests, and rich investors are willing to pay handsomely for those who have access to power. During the 1980s no one charged more than Gray. In the first term of Reagan's presidency, Gray became a rich man.

Robert Gray exudes charm and warmth. He is a dapper man. Like George Bush, he is a man who writes thank-you notes. On first glance Gray, his white hair contrasted with a tanned face and blue eyes, looks a dozen years younger than his seventy-plus years. Gray's voice is full with a flat, but friendly Midwestern tone. His demeanor is formal—almost Nixonian—but without the clumsiness. Gray seems incapable of an awkward movement. He is trim and short. His impeccable manners and ramrod straight posture and conservative tailoring add to an aura of cool grace and old establishment Republicanism instead of small-town, Midwestern modesty.

Although Robert Keith Gray is not a household name outside the Beltway, he became the preeminent lobbyist in Washington during the 1980s. He rose to the top not because of his expertise in government and substantive policy-making experience, but because he knew almost everyone who mattered in town, did favors for people, was a perfect host, and a perfect guest. Gray cultivated Washington society wives, raised money for the Republican party, and took care of the politically powerful because that cemented loyalty and personal bonds. Gray made it personal because that gave him access. In 1981, after twenty-five years behind the scenes, his moment in the sun came with the inauguration of Ronald Reagan. His work on the campaign and as cochairman of the inauguration brought him access to the top levels of the new administration. He cashed in his "access" chips by starting his own firm, which he called Gray and Company. He picked a beautiful old brick building on the canal in Georgetown and transformed the old power plant into offices. He dubbed his new office building "The Power House." The firm combined lobbying with public relations on a *bipartisan* basis.

Gray began with a small staff and a handful of loyal clients. He knew he had to expand his base beyond his strong ties to the Reagan White House, and he knew just how to do it. He bought access by patenting the revolving door. He hired the top staff or the close friends or family of prominent politicians. To gain entrance and insight into the various government agencies and Congressional committees, he hired their former top officials. These people knew the inside because they had been working there for several years and had probably played a role in picking their successors. This created a citywide symbiotic relationship among Congressional committees, government agencies, and lobbyists.

On the public relations side, to ensure credibility with the media, Gray hired reporters and television anchors. For his new, mysterious International Division, Gray hired an assortment of staffers with ties closer to the intelligence than the diplomatic community. Gray hired the best. "I call them my stars. Gray and Company is a constellation of talent and access," Gray often told reporters. But Gray was careful to make certain that no star shone brighter than his own. He succeeded in nurturing an image of being at the top of his profession.

In reality, Gray was in many ways a cipher when it came to the true nature of his personality and beliefs. The fact that he could fill his lobbying and public relations company with Democratic and Republican "stars" demonstrates just how practical a man Gray is. He represented clients who outraged liberals, such as the Catholic Bishops antiabortion campaign. The fact that he accepted as a client an organized crime figure like Jackie Presser, and clients who equally outraged conservatives, such as supporters of *Penthouse* and *Playboy,* corrupt foreign governments like Duvalier's Haiti, never seemed to tarnish his star status.

Gray and Company quickly became the talk of Washington. Gray not only charmed the media, many of them, including NBC, became his clients. Admiring articles appeared in the press about his access to top officials. Clients poured in. NBC News did a flattering profile of Gray. Gray and Company, the new kid on the block, was the envy of its competitors.

Gray succeeded in becoming the most well-known lobbyist in Washington. He eclipsed other public relations professionals and lobbyists by breaking their cardinal rule. He went public with his connections. He became the story. His self-promotion included mentions of his connections and his "access" to people in high places. He traded on his influence. Gray's visibility bothered other lobbyists in town. Besides the obvious competition, his publicity hunting seemed totally out of character for a profession used to operating behind the scenes. The idea of using clients to attract other clients through publicity made no sense to the older, more established influence sellers who were used to only bragging about their political triumphs in private. In other times, it would have been foolhardy. Self-promoting influence peddlers ended up with closed doors and unanswered telephone calls. Not in the 1980s. Gray was a whiz at promoting himself, but he had a knack of stopping just short of being too outrageous.

This book is about what Washington has become. Why does nothing get done in Washington? Why does government seem not to understand or care about the problems of the citizenry? Why are the politicians so concerned about the nuances and the relationships that they have completely lost sight of what they were elected to do—legislate and govern in the best interest of the country?

Today many Americans feel removed from their government. People feel that their governmental institutions no longer understand their problems, and even if they did, are powerless to solve them. They feel helpless and isolated. Nothing seems to change. Nothing seems to get done. Nothing seems to get cleaned up. From Watergate to Koreagate to Debategate to the Sex and Drug investigation to Iran–Contra, to the Savings and Loan and HUD scandals to BCCI, it seems that the same people are doing the same things over and over, and never getting punished—and no one seems to care. The triangle—the media, the government, and the lobbying and PR firms—protect each other. Even in time of war, the White House turned to people like Gray because they can operate without the constraints of public service. Gray's story demonstrates how corporate, government, international and private powers can be marshalled for their own purposes and profit, often at the expense of the public good.

In researching this book I conducted over two hundred interviews with more than a hundred Washington lobbyists and public relations professionals, government officials, legislators, clients of Gray's, friends, and competitors. (My husband, Joseph Trento, conducted some of the interviews.) I wrote about Gray because he and his companies were the ones who rose to power over the last two decades, but other lobbying and public relations firms and Democratic politicians and lobbyists operate similarly. I went to Gray's hometown in Hastings, Nebraska, to research his early years and to the Eisenhower library in Abilene, Kansas, to study his and others' papers written during his White House years. The government documents on which I relied were largely released to me under the Freedom of Information Act. I would like to especially thank Betty Lopez at the Securities and Exchange Commission for the professional way in which she handled my FOIA requests.

I would also like to extend my appreciation to the publication *Vital Speeches of the Day* for granting me permission to quote from the following speeches: "Washington Public Relations—The Next Twenty-Five Years," Robert K. Gray, *Vital Speeches,* January 1, 1975, pp. 172–175; "Getting the

Story and Getting it Right," Robert K. Gray, *Vital Speeches* October 1, 1984, p. 763; "AIDS—We Will Win the War," Robert K. Gray, *Vital Speeches,* November 15, 1989, pp. 297–300. My appreciation also to *The Washington Times* for permission to reprint a "Doers Profile" of Robert Gray.

Of course the most important interview for this book was Robert Gray and I want to thank him for answering written questions. I asked him over the course of two and a half years for an oral interview, but he declined. Eventually he agreed to answer a series of written questions. In the end, he answered a portion of these questions. Mr. Gray gave me permission only to quote his answers in full. Wherever appropriate I have done so. In other cases I have communicated the sense of his answer, especially where it pertains to events of which Mr. Gray had recollections contradictory to those of other participants.

In addition, I greatly appreciate the help of the following people who agreed to interviews, often sharing their time and recollections more than once: Sharon Brooks, Tom Smith, Joyce Ore, Tom Jorgenson, Don Seaton, Jim Bonahoom, Ruth Deveny, Bob Hardin, Harry Borley, Vern Anderson, Jerrold Scoutt, Bob Cowgar, Wesley Jones, Gratia Coultas, Carl O'Neill, Grace and Bob Bauske, Alice and Ray Heley, Dennis Tufte, Warren Bartholomae, Richard Hoffman, Elton Hailey, Walter Heacock, Eddie Jordan, Dr. Frederick J.T. Roukema, Clarence Hope, Senator Carl T. Curtis, Albert Pratt, Bradley Patterson, Clifford Guest, George Worden, Larry Speakes, Sheila Tate, Charls Walker, Fred Korth, James Lake, Tom Korologos, Senator Paul Laxalt, Senator Richard Schweicker, Paul Weyrich, Carl Shoffler, Marvin Liebman, Edwin Paul Wilson, Richard Pederson, Victor Marchetti, Robert Crowley, William R. Corson, John R. Block, Mark Moran, Martin B. Gold, Niels Holchs, Adonis Hoffman, Pate Felts, Barry Schochet, Joan Worden, John E. Lawler, Lyn Nofziger, Richard Allen, John Sears, Stephen M. Johnson, Michael Pilgrim, Bob John Robison, Bette Anderson, Al Regnery, Richard Powers, Carol Darr, Dan Jones, Ambassador Alejandro Orfila, Marta Diaz, Jack McGeorge, Barry Zorthian, Betsey Weltner, Carter Clews, Judith Reisman, James Wootton, Richard Berendzen, Ken Gray, Don Nielson, Robert Thompson, Neil Livingstone, Larry Brady, Charles Pucie, James Gall, Donald Deaton, General Joseph J. Cappucci, Raymond Donovan, Peter Hannaford, Joan Braden, Charles Black, Ted Kavanau, Jeanee von Essen, Jerry Hogan, Chris Gidez, William Phillips, Representative Richard Hanna, Howard Wickam, Anna Chennault, Bernard Katz, Tongsun Park, Henry Preston Pitts, Joe Volz, Norman Larsen, Milton G. Nottingham, Jr., Ronna Freiberg, Donald Fraser, James Hamilton, and John Flannery.

I also want to thank an equal number of people who asked that their names not be revealed, requests that I have honored.

My appreciation to friends who knew that almost every time I called I wanted something and who still answered their phones and came through with many favors—Paul Schlegel, Jack Mitchell, Jay Gourley, and Brad White—and to the reporters and producers who worked on parts of the Gray story and who willingly and encouragingly passed on information they had uncovered—Jay LaMonica and Gordon Platt.

I am grateful to my researcher, Erik Fatemi, who always found the articles and materials I needed, and to André Colaiace, Andrew Clarkowski, and Eric Hillemann at Carleton College who conducted research on Gray's college years for me. Also, my thanks to Paula Murphy and Jean Hort at the Naval Historical Center, who promptly provided information on Gray's Navy years, and the Hastings Public Library, the Hastings Historical Society, the Douglas County Historical Society Library/Archives Center in Omaha and the Nebraska State Historical Society in Lincoln, who helped with the early years.

Special thanks to my friend, Linda Durdall, who has helped me through three books and whose common sense and good cheer eases the process, and to my local librarian, Jeanne Mulcahy, at Samuels Public Library, who gladly verified dates, ordered books, photocopied articles, and rushed orders.

I owe a special debt of thanks to Ronald Goldfarb, my agent, whose idea it was for this project. He promised me it would be difficult and there would be roadblocks—and he was right.

Finally, my sincere gratitude to my editor, Bill Thomas, whose vision, support, and good humor encouraged me during the tough times and whose faith in the project made it a reality; and to my husband, Joe, who helped and encouraged me throughout.

Susan Trento
Front Royal, Virginia
April 1992

WASHINGTON, April 28—President Bush donned a tuxedo, waxed effusive about "a miracle called America," and deftly separated some 4,300 Republicans from about $8 million of their money tonight. . . . Asked today whether donors to the event were indeed spending money for access to Mr. Bush's top aides, the White House Spokesman, Marlin Fitzwater, replied: "It's buying access to the system, yes. That's what the political parties and the political operation is all about." . . . Asked how other, less wealthy citizens could buy into the system, Mr. Fitzwater said, "They have to demand access in other ways."

—Michael Wines, *The New York Times,*
April 29, 1992

BOOK I

SMOKE

1

FROM THE HEARTLAND

"[Nebraskans are] hard-working and God-fearing people. They have everything going for them, except they are separated from the east and west coasts and other countries."

Bob Gray[1]

In temperament and design, Hastings, Nebraska, seems the exact opposite of Washington, D.C. Hastings is a square-shaped town in a square-shaped state. The views people see here are flat farms and endless rows of corn, not sweeping vistas of grand limestone buildings and imposing marble monuments. Hastings, "Queen City of the Plains," sits halfway between Los Angeles and New York. The town was established in 1872, just eight and a quarter miles from the Oregon Trail.[2] It began with three or four buildings clustered around where the St. Joseph and Denver City Railroad intersected with the Burlington Railroad.[3]

The early history of Hastings reads like that of many a pioneer community, with boom and bust years, hotels with names like The Roaring Gimlet and The Howling Corkscrew, a fire that destroyed the downtown's wooden structures, and the ill-fated exploits of three masked men who robbed the grocer, were caught and then lynched. The trains stopped by the gallows so the passengers could watch the bodies swing from the ropes; the hanging judge said that this was "one decision the Supreme Court could not reverse."[4]

In 1907, the Seventh-Day Adventists moved their state headquarters to Hastings and built the Nebraska Sanitarium. That same year, a pleasant, easy-going seventeen-year-old named Garold C.J. Gray moved to Hastings from Long Pine, Nebraska. Some years after moving to Hastings he met the woman with whom he would spend the rest of his life.

Marie Burchess, the daughter of a harness maker, was born in Waunet, Nebraska, and moved to Hastings when she was two years old. She finished

Hastings High School in 1913 and married C.J.; soon thereafter they started their family. Robert Keith Gray, the couple's second son and third child, was delivered by his aunt, Mabel Newburn, in Hastings at 7:30 P.M., on Friday, September 2, 1921. His father, C.J., was thirty-one years old and worked as a mechanic. His mother, twenty-seven, remained at home taking care of the family.[5]

C.J. was a fun-loving, likable man who enjoyed life. It fell to Marie to be the disciplinarian in the household. She was unquestionably the boss. "She was really part of the backbone of that whole family. [She] encouraged all of the children to get ahead. Move ahead. Keep busy," Harry Borley, a lifelong friend of Robert Gray's, said.[6] She was determined for her children to succeed. Marie Gray told the Hastings newspaper that although her husband played an important role in the family, she was the final authority when the children wanted to do or get something.[7]

Marie Gray was active in community affairs, including the Eastern Star, the Red Cross, the Community Chest, and the Heart Fund. She kept the house spotless and raised her children to be neat and clean. "It never hurts a girl to be tidy," she told the *Sunday World Herald* in 1961.[8] Her only hobby was coin collecting.

Religious training was important in the Gray family. Marie, a petite woman, raised her children Episcopalian. They were active in many church activities and functions, attending St. Marks, a classic, miniature gray-stone gothic cathedral with stunning stained-glass windows. Gray served as an acolyte when he was a boy. Education was also stressed by Gray's parents. His younger sister, Jean Miller (she is ten years younger), said creativity was encouraged. Reflecting on her childhood, she told *The Hastings Tribune* that her father challenged the children to be imaginative and to develop ideas that were attractive, but functional. "It was almost a family game, I guess," Mrs. Miller said.[9]

The Protestant work ethic was central to the Gray household. Resourcefulness was always encouraged. When Gray's older sister, Doray, wanted clothes as a child, her mother, instead of buying them, introduced her to the sewing machine. "Like all girls, she wanted lots of clothes and we told her we'd buy the material but she'd have to make them," Marie Gray said.[10] Years later, Doray became a dress designer in Denver.

Although C.J. Gray never finished high school, he was talented and very bright. "If he had an education and more opportunity, he probably could have been—I won't say a great man—but he probably could have made a place in life for himself," Vern Anderson, C.J.'s friend and boss, said.[11] By the late 1920s, C.J. had developed a reputation around town as a talented mechanic through his work as the shop foreman at the Ford garage. He had helped design a gasoline engine that fired at both ends of the piston's stroke. In 1927, Western Land Roller, a company that manufactures agricultural equipment, built its new factory in Hastings. The company hired C.J. to design a new feed grinder called the BearCat Grinder. It was a great success among the farmers.

Life in the Gray house was never quiet and subdued. "There was always something to do. Something to be kept busy. Some kind of games to play," Harry Borley said. "Gray's father was busy most of the time working on inventions or ideas." Borley remembered Gray and his father as being fairly close. "I don't know if you call it adored, but [he] respected his father greatly," Borley said.

The 1920s were prosperous years for Hastings, with the construction of many new plants and buildings. The automobile was just beginning to make an impact on the country, and Hastings had fifteen agencies selling cars to the surrounding communities. But the Roaring Twenties, which never roared very hard in Hastings, gave way to the much darker and desperate 1930s, and Hastings was not spared.

Western Land Roller began marketing the BearCat Grinder around 1929, just in time for the stock market crash and the Depression. By 1931, the company was almost at a standstill.[12] C.J. was one of the few to keep his job with the company, but they could not pay him very much. "He was a very patient person to do what he could do everyday even though he wasn't getting paid very much at that time," Vern Anderson remembered.

C.J. and Marie's fourth child was born in 1931. To survive the Depression years, C.J. invented what was to become a much copied fast-food product, a hot dog enclosed in bread, similar to today's corn dog, but made out of wheat and not corn flour. He took a waffle iron and reconfigured it so that he could place the hot dog on the waffle iron and pour a waffle-like batter around it and bake it. He called his product the "Weenie Waffle." To market his creation, he traded his 1925 T Roadmaster to his boss, Vern Anderson, for a 1926 Model T touring car since it had a heavier rear axle and wheel-and-tire assembly. Next he built a concession stand on a two-wheel trailer to pull behind the car. During the summers and falls, he took time off of work to go to the state and country fairs to sell his Weenie Waffles and earn extra money for the family.[13]

Gray remembers his family as being quite poor, a family of six sharing one can of food with no one wanting to take the last bite. On another occasion his father in an effort to save money pulled his own tooth rather than go to a dentist. In an effort to make ends meet, all the members of the family did odd jobs around Hastings. Nonetheless Gray had warm memories of his childhood and painted a portrait of a loving, close family. His mother pushed the children to work hard in school and encouraged them to set high goals for themselves.[14]

On May 8, 1930, when Gray was eight years old, a tornado hit the town, causing millions of dollars in damage and one death. The natural disaster seemed an omen for the decade. In Nebraska, the collapse of the national economy and the environmental cataclysm of the Dust Bowl combined with devastating results. Banks failed, crops died, plants and stores closed. During Gray's formative years, Hastings was a town in trouble. Young Gray watched his mother go to work as a PBX operator at the telephone company and as a bookkeeper at the Clarke Hotel. Gray remembered spending a great deal of time in his early childhood at the hotel, especially sitting on Santa Claus's lap when he was a young boy.[15]

In many ways the Depression forced Gray's parents to become the reverse of the typical American family at that time. His mother worked and they considered her "worldly." His father, called "a dreamer," cooked, sewed, cleaned, and invented. He converted a 1923 truck into a mobile home. Before radios were common, he built one out of an assortment of tubes, dials, an old oak cabinet, and a car battery. Both parents loved music. Each played the piano and organ, but C.J. also played the coronet, saxophone, banjo, and violin. He was a natural musician and played in the Hastings Band when the town still had summer concerts in the park. He played at both Saturday night dances and in the church orchestra, until the church told him he could not play the same violin he played in the dance hall on Saturday in the church on Sunday morning. For C.J. the choice was easy; he quit the church orchestra.[16]

When Gray was eleven years old, the 1932 county fair included an electrical exposition with an electric fountain, then a technical marvel. The Hastings Water and Light departments combined an electric pump that spewed jets of water with colored floodlights to create a colorful fountain, about the size of a large Jacuzzi, that even today is featured on postcards and in brochures for visitors to Hastings. It was supposed to offer hope for the Dust Bowl years, but the worst was yet to come. The dust storms of 1934 and 1935 devastated the farms and virtually no crops were raised. President Roosevelt's public works projects helped, but unemployment and economic uncertainty dominated.[17]

When C.J. Gray was not designing and engineering farm equipment, he demonstrated the equipment at state fairs, farm shows, and to farmers and potential distributors. He planned the demonstrations well and was so likable that he enjoyed success in selling his products when others did not.[18] C.J. was a natural politician, but had no interest in politics. "I don't think he cared particularly about politics," Vern Anderson recalled. Early on his son, Robert, seemed equally apolitical. The young Gray's hometown friends do not remember him as having any strong political interests either. "I'm not sure that it was the political that exactly motivated him," Bob Hardin, a friend from Hastings, said.[19] Later, when Gray's college friends visited, one remembered C.J. as very conservative, and another, who lived in the Gray household, barely remembers C.J. at all. But both agree that "Bob didn't seem to have any strong political feelings."[20]

By the time Gray graduated high school in 1939 his family had moved from West Sixth Street, where they had been living since he was born, to a home a few blocks away on West Fifth. While he was in college, his family bought a home on West Ninth Street which became the permanent family residence. A pleasant but modest home built on a city lot, the house is a two-story white clapboard colonial with a front porch that his sister, Doray, still decorates for Christmas.

For fun in Hastings, there were home parties. "We had dances in our home," Harry Borley said. Gray also attended Demolay dances and other civic-sponsored youth dances, although from all accounts he never had a steady girlfriend in high school, or later in college.

Bob Cowgar, another friend from high school and college, said that Hastings "was a great place to grow up. . . . Pretty solid citizens. There was only maybe one or two girls in town that you could punch. None of us had any sex through high school." The boys would get their homework done in study hall so that after school they could play baseball or football "or, in the winter, almost every night, we'd go ice skating," Bob Cowgar remembered.

Harry Borley, who has known Gray since kindergarten, remembered him as a good student who never got into much trouble. As far as school, "he was into everything." Participating in extracurricular activities became Gray's trademark.

On June 2, 1939, Gray graduated from Hastings High School. In his graduation picture he is a clean-cut, handsome young man and the only boy daring enough to wear a striped shirt and sweater instead of a white shirt and jacket. He had a full head of dark-brown, almost black, hair, parted on the side and combed straight back, dark-brown eyebrows, an oval face, and a nice smile with straight white teeth. His ears lie close to his head and are almost invisible from a straightforward glance. "Eloquent" is the one-word description under his yearbook picture. Gray was active in the Debate, Hi-Y, Kosmet, Library, Science, and Mixed Glee clubs. He was also in the band and the orchestra and was music editor on the yearbook staff. He was not on the student council and did not receive any academic awards. "He was busy all the time. In school and out of school," Borley said.

Gray remained lifelong friends with some of the other members of the debate team—Harry Borley, Jerry Scoutt, and Bill Cowgar. Throughout high school, they traveled together frequently around the state and country to various competitions and won state and national honors. "This was a big thing in the Middle West in those days," Jerry Scoutt said.

The Hi-Y club was open to all high school boys to create, maintain, and extend, throughout the school and community, high standards of Christian character. Twice a month the club held supper meetings. At one of them, Gilbert Charles, a Navy recruiting officer, discussed life in the Navy. With the war starting in Europe, it made an impression on Gray and the other boys.

In the fall of 1939, Gray and several others from Hastings, including his debate team friends, Jerry Scoutt and Bill Cowgar, started classes at Carleton College in Minnesota. In the early 1940s, Carleton was a small, quiet school, much more conservative than it is today. No automobiles were allowed on campus (they still aren't), so all student life revolved around campus-related activities. The dormitories were separate, with men living on one side of campus and women on the other. "There was a dance on campus almost every weekend or some sort of social event and blanket parties in the arboretum. The arboretum was a big forest preserve on part of the campus. That was the antique version of necking," Wesley Jones, a Carleton alumnus and classmate of Gray's, explained.[21]

The class of '43 had 152 men and 160 women. Everyone knew each other since there were very few distractions besides classes and social events. One of Gray's best friends, Gratia Coultas, remembered their taking the bus to the Twin Cities to shop and go to movies, and Gray playing the bass fiddle in the band for the Saturday-night dances. She used to visit him in Hastings during the summer, and remembered seeing him in Greeley, Nebraska, when he was with a summer dramatic workshop, a little theater group. Although no one remembers him being in plays at Carleton, his college records indicate that he acted in several plays and also directed some. "He was good company," Coultas said. "He was really very nice."[22]

When Gray's friends and classmates from Carleton are asked what they remember most about Gray, they all have one answer: he was senior head waiter in Evans, the women's dormitory. "Bob was one of the men who waited tables. . . . It was a great job. He worked every meal on the other side," Wesley Jones said.[23] Although other male students envied Gray's access to the women, Grace and Bob Bauske, Carleton classmates, said, "He was very businesslike about his job. He did not joke around." He was considered handsome, funny, suave, slight of build, but not a ladies' man. "He was just nice to everybody. . . . Just friendly . . . I know he didn't have any one special girl that he went with," Alice Heley, who worked with him at the dormitory, said.[24]

It was not unusual for students to work their way through college. "We either worked to pay off loans or it was part of a program to finance our education through school," Wesley Jones explained. "We were all poor," Jerry Scoutt said, "He [Gray] had a combination scholarship and work arrangement so college didn't cost that much." Gratia Coultas remembered, "He was working a lot of hours to get through school."

After Pearl Harbor, many young men at Carleton enlisted in the Army or the Marines. But word spread quickly about the Navy's V-7 program, where men were allowed to finish college before entering the service. A small group of Carleton students, including Gray, signed up for the V-7 program. Gray enlisted in the U.S. Navy as an apprentice seaman for officer training in late August 1942. Then he returned to Carleton to finish college. That December, his brother, Donald, married his high-school sweetheart. Robert "attended the bridegroom."[25] Robert would be the only Gray child not to marry.

Gray's college classmates, like his high-school friends, remember him as quite charming and well-liked. "He could make friends easily. He was fun to be with," Alice Heley said. He had slick black hair and was always immaculately dressed.[26] Bob Cowgar, who knew him both in high school and college, said, "He was constantly helpful whenever asked."[27] As in high school, he was an unspectacular student, but was very active in various extracurricular organizations.[28] He was president of his junior class, the ad manager on the school newspaper, the *Carletonian*, a staff assistant for Carleton's yearbook, *Algol*, and a member of the Independent Republicans and the International Relations Clubs.

At Carleton, Gray began to take an interest in politics and government for the first time. Although none of his friends remember him being politically active, Gray said he came under the sway of a professor who was the first female Minnesota state legislator. She convinced him to major in political science. Gray claims that he gravitated towards the Republican party because of his innate fiscal conservativism.[29]

By the time Gray graduated with a B.A. in political science in 1943, his dark black hair had already turned salt and pepper. His college yearbook states: "Bob is the fellow who beats out the rhythms on the bass viol at the dances every Saturday night . . . plus, helping on every committee the college ever created."[30]

After college, Gray, along with the others in the V-7 program, went to Columbia University in August 1943. The first month was the test. Those who passed became midshipmen, and, for the next three months, would be crammed full of navigation and ordinance training. They were called "90 Day Wonders," and graduated as ensigns in November. Gray not only passed the first month test, he also served as the barber for the group.

When Gray was halfway through Columbia, the Navy announced that there were openings in the Supply Corps. With World War II raging in Europe and the Far East, Gray signed up for the Navy Supply Corps Midshipmen Officers' School—a year-long program at Harvard. The program was three four-month terms. Although there were no civilians on campus, the first term was strictly civilian courses in management, statistics, accounting, and sources of supply. Since Gray had been a political science major, the business courses were new to him, so his roommate, Richard Hoffman, tutored him in accounting. Although Gray struggled with his business courses, Hoffman said Gray was "very talented" in other areas. "He was interested in history and art. He was a very sensitive individual."[31]

Hoffman remembered Gray as a talented writer with a good command of the language, and a good speaker. "He's a hell of a speechwriter . . . pretty handsome. Kind of a skinny guy. Slight built. Sensitive. Artistic. Extremely good vocabulary. Exceptional writer. An inspired kind of person. Could do a lot of things. Just involved in lots of things all the time. . . . He had a strong imagination.''

After the first term, the midshipmen were no longer required to live on campus, so Gray, his roommate, Richard Hoffman, and friends Walter Heacock and Elton Hailey, who lived on the same dormitory floor, decided to share an apartment off campus for the remainder of their stay. Heacock found an old mansion, in an historic area on Brattle Street in Cambridge one block from Longfellow's home in one direction and James Russell Lowell's home in the other. They rented the third floor.[32]

Hailey remembers Gray as "very clever." Once in a management course, Gray had to make a presentation. Ahead of time, he planted questions in the audience, among the other students, to impress the professor. "And everybody knew it, of course, but the professor. He [Gray] was pretty clever," Hailey said.[33] Gray also edited the yearbook, "and that was quite a job to get that out when we were under pretty stringent hours," Hailey remembered.

Heacock, Hoffman, and Gray spent weekends hitchhiking through the mountains of New Hampshire and up into Maine visiting places of historical significance. Heacock had a strong historical background, so he guided them through the sites like Bretton Woods, where the 1944 international monetary conference established the World Bank and the International Monetary Fund. In Maine, they visited summer theater and artist colonies along the shore.

Gray rarely went with Hoffman to the dances at Cambridge, which were the easiest way to meet women. Instead, he went with his roommates to concerts to hear the Boston Pops. They went several times to the beautiful mansions in and around Boston when the wealthy residents invited the midshipmen out for the weekend. "But he [Gray] was not looking for girls. He would go along with us, and if the occasion arose, he was very pleasant to be with, but he was not looking for girls," Hoffman said.

Although often the butt of rough military humor, Gray had a sense of humor and enjoyed a good laugh. "He liked the horseplay that went on amongst the guys in the Navy. He was not one to initiate, but he liked it. Enjoyed it. The manly crap that you do with a bunch of Navy guys. Storytelling and all that stuff. He enjoyed the horseplay," Hoffman remembered.

Gray and his class graduated from the supply officers school as ensigns at the end of September 1944. After Harvard, Gray was assigned to Terminal Island near Los Angeles to await his ship, the U.S.S. *Collingsworth*, which was still being built. His roommate in California was Eddie Jordan, whom he had met at Harvard. They rented an apartment in Santa Monica and carpooled the considerable distance down to San Pedro every day.

Jordan remembers Gray as a devoted Democrat and a Roosevelt and Truman supporter. Jordan remembered that the man who drove them every day "was a very rock-rib Republican, and we used to jibe him all the time." Jordan and Gray, when they drove past the Roosevelt School, would salute just to annoy the driver. The first page of the yearbook Gray edited at Harvard featured a full-page photograph of President Franklin Delano Roosevelt. (Gray stated in a written interview for this book that he has always been a Republican, and that any misapprehension that he was a Roosevelt supporter must stem from his abiding respect for all presidents. He said that he has occasionally supported Democratic candidates, and mentioned that he counseled Senator Eugene McCarthy during the 1968 Democratic primary campaign.)

The U.S.S. *Collingsworth*, a troop transport, was launched on December 2, 1944. According to the ship's official history, it was then towed north and outfitted at Vancouver, Washington.[34] Although Jordan and Gray were assigned to different ships, they were both sent to Astoria, Oregon, to train with their respective crews. On February 26, 1945, the U.S.S. *Collingsworth* was commissioned. Gray served as the supply officer. The ship spent the next several months sailing up and down the California coast on its shake-down cruise and for other training. It was during predawn exercises along the North American coast that the crew of the *Collingsworth* were informed of President Roosevelt's death, April 12, 1945.

Fifteen years later, Gray wrote movingly in his memoirs of the emotion of that moment, but the location of the *Collingsworth* had been moved several thousand miles. "I was aboard the attack transport U.S.S. *Collingsworth* in the South Pacific when we were flashed the bulletin about Roosevelt. A dozen or so of us were having a lively discussion when the news jolted us. The room emptied quickly as men found excuses to go to their quarters so they could contemplate, alone, the lasting effect of this development on them, their world, and their war." In reality, the ship did not make it to the South Pacific until several months after FDR's death. In fact, it made it to the Far East just in time to carry the troops home after the war.

By the time the U.S.S. *Collingsworth* reached Okinawa in August 1945, Truman had dropped the atomic bombs on Japan and by mid-August, peace terms were being dictated. The ship saw no action. By the end of August, men were already being transferred back to the United States for discharge. The ship traveled to Saipan, Korea, and China, transporting troops. On November 28, 1945, it left for the United States. From Tacoma, Washington, the *Collingsworth* went through the Panama Canal and was decommissioned in Norfolk, Virginia, on March 17, 1946.[35]

Dr. Frederick J.T. Roukema was the ship's junior medical officer. He remembered that Gray was quiet and kept to himself on the ship, in a departure from his normal pattern of conviviality. "He was more of an intellectual, I guess," Roukema remembered, "a loner and didn't join in too much with the activities of the officers." After the *Collingsworth* was decommissioned, Gray was assigned to his hometown of Hastings. He reported to the Naval Ammunition Depot there.

The ammunition depot was an enormous Navy facility (48,753 acres). The first loaded ammunition came off the production line on the Fourth of July 1943, after the Navy had poured $45 million into the project. Although it was dangerous work (explosions killed several of the workers), an additional $71 million was spent to expand the depot in 1944, making it the largest inland depot in the United States. By the time Gray arrived in 1946, however, the Navy was beginning to deactivate the installation.

The Navy gave Gray's former roommate, Eddie Jordan, his choice of assignments after he stayed in the service an extra six months. With Gray's encouragement, he also chose the depot in Hastings. Gray wanted him to stay in Hastings and start a new business with him when they were discharged. The idea was to launch a baby-diaper service. With the returning GIs and the beginning of what would become the Baby Boom, it seemed like a good idea. This was just the first of many good ideas for new businesses that Gray would have, though none seemed to work as well in practice as they did in concept.

During the summer of 1946, Gray and Jordan worked as assistant supply officers at the depot and lived at Gray's family home until they were assigned housing. Jordan did not feel comfortable in Hastings, so he left after the summer for California. After being discharged from active duty, Gray stayed in Hastings, but maintained his ties to the Navy as a reserve officer. Proud of his service, he is, even today, known to keep his white uniform with gold epaulets hanging in his office.

Gray spent the next couple of years trying to figure out a way to put his new business expertise to use, but none of his ventures worked out as planned. In 1948, he returned to Harvard and received his masters in business administration on June 23, 1949. His thesis was "Small Business— Its Place and Problems in the Future of the American Economy." As in high school and college, he edited the yearbook and wrote a column for the Harvard newspaper, the *Crimson*.

With his new Harvard MBA in hand, Gray returned to Hastings and moved back in with his parents. That fall he began teaching business administration at Hastings College.[36] The second semester he developed a new course entitled "Small Business," on the planning and operation of a small business. He said he added the course because most Hastings graduates would enter commerce through a small-business enterprise. "The course will stress creative thinking because the small business must provide something new, either in goods or services, in order to be successful in the face of competition," Gray told the college newspaper.[37]

The new course was enormously popular. Seventy-one men and one woman enrolled. Gray wrote his own text entitled, *A Case Book for the Organization of the New Business Enterprise*, incorporating the Harvard case-study approach. Outside of two *Readers Digest* reprints, the text was all original material that was mimeographed and handed out to the students.

Tom Jorgenson was one of Gray's students and remembered him as an excellent teacher. "He had a sense of humor that went along with it. It was a fun thing to go to class, and he had a lot of great ideas. Very creative. And he made us be creative in our thinking."[38] Gray was an imaginative teacher. He took his students on a bus trip to Chicago so they could stand on the floor of the Board of Trade and experience firsthand what they were learning in the classroom. Gray also took his students to Kansas City to visit the Federal Reserve and to tour various automotive and other plants. He organized a trip to Independence, Missouri, where he arranged for his class to meet President Harry Truman. He was promoted to assistant professor in February 1950.

Gray was as close to many of his students as he was to other faculty members. He had them help him with odd jobs and chores, like painting his house. Tom Jorgenson still laughs when he remembers how Gray always got the best of him: "The freshmen used to be initiated and we had paddles. . . . Well, I was mayor of the dorm, this old, old naval barracks that was moved out from the big naval ammunition depot out east of town. Eighty guys lived there. . . . One time his sister, Jean, was having a slumber party at the house so Bob said, 'I've got to get out of here.' So we said, 'Well, come and stay at Bronc Hall.' And then he said, 'I've got to be at this meeting. I've got to get up at six.' So we changed the clock around so he got up about two-thirty or so. . . . And then the next morning we were talking about trading swats [paddling each other]. He said, 'Yoggie, I'm going to hit you first. No. I want to hit last.' And I said,'No. No. No. No. I want to hit last.' Well, he always had a method to what he was doing. *Always.* Very cunning and conniving. And so we argued and argued. Finally, he said, 'Okay, I'll hit first.' So I grabbed my ankles and he hit me harder than anybody in the world. And he dropped the paddle and ran out of the room. I couldn't catch him. I never did give him a swat. Oh, he was a rascal."[39]

During the spring, two news stories appeared on the Associated Press newswire about Gray's new methods of teaching. That summer, Gray was a guest lecturer in Industrial Management at the University of Southern California, from August 4 to September 2. During that month an article he wrote on socialism appeared in *The Creditor*.[40] Even from his first job after business school, Gray was proving very adept at self-promotion.

In the early 1950s, Gray's hair was beginning to turn silver around the temples. Looking more mature, he hardly kept a low profile in his home-town.[41] Gray was active not only at the college, where he sponsored a fraternity and worked with the Forensic and Special Study committees, but he was also busy in the community, where he was chairman of the executive board of the Hastings Civic Symphony, an officer in the Masonic Temple, and a vestryman at St. Marks Episcopal Church. In 1951, he was voted

Outstanding Man of the Year by the Hastings Chamber of Commerce. He was nominated by two of his Hastings College students.

The college newspaper, in its gossip column, recounted Gray's activities after the spring society dinner dances in 1951:

> Bob Gray and Dorothy Tirrell were just a wee bit late to the dinner at the Clarke Hotel . . . Immediately after the dinner the couple rushed to Bellevue where Bob shed his white dinner jacket and black trousers for the plaid kilts of a Scotchman [sic] . . . He was featured on the advertising portion of the disc jockey program . . . He threw out Scotch kisses to the guests . . . not real ones you understand, just butterscotch kisses wrapped in cellophane . . . Nothing like being Scotch, even with your kisses, eh Bob?[42]

The following year Gray took his own advice and left teaching to work in a variety of small businesses. In 1952, Gray, still living at home, tried his hand at several ventures in Hastings. Gray managed a Sinclair gasoline station which he co-owned with his friend, Harry Borley. Gray had written a paper on the success of green stamps while in school, so the station offered green stamps to give it a competitive edge. The station eventually failed. "It worked out fairly good until prices [for gas] went out of sight," Borley said.

Gray worked for Phil Bonahoom at his warehouse across the rows and rows of railroad tracks that separate the commercial from the industrial sides of downtown Hastings. Gray worked on other projects, but kept an office at the Bonahoom Seed Company warehouse. Primarily, he helped manage personnel and other tasks for the warehouses that mainly stored government material.[43]

On June 27, 1952, C.J. Gray died after a long bout with diabetes at age sixty-two. On July 3, Dwight D. Eisenhower, the Republican candidate for president, spoke briefly from the back of a train, the "Victory Special," during his whistle-stop tour of the country. It was an unusually cool day and a crowd of three thousand gathered to greet the candidate at the Burlington Station. Standing behind the sign "Eisenhower Special" with Ike was his wife, Mamie, holding a bouquet of red roses. On their left was Fred Seaton, the local newspaper publisher.[44] Gray was not there to see the people to whom he would one day owe much of his success. It was the day of his father's funeral. At 10:30 A.M., services for C.J. Gray were held at the huge, yellow-brick Masonic temple. He was buried in the Parkview cemetery.

Besides the service station and the warehouse, Gray worked in other small businesses. Putting into effect his teachings on marketing new and innovative products, Gray opened Television Mart, the first television store in Hastings. He convinced his boss, Phil Bonahoom, to finance the store, and he managed it. They carried Hoffman and General Electric televisions.

Since television was in its infancy at that time, very few families had television sets. Unfortunately, there also was no television station in Hastings and the reception from the Omaha station was very poor. Eventually, the store failed. "They were a little bit ahead of themselves," Bob Hardin, who worked with Gray, said.

Yet Gray had recognized the enormous potential of television and, according to his high school and college friend Jerry Scoutt, soon tried a different tack. He applied to the Federal Communications Commission (FCC) for a television license for Hastings. It was the perfect solution to his problems. Although Gray does not remember applying for the license, Scoutt recalled handling some of the legal work for the application. Unfortunately for Gray, Fred Seaton, the town's newspaper publisher, was his competitor. Since Seaton was a former United States senator and was currently working for President Eisenhower in the White House, he had substantially greater resources, both financially and politically. Gray experienced the power of politics firsthand. He lost the license to Seaton, but he learned an important lesson. He learned that close connections to powerful politicians was as important to success in business as good ideas and hard work.

Gray then applied for the contract to collect garbage for the town. He put together a very interesting and innovative plan that called for uniformed attendants and brand new, shiny trucks. "Having come from Harvard Business, he had bigger ideas," Jerry Scoutt said. But the city turned down Gray's proposals in favor of an older man who had been around town longer.[45] Gray was very disappointed when he lost first the television license, and now the town garbage contract. ". . . I think that may have been one of the times he realized that if you go out for politics, that you'd better understand," Jerry Scoutt said.

By 1955, Gray was tired of dead-end jobs and thwarted opportunities. The experience with Seaton made him aware of the importance of connections, and perhaps that Washington, D.C., was a more fertile ground for him than Hastings. He was thirty-three years old. He had little money, but he possessed personal characteristics that would serve him well in the political culture of Washington: charm, a strong work ethic, an attractive and clean-cut demeanor, and a desire to please. What he lacked entirely was political, governmental, or bureaucratic experience. But that would not matter.

2

TO THE WHITE HOUSE

When the young man raised in all the solid, basic virtues of the small town
breaks out of his provincial cocoon into the city, he finds its variety
invigorating, its cultural smorgasbord rewarding, its people mix exciting.
        Who's Who in America—Robert Keith Gray's 1980 entry

Gray's experiences with Fred A. Seaton showed him firsthand that political connections count. The television station Seaton controlled, the one that Robert Gray had wanted so badly, began broadcasting in Hastings in 1955. Yet in this defeat Gray saw opportunity. He desperately wanted out of Hastings at this point and Seaton, his former adversary, proved the avenue. On May 12, 1955, Gray sat down and wrote a letter to Fred Seaton in Washington asking him for a job. Gray said in a speech a year later that his warehouse job routinely brought him to Washington and that each time he went, he became more and more "determined" to move to Washington and work for the Eisenhower administration.[1]

Seaton was originally from Kansas, not Nebraska, where his family had helped Dwight Eisenhower get his nomination to West Point. In part because of this old connection Seaton was brought into the 1952 campaign early and was awarded a high-level staff position after Eisenhower was elected.[2]

Although Gray had no family connections to Eisenhower, had not worked on the campaign, and was not politically active, he had learned enough to use his ties to those who did. Seaton, who had just moved from the Pentagon to the White House staff in February, responded to Gray's letter on May 23:

PERSONAL

Dear Bob:

Your letter of May 12 has finally caught up with me. As you may know, I was in Hastings at the time you addressed the letter to me here, and I found it on my desk after I returned.

14

I am very much interested in your desire to take a fling at the problems we have down here, and I shall try to see what can be worked out. I am sure you can be a great deal of help to us if we can find a spot which would be attractive to you.

With best wishes, I am

Sincerely,

Fred A. Seaton
Administrative Assistant
to the President

Mr. Robert Gray
Manager
Phil Bonahoom Warehouse Company
Hastings, Nebraska[3]

Immediately, a four-by-six, plain white index card was completed, and Gray's job request was turned over to Edward Tait, Fred Seaton's assistant who handled White House personnel matters. The card stated that Gray was interested in "SOME POSITION IN GOVERNMENT." Tait suggested possibly the executive director of the Securities and Exchange Commission (SEC). He knew the job was available; he had just left it to work at the White House. Under "Recommended by" the card said "Self-Endorsed."

In Washington, Tait contacted the SEC in July 1955 on behalf of Gray, and, in Hastings, Gray gave notice to his boss at the warehouse. The White House received job recommendations from F.E. Weaver, the Dean at Hastings College, and Phil Bonahoom, the owner of the warehouse, in August on behalf of Gray. On October 6, 1955, Gray wrote to Tait advising him that he had an appointment with Chairman J. Sinclair Armstrong at the SEC on October 10. Gray packed his bags and left Hastings full of hope and excitement. He thought he had the job wired. As he had written Seaton, he was ready to tackle the world's problems.

But after moving to Washington in late 1955, Gray realized he would not get the SEC job. Tait arranged for him to meet with an assistant to Gordon Gray, then the Director of the Office of Defense Mobilization, but that did not work out either. He contacted John Lindsay, the future Mayor of New York, and then a political appointee at the Justice Department, but Lindsay replied: "nothing available in Justice as Mr. Gray is not a lawyer." Gray's white index card was filed away in the General File on November 28, 1955. He found himself in Washington with no job and little prospect of finding one.

Gray turned to members of the Nebraska Congressional delegation in Washington, especially Carl Curtis, a genial, rotund conservative who would later consider Gray a good friend. Ethel Friedlander of the Republican National Committee was also helpful.[4] Curtis was in his first year in the

Senate after spending sixteen years in the House of Representatives. "Bob Gray . . . thought there was a certain job that had been promised him. He came to Washington and the job did not materialize," Curtis remembered. Curtis would not offer Gray a job, but agreed to help him.

Curtis's administrative assistant checked around town for job openings. Throughout the day, Gray went to interviews; at night, he followed up by sending thank-you notes. "If I found out during an interview that your hobby was butterflies, somehow I'd find something about butterflies, an article or card or whatever, to send you," Gray told the *Washington Post*.[5] Finally, in December, Curtis's staff found Gray a job at the Pentagon as Special Assistant for Manpower to Albert Pratt, then the Assistant Secretary of the Navy for Personnel and Reserve Forces.[6]

The Navy assignment was a very low-profile, tedious job that offered little chance for advancement, prestige, or exposure. Gray's job description reads as if it was drafted by a career bureaucrat anxious to punish a subordinate with the dullest assignment possible:

> In his position Gray will review and evaluate the reports of manpower programs and requirements as developed by the Marine Corps commandant, the chief of Naval operation, and the bureaus and offices regarding personnel. He is also responsible for preparing policy statements and basic criteria to influence, assist, and control the determination of manpower requirements and the utilization of manpower by all Navy Department components.[7]

For many reasons, the Pentagon job was not suited for Gray's ambition, personality, or lifestyle. But in other ways the job was a godsend; it gave Gray time and a position from which to maneuver. He had his eyes on a bigger prize, and wasted no time in going after it.

Gray did not give up on Fred Seaton. He made an appointment for lunch at 12:30 P.M. on February 7, 1956. He again went to see Seaton at the White House at 5:30 P.M. April 18. He was back the next morning at 9:30. On Saturday morning, May 5, at 8:00, Gray had breakfast with Seaton before Seaton went to the Virginia Gold Cup Steeplechase races in the nearby Virginia horse country. Five days later, on May 10, Gray was back for a 9:00 A.M. appointment.

The following Saturday, on May 12, 1956, the White House issued a press release announcing "the appointment of Robert Keith Gray, now a Navy Department official, as a special assistant in the White House office." The Associated Press reported, "He will succeed Edward T. Tait whose chief responsibility has been in the field of federal personnel matters as assistant to Fred A. Seaton . . . Tait has been granted an indefinite leave of absence because of illness."[8]

Not long after landing the job at the White House, Gray said in a speech that he got the job through "luck," that he came to Washington "starry-eyed," and that the chances of his getting a job at the White House were "fantastic."[9] Twenty-four years later, an embellished account of Gray's quick entry into the height of the Washington power structure appeared. In 1980, the *Washington Post* reported:

> While he (Bob Gray) was working at his first Washington job, with the Secretary of the Navy, Eisenhower presidential assistant Sherman Adams heard him give some testimony at a Congressional hearing. Adams invited him to work at the White House, dispensing patronage jobs.[10]

In fact, it is highly unlikely that he ever gave Congressional testimony while working in the Navy Department; Albert Pratt did not recall such testimony. In a written interview for this book, Gray offered a different account than the one reported in the 1980 *Post* article. He did not acknowledge asking Seaton for a job, implied that his frequent visits to Seaton's office were due to their developing "close friendship," and that it was Seaton who had been impressed by testimony he had given and recommended him to Sherman Adams.

On Monday, May 14, Gray reported to Seaton's office at 9:00 that morning. Ed Tait said good-bye to Fred Seaton at noon, and Gray was back that evening to say goodnight before Seaton left for dinner.[11] Gray did not have to undergo the usual political and personal background checks for a presidential appointment, including one of J. Edgar Hoover's notorious FBI field investigations, which, especially in the witch hunts of the 1950s, could devastate a man's career. He had an "excepted" appointment, which meant he had been simply detailed to the White House from the Navy. His first official day at the White House was Wednesday, May 16.

Gray, who six months earlier had been unemployed and pounding the street, not only had a job, but was controlling the flow of information about everyone looking for patronage, or political jobs, for the entire federal government. In four three-ring binders—two black and two olive green—Gray had a listing of all federal jobs and how much each one paid. He also had at his fingertips confidential information about some of the most powerful people in the United States. He took to the job like a sponge to water, soaking up every detail, every nuance, every name, and every file.[12]

By White House and government standards in the 1950s, Gray was very young. At thirty-four years old, he was one of the youngest men in the White House, and wrote enthusiastic lines in his speeches about what a wonderful environment for youth existed in the Eisenhower White House. Gray called members of Eisenhower's cabinet "senior citizens."[13] By this time, his salt and pepper hair had turned predominantly white.

Ten days after Gray's White House arrival, a Cabinet shuffle helped propel Gray even closer to the pinnacle of the inner circle of the Eisenhower administration. His mentor, Fred Seaton, was appointed Secretary of the Interior on June 8, 1956. Gray suddenly found himself working directly for the powerful Sherman Adams, the former governor of New Hampshire, who truly ran the Eisenhower White House. Gray was now one of "Sherm's boys," with all "the power and prestige this identity carried with it."[14]

Sherman Adams was a patrician-looking, white-haired New Englander who was the political brains behind the Eisenhower White House. The President's "right-hand man," Adams always seemed prepared with an answer or opinion for his boss; the President took his advice most of the time.[15] Unlike Eisenhower, who had spent his entire career in the military, Adams had worked his way up the political ladder from the New Hampshire legislature, to the U.S. Congress, to the governorship. Much like John Sununu did more than thirty years later with George Bush, Adams risked his political future on Eisenhower in the early New Hampshire primary in 1952.

When it came to political decisions, Sherman Adams gave the orders. He amassed what the press called enormous, unaccountable power. Eisenhower's political interests were, at best, academic. Sherman Adams filled the void. Forceful and abrupt, Adams had almost unquestioned authority in Washington. Arriving at 7:30 A.M. every morning, he ran the White House staff with what was frequently described as "ruthless efficiency." He left secretaries in tears, and often had one-word telephone conversations with some of the most powerful people in Washington; usually the one word was "no." Even to Eisenhower on the telephone, he had no time for hellos or good-byes. He was too busy.[16]

Called "the locomotive among the boxcars in the White House" by the *New York Times* or "the Great Stone Face," "The Iceberg," "The Abominable No-Man," or "The Granite Governor," by others, Sherman Adams treated members of Congress and the media with disrespect, and soon had many enemies on Capitol Hill and in Washington.[17] Drew Pearson, the syndicated columnist, wrote in his diary:

> Talked with Senator Ed Johnson of Colorado about the FCC (Federal Communications Commission) . . . He launched forth in a tirade against the Eisenhower administration as the most graft-ridden in history . . . He pointed out that commission after commission is bent on robbing the public, that the quasi-judicial process has disappeared, and that all you had to do was to know Presidential Assistant Sherman Adams to get TV licenses . . .[18]

"I lived in awe of him," Gray wrote. Every night he went home with Sherman Adams stories to tell his Georgetown roommates.[19] Gray had experienced firsthand what it was like to lose a dream, the television station in Hastings, based on politics. He was ready to learn the ropes so that would never happen to him again. The seeds of his future success in Washington were being planted. He learned at the knee of Sherman Adams, but the lessons were not policy questions or good government or high principles. The lessons were in basic visceral politics.

Gray learned the importance of patronage and partisan politics from Adams, who would get very agitated if he had trouble placing a Republican at a federal agency because a Democrat still held the position. Eisenhower twice urged his cabinet "to place men of their philosophical persuasion in the posts subordinate to them. He warned them of the ease with which they could be made captive by their staffs."[20] Gray learned that politics played the most important role in patronage, and that political appointees who did not toe the party line were "ingrate[s]." He urged appointees to "wield a heavy ax" in firing holdovers from the Truman administration, and argued "for using a wide and partisan broom in effecting personnel changes." He resented appointees who were coopted by their subordinates, usually career federal bureaucrats, within thirty days of their appointments. He lamented that "not the least of the trials of a patronage officer is the futility of trying to explain to a heavy campaign contributor why the fully qualified man he recommends cannot be placed in a position occupied by an opposition holder."[21] "The importance of having those who share the President's philosophy in all posts bearing on policy is not fully appreciated outside of Washington," Gray explained.[22] Already Gray considered himself a full-fledged insider.

One of the first instructions Gray got from Adams was a June 16 memo that said of an administration appointee:

> [He] is incapable of performing the duties of the office which he now holds. It will therefore be imperative that he either be removed or transferred.
> Will you explore the possibility of transfer?[23]

Two days later, Gray responded:

> Chauncey Robbins [who handled patronage for the Republican National Committee] anticipates the political repercussion will be considerable unless we can offer [the appointee] something equal or better. He feels that he is not [underlined twice by hand] a man of great ability; has very strong political support as well as strong support from industry. Robbins said that [he] is one of the few Republicans Mansure appointed; that he has been fully cooperative with the National Committee.[24]

Gray then listed from the White House personnel files all of the job recommendations he had received from Oklahoma.

The important issue here was not whether the appointee could do his job, but if he would pose a political problem if he were fired. It was Gray's job to make certain that the man would not do any damage prior to the election. A year later, Gray wrote a memorandum to Maxwell Rabb, then Eisenhower's Cabinet Secretary, explaining the situation:

> [The appointee] was discharged for disloyalty and for making derogatory statements regarding Floate and Mills. There was also an instance of drinking during an Operations Alert. Following his discharge, Brad Morse, in Saltonstall's office, put him to work in Sumner Whittier's campaign. He was put on this project primarily to keep him quiet during the campaign since GSA was convinced he had taken materials from their files that would cause them embarrassment prior to election day.[25]

Knowing firsthand how partisan the selection process was, Gray would give speech after speech stressing just the opposite.

Gray relished his personnel job. He accumulated and then passed on, as he saw fit, personal, private, and often derogatory information on job applicants to Sherman Adams. Gray did not sugarcoat his reports to his boss. For example, on June 26, Gray sent a memorandum to Adams on a candidate for chairman of the Railroad Retirement Board:

> Jack Martin contacted Senator Schoeppel regarding subject. Schoeppel says [the candidate] is unreliable, controlled by outside interests, dishonest, a plagiarist, and slants his Committee's reports. Further, that Schoeppel will block him if the name is submitted.[26]

Gray also did not refrain from passing on unsolicited information as well. In a memorandum to Robert Hampton, then a political appointee at the State Department, Gray wrote:

> On December 18, 1956 we referred to State papers on Christopher Janus, who was recommended to us, as I believe he has been recommended to you, by several sources for a diplomatic assignment.
>
> In the event that his papers are getting consideration in any degree, I feel I should tell you that one of the members of the White House staff who is personally acquainted with Janus has felt compelled to talk with me about the man and what he considers his definite limitations for an overseas assignment.

Gray, a young man from rural Nebraska, was, through perseverance and luck, working in one of the most sensitive White House jobs. When the magazine, *U.S. News and World Report*, ran a picture in July 1956 of Sherman Adams's staff, the first nationally published photograph that included Gray, he asked for a copy of it for his personal use. It would be among the first of hundreds of photographs Gray would accumulate that pictured him with powerful Washington politicians that were to hang on his office wall. They were mementos that also served to project to others his power through association.

Gray worked as the White House personnel sieve straining the information he accumulated and then passing it on to Adams. "My part in patronage was in the distillation process in which we narrowed down the field for presidential consideration," Gray wrote. He said that for highly sought after positions, it was not unusual to have fifty to a hundred candidates. "Most of these could be quickly ruled out as having no endorsement save their own . . ."[27] When Gray had first written Fred Seaton asking for a job, he was "self-endorsed." In "discreetly" researching candidates for Adams, Gray discovered two disastrous handicaps: one was that the candidate "made no dollar contribution" to the party and the other was that he had the markings of "a New Deal Democrat." Gray's friend Eddie Jordan believed Gray was a liberal, FDR Democrat. "To go from that to Eisenhower/Nixon was something. . . . He became that [a conservative Republican] when he got close to Eisenhower," Jordan said.[28] It appears that if Gray had applied to himself for a job, he would have disqualified his own application.

Gray also kept the files of any additional information sent on to Adams by others. "There are 2,027 Presidential appointments. As there are always some vacancies, and there are many candidates, each with many supporters, Mr. Gray has a busy telephone, a busy staff, and is a busy man," The Omaha *World-Herald* newspaper reported in 1957.[29]

Gray worked with the FBI and the CIA on background checks. He had the authority to order a full field FBI check on prospective candidates. "They cost the government some $600 per investigation and seldom could be completed in less than three to four weeks. . . . Their disclosures, by which were uncovered about the job seekers things they had not told their wives, were an invaluable assist in the selection process," Gray stated.[30] (It will be remembered that Gray himself was not subjected to this rigorous examination of his personal life when he assumed his White House job.) He also called the Republican National Committee as well as state and local party officials for information. He referenced Dun & Bradstreet and Martindale-Hubbell. He spoke to members of Congress and business associates. He looked through civil service and other government files and prepared long, detailed reports. Nothing was sacred.

Although Gray was supposed to be finding people like the appointee who was suspected of taking embarrassing government memos from GSA new jobs in the fall of 1956, he did not miss opportunities to help personal friends as well. In September, Gray sent a memorandum to Sinclair Armstrong, the Chairman of the SEC, (the same man with whom Gray had sought an interview a year earlier) recommending his old Navy friend from Harvard, Elton G. Hailey, for a position:

Hailey is a personal friend of mine. I hesitated to mention this to you on the phone for fear you would feel compelled to give him consideration for that reason alone. Now that you have expressed an interest in looking at his material, I hasten to tell you that he is a friend because I don't want you to think that I would recommend him for that reason only. We attended Harvard Business School together. I feel that his success in the investment field, coupled with his other qualifications, may mark him as the type of staff addition for which you are looking.

Hailey had been, in fact, Gray's roommate in school. Hailey was operating his own greenhouse and floral business in Abilene, Texas when Gray recommended him. Hailey did not get the job at the SEC, but Gray eventually found him one in public information at the General Services Administration. In return, Hailey did not forget Gray's intercessions. In 1960, Gray went with Richard Nixon for a campaign speech in Nebraska. When he returned to Washington, he wrote Nixon a thank-you note and enclosed a check for the plane ticket. When the Associated Press ran a story about contributions Nixon had received from cabinet associates, Elton Hailey called to warn Gray that he was mentioned on the wires.[31]

Nineteen fifty-six was a presidential election year and in June the campaign began to focus on the upcoming conventions. Even though Gray had not helped in earlier campaigns, in 1956 he was eager to make a contribution. Gray went to his first Republican Convention, held that year in San Francisco. Since Eisenhower was unopposed, the convention consisted mainly of parties and gave Gray a chance to meet Republican stalwarts. Gray watched the proceedings with "spellbound fascination." He learned how Sherman Adams carefully staged the important political events.

For example, on the day Eisenhower was to meet with Harold Stassen, the former governor of Minnesota (who was leading a dump-Nixon-from-the-ticket campaign), Gray met with Adams on the sixth floor of the St. Francis Hotel early in the morning to receive his instructions on how to limit press attention of the meeting. As Gray recounts it in his memoirs, Adams said, "Harold Stassen will be coming out of that elevator at nine-fifteen. I want you to meet him; get him by that pack of hounds"—he jerked his thumb in the direction of the large group of reporters and photographers who were waiting—"bring him down here, and set him in *that* chair."[32] (Almost thirty years later, Gray would be controlling a similar convention when another popular president was unopposed for renomination. By then, it was Gray who was giving the detailed instructions to subordinates.)

Gray also was able to pass on confidential information about the Democratic opposition to the campaign. He wrote to Eisenhower's economic advisor, Gabriel Hauge, and to others on the White House staff, on October 5:

From a source which I believe to be reliable, I learned that (Adlai) Stevenson's speech in Montana on October ninth will be completely devoted to conservation of natural resources.

The attached will give you a little advance information on what the Stevenson group has planned.

Gray attached a campaign flier attacking the Eisenhower-Nixon administration's record on conservation. He got the information from a conservation specialist for the Pan American Union who had previously met with Sherman Adams. (Six presidents later, similar memorandums would be uncovered by a House of Representatives Committee in 1983 looking into campaign material stolen or missing from President Carter's files when Ronald Reagan was running in 1980.)

Among the first things Gray did when he reached the White House was volunteer to the Republican National Committee to give political speeches for the president and party. Television was just beginning to compete with live political speeches. Since it was an election year, Gray kept very busy. He traveled all over the United States, giving pep talks to the Republican faithful, never missing an opportunity to make contacts and to promote himself. He was building his own grass-roots organization. He also never missed a chance to go home to Hastings to speak.[33]

On the same day Fred Seaton was appointed Secretary of the Interior, June 8, Eisenhower was rushed to Walter Reed Army Hospital. The White House said it was indigestion, but the next day the President underwent two hours of surgery and ten inches of his intestine were removed. After Eisenhower's earlier heart attack, there were constant questions about his health and whether or not he should seek reelection. The next day, the White House confirmed his candidacy for reelection.

Gray, new to Washington and to politics, was now learning firsthand a crash course never taught in high school or college political science courses. He watched how the White House played down obvious health problems, emphasizing, instead, Eisenhower's vigor, stamina, and hard work when, in reality, he often vacationed, played golf, and took naps in the afternoon. Soon Gray became a participant, giving speeches about how healthy and vigorous the President was. Even after seeing for himself how fragile Eisenhower's health was, Gray continued to emphasize just the opposite.

Gray said in speeches that President Eisenhower was working "longer hours on a heavier schedule on weightier problems" than ever before. He called Eisenhower "the world's hardest working man. . . . I can't speak for the other members of the White House staff, but I can say for myself that I couldn't survive if he were any more a full-time President."[34] When critics called Eisenhower the part-time president, Gray responded that there were demands on the President's time mornings, evenings, and weekends and that the telephone was always close by. Gray gamely explained that even when Eisenhower was playing golf, the Secret Service agents had a walkie talkie hidden in a golf bag.[35]

In Gray's speeches, he always brought personal greetings from the President. In his first speech at Hastings College after his White House job, he said that when he told Eisenhower the preceding Saturday that he would be finishing up his series of campaign speeches in his hometown and that he would be speaking at the college, the President recalled that he had sent congratulations for the college's seventy-fifth anniversary. "He asked that I wish you well in your next seventy-five years," Gray said. Of course, just prior to a reelection campaign, Eisenhower was not focusing on the seventy-fifth anniversary of a small college in Nebraska or having intimate conversations with a low-level aide. In fact, Gray's first meeting with Eisenhower was a year and a half away. But Gray was "thrilled" to be home, and he was going to make certain his hometown knew about his new-found importance.

When the State Department drafted a speech for Gray that said: "It is with pleasure that I greet you here today in this effort, and in behalf of the President extend his greetings and best wishes also," he crossed out these words and inserted: "Let me finish by telling you that the President, when I told him that I was meeting with you this morning, asked me to give to each of you his greetings and his very best wishes in your undertaking. To these illustrious wishes, I hope you will permit me to add my own."[36]

In other speeches, Gray would say that he wished his audiences could see the President at work like he does, studying at his desk, swivelling in his chair or pacing the floor. These remarks were intended not only to enhance the image of a president hard at work, but to also confirm to the audience Gray's insider status. When Gray talked about his personnel job, he said that the President insisted on only the best qualified available men for a vacancy. "Dwight Eisenhower has been the symbol of a new standard of integrity and good government and has attracted and demanded men who subscribed to those ideals," Gray said. An unstated implication was that Gray was a man who passed such high standards.

After the election in November, it was Gray's job to put together information on defeated Republican congressmen and governors and candidates for suitability for job placement in Eisenhower's second term. He accumulated their voting records and other political information on their loyalties to Eisenhower and the Republican party for Sherman Adams, along with comments from Capitol Hill and from others in the White House.

Sherman Adams, getting ready for Eisenhower's second term, had Gray collect from the various agencies lists of people who should be replaced and why and who were possible replacements. He wanted reports on how many Republicans had been hired at the departments. For possible replacements, Gray collected political and biographical information from young Republican organizations about their members around the country.

From the State Department, Gray got a list of Eisenhower's political supporters, who had recommended them, and to which countries they wanted ambassadorships. "Men of wealth are the largest contributors to a political party; to shoulder the load at the major embassies (London, Paris, or Bonn) requires men of wealth. So it should not be too shocking to discover that America's noncareer ambassadors have made political contributions, some of them of impressive size," Gray wrote.[37] (In the early 1970s, Gray would be called before the Senate Watergate Committee regarding its investigations into the selling of ambassadorships by the Nixon administration.)

The list for ambassadors in 1957 read like a Who's Who in American Business. Included on the list was William Paley, the late head of CBS, who always wanted, but never got, an ambassadorship. Paley and CBS anchorman Walter Cronkite were close to the Eisenhower administration, and Gray's friendship with Cronkite proved very beneficial over the years. Gray began learning the value of media contacts.

In January 1957, Gray attended his first presidential inauguration. When Eisenhower took the platform in front of the U.S. Capitol at noon, he spoke of world peace, "the building of a peace with justice in a world where moral law prevails."[38] Gray's White House papers indicate that he was dealing with more mundane issues, with guest lists and who should be included on which list.[39] It was good training. One day he would be in charge of Ronald Reagan's inaugural.

Sherman Adams, a tough taskmaster, was also a good teacher. He was Eisenhower's most valuable political troubleshooter. In a memorandum to Gray on January 26, 1957, he wrote:

> You must give careful consideration to the timing of letters such as you have written Senator [Allen J.] Ellender. You have told Senator Ellender that Mr. Herget will receive 'careful consideration.' You have told Judge Johnson the same. You have told Judge Lindsey that Mr. Herget 'will be given every consideration.' If these letters go out and in the next few days the nomination goes to the Senate naming another candidate, it is quite obvious that substantially no consideration has been given. This is a matter that you want to give careful attention to.

The key is that Gray is not being admonished for writing something that is not true; he is being instructed about the importance of *timing*, which is underlined, by hand, on the memo.

Gray learned that the minute a name for an important post was known, it seemed like everyone in Washington brought out the daggers. "Once a man was known as the front runner, he became the target of criticism fired from all other candidates and the men who backed them."[40]

There were few areas of patronage where Gray did not have some input.

In a memorandum to the head of the General Services Administration, Gray lists what his "informants" have told him about a prospective candidate:

Pro: No bad habits
     If a drinker, is a moderate one
     Has an excellent reputation for honesty, integrity, and citizenship
     Is a church man
     Sold his company to U.S. Steel in a transaction which netted him over a million dollars after taxes
     He is a family man with three children
     Good appearance (6'2")

Con: Over-valued opinion of self
     There is a question as to whether he would stick to a desk job after the prestige wore off
     Believed to be dumb on politics
     Administrative ability has not been put to the test which his net worth would indicate

Our informants have summed up their contributions with statements such as, 'He certainly would be no worse than many we have in government service' . . .

At the Department of Justice, Gray got involved in the appointment of federal judges. "As a group, the most coveted patronage appointments are the federal judgeships. These 'plums' pay at the top of the federal salary scale, the incumbents are appointed for life, and they enjoy dignity, power, and prestige," Gray wrote.[41] On April 9, 1957, Gray warned General Persons, who would later replace Sherman Adams:

I believe you should know that [name deleted] former law partner and his private secretary, while in the Governor's office, have been indicted by the Federal Grand Jury for influence peddling in Federal Housing matters. I would not bother you with these gory details except that [name deleted] indicated in his letter to you that he will be seeing you around the middle of April and under the circumstances I think you might want to soft-peddle on [name deleted] chances for the Federal Judgeship at this particular time.[42]

When Nelson Rockefeller wrote Sherman Adams in support of reappointing a federal judge in Honolulu, Gray went to work. He advised Adams that the judge would not be reappointed because he was a "Truman-appointed holdover," the Hawaiian Republican organization opposed him, the judge had "waged" open battles with the U.S. Attorney, and he had "offended many Hawaiians by being a protagonist of *Alaska* statehood."

At the Department of State, Robert Hampton fed Gray confidential information for his files on a job candidate:

I have checked the records at ICA to determine why he left and found that he was fired for black market activities.

Thought you would want to have this information for your confidential use.[43]

Even the FBI did not hesitate to send Gray copies of their files. Gray accumulated information in a way that would have made J. Edgar Hoover proud. On May 20, 1957, Gray wrote a memorandum to Sherman Adams, enclosing a list of top members of the Eisenhower administration, which clearances they had received (FBI full field, Top Secret, Q Clearance, Crypto, etc.) and the dates. He said:

With the exception of those noted below, we have satisfied ourselves that those on the list are politically discreet:

Vice Admiral James L. Holloway, Jr., United States Navy
Willard F. Libby, Atomic Energy Commission

In his work, Gray was considered gracious, cooperative, and deferential to his superiors. He never shirked responsibility and was willing to accept or volunteer for additional responsibilities. When the Civil Service Commission requested that each department, including the White House, designate someone to handle handicapped issues, Gray wrote, "Happy as I would be to give this additional problem to someone else, I am afraid I am the logical man for the job."[44]

Civil rights and racial discrimination were important issues in the Eisenhower administration. After the 1954 *Brown v. Education* decision regarding desegregation of public schools, racial tension, especially in the South, was growing.[45] E. Frederick Morrow, the only black on Eisenhower's staff, sent a memorandum to Gray asking for an ambassadorship to a "white" country. "It is so obvious to send a Negro to Liberia or Ghana or Haiti, but imagine the thrill that would come from sending a Negro to some South American country, to one of the Scandinavian countries, or to any small country that is commonly referred to as 'white.' "[46] Morrow never got his ambassadorship.

A telling example of the attitude toward and the treatment of minorities in the Eisenhower White House is the following anecdote Gray wrote about in his memoirs. He first explained that when celebrities and movie stars visited the White House—Helen Hayes, Bob Hope, Danny Kaye—high-ranking officials took them to the White House staff dining room for lunch. But when it was Louis Armstrong's turn, it fell to Gray, one of the lowliest staff assistants in the White House, to entertain him. Gray was embarrassed by the luncheon, in part because Adams was sitting at the next table. He wrote at length about what he considered to be Armstrong's loud and boorish behavior. The tone of the passage is painfully patronizing.

> Art [Minnich, assistant staff secretary] asked Mr. Armstrong if his wife had accompanied him on his overseas trips. After the affirmative answer was enlarged upon with a double forte discourse on the value of constant female companionship to the musically inclined, we struck off after gentler topics. Minnich thought he was safe in asking the maestro to name his favorite musical selection. I agreed. This sounded like a question to relax by. But Armstrong said, in a booming voice that stopped all conversation, " 'Sweet Georgia Brown'! When the man say"—he was now shouting—"Old Satch will play 'Sweet Georgia Brown,' Ah just"—and, rising to his feet with his hands grabbing an imaginary horn, he went—"roo-ta-te-toot-ta-too." Silverware dropped by the handful all over the room.

After the Civil Rights Act of 1957 passed, Gray made his recommendations about who should serve on the new Civil Rights Commission and how much they should be paid. Gray took exception to William Kloepfer who had been recommended for the public relations job. Gray wrote, "Mr. Hagerty [the President's press secretary] also has strong feelings about Kloepfer who, he says, was fired by Len Hall [at the Republican National Committee] because of an anti-Eisenhower attitude." Gray recommended that Kloepfer be offered no more than a GS-15 ("his present grade").

Gray also recommended that the one woman selected for a staff job at the Commission, Carol Arth, not receive a salary increase. "While I have confidence in Mrs. Arth's abilities, I question that this position warrants her jump from her present GS-14 ($10,320)" to a GS-16. "Not incidentally," Gray continues, "*only four women out of 533,802* in government service are in the GS-16 grade."

Of course, none of Gray's comments or suggestions had anything to do with civil rights policy or the effectiveness of the commission. He only focused on an individual's political and personal backgrounds and whether or not they fit into his and Sherman Adams's patronage mold.

Requests from members of Congress who were looking for jobs, went through Gray. Congressman Stuyvesant Wainwright II of New York secretly typed himself a letter to Sherman Adams so his office staff would not know he was looking for a military appointment. Former Congressman Edward Boland from Massachusetts also asked the White House for a job. They liked Congressman Boland, whom they considered a moderate, but were afraid if they got him a job, someone more liberal might win his seat in Congress.

Gray learned the art of trading favors. When a congressman's office called Sherman Adams to complain that after seven months Gray had not found the congressman's friend, Theodore Richardson, a job, Gray responded that

". . . following our policy of bending over backwards for [the] Congressman" that he would make arrangements for yet another job interview for Richardson at the Veterans Administration.

Even President Eisenhower's personal choices for positions were researched by Gray. Like Lyndon Johnson after him, Eisenhower used the FBI to check out his friends. Eisenhower sent a memorandum on October 21, 1957 to Attorney General Herbert Brownell, Jr.:

> . . . Burton Mason . . . is General Counsel for the Southern Pacific Company, San Francisco. He was sixty-three in September 1957.
>
> In about 1914 he left West Point under a bit of a cloud, accused of getting unauthorized help in an examination but, as I remember it, the only evidence against him was circumstantial.
>
> . . . I should like to have a thorough FBI report made upon his possible qualifications as a United States Judge. I realize that he is about a year older than individuals should be in accordance with the policy on which we have agreed. But over the years I have thought of him and heard of him as a man of the highest character. Even if we should decide that his experience does not qualify him on a judgeship, I should like to know if the FBI examination would substantiate my opinion.[47]

Gray telephoned a request and received the FBI file on A. Burton Mason. He sent a memorandum to the Attorney General on December 14, 1957 saying:

> . . . While it [the FBI file on Mason] was in our possession, I took the liberty of showing it to Jerry Morgan and we have indicated with paper clips two significant statements in the report: (1) that Mason was expelled from West Point, and (2) that he is a 64 year old man who has 'learned to live with a serious heart condition.' While both of these points will undoubtedly affect your decision, I think you will agree that it will be rather indelicate to mention the second one to the President.

Gray was learning who was important, and why. He knew whom he had to please, and whom he could ignore. Important people could not be ignored, regardless of their abilities or job performance. If someone were unimportant, or below Gray in seniority, he did not hesitate to include derogatory information in his files and memos. Gray wrote on April 2, 1958:

> As an applicant for Under Secretary of HEW, [name deleted] was referred to me by Howard Snyder. He brought with him a 6-page resume of his experiences written in the style of a doctorate of education. He is officious, over-dressed, and annoyingly egotistical. His affectations include wearing a wristwatch part way up his arm on top of his shirt sleeve.
>
> He talked too much and stayed too long.

On November 6, 1957, Bernard M. Shanley, the Appointments Secretary to the President, left the White House to run for the Senate in New Jersey. Gray temporarily took his place. It was a big promotion that put him in direct, daily contact with Eisenhower. It also brought him close to Eisenhower's wife, Mamie. A limousine began picking him up early every morning to go to the White House. It was a perk Gray grew to enjoy.

Only a few weeks after Gray started as Appointments Secretary, President Eisenhower suffered a stroke. It was his third major illness during his presidency. Gray was the first to find Eisenhower, disjointed, sitting at his desk. He remembered the precise time, 2:22 P.M., when he heard the buzzer summon him and he rushed into the office. Eisenhower did not recognize him, and called him by his predecessor's name. The President tried to put his glasses in his suit pocket, but couldn't, and dropped them on the floor. Speaking slowly, Eisenhower dismissed Gray. Gray left not knowing what to do. Luckily, Eisenhower's personal secretary took charge.

Eisenhower had a button at his desk where he could buzz Gray whenever he had a question. When he buzzed, Gray grabbed a notebook and ran into the President's office. Gray even jumped when Eisenhower's dog, a weimaraner named Heidi, accidently pressed the buzzer when she was under the desk. "Ever since, I've been telling folks about the day I answered a summons by a dog," Gray said.[48]

In many ways Eisenhower resembled Ronald Reagan, with whom Gray would become friends twenty years later. They both favored brown suits and came from modest, midwestern backgrounds. They both had health concerns, being the two oldest presidents in history, and they both took naps in the afternoon.

In mid-December 1957, a "rumor" circulated in the media that Gray was going to get the appointments job permanently. The Associated Press and the *New York Times* both ran stories saying: "Robert K. Gray, special White House assistant on patronage, was reported in administration quarters Friday as a 'pretty safe bet' to be President Eisenhower's new appointments secretary."[49] It would have been a major jump for Gray both in terms of money and visibility, but the official appointment never came.

By now, United States Senators were calling Gray for his help and advice. He sent a memorandum to Bryce Harlow, an Eisenhower assistant who handled congressional relations (and who would become a long-time Gray associate), advising him that Senator Glenn J. Beall, Jr. of Maryland was "running both scared and hard in Maryland" and that "he called him to let us know what we might do to guarantee his election . . ." Beall wanted the Pentagon to increase an Army contract at Aberdeen, Maryland. Gray wrote:

> If Defense can be persuaded to act favorably on the Aberdeen request, the Aberdeen Chamber of Commerce will be pleased with the Senator, the Senator will be reelected and we will have once more a Republican Senate.
>
> See how it works! As usual, it is up to you.

Gray's temporary job as Appointments Secretary, a high-profile position, brought him some enviable publicity when *U.S. News and World Report* decided to run an article on a day with President Eisenhower in the White House. On March 4, 1958, a reporter and photographer went to Gray's office, which they used as their "vantage point." Gray's desk sat just to the right of the door leading into Eisenhower's office, much like a guard desk posted to prevent any unauthorized entry.

That day Gray's wooden desk looked remarkably neat, while he sat in his high-backed leather chair talking with Cabinet members and others who were waiting their turn to see the President. There was a credenza behind his desk, a picture on the wall just to the right of his desk, a leather chair with wooden arms and legs where visitors could sit to the side, and behind the chair was a floor lamp, in front of a heavily draped window. Arranged around the rest of the office were other desks where secretaries busily answered phones and distributed paperwork.

Gray was featured in most of the photographs accompanying the *U.S. News* story. His office was called "the White House nerve center." When the day began, Eisenhower's military aide advised Gray, "The boss is in his office." From then on, Gray and his staff screened the President's telephone calls, placed calls for the President, acted like traffic cops for incoming paperwork and greeted officials and staff waiting or dropping by to see the President. "Ceaseless activity," the article said.

Gray provided *U.S. News and World Report* with statistics on the President's schedule: "A White House compilation shows that in January . . . the President had 301 office callers, two dinners, one luncheon, one press conference and made two speeches."[50] Gray had learned how to work with the press, what to tell them, when, and how. He did not know it yet, but he had found his calling. Gray's hometown newspaper ran a story about the *U.S. News* article reminding its readers that Gray would be in Hastings the following month to address the annual convention of Nebraska's Young Republicans. People from around the country started writing the White House asking for Gray's autograph.

Gray watched Eisenhower closely, noting details about his personality and personal characteristics that he would put to good use later, often adopting some of those traits. Gray noted that Eisenhower wrote thank-you notes for everything, and soon Gray was doing the same thing. When Gray's appointment assignment was over, Eisenhower called him in and asked, "Bob, is there anything I can do for *you*?"[51] In later years, Gray would do the same for prominent politicians and their wives, explaining to the press that this was one of his techniques for success.

On March 26, 1958, syndicated columnist George Dixon ran an entire column on Gray. It was among the first of dozens of articles that would follow over the next thirty years, most of which gushed with praise and admiration for the marvel from Nebraska who took Washington by storm. Dixon wrote:

> So rapidly and unobtrusively that few outside Washington have yet grown aware of it, a 36-year-old college professor has become the 'Third Man' at 1600 Pennsylvania Ave. Robert Keith Gray has been elevated to a double role, never entrusted to one man before. He not only screens all the White House patronage, but all of President Eisenhower's appointments . . . This prematurely gray young man is listed only as a secretary. But he has six secretaries working for him. In an average . . . six-day week, they weed as many as 600 seekers after Presidential favors, and more than 300 applicants for audiences with the President.
>
> Only D. W. Eisenhower and Sherman Adams wield more power in the White House. Unless Ike or "Sherm the Firm" intervene, no one gets to see either a job or the President without the blessing of the gray Mr. Gray.

Gray's perceived power did not come from his intricate knowledge of government programs or world affairs, but from his control over the President's schedule. In reality, Gray was not powerful or courageous enough to deny access to the President to any Cabinet member or any of his superiors. The column made Gray feel uneasy, since he knew his true powers did not match the column. "This reference was completely gratuitous and, as completely, untrue," Gray wrote later.[52]

The Dixon column goes on to describe the lady who lives across the street from Gray in Georgetown who "entertains ideas" about the young bachelor. It says Gray has "a delicate sense of humor," when he invites friends to use the swimming pool in his garden, which is "a small well about four feet in diameter." "It will hold about two very friendly people," an unattributed quote said.

Unfortunately, most of the Dixon article was not true. When describing Gray's "remarkable history," it says he taught at Carleton College and then went to USC as a professor in business administration. When he returned to Hastings, he "talked some monied friends into putting up cash, and ventured into the warehousing business. It mushroomed. Now he has thirteen profitable warehouses in Nebraska, Iowa, and Minnesota."

The column went on to report that Fred Seaton noticed Gray's success and mentioned him to Eisenhower and to Sherman Adams, who "induced Gray to take a furlough from warehousing and join the White House secretariat."[53] Gray had realized just how easy it was to manipulate the press. Since they often were on tight deadlines or just plain lazy, it was easy to feed them information with varying degrees of truth which they would run in newspapers without question. Gray's public relations genius, in many ways, stemmed from his ability to shape his own public image.

By 1957, Gray had become a Washington fixture. An attractive bachelor, his most important success in the nation's capital came not just from the responsibilities of his White House job, but also from his entry in the Washington social register. Now he would be included as the acceptable extra man. *Cosmopolitan* magazine ran an article that year about the most eligible bachelors in Washington. Gray made the list. The story surrounds a picture, where Gray is standing, carefully posed, in front of the White House holding a couple of notebooks. Like the other pieces being written about Gray, the article exaggerates his background, saying he was "formerly president of two Nebraska corporations."

What made Gray so attractive to the Washington social scene was his charm, good looks, and, most importantly, his eligibility. The *Cosmopolitan* article says:

> Bob claims the demands of his job prevent him from even considering marriage just now. 'If it happens to me, it'll happen against tremendous odds,' says the handsome Midwesterner, who often works a fourteen-hour day, spends many weekends speechmaking all over the country, and attends countless official functions.[54]

Gray, always concerned about his appearance, spent $1,000 a year on clothes, according to the article. Ironically, Sherman Adams, who would be forced from office for accepting a free coat for his wife, once asked Gray, "Where do you buy your suits? I hope you're working for them."[55] In 1957, Gray's salary was $12,900 a year. *Cosmopolitan* explained that he shared a "suburban" Georgetown townhouse with two other government bachelors, and that he spent his leisure hours "reading, swimming, or painting (one of his canvases—a surrealistic pallet knife painting—hangs in the White House gallery)."

The portion of the article about Gray ended with an anecdote on the difficulties he experienced when he tried to date. It said when Gray did "occasionally" find time for a date, "he asked his personal secretary to hire a waiter for a 'quiet dinner at home.' " She discussed Gray's date with the ten other secretaries in the office who all agreed that they did not like "his lady friend." "Much to Bob's embarrassment, all ten showed up at his home in frilly waitress uniforms to serve his 'quiet dinner.' "

In a newspaper column entitled "Social Climber," the Omaha *World-Herald* wrote on December 1, 1958:

> Robert K. Gray . . . is . . . a leading social light in the Capital. A handsome bachelor, Mr. Gray is much in demand at social affairs. He played host recently at a farewell party for famed hostess, Mrs. Perle Mesta, as she

departed on a trip. His picture, sometimes . . . in white-tie-and-tails, often appears in the social columns of the Washington newspapers.

In 1960 *Look* magazine sent a reporter and photographer to crash Washington parties. In one of the photographs accompanying the article, the reporter, Sue Seay, is pictured with Gray in his tuxedo, both laughing, with the caption: "Someday, I'd like to meet bachelor Bob Gray, Secretary to the Cabinet, again."[56] Nineteen sixty was a leap year, so articles on women in Washington catching eligible men were prevalent. Gray was considered a big catch:

> At the White House, single girls have long eyed the attractive and friendly Secretary of the Cabinet, Robert K. Gray. The 38-year-old White House official frankly admits that he is not going to let Leap Year push some woman into asking him. He's ready to pop the question himself the minute he finds a lady fair who has these qualifications for his affections: "She must be a bit younger than I am, be attractive and, of course, she must be a Republican!"[57]

Much of Gray's success later in life could be attributed to the social contacts and friends he made during his Eisenhower years as one of Washington's most eligible bachelors. He was a regular guest at cereal heir and socialite Marjorie Merriweather Post's parties.[58]

Gray gushed with praise for Clare Boothe Luce during her ambassadorship to Italy. She, too, would become a lifelong friend, eventually serving on the Board of Directors when Gray started his own company. He admired Washington socialite Gwendolyn Cafritz's style, especially her Easter reception honoring the Supreme Court which featured exotic, fresh Hawaiian flowers and live white rabbits in gilded cages. He doted on Perle Mesta's "flamboyant" parties and writes in his memoirs that "the cha-cha was slow to catch on in the capital. The mambo and the samba, the fox trot and a few waltzes made up the most popular program."[59] Gray memorized what was "socially correct." This skill was undoubtedly critical to his popularity and success.

In March 1958, Tom Stevens, a jovial teaser who made the President feel at ease and comfortable, returned to his job as Appointments Secretary, which he had held before Bernard Shanley.[60] Gray had not worked out. Gray believed it was because he was nervous around the President. "Not until later, when I had gone on to the cabinet assignment, did I learn to relax in his presence." With an eagerness to please that must have been painful to witness, Gray "talked too fast," discussed information "tensely," and "sir'd" Eisenhower so many times he made Eisenhower "uncomfortable."[61]

Although Gray had had more personal contact with Eisenhower than many other White House staffers, "few, if any, of these contacts had a substantive bearing on the course of United States policy," according to Gray himself.[62] He had been responsible for who came and who went and how to get rid of lingering guests, but never about what was going on in the meetings. Now, the attention he derived from his access to the President was over. On his personal stationery, his name in script centered at the top, Gray wrote the President a heartfelt, eager thank-you note. He signed it: "Devotedly, Bob."[63]

3

SHERM'S BOY

In politics disuse is often more galling than abuse . . .
Robert Gray, *Eighteen Acres Under Glass*

Not being named Eisenhower's permanent Appointments Secretary was the kind of career blow that might have forced a less determined person out of the White House, but Robert Gray had already proven that determination was one quality he did not lack. Although Gray's tenure as Eisenhower's Appointments Secretary had been less than a personal triumph, he had learned some important lessons on personal deportment around the powerful. He had also learned about the flow of information and people into and out of the Oval Office and how to obtain access to these arteries. More importantly, he had developed a personal friendship with the First Lady; he was beginning to learn that relationships with spouses of influential officials had some very beneficial side effects on one's career.

Although Eisenhower chose not to continue to work with him on a daily basis, Gray's five months as Appointments Secretary were the most important in his four and a half years at the White House. As Appointments Secretary, it was Gray's job to coordinate the President's scheduling with the First Lady. While Gray may have gotten on Ike's nerves, his work while sitting just outside the Oval Office cemented his friendship with Mamie.

Years later, Gray would try to develop the same kind of relationship with another First Lady—Nancy Reagan. Gray does not believe that his friendships with the wives of the powerful throughout his career have given him any special benefits. However, those friendships were a way of maintaining entree to their husbands's inner sanctums. His friendship with Mamie Eisenhower set a pattern he was to follow for the next three decades.

Gray would be at Mrs. Eisenhower's side when she went to Andrews Air Force Base to wave good-bye to the President when he left for overseas trips. In his memoirs, he describes being present at a dress fitting for Mamie Eisenhower with her designer. He details the changes she made for State dinners. He explains how she offered to help him buy a fur stole for his mother at a discount:

> . . . Monday morning at ten minutes past eight Mrs. Eisenhower telephoned. "Good morning, Bob," she began cheerfully. "Mike [her nickname for her sister] tells me you are looking for a fur for your mother. I found a fur-sale notice in my Sunday *New York Times* yesterday, and I'll send one for you to look over. If you are interested in it and have any difficulty, please let me know."[1]

The late Bryce Harlow said Gray comforted Mrs. Eisenhower and protected her from criticism when she was accused of accepting expensive gifts, flying to Elizabeth Arden's Main Chance salon in Arizona with her sister at government expense, and drinking too much (due to the strain on her marriage from the rumors about Eisenhower's continuing extramarital relationship with Kay Summersby). To the contrary, Gray emphasized Mrs. Eisenhower's "deep devotion" for her spouse, her worries when he traveled, and her concern about his health and the pressures of the job.[2]

Gray maintained a close relationship with Mamie Eisenhower, her sister, Mrs. Gordon Moore, and many of their girlfriends long after they left the White House. He knew about their telephone calls and their feelings toward their friends and other family members. He went to their parties, listened to their complaints, and was always very attentive to their problems.

The loss of the Appointments Secretary job took Gray out of the spotlight, but he would not stay there for long. He continued his personnel work and his speeches on the rubber-chicken circuit, speaking to as many groups as he could while he waited for his opportunity to advance.

Once in the limelight, Gray was not content with remaining in the background. Since he knew about all administration jobs, who was leaving, when, and why, he knew that Eisenhower's Secretary to the Cabinet, Maxwell Rabb, had wanted and not received the United Nations ambassadorship, and was planning to leave the administration. Gray suggested to Sherman Adams that they offer Rabb the head of UNESCO as "a fine consolation prize," but Rabb returned to New York to practice law.

Gray made his move. On Sunday, April 27, 1958, within a week of the announcement that Rabb was leaving, White House Press Secretary James Hagerty announced from President Eisenhower's golfing vacation headquarters at the Augusta National Country Club in Georgia that Gray would be the new Secretary to the Cabinet. Although Rabb had handled the politically sensitive civil rights and race relations issues for the White House, Gray was not given this assignment. Instead, he would keep his responsibilities for job patronage temporarily and would also handle immigration issues.

On Friday, May 16, 1958, exactly two years after Gray's first official day at the White House, he was sworn in as Secretary to the Cabinet, immediately after the Cabinet meeting around 11:00 that morning. President Eisenhower held the Bible, while Gray's boss, Sherman Adams, administered the oath. To Adams's right, Gray's mother, Marie, looked on. On the other side stood Fred Seaton.

At thirty-six years old, Gray assumed what proved to be his highest government office: "Eisenhower's Secretary to the Cabinet." It was a title Gray would treasure for the rest of life and would refer to constantly in an effort to reinforce an image of status, acceptability, knowledge, and importance.

"The Washington career of Robert K. Gray of Hastings is being described as meteoric," the Omaha *World-Herald* newspaper stated.[3] There was no mention of Gray losing the coveted Appointments Secretary job in large part because Eisenhower did not like nervous people around him. To the contrary, *U.S. News and World Report*, the same magazine that two months earlier had featured Gray in almost every photograph, reported, "Mr. Gray does not fluster easily. . . . His calmness should prove helpful . . . since President Eisenhower doesn't like jittery people around him, and the President will be seeing alot of Mr. Gray."[4] In reality, as Cabinet Secretary, Gray would only see the President once a week at Cabinet meetings, and, in those meetings, he was not supposed to say a word.

If salary indicates the importance of a job, then Gray's was less significant than others since he was one of the lowest paid in "the White House family," earning $17,500 in 1958. There were forty-five on the staff. Most of the other professional positions, including Appointments Secretary, paid $20,000 or more per year.

The Cabinet Secretariat consisted of Gray, his assistant, Bradley Patterson, and three stenographers all operating out of three small rooms. If one opened the door, there was a room with the three women; Gray's long and narrow office was on the left and Patterson's was on the right.

Gray's contribution to the decor was a little unusual for the White House. He hung a large painting of a reclining nude woman, entitled "Miss Fanny," over his desk. He had to. When he was on two-weeks active duty with the Sixth Fleet, he had admired the painting in a French gallery, but it was too big to bring home. Gray described the painting in detail to his staff. For Christmas, they had Eisenhower's naval aide bring the painting back on the Presidential plane.[5]

The evening that Gray was appointed Cabinet Secretary, he hosted a cocktail party for his predecessor, Maxwell Rabb, at his Georgetown home. Some members of the Cabinet and almost all of the White House staff came. "The group presented Mr. Rabb with the chair he occupied in the White House Cabinet Room at Cabinet sessions," the *Evening Star* reported.[6] Gray enjoyed giving parties and as he became more sophisticated due to his exposure to Washington society, his parties too grew in sophistication. It did not take him long to learn that, in Washington, the best way to guarantee a successful party—one with a large attendance and many prominent people—was to host it on behalf of an influential and popular person.

A few weeks later, Gray was back on the road, enjoying his new status. When he was making a speech in Minnesota, he took a helicopter and landed on the baseball diamond at his alma mater, Carleton College, where he had worked once as a waiter. The college president greeted him "like Santa Claus come to Bloomingdale's" and took him on a brief tour of the campus.[7] Then Gray left, but not before he had his picture taken with the helicopter for the alumni newsletter.

Maxwell Rabb had been the first person to hold the newly created job of Cabinet Secretary. Rabb and his assistant, Bradley Patterson, had developed a routine to prepare for Cabinet meetings and to follow up on decisions reached that was already in place when Gray took over the position. Since Gray was assuming an operation that was already running smoothly, he did not make any substantive changes. He did, however, want to add his personal touch to the Cabinet meetings.

Gray's assistant, Bradley Patterson, remembered one of Gray's first changes. "He was very sensitive . . . that the President was concerned about cabinet officers who talked too long, particularly making a presentation. . . . And Bob was worried about never eating up too much of the President's time, particularly after his heart attack. . . . So Bob rigged up a series of lights. . . . Somehow, somebody leaked this to the *Wall Street Journal*. It goes on the front page."[8]

Gray had set up a system of lights—green, yellow, and red—on the rostrum in the Cabinet room. He may have gotten the idea from his old debating days in high school. If he felt an individual was speaking too slowly, he would hit the green light that indicated "speed up." The yellow light meant that the speaker had "three minutes to go." After three minutes, the red light would flash that it was time to quit.[9]

After Gray's lighting system made the front page of the *Wall Street Journal*, some thought it "smacked of mechanical puppetry." A system of lights flashing in front of high government officials trying to present complex ideas seemed undignified. How could intelligent men debating critical and complicated issues be subjected to such arbitrary time constraints? Gray's idea backfired in full public view. Shortly thereafter, the lights were removed from the rostrum.

The Cabinet meetings under Eisenhower were not informal weekly sessions where the heads of the various departments got together and discussed with the President various problems and solutions. Maxwell Rabb had created a very formal, structured formula that Gray inherited. It made the Cabinet Secretary job time consuming, but not very substantive. It was mainly organizational, according to Bradley Patterson.

Before a cabinet meeting, the presenter would haul his charts (the lettering had to be at least one inch high) and graphs over to a room beside Gray's office on the second floor of the west wing of the White House for a dry run, or full-scale dress rehearsal. Gray and other White House aides would make suggestions and offer criticism and determine how much time would be needed for this part of the two-hour Cabinet session.

The *Wall Street Journal* article criticized the elaborate preparations and the formal procedures of the Cabinet meetings that seemed to overshadow the substance and reason for the sessions. It said that besides the dry runs, there were numerous meetings and position papers that "all but decide an issue before it ever reaches a Cabinet session."[10] It asserted that more and more decisions were being made "behind the scenes" for either the President to simply approve, or he was given a few alternatives from which to choose.

Eisenhower did not really use the Cabinet to govern. According to Washington lobbyist Charls Walker, who was an Eisenhower appointee at the Treasury Department, "The Cabinet meetings were pretty much a waste of time. . . . The Cabinet would meet, but it was a disparate group, and they didn't really concentrate on specific issues. But Eisenhower gave great power to people he had confidence in like Robert Anderson [Eisenhower's Secretary of the Treasury]."[11] (Years later, Robert Anderson would serve on the Board of Directors of Gray's firm.)

The process for the Friday morning Cabinet meetings began with an idea for an agenda item. Patterson and Gray would prepare suggested agenda items for Sherman Adams's approval. "Adams would determine the agenda . . . and his judgement was always very good," Patterson explained. Then "the complex staff machinery grinds into action."[12] Gray would set up a subcommittee of White House aides and executive branch assistants to determine points of agreement, disagreement, and try to find a solution or a list of alternative answers. Once finalized, each agenda item was accompanied by a blue-tinted position paper following a standard format. By Wednesday the agenda for the Cabinet meeting was set.[13]

On Thursday afternoon the Cabinet received their briefing books containing background material on all the agenda items.[14] Preparing these books was not easy. Printing was a very rare commodity, and this was long before Xerox machines. The correspondence staff cut stencils and then the reproduction staff worked all night running off copies, punching one set for the cabinet member's briefing book and providing three unpunched sets for his staff. To collate the copies, there was a big, round table with an electric motor to turn it so that the staff could pick off the pages and staple them.

On Friday mornings at 9:00, the twenty-by-forty-foot Cabinet Room, then painted green, with its huge conference table and leather chairs, filled with men carrying legal-sized black briefing books with their titles embossed with gold lettering. At the meetings, Gray would sit at the table, but he was not a participant in the discussions. "My role during the meetings was a silent one," Gray wrote.[15] Gray never saw the President, except at the Friday morning Cabinet meetings.

There was the Cabinet, consisting of the secretaries of the government departments, and the "Little Cabinet" made up of assistants from these agencies who met right after the Cabinet at 11:30 A.M. At the "Little Cabinet" meetings, Gray and Patterson would go over, in detail, the minutes of the earlier meeting. Sometimes whoever made a presentation would do it again for the assistants. Then Patterson would prepare a Record of Action to indicate decisions reached and any follow-up that needed to be done. The "Little Cabinet" was supposed to follow through on the decisions reached by their bosses earlier that day. Gray worked directly with the "Little Cabinet."

The Cabinet Secretary's job was like a plant foreman's, supervising workers to ensure that they followed through on management's decisions, but not participating in the decision-making process itself. After the cabinet meetings, Gray gathered up the President's black-leather briefing book that had Eisenhower's famed doodles he had drawn during that day's session. Once Gray tried placing a pencil without an eraser by the President to prevent him from erasing any of his drawings, but Eisenhower simply borrowed the pencil from the seat next to him.[16] Gray treasured these sketches and kept them safely in his office, for himself.[17]

While Cabinet Secretary, Gray worked closely with his national security counterpart, Gordon Gray, who handled National Security Council (NSC) meetings. The two Grays would exchange highly secret defense or foreign policy information to determine whether an item should be considered by the NSC or the Cabinet. "Fortunately, Gordon and I maintained the best relations, . . . and referred items back and forth whenever one of us uncovered something which was more properly in the domain of the other."[18] Gordon Gray was one of Robert Gray's connections to the intelligence community and its activities.[19]

Gray's predecessor, Maxwell Rabb, was a well-connected, Eastern-establishment Republican. Prominent people were always coming to visit him. "Danny Kaye would come in and other Hollywood people. They always would come to Max's office. He had a lot of friends and contacts," Bradley Patterson remembered. Gray's visitors, in contrast, were not rich or famous. They were mainly his friends and family from Hastings and from college. Jerry Scoutt said, "When he (Gray) was in the White House, he was always generous with the invitations to come over and have lunch or go swimming in the pool or go to the inaugurals or things like that where he was involved. And he was very considerate of other people. He had a sense for public relations, really."[20]

While Gray did not forget his pre–White House friends, he was not above a little self-aggrandizement in front of visitors. He had his own system of lights installed in his office. He would secretly push a button and a red light would go off. He would then pick up the phone and pretend to be talking to the President. It was a public relations move that never failed to impress his guest, and one he would continue to use throughout his career.

By the summer of 1958, many in the Congress, including several prominent Republicans, were pressing for Sherman Adams's resignation. Adams, who had rubbed many powerful people the wrong way, had accepted many gifts, including a vicuna coat for his wife from Bernard Goldfine, a Massachusetts businessman who was known for contributing heavily to politicians throughout the country. In what was considered an outrageous conflict of interest, Sherman Adams contacted the Securities and Exchange Commission (SEC) and another regulatory agency on behalf of Goldfine after his businesses ran into difficulties.[21]

Few in Washington came to Sherman Adams's defense. His antagonistic persona had made him too many enemies. As the 1958 elections grew closer and the congressional investigation continued, the pressure for Sherman Adams to resign intensified. After a Republican candidate in Maine lost an election in September, the President realized that it was time for Governor Adams to go. Eisenhower had Richard Nixon speak to him. On September 22, 1958, Sherman Adams got into his green Oldsmobile station wagon and drove himself over to the CBS television and radio studio. At 6:35 P.M., sitting in front of a set made to look like an executive office, with an American flag, a desk, and a row of books, Sherman Adams told a national audience that he was resigning his White House job.[22] A little more than a month later, Sherman Adams returned ''unheralded'' to his New Hampshire home, quietly retiring to write his memoirs.

The entire Sherman Adams downfall taught Gray three very important lessons. The first was Adams's removal from Washington's Green Book, the Washington social register and protocol guide. When Adams's political standing deteriorated, so did his social standing. One year Adams was on the top of the list, the next he was not even mentioned. The speed, viciousness, and ruthlessness with which Washington society doted and then dumped on people amazed the young man from the Midwest, where social standing revolved around families and wealth, not politics.[23]

The second lesson was that the media could make or break someone in an instant. Gray realized that all the work that Sherman Adams had done in the past six years would not be remembered. What would be was the vicuna coat and the smell of scandal. Gray did not blame the media; he blamed Adams for keeping too low a profile in the media so that when the Goldfine stories began to appear, the American public knew very little else about the top assistant to the president.

The third, and probably most important lesson, was Sherman Adams's response to the accusations made against him. Gray remembered ''Sherm's boys'' anxiously waiting for Adams to devastate his enemies with a ''cutting" denial. "From the moment he gave, in lieu of the expected refutation, an explanation, his power was on the wane."[24] Repudiate, never explain— that was the key. Quick denials, no excuses.

Gray watched the total disintegration of a once feared and powerful man, both physically and mentally, as Sherman Adams was reduced to a quiet and impotent "shell." Gray felt sorry for his mentor. When others in the White House no longer bothered with him, much less listened to his orders, Gray called Adams and told him he would be proud to have Adams's picture on his wall, and Adams supplied one with the inscription "With regard and affection . . ." Adams would have reason to retract that affection in a few short years.

Gray's White House work and his speeches gave him exposure not only to the Washington press corps, but to media around the country. He learned many valuable lessons especially about what he termed journalists' "devious ways." In his patronage job, Gray watched reporters compete with one another on who could scoop the other on the names of new appointees. They usually tried to trick the stenographers into telling them by floating names to get a reaction or by assuring them: "I just need it for background." When the press learned of the appointment, there would be a search for the leak. Sometimes it could be traced to members of Congress, who might have traded the information for future "credit" when they needed publicity for something later. Eventually Gray concluded: "In politics, of course, you learn to accept press distortions, omissions of your pet points from reports of speeches . . . and, occasionally, some additions to the facts."[25]

Gray learned how to generate articles about himself by telling humorous anecdotes about his White House adventures, even if he had to make them up. One newspaper story opened by saying, "Robert Gray . . . has learned— the hard way—not to joke about speech titles." Gray said that his secretary asked him several times on a hectic day what the topic of a speech was going to be and finally he replied, jokingly, "I am going to tell them how the cow ate the cabbage." When he received an advance copy of the program for his speaking engagement, it said the Secretary of the Cabinet was going to speak to the group "on the intriguing topic of 'How the Cow Ate the Cabbage.' "[26] Cute story, but untrue. In Gray's memoirs, this same story was attributed to Governor Howard Pyle, whose speeches Gray kept in his files for reference, and who had made the off-hand remark and had given the speech in North Carolina.

Gray was fond of telling another anecdote, apparently true. A few days before one of Gray's speaking engagements, headlines across the country carried stories about a Florida airplane crash believed to be caused by a bomb hidden in a briefcase. In the 1950s, a terrorist attack on an American airplane was unheard of. The story caused panic across the country. People were afraid to fly. Bad weather forced Gray to take a bus from Birmingham, Alabama, to Memphis, Tennessee, to catch a flight to Oklahoma City where he was to make a television appearance. "I had to sleep in my clothes, without shaving, and about thirty minutes out of Oklahoma City, I thought that I could at least shave," Gray explained to the newspaper.

Gray took his nonelectric, wind-up shaver out of his attaché case which also contained copies of his resume and some publicity photographs. He started to shave when he realized he might disturb other passengers. So he put the shaver back in his briefcase and walked to the lavatory, which was occupied. While waiting, he rested the case on the armrest and the jar started the shaver. A woman screamed, believing it was a bomb, and Gray's shocked reflexes tossed the case in the air while other passengers sat "white-faced" in horror, believing there was a madman on board. Gray got the case opened and stopped the shaver. No one on the airplane stirred. When the plane landed, he stood up to leave, but no one else moved. "It was an unbelievable nightmare," Gray told reporters.[27]

Self-deprecating humor and clever anecdotes made good copy, and Gray was learning how important favorable press could be. The subtext of such stories was that Gray was important and powerful; the reality was somewhat different.

Gray's file at the Eisenhower Library in Abilene, Kansas, consists of three gray cardboard boxes. Very few of the papers inside deal with matters of policy or historical interest, since Gray's work was mainly administrative, but the papers do reveal he was assigned responsibility for a few substantive issues. One was world refugees from communist countries. It was a difficult cold-war problem. If the United States did not open her arms and borders to people fleeing communism around the world, it would be viewed as hypocritical. But the Soviet Union, China, and other communist countries were planting spies among the refugees. Besides the national security concerns, the cost of resettling the refugees or keeping them in camps was enormous. The United States established a purely self-serving policy. The amount of assistance to refugees would correspond directly with "the degree such assistance directly serves U.S." interests.

Among the first crisis issues to confront Gray was a critical story being written by Harrison Salisbury for the *New York Times* about the problems with the resettlement of the 38,000 Hungarian refugees in the United States who had fled after the 1956 Soviet crackdown. Eisenhower had discontinued the emergency aid program for the refugees at the end of 1957. Salisbury phoned Tracy Voorhees, who worked as a consultant to the White House, about the story, and Voorhees called Gray. Gray arranged a meeting at the White House with the two federal agencies responsible for handling the problem: HEW (now Health and Human Services) and State.

The results of the meeting were a classic example of Gray in action. Those attending decided the best approach was to study the situation. In response to the *New York Times* story, they would commission a survey. It would be their official "counter-offensive." A month later, after the article ran and publicity subsided, the government determined the best way to help the Hungarian refugees was to make them "aware of the assistance opportunities that . . . are available to them."[28] Gray's solution was predicated on a public relations trick, on making it appear that something was being done. Surveys, studies, polls, and commissions would become a familiar White House maneuver, especially during the Reagan-Bush administrations.

Another pressing refugee issue was the constant flow of escapees from Yugoslavia. Gray wrote on July 9, 1958, that Italy and Austria were prepared to handle these refugees in camps as long as they were assured that it was only temporary and the Yugoslavs would soon be sent on to other countries. Gray began working closely with the National Catholic Welfare Conference, which needed an additional $350,000 to help move the refugees to Canada and Australia.[29]

Gray decided to check the situation out for himself. During the fall of 1958, during the time when the controversy over Sherman Adams reached its peak, Gray left for Europe as part of his Navy Reserve commitment. While there, at his own expense, he toured the Yugoslavian refugee camps in Italy and Germany and spent a few days with the Intergovernmental Committee on European Migration (ICEM) and the U.N. High Commissioner in Geneva. Upon his return, he notified people that he had just returned from "Europe on some matters for the President."[30]

The American government officials in Europe saw Gray's visit as an opportunity to increase the White House's interest in refugee problems that were causing great strain, especially in Germany and Italy. Their plan worked—temporarily. Gray was personally moved by the human suffering of the Yugoslavian refugees living in camps, especially the Valka camp in Germany. On October 11, 1958, he sent a letter to U.S. Ambassador David K. Bruce on the deplorable conditions at the camp. "Only the grace of God can have prevented a serious epidemic among the inmates living in unbelievable squalor," Gray wrote.[31]

In a classified State Department memorandum to Gray on October 31, 1958, Robert S. McCollum wrote about the Yugoslavian refugees, many of whom were in the Valka camp about which Gray was so concerned: "Refugees from Yugoslavia are eligible for a 'limited form of assistance which reflects the limited extent of U.S. interest in this group.' "[32] Soon Gray's concern for the refugees not only vanished, but took an adversarial turn.

By 1960 Gray's position on helping the Yugoslavian refugees immigrate to Australia and Canada had totally reversed. "As White House liaison officer for refugee-immigration matters, I am becoming increasingly dubious of the wisdom of continued U.S. contributions to migrant movements to Australia. . . . I urge that we authorize our representatives at the approaching meeting to advise the Australian Government that no further U.S. funds will be available to support Australian migrant and refugee movements after 1961,'' Gray wrote.[33]

Although others in the administration tried to include Gray in their work on refugee issues, he considered it his turf, and was reluctant to share the spotlight with anyone subordinate to him. At the State Department, Robert McCollum, the Deputy Administrator for Refugee Programs for the Bureau of Security and Consular Affairs, suggested that Gray be one of the delegates to a high-profile meeting of the Intergovernmental Committee for European Migration (ICEM) in Geneva, Switzerland. On November 17, 1959, a little more than a year after Gray's first visit to the camps in Italy and Germany, he did in fact speak in Geneva.

Gray did not return McCollum's favor. On the draft press release announcing the Cabinet meeting on the World Refugee Year, Gray scratched out McCollum's name. When Eisenhower's chief of staff, General Persons, asked Gray for information on who should be on the delegation to the ICEM meeting, Gray noted that the "political payoffs" on the delegation were Dorothy Houghton, Dean Sayre (Francis B. Sayre, Jr., Dean, Washington Cathedral), "and a Colonel Hughes whom [Senator] Eastland wanted appointed."[34]

In Gray's response of September 24, 1959, he suggested that Dr. Milton Eisenhower, the President's brother, head the delegation and not Robert McCollum, the government's foremost expert on refugee issues. He wrote that Dr. Eisenhower "would give the Delegation enormous prestige" and would make the other countries believe the President meant business. Again, public relations took precedence over substance. Gray's instinct was to send the person with the best connections, who would project the best image, even if it meant the most knowledgeable person did not go.[35]

Gray spent the summer months in 1958 studying legislation in the immigration and refugee area, and combing through National Security Council files that established White House policy on these issues. Besides handling and referring routine complaints and problems of individuals who wrote to the White House for help, the job also involved coordinating administration policy among the various government agencies. Two of those agencies, the CIA and the Army, were running a massive program to recruit ex-Nazis living in Communist countries and sneak them into the United States as refugees.

Refugee and immigration issues, the only real substantive policy part of Gray's work, was also the one to which he attributed his biggest "disappointment." Despite his best efforts, Gray could point to no major legislative or administrative accomplishments. He was, however, very successful in cultivating contacts and making friends in the international community— people who were always looking to the United States for assistance, and people who could also be very helpful to Gray.

For those interested in immigration issues Gray was an important person to know. The Labor and Immigration Attache of the Italian Embassy asked to meet Gray to ask for the White House's support for legislation to increase immigration quotas for Italians with close relatives in the United States. Gray also worked with the American Committee on Italian Migration to try to help Italians who were being expelled from Tunisia immigrate to the United States.

The Japanese American Citizens League (JACL) gave Gray a citation "for his countless and inspired activities . . . and especially for his cooperation and aid over the years to the JACL in promoting equality of treatment and opportunity for Americans of Japanese ancestry." When Japan "postponed" its invitation for Eisenhower to visit during the summer of 1960 because of anti-Eisenhower demonstrations, Gray phoned the JACL and offered to do anything personally or through his government office he could to help Japanese–Americans who might be subjected to persecution or ridicule as a result of this incident.

Another issue under Gray's purview that drew media attention was the purchasing of orphans, especially from Korea, Germany, and Greece. Gray learned an important lesson when he tried to organize the various federal agencies to effect change. He learned how difficult it is to accomplish anything in Washington, even if everyone "agrees."

For example, Gray worked closely with Elliot Richardson, then an Assistant Secretary at HEW, in an attempt to transfer responsibility for policing the adoption of foreign orphans and ensuring that they received proper homes in the United States, to HEW from the Immigration and Naturalization Service (INS). Gray called a high-level meeting at the White House to discuss the issues. He thought that when the meeting was over, the Departments of Justice, INS, State, and HEW all agreed on the change. Nothing happened, in part, because of opposition from Capitol Hill. Gray suspected the INS Commissioner, General Joseph Swing, of going behind his back to his friend, Congressman Frank (Francis) Walter, the Chairman of the House Un–American Activities Committee. In a memo to Gerald Morgan, General Persons's top assistant, Gray wrote:

> . . . General Swing's friendship with [Congressman] Walter is famous. HEW, State, and Budget all feel now that Swing gave a quick agreement to the group's recommendation [that the responsibility be changed to HEW] knowing that he could steer Walter privately in any direction he wished . . . I recommend that Swing receive a top-level call from General Persons . . . asking if he won't see Walter and urge him to back the change in the legislation which would reflect the Administration's agreed position.[36]

General Swing was a friend of Eisenhower's from West Point days. The test of Swing's loyalty never happened.

Gray also pressed for legislation to increase the number of refugees that the United States could accept; when that effort failed to go anywhere in Congress, he drafted a letter from the President to the Attorney General requesting him to invoke his administrative authority to raise immigration ceilings. This effort was also stymied. The State Department warned Gray, in writing, that he should not try to go around Capitol Hill and affect changes administratively, because the Congress could retaliate in other, more substantive ways. John Hanes, Jr., the Administrator of the Bureau of Security and Consular Affairs, wrote:

> I believe that Mr. Walter would consider it a personal affront and an act of extremely bad faith on the part of the Administration if the clear and expressed intention of the present act were circumvented by executive action. I think there is a possibility that he might be sufficiently mad to cut the legislation off in mid-year when the Congress reconvenes . . . These, it seems to me, are pretty high prices to pay for a short term advantage . . . [37]

Hanes suggested that if Gray decided to go against his advice, the White House should at least wait until Congress adjourned.

Here were important lessons about Capitol Hill that Gray would put to good use when, as Washington's premier public relations expert, he lobbied Congress on behalf of clients. He saw how one person who was friends with a powerful member of Congress could stop a piece of legislation, even while pretending to support it; that short-term advantage could lead to long-term loss; and that if the Executive Branch was going against Congress, it should, at the very least, wait until they were out of town before acting.

Gray also learned during his White House years the power of "grass roots" support and how, if generated correctly, it could be more effective than intragovernmental avenues. Gray laid out his legislative strategy on getting members of Congress lined up and then activating the pressure groups. He wrote in a memorandum to the file on March 6, 1960:

> I see no advantages to a resubmission [of the pending legislation] without change except the advantage of refocusing the effort of those who like to see the legislation passed. We can get the same advantage if we organize interested parties behind pending proposed legislation. . . . It will then be Forsythe's job to organize the private welfare organizations [in support of the legislation] . . .

Gray now knew how it all worked. After the Democrats' victorious 1958 congressional elections, Eisenhower had been afraid the new Congress might return and pressure him for more federal spending, which he feared would increase inflation. Through Gray's office, Eisenhower "directed a massive appeal for public support, centered around his budget." Gray and his staff arranged luncheon meetings with the heads of national associations and organizations. The criteria used in determining who to invite? "Is their mailing list long enough to be worthwhile."[38]

Labor Unions, of course, were not invited. Instead, the Institute of Life Insurance, the National Association of Life Underwriters, the American Farm Bureau, the National Retail Merchants Association, the National Association of Manufacturers, the Kiwanis International, and hundreds of other special-interest business and civic groups joined in at their own expense for mailings, newspaper advertising, and lobbying on behalf of the White House. When the new Congress convened, they were inundated with letters and telegrams in support of Eisenhower's cause. Gray's only criticism of the effort was that it was not sustained.

All through the Eisenhower administration, besides his job and his speeches, Gray maintained a hectic social calendar. Bradley Patterson remembered his dating Honey Bear Warren, one of then Supreme Court Chief Justice Earl Warren's daughters. Gray's Georgetown roommate, Elton Hailey, said Gray came very close to marriage. Hailey recalled that Gray was seriously dating a staff member to a congressman from Texas. "He was pretty close at one point," Hailey explained, "but she married somebody else and that seemed to upset him a little bit for a while." At this point in his life, Gray's closest sustained relationship with a woman was with his mother. Their closeness never diminished. She would visit him in Washington, and he would go to Hastings whenever possible. During 1959, Gray went to New York to see his mother off on a European vacation on the *Queen Elizabeth*.

After Sherman Adams left, there was a dramatic change in personalities and procedures at the White House. His replacement, General Wilton B. Persons, was less interested in administrative details. He had served for many years in congressional relations and that continued to occupy his attention. Cabinet and staff meetings became more and more infrequent, and Persons often ignored Gray's reports on follow-up items that needed attention. "I think subjects of the cabinet were of less and less interest. The meetings were a little bit less frequent. The whole sense of initiative in the administration—taking initiative on things, I think diminished some," Bradley Patterson remembered.

Toward the end of the second term, Eisenhower's popularity was fading, and he was losing interest in the presidency, turning more and more authority over to Vice President Richard Nixon. Many of Eisenhower's top assistants had left the lame-duck presidency. Those who remained were dubbed "undistinguished" and "not a stable of giants."[39]

Those left at the White House were preoccupied in 1959 and 1960 with Richard Nixon's bid to succeed Eisenhower. Gray greatly admired Nixon, and had made friends with his secretary, Rose Mary Woods, when he worked as Eisenhower's Appointments Secretary and the two had routinely coordinated scheduling.[40] In March 1960, Gray flew with Nixon for a speech at the Nebraska Founders' Day in Lincoln. In his efforts to support Nixon's 1960 election campaign, Gray emphasized in his speeches that Nixon had presided over 11 percent of the Eisenhower administration cabinet meetings and 26 out of 217 National Security Council meetings, when Eisenhower was either ill or out of the country.[41] Gray explained to his audiences that he knew what he was talking about because he observed Nixon at Cabinet meetings where he sat diagonally across the table from the Vice President.

Gray called Nixon the "most-experienced" and the "best-qualified" candidate ever to run for the Presidency of the United States.[42] "I came to Washington not liking Richard Nixon," Gray wrote in his memoirs. "I had no reason for not liking him. I had simply joined the large group of my fellow citizens who were swept up in a cliché of the day . . . that had succeeded where smear attempts had failed—'I don't like Dick Nixon but don't know why.' "[43] But after joining the Eisenhower administration, Gray's opinion of Richard Nixon almost instantaneously changed. "In the following years I came to know Nixon personally. I had increasing opportunities to view him in action, and my list grew long with reasons for supporting him as Eisenhower's successor."[44]

Gray was convinced that Senator Henry Cabot Lodge and Governor Nelson Rockefeller had little chance of defeating Nixon for the GOP Presidential nomination. Gray admired Nixon's political astuteness and his willingness to play hardball with opponents. Nixon, who excelled at red baiting, was a dramatic contrast to Eisenhower's "people over politics" approach. After Sherman Adams left, Richard Nixon became Gray's political mentor. Gray praised Nixon's "humility and warmth," adjectives rarely used to describe Nixon before or since.

Gray continued to travel heavily in 1960. He gave numerous speeches around the country, including as many stops in Nebraska and Hastings as possible. Gray has estimated that he gave three hundred speeches and traveled over one hundred thousand miles during his White House years. The Chairman of the Republican National Committee explained, "Since Bob's title was a new one and few people knew exactly what it stood for, we could book him as a White House assistant, presidential aide, or associate of the Cabinet depending on what was requested."[45]

Since 1960 was a campaign year, Gray's speeches became more and more political. His target this time was John F. Kennedy. Gray said "the nation doesn't want a bobby-sox idol leading the Free World. Americans want a man of full, mature, and seasoned judgment. 'Little wonder a movement has started in Washington this week to back Jack Kennedy for President—in 1976.' "[46]

Gray described Nixon as "Washington's indefatigable man" and his campaign " . . . as smoothly synchronized as the finest watch, and as powerful as a bulldozer, running at full throttle.''[47] On the campaign trail, Gray quoted Nixon as saying, "Both parties want more and more, better and better things for America and Americans, but we Republicans recognize that only a socialistic form of government attempts to provide these services from a federal bureaucracy.''[48] It was Richard Nixon's definition of Republicanism. Years later, Gray would blame the loss of the campaign on this definition. He thought it was a losing strategy to say Republicans could provide more for less than the Democrats.

On May 1, 1960, President Eisenhower learned from the CIA that a U-2 spy plane had disappeared over the Soviet Union. Within a week, Khrushchev was using the downed pilot and plane in a propaganda effort against the United States. The recent thaw in U.S.–Soviet relations was over. The White House chose Gray to speak out on these growing national security concerns. His speech on May 23, 1960 was not the usual political variety designed to stir the Republican faithful. This time it made the Associated Press news wire and was carried in newspapers around the country. It reflected Gray's increasing involvement with the intelligence community and his knowledge of classified information. "REDS SPY ON EMBASSY, Eisenhower Aide Says" was the headline in the *New York Times*.[49] Gray said in Scottsbluff, Nebraska: "The incredulously rude Khrushchev is the leader of a political philosophy so devious that even the sanctity of the American Embassy in Moscow has not escaped its espionage." This revelation was designed to offset the criticism Eisenhower was taking in the world press for the U-2 espionage incident.[50]

Gray's writings on the 1960 campaign demonstrate a penchant for putting the best face on things, even at the cost of stretching the truth a bit, or a lot as when Gray wrote in his memoirs of Nixon's relationship with members of the press. Amazingly, Gray maintained that Nixon expertly handled the news media during the 1960 Presidential campaign. "Nearly every reporter can cite an instance to prove Nixon was one of the most obliging men in national news. . . . Nixon worked hard to change some of the deep-dyed prejudices harbored against him by many members of the fourth estate. In the process he learned a lot about a professional newsman's problems.''[51] In reality, Nixon despised the press and did everything he could to avoid them. His poor treatment of the media contributed to the much less critical coverage of Senator Kennedy.

Inside the White House, Gray learned to evaluate policy based on public relations criteria. Ezra Taft Benson was Eisenhower's unpopular Agriculture Secretary. Gray wrote in his memoirs that he thought Benson should have resigned for the good of the party in 1960, because by the time it became apparent that his replacement "was as hamstrung as Benson in solving the problems," the election would be over. But Gray did not communicate his views to Benson. On the contrary, Gray would phone the besieged

Agriculture Secretary to tell him he had just returned from Nebraska where a farmer had told him how much he liked Benson.[52]

Although Richard Nixon was pleased that Benson supported Rockefeller over him in 1960, it fell to Gray to prevent Benson from ruining Eisenhower's public endorsement of Nixon. Since it was difficult to get to the hotel for the endorsement because of the large crowds, Benson was the only cabinet official who made it with his wife. The other members of the Cabinet "gallantly" passed Mrs. Benson to the front of the line with her husband following. "At the last moment the Vice President and Mrs. Nixon emerged from the hotel to find the valued moment of endorsement by the popular Eisenhower about to be soured by the fact they would be sharing the limelight with the politically leprous Benson," Gray wrote.

Nixon turned to Gray and asked, " 'Bob, are we in protocol order?' This is the order in which Cabinet officers are ranked, primarily for social purposes, according to the date of the creation of their department. I replied that we were not, but that it would only take a moment. The shift . . . moved them [the Bensons] out of camera range," Gray remembered.[53] (Twenty years later Richard Nixon would be the one who Gray worried would appear in GOP photo opportunities).

Gray helped Nixon in other ways. In June 1960, Gray gathered from all of the federal agencies "the Accomplishments of the Eisenhower–Nixon Republican Administration" for use in the campaign. Only in the final weeks of the campaign, with Kennedy in the lead by a paper-thin margin, did President Eisenhower actively campaign for Richard Nixon. Gray took to the airwaves to explain the situation. On ABC's "College New Conference," Gray said that Eisenhower's late entry had been planned since the Republican convention the previous summer and was not a result of Kennedy's lead in the polls. Gray said those polls did not reflect the current situation and that he believed Nixon was now ahead.[54]

On election day, 1960, Gray's job was to call the members of the Cabinet to invite them to the President's suite at the Sheraton-Park Hotel to watch the returns. Nixon's narrow defeat was a bitter experience for those present. "Now it was over. And the time for cleaning out, sweeping up, and moving on was at hand," Gray wrote.[55] ". . . The crushing nausea of defeat had settled over the White House."[56]

Gray took away some valuable lessons from the election. He felt that Nixon should not have debated Kennedy, because it gave Kennedy exposure and credibility that he needed at the time much more than Nixon, that Nixon should have focused more on the national debt and opposed increased government spending as his key issue, and that Nixon should have kept the offensive and not tried to defend the mistakes of the Eisenhower administration. He should have hammered away on Kennedy's absenteeism from the Senate, instead of defending Eisenhower's golf outings. He should have emphasized tough leadership rather than defending criticism of the loss of

American prestige around the world. He should have attacked Kennedy about his wealth, instead of defending himself with statements like, "I know what it is to be poor." He should have forced Kennedy to admit to health problems.[57]

Gray has said that his public relations efforts for Nixon would have been four pictures. Two positive ones of Nixon: one with him lecturing Khrushchev and the other with his two daughters eating hot dogs at a baseball game. And two negative ones of Kennedy: one at a Kennedy rally with the sign "WELCOME WALTER REUTHER *AND* JACK KENNEDY" and the other of Kennedy in his top hat at a Harvard reunion with the caption "Senator Kennedy ponders the farm problem."[58]

As others were cleaning out their desks, looking for jobs, briefing their successors, and preparing to leave the White House, Gray was busy dictating his memoirs to his White House secretary.[59] He was ready to cash in. Gray wrote about the personal details of Eisenhower's life—his obsession with golf, his swimming in bad weather, the planting of a tree at the White House, the picking out of gifts for foreign dignitaries. Many others from the Eisenhower administration, including the President himself, eventually wrote their memoirs. But all of them were published long after the administration ended. "A little distance from events and a little deference to those still in office or merely still alive used to be thought in order," Meg Greenfield wrote about government memoirists prior to the Kennedy administration.[60] In the early 1960s, it was considered tasteless and opportunistic to turn around inside information so quickly.

During the transition, according to *Eighteen Acres Under Glass,* Gray met legendary Washington insider Clark Clifford, who was handling the transition arrangements for Kennedy. Gray grew to admire Clifford as a Washington fixer and would soon pattern his career after him, and years later, work with him on various projects.

Before the last Cabinet meeting, Gray suggested: "It would seem likely that the Eisenhower Cabinet sessions would end with some exchanges about our efforts together and their significance as a legacy to the future." Unfortunately, the legacy did not last very long. The new president termed formal Cabinet meetings like Eisenhower's "a waste of time." The last White House dinner was for Eisenhower's "official family," and Gray said it "was a party to end all parties." It ended with everyone singing "Bless this house, O Lord, we pray."

With the end of the Eisenhower administration, Gray's initiation into Washington politics was complete. He had been at the right hand of the powerful, watched power evaporate practically overnight with Sherman Adams, worked with the press and learned how it operated, made impressive inroads into Washington society, knew more about the personal history of powerful Washingtonians than most, had developed a grass-roots organization around the country and had contacts throughout the government, both on Capitol Hill and the Executive Branch, the international community and the private sector.

"Bob had an excellent training, obviously, in public affairs, but he is a very smooth guy. . . . He'll charm the shoes off of you," Bradley Patterson said. Elton Hailey did not remember Gray being particularly downcast as his tenure in the White House ended. "I didn't detect anything like that. He was always planning down the way. Always looking ahead." Between the time Richard Nixon lost and the last Cabinet meeting, Gray had lined up another job. This time it was in an area where "he had a tremendous amount of ability . . ."[61]

4

"THE HONEST LOBBYIST"

Beyond 1960 I plan to continue actively in politics, as a private citizen if nothing else. You can't be exposed to national politics and suddenly withdraw from activity.

Robert Gray[1]

The 1950s had been tough on Washington. The euphoria of victory in World War II was shattered by the Korean War, and the demagoguery of Joe McCarthy. The last half of the fifties featured an aging Dwight Eisenhower presiding over a country that seemed to have lost a little of its national drive. Always considered a sleepy, southern town—vendors by the Capitol and the White House still had thriving sales of confederate flags—toward the end of the decade the city began to awaken. Like other cities around the country, Washington ripped out its streetcars and widened the roads for buses and cars. Labor Unions began building their headquarters buildings, the most powerful, like the Teamsters, located theirs at the foot of Capitol Hill.[2] The American Federation of Labor built its temple a few blocks up from the White House, a not so gentle reminder to the occupant about the biggest voting block of all.

Four new bridges crossed the increasingly polluted Potomac River; lights lit up the Washington Monument at night; neon signs began to proliferate. The main tourist attractions were the White House, the Capitol, the Bureau of Engraving, the marble monuments, and the Smithsonian. There was no Hirshorn Gallery, no Kennedy Center for the Performing Arts, no Air and Space or American History or East Wing Museums, few art galleries. Restaurants were not only bad, almost none offered any degree of ethnicity. The largely African–American city was still governed by White-appointed commissioners, who answered to Congressional committees dominated by Southerners.

The 1960 election ushered in a young President determined to energize the country. The emergence of Camelot on the Potomac, of America's "best and brightest" taking the reins of government to romantically push the country into the space age, excited the city. John Kennedy had joked that Washington was a city of "northern hospitality and southern efficiency." Kennedy's ascension to the Presidency would bring a more dynamic ethos to the capital. Washington was a town about to lead the country in massive change.

The defeat of Richard Nixon meant that Robert Gray had to find a job in the private sector. There was speculation in the press that Gray would return to Nebraska to seek public office. Why else, journalists speculated, did he return to the state so often to make speeches and attend Republican party events? Gray told friends he might run for governor in 1960; he didn't. To a reporter he confided that he might ultimately run for office, but he had no immediate plans. Running for political office in Nebraska would mean moving back to the state, and Gray had no intention of leaving Washington.[3]

In a written interview for this book, Gray elaborated on why he chose not to run for office. "In early 1961 several [people] from Nebraska flattered me with the suggestion that I return to the state and run for governor. I considered it briefly, rejected the thought for three reasons.

I originally had come to Washington not because of an assignment but in search of one. From my first business visits to the Capital I had sensed the fast pulse where assignments had the potential for making vast change, where fascinating people with an eclectic mix of interests were making real contributions. I did not catch 'Potomac Fever' in Washington, I brought it with me.

If I had returned to Nebraska, *if* I had been elected to the governorship, and *if* a vacancy had occurred in the congressional delegation, I could then have appointed myself to fill the vacancy and returned to Washington. But quite apart from that being a shabby reason to ask Nebraskans to give their votes, I already was in the city of my dreams and did not need a circuitous route to get here.

There were two other considerations. I had been in government service for six years and the governorship of Nebraska would have required further financial sacrifice. Further, by then I was heavily involved with Hill and Knowlton's extensive client mix, had found my job gave me the varietal mix and peripheral political involvement.

After more than six years in government in three of the most exciting of White House jobs, my interest in appointitive office was well stated. I have thought it would be a challenge to be an ambassador and certainly would have sought a nomination if I could have served such a posting from Washington, D.C."

Bryce Harlow was a politically savvy member of the Eisenhower administration and a good friend of Gray's.[4] Harlow had helped create Eisenhower's congressional liaison operation, eventually heading it, and remained a close confidant of the President's even during his retirement in Gettysburg. "I will bet you that Bryce was the most popular government official in Washington before he left government," Clifford Guest, who worked at Hill and Knowlton's Washington office, recalled.[5] Both Hill and Knowlton, the international public relations firm, and Proctor and Gamble, a Hill and Knowlton client, offered Harlow jobs.

Heading Proctor and Gamble's Washington office was the better job, so Harlow turned down Hill and Knowlton (H&K), but recommended Gray to them instead. "H&K felt that a man with his experience and wide acquaintances would be a valuable asset, so they hired him," Guest said. "When he came in, of course, he didn't bring any [clients] with him at that time. He came cold from the White House. But he was instrumental in picking up additional accounts, but that came slowly."

The job was a great break for Gray. There were only a couple weeks left before he had to leave the White House and he needed somewhere to go. On Wednesday, January 11, 1961, Hill and Knowlton announced that Gray would be joining the firm as a vice president and director of its Washington office on inauguration day, January 21, 1961. He was replacing Avery McBee, who was very well-liked within the firm. "Absolutely one of the nicest," Guest remembered. The office would never be the same again.

Like Gray, other Eisenhower appointees were scrambling for jobs at the end of the administration. Prior to working at the Treasury Department during the Eisenhower administration, Charls Walker had been an economics professors and a banker in Texas. He had developed an area of expertise and left Treasury to head the American Bankers Association. Gray, on the other hand, had not developed a specialty prior to coming to Washington. Despite his business background, he was not recognized as an expert in any particular field. Hill and Knowlton was not hiring him for his knowledge. They were hiring him because of his connections and charm. They were hiring him for his influence. In Washington, D.C., these characteristics proved more important to success than in Hastings, Nebraska.

When Gray reported to his new offices at Hill and Knowlton, he no longer received hundreds of telephone calls and letters a day, or dozens of invitations to social events or speaking engagements. The White House insider was now on the outside. The new Kennedy administration did not have much use for conservative Republicans, which is exactly how Gray described himself to the press. Now Gray had to maintain his political and social contacts while working from the outside to elect another Republican to the presidency in the next election.

Gray had never worked in public relations, but no one had to teach him. "Actually, he had an instinct. It was natural," Guest said. Like a preacher called to the ministry, public relations was Gray's calling. It reflected the essence of his personality. He knew intrinsically what to do. For example, one of his first requirements was a limousine, not just for luxurious, convenient transportation, but, more importantly, to enhance his image.

But Gray did not yet have what every successful PR man needed—a background with and knowledge of the press. He did not socialize with members of the media or know many of them by name or know what they covered or what their interests were. The people he knew were politicians, government officials, and socialites. A good PR man knew the media, in detail. As Larry Speakes, who worked for H&K, explained, "In the PR business . . . it is important that you know reporters, you know who deals in specific areas, you learn how they work, what they need to do their jobs, what kind of information they need, who it is good for them to talk to; and then when you have a client that has that problem, then you know that reporter, he trusts you, you trust him, and you could call and say, 'You know, Joe, I know you're working on this story and we represent so and so. I wondered if you mind sitting down and hearing him out on this subject.' And they'd say, 'Well, sure, yeah, we've known each other for a long time. I would be glad to listen to him, bring him over.' If you don't know the reporter, maybe you wouldn't get the same treatment. . . . When it boils down to it, there are a dozen people that cover your business on a regular basis, and so you get to know them."

On a personal level, it was lobbying, not public relations, where Gray felt he could be most effective. He knew almost all of the players on Capitol Hill and throughout the executive branch. He could get appointments to see them and present a client's case as well as anyone. That would be much more fun and effective than sitting in an office drafting press releases, monitoring the *Federal Register* and various trade publications, or going to the press club to have a few drinks with reporters. Gray was much more the exclusive F-Street-Club type.[6]

But first Gray had to convince John Hill, the founder of Hill and Knowlton, to let him lobby.

Hill and Knowlton, Inc. (H&K), the world's largest public relations firm, started in Cleveland, Ohio, in April 1927. John W. Hill, a former newspaper reporter and columnist and financial editor of a steel-trade paper, was the founder and the guiding force for almost fifty years. "He was a great man. Physically, a husky man; Indiana farmboy–type. Never finished college," George Worden, who worked with Hill, said.[7] "John was a very, very thoughtful man. High integrity. Tremendous integrity. . . . The staff liked him and were loyal to him."

Up until the 1920s, most American businesses paid little attention to the media.[8] To them, press coverage was not important to profits. In Cleveland, that indifference changed in 1927 when a stock fight at a steel company resulted in the loser shooting himself. The banker who was handling the public stock offering felt the suicide might queer the financing deal, so he asked John Hill to go with him to the *Cleveland Plain Dealer*, for whom Hill used to work, and the wire services, and convince them that the suicide did not indicate financial problems for the company.

After Hill succeeded with the press and the refinancing deal went through, the banker offered Hill $500 a month to handle press relations and helped him recruit other clients. Hill was in business. By 1933, Hill, with little competition, represented prominent financiers, Standard Oil of Ohio, banks, mining companies, railroads, manufacturers and the future head of U.S. Steel.

Don Knowlton was the public relations director for one of Hill's client banks in Cleveland when the bank closed because of the Depression in 1933. Hill invited Knowlton to join him as a partner in his "corporate publicity" business. But it was New York, not Cleveland, that interested Hill. "One of my ardent ambitions was to have an office in New York," Hill wrote.[9] New York, after all, was the corporate and financial center of America and the communications hub of the country. All Hill needed was an East-coast client. When the American Iron and Steel Institute, the industry's trade association in New York, hired Hill to handle their public relations, he opened an office there.[10]

"Knowlton didn't like New York and he didn't want to leave Cleveland and he didn't," Worden explained. In the mid-1940s Hill turned his interests in the Cleveland office over to Knowlton and made the New York office into a new company separate from Cleveland called Hill and Knowlton, Inc. "Nobody's met Don Knowlton," Worden said.

John Hill expanded his company with major national accounts. He succeeded because he truly admired and respected businessmen and abhorred big government, "the welfare state," and labor unions. After the Depression and the New Deal, Hill convinced his clients that increased government regulation and the strength of labor unions were not a temporary setback, but a reflection of long-term public distrust and hatred of American corporations. He convinced them that public opinion had to be changed or more government interference lay ahead. His solution was to let "organized public relations" work as "a shield and a spear" to defend or attack the interest of American corporations.[11]

Hill and Knowlton became one of the few truly national public relations firms; its job was to change the public's view of big business as evil, thus making it more difficult for hostile politicians to act against his clients' interests. For example, the Aircraft Industries Association (AIA, now Aerospace), was one of H&K's largest clients. After World War II, production of military airplanes dropped from over 95,000 in 1944 to little more than 1,400 in 1946. H&K worked to change national policy to convince the public and the President that increased funding for military aircraft was necessary despite the end of the war. Hill wrote, "The nation would be running a frightening risk to allow its air strength to evaporate."[12] Hill was a pioneer in plucking the emotional string of national defense, the heart of American patriotism.

H&K, along with AIA and the Air Force, developed a public relations campaign that fanned aircraft executives out across the country armed with speeches and brochures promoting their new slogan, "Air Power Is Peace Power," organized veterans groups and aircraft labor unions to support increased spending, worked with newspapers and columnists, and played upon cold war fears of the Soviet menace. The result was the Congress voted to increase funding for aircraft procurement and research and development programs, thus ensuring the Air Force as a fundamental strategic force. John Hill credited their efforts with preventing U.S. forces from being "blown off the Korean peninsula without air cover" a few years later.[13] He termed H&K's public relations program "the type of broad national campaign in the public interest that show public relations at its best."[14] In fact, what Hill's campaign demonstrated was that big business could use public relations to get politicians to vote their way.

Thus, almost from the start, H&K public relations efforts were a major player in influencing Washington, in this case also national security, but in an indirect way. Instead of directly advocating policy—to buy more aircraft—the PR campaign explained the dire situation of the aircraft industries and their importance to national defense. It is a fine distinction. But never did anyone from Hill and Knowlton approach a member of Congress asking for support for more military aircraft. Hill did not like to get directly involved in politics.

John Hill ran a very conservative company. He saw himself and his employees as public relations counselors, much like lawyers are legal counselors. Hill did not simply take instructions from his clients and put out press releases. He genuinely tried to advise them. If a company was getting bad publicity because of bad policy, Hill would press for the policy to be reviewed. He "advocated forthrightness" and "fighting suppression," Edward Barrett, then the Dean of the Graduate School of Journalism at Columbia University, wrote in the preface to one of Hill's book, *The Making of a Public Relations Man*. "Hill would advise them on what they should do. That's the counseling part of all this, and he was a genuine counselor," Worden said.

Hill would not represent just anyone. His clients were always *Fortune* 500 corporations. "He was very selective. Not just anybody could hire him, Hill and Knowlton. He turned down a lot of clients. Too small. . . . We have problems [with] the economy of scale. . . . We were too big, even then, to take small accounts," Worden explained. Hill would turn down clients for other reasons, too. If he did not believe in their cause, or if he felt they wanted to "shade the truth," he would not represent them. "He was a very moral man . . . and if he didn't agree with an issue, he wouldn't represent the firm at all," Worden said. "Integrity and service: that to me always summed up the essence of John Hill's philosophy and which imbued the whole company," Clifford Guest recalled.

Hill opened the Washington, D.C., office in 1946, a few years after the AIA moved its operations to Washington from New York. In public relations, Washington was considered a backwater. No major media were headquartered there. Television was still in its infancy. Many newspapers had Washington bureaus, but they covered politics, and public relations clients were mainly businesses and associations. Like other public relations firms, the Washington office of Hill and Knowlton was very small—only three men in the 1950s. It only had one major client, the AIA, to service. Often New York would forget to include them in meetings. "Here's how unimportant Washington was in those days. . . . We would have meetings of the field offices, as we called them, and we'd forget to invite Washington," Worden said.

With the media headquartered in New York, there was little reason for a large PR contingent in Washington to handle the small newspaper bureaus. In the 1950s, the media were mostly print. TV news was in its infancy.

When Gray took over in Washington, the work of his small staff was very routine, sending out press releases and monitoring the media for items of interest to the clients. Although John Hill wanted a higher political profile in Washington, he considered lobbying a dirty business. "Hill felt that 'lobbying meant booze, blondes, and bribes, and he wanted no part of it," Gray told *Washingtonian* magazine.[15] Almost everyone in the country felt the same way. In the 1960s no one really called himself a lobbyist. People were always consultants or lawyers or in "government relations." There had been enough scandals involving lobbyists to give the profession a seedy image.

Hill had a more personal reason to be leery of lobbying. In the mid-1950s, oil and gas interests hired H&K for a PR program opposing federal regulation of natural gas. A separate organization was established to lobby Congress for legislation prohibiting regulation. In 1956, Senator Case of South Dakota stated publicly that two lawyer-lobbyists representing oil interests had contributed $2,500 to his campaign, expecting, in return, his support for the legislation opposing regulation. A major scandal erupted and outraged the nation. A Senate Committee began investigating. They called the president of H&K to testify. H&K was cleared of any wrongdoing, but it was an experience John Hill did not want repeated.

Hill believed that lobbyists or "influence peddlers" who called themselves public relations counselors hurt the image of the business. He also disliked "a specialist in getting names mentioned in society gossip columns."[16] He worked hard to promote a positive image of his profession, and did not want the scandal-tainted occupation dragging down what he considered honest public relations.

But Gray convinced Hill that lobbying could be handled honorably and honestly, and that it would benefit their clients. Eventually Hill let Gray register as a lobbyist. George Worden remembered what Gray told Hill: "I can add a dimension here to your business that you don't have. I know everybody. I know the whole White House scene. I also know Congress . . . and I think it would be a valuable service to offer your clients. That's how all this started."

This combination of lobbying and public relations may have been born of necessity—Gray's lack of specific expertise meant he almost had to tailor a job to fit his talents. But in doing so Gray hit upon a formula that would revolutionize the way Washington debated public policy, and ultimately fundamentally alter the way policy is made. "Bob Gray is really almost a pioneer as far as Washington PR firms are concerned," Larry Speakes said about his former boss.

Before Gray, Washington *public relations* and *lobbying* were two distinct jobs, with two distinct requirements:

Public relations focused mainly on influencing public opinion, the so-called grass roots, in favor of a client's position. Although H&K did not invent "grass roots" pressure, the firm probably used it more often than others. "That was one of his [Gray's] basic ways of operating," according to Clifford Guest.[17]

There are basic techniques some or all of which are employed for almost every client. One of the first tasks a public relations firm does for a new client is to conduct a poll. If the client has identified three problems that need attention, and the PR firm believes three different areas are the real problems, then a poll can help convince the client of the real problems without pitting the PR firm against the client.

In addition, the poll establishes a benchmark so that in a year or so, the PR firm can compare the changes in attitudes and empirically prove what it has done, or not done, for the client on issues that are often very intangible. Additional polling identifies the strengths and weaknesses of the client's position in the public's mind so the PR firm can draft the next year's goals. It helps a PR firm determine who to target—who are the groups that disagree with or have no opinion about their client's position that need to be changed. In the past, polling was contracted to outside firms to maintain a degree of independence and integrity. Today, the PR and the polling firms are often owned by the same company.

In 1960 the American Association of Advertising Agencies hired H&K "to correct what was described as a 'deep-seated emotional distrust of the ethics, believability and taste of advertising.' "[18] What H&K recommended to the association to correct its image provides good examples of many of the techniques it still uses today. First, it told the advertisers not to use advertisements to try to help their image, a natural first choice. The poll had indicated that only a small group of opinion-makers, not the general public, were leery of their ethics and full scale advertising might draw attention to a problem most did not know existed, might be confused with other advertising campaigns that were ongoing, and might weaken advertising's position with some of its media supporters.

What H&K recommended was first, that the association start a new, "thought-provoking" magazine to be mailed to prominent opinion-makers across the country. Second, the association should work more closely with editors and writers "who influence thinking on advertising." This included "closer contact with intellectual publications, cooperation with textbook authors and a flow of reference materials to schools, colleges and major public libraries."[19] Third, the association's best speakers should branch out from speaking only to advertising-interested audiences and to appeal to a broader cross section of nonadvertising groups.

Fourth, the association should sponsor a pilot advertising seminar at a major university. The university would act as both a host and a cosponsor. "Participants will be faculty members from other universities. They will hear and discuss the story of advertising as presented to them" by members of the association. The seminar would be a hot-house for studying the thoughts of the educators and the reaction of the students to the advertising position. Fifth, a further in depth study of a sample of "thought-leaders" in sixteen cities should be taken to determine why opinion-makers have negative attitudes toward advertisers. Finally, of course, the association should start "aggressive" publicity of what was considered its good side— the association's self-policing program—about which most were unaware.

Who were the opinion-makers and why did they dislike advertisers? Religious leaders said advertisers instilled false, materialistic values—that it was wrong for advertisers to lead people to believe that material goods would lead to happiness. Educators said that television promoted products to children and children sat around watching "junky, time-wasting" television instead of either playing outdoors, reading, or doing their homework. Since advertisers demanded the highest audiences, they played to children's lowest common denominator instead of promoting uplifting values. Editors and writers said advertising abused the air waves with stupid, irritating commercials. Government officials were concerned about false claims and promises by advertisers. The PR program was designed to change their attitudes so that their views would positively influence public opinion in favor of advertisers.

Lobbying, on the other hand, concentrated one key person on only a few key politicians or bureaucrats. It is a more personal, individualistic, concentrated effort to try to influence a handful of people to a policy position rather than hundreds or thousands. Lobbyists jobs are to influence Washington's minds. At best they trade in talk. Every piece of legislation, when not actually drafted by lobbyists, is affected in some way by them. They represent every imaginable interest from automobiles to zippers, and they all are trying to either change or maintain the status quo. They want either to get government to do something differently or to prevent it from changing the way it is currently operating.

A "good" lobbyist was someone who was considered a specialist in a certain area and who established a reputation for being an honest expert who provided balanced, reliable information. Before the growth in the General Accounting Office or the Library of Congress or the Office of Technology Assessment or the myriad other agencies set up to provide Congress with nonbiased, in-depth information, the legislators had very few other resources from which to obtain information on how a piece of legislation might affect a certain industry except through a lobbyist. In a 1958 *Cosmopolitan* magazine article, a lobbyist is quoted as saying, "I can't think how many congressman have told me how indebted they were to me for facts I was paid to dig up for them. Why? The congressman would be completely at the mercy of the damn bureaucrats if it wasn't for us furnishing him with information."[20]

But lobbying also had a long history of scandal. For example, in 1913, Colonel Martin M. Mulhall, a lobbyist for the National Association of Manufacturers, said that he had paid off a number of congressmen to do what they were told. By the mid-1940s, the Congress tried to curb criticism of the effects of lobbying by enacting the Federal Regulation of Lobbying Act of 1946, which required any person or group whose primary purpose was to influence legislation on Capitol Hill to register and file quarterly reports of their receipts and expenditures. But by the 1950s, not much had changed.

"We were infants in the 1950s. Absolute infants. Those were the days still when people could walk up to the Hill with a plain white envelope with money in it. . . . Look what happened to Spiro Agnew," George Worden said. Marvin Liebman, then a lobbyist for Nationalist China, agreed, "In my book . . . I was talking about the people I gave little white envelopes to. And there was cash. . . . We used to hand out greenbacks."[21] When Americans thought of lobbyists, they conjured up the image of a man buying a weak congressman a few drinks (booze) and providing him with sexual partners (blondes) and cash (bribes) in exchange for his vote.

In 1955, even though there were thousands of individuals and organizations lobbying Congress, only 579 individuals (a little more than one for every elected representative) and 316 organizations bothered to register. The most prominent lobbyists in Washington were lawyers. The most powerful lawyers were former Roosevelt and Truman administration officials—Abe Fortas, Clark Clifford, and Thomas "Tommy the Cork" Corcoran.

When Gray combined the public relations staple, grass-roots campaigning, with Washington lobbying, as a matter of routine in one office, the effects on the American political systems could not yet be realized.[22] This alliance between lobbying and public relations over the following two decades grew in sophistication and effectiveness, eventually forever changing the way America is governed. The combination of public pressure with money and individual attention began to gel into a permanent structure of individual firms and special interest groups, all gravitating to Washington and moving the political power base farther away from the voters and the political parties, to a group of unelected, unregulated, and unaccountable executives who dramatically and daily influence government. The increased importance of television for basic information, the changes in campaign financing, and the growth in government eventually strengthened the control of this group to the point that today it rivals the power of the traditional legislative, executive, judicial, and media power bases.

During Gray's first week on the job, he created a small firestorm in the press. It was not a good omen for a new public relations executive. *McCalls* magazine issued a press release on the article, "Sherman Adams: The Inside Story," on January 23, only three days after Eisenhower had left the White House. The article was excerpted from Gray's memoirs, which he had been writing the last few months of the administration. Before the Eisenhower administration had finished unpacking, Gray, one of "Sherm's boys," was confirming some of the press's worst fears about Sherman Adams and the administration.

Although the article was in some ways complimentary of Adams, the aggregate effect was devastating. Gray included every personal detail he knew about Sherman Adams, from his famous temper to how much rent Adams paid, to how he awakened to classical music he had selected the night before. He said that Adams's "frigid personality" became buoyant and "good-natured" only during Eisenhower's three illnesses. "Adams, supremely confident in his ability to run the government without interference from the front office, enjoyed the chance to do so." He quoted Adams's secretary as calling him "that impossible beast," and repeatedly mentioned Adams's foul language or "woodsman's vocabulary." Noting that Gray was now in public relations, the *New York Times* said, "Gray pictures the former New Hampshire governor as a humorless and impenetrable taskmaster who was often critical of President Eisenhower and whose downfall in the wake of disclosure of his relations with Bernard Goldfine was traceable to his own penury."

Sherman Adams, who had been run out of town by his enemies, was now being skewered by one of his own. Gray did not limit his criticism to Adams, saying that even President Eisenhower himself joined in the "petty jealousies and plays for power" of the White House staff after Adams was destroyed by the Goldfine scandal. "The President joined in this embarrassing side-stepping by dealing more exclusively on policy matters with members of the

Cabinet and by using less frequently his phrase of five years: 'Check it with Sherm.' "

The magazine article corroborated criticism that Eisenhower was a do-nothing president and that Sherman Adams was really running the White House. "Among the things for which the President had little taste were politics, patronage, and much of domestic affairs. Further, he left to Adams actions that involved the backbreaking volume of tending to details, and the unpopular job of saying no . . ." After Sherman Adams left the White House, Gray wrote, Eisenhower took more interest in the presidency and worked harder.

"Ex-Cabinet Secretary Says President Was Shielded From Major Problems," the *New York Times* subhead read. Gray wrote that Eisenhower responded too late to the 1957–58 recession and to Sputnik, the Soviet satellite, because Sherman Adams kept certain people and papers from the President. The press release said "this was because of Mr. Eisenhower's 'desire to be protected from unpleasant problems.' "[23] In the lead, the *New York Times* said: "Former President Dwight D. Eisenhower was prevented from acting promptly on many major problems because Sherman Adams kept them under wraps until they reached crisis proportions . . ."[24]

Gray modified the line from his speeches that only the best qualified were selected for important government jobs. The reality, he said, was that politics was really "the major consideration." Similarly, contrary to all his "hardest-working president" speeches, Gray wrote that Sherman Adams grew impatient with Eisenhower's leisurely lifestyle:

'Send it up to the Hill and give it to Hagerty for announcement,' he once told me, after I had reported our work completed on an impending appointment matter. I replied, 'We'll have to wait until morning, Governor. The President will not be in his office this afternoon.' To which he snorted in exasperation, 'Good God, is he playing golf again?'

Other members of the Eisenhower administration were furious with Gray for what they considered a tremendous breach of faith. "I'll bet that Ike, after he reads that, will recall that friendly letter he wrote Bob Gray when the old Administration went out," a reporter was quoted as saying in the Omaha *World-Herald*.[25]

The pressure on Gray forced him to take action. In March 1961, Gray flew to California to apologize to Eisenhower for the article. When his memoirs were published on May 18, 1962, they did not contain the negative references to Eisenhower, the names of many of the others mentioned derogatorily, or the negative Sherman Adams quotes.[26] Gray explained in a written interview that the final manuscript was approved by Bryce Harlow on Eisenhower's behalf, and that the magazine excerpt was based on an earlier draft. It would not be the last time Gray edited history.

In February 1961, Gray told the Associated Press that he would be returning to Nebraska in the spring to write his second book and to remain "personally active" in the state. He explained that by spring H&K would be opening an Omaha office and he would be sharing his time between the two offices and would keep his legal residence in Nebraska. His next book was going to be about how to elect conservatives to office. It would be a "how to win" book for conservatives that was supposed to be published in time for the 1962 congressional elections. But the book and the Omaha office never materialized.

Also in February, David Sarnoff, the head of RCA (which owned NBC) announced that Gray had been elected a trustee and vice president of the Heritage Foundation, a conservative think tank in Washington. (Sarnoff was the foundation president.) Gray continued speaking to groups as often as possible, especially in Hastings and other Nebraska towns. In March 1961, his mother, Marie, was named Nebraska State Mother of the Year. Gray had helped put together his mother's winning brochure. Marie Gray said an even greater thrill than receiving the award was her son Robert arranging a conference call, a novelty at the time, with her and all four of her children to offer their congratulations.[27]

Continuing his heavy social schedule in Washington, Gray soon became something like the male equivalent of Emily Post. In January 1962, the second excerpt from Gray's White House memoirs appeared in *McCalls*. It was called, "How Washington Society Goes to a Party." In this article Gray recounts the various kinds of social functions in Washington from Embassy to White House dinners, taking great pain to describe the crystal, china, silver, tablecloths, candles, and flowers. He discussed in detail seating charts and fingerbowls, when to arrive, when to leave and in what order, when to sit and when to stand:

> . . . Men should avoid predinner conversation with the ladies they are to escort to the table. . . . After showing his partner to her place and seating her, he sits beside her, and they engage in concentrated conversation . . . keeping the hostess in their peripheral vision to see when she 'turns the table,' their signal to begin a conversation with the diner on the other side, during the fish course.

The article revived his status as a bachelor in demand around town. "A Washington bachelor can find full-time social occupation," Gray wrote.[28] He was "one of Washington's extra men" whom a "plucky" hostess could call at the last minute when a husband could not make it "so the table will not be thrown out of balance." The Associated Press ran an article and photograph: "BEING BACHELOR IN CAPITAL ALMOST FULL-TIME JOB, WRITES BOB GRAY." The article called Gray "a continuing pet of Washington hostesses.'' When asked what he believed was most important for a wife, Gray responded: ''When I was in college I'd probably have put appearance first in order. . . . When you are a bachelor for awhile, you get more attracted to the solid qualities.''[29]

In May, when Gray's book, *Eighteen Acres Under Glass*, was finally published, he went to Nebraska to promote it. The cover was a photograph of the White House (which is surrounded by eighteen acres) with a magnifying glass over it. The Omaha *World-Herald* called him ''a champion of conservatism.'' He told the newspaper that Republicans had lost the 1960 presidential election because they had ''compromised their conservative principles.''[30]

Looking ahead to the 1964 presidential election, Gray predicted that a conservative ''should be powerful enough to demand the Number Two spot on the ticket if not the Presidential nominee.''[31] Commenting on current politics, Gray said, ''From a public relations standpoint he's [President Kennedy's] a wonder man. His willingness to make jokes about points where he is most vulnerable is very wise.'' When asked about medicare, then still a legislative proposal, Gray responded, ''If it were not for continued promises of Government handouts, people would take care of themselves.''

Gray had no intention of staying out of politics. He told the Associated Press, ''I don't think I'll ever stop being a politician.''[32] After all, he owed much of his success to breaks politicians had given him. He tied his future to the tails of the conservative wing of the Republican party, a wing closer to his geographical roots and the West than to the Eastern-establishment wing. By 1963 he was actively supporting (''103 percent'') Barry Goldwater for the Republican nomination.[33] He hosted a party for him at the exclusive F Street Club in November, the same place where he would entertain Ronald Reagan after his election in 1980.

A couple of weeks later, President Kennedy was killed in Dallas. Gray had just finished correcting the proofs for his new manuscript four days before the assassination. The book was scheduled for January publication and had already been sold to two magazines for excerpts. Unfortunately, the book was not about how to elect conservatives as he had said, but was a critique of the Kennedy administration entitled *The Bandwagon*. The book and the magazine articles were canceled in December.[34]

The new President, Lyndon Johnson, was a Washington insider who knew how the system worked and how to affect change skillfully and quickly. The people of the nation, still shocked over Kennedy's death, were very sympathetic to many of the late president's proposals. On the domestic side, in one year alone there were four housing bills. Federal aid to education increased. Food stamps and the school lunch program became law. Medicare was adopted. The 1964 Civil Rights Act changed the face of the country.

The Vietnam War consumed foreign and military policy. Federal regulatory agencies, especially the Federal Trade Commission, the Food and Drug Administration, and the Securities and Exchange Commission increased in power and enforcement activity.

The staple of Washington PR and lobbying offices became the monitoring of the federal government on behalf of clients. These offices followed what was happening in Congress and in the Executive Departments, monitored the trade newsletters and publications, and filed routine reports with their clients. The Washington H&K office was no exception. Some of the staff would read the *Federal Register*, *The Congressional Record*, congressional hearings, and other government publications to see if there was any information of interest to any of their clients. The office produced newsletters and special reports warning clients of trends. It combed government press releases to see if there were any new federal grants or pilot programs that might be of interest to clients. It developed contacts and sources within the government agencies.

"My specialty with quite a number of our clients was to keep close in touch with those (regulatory) agencies. To try to know, not only what they were doing, but what the trends were, what would be future developments. Then when a company did have a case . . . it was my aim to be able to notify the company before anybody else what was coming and when," Clifford Guest recalled. "In those days the Federal Trade Commission was very active. And I think there were a dozen clients that had quite frequent business with the Federal Trade Commission. You know it was hard to do business and not come across government regulation."

In Washington, public relations is handled differently than in any other place in the country, especially for large, national accounts. Where other cities' bread and butter would be publicity for something like the opening of a new restaurant, in Washington, PR for big clients revolves around issues. When H&K represented the American Petroleum Institute (the big oil companies) in Washington, it did not care what brand of gasoline one bought, only the amount of federal taxes on gasoline and other more broad-based concerns.

When Gray joined the firm, lobbying quickly gained equal footing with public relations in the H&K Washington office, and later surpassed it. Gray encouraged everyone in the Washington office to register as lobbyists even if they only dealt with the media and never went up to Capitol Hill. "We would generally begin on clients that were already in-house to monitor Capitol Hill for them and if there were something that affected them, to alert them on it, and help them deal with it," Larry Speakes said. "But generally, when we identified an issue that was going to require some work for the client, we would devise a program and, of course, the goal was to utilize the media, both in Washington and in their home districts, to present the client's message to them. We would generally begin by deciding who the key members were. You can't lobby four hundred thirty-five people, but there are key people—the committee chairman or a person who has a special interest in this subject, or a senator that might be from the home state where the client had a facility of some type. So we would identify these people and then work both with the media in Washington and many times in the congressman's home district to present the facts. We'd work out fact sheets for the staff. We would arrange meetings on Capitol Hill for the clients to visit with the staffs and the Members of Congress to discuss their issues. . . . You could assist a client in mobilizing a letter-writing campaign.''

But H&K ''research'' was not always so routine. Handled mainly out of the New York office's ''Education Department,'' but working closely with Washington, H&K recruited students to attend teach-ins and demonstrations on college campuses at the height of the Vietnam War, and to file agentlike reports on what they learned. The purpose was for H&K to tell its clients that it had the ability to spot new trends in the activist movement, especially regarding environmental issues. After all, H&K's clients, large chemical, steel, and manufacturing companies, represented some of the worst polluters in the country. Many of its corporate clients were on all the ''dirty lists'' of the emerging and increasingly powerful environmental groups. For example, H&K worked with Proctor and Gamble to keep phosphates in laundry detergent, despite environmental concerns that the chemical was not biodegradable and did not significantly contribute to cleaner clothes.

Gray did not force H&K executives to work for clients to whom they objected. ''It was a big enough operation that if there was some client that you didn't want to lobby for, you could just say so and somebody else would be given that assignment,'' said Liz Carpenter, who worked for Gray at H&K. There were certain clients for whom she would not work, but, on the whole, Carpenter valued her experiences at H&K.

Besides the increase in government regulations, the H&K Washington staff grew because it began to offer more services. When people on Capitol Hill needed something to say, something to hand out—speeches, position papers, Congressional Record inserts, Committee opening reports, floor statements—the lobbying and public relations firms hired writers, often young Ph.D.s with expertise in fields like economics and science, to provide these materials that supported a client's position.

Gray, himself, knew what to do in his capacity as a lobbyist. ''Bob Gray has charm. He plays it smooth. . . . He would come into your office, 'I'd like to talk to you about this and this.' And he would explain his proposition,'' former Nebraska Senator Carl Curtis said. ''He is a genius. He is a smart operator.'' Gray has said, ''Get caught telling an untruth once in this town, and you're through. . . . We have so many clients that we couldn't afford to fudge the facts on a given issue, because we have to be back tomorrow or next week; if an office won't believe you, you are out of business."[35]

Regardless of what a lobbyist might say, walking into a Capitol Hill office and discussing briefly a position with the politicians or their staff and then leaving a fact sheet does very little to change a congressman's position or a vote. And Gray did not routinely go up to the Hill to lobby. Often when he went, it was scheduled more to impress a reporter covering him for the day than a real effort at influencing the outcome of a vote. Gray's effectiveness was based more on his social contacts than his lobbying and public relations skills. His White House experience and society friends gave him access, the lifeblood of a lobbyist, to politicians and government bureaucrats. But although many clients believed he could change the course of events with one word to the right person, he used his access sparingly to ask favors directly on behalf of clients.

In the fall of 1966, H&K promoted Gray to senior vice president. But being a PR man did not command as much respect as being Eisenhower's Cabinet Secretary. To make matters worse, lobbyists still had an unsavory reputation to many people. That year he wrote an editorial defending lobbyists, in which he cited the familiar specter of "booze, bribes, and blondes," but went on to describe the lobbyist as a sort of friendly helpmate to beleaguered legislators:

> In the Eighty-ninth Congress, 18,552 bills were introduced in the House of Representatives; 3,931 in the Senate. Given this volume of potential legislation, it is small wonder our representatives in Government, harried by constituents' demands and by speech commitments and administrative detail, welcome the legislative homework done by lobbyist . . .

> The honest lobbyist is today's best communications link between a Government and a public grown too large to keep in full touch with each other.[36]

Today, the arguments in defense of lobbying are the same. When one thinks about it, it is difficult to come up with new justifications. There is hardly a hue and cry across the country for more lobbyists. Unfortunately for Gray, some of his associates would soon be exposed as the "mercenary villain" or "blackguard" lobbyists he dismissed as exceptions in the editorial—the ones who worked hand in hand with corrupt politicians.

Gray and the Hill and Knowlton Washington office operated on two distinct levels. There were the working public relations and lobbying staff who actually did the nuts and bolt work, and the other, higher profile, higher society staff whose jobs were to maintain influence in the Washington power structure.[37] On a social level, the H&K Washington office also operated on two levels. "Gray keeps himself a social level above most of his associates: Few see him after hours," Joseph Goulden wrote.[38] "Gray would often have strictly social parties at his home or some hotel or whatever, depending on the scope of it. And that sort of thing the staff did not usually attend. . . . I did not attend the strictly social ones. But, of course, we sponsored press conferences, cocktail parties, and that sort of thing for clients [that the staff did attend]," Guest explained.

Gray constantly went to parties and often gave them. It was something at which he was very good, and to which he expended great effort. In 1966 Gray had a party at his home in suburban Virginia for the Ambassador from Saudi Arabia and his wife. "Visitors to the hillside home . . . were greeted by what appeared to be Arabs in full Arabic costume. Turned out they were mannequins. . . . But the Ambassador, unlike the fixtures in their tarbooshes and other Arabia regalia, was wearing a conservative blue suit," the Omaha *World-Herald* reported.[39]

Gray maintained his close ties to the *grande dames* of Washington society including Mamie Eisenhower and her friends. "He plays his social life smooth. . . . We've been to a lot of his parties and it would be filled with women old enough to be his grandmother. Wealthy [women]," former Nebraska Senator Carl Curtis said. "He was the favorite escort of the oldest women, the oldest in Washington. I've met more eighty-year-old women. . . ." "He was especially good with the little old ladies," echoed George Worden, "Bob Gray working a room is a thing of beauty. . . . He'll hit two, three places a night."

Gray's success in Washington was based not only on who he knew. His charm came from his knowledge of people and processes and events. "He's very good at his homework. He doesn't just get by on the . . . empty-suit syndrome. He's not an empty suit by any means. The empty suit gets by with a smile and a shine, you know, because they're usually spotted and you can figure them out quickly. But he's got substance," Worden said.

With the next presidential election approaching, Gray knew who he wanted to support very early—Richard Nixon, his longtime friend, someone he genuinely admired. In 1967, Gray joined a fifty-member Nixon-for-President Committee in Washington.[40] After Nixon was elected, it was a big boost to the office. Nixon himself had complained publicly about the dearth of Republican lobbying firms. Gray often bragged to associates and friends about the increase in clients Nixon's election meant for the office.

"Nixon's victory was the first time that [the] . . . Republican party took control [of the White House] since before the Depression," said John Sears, a Nixon campaign aide and now a prominent lobbyist. "You see, Eisenhower was not really a partisan president. . . . As you look around—it's even true today in this [Bush] administration—you will find some people around even today that go back to Nixon days even though a large segment of them were taken out of commission by . . . Watergate. . . . A lot of the people that have been around [Republican] politics and government at least for any period of time, at least somewhere in their resumes, if they still write it down, there's some kind of experience with Nixon.''

Republican control of the White House was not the only development that resulted in increased business for lobbyists. Nixon added the Consumer Product Safety Commission and the Environmental Protection Agency which dramatically expanded regulatory requirements on business. In turn, the H&K Washington office grew to meet the increasing needs of its clients for help in the nation's capital. ''It was a steady thing. It wasn't a great one-time burst,'' Guest remembered. Gray also brought in clients of his own. ''That's what Gray did best. He was a real rainmaker,'' Worden said.

The arrival of the Nixon administration was a boon to Gray. He was the big gun, ''the heavy hand,'' in the office, and now his longtime friend and his political party were back in power. For the next six years, business would be good for H&K's Washington office—but Gray was not complacent. As long as the firm was dependent on the party in power (and thus the whims of the electorate), it would be vulnerable. His task was to find a permanent power base, by broadening contacts with Democrats, labor, and especially the media. As with his marriage of lobbying and public relations, Gray understood the changing nature of power in Washington.

5

THE PHYSICS
OF POWER

*Nothing quite like H&K exists anywhere else in the city's lawyer-
government-lobbyist establishments. What H&K sells . . . is manipulation
of the governmental process—in Congress, the regulatory agencies, the
executive departments.*
                    Joseph C. Goulden, *Washingtonian* magazine, 1974

At the turn of the decade, Robert Gray
signed a ten-year lease for tenth floor offices located at 1425 K Street in
downtown Washington, D.C. The building bordered on 14th Street which
was still, in the early 1970s, an area where prostitutes openly solicited. Strip
joints were a few blocks down the street from Gray's office and the White
House. "Oh, it was an awful neighborhood," George Worden said, "I
walked out the door one night with a man who was down for a few days
from New York. He turned left and I said, 'Bill, stop!' And he said, 'What
do you mean?' I said, 'You can't turn left—we'll never see you again!'"
    The building did offer an advantage in that Gray's corner office on the
Vermont Avenue side of the building, overlooking McPherson Square, gave
him a view of the White House. While others in Washington kept walls of
pictures with senators and congressmen, Gray kept one with only presidents
and their families. He had come a long way from his first *U.S. News and
World Report* photograph as one of Sherm's boys. Now mementoes of his
friendships with those at the top were prominently displayed, where they
could not be missed by visiting clients, reporters, or friends. "Framed on
his wall is a 1969 letter thanking him for the gift of a musical cigarette box
that 'is the highlight of my office and chief source of curiosity.' It was signed
'Dick,'" a *Washington Post* reporter noted. The gift to Richard Nixon was
a cigarette lighter that played "Hail to the Chief."[1]
    In the early 1970s, the H&K office ran an informal survey of Capitol Hill
aides to determine the most effective approaches for lobbying. They learned,
in order of priority, that old friends, businessmen from the state or congres-

sional district, and ordinary constituents make the biggest impact. Visits are better than letters. Handwritten or personalized letters are better than form letters or preprinted postcards. Letters are better than telephone calls. "One or two mayors and a banker, they make a hell of a lot more impression on a congressman than any presentation I could offer as a Washington PR man," an H&K executive said. "They are more interested in listening to a voter— than one little flack."[2]

"Of course, the old quote from Sam Rayburn, 'When they write you with a lead pencil on a big ten notebook tablet paper, then you pay attention.' We said, 'It does no good to get a bunch of pre-printed postcards and sign your name to them. That is heavily discounted by a member of Congress. But if you assemble the facts, marshal the members of your group, your business, your employees, or whatever and have them compose their own individual letters, then they will stand a lot better chance of having an impression on the Congressman.' So we tried to adhere to that. That the basic form of constituent pressure were best when they were applied as individuals," Larry Speakes explained.

Basically, the PR firm would put together information (fact sheets) instructing the clients what to say and then request they paraphrase the arguments as often as possible. It was more time consuming than simply signing a postcard or form letter, but just as superficial and cosmetic in terms of substance. But it worked.

The lobbyists' goal was to convince the legislator that his home state was desperately concerned about the issue their client wanted pressed. The Washington office of H&K relied heavily on their field offices around the country and on their computerized information system. The computer contained detailed information on each staff person and their families. When a client needed something, the computer would indicate if anyone was from that area or had relatives there. It was far better to have someone local, who knew the media, hand deliver a press release rather than mail one from Washington. More often than not, it was more effective to have an editorial in a politician's local newspaper than in the *New York Times*—not to mention easier to place.

H&K designed a campaign for El Paso Natural Gas much like the one they had run for the advertisers in the early 1960s. Only this time, the campaign was designed to influence legislation—specifically, legislation to supercede a Supreme Court decision barring El Paso Natural Gas from buying Pacific Northwest Pipeline Company. The courts had determined that the merger would mean higher costs to consumers due to less competition.

Now what could a PR firm do to convince the public to support a move that could eventually mean higher costs? H&K drafted dummy, fill-in-the-blank resolutions and distributed them to chambers of commerce in Washington State, the home of Warren Magnuson, the chairman of the Senate committee considering the legislation. It used El Paso wholesale customers, mostly gas distributing companies, whose local utility managers were part of the small-town scene, to help spread the message.[3] It provided state and local officials with background materials and sample letters to send to Congress. It contacted newspaper editors with volumes of canned material; many wrote supporting editorials.

When Senator Magnuson held hearings in his hometown of Seattle, H&K helped provide witnesses, prepared testimony, coached the witnesses and handled the press. "H&K has almost an entire floor of a Seattle hotel for its headquarters, and its flacks were all over the place, holding hands with the press and making sure witnesses friendly to El Paso had their testimony down pat. A very smooth operation," one committee staffer said.[4] The H&K work did not come cheap. El Paso paid H&K hundreds of thousands of dollars that year, but to the company, the price was cheap compared to the anticipated returns. After all, what was a few hundred thousand for good will compared to the $360 million El Paso was paying for the competing pipeline company? The PR and lobbying campaigns were a success, and El Paso Natural Gas completed the deal.

Unlike Hill and Knowlton's Washington office, most public relations firms in the 1970s still did not include lobbying. Some even had policies against it. But Gray heavily promoted his office's lobbying capability. "Our reason for being large and in Washington is because we're government specialists," Gray told the *Washington Post*. "We pick people to work for us who have political backgrounds. And out of our staff of thirty in this office, about one third are registered lobbyists," Gray said.[5] Gray predicted that in the future, most of the other PR firms would become "sophisticated enough" to offer lobbying. He was right. But when he added his favorite line: "It is not 'the bottles, blondes and bribes' way of life some folks fifty miles outside of Washington might think," in many instances, he was wrong.[6]

No longer was Gray only hiring what reporters often call flacks, the traditional staple of PR firms. Gray did not need any more flacks. As Gray said, he wanted more people like himself, people with political backgrounds. Translated, that meant he wanted more socially prominent, politically connected people—more people with influence and access. Only now, Gray, the self-proclaimed conservative, working for the old-line, Republican-identified, business-oriented, New York–based PR firm, began hiring prominent Democrats. Doing so would help insulate H&K from the vagaries of the voters' whims. By the mid-1970s, Gray claimed that there were more Democrats than Republicans in the Washington office.[7] He needed them. Gray's prescience was borne out when the Watergate scandal decimated the elite of the GOP. In a highly partisan world, especially during the Nixon years, Gray expanded the bipartisan nature of his office. Professionally, Gray was not the highly charged conservative Republican he professed to be.

Gray hired Lady Bird Johnson's former White House press secretary Liz Carpenter, one of the most popular Democrats in Washington. He brought in Larry Merthan, former Senator Eugene McCarthy's former administrative assistant. He hired Jerry Blizin, who had worked for Florida Senator George Smathers, a close friend of President Kennedy's, and Larry Speakes, a former aide to Democratic Mississippi Senator James Eastland and a former White House aide to President Gerald Ford. (Kansas Senator Bob Dole asked Gray to hire Speakes as a favor.)

Liz Carpenter was the first highly visible, politically prominent, socially popular woman in the H&K Washington office. It was a big change. "When I came in I had chintz curtains and chintz furniture and it was a whole different look than that heavy, navy blue and gray," Carpenter said. She credits Gray with helping her open doors for women when the women's movement was very active. "I think Bob Gray, even though we were certainly [from] different political parties, we had a great rapport. He gave you a lot of dignity as a woman working there. . . . Now the women's movement was moving, and so frequently I was asked to suggest the names of women for, I guess, the token woman, but we hoped it would be more than that in various companies. And so I did get a lot of jobs for women," Carpenter said.[8]

Gray wanted a "visible" Democrat. "I think as far as being conspicuously Democratic, I certainly am that and I'm not a watered down Democrat," Carpenter said. Gray hired her partly to build bridges to the Democrats but also because she had the magic "access." "I had marvelous contacts all over the Hill, but also with newspapers. I certainly could set up a press conference, if necessary. I could open the door to a story," Carpenter said.

Although Carpenter remembered Gray as "a delightful boss" and "found Hill and Knowlton very generous," she said her work "wasn't hard lobbying so much as opening doors. Maybe the CEO from some company needed to see somebody where I was the best source and so I would call and make an appointment and go with that person to an office. I remember going around the Hill with a lot of people from the Wine Institute. . . . And we were lobbying to try to get the taxes off of that. I remember when Motorola came out with a big product of those telephones that you now see everywhere in people's briefcases. We thought that would be something that congressmen and senators would want to know about in their campaigns. So I took him around the Hill and he demonstrated it. And at this point it was a very new product."

By the mid-1970s, Hill and Knowlton's Washington office had grown from three men to around thirty professionals. Articles were appearing regularly about H&K as the largest PR firm in the world. On Sunday, March 10, 1974, *The Washington Post* magazine, then called *Potomac*, ran a cover story on lobbyists titled: "Influence and Image: D.C. Public Relations," by Rudy

Maxa. He profiled "Six Persuaders," one of whom was Gray, who was featured on the cover.[9] Beginning in the 1970s, Gray would always be among the list of the five most powerful public relations executives or lobbyists. While other names floated on and off the list, Gray's would remain for the next two decades, his image growing in stature and importance.

Yet when veteran Washington reporter Joseph Goulden canvassed his sources on Capitol Hill, in the law firms, the regulatory agencies, and the media about Gray's operation in the mid-1970s, he discovered that they knew about H&K, but had not really had much direct contact with them. "So what does H&K do—if anything—to warrant its reputation for being the superpower of Washington public relations?" His answer was the reputation of Robert Keith Gray.[10]

When asked about H&K's "low visibility," Gray said, "We're in business to publicize other people, not Hill and Knowlton."[11] That, of course, is the standard PR/H&K line. But the growth and success of H&K's Washington office was directly linked to Gray's high profile, and he never stopped promoting himself. "Absolutely," Worden agreed. It was a very effective personal PR campaign that seemed to work as far as bringing publicity and clients to the firm. But it began to cause concern at H&K headquarters in New York.

New York's concept of public relations was different from Gray's approach in Washington. Gray's ideas and suggestions about how to improve the operations of the business were often rejected. In Gray's mind, New York was restraining him. Gray had big plans and New York always seemed to be stifling them. "They kept sending people down trying to get him back on track. He had ideas like, 'I want to buy a building here. Stop paying rent.' Nobody in New York would buy that. Of course, he was absolutely right," Worden said.

People in the New York office were upset that Gray would not always check everything out with them. "There's a lot of competition in those companies. Everybody didn't love Bob Gray. . . . They were trying to find things that were wrong. [People were] jealous of him," Liz Carpenter remembered. New York also did not understand the big parties he was always hosting.[12] They kept a close eye on him and tried to stop him whenever he tried to do something on which they did not agree.

Gray defended his approach to his work. "Most of the important work in this town is done either early or late anyway. . . . How could we survive without the evening social events, and the chance to talk with someone over brandy? You can get to a person without going through a secretary or worrying about a schedule. Much of what we do relies upon that sort of personal contact," Gray told *Washingtonian* magazine.[13] "Gray was very much on the social circuit and knew a lot of people through his social contacts. He'd put on dinners and things," Larry Speakes recalled. Another H&K executive said, "I never knew Bob Gray to go on the Hill and lobby on anything. Never. He socialized with them [Members of Congress], but he didn't lobby them.''

Prominence as a lobbyist takes more than social connections; it takes rich and powerful clients. Hill and Knowlton had them. Oil—the American Petroleum Institute and member companies. Steel—the American Iron and Steel Institute. Pharmaceuticals—Miles Laboratories. Aerospace—Aerospace Industries Association of America and member airlines. Consumer Products—Proctor and Gamble. Communications—National Association of Broadcasters.[14]

Gray was fond of boasting that H&K clients represented 14 percent of the GNP of the country. "There is hardly a congressional district or a state in which we do not have a client who is a big employer, and by that I mean of significant size in the district or state," Gray said in 1974.[15]

Gray was involved in the solicitation of new clients and monitored some of the accounts, but did not work directly on most of the accounts. He was not a "hands on" manager, especially with the older, more established executives and clients. "Gray participated in almost all new business presentations," according to Speakes. H&K would go to the company or trade association and make a presentation on why they were the best for the job. "If we got the business, then Gray would appoint an account executive, probably the one who had developed the communications plan, the PR plan for the them [the client], and then you would take one or more people that were junior account executives that would work on that with you. Gray sometimes was hands on enough that he would ask you how is it going and 'tell me what's brewing with them,' that kind of thing," Speakes said.

PR firms have, like lawyers, traditionally billed by the hour. There were some flat fees, but very few. Most clients paid large fees (in the 1970s, $50,000 per year), and H&K billed them by the hour against that fee for the work they performed and for expenses. The account executives kept their time carefully blocked out in fifteen-, thirty-, and sixty-minute intervals for the day for billing purposes. "The pressures at Hill and Knowlton, as they are with any agency or probably a law firm, too, is to be ninety percent available. You have to account for seven hours a day and to be able to put down on paper that 'I worked three hours for client X and three for client B and one for client C.' And that was sometimes difficult," Speakes said.

What do large companies get for their thousands of dollars? One example was H&K's work on behalf of Proctor and Gamble in the 1970s. Competitors petitioned the Food and Drug Administration (FDA) to prevent Proctor and Gamble from labeling their new product, Pringles, as a potato chip. Clifford Guest had been monitoring the FDA and knew who the players were. George Worden took cases of the red, tennis ball–shaped containers to the Press Club to hand out to reporters. Containers also poured onto Capitol Hill. Proctor and Gamble eventually won the fight, and the perfectly shaped, neatly stacked, processed chips were allowed to fill grocery store shelves along side their crooked, crumpled cousins.

Also on behalf of Proctor and Gamble, the Grocery Manufacturers Association and others, H&K helped to defeat the proposed Consumer Protection Agency back in the 1970s when many in the country were actually calling for more government regulation and protection. In those days, there was no overriding concern about federal deficits and government spending. If there was some newly identified need, the Congress did not hesitate to spend the money.

H&K did not always win, and it was quite capable of throwing back a smaller client into the lake of the unrepresented for a larger one. When the National Association of Broadcasters (NAB), which represents commercial television, set aside an estimated half a million dollars for a campaign against cable television, H&K discarded its smaller cable account. NAB was fighting against deregulation that, among other things, would have allowed cable, still very much in its infancy, to broadcast certain sports programs and movies. NAB eventually lost that battle, but the two competitors have never stopped fighting over dominance of the airwaves in the halls of Congress and with the regulatory agencies.

With the onset of the Nixon administration, many of Gray's former Eisenhower associates were back in positions of power. Nixon appointed one of Gray's former "Little Cabinet" contacts, Elliot Richardson, as Secretary of Health, Education, and Welfare. Once during a fight against legislation an H&K client opposed, Gray commented to an associate that he was going to "wear out my welcome" with the HEW Secretary.[16] The biggest fees went to the most well-known firms with Cabinet-level contacts, and Gray worked hard at cultivating high-level government officials.

Gray had mastered the subtle art of nurturing his political relationships, which meant that, although he kept a high personal profile, his professional side did not get exposure. "You can't tell some of the things he does, though, that's the beauty of that," George Worden explained. "A Nixon Cabinet officer was about to make a mistake that would have cost him not only his job, believe it or not, but his career. And Gray talked him out of doing it. It had to do with money, as is often the case. I was in Gray's office when the phone rang and it was the Cabinet officer and Gray didn't ask me to leave. . . . And I could hear the whole thing. He was doing all the talking because he was talking this guy out of something and he succeeded. . . . And he turned to me and he said, 'How do you like that. Unbelievable. Wow, that was close.' Now that guy owed him. And when he [the Cabinet official] went home that night and woke up the next morning [he thought]— 'Boy, Gray saved my life.' Now suppose Gray went to see that Cabinet officer . . ."

When the White House asked for bids from PR firms for a project, Gray offered to do it for free. Collecting political chips for the next political poker game was good business. He cultivated Congress as well as the White House.[17] Gray provided friendly members of Congress with free speeches and research. A Senate staffer uttered a memorable line quoted in Goulden's 1974 profile: "Gray has some guys up here—Bill Brock and Paul Fannin, to name two—who would give readings from the phone book on the floor if he asked them."[18] Gray did pro bono work for the Postmaster General and gave free, informal PR advice to those at the top of government. In return, he got favors for his clients. "I think we were hired to promote a postal stamp—a new stamp at one time. . . . Montgomery Ward [an H&K client] was seventy-five years old and they [the Post Office] put out a stamp," Liz Carpenter remembered.

By 1974, Watergate was in full swing. Gray was squiring his longtime escort Rose Mary Woods around town. He had known her since his days as Eisenhower's Appointments Secretary. Woods was Nixon's secretary, and had been called to testify before the Senate committee investigating what caused the famous eighteen-minute gap on an important Nixon White House tape. Gray could sympathize with Woods. He knew from personal experience how it felt to be called before the Senate Watergate committee and grilled.

On March 21, 1974, Senate Watergate committee lawyers interrogated Gray, under oath, in a small, windowless, basement room in the Dirksen Senate office building. The committee was probing Nixon administration promises of ambassadorships in exchange for campaign contributions. "I recall one client we had and Gray was instrumental in getting him considered for an ambassadorship," Clifford Guest said. The donations-for-ambassadorships scheme was a very elaborate system. Some officials within the Nixon campaign had actually categorized the positions for a certain amount of money based on the importance, prestige, and location of the country. Gray had come a long way since the 1956 Eisenhower campaign where Sherman Adams was instructing him how to control and manipulate politicians and the press. Now on the outside, he was expected to do much more than give speeches and design inaugural souvenirs. He was expected to raise money, lots of money.

Gray explained to the committee that his work in the 1972 campaign was just a continuation of his involvement in four previous presidential campaigns "just as I am constantly involved in congressional fund raising. It is part of my interest in politics and the role I continually consign."[19] Gray said that Maurice Stans, Nixon's campaign finance chairman, told him, "Gray, I hope you will be as active as you have been in the past, trying to find money where you can. . . . If you can find anyone who wants to give, by all means corral him."[20] And who better for Gray to lasso than H&K clients and society friends?

Gray described his client, Roy J. Carver, the owner of a midwestern company, as a man "who has become very wealthy in a relatively short period of time, and in many ways has outgrown Iowa" and who wanted "to get better visibility in Washington."[21] What was the quickest way for a rich, midwestern businessman to get to be known in the nation's capital? Hire Gray, the insider, who could tell him exactly what to do.

As a first step Gray had Carver sponsor the annual Meridian House Ball, a charity fundraiser. Carver donated $10,000 to pay for the expenses, so the ticket sales could all go to charity. H&K made certain he got publicity for his good deed. Another Gray suggestion was for Carver to try to buy a baseball team for Washington. "It seemed to us that if we could buy the Senators and bring them home, that would be as good a way for him to have instant acceptance and notoriety in Washington as anything we could get him to do," Gray said.[22]

Lastly, Gray recommended that Carver "might like to make a contribution to the Republican party. By this point I knew of his wealth—he is a man who has not one but two jet planes . . . and so I decided that he . . . was worthy of a conversation with Stans . . . The only thing I know is that during the campaign he would call every so often to find out what other people had given, who was top money man at the moment, because he, particularly in the final weeks, got very anxious that he be on record as having given more than anyone else. . . . He likes to be first in what he does, and he was determined in the final weeks to be first if he could," Gray told the investigators.[23] Carver donated $257,000, but did not come in first. Others contributed millions.

Based on Gray's own memoirs, he did not see anything wrong with rich contributors getting ambassadorships, and so when David Dorsen, the Watergate investigator, asked him: "At any time did you and Mr. Carver discuss possible service by him to the government?" Gray responded, "Yes. He was anxious to be an ambassador, and I told him that in the terms he was thinking that he would certainly have a right to be considered, but again I gave him the pat speech I had always been drilled to give—that no one but the President could promise him an ambassadorship; and all that any of us who worked in the campaign could do was to tell him that his qualifications would be considered."[24]

Gray admitted that Carver's desire to give the most money correlated with his desire for an ambassadorship. "I cannot imagine that he would have given those kinds of monies without that belief," Gray said.[25] When asked about Carver's diplomatic qualifications, Gray replied, "He is a great believer in the free enterprise system and a very good example of how effectively it can work."[26]

Another subject of the inquiry was a social friend of Gray's, John Safer, a Washington lawyer who made a great deal of money in real estate and retired early to "become a sculptor and patron of the arts."[27] Gray introduced him to Maurice Stans. "He [Safer] did tell me what he wanted to do if he could was to be considered for an ambassadorship," Gray said. Gray explained that he did not make any promises, but agreed that Safer "appeared to be eminently qualified to be an ambassador."[28] Safer contributed $250,000 and Carver had several postelection interviews at the White House and the State Department. Neither received an ambassadorship, and the investigation did not focus heavily on Gray's activities. (Herbert Kalmbach, Nixon's personal attorney, went to prison as a result of the investigation.)

Although Gray had insulated H&K from the repercussions of the Watergate scandal by reaching out to Democrats, the fall of Richard Nixon was a personal blow to him. Gray let reporters know that he remained close to Richard Nixon, despite the President's resignation. "People who know him say he enjoyed access to the former President's ear—via phone and quiet personal visits—even during the final isolation of Watergate," *Washingtonian* magazine said. One of Gray's associates told the magazine that after Nixon's resignation, "Bob took this damn hard. After all, he and Nixon had been friends for twenty years, and it's bound to hurt." Liz Carpenter said, "I was there in Watergate and Bob was a good friend of Rose Mary Woods, and I think he was the shoulder for all that White House crowd to cry on. Very good friends over there during that period. He went to dinner a lot with President Nixon. And I don't fault him for it. God knows the President needs friends. And I think it produced business for Hill and Knowlton because he had contact."

But Gray never really stuck his political neck out. He had learned to cover his bases. "Bob Gray has been friends with Jerry Ford almost as long as he knew Nixon. And Bryce Harlow was one of the first people Ford called to the White House. And Bryce and Bob talk almost daily," an associate said.[29] Gray's strategy of broadening the firm's political base paid off. "You know administrations change," Carpenter explained. Despite Watergate and his closeness to Nixon, "he [Gray] had a lot of bounceback," Carpenter continued. "It doesn't matter who's in the White House—we have this town wired in both parties. I think you could say that H&K has institutionalized public relations in this town," a H&K staffer said.[30]

Partially as a result of the Watergate scandal, the 1974 congressional elections brought in a wave of young, maverick Democrats ready to challenge the old ways of doing business. These young turks, coupled with many of the post–World War II Democrats tired of a seniority system they could never control, went into secret Democratic caucuses and kicked out three committee chairmen. From then on, congressional committees, instead of being run by strong chairmen, were democratized. Some members of Congress even saw themselves with responsibilities to their committee assignment and not just their district or state or party or speaker or president. The United States would never be the same again. And neither would lobbying.

Washington lobbyist Charls Walker described the importance of the changes: "In those days [the 1950s], you could deal with a few leaders in the Congress because of the seniority system. You take the Ways and Means Committee, if you had a tax bill. In the fifties or sixties, if you had an issue and you had the agreement of the Speaker of the House, [Sam] Rayburn, and the top Democrat and Republican—if you did, your work was pretty much done. You did not have to worry about the other twenty-three members of the committee. [Today] you've got to lobby all the members of the committee on both sides of the aisle."

A few days before the 1974 congressional elections Gray addressed the Washington chapter of the Public Relations Society of America. His speech was titled: "Washington Public Relations, The Next Twenty-Five Years."[31] In the speech he described Hill and Knowlton's role in the evolving practice of intense lobbying for individual corporate clients.

> There will be those who will say that Hill and Knowlton helped to start it all when we gave a hand a few years ago to a client in obtaining a $50-million loan from the United States Treasury. And whatever its beginnings . . . many businesses today have come to accept that government is the logical answer to their needs for cash, as in the case of Pan Am; for reorganization, as in the case of the railroads; or for protectionism as in the case of the glass manufacturers . . .

Gray went on to predict a sort of partnership between business and government, as business realized they could sway legislative and regulatory policy—with the help, of course, of firms like H&K. "It suddenly becomes apparent that businesses accept . . . even welcome, incursions by or partnerships with government that would have been cause for revolt a very few years ago."

"Power of any kind is like physics; you can't create it or destroy it. It's there somewhere. So when you take it from some hands that have it, it doesn't just disappear. It doesn't just get evenly distributed. It falls into other hands," Washington lobbyist John Sears said. Gray saw the enormous growth, change, and instability in government as an opportunity for public relations and lobbying to grow. He recognized the power vacuums and moved to fill them. "Change means opportunity for growth. And great change means opportunity for great growth, especially in public relations and in governmental affairs. And if we think fast as well as smart, then you and I are on the threshold of something very big."

With the increases in government came increases in the organizations that depend on or are affected by it. As Gray predicted in his speech, most national associations began to move their headquarters to Washington. The number of trade publications and newsletters grew. Washington bureaus of network television and newspapers expanded. Washington began to develop into a media center in its own right, replacing New York as the center of the breaking news universe.

Senator Carl Curtis experienced the changes firsthand. "Even before I left Washington in January 1979, I was faced with two or three committees meeting at exactly the same time almost every day. . . . Not only does he [a senator] do a poor job in those committees, but he never has the time to listen to the debates, neither does he have time to read the record. He's working hard, probably twelve or fourteen hours a day. The bell rings, he drops his committee work. He rushes to the floor. He goes to the door— 'What's this about?' Somebody says, 'Well, this is for orphans' or 'this is for education.' He [the senator] may doubt it. He thinks, 'How can I manage this so I can vote no and go out and defend my position . . . and so he ends up voting for it. And he's neither read the legislation. He hasn't read the debate. He hasn't listened to the debate. That's what I'm referring to as big government falling under its own weight.''

To reform the campaign financing laws after Watergate, the Democrats created Political Action Committees, or PACs, which set limits to amounts individuals could contribute to a candidate and required public disclosure of contributors. To the Democrats, this reform made sense because their largest contributors were labor unions and they raised money through numerous small contributions from union workers, rather than through a few large contributors, as the Republicans did.

But it did not take long for Republicans, special-interest groups, and businesses to overtake the system. "They [the Republicans] found out that there were an awful lot of people that they could get money out of that they never asked before. Even in '76 Republicans had the financial advantage. Democrats found that this new law they had written made it very difficult for them to raise money,'' Republican strategist John Sears explained. Keeping with a theory of his that power is like energy and can neither be created nor destroyed, Sears said, "So when you took the power of large contributors out of the process, what you did, unfortunately, is you armed special interests . . . of all kinds, not just Republican, but with Democrats, too . . . with power they have never had before and they quickly saw that.''

In the past the feeling was "some rich guy might get something out of the process that he didn't really deserve because of all the money he gave. Now we created a situation where special interests clearly did not have in mind the general good of the majority,'' Sears continued.

The PAC–leveraged special interests went beyond giving money to candidates who supported their cause, but began to reverse the process. No longer would candidates say what they thought about the issues and then the contributors decided who to support. To raise money, special interests had to identify their constituencies—by name and address. They now could marshal their forces for votes. Soon special interests were sending out "candidate questionnaires" demanding to know the candidate's position *before* they donated money—and, more importantly, actual votes.

"The poor candidate now had no protection," Sears explained. In the past, the few leaders who controlled the process, the powerful committee chairmen and the political parties, could insulate a candidate from these pressures. After all, there was no real need for these groups and individuals to bother the candidates if the candidates did not want anything from them. Before PACs, campaigns did not cost so much, so contributions were not as critical as they are today. Often members of Congress thought getting a mailing list from a lobbyist was as important as a contribution. That made it easier for candidates to go out and say what they thought. The political parties were powerful enough not to have to deal with everybody who walked in the door, so the special interests were more effectively closed out of the system. In the mid-1970s, campaign and congressional reform took all of that away. Now special interests went directly to the candidates and discussed money and votes.

Soon the nation had candidates from president on down who avoided saying anything, especially anything that might unnecessarily challenge a powerful special-interest group. They refused to take positions unless they were forced into it. And when they finally took a stand, they were discussing issues like the right to an abortion, which is an important issue, but that provides little real information to the voter about whether or not a candidate would make a good president or legislator.

The reforms created a whole new cottage industry in Washington. The more money special interest could raise, the more influence they could buy. "You have got so many special interests that are so effective now. They are so loaded up with lobbyists and they are so effective and productive campaigning against you in your home town . . . it's scary. A lot of them [politicians] run scared," former Nevada Senator Paul Laxalt said.[32]

Senator Laxalt blames himself and other members of Congress for creating thousands of these monsters. "You know where it started, I think? . . . Probably with the Panama Canal. I had a part in that," Laxalt said. Many senators worked with conservative special-interest groups on letter-writing campaigns and phone calls opposing the Panama Canal Treaties during the Carter administration. "Then common situs picketing was another one," Laxalt remembered. This legislative proposal was Custer's last stand for the once all powerful labor union lobbies. "That is when all the business people around the country—they flooded the White House with billions of pieces of mail. . . . And I look back now and I was [part of] one of the moves to getting that outside effort. They had created a monster. . . . Now everybody does it," Laxalt lamented.

Now United States Senators, the upper body, were working with outside special-interest lobbyists using grass-roots, public-relations techniques to pressure their own colleagues. In the past, that simply was not done. No one went into a home state or district and organized interests against incumbents, especially not their own colleagues. "And now it's common play. It just wasn't [then]. . . . Stay out of my backyard," Laxalt explained.

The United States, already a country of individuals—a country with no common culture, a country founded on individual freedom—was now losing faith and confidence in its institutions, both public and private, where it once looked for a portion of the truth. Now these institutions were proven to one degree or another less credible. Now there were many, many places to go for information and guidance instead of a relative few. To make matters worse, an individual seeking advice believed or was taught that each institution now had only its own self interest in mind. "The greater good," "the public interest," was gone.

Today, people in politics, both inside and out of government, and the media address their own constituencies—their own special interests. Each leader speaks to his own constituency to keep up his support without being constructive on how to solve any problem. The answers to questions have been predetermined by the special interests. And the "leader" now either caters to that constituency or to a coalition of constituencies to stay in power.

Where would the nation turn next? Whenever everything else is beyond individuals to figure out, they judge candidates on their character rather than their views. That is why campaigns became the business of who you are—what kind of person you are—rather than where you stand on the issues. In the past, that was always an ingredient. Today, it is the whole recipe.

Watergate ushered in other dramatic changes in government that changed the face of lobbying and public relations. Government "sunshine" laws opened up meetings and other processes to the public. Freedom of Information and privacy laws were enacted. But perhaps the biggest change was the elimination of lobbyists' best justification for their existence. One prominent Washington lobbyist said, "Information is the major change. When we started this business, few people had information. The administration, the executive branch and the lobbyist—by lobbyist you're to put in parenthesis, the industry. The lobbyist representing the sugar industry had all the sugar information in the world. Then the information explosion occurred and because of Watergate and because of Vietnam—not because . . . perhaps cause and effect—the Hill felt bamboozled that they did not know that these things were going on. And they said, 'We'd better get into the twentieth century.' And they created the Office of Technology Assessment, they created the Congressional Budget Office . . . and they created their staffs by the tons and now they can press a computer and they can get the same sugar data that I have instantly. . . . So the lobbyist now has become, not irrelevant, but the lobbyist has to work harder because that guy has the same information and he is not the monopolistic guru of all that's holy in his data that he presents.''

The Congress was no longer dependent on the "good" lobbyist to provide information, but they were now almost totally reliant on them for money. Soon many members of Congress did hardly anything else but raise PAC money from lobbyists. The balance of power was quickly shifting to forces outside government, most of whom worked for the highest bidder.

Times were rough for Republicans in the mid-seventies. Besides the new group of maverick Democratic congressmen elected after Nixon resigned and Gerald Ford took office, one poll showed that fewer than 20 percent of the country characterized themselves as Republicans. The Party's popularity was at an all time low. To make matters worse, a man considered an ultraconservative, even a right-wing nut by many in Washington, was daring to challenge the sitting president for the Republican nomination. Ronald Reagan's supporters in Washington in 1976 would have filled a telephone booth. Amazingly, Gray was one of them.

Gray has always maintained that he first noticed Ronald Reagan at the 1968 Republican convention in Miami when Reagan made his initial bid for the presidency. That is not surprising. Many of Reagan's West-Coast supporters, including Justin Dart, Holmes Tuttle, and Walter Annenberg, were also intimates of Dwight and Mamie Eisenhower. Dart had raised $3 million for Eisenhower and the Republican party in 1958 when Gray was Cabinet Secretary. On March 13, 1967, Eisenhower met Ronald Reagan at Eisenhower's Eldorado home in Palm Desert. On July 26, 1967, Eisenhower spoke to Reagan on the phone, encouraging the then governor to stick to his job in California and not to run for the presidency in 1968 because Reagan was "not far enough away from [the] entertainment world yet." Reagan agreed, but entered the race anyway.[33]

What Gray saw in Reagan, that others in Washington did not, was the charm that made him an attractive candidate.[34] In 1974 James Lake, who was running Reagan's California Washington office during Reagan's last year as governor, was having lunch at the Palm restaurant with Arthur Silverman, who was doing some work for the California Wine Institute, an H&K client. Gray and Lake had never met, so Silverman introduced them. When Lake mentioned that he was working for Ronald Reagan, Gray said he was a big fan of Reagan's and would like to get together with him because he was such an admirer.

Lake arranged for Gray to go to California and meet Nancy and Ronald Reagan. From that moment on, Gray worked hard to develop the relationship. According to Reagan aides and H&K staffers, Gray routinely wrote the Reagans with ideas on different ways to conduct themselves in different situations. He suggested phrases they could say and issues Reagan should consider. He sent them clippings from newspapers and magazines that might be of interest. He became their friend and partisan. During the 1976 campaign, Gray ran advertisements with his own name, supporting Reagan and opposing Ford in Nebraska. "I always appreciated that he was willing to stick his neck out like that, even though it was in Nebraska that he did it," James Lake said.[35]

Gray kept a lower profile in Washington. "I don't think he was anti-Ford. I think he was genuinely enthusiastic about him [Reagan]," Carl Curtis explained. "He [Gray] was sympathetic," John Sears, Reagan's campaign manager, remembered. "Like most people in '75 and '76, he was more involved the next time [1980]. But he was sympathetic, and he helped in some small ways. It was understandable."

Lake also introduced Gray to Nancy Reynolds, a longtime Reagan friend and supporter, and they became friends and eventually next-door neighbors.[36] Whenever Gray went to California, he made an effort to see Reagan. When he heard Reagan was coming to Washington, Gray did what he does best—he threw a party. "I think that Reagan and Bob Gray sort of wowed each other. The Reagans and Bob Gray hit it off. Before Reagan was president, he'd be coming to Washington for some event. Bob Gray may throw a party entertaining Mrs. Reagan and, as I say, he had a lot of ability," Carl Curtis said. Gray joined Citizens for the Republic, Ronald Reagan's political organization.

PR executives know they would be out of business if there were no bad times. "As Bob Gray used to say, 'Don't wait until your shirttail is on fire before you come, because then it is too late. The time to do it is to build your good will and to build your image when times are good. Then when you do have the inevitable rough spots, then you've got a reputation that prevents you from being a Johnson and Johnson and Tylenol,'" Larry Speakes said. In 1958, Gray had watched Sherman Adams disintegrate, partly because he felt Adams had not generated enough good will to sustain him through the bad times.

In the 1970s H&K had several crisis clients. One was the "Calorie Control Council," a group of soft-drink companies that were desperate to prevent the FDA from banning cyclamates and saccharin, sugar substitutes, in diet drinks. Much like the alar-in-apples controversy in 1990, there were reports and fears that these sugar substitutes were cancer-causing agents. "There were a lot of clients that had regulatory situations to deal with. Of course, the saccharin issue was an FDA [Food and Drug Administration] issue," Speakes recalled. The FDA did not prohibit the use of these sugar substitutes in soft drinks.

Perhaps the biggest PR crisis—ever—was the Three Mile Island crisis, when the nuclear reactor began to melt down in Pennsylvania in March 1979. When Robert Dilenschneider, who eventually became the head of

H&K, worked out of H&K's Chicago office, he had based his career on working for utility accounts. At one time, according to George Worden, H&K represented nearly a dozen utility companies. Dilenschneider developed a basic PR plan, which, with some localized variations, he used to recruit utilities across the country for H&K.

This plan would have been fine for normal public relations problems, and H&K was well established in Pennsylvania; they knew the media players and the state and local officials. "But what we didn't know was what a nuclear disaster was like. Nobody knew. When we got there Three Mile Island had one telephone line. It went into the manager's office. Why do you need another phone line? The only one anybody talked to was the manager, and the only one who could call out was the manager," Worden said.

Metropolitan Edison, the utility operating TMI, did not bring in H&K for almost a week. "They were sinking! They weren't talking to the press at all, so anything we did was an improvement," Worden said. Some H&K executives laughingly tell the story, probably apocryphal, of one of the first suggestions made to handle the crisis. Supposedly they suggested a hotline telephone number for the public to call for information. "But we don't have anyone who could man the telephones. We don't know what to say," the Metropolitan Edison officials protested. Their H&K advisors were ready with an answer: "Take the phone off the hook."

If the biggest crisis was Three Mile Island, then, by far, the biggest account was the American Trucking Association (ATA). With the Carter administration in 1977 came the push for deregulation of the trucking and airline industries. ATA hired H&K's Washington office to oppose trucking deregulation. At the time, it was the largest public relations and lobbying campaign ever undertaken. "We (H&K) had two offices at one point in there [Washington]. We had those who were working on the American Trucking Association account and those who were not. That was the largest single account that H&K may have ever had anywhere. They had an unlimited budget," George Worden said.

When Sheila Tate (later Nancy Reagan's press secretary) arrived at H&K in Washington in the summer of 1978, the office had remained constant over the decade at around thirty-five people. By the time she left in 1981, it had ballooned to ninety. "One of the main reasons was the American Trucking Association account," Tate remembered. "We used to Xerox the checks that were sent once a month and stick them up on the wall to remind ourselves. Billing, on occasion, reached $300,000 a month." Quite a dramatic increase from John Hill's $50,000 annual retainer.

H&K divided the country into seven regions with seven states to a region. There was an office for each with at least two staff people working full time on the account. Tate supervised the regional offices. In the Washington office, she worked with John Jessar, a veteran H&K PR executive whom

George Worden had brought down earlier from New York, and eventually they hired twenty more people. It was a close-knit group that worked independently from the rest of the office and reported directly to Gray. "He was an arm's-length guy. But he had to watch this account because it was so big," Worden explained. Within a few months, the ATA staff filled a New-York-telephone-book-sized notebook with press clipping they had helped generate.

The deregulation fight was a bruising two-year battle. ATA—and H&K— eventually lost, although the truckers received some concessions. But the battle had profound effects on lobbying and PR in Washington. "It elevated public affairs to much more of an ongoing government public relations function," Tate said. "I think the kind of money the truckers poured into this and their willingness to try some new things has had a lasting effect on the public affairs business in town. There are a lot more big, big accounts like that."

Despite the fact that H&K's Washington office was running the largest account in the country, the strain between it and the New York headquarters remained. Sheila Tate called the relationship "disquieting." "We were running the biggest account in the country and New York never even came down and met our clients."

By 1980, the ATA account was drawing to a close and H&K had to start laying off several people. Besides facing large staff reductions and a tight budget, Gray and his executives encountered another, more painful blow. J. Walter Thompson (JWT), a large advertising agency in New York, offered to buy Hill and Knowlton.

To the layman, the animosity between advertising and public relations executives is confusing. After all, both represent companies and try to package their client's image and products to sell them favorably to the American public. But the hostility is palpable. "They are a subspecies," Worden said of ad executives, "They're awful. They're awful. They're awful. What a way to spend your life. Here is all this creative talent: the art director, the copywriter, the account executive, all spending months so they can create lies?"

Gray opposed JWT buying H&K; many H&K employees agreed that it was a mistake. "Gray fought that very hard and I agreed with Gray," Worden said. Many H&K executives believed that if they were engulfed by a much larger, alien company, that they could no longer counsel their clients in good faith. "Then they can't say, 'This is Hill and Knowlton's opinion,' with one hundred percent safety because somebody owns us. And of all things, an ad agency," Worden continued. "It was the world's worst merger. The advertising dog wags the PR tail."

Some H&K executives, including Gray, tried to buy H&K themselves, but they could never compete with JWT's lucrative offer, and Gray could not devote all of his attention to fighting the takeover. After all, 1980 was a presidential election year. As in every presidential campaign since 1956, Gray had no intention of standing on the sidelines waiting to see who won. He wanted to be in the middle of the action. Although he was considered a friend of Ronald Reagan's, he was not one of the California crowd, nor one of the leaders of earlier campaigns. He was not close to John Sears, James Lake, and Charles Black, who were running the campaign. He had to figure another way to get inside, and it did not take him long to get in the door.

6

ELEVATOR BUDDIES AND RICE BROKERS

No one cares what you are. There's no Democrats or Republicans inside the Beltway at all. They're all the same.

—Edwin P. Wilson

Power in Washington," Bob Gray once told a Cable News Network reporter, "is as much perception as reality."[1] There was a perception in Washington that Gray had ties to the intelligence community that went back to his Eisenhower days; this was not an idea discouraged. After all, if Gray was plugged into the netherworld of spooks, letting it be known could give him an aura of having an insider's edge, a tremendous advantage in the competitive world of lobbying and public relations. "We often wondered if he, at some time way in the past, had some CIA connection. Very strange people would be involved with him," said Sheila Tate.[2]

Clearly Gray had worked with the FBI and CIA on classified refugee and personnel matters during his White House days. But his selection to join the Washington office of Hill and Knowlton put Gray at the heart of a company that employed people with CIA ties. According to Robert T. Crowley, who for years called upon American corporate chiefs asking them to provide help to the Central Intelligence Agency, Hill and Knowlton "was long ago housebroken by the CIA."[3]

Hill and Knowlton literally wrote the handbook on international public relations. John Hill opened the first international office in London, in the mid-1950s. Soon H&K had offices all over Europe, eventually all over the world. "I used to kid at Hill and Knowlton about our office in Kuala Lumpor, because nobody would tell me what it did, and I swore it had to be a CIA front. That's [the] only reason [to have one there]," George Worden said.

Hill decided to open overseas offices for his public relations firm on the advice of friends, including then CIA Director Allen W. Dulles, according to Crowley.[4] "Hill and Knowlton's overseas offices were perfect 'cover' for the ever expanding CIA. Unlike other cover jobs, being a public relations specialist did not require technical training for CIA officers," Crowley said.

The 1974 *Washingtonian* magazine article mentioned the connection: "In at least two instances people watching H&K's foreign work saw spooks in the background. A former operative of the Central Intelligence Agency says H&K was retained by the CIA in the 1960s to help arrange U.S. tours by Iranian officials at a time when Iran needed a PR boost. Later H&K did very discreet press work for the CIA to discredit South Vietnamese students living here who opposed the Diem regime. Another former CIA man says, 'Rattle some of those foreign offices of H&K, and you'll see some [of] our people jump.' "[5]

According to Crowley, the CIA used its Hill and Knowlton contacts "to put out press releases and make media contacts to further its positions." That activity by the CIA was in itself unlawful. The CIA is prohibited by law from disseminating propaganda domestically. According to Crowley, Hill and Knowlton employees at the small Washington office and elsewhere, distributed this material through CIA contacts working in the United States news media.

Reporters were paid by the CIA, sometimes without their media employer's knowledge, to get the material in print or on the air. But other news organizations ordered their employees to cooperate with the CIA, including the San Diego-based Copley News Service.[6] But Copley was not alone, and the CIA had "tamed" reporters and editors in scores of newspaper and broadcast outlets across the country. To avoid direct relationships with the media, the CIA recruited individuals in public relations firms like Hill and Knowlton to act as middlemen for what the CIA wanted to distribute.

This cozy relationship between the CIA and the media put reporters who had accepted planted stories early in their careers in vulnerable positions, when such activity was looked upon more critically later. Many of these reporters who had been on the CIA payroll had been promoted to top positions in the broadcast networks and the country's most important newspapers. The fact that a PR man like Gray might have knowledge of something that could conceivably damage the career of a major Washington correspondent or news executive could cause them to have second thoughts about running a critical piece on the PR man or one of his clients. This knowledge would give the PR executive yet another tool in his dealings on behalf of clients with the media.

These longstanding Hill and Knowlton intelligence ties and CIA–linked reporters' fears that Gray might know about them might partially explain why Gray has escaped close media examination, even though he was questioned about his or his associates' roles in one major scandal after another during his long Washington career. Gray was involved with some of the intelligence community's most notorious figures for almost three decades.

When asked if he knew a man named Ed Wilson, Gray acknowledged only that at one time both men were "elevator buddies."[7] There was considerably more to their relationship than sharing office space, however, and the nature of that relationship tells much about the other side of Gray's power in Washington.

The very idea that the respectable Gray and America's most notorious CIA renegade were friends and business associates would seem unthinkable to many in Washington. Edwin Wilson currently resides in the K Unit, the most secure prison entity in America, located at the United States Federal Penitentiary at Marion, Illinois.

K Unit is located through the infirmary and a right turn down a dark, lime-green, industrial staircase illuminated with fluorescent lights. In this surreal basement facility, the most notorious criminals in America are kept in solitary confinement under the tightest of security conditions. On the K Unit are KGB spy John Walker, Israeli agent Jonathan Pollard, and Bernard Welch, the burglar/murderer who terrorized Washington. It is among these men that Ed Wilson, Gray's business associate, fellow club member and traveling companion can be found. Wilson has been convicted of selling tons of plastique (explosives) to Libya and plotting to kill Justice Department prosecutors and witnesses against him.

A decade ago, Wilson greeted his visitors at his home, the 3,500-acre Mount Airy Farm in the heart of Virginia horse country. Here he entertained top CIA and government officials, congressmen, and senators with crystal and fine china. They, like Gray, were his friends.

Wilson is an enormous man, standing six feet, four inches tall. His large face with thick brown eyebrows and thinning white hair looks pale. His prison uniform is khaki pants, a khaki shirt, and a white T-shirt. He has lost sixty pounds and his pants are too big for him. His jailers, of course, will not let him have a belt.

It was hard for Wilson to believe that anyone would travel all the way to Marion to ask him about Gray. No one has asked him about his friendship or business dealings with Gray in the past. What prompted Wilson to speak on the record about Gray was that Gray had business relationships with people involved in a private intelligence network that Wilson ran for the CIA and that eventually betrayed him. Gray used to tell Wilson that every client "has a great story to tell." But Gray never answered Wilson's pleas to help him tell his side of the story.

Wilson claims that Gray's connections and influence could have kept him from ever being sent to prison. According to Wilson, Gray could have confirmed to the world Wilson's connections to U.S. intelligence in the late 1970s. The heart of the government's case against Wilson was that he was a CIA renegade acting on his own. "With one phone call, he could have solved my problem. . . . He knew I was working for U.S. intelligence . . . That's why I don't have any respect for the guy. He could really help me if he wanted to. But he didn't do it because he didn't want to get involved. That's the way he is. He's not going to do anything to help anybody. Now if I walked in there tomorrow and said . . . I own XYZ Company and I want to pay you to give me some introductions, he'd do it,'' Wilson said.

For whatever one thinks of Wilson, scores of witnesses confirm that Gray and Wilson were much more than just "elevator buddies." Ed Wilson is one of the irrefutable links between Gray and CIA figures. Gray's relationship with Wilson is a fascinating example of how Gray combined the world of lobbying and public relations with the world of intelligence. Why would a lobbyist and PR man like Gray have anything to do with someone like Wilson?

Wilson was the CIA's top front man. The CIA used him to set up businesses that would give agents cover in dangerous foreign assignments. Wilson was so good at his job that he ended up becoming a business genius, eventually amassing a real estate fortune in excess of $20 million.

In many ways Wilson and Gray were much alike. Wilson, like Gray, was a quick study and, like Gray, was very interested in making money. Personally they were opposites. Wilson was the quick-witted former labor organizer; Gray, the Harvard business school social climber. Both wanted money and connections beyond their professional roles in life, but Wilson's relationship with Gray had more to do with the intelligence business than his desire to make money.

When Wilson and Gray first met in 1964, both men were lobbyists and both had terrific connections on Capitol Hill. Wilson had returned from an assignment in Europe in 1963 where he had worked under cover for the CIA as an American Federation of Labor (AFL) organizer. When Wilson came back to the United States, to preserve his CIA cover, he continued to work as an AFL lobbyist, picking which congressional candidates the union would fund. Wilson entertained liberal Democrats like Tip O'Neill, who were Labor's Capitol Hill advocates.

Wilson's job as a union lobbyist stemmed from the longtime relationship between the CIA through CIA officials like James Angleton and then AFL head George Meany. Although such domestic operations were illegal, Wilson supervised the funding of campaigns for the 1964 congressional elections. As head of the Washington office of the Seafarers International Union, Wilson had more than a million dollars in contributions to hand out.

The checks Wilson handed out launched his long relationship with members of Congress. The nature of these contributions also illustrate why the Democratically controlled Congress ten years later would think Political Action Committees (PACs) were such a good idea. In the end, Wilson distributed checks to ninety congressmen and senators for $50,000 apiece. "We handed out, I think it was a million and a half bucks in that campaign.

I was a popular guy up there for a while," Wilson said. But Wilson's popularity on Capitol Hill was beginning to worry his CIA bosses.

According to Wilson, the traditional method of planting CIA operatives was to place them with established companies. This was done through a CIA organization called Central Covers Division. If the agency needed to place an operative in, for instance, South America, they would find a company that had operations on the continent and approach them with the proposal to plant an agent. This practice was cumbersome: The agency had to brief the senior officers of the company, and the company had to take the time to train the agent in their procedures. On top of that, the agent's cover was vulnerable, since it could be obvious to the agent's coworkers and business associates that he was spending most of his time on suspicious noncompany business.

Wilson came up with a simpler approach. He approached small, little-known companies and offered them services in foreign markets if they would provide him with documents saying he was an official representative. "Christ, I had three or four letters from three or four companies down there . . . I had all kinds of covers; nobody knew anything," Wilson said.

"My relationship with Bob was really kind of unique. I had a friend of mine who's got a big commercial art firm in Washington [Howard Wickham] and he had done some work for Hill and Knowlton. At my request he introduced Gray and I," Wilson explained. At the time Wilson was running Maritime Consultants, the first of many CIA front companies.

Howard Wickham not only remembers introducing Wilson to Gray, he remembers the two men becoming close business associates over fifteen years. "For Gray to claim that he and Wilson were just 'elevator buddies' is absurd. Those two did a lot of business together," Wickham said.[8]

Wilson's immediate motive for meeting Gray was to discover the relationship between Gray and a young Korean named Tongsun Park who first came to the United States in 1956 to attend Georgetown University. Park subsequently dropped out of college, but for a college drop-out he was rubbing elbows with some of the biggest names in Washington society, thanks largely to introductions from Gray. Park came from a family with long ties to Korean intelligence, and American oil companies that did business in Korea.

By 1965 the CIA became interested in young Park because, with Gray's help, he had formed a new, exclusive social club named The George Town Club after its location. Park had been working on organizing the club for years. He was loading his new social club with founders, members, and management with ties to U.S. intelligence. Park put up the money and, with introductions from Gray and others, recruited "founders" for the club like the late Marine General Graves B. Erskine, who had an active intelligence career.[9] Anna Chennault, the powerful advocate in America for Nationalist China, became a force in the club. Others followed, and most, like Gray, had the same conservative political outlook, connections to the intelligence world, or "congressional overtones."[10]

Gray's ties to right-wing Asians like Chennault and Tongsun Park had deep roots. Gray had been critical of President Eisenhower for never being partisan enough. Perhaps that is why Gray embraced wholeheartedly the powers behind the China Lobby, like Chennault. The China Lobby, which fought against the recognition of Communist-mainland, or "Red" China, was quite militant and prone to make vicious attacks on the patriotism of anyone who found fault with Chiang Kai-shek, the leader of Nationalist China, or his corrupt regime. One reason Gray was attached to the lobby was that they had long been behind the funding of Richard Nixon's various campaigns.

Peking-born Anna Chennault was at the height of her powers in Washington when Gray introduced Ed Wilson to her. Decades before, at age twenty-three, she was a would-be journalist who began a love affair with a onetime American stunt pilot named Claire Chennault. When they met, Chennault commanded the Flying Tigers, an "off the books" force of "volunteer" American pilots who were flying for Chiang Kai-shek fighting the Japanese during World War II. Eventually Chennault left his wife and eight children and married his young Chinese mistress.

The Chennaults, Claire and Anna, served as symbols of Chiang's "free China." General Chennault became a front man for various CIA activities, including the CIA's first airline, Civil Air Transport (CAT), set up after Mao Tse-tung defeated Chiang and drove his forces from mainland China to Taiwan and surrounding islands. CAT played a major role in moving Catholics from northern Vietnam south to form the Republic of South Vietnam. Unfortunately, there was a far darker side to the Taiwan and South Vietnam relationship. According to William R. Corson, a former Marine officer and CIA official who spent years in Asia, "Much of Chiang's former army—the Kuomintang—were resettled into Burma where they joined in the heroin trade. . . . The alliance between Taiwan and South Vietnam was based on profits from opium and heroin."[11]

Anna Chennault moved to Washington after her husband died in 1958 to become a major proponent on behalf of tiny Nationalist China (Taiwan) and the corrupt, but anti-communist governments of South Korea and the Philippines as well. Her friends in government circles at the time included President Park Chung Hee of South Korea, President Ferdinand Marcos of the Philippines, and President Nguyen Van Thieu of South Vietnam.[12] Chennault became the international Vice President of Flying Tigers, another CIA-backed airline named after her late husband's former outfit. Over the years, Flying Tiger Airways would evolve into World Airways, and Gray would become a board member.[13]

Prior to the 1971 opening of relations between the United States and the People's Republic of China, Mrs. Chennault was the most visible symbol of what was then the most powerful special interest group in Washington. Crossing the China Lobby that she symbolized meant political suicide. The China Lobby was considered far more powerful than the Israeli lobby is today.

In many ways Anna Chennault represented the interests of the CIA and Richard Nixon, as well as Nationalist China and similar regimes in the Philippines, South Vietnam, and South Korea. She has said her relationship with Gray "was just a social one."[14] But she was involved with Tongsun Park and Gray in The George Town Club. As Gray himself has said, it is often hard to distinguish in Washington between where social connections begin and business transactions end.

Anna Chennault, who along with Gray was one of the original founders of The George Town Club,[15] played a vital role in the defeat of Hubert Humphrey and the election of Richard Nixon in 1968. Mrs. Chennault raised $250,000 for Nixon and Agnew. John Mitchell orchestrated putting Chennault in a major GOP finance job. Gray arranged bringing Mamie Eisenhower and Anna Chennault together to head "Women for Nixon–Agnew." But Anna Chennault's role in the campaign was much more sinister.

FBI wiretaps later revealed that on October 30, 1968, Anna Chennault, a naturalized American, tampered with American foreign policy. Lyndon Johnson had dropped out of the presidential race the previous March after an electoral debacle in New Hampshire, and he was in the midst of serious negotiations with North Vietnam. Johnson offered to suspend the bombing of North Vietnam in exchange for peace talks. This policy seemed to be paying off, and there seemed to be good prospects for peace negotiations which were due to begin in the closing days of the presidential campaign. To Richard Nixon, in a close race with Hubert Humphrey, that was devastating news. It could easily cost him the election.

President Johnson kept Humphrey, third-party candidate George Wallace, and Nixon informed about the peace negotiations.[16] According to Nixon aides, Chennault had been pressing the GOP standard bearer to convince South Vietnam's president Thieu not to attend the peace conference. Despite Johnson's seeming openness, Nixon refused Chennault's suggestions that he meet secretly with South Vietnam's Ambassador Biu Diem. That is why Chennault herself met with Ambassador Biu Diem on October 30, 1968, just a week before the election and gave him a message for President Thieu she said came from Nixon. The message said that under no circumstances should Thieu carry out his promise to take part in the Paris peace talks scheduled to begin the next week, because Chennault claimed he would get a better deal from Nixon if Nixon were elected president.

Chennault's actions were recorded on FBI wiretaps which monitored Biu Diem's telephones and offices. FBI Director J. Edgar Hoover informed President Johnson, who told an angry Hubert Humphrey about the incident. Under law, Chennault had committed a felony. But Hoover, a close friend of Chennault's and a Nixon supporter, convinced President Johnson that to provide the transcripts and tapes to charge Chennault would reveal that the United States was bugging our South Vietnamese friends.[17]

Predictably, Nixon denied any knowledge of the incident. But in 1974 Anna Chennault told the authors of *The Power Peddlers*, "Whatever I did during the campaign, the Republicans, including Mr. Nixon, knew about it . . . I made it clear that I was speaking for Mr. Nixon, and it is clear that the [South Vietnamese] ambassador was only relaying messages between Mr. Nixon and Mr. Thieu. We did nothing but relay messages."[18]

To make matters worse, the CIA later discovered that Chennault also had gotten Presidents Marcos and Chung Hee Park to press Thieu not to attend the peace talks. In the end, the China Lobby triumphed. Nixon won, and a final "peace" in Vietnam was not negotiated until 1973. Chennault helped end Hubert Humphrey's presidential hopes by sabotaging LBJ's "October Surprise."

Another frequent guest at The George Town Club was William Casey, a brash New York businessman who was appointed Nixon's head of the Securities and Exchange Commission. Both Casey and Gray had worked in the Nixon campaign. Whatever one thinks of the plausibility of the "October Surprise" scenario (there is an ongoing congressional investigation into the matter), Anna Chennault's actions in 1968 bear a startling resemblance to what people in the Reagan campaign were accused of doing during the 1980 campaign.

Tongsun Park was no ordinary student when he first came to Georgetown. He was a trained Korean Central Intelligence Agency (KCIA) officer who had been assigned to infiltrate the American political scene as an "agent of influence."[19] More importantly, Park came from one of the most powerful families in Korea. They owned oil tankers, a huge rice business, and were politically well-connected.

By the time The George Town Club was in full operation, Tongsun Park, backed by the KCIA, was the exclusive broker for American rice sold to the Korean government. The major American rice-producing states, California and Louisiana, had to pay Park possibly illegal commissions totalling between two to five percent of each transaction to get Park to buy from them. At the height of his power, the congressional investigation that looked into his activities estimated Tongsun Park earned $11 million in one year in illegal rice commissions. In turn, Park used some of the money to bribe influential members of Congress and to pay the enormous costs of subsidizing The George Town Club.

Because South Korea received vast amounts of United States aid, Park used the introductions arranged by people like Gray and Chennault to lobby congressmen and senators to make certain that low interest government guaranteed loans went to domestic rice producers who paid him off. In addition, on behalf of the KCIA, Park lobbied for support for foreign and military aid to South Korea, especially after the United States abandoned South Vietnam and some government officials began to criticize South Korea's human rights record.

According to Henry Preston Pitts, Jr., who had worked for Gray at Hill and Knowlton and whom Gray had recruited as a founder of The George Town Club, Tongsun Park exuded charm. "I do think Bob introduced Tongsun to many of the people who then became founders of the club. . . . I knew more people than Bob. Bob knew them on the political side, and I knew them on the social side and Tongsun was rather socially inclined. He really wanted to be big dog and he was for a while."[20] Pitts said that the Club was in tough financial straits "for ages. If it had not been for Tongsun, the club would not have survived. Tongsun subsidized the club. Remember this city is club poor. There are too many clubs in this city. When I joined I said to Tongsun, 'Ye gads, you're really going up against the wall because there are so many clubs,' and he said, 'Well, I'll sort of take care of the club until it catches on,' which indeed he did."

Pitts said that Park "thoroughly enjoyed being in the company of important people. The more important the better. He loved it. It was his ego trip, and he could afford it." Ed Wilson and Milton G. Nottingham, the first president of The George Town Club, agreed that Park fancied himself a socialite. He would refer to himself as the next Perle Mesta. Anna Chennault was one of his favorite dates. Wilson recalled that Gray and Park entertained most of Washington society at The George Town Club, including the late Marjorie Merriweather Post. Gray would arrange to invite senators and congressmen down to Mara Largo, her vast Palm Beach mansion. Ed Wilson said he sometimes went on these trips. "Mrs. Post used to come in quite a bit because Gray was very close to Mrs. Post. When she went down to Florida to her big mansion down there, he [Gray] used to fly senators and stuff down there and they had contact. I don't think it was business, just social. I used to see her all the time there."

While Gray was one of thirteen founders of the club, Milton Nottingham and other club members agree Gray was the driving force behind the membership campaign.[21] The club's early board meetings were held in Gray's office at Hill and Knowlton. Wilson believes that Gray got involved because the club was the perfect atmosphere to entertain those he was trying to influence. One of the first things Gray did after he met Wilson was sponsor the CIA man for membership in The George Town Club. Gray had done the same for others before Wilson.

Wilson and Nottingham said it was obvious that both Park and Gray planned to use the club to extend their influence on Capitol Hill. Wilson said The George Town Club was designed for the powerful to conduct business in comfort and relative secrecy. Park made certain that even his club manager had an intelligence background. Park turned to the International Youth Federation for Freedom, a longtime CIA front, to hire George Town Club manager Norman Larsen.[22] Larsen remains the manager of the club today. His previous job before working at the club had been at one of H. L. Hunt's right-wing foundations.

Wilson liked The George Town Club because "you don't have to pay any check; you just get up and walk out and they bill you. You never know what it cost you." That was also the feature that made it a watering hole of choice for scores of congressmen, senators, first ladies, presidents, and their children. Wilson said that he used The George Town Club to entertain friends from the CIA. "It was an impressive place," he explained.

Tongsun Park was the reason behind Wilson's effort to get to know Gray. One of Wilson's assignments for the CIA was to examine exactly what Park, who the CIA understood was linked to the KCIA, was doing entertaining some of the most powerful people in Washington. The George Town Club seemed to be the center of these activities. Wilson was to report back to the CIA on Park. He believed their interest in Park was straightforward. "The U.S. has fifty thousand troops in Korea. We're giving them tens of millions of dollars worth of equipment. . . . The Agency wanted to know what the Koreans were up to," Wilson said.

The CIA, according to former intelligence officer William R. Corson, "grew concerned with the monster the China Lobby had become."[23] Corson said that the Agency was worried about an alliance between South Vietnam, South Korea, the Philippines, and Nationalist China. "Mrs. Chennault and her cronies had orchestrated this alliance and the fact of the matter was our foreign aid money was being used to pay for lobbying and influence peddling back here."

Gray "used The George Town Club as an extension of his office; he was there almost every lunch because he had his own chauffeur. . . . He kept that chauffeur and that car telephone going all the time. The chauffeur would drop him off, him and the client, and then he'd call the chauffeur on the phone and he'd come in and pick him up. . . . Of course, if he wanted Park to meet him, why Park would show up before the meal when Gray and a politician had drinks downstairs. And I'm sure that Park got some good contacts out of it," Wilson explained.

Clifford Guest, who worked for Gray at H&K, confirmed Wilson's memories. "That was an impressive place. So very often we would take clients over there and Gray, himself, did." Although Guest usually "confined himself" to the press club, it was at The George Town Club that he met Tongsun Park. "He was an operator," Guest said.

After the CIA assigned Wilson to keep an eye on Tongsun Park and Gray, it did not take Wilson long to realize that Park was using The George Town Club not just to entertain the powerful, but to collect as much information about their personal lives as possible to feed back to KCIA Director Kim Hyung Wook in Seoul. Wilson reported to the CIA that Park and Gray worked hand in hand in organizing parties to influence and entertain Washington's most important people. Park was so important he did not report to the KCIA Station Chief in the Korean Embassy in Washington, but directly to Seoul. Wilson later learned that Park received his communications from Seoul through Korea's Ambassador to the United Nations.

California Congressman Richard Hanna's friendship with Park began when he joined The George Town Club.[24] "I came to the club when it was in bad shape. Its financial status was very weak. . . . I told Park, 'You have got kind of an in group here that doesn't care whether you get any members or not. They like it the way it is.' They wanted to have it as kind of a cozy thing. There were older people involved in it like Anna Chennault. So I said, 'If you really want to make this place pay, you've got to kind of get it opened up.' So he said, 'Can you get me some members from Congress?' I said, 'You don't want too many members from Congress. They don't spend any money. What you want to do is to get the lobbyists. Because they're the ones that have the money to spend and they'll bring the Congressman to the club.' I got him his start among the lobbyists, because I knew them very well."

Hanna was right. The dozen lobbyists he brought in did draw congressmen looking for free meals and entertainment. The relationship between Park and the powerful California congressman evolved into a comfortable friendship. Ironically, Hanna found himself lending money to Park, even though the Congressman was becoming enmeshed in the middle of an elaborate scheme, hatched by Korean President Park Chung Hee, to spend more than a million dollars to influence members of Congress and other government officials. When the scheme became public as "Koreagate," Hanna ended up in jail. Hanna now says of Park, who was given immunity when the scandal finally surfaced, "He should be in the slammer or someone should have shot him a long time ago."

Hanna said that Gray, whom he got to know through Park, did lobby him on a matter concerning Korea. "He represented Pfizer Pharmaceutical. They had a contract with a Korean firm for making a particular medicine. There was a beef on about the production. The contract they had called for a certain volume. The Korean government had granted a license to another firm to come in competition and therefore their volume went down and they were screaming that was against the contract. They wanted me to intervene for them."

Gray would tell investigators looking into Park's activities, as well as reporters, that his dealings with Park were only social. In a written interview for this book, Gray said, "I never have had any professional, commercial, financial, or business relationship with Tongsun Park. I first met him after our firm had been recommended to him to promote Miss Korea in the Miss World contest. I met with Park, told him so far as we knew these decisions were not based on press or public notoriety and therefore there was little we could do to be of help to him. My original meeting with Park was in The George Town Club, which was then under construction. I assume it was his idea to start the Club, but as I say it was nearing its final completion when I first saw it. I have no idea how much money it took to get the Club started; I did not raise a penny for it nor was I asked to do so. I was not aware the Korean government was providing funds at the time nor am I aware now that it did so. Similarly, I do not know nor ever have I known that Park was acting as an agent for Korean intelligence."

Documents show, however, that Gray was on the Board of Directors of Park's Pacific Development Corporation in 1968. Park used Pacific Development accounts to make payments to Hanna. What is also clear is that Gray's relationship with Park brought a major $300,000-a-year (plus expenses) South Korean account to Hill and Knowlton. The Korean Traders Association, representing some 1,200 Korean firms, hired Hill and Knowlton to help offset bad publicity the South Koreans were getting in the United States. Hill and Knowlton dropped the contract after a congressional investigation revealed that the KTA was associated with the KCIA.[25]

Very little came out of Wilson's association with Gray early on, but Gray's role in the 1968 campaign and Nixon's victory meant that the Hill and Knowlton executive would become a major player with the new administration. Wilson quickly realized that Gray's access was very good in the Nixon White House. Gray used his access to try to help Wilson get a job in the Nixon administration. Gray made all the arrangements, but it was up to Wilson to sell himself. Wilson wanted to be Assistant Secretary of the Army for Defense Logistics. For a man with Wilson's instincts and ability, the job of Army purchasing agent, with all the contacts one could make, could prove very lucrative.

Gray and Tongsun Park, two of the founders of The George Town Club, held a birthday party for former first lady Mamie Eisenhower at the club. Wilson said that at first only the Nixon Cabinet was to be invited to the party. But Wilson convinced Gray to expand the guest list: "At that time I had talked with some of my friends, so I was trying for Assistant Secretary of the Army job in logistics. I wanted to get on friendly terms with the then Secretary of Army. So we invited the Secretary of the Army to this deal— he wasn't part of the Cabinet, but we invited him and his wife anyway."

Wilson also had hoped that Gray would put in a good word with Secretary of Defense Melvin Laird but, according to Wilson, Gray, following his customary procedure, did not actively promote Wilson's cause. Gray would make the introductions, it was up to Wilson to do the rest. Gray seated Wilson across from the Secretary of the Army and their wives across from each other. The birthday party was formal, of course. Gray had a photographer with a Polaroid camera and dresses and men's hats and jackets from the 1890s. Everybody had their pictures taken in the costumes and took the pictures home to keep as party favors.

The Army Secretary had a good time, but Wilson did not get the job. He blamed Gray. "He just won't ask for the order, so to speak. So that's basically how most of the lobbyists work. . . . Gray was no different. He was not about to use an IOU up for me."

In 1968 a bizarre incident forced Wilson to leave the CIA and work under deeper cover in the corporate world. The CIA claimed that Wilson was fired from the Agency for misrepresenting ownership in a CIA-controlled company as his own in an attempt to get a bank loan. Wilson disputes the CIA's account. He claims a Soviet agent in Senator James Eastland's office tried to recruit him; he reported the contact but his cover as a lobbyist was blown. Wilson's carefully nurtured secret identity was of no value to him now. While the CIA officially separated Wilson from the Agency, he continued to work for them as a deep cover operative with several business fronts. Wilson needed a new business venue unconnected to Maritime Consultants, his CIA-backed operation. Gray was the solution to Wilson's problem.

Between 1968 and 1971 Wilson and Gray talked about a number of business ideas, but it was not until 1971 that Wilson moved his offices to the tenth floor of 1425 K Street, where Gray had signed a ten-year lease for office space for Hill and Knowlton. "They had just opened there and I rented space in the same area. . . . So I had a firm. I was just leaving CIA and going with Navy Intelligence at the time," Wilson said. Wilson was setting up a series of new front companies for a secret Navy task force— Task Force 157.[26] One of them was Consultants International, and Wilson asked Gray to be on his Board of Directors. "He was on the Board of Directors of this company. We had an agreement that anything that Hill and Knowlton didn't want, they would throw to me, you know, so that I could make some money out of it, and Bob and I would share that. . . . I set up Consultants International fairly soon after I met Bob Gray because I wanted him to be a partner in this thing and I needed my company if Gray wanted to have a piece of the action."

The arrangement Gray made with Wilson was unique. According to both Wickham and Wilson, Gray agreed to steer business in which Hill and Knowlton had no interest to Consultants International. In exchange, Gray would be paid half of all the profits from clients he generated. To be near Gray, Wilson had rented a small space (one thousand square feet) in an adjoining suite to Gray's Hill and Knowlton offices. Wilson soon realized this may not have been a great move. Because his operations were often many time zones ahead of Washington, he and his secretary came to the office at unusual hours. Late at night, the street in front of the building Hill and Knowlton and Wilson shared was a parade ground for prostitutes.

Wilson said, "I used to look out the window there on Vermont Avenue and see these girls out there at three or four in the morning."

According to Wilson, before he could put Gray on the Board of Directors of Consultants International, the CIA had to approve their business arrangement. Wilson said when he checked on Gray with the CIA's Office of Security in 1970, he discovered that Gray had already been cleared by the spy agency—that Gray had previous clearances. Gray remained on the Consultants International Board for five years.

Many Gray employees liked their new neighbor. Clifford Guest said he "thought that Ed Wilson was one of the nicest guys I'd ever met. . . . He had a great personality . . . We knew he had been CIA. And all we knew was that he was supposed to be in the export business. And you thought nothing of that because lots of people were. But Ed would be around our office. He'd use the Xerox machine and come around and talk with everybody. Everybody liked him."

Another former H&K executive confirmed these recollections. "Gray was on Ed Wilson's Board. . . . He was a genial fellow. Big, lumbering moose of a man. I know vaguely what he did. I mean I knew he used to be CIA. Everybody seems to know if you used to be with the CIA. He had the tackiest, sleaziest visitors you ever saw."

Wilson's office was directly adjacent to the Hill and Knowlton offices. Some former employees believe that even if they were not certain about the specifics of Wilson's operation, Gray had to know since he was on the Board of Directors. Gray also discussed with Wilson his real estate investments. Wilson said he advised him against buying six condominiums at Rehoboth Beach, which, at the time, had been overbuilt and were selling for low prices.

Gray categorically denies either being a friend or business associate of Ed Wilson. "Edwin Wilson was a fellow tenant at 1735 K Street NW, when Hill and Knowlton's offices were in that building. I was never in Wilson's offices but did over a period of two years have nodding and speaking acquaintance with him in the elevator. When the 1735 K Street building was sold to the National Association of Security Dealers, all tenants of the building had to find alternative space. Wilson asked me one day in the elevator where we were heading, added our destination to the locations he was considering and eventually selected the same building as we. Again—this time for a period of over two years—I saw Mr. Wilson from time to time in the elevator. I discovered after the fact that Mr. Wilson had made me a director of one of his companies. I never was asked to become a member, never received notice of any meeting, never attended any. Let me state the facts clearly. I never was involved in any transaction or business relationship with Ed Wilson. I never attended any meeting. I never even knew in what business he was involved. He used my name without my knowledge or consent."[27]

Wilson certainly learned about Gray's operating procedures and business practices. By 1972 Gray had been very effective at attracting clients and exploiting his connections to Richard Nixon. "At that time Hill and Knowlton's clients represented 16 percent of the Gross National Product. That's a lot of people; that's a lot of clout, you know. I think they had Buick, they had Bud Engineering, they had American Airlines. . . . They also had a lot of overseas clients," Wilson said.

Wilson explained how Gray used the access: "Let's say American Airlines had a problem with their flights overseas. Under the American system, airlines don't get to do their own negotiations, the State Department does. So it's very important for them to have high-level input into what goes on in those negotiations, more than just filing a few documents. They want to be able to get the guy when he comes out of the room and say, 'Listen, we need this and this and this.' They need that personal contact, and that's what Gray sells," Wilson said.

Wilson found activities at 1425 K Street tumultuous at times. After the State Department's Passport Office moved into the building, Wilson and Gray found their clients having trouble getting into the building for security reasons. "Then to make matters worse, on the floor just below us—they put the Watergate Commission—the whole thing," Wilson said. Wilson said the added security made normal business so untenable that he quickly figured out how to break his lease and move out of 1425 K Street.

After Gray introduced Wilson to Anna Chennault and her companion, Roosevelt confidant Thomas "Tommy The Cork" Corcoran, Wilson socialized with one of the most powerful couples in Washington in the 1960s and early seventies. Wilson says she did not marry Corcoran because she didn't want to lose the Chennault name. "He [Corcoran] was really a powerful guy from the Roosevelt days on, really powerful guy. He and Clark Clifford ran Washington; I mean literally. He was far more powerful than a Bob Gray because he really made policy. They'd call him in to get things done for the Administration."

Corcoran bought Chennault a large, expensive apartment in the Watergate condominium complex overlooking the Potomac River. Gray brought Wilson over to her Watergate apartment so Wilson could volunteer his services to assist in the 1970 reelection of California Senator George Murphy. Wilson attended fundraisers for Murphy's reelection several times at Chennault's apartment. Despite Anna Chennault's role in getting Richard Nixon elected in 1968, it was clear that both Pat Nixon and Henry Kissinger did not care for her. This was of course also the time of Nixon's China initiative, whose outcome was odious to the Taiwanese. By the end of Nixon's first term, relations between Chennault and the Nixons had cooled considerably.

What motivated Wilson to work for Murphy was that Wilson wanted to do business with the government of Taiwan and helping out a friend of Chennault's could clear the path. Specifically, Wilson was interested in selling the Taiwanese air filtration systems for huge defensive tunnels the Nationalist Chinese military had constructed on the offshore islands. For Wilson, it was a potential multi-million-dollar deal. He met with their military representatives and during the session brought up the sensitive issue of Nationalist China being replaced by Communist China in the United Nations. "I met the Taiwanese and the generals and the admirals and I told them, I said, 'You guys are about to get kicked out of the United Nations, and you have some terrible publicity. Why don't you meet a good guy like Bob Gray and Hill and Knowlton, the biggest commercial public relations firm in the world.' So I introduced them to Bob, and they sent back messages back and forth and they said, 'Yeah, we'd like Hill and Knowlton to represent us.' So Bob thought that was really great." Wilson thought bringing Gray to the Taiwanese would help him with both parties.

According to Wilson, two important events took place at the same time. Gray told Wilson that he had learned from his own sources within the CIA that Wilson was a CIA agent. Wilson confirmed it to Gray. "In the end I had to tell him, because I asked him to help me on a couple of things. I had to tell him. He didn't seem to mind. . . . I realized he didn't mind because he had known all along. I had to tell him eventually because I knew he could check me out real easily."

The second event was that Gray and Wilson traveled together on an eighteen day trip to Nationalist China (Taiwan).[28] "We met Chiang Kai-shek and we met his son and we flew out to Quemoy and went through all the tunnels and all that crap. While we were there . . . [we] met with the joint chiefs of staff and got really briefed up on how we were going to represent them," Wilson said.

As Wilson tells it, when Wilson and Gray were on Quemoy, one of the islands, the Taiwanese gave both Wilson and Gray beautiful Chinese porcelain vases. When they returned, Gray's was broken. "He kind of put the arm on me," Wilson remembered. "I had to give him mine. I hated that. I loved that vase." Wilson also recalled that while they were in Taiwan, Gray ordered a Chinese rug with H&K emblazoned in the middle. When it was delivered to the office after they returned, Gray proudly unrolled it only to discover that the initials were backwards. An embarrassed Gray had to put a coffee table over the initials.

While Gray and Wilson were still on Taiwan, Henry Kissinger was orchestrating the breakthrough diplomatic opening between the United States and mainland China. Gray had to find someone else acceptable to the old China Lobby to head the campaign to make certain Taiwan remained "America's China." After Senator George Murphy lost his 1970 reelection bid, he had gone to work for Hill and Knowlton. According to Wilson, Gray set up a separate company called GM to handle the Taiwanese account. Since Anna Chennault trusted Murphy, Gray put the ex-senator in charge of GM to work on the Nationalist Chinese account. Just what Gray's motivations were are hard to fathom. Wilson says he now suspects Gray had close relations with the CIA, and may have been asked to sabotage Nationalist China's efforts. It was no secret that George Murphy was not a hard worker and did not impress his colleagues nor Wilson. "I'll tell you, my impression of Murphy and being in a lot of meetings with him, he couldn't hold a train of thought. He really wasn't a very smart guy. You'd get in a goddamn meeting and he'd get off on a story on Carole Lombard . . . Murphy was like that. You never could concentrate on anything. I think somebody had got a hold of him and just pushed him out to be a senator, pushed him up. Then once he got there, he believed his own crap and really thought he was something."

According to Wilson, the only profit on Murphy's ill-fated lobbying was $30,000. Wilson, who had set up the entire operation, asked Gray, "Hey, where do I come in? I've spent a lot of money on this thing, a lot of time." Wilson said Gray offered him 10 percent of the profits on the account. When Wilson learned his share of the profits would only amount to $3,000, he told Gray to keep it.

The 1974 *Washingtonian* magazine article said: "On the eve of Richard Nixon's Peking visit an H&K flack persuaded a wire service correspondent to file a story saying the President intended to reaffirm U.S. support of Chiang Kai-shek. The wire service did not use the story—to the profound relief of the writer, for Nixon said no such thing. The reporter still wonders why the H&K man pushed the story, although he suspects he acted on behalf of a client, business or otherwise."[29]

Specifically, Murphy's job was to lobby in support of keeping Nationalist China (Taiwan) in the United Nations and keeping mainland China out. Murphy's performance for his client was not impressive. "He just doesn't understand how to operate. I think by that time he was a little senile, and the Chinese (Taiwanese) got kicked out of the United Nations. Murphy didn't do anything," Wilson said.

Taiwan would be the first of a number of instances in which Gray accepted or solicited foreign clients whose objectives appeared contrary to those of his friends in Republican administrations. This seemed puzzling given his seeming closeness to the Nixon, Reagan, and Bush administrations, and his repeated statements that before accepting a foreign client he would check with the United States government to ensure that the goals of the client were in the best interests of the United States. Many who know Gray conclude that he is simply a businessman willing to take almost any paying client. Others believe, however, that he has reasons other than the bottom line. Wilson speculates that, as to Taiwan, the intelligence community may have used Gray. "I think it is likely that they got him to take on clients they wanted to keep an eye on. What happened to Taiwan was exactly what the Nixon administration wanted." Gray, however, says that the government has never asked him to represent a client.

Tongsun Park's career as a rice broker and Washington socialite was interrupted when The George Town Club and some of its guests became the center of the scandal known as Koreagate. The scandal might have broken earlier, but as the record shows, the Nixon Justice Department's Internal Security Division, then under Robert C. Mardian, ordered lawyers looking into the activities of the Reverend Sun Myung Moon, Tongsun Park, and the KCIA to drop its investigation under orders from Attorney General John Mitchell (the same John Mitchell who, according to Anna Chennault, had relayed the messages from Nixon to Anna Chennault to keep the President of South Vietnam from the peace negotiations).[30]

Just as Koreagate was about to break, one of the more honest members of Congress was deeply involved in an investigation of human rights abuses by various regimes. Minnesota Democrat Donald Fraser did not hang out at The George Town Club nor accept bribes from KCIA front men. His abiding interest was human rights, and he was painfully aware that South Korea had an abysmal record.

Tongsun Park had come to his attention through employees of the Korean Embassy in Washington who had defected and were supplying Fraser's staff with information about how the KCIA terrorized government opponents who had fled to this country. Although Fraser was looking at KCIA's operations in the United States, Justice Department officials in the Ford administration asked Fraser not to force Tongsun Park to testify at his hearings. Fraser dealt with Justice Department lawyer Paul Michel, who in August 1975 asked Fraser not to scare Tongsun Park by subpoenaing him, because Justice felt he was going to cooperate with them.[31] Fraser, a trusting man, agreed. Michel thanked him and promised to get back to him in a week. On September 30, 1975, Park fled to London and Fraser was without a key witness. Fraser was incensed; he felt he had been taken.

Fraser's subcommittee had no jurisdiction over the fact that the KCIA was paying off members of Congress. These payoffs were not being made just by Park, but by other Koreans as well on behalf of the Park Chung Hee regime.

To make matters worse, the KCIA had a female agent, Suzi Thompson, better known in Korea as Sook Nai Park, working in then Speaker Carl Albert's office as his personal assistant. Two Democratic congressmen involved in the scandal, Robert Leggett and Joseph Addabbo, were investigated by the FBI not only for taking bribes from Park, but also, in the case of Leggett, for sleeping with Suzi Thompson.[32] No charges were brought against either Leggett or Addabbo.

In addition to investigating Tongsun Park, Fraser was ready to produce Korean defectors who would detail how the Reverend Sun Myung Moon was a KCIA agent who had close ties to the Nixon and Ford administrations. Two of Moon's top aides in the United States, Colonel Bo Hi Pak and Neil

Salonen, refused to testify before Fraser's Subcommittee on International Organizations.

By 1976 Fraser had a very important witness he wanted to call. Kim Hyung Wook, the former KCIA boss, had immigrated to the United States in 1969 with great wealth. For more than a year the KCIA had been trying to shut Wook up through apologies, bribes, and job offers. He rejected them all. The agent assigned that task—Sohn Ho Young—grew fearful that he would be punished when the KCIA suddenly recalled him to Korea. Instead of going home, he met secretly with members of Fraser's staff and decided to defect. Elaborate arrangements were made to keep his defection and plans to testify before the subcommittee secret from the KCIA. Congressman Edward Derwinski, the ranking Republican on Fraser's subcommittee, was briefed on the arrangements. Within an hour of that briefing the KCIA knew what Sohn Ho Young was up to. Unfortunately for Derwinski, so did the FBI, since they had bugged the South Korean Embassy phones. Derwinski did not deny calling the Korean Embassy, with whom he was in frequent contact, but denied any wrongdoing. The FBI managed to rescue Young and his family the next day. Within an hour of that rescue, the KCIA sent agents to Young's house, only to find it empty.

Derwinski was never linked to bribes, but he was an almost mindless supporter of Park Chung Hee. No indictment was made because, once again, like the Chennault case, embarrassing national security practices would have to be revealed. Derwinski refused to answer any questions before a federal grand jury which was targeting him with an obstruction of justice charge. He hid behind a clause in the Constitution that grants congressional immunity.

Derwinski got away with his leak to the KCIA. Jurors in the KCIA grand jury filed a special sealed report to the court stating that they were convinced Derwinski was guilty. Judge William Bryant thought the evidence so convincing he passed it on to the House Ethics Committee. But the committee took no action. Derwinski went on to be repeatedly reelected to Congress.[33]

The Koreagate scandal broke open in 1977 on the front pages of the *Washington Post* and five investigations were opened. Of the dozens of congressmen and senators who enjoyed Tongsun Park's hospitality at The George Town Club and who became implicated in the Koreagate scandal, only one of them ever served time in prison. Former California Congressman Richard Hanna, who had reveled in singing his songs at George Town Club birthday parties like the one Park gave for Tip O'Neill in 1974, fell the hardest. Hanna pleaded guilty and spent a year in prison. Others, like former Louisiana Congressman Otto Passman, escaped conviction. Passman took advantage of a legal technicality to get the venue changed from Washington to his home district, where he was acquitted.

The Ford administration, with close ties to Korean intelligence, and the leadership of the democratically controlled Congress, who had been compromised by the KCIA, had little heart in the effort to get to the bottom of Koreagate. Justice Department lawyers treated Park, the fugitive, more like a head of state than a potential felon. More remarkably, even after Park and Moon's activities were revealed, the Ford Justice Department refused to force Moon and his colleagues to register as foreign agents. After all, Moon headed a religious institution.

Eventually Park agreed to talk to U.S. authorities, but only after a complete granting of immunity and a guarantee that he would not have to testify before Fraser's subcommittee. This time it was Park's friend, Tip O'Neill, the new Speaker of the House of Representatives, who asked Fraser not to issue a subpoena to Park. Instead, Park appeared before a decidedly gentler House Ethics Committee.

Despite the new Carter administration's desire to get to the bottom of Koreagate and to get American troops out of South Korea, the KCIA prevailed. Park was welcomed home to Korea as a success in America and now travels freely to live and do business in Washington, and American troops are still in South Korea. As for Congressman Fraser, he lost reelection, and is the mayor of Minneapolis.

As for Gray, his close friendship with Tongsun Park went sub rosa when Park fled the country to avoid arrest in the Koreagate probe. According to both Wilson and former George Town Club President Milton Nottingham, Gray deliberately distanced himself from Park. Gray managed to escape adverse publicity in the subsequent probes of his friend, despite their George Town Club association. More importantly, South Korea's intelligence operations grew stronger, not weaker in the aftermath of the scandal. Working in tandem with Park's efforts in Washington, the KCIA kept tabs on Korean dissidents and American politicians using the Reverend Sun Myung Moon and his top aide, Colonel Bo Hi Pak, to provide a network of businesses all under the auspices of the Unification Church. According to former CIA official Tullius Accompura, Moon and Pak have been under "KCIA control from the very start."

Moon may really believe he is a deity, but his wealth which buys him his power has a less-than-holy basis. During the Nixon administration, when Melvin Laird, a good friend of Gray's, was Secretary of Defense, the Pentagon granted Moon the exclusive right to produce the American M-16 rifle in Korea. This arrangement gave tremendous impetus to Moon's arms business, the portion of his empire that generates the most revenue. Gray had no problem accepting money to represent supporters of the Reverend Moon and his Unification Church when Moon was indicted for tax evasion several years later.

By 1976 Ed Wilson, tired of the problems in renting next to Hill and Knowlton, had moved his various front companies to a townhouse in Washington, but his relationship with Gray did not end. When Wilson began doing business in Libya, he suggested that Gray be the representative for Libya and the Qaddafi government. Wilson said, "He wouldn't take it. I tried like hell to give it to him. That's why I was in contact with him."

In Wilson's account, Gray did not say no because he felt Libya was a terrorist state and an enemy of the United States. He said no because Morocco and Saudi Arabia were H&K clients at the time, and relations were tense between these countries and Libya. When Anwar Sadat took over Egypt after Nasser, who was a close friend of Qaddafi's, died, Qaddafi tried to become the new Nasser. "I tried like hell to get Bob to do it because he could have really done something for them because at that time, Qaddafi wasn't as crazy as he is now or was shortly afterwards," Wilson said.

Gray confirmed Wilson's overtures to *Forbes* magazine in 1982, leaving the impression that he turned down Libya for political rather than financial reasons. "When the Libyans wanted something they came to Robert Keith Gray, a man with those almost invisible connections and that access to the mighty that add up to *influence* in Washington. They know his name in Tripoli. Gray was an acquaintance—'an elevator friend,' says Gray—of Edwin Wilson, the ex-CIA man hiding out in Libya and now under indictment for selling arms to Qaddafi. . . . Bob Gray is no fool. He turned down the Libyans. 'Wouldn't you have?' he asks *Forbes*."[34]

BOOK II

THE POWER HOUSE

7

THE DILIGENT DYNAMO

Bob Gray is a Washington fixture and a Washington phenomenon.
                                                    Washington Post[1]

If 1980 was an important year for the country, it was a watershed one for Robert Gray. Professionally, he was confronting what he considered a hostile takeover of his employer—although that term had yet to become commonplace. Politically, it was a presidential election year, the outcome of which would presage momentous changes for the country, and catapult Gray to the height of his power and prestige.

Ronald Reagan was running against George Bush, John Connally, Robert Dole, and Howard Baker for the Republican presidential nomination. Gray had already pitched his tent in the Reagan camp; in fact, he had worked hard at developing a relationship with the Republican candidate. He was not one of the Washington insiders or political pros running the campaign, nor was he one of Reagan's close friends. In February, that all changed; a new group took over—a group with whom Gray would feel much more comfortable.

John Sears's current office in downtown Washington today is notable for its security apparatus. The doors are locked. A surveillance camera scans the visitor. Sears, a distinguished-looking man with gray hair, professorially discusses Washington like an ivory-towered political scientist rather than an inside player. Today, he is best known for representing South Africa, but in 1980 he was Ronald Reagan's campaign manager. Holding his cigarettes like a European, he declines to comment on the reasons he was fired from the 1980 campaign. But others say it was because he was spending too much money and had forced out Reagan's California team—Lyn Nofziger, Mike Deaver, and Martin Anderson.

James Lake, one of Sears's top assistants, explained what happened:

"There had been real internal conflicts between Lyn Nofziger and John Sears and Ed Meese and John Sears. Reagan had to do something. It was just really intolerable. It was an unworking environment. Lyn Nofziger had actually quit the campaign earlier, but he was outside stirring up trouble, and Ed Meese was in the campaign and knows nothing about politics and was causing trouble. . . . Ronald Reagan couldn't understand why we couldn't get along with Ed Meese. He trusted and liked Ed Meese and Meese had been with him for a long time and he just felt more comfortable with Meese than he did with Sears. It was primarily a choice between Sears and Meese which Reagan made. . . . So Ed Meese put together bringing in Bill Casey, and he and Lyn Nofziger and others sort of outside orchestrated this takeover."[2]

After Reagan lost the Iowa primary to George Bush, the anti-Sears forces made their move. The anti-Sears forces agreed that William Casey, known for his financial acumen, would be the best person to straighten out the finances and head the campaign. Richard Allen, who handled foreign affairs and national security issues for the campaign, remembered that it was he, Richard Wirthlin, Reagan's long-time pollster, and Peter Hannaford, a public relations man and Reagan friend, who were instrumental in pushing William Casey to replace Sears.[3] On February 26, the day Ronald Reagan won the New Hampshire primary, Reagan fired Sears and put Casey in charge.

William Casey had worked in 1979 with Charles Wick to raise $800,000 for the Reagan campaign in New York. Wick, a former booking agent for bands, had made his fortune in nursing homes and had coproduced a movie in Hollywood (*Snow White and the Three Stooges*). He and his wife, Mary Jane, were very close friends of Nancy and Ronald Reagan.[4] Casey was also very close to New York conservatives like former Treasury Secretary William Simon, and William Buckley often bragged that Casey's advice had saved his magazine, *The National Review*, in the 1950s.[5]

When Casey was asked to review and evaluate Reagan campaign expenditures, he found them enormous and perilously close to federal spending limits. Lyn Nofziger, who was brought back into the campaign, said that Casey had "never done any national campaign, but by this time Sears and Black had just about bankrupted the campaign . . . in terms of having spent most of the money that you could spend under the law until the general election started. Casey came in and he fired people left and right and put a real down hold on expenses."[6]

Gray as yet had no official role in the campaign. Allen said at that point that "Bob Gray didn't do anything. Bob Gray was nowhere around. Then he gradually grafted himself to the campaign."[7] With Casey's appointment as campaign manager, Gray had the opening he needed to work his way inside the campaign. Gray had known Casey since Casey's appointment during the Nixon administration as the chairman of the Securities and Exchange Commission.[8] Both men were great admirers of Richard Nixon who had stood by him throughout Watergate.[9] Both had connections with the intelligence world, Gray from his Eisenhower days and Casey since his OSS days during World War II.

After the Republican convention in Detroit, where Reagan picked George Bush for his vice-presidential running mate, Casey moved the campaign headquarters to Arlington, Virginia, in the suburbs of Washington. At these headquarters, James Baker, George Bush's campaign manager, was a special advisor in charge of preparing Reagan for the presidential debates, Richard Wirthlin was the pollster, and Edwin Meese was the campaign chief of staff. Casey brought in two Richard Nixon supporters, both of whom also happened to be friends with Korean businessman Tongsun Park: Bill Timmons, who had worked in Nixon's White House congressional liaison operation and had gone to Georgetown University with Park, was in charge of campaign operations. The other supporter was Gray, who headed the communications office.

The word given to the press for the sudden appearance of Gray at campaign headquarters was that Reagan's longtime advisor and press secretary, Lyn Nofziger, was not up to the job. Nofziger wore wrinkled suits and was outspoken, disarmingly candid, and combative. Some of his advice to Reagan, like Reagan's statement that President Carter had opened his campaign in the birthplace of the Ku Klux Klan, had met with criticism and bad publicity for the campaign. On the other hand, Gray, the freshly pressed-suit, slick, and ever cautious public relations professional, had prepared a twelve-page memorandum for Reagan on the flaws in the campaign's internal communications system. Gray offered to take a leave of absence from his job at Hill and Knowlton if Reagan gave his personal approval to rectifying the problems that Gray had identified in his memorandum.

"Bob Gray was nothing in seventy-six [in the Reagan campaign]. Well, he may have been some kind of an advisor or some damn thing. Self appointed. He had attended two or three of our meetings and so forth, but he wasn't in the campaign as such, he was with Hill and Knowlton," Lyn Nofziger remembered. "In 1980, Casey brought him in . . . to kind of conduct the public relations part of it," Nofziger continued. "Casey's excuse was that I was always on the road and, therefore, he needed somebody here. I said, 'If you had given me the money that you have given to Gray.' What happened is, Casey wouldn't let me hire a half a dozen people. So Bob came in in the last part of the campaign . . . and Casey and I had a big fight over that because he did it in a roundabout way. He wasn't very forthright in what he was doing. . . . Until he [Gray] all of a sudden showed up there, he was not part of any of the day-to-day activities of the campaign."[10]

Even though H&K's Washington office was experiencing financial difficulties, H&K did not mind Gray leaving to join the campaign. After all, if Reagan were successful, Gray's work would prove lucrative for the PR firm.

"We thought it would be good for Bob, and, therefore, good for Hill & Knowlton, and that afterward he would come back and straighten things out," Loet Velmans, then the head of Hill and Knowlton, told *Regardie*'s magazine.[11]

Gray brought John Jessar, Larry Speakes, Charles Crawford, and others with him from H&K to work on the Reagan campaign. Jessar, Speakes, Crawford, a lawyer-volunteer named Daniel Jones, and Nancy Reynolds, a friend of Gray and Reagan, sat in a large bullpen outside Gray's small office on the fourth floor. Speakes worked as liaison with his old boss, former President Jerry Ford, coordinating campaign appearances with issues and media relations. Gray was doing the same, in a less obvious way, with the outcast Richard Nixon, whom he still regarded as "the most brilliant president we've had."[12]

Dan Jones was the only person in the communications office who neither worked for H&K nor was a personal friend of Gray's. Jones, a conservative Republican, had been brought into the campaign by Lyn Nofziger. When Jones arrived a month earlier in mid-August, the communications office on the fourth floor was empty. He spent the first couple of weeks moving furniture, arranging the office, and meeting others on the campaign. Ed Meese personally took him around introducing him to everyone on the staff. Meese liked him because he was a lawyer and a volunteer. Jones went to New England at the end of August, and when he returned things changed dramatically. Gray and a retinue of Hill and Knowlton staffers and friends had arrived and taken over the communications operation.[13] In the bullpen area there were tables and desks pushed together forming a long platformed-shaped desk in the center, with Gray ensconced in the interior office.

There was friction between Jones and the H&K people, in part, because Jones, who considered himself a good writer, made the mistake of criticizing Crawford's writing ability in conversation with Gray. "Not knowing all the connections, and being very naive about everything and everybody," Jones told Gray that he would like to write more, to have more responsibility, and, in fact, he thought Charles Crawford was not very good. "And that's when he [Gray] got a little huffy and said, 'That Chuck Crawford, he has the most creative mind I've ever met in this business.' He was very defensive. . . . And I thought to myself later, 'Gee, I don't think he [Crawford] can write at all. . . . Maybe he does have some other talents that I don't know about.' In any case, I realized that I was the little man out," Jones said. "Everyone else knew each other and all had grand plans for the new administration, and I frankly wasn't part of that group."

Jones worked every afternoon from around three or four in the afternoon to about seven or eight at night. He mainly wrote op-ed pieces or articles to which others attached their names, among them actress Arlene Dahl, Charlton Heston, Richard Allen, and Frank Sinatra. The one that got the greatest attention was one for William Simon, Nixon's former Treasury

Secretary. "Bob Gray would have an idea or two on what I should write. Other times I initiated it entirely," Jones said.

Casey's "operations center" in Arlington centralized speech writing, issues research, crisis management, and media and public relations for the campaign. Gray was now on the inside, but he was still not a Reagan insider. "He wasn't tight inside," former Senator Paul Laxalt, Reagan's campaign chairman, said. Gray was one step removed from Ronald Reagan's closest advisers; he derived his authority as a deputy to Casey. "There was no question that Casey was in charge. . . . And maybe you'd say a close second was Ed Meese. But the second level below them was Jim Baker and people like maybe Wick. And then below that was Gray," Jones explained. Although Gray had known them through his efforts on early Reagan advisory committees, through the course of the campaign Gray became friends with Ed Meese, Max Hugel (an old friend of Casey's), Charles Wick, and Richard Wirthlin.

Casey took many of the public-relations responsibilities from Nofziger, who was with Reagan on the campaign plane, and gave them to Gray. "There was a little bit of friction, too, between the Gray people and the Nofziger people. You know, 'What are these people doing here? Why are they coming in at the last minute' type of thing?" Larry Speakes remembered.[14] There was also animosity between campaign headquarters and the campaign plane.

Not long after Gray arrived, someone in the Arlington "high command" commented negatively about Nofziger and positively about Gray to the *New York Times*.[15] " 'Not everybody's been totally happy with Lyn,' the campaign official" told the newspaper. In contrast, the article said: "Mr. Gray has sought to issue quick responses to controversies before they drag on for days. For example, it was his idea to notify the networks of an equal time protest before President Carter had even finished his recent news conference in which he opened with a statement widely criticized as a campaign pronouncement. 'Under the old arrangement with Lyn on the plane, that would not have happened at that clip,' said Mr. Gray, who insists that his being hired was not a slap at the press secretary."

Gray also told the *Times*, "I cannot imagine any staff member who knows Ronald Reagan who thinks it would be wise to keep him away from the press or the public."[16] Of course, that is precisely what William Casey himself demanded. The campaign had designed a public relations effort that would give maximum exposure to staged campaign appearances, and little to in depth questioning from reporters. In fact, some campaign aides told the *New York Times* that Casey badgered them about talking too much with reporters.

There were two major events on which the Reagan–Bush campaign thought the election hinged. One was the single debate scheduled between President

Carter and Governor Reagan for October 28, a week before the election, in Cleveland; the other was the possible release before the November election of the Americans being held hostage in Iran. As a result of these concerns, the 1980 presidential campaign produced two related scandals. Like Watergate and Koreagate before them, Gray was questioned about his, or his associates' role in both.

The first, "Debategate," was the "pilfering" of Carter administration materials, especially the President's national security and foreign affairs briefing book, by the Reagan campaign.

Exactly how the briefing book went from the Carter White House to the Reagan campaign organization has never been determined. Several scenarios have been advanced.

Robert Crowley, a former high-ranking CIA official, believes that Robert Gates, then a mid-level CIA analyst, gave a copy of Carter's briefing book to the Reagan campaign.[17] Gates had joined the White House staff at the beginning of the Ford administration and remained there during Jimmy Carter's years in office.[18] According to William Corson, a former intelligence agent, Gates served with another aide, Lt. Colonel William E. Odom, who, like Gates, mysteriously prospered as an ex-Carter official in the politically charged Reagan era.[19] Corson, a former marine officer, was a mentor to Lt. Colonel Oliver North during the Reagan years and was in a rare position to understand how quickly these Carter officials advanced, in part, because he had held Oliver North's job in earlier administrations.

According to Corson, Gates was assigned as the official Carter White House liaison to the Reagan election campaign. Corson says Gates's responsibility was to brief Casey on intelligence and foreign policy matters partly to make sure Reagan would not say something to jeopardize national security and partly because Carter did not want to be accused of manipulating information at his disposal for political purposes. "So Gates had a reason to be going over to Virginia to talk to Casey and or Baker. No question about it," Corson said. "There is no question Gates had access [to the briefing books]. There is no question Casey got it," Crowley believes.

According to Corson's version, it was in this capacity that Gates obtained the portion of the briefing papers for President Carter on foreign policy and turned them over to the Reagan campaign. The briefing book was put together in the Old Executive Office Building. There were foreign and domestic parts to the book, and it was the responsibility of Carter aide Stuart Eizenstat to coordinate and produce the briefing book. The international material could not be finalized without the signature of Zbigniew Brzezinski, Carter's National Security Advisor.

In Corson's scenario, on the day the foreign policy section of the briefing book was stolen, Brzezinski was at a long lunch at the Metropolitan Club. While the National Security Advisor was out to lunch, then Lt. Colonel

William Odom, a National Security Council aide, took the document out of the Old Executive Office Building to be duplicated. "There's a quick printer that's in the building where Hogan and Hartson [a Washington law firm] are. That's where they did the duplication." Corson says Odom then gave the document to Gates. Since, according to this scenario, Gates had reason to be seeing Casey on a regular basis he could pass over the material to the Reagan campaign without arousing suspicion.

These men—Gates and Odom—quickly rose to high positions in the Reagan administration. Odom became Assistant Chief of Staff of Intelligence for the Army, was promoted to brigadier general, then given another star, and finally ended up as head of the National Security Agency. Gates moved up quickly in the CIA, becoming Associate Director for Intellgience then moving up when Max Hugel, Casey's friend, became Director of Operations. Gates was confirmed as Director of Central Intelligence (on his second nomination) in 1991.

A difficulty with this version is the placement of Gates in the White House in the late summer and fall of 1980. Gates served in the NSC at the Arms Transfer Policy office for and with Robert Kimmitt (now U.S. Ambassador to Germany) during the Ford and Carter administrations. According to Gates's official CIA biography, he left that office in late 1979. Zbigniew Brzezinski's book *Power and Principle* has Gates leaving in December 1979. White House official Douglas Davidson said Gates did not leave the White House payroll until March 1980, when he returned to the CIA payroll as a special assistant to Admiral Stansfield Turner, Carter's Director of Central Intelligence. That date does not jibe with Gates's CIA biography, but it has him leaving the White House well before the general election.

On the other hand, Turner, who was extremely unpopular with career CIA officers, having fired hundreds of them, kept his office not at CIA headquarters in Langley but at the NSC offices in the White House. This means that Gates would have been in and out of the White House all the time, even during the general election campaign, when the briefing book was stolen. An assistant in Brzezinski's office said that Gates was constantly coming into their offices up through the end of the Carter Presidency.

Some individuals with knowledge of the briefing book transfer assert that it was Gray, not Casey, who was the direct conduit in the Reagan campaign. Michael Pilgrim, a veteran security expert who worked on the 1980 campaign, stated flatly that a former Ed Wilson operative, Neil Livingstone, acted as a kind of ex-officio "operations manager for Gray" on the campaign. Livingstone downplayed his role in the campaign, and said that his being hired later by Gray in a top level job was coincidental. Pilgrim, who worked with Livingstone at an Ed Wilson company, insisted that Livingstone was heavily involved in the campaign.[20]

Pilgrim asserts that it was Livingstone who got the briefing book, possibly from Gates, and passed it on to Gray. Pilgrim claimed that when the Carter briefing book came over to the campaign, he remembered seeing the book having a notation on the cover beginning with the letter "B." Pilgrim said that people assumed the "B" was Bill Casey. "As I remember the notation . . . it's Bob not a Bill. Everybody assumed that it is Casey and it's not, it's Gray." Pilgrim remembers seeing Livingstone's handwriting on the briefing book. Pilgrim claimed that his information is based on first-hand knowledge from "sitting in the meetings where that was discussed and those documents were present."*

Pilgrim also pointed out that Livingstone, like Gray and Bill Timmons, who also worked on the campaign, is a "close friend of Tongsun Park," the South Korean influence peddler and intelligence agent whose ties with Gray are detailed in the preceding chapter. In addition, Pilgrim, a William and Mary College graduate, explained that Neil Livingstone and his wife, Susan, both knew Robert Gates since they were all at William and Mary together. Livingstone denied he participated in the 1980 campaign except for an occasional Madison Group meeting of advisors on foreign policy issues, but he confirmed that he knew Gates at William and Mary and that he was friends with Tongsun Park.

Robert Kimmitt, who worked with Gates, also has been mentioned in conjunction with speculation as to who leaked the briefing book from within the White House. Democratic Senator Claiborne Pell of Rhode Island asked Kimmitt directly during Kimmitt's confirmation hearing for the ambassadorship of West Germany (now Germany) whether he passed the briefing book to the Reagan campaign, but Kimmitt denied doing so and nothing came of the line of questioning.

In 1980, Carol Darr, a lawyer, was assistant counsel to the Carter–Mondale campaign and a friend of Charles Crawford, whom Gray had brought with him from H&K. She said that Crawford told her a couple of weeks before the October 28 debate that the Reagan–Bush campaign had the Carter debate briefing book. She said at the time she did not believe him, but told her boss, Tim Smith, about it. Smith assured her not to worry, that it was probably just a friend trying to plant disinformation. He explained that there were only a few copies of the briefing books and that they were closely held. Smith later said he remembered the conversation, but not what was specifically said. In 1983, Charles Crawford denied either telling Darr anything about the Carter debate briefing book or knowing anything about it.

A Reagan campaign aide, Mark Ashworth, who operated the Xerox machine, said that during the second or third week in October that Crawford had asked him to copy what he remembered as material on domestic and

---

*As this book went to press a Gray spokesman wrote, in response to my question, "Mr. Gray vehemently denies any suggestion that he had anything to do with the delivery of any Carter briefing book to the Reagan campaign."

economic issues from either the Carter White House or the Carter–Mondale campaign. Crawford denied seeing any Carter material during the campaign or asking Ashworth to photocopy any of them.

But there are other instances that show that Gray's communication operation in the Reagan campaign received nonpublic information from the Carter White House. For example, Dan Jones relates how one evening, in early or mid-October, John Jessar, one of the H&K campaign workers, received a telephone call from the security desk in the lobby of the building explaining that a man was there with a package. Jessar asked if someone could go down to receive it and Jones volunteered.[21] The man Jones met in the lobby was white, about five feet, ten inches tall, with short brown hair, no distinguishing ethnic characteristics, about thirty-five years old or older, wearing a khaki uniform. Jones thought he was not well-educated but was well presented, clean shaven, and neat. He handed Jones a large, brown envelope with a metal fastener on the flap. It had no writing or addresses on the outside.[22]

Jones thought the man was an Air Force sergeant, possibly a courier in the Pentagon motor pool on his way home from work. They talked for a couple of minutes. The "Sergeant" commented that he did not like Carter's military budgets and wanted to help the campaign. He wrote his home telephone number on the envelope if Jones needed to get in touch with him in the future.

Jones went back to the bullpen and opened the envelope. Inside was about an inch of papers. Something fell out—a copy of a handwritten "get well soon" note from President Anwar Sadat of Egypt to President Carter, written in English and beginning "Dear Jimmy." Jones exclaimed to Jessar "I think we have a mole in the White House!" but nobody seemed to pay any attention.[23]

Also in the envelope was an October 3, 1980, White House Press Office release entitled "Inflation Report," an October 2 Office of Management and Budget document titled "Analysis of Republican Budgetary Goals," an October 10 Anne Wexler and Al McDonald memorandum for the Cabinet regarding "Economic Information" and about fifty other pages. Jones wrote "*Bob*—Report from *White* House *Mole*" on top of the October 10 memorandum. On the second page of the memo he wrote, "*Bob*—Expect this line of attack next week, Dan."

"There was a lot of interesting stuff in it. At that point I probably coined the not so artful, and not terribly original phraseology about having a mole in the Carter White House," Jones said.[24] Jones put all the documents in an envelope on Gray's desk. Later he asked Gray about them and Gray responded that he had no interest in the identity of the mole.[25] But across the Wexler-McDonald White House memo was typed "To: William Casey (for transmittal to Martin Anderson)" which Jones took to mean that Gray "passed that document on to Casey." Gray told the *Washington Post* in

1983 that it was probable that the document passed from his office to Casey to Anderson, who was then Reagan's top domestic advisor on the campaign plane.

Jones believed that Gray then told him to write an op-ed piece based on one of the documents entitled "Guidance on Unemployment Rate and Producer Price Index in September." Jones drafted an article entitled "Little White Lies." Gray suggested adding the word "House" to the title making it "Little White House Lies." Jones read the piece to former Treasury Secretary William Simon over the phone. After deleting some criticism of Charles Schultze, President Carter's then Chief Economic Advisor, William Simon, agreed that the piece could be sent out under his name.

Two weeks later, on Friday evening, October 24, 1980, the sergeant again called Jones, by name, at 6:30 P.M. in the communications center and offered to drop off more information that evening. This time Jones met him at his car outside campaign headquarters. He was driving a dilapidated blue sedan with a damaged right front fender that was full of trash and beer cans. Still in uniform, the sergeant did not get out of the car, but leaned over and handed Jones from the passenger-side, front-seat window another thin envelope. They exchanged pleasantries, and the sergeant made a U-turn and left. Inside the envelope was another Anne Wexler/Al McDonald memorandum dated that same day to the Cabinet.

Later that evening, Jones ran into Casey in the men's room. After exchanging pleasantries Jones related to Casey the story of the mysterious Air Force sergeant. Casey responded, " 'Well, that's good Dan.' He had seen my memo, I had written a copy to him, on Little White House Lies. He liked it and he said he did. And he said, 'Dan, what we really need— what we'd really like to get—an itinerary for the President for the rest of the campaign." Jones responded, "I'll see what I can do." [26]

Jones then called the sergeant and asked if he could get a copy of Carter's campaign schedule. The following Monday, October 27, in the evening, the sergeant called and read Jones the schedule over the telephone. It was a detailed itinerary that covered the rest of the campaign. Jones immediately typed up the information in a memorandum for Gray, Casey, and Meese. The memorandum said: "According to latest information from reliable White House mole [at] 6:30 on October 27, the following is President Carter's itinerary for the remainder of the campaign." Jones added at the end of the memo: "Attached is recent White House memo re: certain economic information." He attached the October 24 Wexler/McDonald memo that outlined the positions Carter administration officials should take in discussing current economic trends and statistics. [27]

Just as soon as Jones finished typing the memo, he hand delivered a copy to Casey. "I typed it up myself. No one else saw it. I took it directly to him. There was nobody else around so I just walked into his office. I didn't sit down, but I remember him very, very clearly because I was a young and impressionable young kid and here's this great, august presence. He said, 'Well, we know some of this but not all. . . . That's great, Dan. That's great. It's exactly what we needed.' "[28]

Jones also put a copy of the schedule on Gray's desk. Curiously, neither Gray nor anyone in the bullpen ever asked Jones about his "mole"—who he was, how he got his information, or whether he could get something for them. Besides Casey, no one ever asked Jones to request any information from his source. Gray told the *Washington Post* three years later, "I do remember we had information as to what his (Carter's) itinerary would be. I do remember that. . . . The President's going to Pittsburgh. Steel is obviously an issue. Let's see if we can get someone to meet him at a plant and cause a rhubarb or something."[29]

When asked in 1983 by the House of Representatives Subcommittee investigating "Debategate," Gray said that he did not recall receiving either of Jones's October 24 or October 27 memoranda, did not remember the note about a "White House mole," and did not remember routing the memorandum to Casey with a note indicating that it should be forwarded on to Martin Anderson on the campaign. When asked by the *Washington Post* whether or not he got Jones's memos, Gray said, "I don't have any doubt," that he received them, but he did not remember them. "I attribute that to the speed of the campaign. . . . It made such a slight impression on me that I didn't even recall it."[30]

The Subcommittee found copies of President Carter's and sometimes Mrs. Carter's schedules in Gray's and others' files. Gray wrote a memo about the schedules to Bill Timmons who was sending "Truth squads" to where Carter or his surrogates were speaking. An October 4, 1980 Gray memo said:

> Attached is such schedule as our office has been able to obtain of Carter's plans for next week. Perhaps this adds some information to what you have.
>
> Of course you will be alerting the appropriate local and state organizations and where possible getting the Reagan poster bearers to prevent a show of absolute unanimity.
>
> One point which may not have occurred is this: If we could have your local people indicate to us the issues of great controversy in areas where Carter is going to appear, we can have some impact on his local press conference and on the press covering the town meetings of which he is so fond.

Although Gray wrote the memorandum to Timmons, he told the Subcommittee in 1983 that he could not identify the source of information on the Carter itinerary. He said he did not instruct anyone to obtain materials from the White House on the President's schedules and thought the materials found in his files came from public sources, although the Subcommittee determined that the information in Gray's memos had not been made public.

There were other indications in Gray's and Ed Meese's files at the Hoover Institution that indicated that Gray was getting nonpublic information from a source in the Carter White House. In a one-page memorandum dated September 19, 1980 to Robert Garrick, who was also working on the campaign, with copies to Meese and Casey, Gray wrote about a scheduled speech by President Carter before the steel industries and labor representatives. The memorandum said:

> From an excellent source:
>
> President Carter is now set to make his big steel presentation on September 26 before an awesome assemblage of steel industry and labor in a White House meeting. Drafts of documents are being given to him over the weekend. Eizenstat has the ball.
>
> RR's schedule next week does not put him in any steel area with the thin exception of Texas where both U.S. Steel and Armco have plants.
>
> For your consideration here are some facts I can verify wearing my previous, salaried hat: . . .

The memo goes on to provide various information and statistics about the steel industry. But, because of the phrase "From an excellent source," the Subcommittee suspected that Gray had a source inside the Carter White House though they were unable to determine if this was the case. In his sworn affidavit Gray said he could not identify the source, but in his interview with the Subcommittee he said his source might have been inside the steel industry. Knowing Gray's and H&K's longstanding ties to the American Iron and Steel Institute, that explanation seems plausible.

Some of these campaign materials and more were found by a souvenir hunter in the dumpster behind campaign headquarters after the election, which he turned over to Martin Schram, then a *Washington Post* reporter, in 1983. Among the papers was a memo from Gray to Casey on how television producer David Susskind was going to endorse Reagan at a news conference, but Gray's public relations staff "were unable to encourage the media to attend."[31] Gray told the *Washington Post* that the Susskind memo was "especially embarrassing to have that get out."

The second scandal was called "the October Surprise." (For a fuller examination of this incident, see Gary Sick's *October Surprise: America's Hostages in Iran and the Election of Ronald Reagan*). William Casey was obsessed with the possibility of losing the election if Jimmy Carter managed to get the American hostages being held in Iran released before the election in November. To monitor the situation, Casey told reporters on July 15, 1980, that he was establishing "an intelligence operation," staffed mainly with retired CIA and military officials, to monitor the situation.

In 1991, Gray told ABC's "Nightline," "We [the Reagan campaign] were afraid that the hostages would be released just days before the election and would have a real extraordinary event or impact on the election totals. This was early in the campaign. One of the great questions was whether or not the President [Reagan] would be able to win. . . . When I got into the campaign in September, he was really behind in the polls—I mean President Reagan. . . . Early on we were very concerned because we thought it, the campaign, was going to be a close one and if the hostages were released in a matter of a couple of days before the election, it could have an extraordinarily heavy impact against Ronald Reagan. That's where the October Surprise came in."

According to Sick's book, Casey began negotiating with an Iranian cleric to not release the hostages before the November election in two meetings in Madrid in July and August 1980.[32] On July 23, a Robert Gray registered at a hotel in Madrid, according to ABC's "Nightline." In 1991, a confused and agitated Gray denied that it was him and produced a passport to prove he was not in Madrid with Casey in 1980. That show of evidence ended the debate with "Nightline." However, that did not end the inquiries into the October Surprise or of the possibility that Gray might have played a role. As of May 1992, a congressional investigation of the accusations against the Reagan campaign was ongoing. One of the areas of inquiry the congressional investigators were exploring was Gray's possible role in the Madrid meetings. And ABC did not completely abandon their efforts. Network reporters followed through by showing a photograph of Gray to people at the hotel, who said they recognized him. Marta Williams Diaz, who worked for Gray when he opened an office in Madrid in the mid-1980s, reported for ABC on Gray's possible presence in Madrid with Casey. She believed that the Iranians, along with Gray, stayed at the Hotel Plaza, until Casey arrived and moved the meetings over to the much plusher Ritz Hotel.[33]

But what about the evidence of Gray's passport? Does it not necessarily rule out the possibility that Gray was in Madrid on the relevant dates? Perhaps, but several former employees of Gray's believed that he had more than one passport, and one employee claimed to have seen more than one. On the other hand, a Gray spokesman called the notion that Gray was in Madrid on July 23 and 24, 1980, "preposterous," and said Gray vehemently denied having more than one passport, adding that he did not understand how anyone could think that that was the case.

One of the congressional investigators who went to Madrid, among other things, to check on the allegations against Gray, termed his trip "successful." The congressional investigation will, one hopes, clarify many of the questions surrounding the allegations about the Reagan campaign. What is clear, however, is that the possibility of a pre-election release of the U.S. hostages in Iran was a near-obsession of the Reagan campaign organization.

Every morning at 6:00 there was a meeting to discuss the hostage situation in an apartment building in the Virginia suburbs, where many high-level Reagan campaign aides were staying. At campaign headquarters, Gray attended the meetings for the deputy directors held later in the mornings to discuss this and other campaign concerns. He strongly denied that there were any negotiations with the Iranians. "Those of us who were his deputies met with him [Casey] at seven in the morning every morning for a staff meeting. I usually went to dinner with him at midnight and then the next morning at seven o'clock—that was Saturdays and Sundays for two months time right straight through. And I know if there had been some other attempt on his part [to prevent the hostages from being released] or some knowledgeable information on his part, he would have shared it with us. There'd have been no reason for him not to. He was sharing everything else in the entire campaign."[34] Another source who worked in the bullpen thinks Gray exaggerated his closeness to Casey in this account.

But what is clear is that Gray did participate in discussions involving sensitive intelligence matters. For example, in an October 2, 1980 memorandum to Ed Meese from Robert Garrick, who was supervising a group of retired military and CIA officers, regarding the deputy directors' meeting that day, Garrick wrote:

> Discussion—The meeting went more than one (1) hour with considerable discussion on the Governor's briefing by the CIA. The majority agreed that it should be canceled. However, if the Governor did not agree, it was then decided that from a press viewpoint we should make the appropriate moves to control the situation. RR should call his foreign advisors in prior to Noon; the event is set for Saturday 4 October and make it a press situation. He should ask to be briefed in the late afternoon, thus, in part eliminating major news coverage of the CIA briefing. The entire issue came into focus as Bob Gray and I agree, that if RR takes the CIA briefing then in the future anything he might say relative to foreign policy, et. al. could be played back by Carter's people as a violation of security . . .

Technically Robert Garrick, a retired naval reserve admiral, was in charge of the campaign staff monitoring the October Surprise, but in reality Stefan Halper, who had worked for George Bush, supervised the day-to-day activities. In 1983 Gray told the House Subcommittee looking into the missing Carter debate material that Garrick had headed "the 'October Surprise' group, provided information and drew on a wide variety of sources."[35] Gray confirmed to "Nightline" that Garrick had a team of retired CIA and military officers monitoring official actions to determine if a release of the hostages was imminent. "We were trying to find out what was going on, trying to stay as current in all facets of the campaign," he said.

WLS, an ABC-owned station in Chicago, announced on October 15, 1980, that there were secret negotiations going on between the Carter White House and the Iranians for release of the American hostages. The discussions were to provide Iran spare military parts for their war with Iraq in exchange for the hostages. The Reagan campaign thought the hostage release was imminent and planted the story.

In a file marked "Hostages" with the campaign material at the Hoover Institute, the House Subcommittee found an undated memorandum from Gray to Ed Meese marked "Confidential." It said:

1. As we reach for contingency plans re hostages we should keep in mind our ability to sow a story or start news trends by non-attributable comments to newsmen. If we leak to news sources our knowledge of the Carter-planned events, spelling out what Carter will do to make a media event of the release-phased return to the states, a White House event, ticker parade, possible use of Mondale, etc., we can get the press saying Carter is politicizing the issue, following his media plan, etc.

2. In contrast to our famous anonymous Reagan aide quoted in Lou Cannon this morning, we should be saying the hostage resolution will not be making any difference in the vote, does not change the overriding issues of the campaign, etc.

3. After the Governor joins in the rejoicing "that our long wait for resolution of this issue is finally over" we should be taking the approach "we cannot allow this happy moment to divert us from our mission to tell the American public about the Carter record, etc."

4. After the hostage return the Governor should "recognize I now have an even heavier responsibility to redouble my efforts to spotlight the Carter record. If I do not the voters might—in a momentary happiness—make a decision they would regret for another four years."

It was classic Gray. Even though the campaign had a whole working group devoted to a possible hostage release, Gray's advice was for the campaign to assert that the release of the hostages would have little effect on the outcome of the election. He advised the campaign to take the offensive, to try to offset the euphoria caused by a hostage release, rather than wait to respond to the situation. Gray knew that if the campaign had to respond, it was already too late.

Because of the wording "our knowledge of the Carter-planned events," the Subcommittee believed the Reagan campaign had inside information about Carter's efforts to release the hostages. Peter Hannaford, who worked on the Reagan campaign, told the Subcommittee that information regarding Carter White House negotiations for the hostages "came to the Reagan–

Bush campaign in late September 1980.'' Gray told the Subcommittee that he did not remember the memorandum and did not believe that its wording indicated advance knowledge by the campaign of Carter's actions. But the Subcommittee wrote, ''At the least, however, this document shows that Gray advocated obtaining information about the hostage crisis not available to the press and the public and using such information for the campaign's advantage.''[36]

Right up until the election, no one in the Reagan campaign relaxed. Casey ordered thousands of dollars of television commercials prepared just in case the hostages were released at the last moment. No one could believe that Jimmy Carter would lose so badly. Whether it was a true landslide or not is a subject of debate, but for people like Robert Gray whose livelihood depended upon who was in power, not how much support they had outside of Washington, Reagan's ascension was very happy news indeed.

Gray's public relations instincts quickly surfaced after the campaign, as he portrayed himself as an integral part of the 1980 Reagan campaign. Gray may have made contributions in public relations and communications or in receiving information from the Carter White House or in planning for a possible early release of the hostages, but the main focus of any campaign is on the candidate, and, according to one campaign source, Gray only saw Reagan once during the campaign.

On November 13, Gray was presented with the 1980 Distinguished Nebraska Award from the Nebraska State Society at a dinner.[37] The next day, the Reagan transition office announced that President-elect Ronald Reagan had appointed Gray to cochair the upcoming inauguration. The next two and a half months were filled with parties and celebrations for Gray, by Gray, and including Gray.

Two weeks after the election, Gray put one of his most developed talents to use. With Nancy Reynolds, Gray hosted a welcome-to-Washington party for Nancy and Ronald Reagan. He held it at the exclusive F Street Club, the same club where Dwight Eisenhower had held the last social gathering of his cabinet and on which Tongsun Park had patterned The George Town Club.

In the interest of time, Gray and Reynolds sent out telegrams instead of written invitations. Most did not respond, thinking it must be a joke since many of the guests were Democrats, including then Washington Mayor Marion Barry. Other guests, like then American University President Richard Berendzen, soon became Gray clients. After dinner, the guests gathered around the fireplace and listened to Ronald Reagan tell old Hollywood stories. It was a perfect evening. Nancy Reagan was impressed.[38] ''He's a great party thrower. And a great man-around-town. He's the kind of person who was able to influence Nancy Reagan. If you get close to Nancy Reagan, then all the social stuff follows,'' Lyn Nofziger explained.

In return, friends had a testimonial dinner for Gray. Reagan confidant Senator Paul Laxalt was full of praise for the Hill and Knowlton man. "Six weeks before the campaign was over the Reagan campaign was in chaos."[39] Laxalt proclaimed that Gray's restructuring of the internal communications system for the campaign had helped elect Reagan, "as much as anyone."[40] The Senator recalled that Gray had helped him prepare for his nominating speech for Reagan at the Republican convention by "diplomatically telling me it was not all that good."[41] But despite Laxalt's public praise of Gray, he did not consider Gray a close friend of either himself or Ronald Reagan. "He never was really an insider," Laxalt said when interviewed for this book.

During the Reagan transition, while many who worked on the campaign scurried and dueled for top jobs in the new administration, Gray settled for cochairman, along with his and William Casey's friend Charles Wick, of the 1980 Reagan inaugural. It was a perfect job for Gray. After all, there was no better party giver in Washington than he, and the Inauguration is one gigantic celebration. "It's not a job I'd ever want. But when you're substance free, it doesn't matter. I mean you take whatever comes in . . . ," Richard Allen, who became Reagan's National Security Advisor, said of Gray's postelection role.

As a result of Watergate, in 1974, the Congress enacted major campaign reforms that provided federal funding for presidential elections and limits on individual campaign contributions. By the 1980 presidential campaign, every loophole in the law had been discovered and sophisticated efforts to pour money into the campaign were underway. Wick was a major player in one of them—an operation to raise what is called "soft money" or money not contributed directly to the candidate, but through the state and national parties to avoid campaign limits and, more importantly, to avoid reporting it. Wick raised millions from Reagan's California backers and others, and besides cochairing the inaugural with Gray, Wick became the head of the United States Information Agency, with Bill Casey's help.[42]

After the election, Wick's fundraising machines continued to generate huge amounts of money. Gray and Wick established the Presidential Inaugural Committee, which included the Inaugural Trust Fund that accepted corporate and individual contributions up to $30,000. If one was a corporate executive or wealthy investor looking to make friends with the new administration, contributing to the inaugural fund was certainly a nice first step. At the time, the Inauguration was the most expensive in history; no expense was spared. The Inauguration was supposed to cost $6 million; it cost over $16 million. Gray said of this spectacle, "This was free enterprise at its best."[43]

With Gray and Wick in charge and money as no object, the Inaugural festivities were the most lavish ever seen in Washington and in the rest of the country. It was quite a contrast from Jimmy Carter's four years earlier, the "people's inaugural," which was Jacksonian in nature. Carter invited every American to come to Washington. Almost anyone could get a twenty-five-dollar ticket to inaugural balls that were more like parties than opulent dances. Carter declined to wear formal attire, but wore a business suit, and walked the parade route rather than ride in a limousine. But in 1981, Ronald Reagan wore formal clothes and waved from a limousine along the parade route. Tickets were tightly controlled for the one-hundred-dollars-and-up invitations to the festivities. Washington noticed immediately the dramatic change not only in appearance, but also in attitudes. The rich were no longer discreetly hiding their consumption, but were truly coming out in the open. "We want to get the administration launched in a memorable way," Gray told the *Washington Post*.

Gray's Reagan Inaugural ushered in not only a new president, but a new philosophy of government in the country. "It is a new era" were words spoken often by Reagan supporters. No longer would the Robin-Hood attitude of taking from the rich and giving to the poor prevail. No longer would government be seen as a means to protect the small investor or the consumer. The rich and the business community were now in charge. Federal agencies whose missions were to protect Americans from unscrupulous business and financial practices, from unfair trade, from environmental pollution were now supposed to reduce paperwork, cutback on the bureaucracies' "waste, fraud, and abuse," and on regulations on banks and businesses.

In addition to the rich, millions of middle-class, conservative Americans who supported Reagan because of his "family values" and "less government" rhetoric saw this administration as their chance at power. The new Departments of Education and Energy would be abolished. Abortion would be outlawed. The Inaugural theme, "America—A New Beginning," was more prophetic (and annoyingly redundant) than anyone at the time realized.

The Inaugural took enormous amounts of planning, and, like any undertaking of this magnitude ran into innumerable snags. On December 10, 1980, the *New York Times* ran Gray's preview of the Reagan Inauguration. The reporter said Gray "seemed to be in a bind." First, Gray's idea for the marching bands in the Inaugural parade to carry flags instead of guns "backfired (the military didn't like the idea one bit)." Next the congressmen and senators were complaining because they were not getting enough tickets to the balls and other festivities.[44]

Mark Moran, who later joined Gray when Gray started his own company, was recruited by Gray to work on the inaugural. Gray phoned the partners of Moran's law firm and suggested they might want to volunteer a counsel for the President's committee. "It was the most incredible accumulation of people in a short period of time who didn't know each other and were expected to accomplish [a tremendous amount], in a very, very short period of time—three months—that I had ever seen. You bring five thousand people together, most of them don't know each other, ninety-nine percent of whom have never been on an inaugural [committee] before; they have three months to carry off twelve hundred events.''

Other thorns in the inaugural side were issues of what to do if former President Richard Nixon, still an outcast from Watergate, decided to attend. Gray, Nixon's longtime admirer, would know what to do. Or, what if Carter refuses to wear formal attire?[45] Neither proved to be problems.

One of the keys to Gray's concept of public relations success and the means to achieve it was his absolute belief in the power of television, and he adhered to this belief in the inaugural planning: "We're concentrating entirely on television," Gray told the *New York Times*. Even high school bands were selected for their telegenic qualities rather than down-home enthusiasm. "We've selected units on the basis of what will really portray well on television," Gray told the *Times*, "rather than letting anyone who wants to be in the parade do so." Gray was not leaving any detail to chance. The fewer but better bands and floats were told to make brisk, energetic presentations. The marching units were actually asked to shorten their paces from the customary thirty inches to twenty-eight inches. "Our parade will be action-packed, distilled," Gray said.[46]

Gray's use of television was unequalled. "Every event has a TV mode to make sure it will get across to the country," he said.[47] Not since his days trying to sell television sets in Hastings was his enthusiasm about the medium so publicly apparent. Every event over the almost week of festivities was geared to television. For example, the normally private luncheon between the new President and members of Congress after the swearing-in ceremony was scheduled to be televised and was termed in an inaugural committee press release as a "major set piece" devised "to demonstrate the importance the President-elect places on good relations with Congress."[48]

Reagan's election confirmed Gray's belief that the main key to success was communicating effectively on television. That was true with a client or a president, independent of whether or not they were good or right or capable or honest or reliable. "He [Reagan] can communicate better than anyone I know. And the ability to communicate is going to go a long way toward a good presidency. If a politician is a communicator, he's a leader, whether good or bad. All recent presidents history has judged as effective have been communicators," Gray said.[49]

For the first time "Mini-Inaugural Balls" were scheduled for more than a hundred locations across the United States (including the Holiday Inn in Hastings, Nebraska) and one in Paris, France, for Americans living abroad. At these locations, those attending were supposed to be linked by large-screen, closed circuit television to the nine balls in Washington at a cost of $2 million. Most of the screens were to be larger than those in movie theaters so those attending would feel part of the celebration in Washington.[50] At the mini-balls the participants would dance to the big dance bands playing at the balls in Washington. ''The neat thing about it is that they're going to be dancing to all the bands here,'' Gray said.[51]

On December 15, the *Washington Post* ran a feature article about Gray, the ''Inaugural Insider.'' The reporter followed him around town and Gray, true to form, had a full schedule, meeting with and talking to politically and socially prominent people from sun up to sun down. Unlike the *New York Times*, the *Post* did not find Gray harried or harassed, but cool and collected:

> Gray hits the ground running. He has a habit of doing a sort of skip when he sets off, as though to gather momentum. . . . 'Get me Walter Cronkite at the Madison,' he tells his secretary. They arrange their drink (together before dinner). '*Ciao*,' he says as he puts down the phone.

> The layers of his life and career fall neatly into a *mille-feuille* of friends, contacts, politics, and lobbying. . . . 'He knows everyone in town,' said Liz Carpenter, who is now chief spokesperson at the Department of Education but worked for Gray at Hill and Knowlton. 'And he's probably danced with his wife.'[52]

The article portrayed Gray in glowing terms, from his arrival in the nation's capital from Hastings, to his successful career in cultivating the Washington establishment. His day had been planned down to every manageable detail to have that effect. For example, his phone call to Walter Cronkite, the godfather of broadcast journalism, gave him instant credibility—after all, if Walter Cronkite is a friend, Gray must also have integrity and honesty. Despite brief mentions of Gray's being questioned by Watergate and Koreagate investigators, the article was a perfect tribute to the public relations executive, especially in getting his age wrong—fifty-five instead of fifty-nine.

Gray was in his element heading the Inaugural. He relished the perks of the job like the special inaugural license plate *No. 1* for his limousine. Not since his days sitting outside President Eisenhower's door had his office received so many phone calls (850 a day) and letters (2,000 a day). The job made the kinds of demands on Gray on which he thrived. But like the short-lived Appointments Secretary job in 1957, the Inaugural job only lasted a couple of months. But he would use it, like his Eisenhower appointment, to enhance his image and the perception of his power.

In early January 1981, Gray left his inaugural planning for a quick trip to New York. He attended a ''private party'' hosted by Mildred Hilson, one of Mamie Eisenhower's friends, for her good friends George and Barbara Bush ''to wish them luck.'' The Vice President–elect and his wife were neighbors of Hilson's in the Waldorf Towers when Bush was U.N. Ambassador. It was a black tie dinner, of course, just the kind that Gray had enjoyed describing in detail in his memoirs.

The guest list of sixty-two ranged from Gray to New York Mayor Ed Koch. Several on the list, including Hilson and Beverly Sills, would one day serve on the Board of Directors of Gray's new company or help his company in other capacities, like the former deputy director of the CIA under Richard Nixon and future UN Ambassador Vernon Walters, and Emil Mosbacher, chief of protocol under Nixon.[53]

Before the dinner ended, there were toasts to the guests of honor. Gray, always the perfect guest, arose and gave a toast to the new Vice President. Hilson, whose husband had made his fortune as an investment banker and who was an advisor to Eisenhower, told the *New York Times* that she had been "very royally" invited to the inauguration. She was, after all, the type of person who had every reason to celebrate the new administration.

"I remember sitting the night before the Inaugural in Bob's office there and thinking to myself, 'This is going to be the first time in the history of the United States the inauguration isn't going to take place. There's just too much to be done. It's just not going to come off. But it was absolutely amazing. Things just clicked, clicked, clicked. And it was remarkable, organizationally, and the credit has to go in large part to Bob for that. He really was the engineer of the whole thing," Mark Moran said in praise of Gray's efforts.

Ronald Reagan's 1981 inauguration was one of the most memorable in history. The patriotic theme of his campaign was carried through with American flags, red, white, and blue banners, and patriotic and, often, religious songs saturating the nation's capital. The crowds were enormous— most excited and full of patriotic pride, seeing Reagan as a great leader who would return America to prosperity and military strength. But what made the biggest impression on Washingtonians was the opulence and extravagance of the "rich Republicans."

Gone were the blue jeans and flannel shirts, the country western music and brown bag receptions from the Carter years. Washington now was Hollywood stars, big bands, furs, limousines, and luxury. The *Washington Post* reported:

> . . . this Reagan bunch of 1981 brings its own unmistakable stamp. Mink has come out of the closet. The only thing liberal about their limousines is the unending number. They are overwhelmingly white and middle class. Many are monied . . . and they epitomize the true believers of American politics.

> To a degree unseen at recent inaugurals, ostentation has been their hallmark this week. From it all, the uninitiated might be deluded into

believing there are no more Harlem, no more migrant lettuce pickers, no more economic pinch . . .

The Reaganites' private planes sat wing to wing at National Airport. Some of the imported limos were as big as buses. A group of Indiana Republicans came by rail, in the opulent private car once owned by J.P. Morgan, fat cat nonpareil . . .[54]

"It was a Hollywood-style inauguration, there's no question about it, but the money came from private sources," Mark Moran said. "I mean the American people have a right to expect some kind of splendor."

More than anything else, Washington was becoming a public relations man's dream. The theory that if a story did not appear on television, the problem did not exist, was going to become a reality over the next decade. Television would become a governing tool in the hands of men like Michael Deaver, who planned Reagan's public appearances to the last detail with television in mind. No longer would network anchors like Walter Cronkite remind Americans how the country was slipping in its place in the world— as they had nightly during the hostage crisis. Gradually, images would prevail over substance, to the point where White House pollsters would be brought in before policy decisions were made.

But it was not the pageantry, patriotism, or glamour that captured the attention of America on Reagan's Inaugural day. It was the release of the American hostages in Iran. As the day progressed, news of the impending hostages' release unfolded. While Carter and Reagan were having the traditional tea at the White House, news reports said that the hostages were on buses heading for the Tehran airport. By the time Reagan completed his Inaugural address, the hostages were on their way to Wiesbaden, Germany. "The hostages were coming home just as his presidency was beginning. For that moment, at least, it seemed possible to believe his appeal for a national renewal had more than rhetorical meaning," the *Washington Post* said.[55]

True to Gray's promise, the 1981 Reagan inauguration was a television extravaganza. The hostages' release and the activities in Washington kept the television networks struggling to keep up with the stunning developments and spectacular pictures. "It is certainly one of the great dramatic days in American history," Gray's friend Walter Cronkite said on the air.[56] ABC showed a split screen with Reagan signing his first official act, a hiring freeze for federal workers, and the hostages disembarking from the airplane for their first real taste of freedom. At the time, it appeared to be the result of circumstances beyond a public relations man's wildest dreams; today, even ABC questions the perfect timing.

Although Gray accomplished his goal of making the Inaugural the most telegenic ever, the overall success of his efforts quickly came into question. There were problems with the television cable links to the "mini-balls." And the Inaugural Committee had to refund in excess of $450,000 to hundreds of people who either did not receive tickets or who were turned away after waiting sometimes hours in long lines for festivities that were oversold. "We simply underestimated the demand for tickets," Gray told the *Washington Post*.[57] The newspaper reported that while Gray's excuse that "unexpected" demands for tickets may have contributed to the refund problem, confidential committee memoranda and sources indicated that "poor management, politics, and finally, panic" also played major parts in the "ticket fiasco of 1981."[58] Ironically, even the tickets for Gray's good friend, Ed Meese, the new White House Counselor, were lost.

Gray explained that many Republican officials had missed the deadline to send in the names of people who should receive invitations and so by the end of December the Inaugural Committee was already behind. To compensate for lost time, the committee set up phone banks to take orders for tickets; callers could use charge cards to pay. Although the invitations said exactly how many invitations the caller could order, unfortunately, the phones were manned by salesmen instead of trained volunteers. The salesmen asked how many tickets the caller wanted and then marked down that number. Soon, bags full of mail started arriving with ticket orders. By mid-January when the phone banks were shut down, the Inaugural events were hopelessly oversold—some to VIPs who had paid thousands for special events.

Although Gray had run "the costliest inauguration in American history" and was now overseeing the largest refund, he said that the refunds would not prevent the Inaugural Committee from netting a "good profit."[59] Over time, memories of the "ticket fiasco," the long lines, and the snubbed VIPs would fade, and Gray, the PR man, would promote his efforts as the first Inaugural not only to pay for itself, but also to turn a profit.

Two driving forces in Gray's life, politics and his profession, gave him the reasons and the means to make dramatic changes in his life. During the last six months of 1980, the Washington H&K office lost more than half a million dollars. When trucking deregulation passed and the American Trucking Association (ATA) account dropped back to the normal $5000 a month from as high as $300,000 a month, Gray did not move quickly enough to cut back the staff to balance the loss in revenue. The ATA account, at that time the largest in the history of H&K, had made the Washington office the biggest in the city; now it made the office start hemorrhaging money.

When JWT Group, which owned the New York advertising company J. Walter Thompson, offered to purchase H&K, Gray was the only H&K director on the board to vote against it. The former head of H&K, Loet Velmans, said he had gotten assurances from JWT that they would not interfere with H&K's operations or decisions. But Gray did not trust the arrangement. "Before the sale I felt like a proprietor. I knew where every postage stamp went," Gray told *Regardie's*. "Then we became just one small part of a huge corporation.'' Gray's efforts to put enough money together to buy H&K failed. ''Damn greed made them [H&K] take the money and run,'' Gray told *Forbes.*[60]

In July 1980, the same month as the Republican National Convention in Detroit nominated Ronald Reagan for president, JWT Group Inc., acquired 100 percent of the stock of Hill and Knowlton, Inc. Almost a month earlier, on June 30, Gray had been promoted to one of the Vice Chairmen at H&K.

With the end of the American Trucking Association account and the merger with J. Walter Thompson, Sheila Tate and John Jessar, who had worked full time on the account, started talking with Gray about setting up their own PR firm. Although Tate would eventually end up at the White House, she, Jessar, and Gray began planning the move in the fall of 1980.[61]

The idea was for Tate and Jessar to do the work, and for Gray to finance the company. Gray's salary was $82,500 a year in 1979, a good salary, but hardly enough on which to finance a new business alone. Luckily, even though H&K had not let Gray buy a building, he had invested in real estate in the Washington area and had other small businesses, including a small venture capital firm. Also, through his purchases of H&K stock, he owned 9 percent of the company. Gray agreed to provide the money, through his investments, stock, and bank loans, and Tate and Jessar agreed to provide the expertise. They began seriously discussing breaking away from H&K about the same time Gray and Jessar went to work full time for the Reagan campaign.

Gray had every reason to want to leave H&K. Besides the merger, the H&K Washington office was drowning in a pool of red ink after the American Trucking Association account wound down. After Reagan won the election and the Senate went Republican, there was an urgent need in Washington for Republican-oriented firms. For Gray it made perfect sense. With another Republican president taking office, the political atmosphere could not have been better. His contacts in government were never better. Virtually all of the people with whom he had worked on the campaign were taking high-level positions in the new administration. Gray helped Larry Speakes get a job on the transition staff, and, eventually, Speakes became Reagan's press secretary. Speakes helped another one of Gray's H&K staffers, Landon Parvin, get a job in the White House speech office. And Gray helped Sheila Tate win her job as Nancy Reagan's press secretary.

Gray loves to tell the story about how he decided to start his own firm. He said that he was sitting in the grandstand listening to Reagan's inaugural address when the President declared it was a time for new beginnings. ''I heard the president talk about a great new beginning for this country,'' Gray said, ''and I thought it was time for a great new beginning for me as well.''[62] Gray wrote his letter of resignation and left H&K, exactly twenty years after he had taken the job during the last few weeks of the Eisenhower administration. The inaugural story and the timing were good public relations—an interesting anecdote, timed for effectiveness, but less than candid.

Sheila Tate said they had planned to start their own firm regardless of who won the election. "Absolutely. It was not dependent upon the outcome of the election. That's part of the myth that [Gray] built up, the new beginnings and stuff. That's all bull," Tate said. But with Reagan winning the election, the timing could not have been better. "Oh, it was perfect, but, I think it would have worked anyway. Maybe it wouldn't have been quite so glitzy," Tate explained.

The long-felt animosity between H&K headquarters in New York and Gray and the Washington office was reflected in Loet Velmans's criteria for selecting Gray's replacement at H&K. "I wanted to get back to teamwork. I wanted someone respected throughout the company, someone who knew Washington, someone who knew Hill and Knowlton and what it stood for, and someone who was not a prima donna."[63] Bob John Robison, Gray's H&K successor, said that Gray took files with him when he left. Gray insisted they were only personal files. Robison said he had to rebuild the reputation of the Washington office since the other H&K offices had lost so much faith in the Washington office that they had quit referring clients and began going to Washington themselves to lobby, bypassing the H&K Washington office. Uncollectible bills of eighty thousand dollars had built up because of dissatisfied customers.

In fairness to Gray, he had been in charge of the Washington office for twenty years during which time it had not only grown in size, but also in stature. By the time he left, H&K headquarters were convinced that a Washington presence was critical to the success of the company. Loet Velmans had called Washington, "the jewel in our crown."[64] "There was a great flurry of activity" when Gray announced that he was leaving H&K, George Worden recalled. People from the New York office flew down several times asking Gray to stay.

One of Gray's last official acts before he left H&K was to sign a lease for new offices in the hottest new building in town. H&K was moving from a modest building in a marginal neighborhood to palatial splendor. The offices went from 12,000 square feet costing $84,000 to 40,000 square feet costing more than $900,000. The space had a 125-seat theater-style conference area, a modern video studio, three fully equipped kitchens, a private bathroom for what was to be Gray's office, all filled with stuffed furniture and expensive prints, but Gray left H&K before he could enjoy the new office.

Soon after William Casey took over as CIA director, in early 1981, he called in many of the old timers, the men who had run the Agency during its heyday when spies were still considered heros like James Bond and not jokes like Boris and Natasha. He called in Robert Crowley and Joe Kirschheimer, who had worked together providing cover for CIA operatives in

American businesses throughout the world in the 1960s and 1970s. On the seventh floor at CIA headquarters, they briefed the new CIA director and the deputy director, Bobby Ray Inman, on new approaches to using American corporations and on offshore commercial developments having to do with natural resources.

Crowley had prepared a letter for Casey with several points that Casey should keep in mind before he began reinstituting many of the programs that had been eliminated over the past several years. The list was not insulting, but it was on the edge. The course was Basic CIA Cover 101, and explained that the world had changed since Casey was involved in intelligence and that there were many surprises out there now. But Casey was full of energy, and he was eager to get the place going again. He wanted to reinvigorate the CIA with the kind of World War II excitement and electricity that Casey so fondly remembered. Robert Gates was not initially present at the meeting, but soon Casey was buzzed on the intercom, and Gates sat in on the discussion.

Casey told Crowley that he wanted to start using American companies again. Crowley protested, reminding the director that the world had changed in the mid-1970s. Besides the new oversight committees in Congress, the Securities and Exchange Commission laws now criminalized unreported corporate liaison with the CIA. "If the stockholder rises up in the back of the hall at the meeting and says, 'Do we now, have we ever,' the chairman damn better tell the truth because they criminalized it," Crowley said. He explained that the laws criminalizing secret CIA/business liaisons brought with them a new breed of trustees who were not the old majority stock holders, like Henry Ford or David Rockefeller. Instead, they were paid hands employed under contract by the Board of Directors, and they would be idiotic to play with the CIA. "It was just absolutely beyond the pale. If a guy agreed to play with us, we don't want him," Crowley said. Unless the CIA owned the company outright, there was no way to do it. Casey brushed aside Crowley's objections, indicating that Casey himself knew many businessmen who would be happy to do favors for the CIA.[65]

To the end, Casey kept talking about how businesses represented all kinds of opportunities for the CIA. The former SEC chairman thought he knew how to get around the new laws. He said that he knew everybody and could get to everybody and nothing was beyond him. He said there are many things that are seen and unseen and not understood except by him. "Casey was ineducable. You could not tell him anything. He knew everything," Crowley said.

On March 1, 1981 Gray opened the doors to The Power House, a building he had bought near the C&O Canal in Georgetown. He started his new company with fifteen former H&K staffers and three former clients— Motorola, ATA, and American Iron and Steel, one of John Hill's first clients when he started H&K. Within a few months, eight more H&K staffers joined the firm. Soon it became the largest privately owned public relations and lobbying firm in Washington, largely due to very lucrative foreign clients. But as Gray never hesitated to explain, before he took on a foreign client, he always checked first with his good friend, William Casey.

8

HOLLYWOOD
ON THE POTOMAC

*The important thing is that over a period of 25 years Gray has become
part of Washington, of its public social life, of the political inner circle,
and the Capitol Hill machinery that grinds out legislation oiled or altered
by lobbyist like he.*

Washington Post, 1980.[1]

Ronald Reagan's presidency and a Re-
publican-controlled Senate created the perfect political environment for
Robert Gray's new firm. He would take his years of Washington experience
and apply it to his own company. For the first time since he left Hastings,
Nebraska, twenty-five years earlier, he was starting his own business where
he would no longer be on someone else's payroll. But this time, he had more
than military service and business school as background. Unencumbered of
many of his Hill and Knowlton superiors' restraints, Gray now had a chance
to succeed or fail on his own. "When he opened up Gray and Company,
school was out. Now he could do anything he wanted," George Worden
said.[2]

Gray's high profile position of cochairman of the Reagan inauguration
helped bring in business. "With the new Administration coming in, [there
was] a lot of jockeying around to get in, if you will. And people like
[Armand] Hammer, half of whose lives depend on his being able to call the
President at the White House, this is a big thing, and sixty thousand dollars
or one hundred thousand dollars is nothing," a former Gray and Company
vice president said.

James Lake, a Washington lobbyist who had been one of Reagan's early
campaign workers, explained why Gray set up his own firm: "He did it to
take advantage of his ability and access and the perception of his access that
people would have as a result of his highly visible role in the campaign. . . .
He had access, but no matter how much access you have, sometimes
perception is greater access. Having people perceive that you have access is

as important as the access itself in generating clients. Bob Gray is absolutely masterful at what he does."[3]

The first thing Gray did that H&K had previously prevented him from doing was buy a building. Gray located his new offices not on Capitol Hill, like many of the labor unions had done twenty years earlier, not on K Street, Washington's business district where most of the law firms are, but in a beautiful old brick building on the canal in fashionable Georgetown. Gray paid $750,000 for the nineteenth-century building, a former power plant that had once provided the energy to move Washington's old street car system, which had been removed in the 1950s to make way for automobiles. With its towering, but long dormant, smoke stack, Gray's new headquarters was imposing. His gray and silver stationary simply read: The Power House, Washington, D.C.[4]

It was the perfect location from which to carry out the carefully crafted illusion of power, access, wealth, and influence: The openness, the glass, the blown-up photographs of the Reagan Inaugural or Gray with the Presidents. Visitors immediately felt dwarfed as they entered and saw the arched twenty-five-foot windows that soared in the open atrium to the thirty-five-foot open, iron-beamed ceiling. Clients were impressed with Gray's large office and the huge conference room. "[Gray] formed a dynamite company in a very incredible setting. [The] Power House was just a unique setting at the time. Now if you look at it, it looks worn and obsolete. But at the time, . . . [it] was really a sexy place—a great big open building," Pate Felts, a Gray and Company senior vice president, said.[5]

The 6400-square-foot, three-and-a-half story building was thrilling, but it was not conducive for work. Its purpose was not to provide a quiet atmosphere where professionals could think quietly. Its purpose was to impress. In the center was the "communications center." By today's standards it would seem a little silly. But in 1981, it was impressive, especially to the uninitiated. The white room housed three television monitors, two wire service machines, a telecopier (the forerunner to fax machines), a teleprinter, a word processor, and four clocks giving the times in Hawaii, Los Angeles, Chicago, and Washington. Later, the times would be changed to international time zones to reflect the increasing importance of international clients and Gray's new International Division.

In setting up his new company, Gray put his Harvard MBA to the test. Instead of the company buying the building, furnishing, and equipment, Gray used a leasing company he had set up earlier, Keith Leasing Corporation (KLC), which had mainly leased automobiles and trucks, to purchase the typewriters and furnishing and other equipment and lease them back to Gray and Company. In effect, Gray and Company's only asset was the people who worked there. The rest of the assets belonged to Gray. "He set up the Gray and Company structure very shrewdly. He had a leasing company, leasing cars, office machines, and so on. Gray and Company leased stuff from his other companies. He got an awful lot of money several different ways out of Gray and Company. Nothing illegal, but very, very shrewd and productive in monetary terms,'' a Gray and Company vice president explained.

Gray was not cheap, either for his clients or with his staff. "Gray always went first class in everything, and that was part of the appeal of the firm, both to the people who worked there and to the clients and to the outsiders. They would come in and see the Power House, and the Power House was a very dramatic kind of place,'' said a Gray and Company senior vice president.

In many ways, there has never before or since been an operation in Washington quite like Gray and Company. It was set up at the very start to combine lobbying and public relations equally in one operation. "Traditionally, public relations and lobbying were two distinct entities. There were firms that did public relations and there were firms that did lobbying. And the two were not generally related. Bob decided that the two were really, at least in Washington, very related disciplines. That public relations could be used to build the base of support that lobbying then translated into legislative action. And there is a lot of truth to that. . . . In order to get your views across in the Congress and to affect public policy, it's important to deal directly with the staff, members, and all that make those decisions. But in order to really shape their views in a particular way, you need that foundation of public support. These guys are mostly motivated by what they see as their political best interest. If you can generate a public feeling about a particular issue, it can be of tremendous assistance in any lobbying effort,'' said Mark Moran, who worked as an attorney at Gray and Company.[6] Gray sold the concept by hiring top-notch, well-recognized people and dividing the firm into a public relations operation, a government relations operation and an international division.

From the day it opened its doors, Gray and Company made a big splash. It became the talk of Washington. It was a glamorous, high-profile operation that attracted some of the most talented professionals in town. "Oh it was good. . . . It had cachet,'' said a Gray and Company vice president. "If you could get to Gray and Company, that was a great credential. And everybody knew it. They didn't know Edelman, although it was the biggest independent PR firm at the time. But Gray was Mr. Washington and everybody wanted to go there.'' Mark Moran agreed: "A lot of people saw it as a stepping stone.'' "It was the premiere organization of that type in this town and maybe in the country. . . . It certainly had go, go. . . . There was flash,'' said Adonis Hoffman, who worked in the International Division.[7] It was "the hottest shop in town,'' said a senior vice president of the firm.

Gray started with John Jessar, who had worked with Sheila Tate on the American Truckers Association account at H&K and had been part of the original planning of the new company, John Cevette, who was his attorney,

Jim Jennings, a former Episcopal priest who had worked in the Nixon White House and whom Gray had hired at H&K, and Charles Crawford, another former H&K executive who, like Jessar, had also worked on the Reagan campaign and had helped with the Inaugural. "There were a few of us who left Hill and Knowlton and went with him," Betsey Weltner, who worked for years as Gray's personal assistant, said.[8] "Maybe six of us. We were phenomenally successful, mainly because . . . of his contacts, [the] reputation he had for being able to access the Reagan administration, his friendship with Reagan and Cabinet Secretary (Ed) Meese."

But Gray also knew that Washington was a two-party town and in order to prosper, he had to hire high-profile, politically connected Democratic executives to balance his conservative Republican credentials. He hired Gary Hymel, who for years had worked as Speaker of the House of Representatives Tip O'Neill's top aide, and Bette Anderson, a former high-ranking Carter administration Treasury Department official. To complete his power base, Gray also hired socially prominent Washingtonians and the wives and families of the powerful. "A lot of wives," former H&K executive Sheila Tate said.[9] "Noreen Fuller [the first wife of Vice President Bush's former Chief of Staff Craig Fuller], Nancy Thurmond [the wife of Senator Strom Thurmond, then chairman of the Senate Judiciary Committee], and Joan Braden. She stirred up quite a controversy. But there were a lot of those kinds of people with very low salaries," Sheila Tate recalled.

In addition to keeping the wives of the powerful happy and busy, hiring them was good business for Gray. Not that they knew the PR and lobbying business, but they contributed to his illusion of access that was the foundation on which he built his firm. "But he gets the name recognition. He'd get people who didn't know how to do anything. . . . It was more illusion than reality," Tate explained.

Gray called them his "stars." "This is the star thing. Hire an ambassador, hire a cabinet officer, hire from the White House. And then nothing's in their in-box. They don't have anything to do," George Worden said. "Gray always hired people to give him prestige," echoed a Gray and Company senior vice president. Some of the stars were seasoned professionals; others were hired for their contacts.

One star was Joan Braden. "Need a favor from Henry Kissinger? Call Joan Braden, yet another [Gray and Company] employee. A prominent Washington hostess with many highly placed friends, she regularly counts Mr. Kissinger among her dinner guests," the New York Times wrote.[10] Two of Braden's friends gave Gray and Company not only its biggest, but also its most prestigious accounts: The Kennedy Center for the Performing Arts and Canada. (Eventually Gray and Company lost both of them.) She recruited the Kennedy Center from her friend Roger Stevens. At the time, it accounted for approximately 23.6 percent of the company's revenues.[11]

In a move similar to the use of his leasing companies, Gray set up a separate advertising company, Power House Communications, in the Flour Mill next door and instructed his employees to steer advertising business there. The main account was the Kennedy Center. Things did not go well. "They were awful. I tried to get them to come in and have meetings and come up with a poster design and I finally gave up and went out and found an artist to design this poster. I never thought they were very good, and other people got upset," one Gray and Company vice president said. "After they lost the Kennedy Center account, which they did lose, they had to let go a bunch of people at the advertising agency because that was their big client."

Next Braden went to another friend, then Canadian Ambassador Allan Gotlieb. It was the perfect example of Gray hiring "stars" who could bring in accounts, but who had no real public relations or lobbying experience. Often once the account was secured, it was turned over to young, low-paid account executives. That is what happened to the Canadian account. To make matters worse, Canada was considered a fat cow account to soak. "The Canadian account was a bottom line account. Everybody who could fancy the slightest reason for piling on, piled on," Joan Braden said in her book.[12] "Why were six people from the press department attending a conference in Ottawa? Why not two people or one person?" Braden wondered. When she complained, she "became a 'goddamn woman who happens to know the ambassador socially and thinks she knows public relation,' " Braden wrote.

Finally, it all ended publicly and with great embarrassment. Gray and Company sent a press release on behalf of Canada to the *New York Times* that misspelled the Ambassador's name, the name of the reporter, and the name of the Ambassador's guest for the luncheon the press release was promoting. The *Times* ran a story that Gray and Company, Canada's publicists, could not even spell the names correctly. Canada canceled the contract with Gray and Company and Joan Braden quit.

In the case of Nancy Thurmond, Gray first tried to hire her, but that obvious attempt at influence peddling bothered even Washington. Instead Gray relied on his old pattern of being helpful and available to wives of the powerful. The *Times* profile provided a nice tableau of this practice: "Nancy Thurmond is sitting in Bob Gray's office. 'I just had a meeting on Project Hope,' she is saying, referring to her favorite charity ball. 'It was the unanimous feeling of the group that you'd be wonderful to do the publicity.' 'Sure,' Mr. Gray says without hesitation. 'I'd love to.' He also agrees to assist Mrs. Thurmond with a few other charity chores. Later, after she leaves, he shares a trick of his trade. 'You see,' he says, 'I always ask if I can do anything to help.' . . . Mr. Gray wants Senator Thurmond to help him get a client's bill through his committee. Meanwhile, he will help the Senator's wife with her charity ball."[13]

A *Washingtonian* magazine article published in the same period underscored Gray's emphasis on the impact of personal favors. " 'I try never to conclude a call with anyone in government or the press or the legislative branch without asking if there is some way I can be of help to them,' says Bob Gray. 'The reason people return anybody's call in this town is because that person has a reputation for not coming at them with nonsense, for coming at them with things that can only be solved on their level, for representing worthwhile causes and articulating them appropriately and honestly. And if there is a downside, letting them know what it is.' "[14]

Gray argued that he was not selling access, that "any well-meaning citizen" could call the White House and arrange a function. Upon further reflection, he added, "The more I think about it, the more I realize how much that's just the way the world goes. For example, the *Washington Post* gives the editorial board briefings with experts on important matters. But let Joe Beercan from Dubuque, Iowa, come in off the street, and he wouldn't get to see the subscription editor. . . . The marketplace is the marketplace." Gray explained that his entree to the White House came from "having been around the track for twenty-two years."

Gray divided his company into four divisions: Government Relations (lobbying), headed by Hymel; Public Relations, headed by Jessar; and International, headed by Crawford. The fourth handled the financial and accounting aspects of the firm. He started with sixteen employees. As clients poured in, Gray and Company grew. The Power House quickly filled with account representatives, young professionals who wanted a chance to break into the business. Visitors were impressed by the crisp, well-tailored staff, always busy, hurried, and attractive. Soon the staff spilled over to the Flour Mill, a neighboring office building.

Besides former employees, several clients from Hill and Knowlton jumped to Gray and Company the day Gray opened the door.[15] It did not take long for dozens more to rush through the door. Gray was very good with clients. "Bob Gray greets you as though you were the one person in the world with whom, at that particular moment, he most wishes to converse. Just as you are beginning to converse, he greets somebody else in precisely the same manner. For nearly seven years I watched him bowl over hundreds of people—clients, government officials, employees, even friends. They all get the same treatment and it is charming, intelligent, seemingly guileless, and effective," Joan Braden wrote in her memoirs.[16] "He had unbelievable charisma. You should see him in a presentation; he was just awesome," Betsey Weltner agreed.

Yet Gray rarely worked on client accounts he recruited. Gray and his "stars" recruited big accounts, but the real work was done by the young, inexperienced, low-paid staff. The number of clients and staff grew so quickly that before the company could really get established, Gray was already losing control. When Gray went to pitch a prospective client he took with him a senior person to whom the account was assigned. The senior account executives typically were responsible for a group of several accounts; so although Gray often was the one who persuaded a client to sign on, the actual work was done by people two or three (or more) levels down. "Gray's not going to be around much on any one account. Only at the beginning and only as a fire engine—tell me when things are bad in production, if something's bad, let me know. If it's good, don't bother me. Send me copies of the letters, of the reports, which is fine. Fine. . . . He's not into any nitty gritty. . . . He's not involved in any day-to-day work except at the outset of the account, the beginning," George Worden said.

The least prestigious accounts or the ones that did not have a lot of money got the least attention. "I think they sort of decided who their favorites were and gave them really neat accounts and gave them a pretty good reign on them; then they'd give accounts they didn't want to deal with to other people," a Gray and Company vice president said.

The arrival of the Republican power structure in Washington reinvigorated the social scene in town. And there was no better party goer or thrower than Gray. Much of his success could be attributed to his long-maintained social ties. "He wears out a tuxedo each year, and at the rate he is partying, Robert Keith Gray may just have to begin to replace that black-tie uniform every six months," the *New York Times* said.[17] It was the perfect way to enhance his already polished image of success, charm, and power and to maintain the contacts he had made during the campaign and the Inaugural.

"There is no doubt he was in that league, the A-list league or at least the B-list league both in Congress and the Administration," said a Gray and Company vice president. Cabinet officials, members of Congress, and prominent members of the media often came to parties and receptions he set up. Besides, Gray really enjoyed entertaining, and he was good at it. Gray insisted that if the Democrats had won the elections, he would have approached them in the same way. "If the Democrats had been elected my first job would have been getting acquainted with the new people in town— doing my homework—moving in as fast as I could," he told the *New York Times*. He described himself as a "political animal but not a partisan animal." The way Gray knew best how to move in fast was "the party scene at which he is a master. He says: 'I never go out socially but that I don't come back with a new idea or a new contact—it's just a matter of everyone stretching out the business day.'"[18]

Adonis Hoffman, who worked in the International Division, said Gray "was like quicksilver. . . . I found Bob was a person who was always up, always on, seemingly always alert, and, I think, always looking for a business opportunity. That was my sense." Larry Speakes explained how Washington operates: "I think a lot of it is relationship. You know the business doesn't end at five in Washington. It goes till the cocktail party is over. . . . So it is sort of who you know and politics. If you scratch my back,

I'll scratch yours. I think that happens to a certain extent in Washington in everything—in government and out of government.''[19] Bette Anderson agreed, "You do more business at night than you do any place else in that kind of business, you really do.''[20]

Gray, always attentive to the often neglected wives of the powerful, threw a party at the elegant Decatur House for Mary Jane Wick, the wife of his Inaugural cochairman, Charles Wick, who now headed the United States Information Agency. The press noticed his attentiveness. *Dun's Business Month* wrote, "In the evenings, the natty bachelor is off to a whirlwind of parties—sometimes as many as three a night—to which he often squires the wives of . . . powerful Republicans. . . . 'I go because that's the way business is done here,' says Gray, who reportedly wears out two tuxedos a year. Marvels a former White House aide: 'He's a genius at making the Washington social scene work for him. Whoever thought of working the wives?' ''[21] Gray had—ever since Mamie Eisenhower.

In May, at the Power House, Gray held a seated dinner for 120 for Sheila Tate, his former H&K account executive, whom he had helped get the White House job as Nancy Reagan's press secretary. The office furniture and typewriters were loaded into vans and driven around the city until the party was over. He planned a September "stomp," a slow square dance, to honor Nancy Reynolds, his and Nancy Reagan's friend, and had a party for former Ambassador Clare Boothe Luce, who served on his new company's Board of Directors.

In turn, the Secretary General of the Organization of American States, Alejandro Orfila, who had known Gray since his Eisenhower years, hosted a dinner for Gray, celebrating his new public relations and lobbying firm. "He knows everyone in Washington—he's introduced me to a lot of people," Orfila said. "He's helped open a lot of doors for me.''[22] Two years later, Gray hired Orfila to be the second in command at Gray and Company. At the dinner, Reagan's new Secretary of Health and Human Services Richard Schweiker, who had known Gray when he was a Pennsylvania Senator and for whom Gray had thrown a party, explained to the media that Gray did not get a job in the new Reagan administration "by his own choice. He could've had any job he wanted." But Gray responded modestly, "I want to be as supportive as possible from the outside. There are so many people who are more qualified.''[23]

In July 1981, Gray threw one of the most extravagant parties of the year in honor of Nevada Senator Paul Laxalt. For this post-Fourth-of-July celebration Gray spared no expense. It was held beneath a huge circus tent at the foot of the Mall in Washington, with the Capitol Building projecting the perfect backdrop. From beginning to end, the carefully planned event emphasized the public relations message Gray wanted sent. The hand-painted invitations carried out the circus extravaganza theme by announcing that the party was in honor of the man "who brought the elephants back under the big top.''[24] The 250 black-tie and evening-gown clad guests enjoyed strolling musicians, as they dined on gazpacho and cold tenderloin of beef. Attendees were seated around circular tables covered in peach linen ''with iridescent geodes (borrowed from the Smithsonian) as crystal rock center-pieces.''[25]

Betsey Weltner, Gray's personal assistant, described the party as ''unbe-lievable . . . we had to get special permission and go through all kinds of rigmarole to get to put a tent on the Mall. That's an example of the kind of thing he would do. I think it cost about twenty thousand dollars. Probably would cost a lot more to get that now. But the inside of the tent looked like a French restaurant. I mean we had to bring everything in. We had to bring in lavatories. We had to get really nice ones. They weren't like port-a-johns. They really looked like the kind in a restaurant. We put flowers in them and rose petals—the whole bit. The reason that sticks in my mind is because almost every member of the Cabinet was there that night plus people in the media, like George Will and people like that, sort of the ultra-nova stars, media stars, like [Rowland] Evans and [Robert] Novak. That type who were there. Then all the older kind of media establishment. The minority leader, Bob Michel. There was a lot of pizzazz. A lot of glitz. . . . It certainly gave an impression to the clients who were there. I remember when Alexander Haig [then the Secretary of State] walked in. That was a real big deal. You know how it works in Washington. The way you get important people to come to your party is to have it in honor of someone and then invite all their friends.''

When the *Times* asked Gray why he had suddenly become one of Washington's leading party givers, he replied, ''to return those lamb chops.'' But the reporter knew better. ''It isn't quite that simple. Mr. Gray is known here as something more than a frivolous playboy. Partying for him is serious business. He has ideas and clients to sell.''

The party was to honor Paul Laxalt, then a United States Senator, but more importantly Reagan's former campaign chairman and close confidant. Although Gray and Laxalt were not close friends, Gray's throwing the party on Laxalt's behalf created the image that they were. Equally helpful to Gray, no prominent or powerful person in Washington would turn down an invitation to honor Laxalt. Thus the party drew an ''almost embarrassing display of power''—nine Cabinet members; the new White House power brokers, James Baker, Michael Deaver, and Edwin Meese; senators, con-gressmen, diplomats, and prominent journalists.

In keeping with Gray's bipartisan efforts, a few Democrats were also invited including Anne Wexler and Stuart Eizenstat, Jimmy Carter's former domestic advisors. At the time, they did not know that their White House memos and briefing books had contributed to putting ''the elephants back under the big top.''

The guests publicly proved that Gray had access to some of the most powerful figures in Washington. It was great for business. Gray and Company lawyer Mark Moran explained why Gray placed such an emphasis on parties. "It was to create the illusion of influence . . . to actually create the image. It has two effects: one, it does give you some degree of influence. If you throw a party for some senator and have five thousand of his closest friends in Washington there, he's going to return your phone calls the next time. But also, it gives you the even greater benefit of everybody seeing you throw the party for this guy and assumes you're really close buddies, and then they see the other five thousand people that come and assume they're your close buddies, too. And it enhances your image as well. It has a dual purpose."[26]

With the new President a former Hollywood actor and a master communicator, Gray was in his element. The pageantry and the parties of Gray's early days in Washington were back. It was as much a reason for his success as anything. And he thrived on it. "Hollywood on the Potomac . . . Bob made this, in a sense, Hollywood on the Potomac. That's the view he took of it," Moran said.

To the more serious professional, the parties and The Power House seemed more like Alice in Wonderland than an earnest attempt at lobbying and public relations. One of those professionals was Barry Schochet, a Gray and Company vice president. "From day one I was troubled with that. It didn't seem like it was real. [Gray and Company was] a lot of fluff, but no substance, and we would have meetings about clients and it was really straight public relations, you know, party-oriented stuff. . . . The short period of time I was there, what we were trying to do was so speculative and so crazy that it just didn't seem serious."[27]

Gray had become the personification of the successful, nongovernment Washington insider. His melding of public relations and lobbying had vaulted him into the heights enjoyed by only a few people like Clark Clifford, but unlike Clifford, Gray had no policy expertise to sell. And there were drawbacks to the firm's attempt to do everything at once. "In the Washington world of consultants and high-powered players, [lobbying and public relations] get meshed together. . . . Bob Gray is the quintessential example," Adonis Hoffman said. "I think on balance, when you kind of try to put everything in one bowl and serve it up, you invariably lose something. And perhaps a little bit of the substance was lost. You know, the clients are always the best judge of that." And despite the parties and glowing press coverage Gray and Company had a high client turnover, Hoffman and others confirmed. Bette Anderson, one of the most senior women to work at Gray and Company, eventually left unhappy. "My entire background was too substantive, and I can't deal with the never-never land."

Gray was not lazy or careless. He was very successful because he worked hard at providing a service that people wanted—access to the powerful. If a client needed access to the Executive Branch and/or Congress and did not support the party in power, or worse, had supported the opposition, to some, the quickest way to move from the outside in was to buy in. For many clients, if just meeting high-level political figures was their goal, then Gray and Company provided a real service. However, most clients who hired the company thought they were buying much more. They thought Gray and Company would solve their problems with government. "People thought that Bob Gray had the silver bullet. That if you had a problem on the Hill, if you had a problem at the White House, [if] you had an image problem you needed corrected in the media, [if] you needed media coverage, [if] you had a story you wanted to tell and you couldn't get anybody interested, call Bob Gray to fix it. And we did. We fixed it, a lot of the time," a Gray and Company senior vice president said.

But many came away disappointed. Although Gray was friends with Ronald Reagan, Ed Meese, Cap Weinberger, Richard Schweiker, Charles Wick and others in the administration, that did not necessarily mean that he would ask for a favor on behalf of the client. "One or some or sometimes all would show up at a party, and you could shake their hands and say hello to them. He [Gray] threw a lot of parties. You would go home satisfied if you had any doubt that he actually knew these guys and now you were shaking their hands. He might even have an opportunity to say to one of them who you had a problem with, 'Listen, I've got this problem.' And they would say back to you, 'Boy, that's very interesting. Have somebody see Zilch on my staff.' You go see him. It's all a charade, though. Zilch isn't going to do anything more for this guy than he would have gotten if he could find a way to get to him anyway," explained Washington lobbyist John Sears.

Gray rarely personally worked for a client—sitting down and drafting a proposal or PR campaign, pounding the hall of Congress or the Executive Branch. His contributions were much more social in nature. "It was much more 'I'll get you together at a party.' Much more that kind of stuff," Sheila Tate said. "I think the people with the serious issues went elsewhere. You look at who his clients were. They were people like [Shaklee]. They wanted to be more visible on the social circuit. For an awful lot of people, that's all they wanted," Tate explained.

Gray had cultivated his social and political connections since his Eisenhower years. He now began calling on them, hoping to generate clients for his firm. These contacts could get him accounts in various ways. Estee Lauder's son, Ron Lauder, was an assistant secretary of defense at the Pentagon and a friend of Gray's. Gray and Company handled a portion of the Estee Lauder cosmetic account for a while. Once the firm had gained the account, some of the professionals at Gray and Company did not feel that Estee Lauder got its money's worth. "Estee Lauder did some big promotion up in New York and [Gray and Company] got involved in the press conference up there and it was something like forty thousand dollars for the press briefing lunch. It was a ridiculous amount of money to spend for announcing these scholarships that they were doing. It was just insane; it should not cost that much," said one former Gray and Company vice president.

Carter Clews worked in the Public Relations Division. By his recollection there were difficulties that made the exorbitant charges seem even worse. "We charged Estee Lauder forty thousand dollars for one press conference and luncheon. Charges were just beyond belief. . . . I know that there was some unhappiness there when they found out that there were dead people on the media list. They felt like for their money, they should have live correspondents. [Gray and Company] supplied them with a media list of who was contacted and invited and all and they knew that one or two of them were dead and they resented that."

Gray did not waste his access by constantly asking for favors, especially for small or less profitable accounts. It often depended on the bottom line. "He had great connections, but he was really reluctant to call people, which to some extent is understandable because you don't want to take advantage of a friendship, but people hired him because of his connections," said a Gray and Company executive.

Former HHS Secretary Schweiker, now himself a lobbyist, thought highly of Gray's abilities. "He's a good lobbyist and he's very credible and he does stick with the rule that I lay down that the information has to be credible or you won't be welcome back. Bob, I think, prides himself on that, too. I think he understands that because of his own government experience. I think he's a very good, constructive lobbyist." But Schweiker did not remember whether Gray had ever spoken to him on behalf of a client when Schweiker was running the largest department in government. "Oh, we surely talked during that time because we're good friends. Let me say this, over the course of my career he certainly has. . . . Whether he was in to see me when I was Secretary, I don't know."[28]

As with so many other aspects of Gray's life and business, his longtime efforts to maintain a relationship with Ronald and Nancy Reagan paid off more in terms of perception than reality. "He was not close to them [the Reagans] personally while the President was in the White House. But he had been labeled—the line was that 'Gray and Company, with close ties to the Reagan administration.' You would see that in every story. And yet, he personally went to one event, the President's birthday party in 1981, and he hadn't been invited to anything again—to which many believe Mike Deaver was involved. There was some jealousy there," a former White House official said.

Gray's link to the White House was Ed Meese. "Yes. Very, very strongly Ed Meese," the White House official confirmed. "He [Gray] was friends with the Reagans and all that, but he did not have a lot of contact with them.

I think he mainly dealt with Ed Meese,'' said Larry Speakes, who was Reagan's deputy press secretary in the early 1980s. A senior Gray and Company executive insisted that Gray's closeness to the President and others was often faked. "He completely faked his closeness with a number of senior administration officials.''

Whether or not Gray was personally close to Reagan really did not matter. What was critical, however, was for Gray to have a close relationship with one of Reagan's top advisors. "It's always the case with Ronald Reagan that the close staff has the greatest access and has the most influence. And almost no one coming in from the outside had the ability to persuade Ronald Reagan to do anything. He depended on what the staff would think was proper or good. So that if . . . Bob Gray went in to Reagan and said, 'Here is a great idea, Mr. President, you should do this' . . . he'd say, 'Yeah, . . . that's a great idea. What do you fellahs think?' Meaning Meese, Baker, and Deaver. Well, if you could get their support, then Ronald Reagan would probably go for it and if you don't get their support, he's not going to go for it,'' James Lake explained.

Gray told *Washingtonian* magazine that he dealt mainly with Ed Meese at the White House because his business chiefly involved domestic issues. "I bend over backward to make sure I don't bother [him]. I know our relationship is good because I don't abuse it. . . . I feel very comfortable going to him even later in the same day that I've talked to him,'' Gray said about Meese.[29] Although Gray had known Ed Meese since the 1970s, the first time he had worked closely with him was during the 1980 campaign. He did not meet Meese's wife, Ursula, until after the election. But soon they became the closest of friends.

Ed Meese was the only one of the three top aides to Reagan who would be impressed by Gray. James Baker came from a rich, socially prominent family and had headed Gerald Ford's 1976 presidential campaign. He did not need any Washington introductions either politically or socially. Michael Deaver, a skilled PR man himself, could see right through Gray's carefully crafted illusion of power and access. But Ed Meese was new to Washington, came with little money, and was vulnerable to overtures of introductions to the "right" people, to offers of kindness and friendship during his times of trouble. He was just the type of person to whom Gray could ingratiate himself, and he held the power with Reagan that would make Gray's time and effort worthwhile. "You know, if you can do something for Gray and he likes you, Gray is a very generous person,'' Carter Clews, a Gray and Company senior vice president, said. "There is friendship and then there is making a buck,'' another Gray and Company executive agreed.

The Meeses's financial difficulties were no secret. *The Washington Post* wrote about it on the front page of its social pages: "She [Ursula] has worn borrowed evening clothes to fancy dinners because the family finances are tight.''[30] Gray knew, like other successful lobbyists, that the most effective way to influence powerful politicians was to become their friends. As a friend, he had one of his clients create a job for Ursula Meese. "Ursula Meese was hired only because she was married to the Attorney General [Meese was the Counselor to the President at that time]. There was absolutely no question about that whatsoever. I was there when she was hired and I remember the terms of the agreement and it was clear," a senior Gray and Company executive said. Ursula Meese took the job, she told the *Washington Post*, for strictly financial reasons. "For Ursula Meese, the concerns about money come first. . . . Their debts, she says, are 'very large. . . . We take loans to pay house payments.' "[31]

Gray convinced Texas millionaire William Moss, a client, to create the William Moss Institute, a philanthropic foundation to poll Americans about their concerns for the future. It was associated with American University, another Gray client. The Foundation was inaugurated when Ursula Meese needed a job. Gray recommended Ursula Meese for director of the institute at $40,000 a year, a nearly 40 percent increase in the family's income (Ed Meese's salary was $61,000). It was not a job that she particularly wanted, but she needed the money.[32]

Former American University President Richard Berendzen was privy to the circumstances and recalled what transpired:

"Bill [Moss] is a personal friend of Bob Gray's, and I think probably hired Gray and Company. As a matter of fact, as I recall he definitely did, to advise him about the Institute. Gray was doing consulting with us, too, at that time. One day Bill and Bob Gray and I met and Bob said, 'You know I've got an idea. There is this lovely lady in town, Ursula Meese, her husband is Ed Meese,' who was at that time the chief aide to the President and the press was calling him the de facto President of the United States. . . . As far as I know, Bill had never met Ursula Meese. I never had. And so Gray set up the meeting and the three of us met at the Watergate."[33]

The Moss Institute not only paid Ursula Meese; in turn, as the Institute's director, she authorized payments to Gray and Company, in 1982, of $115,933 for "Institute set up costs; costs incurred to plan surveys and coordinate activities in connection with identifying and implementing the institute's research and educational activities." Two years later, when her husband was nominated for United States Attorney General, this arrangement brought inquiries from the special prosecutor appointed to investigate Meese's finances (an investigation that did not lead to formal charges). When questioned, Gray insisted that despite his close friendship with the Meeses and the public articles about their financial difficulties, he did not know "there was a financial problem . . . but, people, when they come to government service, usually have a hard time making ends meet."[34] But Berendzen told the *Post* that when Gray recommended Mrs. Meese for the job, "I raised the question of whether it would raise too many political questions."

Berendzen said about Ursula Meese, "What can you say. She's like somebody that lives next door to your mother. I was quite taken by the woman because I don't know what I had expected, but this was all the image of the affluent, highfalutin Reagan Republican administration . . . and I meet Ursula Meese and her kind of half worn-out cloth coat and she's, you know, Let's-go-out-and-have-a-hot-dog-and-go-to-Sears–type person and just could not be more unpretentious. And I could be wrong, but I think the Bob Gray involvement was that he'd been at a dinner or somewhere and she had just mentioned, 'I'd like to get a job somewhere.' And a couple of days later, he bumps into Moss and says, 'Ah ha'—Being the right guy at the right place with the right people. So she works at the Institute and the funding is provided by Moss."[35]

Gray was there when the Meese family needed assistance. During the summer of 1982, when the Meeses's college-aged son, Scott, was killed in a tragic automobile accident, Gray comforted the family. He offered them every kindness, and, in return, Ed Meese was a loyal friend and, when possible, returned the favors. "Gray and Meese were close," one of Gray's employees recalled, "Gray did quite a bit for Ursula. Bob Moss set up that foundation tied to AU that hired her, Ursula Meese. Gray had a hand in that. Gray also, as a result of that, had AU as a client for a while. I worked on that account."

Ursula Meese's job, and the foundation, eventually disappeared. "It ended because they never could quite figure out what they were going to do," Berendzen confirmed. "It was not a bad idea—the public really doesn't know what the future holds—but we could never figure out how to make it work. The other big problem that Bill [Moss] had was that he couldn't get money. Bill had hoped that he could round up a bunch of his friends. All he wanted to do was put in the seed money."

Meese was not the only Reagan administration official whom Gray helped when needed. "Do you remember when Casey was under severe attack? [In 1981, then Arizona Senator Barry Goldwater called for Casey's resignation because of some of Casey's past business practices] . . . I remember Gray talking to him on the phone and I literally wanted to throw up on the carpet. 'Mr. Director, we are supporting you 100 percent.' I mean, he kissed his ass all the way through that stuff because he was clever. He knew that when somebody was down and he dropped all sorts of innuendos that he was helping him here and he was going to do this and that. And he was going to provide this type of support. Well, hell, when Casey rehabilitated himself, he's not going to forget that," a Gray and Company vice president said.

Buying influence with the powerful was easy. For example, Gray had known Caspar Weinberger for years. Reagan's new Secretary of Defense had been Richard Nixon's Secretary of Health, Education and Welfare. What did Weinberger need? A job for his son. "Yes. Junior. He was [a] nice, ineffectual young man," said Neil Livingstone, who was a Senior Vice

President at Gray and Company.[36] Gray paid Caspar Junior two thousand dollars a month, and when Gray's clients needed something from the Pentagon, Gray and Company went right to the top.

On the surface, Gray and Company was a glamorous, high-flying, seat-of-the-pants operation that almost everyone in town seemed to admire. Internally, the infighting was enormous. Gray, some staffers felt, did not demonstrate great loyalty to his employees. "Bob had an attitude about staff that it doesn't matter how you treat them because you can always find somebody to take their place. I have heard him say that it doesn't matter. Nobody is indispensable. We can always find somebody to take the place of anybody. And that was very much his attitude. It's hard-pressed to find somebody in Washington that hasn't worked for Gray at one time or another," said Mark Moran.

Gray and Company's treatment of the staff resulted in a high turnover rate. "It must have been at least one hundred people who left unhappy, that's for sure . . . it was a nightmare. It was a horrible place to work," one Gray and Company vice president said. But it did not matter. The company's image was so great that people were literally waiting in line to get jobs. "I mean I got generals and admirals and ambassadors and sub-Cabinet officials—I mean we were riding so high everyone wanted to come over," Neil Livingstone said. Gray's nephew, Ken, who worked at the firm, remembered people handing him resumes and asking for jobs at bars in Georgetown. One Gray and Company executive said, "I always felt that Gray just took you in, milked you, and then [when] you were done, threw you out."

"It was a very tough environment. It was very fast-paced. There was enormous pressure, and there was pressure on people at the top because of the substantial amount of revenues that they had to either generate themselves or service if they were making those very high salaries," a Gray and Company senior vice president said. When an employee negatively affected the bottom line of the company, regardless of the reason, the staffer was quickly let go. On at least one occasion client pressure or the presumption of client interest led to the dismissal of an employee.

For most of the 1970s, Barry Zorthian, an Armenian-American, had been a vice president with Time, Inc. Prior to that, he was best known for his defense of the Vietnam War as the government's chief spokesman. While working for a business association, Zorthian volunteered for the Bush campaign in 1980 and later for the Reagan/Bush campaign. There he ran into Gray whom he had known earlier, though not well, because of his *Time* magazine job. Zorthian also helped on the Inaugural and kept in contact with Gray throughout the year. In late 1981, when Gray and Company was rapidly expanding, Gray took Zorthian to lunch and offered him a job.

Ron Lauder, the Estee Lauder offspring and a government official at the time, had recommended Gray to the government of Turkey. It was the beginning of the end for Zorthian.

Although Zorthian was never very active in the Armenian-American community, in late 1983 the Armenian Assembly, a group established to remind Americans about the deaths of over a million Armenians by the Turks between 1915 and 1923, asked Zorthian to serve on its Board of Directors starting in 1984. A small ethnic newspaper, the *California Courier*, with a circulation of about 5,000, carried a short article mentioning that Zorthian was a vice president at Gray and Company which represented Turkey.[37] The long animosity between Armenia and Turkey, which denies that Armenians were systematically killed, bubbled over when a Turkish newspaper correspondent saw the article and ran a story in Turkey saying, "The Turks Realize That They Have Left to an Armenian the Job of Promoting Them in America."[38]

Several former Gray and Company executives thought someone inside the firm, a competitor of Zorthian's, leaked the story to the Turkish press to try to get rid of Zorthian. "There are some strange people in that shop. They would cut their mothers's hearts out for an extra buck," said one.

Members of the Turkish parliament began questioning the government, and the government complained to their Ambassador, who had hired Gray and Company. Gray was on vacation in Acapulco when the Turkish Ambassador, His Excellency Dr. Sukru Elekdag, called. He was furious. Alejandro Orfila, who was the new Vice Chairman of the company, spoke to Elekdag. According to Zorthian, Orfila told him the Turkish Ambassador said, "I hired you guys to help me and my political problems, and instead you're creating problems for me. . . . You must do something drastic that I can report back to my government or else I'll be forced to cancel my contract."[39] When Gray returned and was confronted with the situation, he went to Zorthian and asked, "What the hell's going on?" Zorthian tried to explain that he had never worked on the Turkish account, had never said anything derogatory about Turkey, and that his opinions regarding Armenian positions and causes were strictly private and personal, not public or professional. His protestations did not seem to matter. If it was a choice between a Gray and Company executive or the possible loss of a client, the decision was easy. It fell to Orfila to fire Zorthian.

Articles about Zorthian, a well-known figure in Washington media circles, appeared in the newspaper. At first Gray said that he had fired Zorthian because he was ineffective. Later, to the Associated Press, Gray admitted that it was because of the Turkish government. When asked about the matter for this book, Gray wrote that Zorthian was terminated because of his conduct; he had publicly expressed an opinion that was counter to the firm's public relations efforts for Turkey.

Zorthian pursued the matter with the District of Columbia Human Rights Commission on the grounds that he had been fired based purely on ethnicity.

The Commission agreed with Gray and Company that Zorthian had been dismissed for his conduct rather than for his ethnicity.[40] Since he had found another job shortly after leaving Gray and Company, it would be difficult to show damages if he pursued the case in court, so he dropped it. Within Gray and Company, said one senior vice president, the incident underscored the toughness of the corporate politics. "Barry Zorthian left under a cloud. The fact of the matter is there was a huge corporate power struggle and when they wanted to get rid of you, they PR'd you out of there and dumped on you."

Inside the firm, it was very competitive. Gray had made promises to many executives that went unfulfilled. Within the first few years, two of the top four executives who had started Gray and Company, John Cevette and John Jessar, were forced out. Charles Crawford and James Jennings survived— Jennings because of his personal closeness to Gray, and Crawford because of his willingness to be tough on employees and to fire them so Gray could remain the soft touch. "A lot of people underestimated Gray, and they particularly underestimated Crawford and Jennings. There's still a lot of people—very senior, important sort of household-word people—in this town who came to Gray and Company convinced that they were going to take over, that they were going to be the right-hand person under Bob Gray. And those people are still walking around with knives in their backs, or, in some cases, in their chests. Because Jim and Chuck were very, very, very good, not only at how to run that business, [but] how to kind of protect Gray," a longtime Gray and Company executive explained.

Not all Gray and Company employees felt like commodities. Some were happy. Niels Holchs is young, politically conservative, and a top aide on Capitol Hill to Kentucky Senator Mitch McConnell. He did not get the job because he came from Kentucky, or worked hard on the Senator's campaign. He got it because he was a lobbyist at Gray and Company. In that capacity, he met people in the Senate who recommended him for the job. He cut his teeth in Washington during a time when lobbying and public relations became respectable—became careers for which to strive. An admirer of Gray's, he believes that lobbyists serve a vital function in government and that Gray should be credited with opening up the process. He believes that lobbying is good. Certainly, his own career success depended on lobbying. As a young professional whose views were shaped in the 1980s, Holchs's perspective on Capitol Hill is roughly analogous to the attitudes of young Harvard MBAs who flooded Wall Street during the period.

"When you get beyond the perception of Gray and Company, when you get down to the work and what you are providing your clients, the culture was one of hard work in developing arguments and trying to help your client succeed at their objective as their representative. A lot of clients stayed and they obviously felt their consultant was doing a good job. It certainly wasn't a perfect firm; I am not going to paint a rosy picture. But all in all, there was a culture there that I think was very helpful to the lobbying business being looked at in a different light. We were all proud to work there and to be called lobbyists. The lobbying profession, I think, had had quite a sordid reputation, and we were proud to be a lobbyist at Gray and Company," said Holchs.

The common wisdom that there are no Republicans and no Democrats inside the Beltway in Washington is typified by Holchs, a product of Gray and Company's bipartisan training. "All the Democrats that I worked with at Gray and Company, even though I am a Republican, are all going to be lifelong friends. You learn from their experiences; they learn from your experiences. There was a tremendous synergy between people from different disciplines and different backgrounds. Gray attracted a tremendous amount of talent from all sorts of disciplines. We had reporters, we had press secretaries, we had conservative Republicans to liberal Democrats. We had a whole variety of people. Stars and nonstars. Indians and chiefs. It really was a melting pot of America."

Holchs is the type of young congressional staffer that lobbyists love. Besides being one of their own, he looks to lobbyists for his information. He believes that they are providing a real service. In short, he looks to Washington, not the people back home, for answers. It is a Washington-knows-best attitude that is pervasive throughout the city. "One frustration that we all have is that a lot of people outside of Washington don't spend half as much time as we do on these issues, so you have these people who are not as informed as they ought to be about not just the process, but the individual issues that make up that process. I think if people spent an hour a day reading the paper or even twenty minutes a day learning about what is happening in Washington, they would be much better able to help their members of Congress," Holchs said.

That does not mean Holchs does not try to please his boss's constituents back home in Kentucky. But instead of considering that public relations campaigns just possibly prey on people with too little time or interest to study an issue by simply reducing a complex problem to simple, usually emotional, often self-interested slogans, he believes that PR campaigns are a public service that help educate his constituents. *That special interests are good.* "You know, we are all involved with special interests and so when the media tags it 'special interest,' we're talking about America," Holchs said. He represents what many on Capitol Hill have become.

Holchs's view of "revolving door" controversies is similarly indicative of the new Beltway culture. Government officials who stay in office for brief tenures, then switch to lobbying firms where they can trade on their contacts and knowledge of government policy, are an increasingly common species in Washington. Also common are people like Holchs who shuttle between staff jobs on Capitol Hill and lobbying firms. Rather than seeing the phenomenon as indicative of slippery ethics in Washington, Holchs thinks "the revolving door" contributes to good government. "Most criminal defense lawyers used to work in the U.S. Attorney's office or the District Attorney's office. That's where you gain the expertise. We have citizen government in this country and you can't afford to stay in government your whole life, nor should you. So you develop a certain amount of expertise which is useful to somebody who is trying to affect a decision in this town." To Holchs, and many others like him, working in government is just a training ground, a graduate course to help along a career. It is a means to an end—often a very lucrative end.

By the 1980s the Congress was moving beyond simply relying on special interests, on lobbyists, to support and fund their campaigns. Now they were demanding that the special interests also serve up their constituents—now lobbyists had to convince legislators' constituents first and then the representatives could vote their way. Gray had truly pushed the edge of the envelope. Now lobbying and law firms were either hiring or seeking public relations help to gather the required grass-roots support. A true "synergy" had reached fruition.

Gray had anticipated this trend and with its "one-stop shopping" approach that combined lobbying and public relations under one roof, Gray and Company revolutionized the business of what Holchs calls "advocacy."

Gray's goal of combining lobbying and public relations into one firm was not pursued in order to improve government or to make the profession more open and honest. The reason he did it was to make a profit. "The company's concept at the time was, 'We're a one-stop shop, and you don't have to go anyplace else for anything,' " Adonis Hoffman said. Like setting up leasing and advertising companies to maximize profit, the combining of lobbying with PR was an economic decision. The bottom line was the deciding factor in almost every decision at Gray and Company. It offered one-stop shopping ostensibly as a convenience or a service for its clients, but by doing so the company also could keep all the money.

John Hill's philosophy of client service, public relations counseling, in which H&K would drop a client if it did not adhere to its advice, and maintaining only blue-chip clients, was abandoned at Gray and Company. The company took just about any client that walked in the door, regardless of how controversial or shady its reputation, if it could pay. "Bob Gray's famous statement was everybody always deserves representation. That was from his perspective because he got a piece of all the representation," explained Barry Schochet, one of Gray's vice presidents.

Gray frequently employed analogies from the legal system to defend his representation of controversial clients. In a written interview for this book, Gray asserted that, as in a judicial proceeding, controversial clients deserve public relations representation because the court of public opinion operates in a like manner to the legal system.

One of the senior vice presidents at Gray and Company thinks this is a rationalization. "Anyone can justify anything. I can justify if I saw a chance to make money from a very unpopular client, I could justify why they needed my representation. One of them would be: Everybody is entitled to representation. I don't think you can say that about lobbying because what you're doing is really an extension of yourself. It's your reputation that you are putting on the line. I am trying to put myself in Gray's shoes and trying to justify something that I want to justify. It's easy to do. You can convince yourself that you are doing the right thing because you want to do it so bad. Why do you want to do it so bad? Dollars."

Gray adopted Hill and Knowlton's and other PR firms' practice of charging clients by the hour, but he added an extra charge. Instead of requiring a retainer against which hours were billed, Gray and Company established a minimum retainer and then billed by the hour above that amount. In effect, the retainer meant nothing more than a client's telephone calls would get returned, and he would still have to pay for the call.

These billings were not insignificant. Gray charged $350 an hour for his time.[41] Clients were willing to pay such high fees because they believed they were buying access to the highest levels of government, in part because Gray recruited his "stars" to create that impression, and because Gray sold the "one-stop shopping" capabilities of Gray and Company. "Bob was very effective in saying, 'Well, that added dimension is we not only have the best people to lobby, but we can help shape public opinion.' So on critical issues, people were willing to pay [a] premium," said Mark Moran.

Gray recruited "stars" because they either provided access to the powerful or they could attract lucrative clients. He pressed powerful people to join his firm or offered favors to the powerful. "There was a great deal of emphasis placed on bringing in new clients, particularly at the senior levels," Adonis Hoffman explained. "There was a general expectation that most professionals would spend a fair amount of their time on developing business for the company."

In order to justify their salaries Gray and Company employees were pressured to either produce clients or bill a great many hours. "In our business there's a basic three-to-one or three-and-a-half-to-one ratio between compensation and ability to bring in. In other words, somebody who's a one-hundred-thousand-dollar-a-year person compensation has to either bring in or bill out three hundred thousand dollar a year in order for the firm to break even. That's where the pressure has to do with figuring out how much money you can make at the firm to cover your salary and all the overhead. [Especially] as you get up into the more expensive people, and they had a lot of expensive people there,'' a Gray and Company senior vice president explained.

There were large discrepancies in salaries in the company. Gray, the chairman, made more than $400,000 a year, a dramatic increase from his $80,000 salary at H&K. The next level of management made between $70,000 and $120,000. Below that, where most of the employees were lumped, the salaries were much lower. Even by today's standards, Gray's charges and salary were high. One Gray employee estimated that it cost $5,000 a month retainer just for clients to have their calls answered. "Standard rates even now in PR firms run about probably thirty-five dollars or forty dollars an hour for secretarial and a minimum of seventy-five dollars to two hundred dollars an hour for the so-called professional staff," Larry Speakes said. "At Hill and Knowlton, I think we didn't want to do anything for less than fifty thousand dollars a year. That was not a retainer. You simply billed against that."

A lot of the money Gray and Company took in went to overhead, which was enormous, especially given its chairman's fondness for parties and limousines. Gray and Company billed clients for everything. Nothing was free. "He bought wine at Christmas for all the clients and then billed them for it plus the mark up. . . . He never missed a thing. The Xerox paper was marked up. They were charged for the time for the Xerox, charged for the paper, and handling charges. I mean it was just unbelievable. Every client. Every client. He was a heck of a businessman," Carter Clews said.

The pressure on Gray and Company executives to bill clients was especially pronounced if the clients had a lot of money at their disposal. "You'd see hours pop up any time a client had money, you'd see hours pop up from nowhere. I remember [one executive] pointed out that no phone call takes less than an hour. 'Always keep that in mind,' he said, 'once you pick up that phone, that's an hour. It doesn't matter how long you talk.' That is the kind of thing they'd do," Clews explained.

The exorbitant charges made some uncomfortable. "I think there's a degree of venality on the part of Bob and lack of integrity which always took me aback. A lot of it he would justify as being a businessman, but there was very little real basic principle and an awful lot, to me, of over charging. If I were a businessman and knew what I know, Gray and Company is not a firm I would hire," a Gray and Company senior vice president said.

Another Gray and Company vice president remembers a client being billed for expenses associated with a party to which he was not even invited. She said wine bought as Christmas gifts for clients was secretly included in their bills the following month. She even maintained that Gray's practice of taking clients' children to the circus each year, for which the company got credit in the press, was eventually charged back to the clients.

Such questionable charges, which were and are applied at other firms besides Gray and Company, go unnoticed by clients because Washington is such alien territory for them. "It's not only excessive in many cases, it's virtually obscene," said one Gray and Company executive. "A lot of clients are paying ten, twenty, thirty, forty thousand dollars a month here for things that just aren't worth it. I recognize if you solve some problems that means millions of dollars difference to a client, that's one thing. But a lot of this is all show. Clients could set up their own offices; clients can call. A CEO can call a senator's office and get an appointment; he doesn't need me to call for him and get an appointment at five hundred dollars an hour. But he does. It happens every day. One of the troubles is business and virtually all organizations in the country are afraid of Washington. They don't understand it. It's a mystery to them. I've seen CEOs here who run big corporations and run them very well come down here and they're almost naive, tenderfoot, really. They do not understand the Washington puzzle. Foreign countries particularly get hurt badly and pay a lot of money for it. I've seen foreign countries paying up to fifty thousand dollars a month for virtually nothing."

Former Gray and Company Vice Chairman Alejandro Orfila is Argentinean. "The word billability is a word that I learned in the English language at Gray. It was so foreign to my mentality. In fact, I joke with my fellow Latins, 'You have no billability.' Imagine that drinking coffee for three hours after a bullfight or whatever and discussing how billable we are. . . . I was totally foreign to that operation."

"It worries me," George Worden said. "I was brought up by John Hill. Nobody wanted to lose money, certainly Hill, and he never did. But his first thing was serve the client well. This bottom [line] thing is awful. You can't focus on doing a good job for the client if your supervisors are saying constantly, 'I want you and your group 100 percent billable,' and, 'You're not billing enough on X accounts.' 'What do you want me to do, fake my timesheets? Is that what you're saying?' I remember when if you faked a timesheet you'd be fired. No discussion. Out! You were cheating. It's like reaching in the guy's wallet and taking his money out. We joined the greed group of the eighties."

If there is one aspect of Gray's public relations career on which almost everyone in Washington agrees he is a genius, it is his own self promotion. When he courted the media, he left nothing to chance. Gray had personal aides or special assistants among whose primary responsibilities were to get him favorable publicity. "Gray and Company was never as good at helping the images of its clients as it was at shaping the image of Bob and Gray and Company. That was the best public relations job they ever did," Mark Moran said.

Gray and Company worked very hard at positioning the firm's image. They courted mentions in the press, especially in the *New York Times* and the *Washington Post* style sections. High social visibility was encouraged, especially among the top tier people like Frank Mankiewicz, Alejandro

Orfila, and Joan Braden. The constant appearance of such well-known Gray and Company "stars" at social and political functions and the drum beat in the press contributed to the firm's image as the most talented and well-connected in town.

Then there was Gray himself. "Gray being seen at five or six different cocktail parties every evening. Gray wearing out two tuxedos a year. Gray going a mile a minute. There was a good deal of sort of magic and mystery to how the whole thing worked," marveled one of his senior vice presidents. This image fed on itself, in no small part because the peripatetic, charming, well-connected lobbyist made good copy.

John Lawler, another Gray and Company senior vice president, elaborated: "The thing that you have to look at is that the press loved to write about Bob because Bob is a star. Bob didn't write about himself. . . . The press loved to do it and it fed on itself." When the *New York Times* wrote about Gray in 1982, he carefully orchestrated the day the reporter covered him as he had done so many times before. Clip files on Gray are filled with stories like this:

> His hair is silver-gray, his suits are impeccably tailored, and he is always in a hurry, now darting into a Capitol Hill reception, now zipping through town in his chauffeured limousine, now hastily conferring with one of his . . . staff. 'Get me Jim Baker,' Mr. Gray calls to his secretary. . . . It is safe to say that Mr. Gray can get just about anyone in town on the telephone, maybe even the President now and then. . . . Just now, he is talking to Mr. Baker. 'James!' he booms. 'How are you doing? . . . We want to help you anytime we can on the outside. You know that.' Then, Mr. Gray brings up the real reason for the call: Mr. Reagan's minimum profits tax. . . . Mr. Baker offers some suggestions that Mr. Gray keeps to himself. Then Mr. Gray thanks him, adding, 'Please keep in mind anytime we can be of help.' He hangs up the phone and telephones Robert B. Peabody, president of the American Iron and Steel Institute, one of his clients. 'Bob,' he says, 'how're you doing? I just had a telephone call with Jim Baker on minimum profits . . .' "

It was all part of the show—all part of the hazy fog of public relations that blurred the lines between reality and hype. Just as Gray had planted questions for other students to ask him in college, or had his secretary interrupt him with fake telephone calls from the President when he was cabinet secretary in the White House, at Gray and Company he stage-managed impressive-sounding calls. "A reporter would walk in and he would instruct his executive assistant to come in and announce that there was a call from the White House. Totally fabricated. Absolutely. They would come in and they would say, 'Mr. Gray, Mr. Meese is on the phone,' and he would pick up a dead line or a line that was set up by the executive assistant, carry on a conversation of four or five short rapid sentences as though he was in constant communication and hang up. And then, of course, the reporters, dazzled, would then report that a White House phone call came in," explained one Gray and Company executive.

"You know there was just tons and tons and tons of stuff that he did to create truly a Wizard of Oz [atmosphere]," said one staffer. But no one ever publicly threw back the curtain to reveal the little man desperately maneuvering the levels that brought him power and wealth. In reality, Gray did not call top Reagan administration officials on behalf of clients routinely, and he was not close to James Baker, and even if he were, the telephone call hardly affected White House policy. At the $350 an hour the American Iron and Steel Institute was paying, his call to James Baker did not mean much. "His relations with the President were very good. His relations with people under the President were not good at all. For example, Mike Deaver would not return his calls. Let's say there was no love lost between the two of them," Mark Moran said. "The same way [with James Baker]. And I can guarantee you that Don Regan and his people did not go for Bob." Edwin Meese was Gray's principal contact in the administration.

In truth, it did not matter if Gray could get Ronald Reagan on the telephone or not. According to Washington lobbyist John Sears, whatever access Gray had to Reagan did not mean much. "You could go in and see Reagan and even if he said yes, which he might do, you'd have no idea if you were going to get that. He wasn't the guy who made the decisions. So access to Reagan was worth zilch. The fact that he was acquainted with Reagan was not very valuable in fact. . . . What power really is is a perception in this society. It's not worth the money [people pay to get the access]. It's an illusion; it's not a real thing."

But Gray successfully traded on his White House and congressional connections to attract clients.[42] "Bob used to get accused of that all he did was sell access. Well, maybe that is what he did. But that's the service he had: to get people to individuals that they couldn't get to themselves . . . that was what Bob Gray learned from that process. He was and is very good at it," Bette Anderson said.

To many in Washington, Gray's openness, even brashness, in soliciting clients through self-promotion of his political clout was disturbing. Gray seemed to be blatantly offering it as a service. *TRB* wrote a scathing column in *The New Republic*:

> Robert Keith Gray, a longtime public relations heavyweight and man-about-Washington, founded his own company after cochairing the festivities surrounding President Reagan's inauguration in 1981. Less than three years later, it is already the largest lobbying firm in Washington. Gray's firm has broken new ground in the brazenness with which it presents itself as selling, not legal services or even public relations, but connections pure and simple. And Gray, in the role of Mephistopheles, has made a dazzling series of conquests.

The columnist went on to list the prominent Washingtonians who had been recruited to the Power House "coven." He was appalled that Alejandro Orfila, the former head of the Organization of American States, would go to work at Gray and Company when he was already quite wealthy and did not need the job.

> What usually drives good people into the world's second-oldest profession is a yearning for fleshy pleasure far more modest than the ones Orfila already enjoys. After living on government salaries, surrounded by people who make a lot more, they long for a taste of affluence. . . . When somebody as obviously status-conscious as . . . Orfila goes to work for Gray and Company, when he could just as easily do nothing at all, it means that being an influence peddler for hire is no longer merely respectable. It has become positively prestigious. My son the lobbyist. You know, Alejandro, your father and I were really worried for a while. It looked as if you were going to waste your life as head of an international organization dedicated to preserving peace and alleviating poverty. But at last you're doing something your parents can be proud of. Thank goodness for friends like Bob Gray.[43]

Before the 1980s, before Reagan, lobbyists never flaunted their close association to politicians. They operated quietly, behind the scenes. As Sears related, "They had to because in the former times nobody would allow themselves to be billed as a friend. . . . To give the impression, in other words, that since Bob Gray is a friend of mine, I might do something for him when I might not for others. If Bob Gray actually did that in public in the old days, he would not hear from me again. So you didn't do that." The ability to sell influence and access goes both ways. If the politicians just as publicly denied access as lobbyists flaunted it, there would not have been such a parade of influence peddlers down Pennsylvania Avenue. But under Reagan, government favors were commodities to be sold in the best spirit of capitalism and free enterprise. Influence peddling became commonplace. "The idea did not shock anybody: If I am an office holder that people who knew me might be able to talk to me better than those who did not. . . . For a lot of reasons, some of which are just not very nice things about all of us, people today, not only in public life, but in business or anything else, we have a certain lack of integrity now," Sears said.

Within a year of opening its doors, Gray and Company had become "the most sought-after public relations outfit in town."[44] It was billing at $9 million a year; it had more than sixty clients; and the number of employees had swollen to eighty-three. "In the 1940s, [a client] might have sought the services of Thomas G. Corcoran, one of the 'brain trusters' of the New Deal and a top-notch lobbyist. In the 1950s and 1960s, the choice might have been Clark Clifford, a sage, quiet-spoken lawyer and adviser to Presidents.

In 1982, the man is Bob Gray," the *New York Times* wrote.[45] Gray could not have been mentioned in more appropriate company.

None of the problems at Gray and Company seemed to matter. Although employees were constantly leaving, there were plenty of applicants lined up to replace them. Although clients continually dropped the company, new ones poured through the doors. The firm was so successful, due largely to Gray's self promotion, it did not even have to spend much time and energy on preparing detailed proposals and soliciting new clients. "They figured they didn't have to do them. Most PR firms will do a proposal if you want to pitch a new client. It involves doing research, getting to know something about the potential client, what the needs are. You talk to a lot of people to try and figure that out and do a fairly long proposal kind of geared to what you can do for them. They didn't do that there. They had two- to three-page proposals because they figured they didn't need to; they were so good, people would just come to them. Surprisingly enough, it did work. People did walk in the door and not blink an eye at paying ten thousand dollars a month for a retainer plus not be billed against it," a Gray and Company vice president remembered.

Gray and Company grew dramatically over its first four years. It promoted itself as the largest public communications firm headquartered in Washington. By December of 1984 a tremendous flood of business was flowing into the firm, much of it from overseas. The go-go ethos of Gray and Company meshed perfectly with that of the "Reagan Revolution." By the middle of the Reagan years, Gray and Company was at its height of power and prestige. "It was clearly reflective of Washington in the eighties; a lot of glitter, very little substance, high-flying, overpriced, undersubstanced; clearly not as much substance as there was blue smoke," Mark Moran said.

If the firm thrived in the freewheeling atmosphere of the eighties, it also suffered from the cavalier attitude toward public service that characterized the decade. "These people are not providing access, they are peddling influence. They are being paid to open doors to the White House and Senate. I don't care what anyone else calls it . . . I think that it is immoral," Carter Clews said.

"[It] was a company without a moral rudder," Sheila Tate said, discussing the firm's controversial clientele. "I think you can be successful and still have limits to what you'll do. I don't think you have to take everything that comes down the pike. But I do agree there was sort of lack of any kind of internal control in the Gray organization that led them to just take anything, do anything. That's what made John [Jessar] so unhappy. They would hire someone and hand him to John and say, 'Here's your new deputy,' and he didn't even know who they were. They would be some old CIA person, and it scared the hell out of him. He never knew what half of these people were doing."

To Tate, what happened at Gray and Company, and to her old friend and colleague, John Jessar, was sad. Jessar and her dream of setting up a top-quality operation was never realized. "I think he [Gray] had a chance to form a company that would have been exciting, that would have also produced quality work and had quality clients," Tate said. But in the end Gray and Company became "sort of an out of control situation," Tate said.

In the mid-1980s Gray and Company was a Washington sensation. Nothing seemed beyond the company's grasp. One Gray and Company alumnus recalled the firm's heyday in a tone almost wistful, elegiac: "We did a hell of an effective job both on the legislative stuff and on the PR stuff, but we always got our names in the paper, too. People liked being around us. Reporters liked being around us. People liked having Gray and Company people at their parties because we were thought to be well connected, be sexy in the Washington sort of sense that we had stories, we knew what was going on, we were high-profile. We were working for foreign governments, we were working for major corporations. We were wired into the White House, to the Reagan administration. We had people on the Democratic side, and they knew everybody. We were wired in with [Ted] Kennedy and [Gary] Hart and those people on the Hill. We were wired in with Dole and Reagan and Bush downtown. It was just thought that we were almost part of the political power structure ourselves."

When asked how much of Gray and Company's image was real, and how much was illusion, the executive gave an answer that goes to the heart of why Americans around the country have become so distrustful of Washington. "Perception is reality. That's a circular answer, but there's no way to answer that question. We were real. We were thought to be real because we were thought to have the influence, and the access, and the power, and the understanding of how much the system worked, and we did have all those things. It became almost a self-fulfilling kind of myth that the more people gave us credit for doing things, the more influential and effective we became. What I am suggesting to you is that if you're writing a book about the nineteen eighties and Gray and Company and PR, you may have to live with the fact that there is no answer to the question of was it real or was it just hype to protect his own veneer. But that's the story. The story is it didn't matter. It didn't matter to people here, and it didn't matter to the clients, and it didn't matter to the media, because everybody was playing the game."

9

THE OTHER SIDE

This story has got drugs, sex, and rock and roll.
—A Gray and Company senior vice president

On a sunny but cold Sunday morning, December 21, 1980, Robert Gray ate breakfast with his longtime companion, William Austin, and left his house for a meeting about the upcoming Inaugural. About a half an hour later, the Arlington County Fire Department responded at 10:18 A.M. to reports of smoke pouring from Gray's secluded two-story brick and slate-roofed house. By the time they arrived, the west side of the house was a mass of flames. Gray had lived at the house for twenty years—ever since he had left the Georgetown townhouse he shared with his college friend, Elton Hailey, and another bachelor in his early days in Washington.

The fire, believed to have started from a woodburning stove in the kitchen, spread quickly to the hallway, the sauna bath area, and the den. The blaze started burning into the upstairs bedroom doors and windows and burned away the door and window into the living room, damaging the chairs, sofa, several antique pictures, and antique roller tapes for a player piano. Within ten minutes after the smoke was noticed by a neighbor, the rooms were gutted. Gray's dog, Opey, died of smoke inhalation.

The entire first and second stories suffered heavy smoke and water damage. The firefighters broke a number of antique vases and plates accidently when they responded to the alarm and started ventilating the house. Other hanging antique paintings and antique paneling suffered heavy smoke and water damage. Gray's entire wardrobe was heavily damaged by smoke.

"He's not an acquiring type of person, but that house was very personal to him," an aide at Gray's office told the *Washington Post*. Gray did not comment on the emotional impact of the fire, but lamented that it had ruined a number of expensive items, "including a portrait of Andrew Jackson as a young man, English oak paneling dating back to 1402 that Gray brought from France to line his den, and political memorabilia from his years in the

White House as President Eisenhower's appointments secretary and later secretary of the cabinet."[1]

The damage was estimated at $350,000–$500,000 for contents and $150,000 for the building. Gray's assistant, James Jennings, told the fire department that Gray had had an appraiser from Adam Weschler and Sons appraise many of the items and Preston Pitts had done a picture history of the house. Jennings made a tape recording of damaged articles and he and Bill Austin boxed up the remaining valuable items and removed them from the house, since the house would be open that night due to the damage.

Gray told a Nebraska reporter that among the items he had lost was a painting by Dwight Eisenhower and most of the manuscript of a book he was writing. Gray had told the *Washington Post* earlier that month that he was writing a book called *January River* about an art theft.

Chuck Hagel, who worked on the Inaugural with Gray and was formerly from Hastings, told the local newspaper that Gray was at an Inaugural committee meeting the morning his house burned down. When the fire department notified him, he left the meeting and returned a few minutes later and continued the committee business. When someone finally asked how bad the fire was, Hagel quoted Gray as saying, "Well, there's not much to tell. It was gutted, but there's nothing I can do about it now," and he went on with the meeting. Hagel said he was told that Gray's house had a fine antique collection and that the damage was around half a million dollars.[2] Former Senator Carl Curtis was also at the same Inaugural meeting the morning of the house fire and similarly recalls how calm Gray was.[3]

As always, Gray returned to Hastings for the Christmas holidays. At a press conference in Nebraska, Gray said that he had made it clear when he was with the Reagan campaign that he did not want a job in the new administration. Reagan "must have thought that it [cochair of the inaugural] was a good job for someone who didn't want a long-term job," Gray told the *Hastings Tribune*. Gray said during the campaign there had been rumors that he would be either the press spokesman or the chief of protocol and that Reagan had talked to him about joining the administration in some capacity, but he had declined. "The place to have fun in the next four years is going to be outside of the administration," Gray said. "Those are a bunch of workaholics."[4] But Gray did not turn down jobs in the new administration because of the amount of work involved. He had many other reasons for not wanting to work inside government.

Robert Gray's anger over J. Walter Thompson taking over Hill and Knowlton did not dissipate after he left to form Gray and Company. To the contrary, the animosity grew. Some at Hill and Knowlton felt that Gray had raided the cream of H&K's Washington office—the best accounts and the best employees. There was also bitterness because some felt Gray had left the office in bad shape—with a large deficit and expensive new offices. "He took six months off from Hill and Knowlton with full pay to involve himself in the Reagan presidential campaign. [It was] clearly understood by the people at Hill and Knowlton that were that campaign successful, that the rich rewards would come back to Hill and Knowlton. What he did, of course, was that thirty days after Reagan assumed the Presidency, he basically turned his back on Hill and Knowlton and opened up a competing firm taking from them enormous numbers of their clients, and he pulled all the staff people that he wanted to pull," remembered a Gray and Company executive, "then he sues them."

The hostility between Gray and H&K boiled over into a legal battle. In August 1982 Gray sued JWT Group, Inc. for violating securities laws, for fraud and deceit, and for negligent misrepresentation in connection with the merger of H&K with JWT in 1980. Gray asked for ordinary and triple damages totaling $4.2 million and punitive damages of $5 million. In his case Gray argued that he had opposed the merger, but that the agreement was accepted over his objections because the "defendants made material misstatements of facts in connection with the merger." Gray was referring to a scandal regarding JWT's television program syndication unit, which involved $30 million worth of falsified computer entries over several years, information that had been made public earlier in 1982. Gray's suit said the H&K merger was accepted based on JWT's statements that its 1979 audited figures were accurate and that the defendants either knew these statements were false or misleading or "acted with reckless and grossly negligent disregard for the truth or falsity thereof."

JWT Group's stock plummeted after the syndication unit scandal became public, falling from $32 to the $15 range. Gray had gotten 33,432 shares of stock in the JWT merger in July 1980. By mid-1982, it had lost half its value. JWT Group responded that it would "vigorously defend against the allegations."[5]

The public relations industry is a small community and H&K was a very close, personal firm. Gray's lawsuit was quickly reduced from legal arguments to personalities. According to George Worden, much of the animosity stemmed from Gray's anger at Loet Velmans, then the head of Hill and Knowlton, because of Velman's support for the merger.[6] On top of all this, the JWT merger prevented Gray from realizing one of his most cherished goals. "Bob sued, that was one of the reasons he left to start his own firm because he felt he had really got screwed by J. Walter Thompson and that they had significantly undervalued his stock. Bob's objective always was to buy Hill and Knowlton out. That's what he wanted. That's the ultimate purpose. He actually, at one point, put a group together to do that. Then when it became impossible—they wouldn't sell to Bob—he had a choice. He could sue them or not," said Mark Moran.[7]

In response to Gray's lawsuit, JWT Group filed a countersuit against Gray. Moran, who at times was a legal intermediary between Gray and

Company and Hill and Knowlton, believed Gray had been treated unfairly by Hill and Knowlton. "He didn't get what he was supposed to have because they thought the monopoly money was real. They didn't have a countersuit. The lawyer talked to me. I went down and did depositions. J. Walter Thompson's [lawyer] was harping around, [but] there wasn't anything to say. They didn't have a suit. He [Gray] didn't start anything, they did." George Worden agreed with Moran's analysis. "They are the ones who had the crook on their payroll," he said.[8]

These two painful episodes, the fire and the lawsuit, were to have very unpleasant ramifications for Gray. A conservative Republican stalwart since the mid-1950s, he would be faced with the possibility of revelations about his private life that could endanger his relationship to the ideological right and with his conservative clients.

In the early 1980s Carl Shoffler was a top detective with the District of Columbia police department who had followed organized crime and vice activities in Washington for years. Rumpled and affable, he reminded people of TV detective "Columbo" and was a popular source for reporters. In 1972 Shoffler was the first police detective on the scene of the Watergate burglary. Shoffler's personal life was about as far away from the glitz and glamour of official Washington as one could get. He is not active in politics and does not socialize with high-powered friends. His world was family, kids, sports, and trying to be a good cop. Shoffler would seem to be little more than a gnat to a man with Gray's connections. But Shoffler was an unrelenting detective; he did not let things go easily. In the spring of 1982 Shoffler came into Gray's life. His arrival was unwelcome.

Shoffler got a tip from the insurance company investigating the December 1980 fire at Gray's house that some of paintings Gray had reported as destroyed were later allegedly seen at Gray's Rehoboth, Delaware, beach house. Shoffler pulled the Gray file and began to investigate. Shoffler found no evidence of insurance fraud, and the insurance company never pursued the matter. But the insurance matter led Shoffler to more disturbing allegations. Both Shoffler and Neil Livingstone, who had recently gone to work at Gray and Company, had a mutual friend, Mike Pilgrim. Shoffler, as part of his investigation, asked Pilgrim for information. Shortly thereafter Livingstone learned of the investigation. Livingstone then went to Gray, told him about the probe, and offered to try to help. Livingstone was convinced Shoffler was moonlighting for H&K, since the lawsuit battle had just begun.[9]

Gray had lived a secret, private life in his decades in Washington, and he had a terrible fear that that lifestyle, if exposed, would harm his carefully constructed public image. Now he learned from Livingstone and others that Shoffler was investigating his personal life going back years. Gray was convinced that Hill and Knowlton was responsible for the probing, that they were looking for an angle against him. Those in the know at Gray and

Company feared Hill and Knowlton was attempting to obtain a gay companion's deposition. That Gray was gay was common knowledge within his firm, as was his fierce determination to keep it from becoming public.

Shoffler had nothing to do with Hill and Knowlton. The extraordinary allegations Shoffler had received were that Gray's button-down world of Republican politics, conservative business clients, and high society events turned into weekend sex parties with young men where drug use was common.

In June 1982, the FBI began investigating allegations made by a male congressional page (a high school student working for the Congress, usually as a messenger) that he had been solicited by a congressman, and that several of his fellow pages had told him about sexual activities with members of Congress. A couple of weeks later, on July 1, Congressman Louis Stokes, the chairman of the House of Representatives Committee on Standards of Official Conduct, known as the Ethics Committee, announced that the Committee was joining the FBI and local law enforcement in their investigations. Stokes said the Ethics Committee would widen the scope of the investigation to include a range of alleged irregularities on Capitol Hill including sexual relations between pages and congressmen and charges that a cocaine and marijuana ring operated in Congress and used pages and congressional employees as couriers.[10] Stokes appointed Joseph A. Califano, Jr., as the Special Counsel to the Committee to handle the investigation.

Gray's name first surfaced as the result of an anonymous tip to the House Ethics Committee accusing Gray of using drugs and sexual activity to lobby congressmen. Richard Powers, an investigator who received the call, wrote a memo to Califano. Powers and other staffers could not find the memo when they looked for it later.

On July 21, 1982 Donald Purdy, an Ethics Committee counsel, and Jack Moriarity, a former D.C. police officer whom Shoffler admired, and who then worked as an investigator for the Committee, interviewed Shoffler regarding his knowledge of sex and drug related matters on Capitol Hill. During their conversation, Purdy excused himself and left for another appointment. Shoffler and Moriarity kept talking and in the course of Shoffler giving Moriarity some sex-related leads, Shoffler told him that the Committee should take a close look at Robert Keith Gray, a prominent Washington lobbyist and associate of key Capitol Hill and administration leaders, including the President.

In a memorandum to Shoffler's Washington Police Department superiors, Shoffler wrote of the meeting:

> Over the past several years, the undersigned has received information suggesting corruption on the part of Mr. Gray. Briefly, the allegations indicate that he is gay . . . ; that he has used and supplied narcotics; that

he has thrown wild drug and sex orgies at . . . Rehoboth Beach; that he was affiliated with the infamous Ed Wilson; that he was used by the CIA. As a result of his past connections in the aforementioned areas and his close association with President Reagan, his conduct has to be suspect in light of the fact that he ended up with the foremost lobbying firm presently operating in D.C.[11]

Shoffler told Moriarity of the above allegations and added that two individuals, a former Immigration and Naturalization Service official at the Justice Department who had worked for Congress and was now a consultant, and a photographer who worked at a Washington photographic studio, were reputed to be running a male prostitution service on Capitol Hill. The consultant was on the payroll of the Diamond Shamrock Corporation, a Gray and Company client. Shoffler left believing that he had met his responsibilities and that the Committee would now take over and continue to investigate these charges.

Six weeks later, on September 1, Shoffler was shocked to receive a telephone call around 10:30 at night at home from Mike Pilgrim asking him if he were investigating Gray for Hill and Knowlton. (Gray, who believed that H&K was set to depose individuals with information about his private life for the lawsuits, thought Shoffler was working for his former employer.) Livingstone had called Pilgrim in a panic asking him to find out what was going on.

Shoffler assured Pilgrim that he was not investigating Gray and hung up the phone. He was stunned. How did Livingstone find out that Shoffler had received allegations about Gray?

The next day, at around 10:15 in the morning, Shoffler received a telephone call from Tom Fortuin, who identified himself as Gray's attorney. Fortuin explained to Shoffler that he was a former New York City prosecutor and therefore had a law enforcement perspective. He assured Shoffler that he personally reviewed all of Gray's business dealings and that he was comfortable with them. Fortuin then explained that if Shoffler were investigating allegations on Gray, any leak of the investigation would prove disastrous for his client. Fortuin said he was calling from California, but when he returned the following Tuesday, September 7, he would make his client available for an interview. He felt that Gray would be able to dispel his involvement in any allegations. He said Gray would admit that he was gay, but that the "drug abuse" allegation was wrong. At the end of the conversation, Fortuin said he had gotten Shoffler's name from Jack Moriarity.[12]

Shoffler sat stunned at his desk. He and Moriarity had both worked for years for the police department. Moriarity had a reputation as a clean, honest, hard-working cop. Shoffler had trusted Moriarity with his confidential information about Gray. The last person he thought Moriarity would tell was Gray's lawyer. Shoffler felt sick and hurt.

A few minutes later Shoffler received a phone message from Moriarity. Shoffler called him and asked him why he had given Gray's lawyer his name as being involved in the investigation. Moriarity asked to meet Shoffler to further discuss these matters. At around 11:30 that morning, Shoffler met with Moriarity at a cafeteria in a House of Representatives office building. A few minutes later they were joined by Richard Powers, a former New York City homicide detective who was Moriarity's business partner. Moriarity and Powers had a private investigations firm which had been hired by the Ethics Committee to work on the sex and drug investigation.

For the next thirty minutes, Powers and Moriarity questioned Shoffler. Powers asked him if he knew J. W. Thompson. (The name had no meaning at the time to Shoffler. He did not know that J. Walter Thompson owned Hill and Knowlton or about the lawsuits.) Again they wanted to know whether Shoffler was investigating Gray while moonlighting for Hill and Knowlton. Again Shoffler said no. Then to Shoffler's horror, Moriarity explained that the private detective firm he and Powers ran not only worked for the Ethics Committee, but it also did work for Gray as well.

Moriarity said that to their knowledge Gray was not involved in any improprieties, and that Fortuin had an impeccable reputation and was a good person to know. Powers said to Shoffler, "Carl, you're not going to be a policeman forever; you've got to get to know people like Fortuin."[13]

In commenting on Gray, Moriarity said that while he may be gay, his private life should not be subject to improper scrutiny. Shoffler agreed, but insisted that if his personal lifestyle had a direct bearing on his business, it should be investigated and that is why he had brought Gray to what he thought was the Ethics Committee's attention in July. In reality, he now realized that he had brought his information to individuals on Gray's payroll as well. Moriarity explained that there was no indication that any of Gray's private conduct caused a conflict with his dealings with public officials.

Shoffler asked Moriarity what came out of the information he had provided on the alleged male prostitution ring whereby Gray purportedly knew its operators, the consultant, and the photographer. Powers told Moriarity that he had seen the two names that Shoffler had provided on a report and Moriarity said he would get back to Shoffler on what came out of the allegations.

Then an awkward situation got worse. After small talk about several of the cases they had worked on, Powers asked Shoffler if he would be interested in moonlighting for them. Powers explained that Gray was a valuable client, that he paid thousands of dollars for simple tasks—$2,000 on one occasion to have a car released from impound or $2,100 to have a civil subpoena served. Their private investigations agency worked for Gray's leasing company, and they were paid very well for their services. (Gray and

Company sources confirmed Powers and Moriarity performed such services.) Powers said that Shoffler could handle some of the minor tasks that their Committee work now prevented them from completing; in return, Powers would pay Shoffler fifty dollars an hour.

Shoffler replied that police department rules had not changed, that it was illegal for him to moonlight in this manner. Powers responded that Shoffler could be paid any way he wanted, under the table or above. Moriarity interjected that Powers's comments were not meant as a bribe, but just that their accountant could handle payments in a way that would not cause any IRS problems. Moriarity, who appeared to be uncomfortable about the entire matter, insisted that the job offer was just a benevolent gesture and it had nothing to do with Gray.

Whether or not Powers intended his offer of employment to be a bribe on behalf of Gray, Shoffler took it as such. He reported the incident to his superiors and to the U.S. Attorney. He told them that he had been accused of moonlighting for Hill and Knowlton, that he had not been told about Moriarity's relationship with Fortuin and Gray, when he met with Moriarity in July, that allegations he had made may have been suppressed, and that Powers had offered him a job.

On September 15 and 16, the highest levels of law enforcement, the Drug Enforcement Administration, the FBI, the Metropolitan Police Department, and the U.S. Attorney's office held meetings on what to do about Shoffler's charges. The general consensus was that an investigation had to be conducted since allegations were made of drug abuse by congressional employees, whose alleged association with Gray had surfaced as a collateral issue. These law enforcement agencies decided that all future contact among Shoffler, Moriarity, and Powers be recorded either by tape or by Shoffler wearing a wire. In addition, top DEA management would give frequent briefings to high-level members of the Justice Department on this matter.

On September 20, in the afternoon, the DEA informed House Ethics Special Counsel Joseph Califano that a confidential inquiry was underway and that there was reason to suspect that two of the Committee's investigators may have engaged in conflict of interest situations regarding Gray. The DEA asked Califano not to take any action pending the Justice Department's development of the probe. That same day Shoffler received a strange telephone call from Moriarity asking for his advice on how to counsel an elderly woman who lived alone and who wanted to sell some diamonds and other jewelry. Shoffler gave some perfunctory response, and then asked Moriarity again about what had happened with his information on the male prostitution ring. Moriarity responded that he would look into that later in the day since he was taking depositions from Senate pages that afternoon.

By September 22, it seemed to Shoffler that one thing was clear. The allegations he had received about Gray were not being kept confidential. That evening when he was leaving police headquarters, Al Lewis, a veteran police reporter for the *Washington Post*, approached him and said that he had heard that Shoffler was working on the drug abuse investigation on Capitol Hill and then asked, "What's this business about you being offered a bribe by a lobbyist?" Lewis assured Shoffler that he could speak freely because Lewis had cleared their conversation with Shoffler's boss. Lewis asked him several more questions regarding the investigation before Shoffler and another investigator walked away. Shoffler warned Lewis that many of his facts were incorrect, but it was clear to Shoffler that Lewis knew about a large portion of the Gray investigation. Shoffler believed that Lewis knew Moriarity, but later learned that he was wrong. Another reporter at the *Post* told him that Lewis had either seen a confidential memorandum Shoffler had written on September 9 or had been briefed extensively about it. Shoffler was feeling more and more uncomfortable about the whole situation.

On September 21 and 22, Shoffler's phones were wired to tape any incoming telephone calls from either Moriarity or Powers. By September 23 it was apparent that Moriarity was not about to call Shoffler and therefore Shoffler called Moriarity. Shoffler told Moriarity that there may be a problem because he had told Detective Michael Hubbard who was working on the Capitol Hill investigation about their earlier conversation. During this call Moriarity did not object when Shoffler referred to the Gray conflict of interest matter. Shoffler told Moriarity about the *Post* reporter's inquiries the evening before and asked if he had been contacted by the press. Moriarity said no. Shoffler said that the press now had the story that Gray was their client at the same time they were working for the Ethics Committee. Moriarity told Shoffler not to worry, that everything was under control.

After this undercover telephone call to Moriarity, the DEA notified Califano and around 6:00 P.M. on September 23, Califano suspended Powers and Moriarity indefinitely for a violation of Committee rules concerning the disclosure of information to anyone outside the committee. Moriarity had disclosed on one occasion to his immediate supervisor that in the past he had worked for Gray. However, during a recent staff meeting when Gray's name was discussed, neither Moriarity nor Powers said anything. More importantly, the disclosure to Fortuin that Shoffler had information on Gray was a direct violation of the Committee rules and a violation of the Committee's assignment contract with Powers and Moriarity. Their suspensions became public on September 26, 1982 in the *New York Times*.[14]

To pursue the allegations Shoffler had received about Gray, the DEA needed more information. Shoffler provided them with copies of articles about Consultants International, Ed Wilson's company on whose Board of Directors Gray had served. He showed them documents about Gray being questioned in 1974 by Senate Watergate lawyers looking into large contributions to Nixon's campaign by people being promised ambassadorships. He showed them articles about the Koreagate hearings in 1977 and 1978 when Gray also came to the attention of investigators because of his close association with Tongsun Park, especially their founding of The George Town Club. Koreagate investigators questioned Gray about a gold Rolex watch Park had given him.

In 1977 the House Ethics Committee, the same committee now looking into the sex and drug allegations, had hired Leon Jaworski as the Special Counsel for Koreagate, who then hired and authorized seven special staffers who could take depositions from witnesses. One of the Koreagate Seven Special staffers was Thomas M. Fortuin, then in his early thirties. Fortuin, a friend of Roy Cohn, was working as an Assistant U.S. Attorney in New York when Jaworski hired him for the Committee.

Fortuin brought an investigator with him to Washington to work on the Koreagate probe—Richard Powers, with whom he had worked closely on several investigations and who had twenty years of experience on the New York police force. Both men were originally from New Jersey, and both would soon work for Robert Gray, whose activities, along with those of Tongsun Park's many other friends and associates, they had been hired to scrutinize in the Koreagate investigation. Powers would become one of several ex-policemen who would work for Gray's companies, according to Gray and Company sources.

Gray had also reestablished ties to the principal of the Koreagate scandal. Tongsun Park, who had fled the country to avoid prosecution and later received immunity in exchange for his testimony, was back in Washington operating freely as if nothing had happened. In 1981, he sent his friends in the Washington area Oriental calendars with a personal message saying that it was not only a new year, but also a new beginning.[15] Soon he was again a regular at The George Town Club, and was often seen around Gray and Company, where he was referred to as "T.P."[16]

Many Gray and Company executives continued to use The George Town Club, often in Gray's name, since he was on the club board. But those more sophisticated in the world of intelligence knew better than to use the club. "I know he [Park] owned part of The George Town Club and Pisces. . . . These are places that I despised. I have never been to Pisces, knowingly, that I remember. I've been to The George Town Club. I don't like either, and I watch for the microphones," said Richard Allen, Reagan's former National Security Advisor.[17] As with the investigation into the sale of ambassadorships, Gray would emerge from the sex and drug congressional investigation shaken but unscathed; no formal charges of wrongdoing were ever brought against him.

No information emerged that Gray had offered sex or drugs in an effort to influence legislation. But there still remained the question of Powers's and Moriarity's dealings with Shoffler. The Ethics Committee called Neil Livingstone to testify on how he had gotten the information that Gray was under investigation. Livingstone told the committee that he had learned of the investigation from police sources. "I had tried to protect Bob on a couple of things, because I knew the cops around town and the cops would tip me off on stuff," Livingstone said. "He [Gray] was under investigation—it is not a secret—during the Capitol Hill ethics deal [the sex and drugs scandal]. The cops told me that there was an observation post over in the Flour Mill and some of Gray's records had been pulled downtown and I informed Gray of that. . . . I was then subpoenaed to the Hill to say, 'How did you know this stuff?' I had to go before the Ethics Committee and my friend who told me said to use my name. . . . So I said, 'Look, I got a lot of friends in the police department and they just tipped me off.' "

Although Livingstone's testimony seemed to minimize the impact of Carl Shoffler's allegations, Livingstone still spoke of the policeman's investigation as if Hill and Knowlton were behind it. Livingstone continued, "He was doing it, I believe, for some other purpose. I don't know what it was—irrespective of what later turned out to be this investigation over improprieties with sex and drugs and so on—the so-called Page Boy [scandal]. That's what it became known as, trading these favors for politics. All I can say is I was subpoenaed on that because it came back, 'How did they find out?' They found out because I had been tipped off. I was subpoenaed, met with Stokes's committee, didn't have much to say, and they thanked me for my testimony and that was it. . . . Those things were kept so quiet within the company. I was told not to talk about the fact that I was subpoenaed or anything."

When asked if he remembered the Capitol Hill sex and drug investigation, Mike Pilgrim said, "Sure. Got me, Shoffler, and Neil all in a lot of trouble. Yeah, I remember that real well. . . . Gray and Company had in their employ a couple of people that tried to bribe Shoffler." Pilgrim disputes Livingstone's claim that he had other sources in the police department. "If Neil had an informant in the Metropolitan Police Department other than what I was telling Neil . . . I would be amazed."

Eventually, several Capitol Hill employees were arrested on drug charges. No charges were brought in connection with the alleged male prostitution ring. "Substantial evidence" was found that three former congressmen used cocaine and other drugs while they were in office. The Ethics Committee reprimanded two congressmen for sexual relations with pages. The supervisor of the pages was accused of having sex with a page. No action was taken against Moriarity or Powers. After Livingstone's testimony cleared them of leaking to Gray, they were reinstated by the Committee and helped complete the investigation, although the blemish remained on Moriarity's once spotless reputation. Shoffler worked on other cases and eventually helped the Meese Commission on Pornography with its investigations. He believes that his investigation into Gray and his work for the Commission hurt his career. Eventually, he retired from the police force.

The investigators on the sex and drug case were not only told to stop their work, but they were discouraged from pursuing any further investigations in these areas in general. In part this happened because the historical persecution of gay people was lessening, and some saw these investigations as motivated by cruel prejudice. But the investigators themselves vehemently denied this interpretation. "I'm not looking into sexual activity of people because I'm some sort of censor, I'm looking into a situation here where if a lobbyist wants to use hookers to influence legislation, there's a pool of talent he draws from. There are certain madams in town that they make connections with. By simple logic if you're in the business of influencing people with male prostitutes or kids, there has to be that supply chain. So by looking into these rings, we were trying to identify that aspect of it. If you're an intelligence service, foreign intelligence service or a friendly intelligence service or a corrupt lobbyist or an organized crime entity, and you want to influence political figures in Washington, D.C., the bottom line is you're all dipping into the same pool. I felt that if I identified all the operators and some of the people who actually do the work in male prostitution rings, we could begin to have that first step toward saying, 'And who else is using your services?' [If] we start to identify some of the clients, it's possible we would find the suppliers for intelligence, organized crime, and lobbyists. But that all got sort of twisted, turned, stomped on, and knocked out by what happened with the Ethics investigation. . . . It became unfashionable for investigators to be looking into massage parlors. They turned the screws on us, you know. The gays got up in arms and said, 'Hey, this is spying on our community,' etc. It all came out of the Hill investigation," one of the investigators said.

Since Gray did not work on Capitol Hill, he was beyond the scrutiny of the Ethics Committee. Gray, Crawford, and Gray and Company attorney John Cevette independently verified the fact there was a Justice Department investigation into Gray. The Justice Department (the DEA and the FBI) did not take any action against Gray. According to Livingstone, Crawford told him that one of those individuals spoke to the U.S. Attorney about the matter, and that the U.S. Attorney then talked to the D.C. police department and the matter was closed.

Like the two levels of employees at Gray and Company, the socially and politically powerful executives and the day-to-day workers, there were also two levels based on knowledge of or participation in Gray's personal life. Those who were privy to Gray's personal lifestyle operated at a much higher level than those who did not. "The real hierarchy was a group of gay men who were closely associated with Gray. Those are the people who knew everything. And then, frankly, most of those business decisions were made at Gray's beach house in the summer time in Rehoboth Beach," a Gray and Company senior vice president asserted.

When Charles Crawford hired Neil Livingstone at Gray and Company,

Livingstone was on the second level. "At that time, I was in the next tier of people within the company, so if it got into these kinds of areas that related to the chairman's private relationships, the door was effectively shut," Livingstone said.

When Pilgrim tipped Livingstone off about Shoffler's investigation into Gray, Livingstone effectively traded this information to reach the top tier."Friends tipped me off that there was surveillance. There were two surveillance places, maybe it was only one at the time, and later we found out there was a second one, and that Gray's file had been pulled on the fire. It had been pulled downtown; someone was obviously digging. . . . I raised it with Gray and Crawford and the counsel of the company [John Cevette]. They had a meeting. I told them what I knew," Livingstone said. "Gray trusted me after that. It marked my rights within the company in some respects. I was a loyal guy. It may sound crazy, but I didn't know much about Bob. I didn't know about his personal life, not that those things are even relevant or important, but they became very quickly. It was kind of the game you played in the company. Someone would say, 'Well, you know about _____?' 'Oh yeah sure.' And then you'd have to go find out what the hell they were talking about."

Pilgrim confirmed Livingstone's assessment. "Neil would be the next to last person to admit that he owed somebody for that. But, yes, that cemented his relationship with Gray and also cleared a little water, if you will, for he and Gray because it acknowledged to Gray that Neil knew his gay background, connections, and vulnerabilities without having to confront him. It was all accepted as, 'Look, we've got a political vulnerability here; not my question, not my call. Here's what the facts are; you've got a problem, Bob. You handle it at a level I can't.' And he did. Gray ultimately took care of his own problem there, but it gave Neil the insight into Gray's character that Neil honestly [did not know] . . . That also convinced Gray that here's a guy that could be trusted to carry the political water regardless of how dirty."
". . . Everyone [was] saying to me, 'You're a great guy for having been able to do this,' " Livingstone said.

Conservative lobbyist Paul Weyrich, whose foundation sponsored a study entitled *The Homosexual Network*, believes the compulsion to hide one's lifestyle puts powerful people in vulnerable situations. "An indiscretion from time to time is going to occur. But if it's a constant lifestyle, then you have considerations that you otherwise wouldn't have because somebody knows how to get you. If you want to get certain people, supply them with a blonde . . . or a young boy, if you are talking about other people, that's the way to get what you want. Well, if you know that about people, then it's going to affect the climate of the relationship, particularly if the people involved on the other end are not people of integrity."[18]

Gray's secretiveness about his sexual preference continually caused him difficulties, allowing rumors to flourish both inside the company and out. There were always stories flying around Gray and Company that various publications were planning scandalous exposés on Gray's personal life. At one point it appeared that one of Gray's former lovers was talking to the press, which caused great anxiety at the upper levels of the firm. Gray had to worry not only about the mainstream press but the alternative press, supermarket tabloids, and extremist publications like *The Deep Backgrounder*, an ultra-right-wing tabloid affiliated with the fringe group "Liberty Lobby." The July/August 1982 issue of *The Deep Backgrounder* featured an article entitled "The Gay Gray Powerhouse" that characterized Gray's homosexuality as "the worst-kept secret in Washington." "The firm lived in constant trepidation that at some point the chairman's private life would appear in the *Post* or someplace. As I became more critical to the company—joined the management committee—I got involved in decisions," Neil Livingstone said, adding that he was often "brought in [for] my advice on sensitive matters. Also, I was the guy that had the friends around town in law enforcement and so on. So there was always the concern that something like that would come out that would be very embarrassing to the company and could seriously damage business."

The closest anyone came in the establishment press to reporting on these allegations was Rudy Maxa in a 1983 *Washingtonian* articled entitled "Wired," which featured a half-page picture of Gray across the top sitting in his Power House office:

> Gray . . . predicted Gray & Company would soon become the nation's largest independent . . . PR firm. . . . But lately Gray has had a public-relations problem of his own. At least one hate sheet has labeled Gray gay, and in her *Washington Times* gossip column, Diana McLellan hinted the *Washington Post* was readying a bombshell of a story touching on Gray's private life. The *Post* is not preparing such a piece, but Gray says the innuendoes have caused him great anguish, and he initially declined to be interviewed for this story because he'd heard the article would dwell on his 'lifestyle' and 'after-hours.' Gray said the gossip had reached such a gutter level that earlier this year a reporter called his office to ask if it was true that he had had sex in a limousine during Reagan's inauguration celebration. . . . Gray . . . protests he works eighteen-hour days on his business, leaving his social life empty.[19]

When the article came out, even those gentle references to his sexual preference deeply hurt. "I have seen Gray cry on two occasions. One was an article in the *Washingtonian* in the early days," said one Gray and Company executive.

Several other journalists looked at Gray's private life but never reported it. The "bombshell of a story" that Diana McLellan mentioned never ran in the *Washington Post*. The *Wall Street Journal* also supposedly prepared a similar piece that never saw publication. Gray defended himself against the political vulnerabilities of his lifestyle by using the best law firms in Washington to scare off journalists who he feared might write about his private life. Some Gray and Company employees asserted that the firm also took steps to ensure that reporters spoke only to top-level employees.

One law enforcement official who had investigated Gray and had been contacted by several reporters believed there were reasons, besides the legal ramifications, that kept the *Post* and *Journal* stories from publication. "There might be a little bit of politics being played, too, because both those organizations are in the business of supplying daily news tips and a lot of the people with possession of those tips would be affected. And it's like the cop with the informant. He makes a really good narcotics case [for you], but you also know he's dabbling. Now do you go after him or do you look the other way while he's feeding you [information]? It's how you handle it as an individual or an organization that determines ultimately your integrity."

There were at least two reasons why Gray wanted to protect his personal lifestyle from public disclosure: the possibility that business clients would leave the firm and that his conservative political friends would not understand. Growing societal acceptance of homosexuality did not extend to the individuals and groups which Gray depended on for his livelihood. "Corporations are pretty conservative and they're not going to hire somebody they think's got a lifestyle that's not in keeping with their viewpoint of what it should be, and I think it would have been also dangerous politically, for a lot of his political friends to be knowing, to be friends or consorting with a homosexual. But they had to know. Not the corporate clients. I don't think they would know, but certainly his political friends should have figured it out somewhere along the line; they had to hear the rumors because all of us hear them," said one Gray and Company vice president. Neil Livingstone agreed that the disclosure might hurt business. "I think it would be shocking, though, to most of these corporations who hired him and foreign governments if they were to know that. I don't think they would want to be associated with that still."

Gray's sexual preference would not be an issue if it did not affect his business, both how it operated and what it did. "Bob's personal relationships had a very definite effect on the operation which, in my opinion, led to a lot of major problems we had. . . . It did definitely come into the office. No question about it," said Gray and Company attorney Mark Moran.[20] "Business and personal were so intertwined," said another Gray and Company executive.

Although outside of Washington, Gray was not a marketable commodity, he almost immediately decided to expand his operating base. First he opened an office in New York. A Gray and Company brochure mentioning the New York office said that it was the first of a "national network of Gray and Company offices and other affiliates." In reality, the New York office was one or two people who were told they could use the Gray and Company name to get business if they shared the profits.

Next Gray opened an office in Los Angeles. He did not have the connections in Los Angeles necessary to launch a successful public relations operation. He hired a young man to head the office, who, people within Gray and Company maintained, was a sexual partner of Gray's. The young man in charge of the office was in his twenties at the time.

The Los Angeles office did not last very long. "We spent enormous amounts of money and didn't accomplish anything," Moran recalled ruefully. "That was an expensive mistake," agreed another Gray and Company official.

Gray's housemate, Bill Austin, was considered a person to be reckoned with by several Gray and Company employees. Austin was a designer and interior decorator who designed the changes to the offices, but many at the firm felt he wanted to play a larger role in the doings of the firm. "Bill always wanted to be involved in the company. . . . I think Bill was always worried about his image to Gray and that Gray had all these advisors and Bill was not one of them. So you had to be careful when you did anything to cover your behind because Bill was always on you looking for a weak spot. . . . Bill was part of the equation, and you had to deal with him," a Gray and Company executive recalled.

Austin ran the leasing company and other Gray businesses separate from Gray and Company. He was a talented designer and designed not only the offices, but also Gray's homes. Particularly stunning was Austin's work on Gray's Rehoboth beach home. In 1990 Gray put the home up for sale. Sadly, Bill Austin had contracted the AIDS virus.

One weekend in 1981 Gray invited one of the young Gray and Company staffers down to the beach. A very elaborate dinner table was set to entertain twenty people, including several other prominent PR executives who owned major Washington public-relations agencies. Often business was conducted in private on weekends within this community. During the dinner party Gray suddenly disappeared with the young staffer and they had sex.

A few weeks later the young staffer's supervisor complained that his job performance at Gray and Company was unacceptable. The staffer was late for work, and he was not doing much work when he was there. "He's literally figuring at this point, having slept with the Chairman, he doesn't have to do anything anymore," explained a Gray and Company executive. The supervisor was given permission to fire the young staffer, but that did not end the matter. The young staffer filed a complaint against Gray with the D.C. government. The complaint was detailed and graphic. If it were made public, it would be explosive. "The complaint described second by second the sexual act that he committed with Gray," remembered a Gray and Company executive. "I mean, I read that and I said, 'Oh shit. How are we ever going to get out of that one?' " Other employees recall the incident in similar detail.

Gray and Company retained its outside law firm to handle the complaint. The law firm was successful in getting the file sealed. The young staffer settled for $3,000. Over the years Gray ended up spending over a million dollars in legal fees and settlements, partly in an effort to try to keep his private life secret. Many felt that the reason Gray never sought a post in the Reagan administration was that he knew he risked exposure from background investigations. Gray's obsession with keeping his lifestyle private did not stop him from allowing it to interfere in his company which, after all, was a public relations firm. This was the paradox at the heart of Gray's tremendous success; he was paid to create images for his clients, yet he was forced to expend enormous effort to maintain his own image with those very clients. Certainly his conservative politics made the problem more acute, but even had Gray been a liberal Democrat, acknowledging his sexuality in public would have been unthinkable until the 1980s, if even then.

As in most companies, several gay people worked at Gray and Company. Whether or not that constituted any problems with regard to conservative clients or opportunities for advancement differed depending on individual perspectives. "Gray had all these property leasing and auto leasing businesses and so on. And they were often housed in proximity to us and they were all run by these guys that none of us knew much about. [Many] were . . . obviously gay. But within the company itself, it was a very strong impetus to have married guys, married women, if you will, as the kind of executive profile that we were looking for because we wanted to combat, because we had a couple of very visible gays—it wasn't that we had a lot of gays, but we had some very visible gays; of course, obviously, the chairman," Livingstone said.

Within the firm rumors and cruel jokes were common among heterosexual staffers, who called young gay male staffers "Gray's boys" or "the network." Nasty stories about the bathroom at the Power House and the weekend Rehobeth parties were bandied about.[21] Yet almost all heterosexual employees interviewed felt that Gray never exhibited favoritism or personal pressure because of his sexual preference. (Gay staffers who were included in Gray's personal life differed on the effects his lifestyle had on the company.)

Public relations and lobbying are very competitive businesses in Washington. To protect the company from potentially harmful rumors "there was a conscious decision made within the company, a corporate decision, which we were able to hold the door on for a long time of the kind of person that we wanted in the company, and that kind of person was different than the chairman. There was a certain suggestion that there were a lot of gays at the firm. I don't think there are probably any more gays at the firm than in any other group. It was just they were more visible," Livingstone said. "Bob never imposed anyone on us." "It was a nonfactor for those of us who worked for him," said another executive.

James Jennings, the former Episcopal priest whom Gray had hired at H&K in the 1970s, became Gray's closest confidant and most aggressive protector. "Basically Jim and Bob, they act almost as one," one Gray and Company staffer recalled. The two men shared an ability to charm and a capacity to play rough. Jennings spent a lot of effort protecting Gray's secret. "Jim Jennings would play the alter ego for Gray's personal life," Livingstone said. "I think Jim Jennings protected Bob much as the people who are very close to Bob in the inner circle protected him, the way Jennings's staff would protect the chief executive or a president. And it had less to do with Bob, than it did simply with him as the company," another Gray and Company senior vice president said.

Few in the United States had heard of AIDS in the early 1980s, but many at Gray and Company quickly became aware of this horrible illness, when one executive's longtime companion died of the disease. "People were always talking in hushed tones about [the executive's] 'special friend,' " said a Gray and Company vice president. "AIDS when it started out was a no-no subject among the firm. When [his] boyfriend died that was the first person that I ever heard of dying of AIDS," said Livingstone.

Around Washington, rumors about Gray's lifestyle were not uncommon. Al Regnery, who headed the Office of Juvenile Justice and Dependency Programs at the Justice Department in the early 1980s, said, "There were all these rumors that I used to hear [at the Justice Department] about Gray and his homosexual parties and all this kind of stuff." A Gray and Company senior vice president said, "I used to get asked about it all the time, when I was working for him. So did most people at Gray and Company. My friends used to ask me all the time. But the way I handled it was by saying, 'I don't know; I've never seen any demonstration of it. I've never seen any evidence of it. It may or may not be true. It is none of my business nor is it any of his business what my views or behavior is in that regard.' " Others were not so kind, demonstrating how savage Washington infighting can be. A prominent Washington lobbyist, a Gray competitor, said, "Of course, you know he's known as Bob Gay. He could never pass the scrutiny [of a security clearance] . . . That was why Gray settled for cochair of the inauguration and never sought a job in the Reagan administration."

Despite the prevalence of the rumors that Gray was gay, the man himself seemed to believe that he had succeeded in suppressing the information. Despite the fact that his competitors could use it against him, and despite his fear that public exposure would hurt the firm, he has continued to allow his private life to become intertwined with his business. "He was kind of an illusion. I mean who didn't know it? Everybody knew it. [But] he didn't think so," said one Gray and Company official.

Despite the rumors, most people, especially his clients, did not know about Gray's lifestyle. When asked if it was common knowledge in Washington, a Gray and Company senior vice president disagreed very strongly, then sarcastically continued, "Okay. So it is common knowledge then and his career has been ruined. His company went down the tubes. Nobody will retain him. Nobody wants him around. Everybody is embarrassed by it. Part of the success story is given the fact that everybody knew, why didn't this have any impact on Gray, on the business? Times have changed. Some [clients] would have [known]; some wouldn't. I'm not sure that people cared one way or the other about it. It was a nonissue to the employees and the staff, nonissue to the clients, and it was so widely known that nobody even sort of waited around for the story; it is never going to run; it is never going to happen. In this town, that particular lifestyle is a lot more widely shared than is commonly believed to be the case, even, and especially among people in power. So that where do you stop? . . . Apparently, the town decided it wasn't a story."

Just as Gray and Company publicly reflected the glamour and prestige of Washington, privately it also mirrored part of the city's darker side. Washington is a city of many contradictions. It is a place where people can fight publicly during the day and be best of friends at night, or just the reverse. Democrats are best friends with Republicans. Labor lobbyists are best friend with business lobbyists. Conservatives with liberals. It is a city based on power, and thus on illusion, leaving contradictions that are enormous. Perhaps that is what Gray, on a personal level, best represents. "Well, I think in many ways if you can reduce [Washington], at least the political end of it to a person, you probably can reflect most of those contradictions into Gray. He was enormously successful [as] the product of that environment and at the same time he was a victim of the environment," said a Gray and Company executive.

"He's a man of enormous, absolutely enormous contradictions. He's a conservative Republican who espoused all of the conservative ideas of Reagan, and yet he was clearly homosexual. [A] friend of mine not all that long ago said one of the true ironies [is] that Bob Gray supported Ronald Reagan [who opposed] . . . funding of AIDS research and education and every other thing while at the same time his lover was dying of the disease. He has a terrific ability to move through tremendously different societies and be successful," said a high-ranking Gray and Company official. The contradictions "are absolutely mind-boggling."

10

"FIRST FLACK"

I am not at all fond of public relations to be honest with you. I think it's ninety percent blue smoke in the air. And I think that it's not very efficient. Most of the public relations activity that is done is done by the public relations firms on their clients, not for their clients, and that's the truth. They're much better at representing themselves to their clients than they are at representing their clients to somebody else. And that's my opinion across the board.

Mark Moran, a Gray and Company lawyer[1]

Mr. Gray is a man of utmost precision. He has not survived in Washington for almost thirty years by being incautious.

The *New York Times*[2]

Within fifteen months of its inception, Gray and Company had become the most successful, most profitable, most high-profile public relations and lobbying firm in Washington, largely due to Robert Gray.[3] Gray's ambition and skill had taken him far from his Nebraska roots. Gray and Company's phenomenal success gave Gray a level of influence that many an obscure congressman would envy. But Gray himself was not committed to furthering any political or ideological agenda. Gray was happy to provide favors for powerful friends, but these relationships did not operate on a strict system of mutual reciprocity, especially if a person in power wanted something that was inimical to a client's interests. The list of Gray and Company clients, furthermore, included a number of companies, organizations, and countries whose agendas contrasted sharply with the conservatives in the White House. Gray's flexibility in accepting almost any client who walked through the door led to some campaigns that were, to say the least, anathema to movement conservatives. Yet because of Gray's relentless cultivation of powerful officials, and the peculiar nature of Beltway relationships, he never suffered for his ideological apostasy.

The crusade to protect society from the supposedly deleterious effects of pornography clashes head-on with the rights of others to produce and consume it. The result is a complicated battle that ensnarls social and legal scholars in a maze of paradoxes and ironies that is lost on most Americans. The unusual alignment of liberal feminists with right-wing ideologues, or civil rights groups with smut peddlers creates strange, and often tentative, alliances. Into this morass stepped Gray and Company. Its performance on this one issue typifies Gray and Company's ability to cross all lines. The saga of the Meese Commission on Pornography shows how the company conspicuously used its bipartisan nature, its friends in high places, its manipulation of a sympathetic media and other forces on behalf of its client. It shows how PR firms refocus the debate to issues more sympathetic to their clients. It shows Gray's company attacking a position in which he supposedly believed, and one which his most powerful friend certainly espoused. Finally, as a sad postscript, it shows how these media and legislative campaigns can devour human beings not skilled in Beltway maneuvers, leaving them discredited: in this case out of work and out of money.

In 1980, Ronald Reagan's deepest support came from the conservative movement, to which Gray had often espoused membership. Reagan's political strategist, Lee Atwater, used to gloat that Reagan would get thirty-five percent of the vote regardless what he did. "He could get caught screwing somebody on Fifth Avenue in New York City and still hold thirty-five percent of the vote," Senator Laxalt said. Reagan fanned the ideological right's anti-communist fervor, their calls to shrink domestic government programs, to eliminate abortion, and to strengthen family values. Of all of Reagan's top supporters, Ed Meese, Gray's closest friend in the administration, was their champion. He, more than anyone else, hired and supported conservative activists and their causes.

The Reagan economic programs were pushed through Congress quickly— tax cuts, deregulation of industries, military spending increases—efforts that mainly benefitted the wealthy establishment Republican constituency: corporations, bankers, builders, defense contractors, savings and loan executives. The conservative agenda was sacrificed. The social agenda never received the expenditure of executive clout needed to implement such controversial positions, and many conservatives blamed some of the people who surrounded Meese, including Gray. The conservatives felt that some of Meese's associates were more interested in profiting from their friendships with Meese then in helping him further the movement agenda. "Certainly Gray seemed to be a good example of that. He did do their [the Reagans'] first Inaugural, and he played heavily on his relationship with Meese and Mrs. Reagan. His access was for sale, which seemed kind of inconsistent to the most ideological President or the most rhetorically ideological President that the country had elected in years. That people that surrounded him seemed to be able to get around their ideology if it meant that they could make some money," said a former, conservative Reagan political appointee.

Many blamed Meese's wife, Ursula, for the problems. "I think Ursula was the one who had to make ends meet, and I think that's what the Moss deal [the job Gray arranged for her with the Moss Institute] was about. They were just trying to make ends meet. To live at sort of the upper-middle-class level in the Washington area today is horrendously expensive. Ursula was more sensitive to that than he was. He was just a busy guy, just kind of involved in everything, and there were people who took advantage of the fact that there was a need and that they were easily befriended," said a Reagan Justice Department official.

Gray was just the type to impress Meese. "At the heart of a lot of his [Meese's] problem [was] essentially social insecurity, that the people who preyed on Ed Meese bet on the fact that Ed didn't feel comfortable in the real establishment social world. Ed was kind of a grown up young Republican Kiwanis. He wasn't a natural for the Georgetown cocktail, dinner party set. He just wasn't. So people who had that kind establishment flavor, albeit conservative establishment flavor, as Gray was, he was impressed," explained a former Meese staffer.

Under Reagan, domestic social issues were quite important to the movement conservatives but the White House realized how politically volatile they were. "The decisionmaking, I think, a lot of times was pragmatic, not sort of a two-faced ideological decisionmaking. And if a Gray could come in and make pragmatic arguments about why you don't want to overdo, they would listen to him," said a Reagan political appointee. Although Reagan and Meese constantly espoused the philosophy of the right, the conservative agenda was never truly pursued, a victim of the reality of Beltway politics. The travails of Judith Reisman make a good case study of why this happened.

Judith Reisman, Ph.D., had a background in music and performance art. She had written children's songs for PBS and Captain Kangaroo. In the mid-1970s, she returned to college and received her Ph.D. in communication from Case Western Reserve. While completing her graduate work, she started looking at pornography: the relationship between pedophiles and what they were reading. She came to believe that there was a relationship between juvenile sex abuse and the use of children in pornography. A Jewish feminist, she left for Israel to teach and began doing research on Alfred Kinsey, the father of sexology. Occasionally she travelled back to the United States to discuss her work.

One night, in 1983, she was on a local radio show in Washington where a Department of Justice official heard her talking about connections between sex education, sex educators, and the pornography industry. She had recently created quite a controversy with allegations about Kinsey's work, especially as it related to children. She thought he was a fraud and, worse, had employed and had relied on pedophiles for his research. Her views ran counter to everything professionals in the field of sexology had learned and stood for. It was like telling physicists that Albert Einstein was a fraud and that every theory on which they had based their careers was wrong, and, worse, immorally obtained.

Although her opinions were discounted by most professionals in the field, they struck a common chord with the conservatives now heading the Justice Department, especially those opposed to sex education in the schools. They called her and asked if she could back up her views with concrete evidence. She went down and showed them her work. They looked it over and told her that they were very interested in her returning to the United States and doing further studies for them. Reisman was inclined to accept, but sought assurances that they would back her up. According to Reisman they agreed, saying, "Yes, we're behind you all the way." Today, she laughs and says, "And they were behind. W-a-y behind. When the bullets started flying, I said, 'Wait, I don't want you behind me, I want you in front of me.' "

The Justice Department's Office of Juvenile Justice and Delinquency Programs (OJJDP) told Reisman to apply for a grant as they had discretionary funds available. She did apply and won the grant without competition. It was the right wing's first real volley on the pornography issue, and it did not go unnoticed. Reisman had no knowledge of the infighting between the liberal bureaucracy and their new conservative political bosses. She thought she was in the right spot, that OJJDP was the perfect place for research into the effects of sexually explicit magazines on child exploitation and abuse. The grant eventually evolved into a project where researchers catalogued activities involving children, crime, and violence in pictures and cartoons found in *Playboy*, *Penthouse*, and *Hustler*. It made the publishers of these and other magazines very nervous.

"The people that initially attacked Judith Reisman really were out to get Al Regnery [the new head of OJJDP]. Al came from a conservative background. He had made it pretty clear that he wasn't going to continue to give the grants to the same left, liberal network that had been getting the grants out of that office over its history. All Judith really amounted to was kind of a juicy target. Here's somebody that wants to look at *Penthouse*, *Playboy*, and *Hustler*. . . . So the fact that we were looking to give her a grant just was kind of irresistible to these people," said James Wootton, Reisman's boss at OJJDP.[4] "She was a convenient target to try to get to Meese and ultimately to Reagan. And she had no idea."

Reisman moved her family to Washington to begin her work. The Justice Department told her that she needed an academic institution to sponsor her grant. Her publisher at the time, Jack Martin, was on an Advisory Board of American University (AU) and encouraged her to take the large research grant, $734,000, there. All she wanted was a quiet place to do her work. She met with the vice provost, who seemed very excited. Since the grant would go to AU and not to Reisman, the university carefully checked her academic credentials and the feasibility of her project.[5]

OJJDP approved the grant in December 1983 and sent it to Congress for approval, where it breezed through over the Christmas holidays. But just as the money was made available to begin the research, American University began to hesitate. AU officials said that it had gotten calls from Jack Anderson and from Congressional staffers who said that there was a possibility that the grant was illegal because there had been no competitive bidding. It took two more months before the University finally signed for the grant, and only then after pressure from a top Meese aide at the White House.

When Reisman finally began her work, there was no welcome party, no photo opportunity, no press release, even though she brought with her American University's largest federal research grant. "It was very tangential, sort of side operation. She didn't teach any classes. She had no students. She was over on Wisconsin Avenue, a mile away from the main campus in a small office over there," recalled former American University president Richard Berendzen.[6] Although Reisman had expected resistance from traditional sexologists, she was not yet suspicious of AU's lack of support for her. She thought it was not intentional, that they were just incompetent. She was wrong.

During her first month investigative reporter Jack Anderson wrote a critical column. The second month, in April, the Congress held hearings on OJJDP. Then an internal Justice Department memo was leaked to the media stating that Reisman's grant could be done in-house for $60,000. In July, there was a flurry of bad publicity on Reisman, personally, and on her grant. In August, senators Arlen Specter and Howard Metzenbaum held hearings on her grant. They said they had received complaints that Reisman was not rational, that she was an incompetent researcher, that she was a right-wing nut who was being paid to look through dirty magazines, that she had falsified her academic credentials, and that she was nothing more than a songwriter for Captain Kangaroo. Reisman had not falsified any of her credentials, and the other characterizations were designed for a deliberate effect.

No one would help Reisman prepare for the hearings. She had no media training or a lobbying firm to coach her for her congressional debut. She thought the hearings would be unbiased, fact-finding procedures. She was not prepared for the hostile questions or the attacks on her credentials. She did not realize that the politicians were posturing for the press or that she could not sue them later for slander. The hearings undermined the public's faith in her work, and worse, frightened her staff, some of whom quit.

Berendzen was also called to testify. "In due course her work began to get very controversial. It got controversial because allegedly the funding was somehow a special favor of some sort to the Meeses or something. To the best of my knowledge, the Meeses knew precisely nothing about it," Berendzen said. "It was people trying to make connections where it is all in their minds, not in reality."

Reisman had no idea that the charges made against her, once they appeared in the media and in the congressional record, would take on a life of their own. From then on, anyone wanting background information on her would look to these sources and be convinced that what they were reading was true. "These things have a way of taking on a life of their own. Everybody gets the idea that this person doesn't have credibility or that their credibility is vulnerable, which is more really the case with Judith, and so everybody gets down on them, kind of group-think," Wootton said. She began receiving hostile inquiries from the media. The antagonism against her grew. AU wanted to drop the grant unless someone else was put in charge. She and OJJDP said they would sue.

President Reagan announced the formation of the Attorney General's Commission on Pornography on May 20, 1985. Ed Meese, recently appointed Attorney General, was in charge. "Pornography" is often considered a red flag for censorship. The Commission sent shivers down the collective spines not only of pornographers, but also civil libertarians and others concerned about First Amendment issues. The concern that the Commission's work and the conservative attack on pornography could result in censorship became a reality in April 1986, when The Southland Corporation, then owners of 7-Eleven Stores, decided to stop selling *Playboy* and *Penthouse*. They cited Reisman's work as one of the bases for their decision.

No longer were Reisman and the Meese Pornography Commission pesky problems. They were now costing these magazines money. It was time to take drastic action. It was time to hire Gray and Company.

Reagan administration policies, especially on conservative issues, were often inconsistent with the President's rhetoric. While Reagan was espousing pro-family values, his administration did not move in substantive ways on these issues. Why? "Vested interests derailed political commitments," a Reagan Justice Department official said, "Bob Gray was in the business of representing vested interest. There was money at stake for them. They were willing to pay him a lot of money."

Specifically, *Playboy* and *Penthouse* hired Gray and Company to discredit Meese's Pornography Commission.[7] Now Gray's company was working to "discredit" Gray's friend's commission. Gray and Company proposed creation of a "broad coalition" of people and groups to provide opposition to the proposals and conclusions of the commission. This new association would be called something like "Americans for the Right to Read" or "The First Amendment Coalition." Such an organization, the proposal went on, "would assist in countering the idea that those who opposed the commission's efforts were motivated only by financial self-interest or were "somehow 'pro-pornography.' "

This was the front organization for the campaign. The proposal also outlined high-pressure lobbying tactics of the most cynical kind.

> Quiet efforts should be undertaken to persuade the Attorney General, the White House, and the leaders of both political parties that the forthcoming report of work of the Commission is so flawed, so controversial, so contested and so biased that they should shy away from publicly endorsing the document. The more doubts that can be created about the objectivity and validity of the Commission's findings and recommendations, the more difficult it will be for anti-pornography crusaders to use the reports as an effective tool for achieving their objectives.

Last, but not least, an intensive propaganda blitz was proposed, featuring "advertorials" and "placing spokespersons on national and local television and radio news, public affairs, and talk shows, holding a series of news conferences in major cities across the country" and to follow up with politicians to point out any "misrepresentations" and "errors" the media might have made. Since the media was predisposed to accept the coalition's arguments, the media campaign was the easy part.

Dealing with Judith Reisman was not much more difficult. She had already been battered by bureaucratic and political sniping. So the groundwork had been laid for Gray and Company, whose proposal included this chilling sentence in a section outlining long-term strategic goals: "A way must be found of discrediting" people and organizations whose activities threaten publishers' businesses. Since Reisman was without political savvy and lacked allies even at the University at which she worked, she made a most appealing target for "discrediting." Gray and Company charged The Media Coalition between $50,000 and $75,000 per month for the campaign. For this particular account, much of the cost was borne by *Playboy*; *Penthouse* also provided funding.

The larger Gray and Company strategy involved underplaying the pornography element of the controversy and refocusing media and political attention onto First Amendment issues. A Gray and Company executive explained how the people who worked on the account came up with the name of the new front group. "You sit down with a sheet of paper and some very smart, crazy, creative people, and you play with words. You try to come up with an organization whose name will be as attractive to as many people as possible and sounds like something you'd like to be involved in and support. We played around with words like liberty, speech, freedom, constitution, Bill of Rights, American, citizen. By the time you work all that through, you come up with Americans for Constitutional Freedom. You register the name. Register with Congress, if you're going to lobby."

Not all Gray and Company employees were so enthused about the account. Carter Clews objected to working for what he felt were pornography magazines, but his protests were overridden. "They said, 'You don't have any choice. When you work here, you serve all the clients.' [The Americans for Constitutional Freedom] was one of those covert activities that Gray and Company was so good at setting up—dummy front organizations."[8]

Aside from standard PR and lobbying techniques like press conferences, testifying on Capitol Hill, personal lobbying of congressmen, and hiring spokespeople for The Americans for Constitutional Freedom, Gray and Company got personal. "We attempted to call into question the motives, motivations, the values of the people on the Commission, raise questions about their own backgrounds. Tried to shoot holes in the report, itself, and in the hearing process," explained a Gray and Company executive, who worked on the account.

The campaign was a smashing success. Remarkably, when the Attorney General's Commission on Pornography issued its report in July 1986, Meese, himself, encouraged by Gray, disavowed it. He turned his back on his own commission. The former California prosecutor, renowned for his toughness, actually agreed to stand up in public and say that *Playboy* and *Penthouse* were not obscene. He said he had read *Playboy* in his youth. The Gray and Company account executive explained the tack Gray took with Meese. He characterized Gray's advice as being, " 'Mr. Attorney General, you need to back away . . . because this is not doing you or the administration any good. You're going to end up looking like a fool. So why don't you just skip and go away while nobody is looking?' "

Meese responded to Gray's advice. "As soon as he was made to see the folly of it, he very quickly disengaged himself," the Gray and Company executive said. But while his backtracking may have kept the Reagan administration out of an ugly battle it could not win, Meese's personal credibility was damaged. "It made Meese a laughing stock," the PR man chuckled.

In the meantime, AU made efforts to rid themselves of Reisman, and the new head of OJJDP refused to publish her final report. She was told she was "damaged goods here in Washington." "One of the things that you have to live with in this town is you're in one of two situations. You've either got the resources to fight the scurrilous attacks or you don't. Judith didn't," Wootton said. After spending years developing an expertise and doing what she thought was an excellent job in the public interest, Reisman had been thoroughly discredited and felt helpless to do anything about it.

Reisman was bitter about the experience. "I'll never work again. Universities will never hire me. I am unemployable at this point. I should be teaching at a college, teaching people how to critique and how to read this stuff, how to teach about it, how to show the kids the way they're being manipulated. That's what I should be doing. And I can't do it,'' she said. Whatever the merits of her research, this was a harsh fate for an academic who saw herself performing a public service. The right wing helped some, but after all, politically, she was a Jewish feminist, hardly someone who would have been welcome or happy at conservative institutions like the Heritage Foundation or Liberty University.

A former Justice Department official tried to explain that the attacks were not personal, and that Reisman was not the only victim. "It isn't just Judith. It's whoever's not going to help you. People don't want to support anybody who's not going to help you get the money and power and access. And the minute you are an impediment to that, they're not going to help you because they can't afford to be associated with you. It's just the way this town works.''

Today Reisman still appears occasionally on talk shows and as an expert witness for law enforcement in pornography cases. Many in law enforcement say she is often the only person willing to come forward and testify on the subject. The ultimate irony is that a woman who wanted to express her views was browbeaten by those ostensibly supporting First Amendment freedom of speech.

As for Gray and Company, it did not, as one might expect, pay a penalty for helping to discredit the Attorney General's pet commission. Indeed, the firm received its own grants from the Justice Department to promote some of the department's other programs. "But that again is something which I think the general public does not understand on two levels. One is that a public relations firm may represent, as it turns out, almost opposing sides. . . . Second, in this city, and I don't know why the press can't understand this, Republicans and Democrats, liberals and conservatives, will work together on the same issue. They may stand in the hall of the Senate and shout at each other and then that night have dinner together and be the most jovial friends. That's the way it works. People try to put people in these stereotypic boxes and it doesn't work,'' Berendzen said.

Berendzen's experiences with Gray and Company extended beyond the Reisman affair. Gray and Company were, in fact, AU's PR firm for a time. "We [American University] looked around town and Gray and Company was, I think, the preeminent place certainly in those days. . . . extraordinarily well-connected, also very expensive. Bob Gray is about the most gracious, charming person you could ever meet. He is an extraordinary human being,'' Berendzen said.

Almost simultaneous to Reisman's grant, Adnan Khashoggi, the wealthy Arab arms middleman and a key Iran–Contra figure (and another Gray client), gave American University $5 million to build a new sports arena. Gray and Company liked to take credit for the contribution, though Berendzen denied that the PR firm had anything to do with it.

The Media Coalition account was certainly not an isolated case of Gray and Company attacking the positions of the administration he had helped put into power. His actions began to attract hostility from the right wing. "What I object to are the prostitutes, the people who are hired [guns]. They have no particular philosophy. They will take on any client. They'd take on you if you could afford it, and two months later they [would] take on someone who is exactly on the opposite end of the spectrum. They are only there for money. They don't believe in what they are representing. There is no connection between their personal belief and what they are representing. They do not have any integrity in that regard. Plus, they take people's money in huge amounts and do not do the work," said conservative lobbyist Paul Weyrich.[9] "It amazes me how people, once they get their name in the paper and get a certain reputation, will end up getting a lot of money. It's unbelievable."

Gray's equation of PR–lobbying assistance with the constitutional right to an attorney led the firm to accept some clients more scrupulous firms (and certainly John Hill) would have blanched at. When the Supreme Court was deciding whether or not to review the tax fraud conviction of the Reverend Sun Myung Moon, supporters of Moon hired Gray and Company to lobby the court. It was a first in Washington. In the past, the courts, especially the Supreme Court, had been considered off limits to lobbying. But for Gray and Company this was a million dollar account, and the firm had no qualms.[10]

Like Americans for Constitutional Freedom, a fake front was established for Moon called the "Religious Liberty Foundation." Gray and Company generated pressure on the Solicitor General, the Justice Department's and thus the American public's representative before the Supreme Court, to file a brief in favor of Moon.

The Supreme Court did not overturn Moon's conviction and the religious leader went to prison. Although Gray's efforts did not prove successful, the connection to him did prove controversial both inside and outside Gray and Company. "Gray tried to get Moon in as a client at one point, and there really was a heated discussion. And I must say Joan Braden, bless her soul, and a couple of others of us that argued very strongly against it," said a Gray and Company vice president.

When asked by *Time* Magazine, Gray insisted he did not take each and every client that walked in the door. Remarkably, the two clients he used as examples were Libya, which he had wanted to represent, and the Reverend Sun Myung Moon, whose supporters he did represent.[11] Furthermore, it often was not Gray who decided whether or not to take clients. What prevented the company from taking the most extreme fringes were outcries from the majority of the executives or advice from the CIA. "Yes, he knew Bill Casey. On those instances where there might be a controversy, he may have called Bill Casey," said Mark Moran. "There was a big discussion over Libya which was probably one of the ones where he did go to Casey.[12] But that was shot down internally; there was not a single—well, there may have been one staff person, but of the executives, all shot that one down. We could see that was a no-win proposition. South Africa was another one."

The Teamsters Union, then headed by mafia-connected (and FBI inform-ant) Jackie Presser, was one account the firm did not hesitate to take on. Presser, a former car thief and one of a long line of corrupt Teamster officials, saw in Gray not just an effective lobbyist but a man who could confer on him a social and political acceptability the rough-edged union man admired.

Physically, the two men could not have been more different—Gray, petite, slim, and impeccably groomed; Presser, an enormous man weighing over 300 pounds. "Most of what went on was Bob dealing with Jackie directly; Jackie dealing with Bob. That was the odd couple. Jackie just liked Bob a lot. For some reason Jackie just worshiped the ground Bob walked on. You know why? Because Bob was sort of the image of respectability and elegance and grace and represented polite Washington society. And he accepted Jackie," Moran said.

Gray worked hard at maintaining the relationship. In Washington, Gray held a fiftieth birthday party for Presser at The Palm restaurant, known for its caricatures of famous people on its walls. At Gray's behest, Mark Moran performed a service that typified the Gray touch: "I arranged to get Jackie's picture put up at The Palm where we had the birthday party. My secretary arranged to have the artist flown down from New York. We arranged for the table, and then we waited to see if Jackie picked up on it. He didn't see it. Then they brought in the cake and they brought in the presents and the whole deal. Then Bob showed it to him, and Jackie went bananas. He thought that was the greatest thing," Moran remembered. "I was there at that one. I tried to keep my back to the wall, though, and face the doorway. It was kind of ironic. They put it [the picture of Presser] next to the picture of Eugene McCarthy with the White Knight dressed in a White Knight's suit. Right next to him was Jackie Presser. They couldn't have picked a better place."

The picture was the kind of detail Gray knew would make Presser feel appreciated, special, and "cement the relationship" between Gray and Company and the Teamsters. Gray was also very good at getting Presser included in many Washington events. Sheila Tate remembered one of the parties: "That [the Teamsters account] was a communications thing, though, really, and I couldn't believe that he [Gray] was associating with them. I went to a big dinner party up on the Mall that Gray had when I was at the White House and I sat next to Jackie Presser. The most charming man I have ever talked to. Tish Baldrige [former Commerce Secretary Malcolm

Baldridge's sister, who used to be Jackie Kennedy's social secretary and Clare Boothe Luce's administrative assistant] was on his other side and at the end of the evening she gave him her unlisted phone number. When he came to New York, she had some lovely women friends she wanted him to meet. He was so charming.''

But not everyone thought Presser was charming. ''The guy looked like a frog to me. He was a distinctly unpleasant person, and the thing that made it more alarming was that you knew that he had a reputation for carrying that unpleasantness to extremes if you crossed him,'' Carter Clews said.

If Presser were charming, those who surrounded him were not. ''They brought me over one day to talk about security. They were goons and I thought they would be sophisticated like John Gotti and real sophisticated guys. They weren't at all,'' Neil Livingstone remembered.[13]

Mostly Gray and Company employees made fun of Presser and the Teamsters behind their backs. ''The guys that worked on that account used to make me cry and laugh at some of the stories. They'd get called into some of these hotel-room meetings and some guy would be standing outside the door. You know, sitting outside the door in a chair guarding [the door]. There was one woman who worked on the account with this one guy [who] was complaining about such a bad image problem. He said, 'You know, people think we're thugs.' She said, 'Well, guarding the doors and everything.' And he said, 'We're not guarding the doors. We're audiovisual men.' So when we'd see somebody, 'Hey, audiovisual men,''' Sheila Tate said laughing. ''But we used to find a lot of comedy in most of it. You have to.''

Moran heard a similar story: ''There was a story that my friend Chuck Crawford swears is true, that when Jackie Presser first came to talk to Bob about representing the Teamsters, he arrived in this big black limousine and these two big gorillas—six-foot-five, three hundred pounds—preceded Jackie into the building. They all went up to Bob's office and sat down. Here's Bob—this diminutive little guy—Chuck Crawford, who's five-foot-six or eight, and Jackie who weighs three hundred pounds and these two big guys with, as Chuck says, bulges under their shoulders, and Chuck, being number two, says, 'Oh, and who are these gentlemen?' Jackie says, 'Them's my audiovisual people—the one on the right punches your lights out, and the one on the left rips your vocal chords out.' He swears that's a true story. That became a running joke: 'Tell Jackie to bring his audiovisual people to the meeting.' ''

Duke Zeller, who, like Gray, is gay, had worked for Gray at H&K, then for Gray's friend Senator George Murphy, and later for Senator John Warner before he went to work at the Teamsters. Under Presser, Zeller was promoted to Director of Communications. One Gray and Company executive in a position to know said that Gray and Company was making payments to Zeller. When another executive learned of the payments, he confronted Gray. An agitated Gray called in his attorney and assured the executive that he had only loaned Zeller money for him to build his swimming pool and that Zeller was paying the money back.

"That account caused us a lot of trouble, of course. It was very controversial. You had the Justice Department investigating Jackie. Meese is heading the Justice Department, and Bob is Meese's good buddy," said Moran. Despite these serious problems, the Teamsters remained a long-term account, one that sometimes paid as much as $15,000 to $20,000 a month. Gray says that his only business dealings with Presser were through Gray and Company or Hill and Knowlton, although a former executive at both firms says that Gray even tried to go into business with Presser, despite his ties to organized crime. The former executive asserted that Gray and Presser set up a company called Member Services Corporation, but it was never activated. Presser remained a client until he died—"to the bitter end," Moran said.

Another controversial Gray and Company client was a small, high-tech, California firm called Helionetics, which was involved in laser and solar research and development. In 1983 Jeff Gerth of the *New York Times* reported that Helionetics had given or offered millions of dollars of stock to Edward Teller, the nuclear physicist who was the father to "Star Wars," the Strategic Defense Initiative (SDI), whom Gray had known since the Eisenhower years. The company had offered stock to William Simon, the former Nixon Treasury Secretary, and gave stock to Gray prior to Reagan's Star Wars speech in March 1983, when the President announced increased spending on scientific development of defense systems to shoot down nuclear missiles. Lasers were one of the promising new technologies. The week of the President's speech, Helionetics's stock increased 30 percent.[14]

Gray said that Gray and Company was Helionetics's representative to the federal government, and that it also did PR work for the firm. Dr. Teller's endorsements of Helionetics's products were contained in its advertisments. The White House Science Advisor said that he did not know that Teller had an interest in a company that might benefit from Star Wars. In 1982, Helionetics had won a noncompetitive contract to provide the White House with "ultra reliable communications for the President of the United States and his staff." Mike Pilgrim, a security expert familiar with the agreement, said, "When was the last time that you heard of a private firm providing the President of the United States with secure communication?"

While Reagan and Teller certainly believed in Star Wars, few in the Washington establishment did. The murky dealings between Helionetics, the White House, and the recipients of Helionetics stock, including Gray, were symptomatic of the enormous amount of taxpayer money poured into an essentially worthless program.

Gray and Company also represented Univox, a minority-owned business based in California. Univox's owner, John Grayson, had worked as the Deputy Director of the Commerce Department's Office of Minority Business

Enterprise during the Nixon administration. He knew how the federally funded minority business programs worked from the inside out. By the early 1980s, his company was one of the Defense Department's largest minority contractors. For years, Univox had received sole source contracts for a water purification system for the Army. In the early 1980s, the Army notified Univox that it was going to competitively bid this contract in the future. There were complaints about the company's "shoddy" performance, and assertions that the quality of the units was poor. Despite the two-year warning, Univox could not compete successfully with other small businesses, and lost the contract.

Since free-market competition failed, the company decided to try Gray and Company instead. "I think Lauri [Fitz, a Gray and Company executive] brought him to Gray, and Gray got him into [the] Republican Eagles. He was a big high roller. A beguiling guy," Neil Livingstone remembered. "He had a government contract to do water units for the Pentagon, these self-contained water purification units that you would drop by air and so on. We wanted to make them part of the AID [Agency for International Development] thing to bring fresh water to underdeveloped countries as well."

Gray wrote a letter to then Army Secretary John Marsh in support of his client. A Gray and Company executive, Larry Brady, once an Assistant Secretary at the Commerce Department, arranged a meeting for Univox with James Ambrose, the Under Secretary of the Army. He wrote a follow-up thank-you noting that William Bolger, the former Reagan Postmaster General, "sends his best." Across the letter, Ambrose wrote in long hand: "One hundred and sixteen grand for a six hundred gph water purifier sounds *huge*. Even in Washington, you can still buy a *whole house* for that. Why does it cost so much?" It didn't. The new company that eventually won the contract produced the units for $40,000 less per unit than Univox, saving the Pentagon more than $11 million.

That did not stop Gray and Company or Univox's congressional supporters. Mervyn Dymally, then the head of the Congressional Black Caucus and in whose district Univox was located, became the company's champion. A former Dymally staffer, Adonis Hoffman, was working at Gray and Company. In tandem they pressed for Univox to get an even bigger contract than the one it lost. Dymally even prepared an amendment to help Univox receive consideration. The Pentagon again rejected the pressure.

In the meantime, the Commerce Department loaned Univox $2 million to improve its capital formation. Despite the fact that Univox had certified that it was "financially struggling for its survival," its owner used these monies for "personal enrichment," according to the Commerce Department's Inspector General's report. On the day it received the loan, Univox paid off Grayson's $275,000 personal loan. Univox paid $13,000 for season tickets to Los Angeles Lakers games. Grayson owned an $80,000 Rolls-Royce (the insurance ran $269 a month), a $304,701 townhouse on Capitol Hill in

Washington, and a suburban Washington condominium used for his many lobbying trips. The company paid $1.1 million to questionable consultants whose work the company could not document. In 1987 Univox filed for bankruptcy.[15]

Perhaps no lobbying effort could save Univox, but Gray and Company was successful with other clients needing Pentagon assistance. One of its biggest triumphs was helping Beretta, an Italian company, obtain the Army's handgun contract. It also helped Martin-Baker Aircraft Co., Ltd., a British firm, compete for an ejection seat contract for the Navy's FA-18 plane.

In 1938 the Congress, concerned about foreign governments trying to take advantage of the openness and freedom in this country by unduly influencing American democratic institutions through lobbying and propaganda, enacted the Foreign Agents Registration Act (FARA). The law was amended in 1966; its stated purpose was:

> . . . to protect the national defense, internal security, and foreign relations of the United States by requiring public disclosure by persons engaging in propaganda activities and other activities for or on behalf of foreign governments, foreign political parties, and other foreign principals so that the Government and the people of the United States may be informed of the identity of such persons and may appraise their statements and actions in the light of their associations and activities.[16]

Any person or organization representing a foreign interest in this country is required to register with the Criminal Division of the Justice Department and provide information about its work. It is illegal for a foreign principal or his agent to make political contributions or for a United States government official to act as a foreign agent.

For years FARA has been criticized for not being stringent enough to protect America from foreign interests. Many lobbyists do not even bother to register, and those who do provide only the minimum required information. When violations are discovered, little action is taken. By the mid-1980s, the once-feared "foreign influences" flourished in Washington. The outrages revealed in the Koreagate scandal were forgotten, as were the bribes accepted by congressmen and senators in meetings with FBI agents posing as Arab sheiks—Abscam. As these scandals passed quickly from memory lobbyists rushed to sign up foreign governments as clients, with no real outcry from the media or the public.

Gray cheered these developments in a speech given before the Chicago Council on Foreign Relations in 1984.

> In Washington, D.C., the societal, political and communications nexus of America, interests that span the globe are beating a path to the most sought after people on Earth—the American voter. From within the U.S.,

Americans are accustomed to being courted by merchandisers and politicians. Now, from all over the world, American citizens are sought after for their dollars, opinions, taste preferences, political sympathies, and support.

Representatives of nations and island-kingdoms, business leaders, and multinationals all plead their cases, build coalitions, and seek to influence American public opinion and policy. Everyday I witness a cataract of foreign lobbying, in the broadest sense of the word, running down Pennsylvania Avenue clear out to the Iowa State Fair. It is exciting. It is promising. It is flattering . . .

These international contacts are so all-pervasive as to be hardly newsworthy. In fact, politicians from both the far left and far right almost have stopped issuing their traditional warnings of "undue foreign influence" or 'international conspiracy.''[17]

Niels Holchs, a Gray-trained lobbyist and now a congressional staffer, agreed with Gray about the benefits of American lobbyists working for foreign clients. "Foreign countries need to understand how America works, so they may want to hire a firm to help them with that. It is a process of representation," Holchs explained. "If you got arrested for drunk driving and all of a sudden you were before a court of law, wouldn't you want to hire a lawyer to guide you through that process if you were unfamiliar with that process? There is nothing any different than coming to Washington; America works differently than your country, and there is no reason why you might not want an American to try to help you work through the American political process any more than if you were an American company or even an American embassy in a foreign country. You might want to use somebody that is familiar with local customs and local standards. Washington is—I mean, we're involved in everything. It permeates peoples' lives in this country and it permeates peoples' lives outside of this country. As long as Washington has a lot of influence, there is going to be a need for people who understand this process. They say that Washington is forty-eight square miles surrounded by reality. I think it is a complicated town to understand and work in. So there is always going to be a need for people who understand that, just like there is a need for people who understand how the District Court of Appeals works," Holchs said.[18]

Conservative Washington lobbyist Paul Weyrich disagrees. "It's the mythology of Washington that you have to work through these people [lobbyists] because the place is exotic and unapproachable, and you cannot possibly find out how to get stuff done. And that is just not true. But, you know, the people from the committees and the agencies who get hired for these lobbyist positions help perpetuate the myth."

Holchs, Kentucky Senator Mitch McConnell's top aide, even feels that some of the FARA provisions should be *weakened*, not strengthened. "If we go to a global economy, and sort of a world market instead of just the United States, I think we are going to have to look at changing that law a little bit. If a foreign corporation buys a plant in Kentucky, they shouldn't be treated any differently than another American constituent. Under current law, if you are a foreign company or an official of a foreign company, you can't participate. So you are saying that employees of Toyota Motor Company, American employees, can't participate in a political system through their company, but across the state, employees of Ford Motor Company can. That, to me, is a dumb idea. Some of these rules that we have, you know, we need to rethink a little bit," Holchs said.

Gray and Company took almost every foreign client that knocked on the door and was willing to pay. "We might take a Communist government if one of those Eastern European ones [asks]. It's a business. We're mercenaries," Charles Crawford, one of Gray's top assistants, told the *Washington Post* in 1984.[19] "We represented a vast number of foreign governments and companies, and one day I could be talking about U.S. foreign assistance to a specific country, the next day I could be talking about the sale of jets that were manufactured by a foreign company and attempting to be sold to the United States," remembered Adonis Hoffman. "He [Gray] has a lot of foreign clients. And they're willing to pay because they're getting something from the government," said former Nebraska Senator Carl Curtis.[20]

The potential for conflicts of interest between domestic and international clients was enormous. "One of the things at Gray and Company that I used to have problems with is if you had a domestic client with one business, but you had an international client you wanted to get on, it was alright to take both of them. Well, now let me tell you, the field is not quite that clearly drawn," said Bette Anderson, a Gray and Company senior vice president.

Trade is the critical issue to Far Eastern clients like Taiwan, South Korea, and Japan. Increasingly rich Asian countries became the profit center for Gray and Company. "The Korean government did not get any foreign assistance, per se, from the United States government, so we were talking about trade preferences—the generalized system of preferences (GSP)—in which Korea was a participant at the time," said Hoffman. Gray and Company worked with the Commerce Department, the U.S. Trade Representative's office, and with members of the Ways and Means Committee in the House and the Commerce Committee in the Senate to ensure Korean businesses continued to receive special trade concessions. "The major effort on Korea was to ensure that their GSP status was preserved and extended for a period. At the time, there were several pieces of legislation that were introduced to completely do away with the preferences, given the large trade deficit with Korea," Hoffman said.

"So our mission was twofold: to make sure that those bills did not become successful and two, to make sure that the GSP was extended. Fortunately, we had the U.S.T.R. on our side, and the administration, and that effort was successful on behalf of the Koreans. On the other hand, I was very much aware that there were human rights problems with the Koreans. . . . But in terms of it being, to a certain extent, a democracy, there were at least assemblages of open elections and a very active opposition. So, I mean, it wasn't like it was a completely aggressive regime. I don't mean to sound like I turn a blind eye to human rights abuses, but our charge was to make sure that the trade relationship between the two countries remained in tack,'' Hoffman said.

"Free trade" became the buzzword for lobbyists working for foreign governments, even though most of these countries did not practice free trade. "My personal philosophy is that of free trade. We in the United States cannot advocate closing our own borders as protection and expect to have open trade relations with other countries," Hoffman said. As for the protectionist policies of countries that exclude American products, Hoffman was sanguine. "Granted, there is a deficit. I don't want to get into defending certainly the Japanese or the Koreans for their trade practices. I think there's some historical and economic reasons why their trade doors are not as liberal as our own. On the other hand, I think that we shoot ourselves in the foot in terms of the international environment and in terms of U.S. industry if we don't look beyond our own borders and try to at least encourage a system of two-way trade. And so with that background, it was certainly personally very easy for me to argue that the Koreans should be extended some preferential treatment."

Niels Holchs agreed: "To some extent, the Japanese have influence in this country because the American consumer likes Japanese cars, Japanese products. The consumer likes to have this freedom to choose between an American product and a foreign product. So the American consumer shares a philosophy with many members of Congress that happen to benefit the Japanese." Today, Hoffman, like Holchs, has left lobbying and is now a congressional staffer on the Foreign Relations Committee.

Some lobbyists who rely heavily on foreign clients insist that they do it because American business does not want to pay for Washington representation. But Tom Korologos, whose firm says it does not take foreign clients, insisted, "American business pays through the nose for representation in Washington. . . . Any client that you have to explain or justify is not a good idea to have hired in the first place."[21]

Former Senator Laxalt, now a lobbyist, also avoids foreign clients. "In my own case, for our shop, now I've pretty much laid down a policy to stay away from foreign governments. To stay away from them. They're dangerous."[22] His reluctance is such that he disapproves of the practice even if a lobbyist checks with the State Department and the CIA before taking on a foreign client. "Oh they probably rationalize it. You know, 'I have an influence on this country's policies so that it coincides with our own policies so it's beneficial.' There's no better rationalizer in the world than a lobby-ist,'' Laxalt said.

''We scrub clean dirty reputations,'' a Gray and Company PR executive once explained, without flinching. One of the more notorious dirty reputa-tions they tried to sanitize was that of American fugitive Marc Rich. A billionaire, Rich fled to Switzerland in 1983 to avoid a sixty-five-count criminal indictment. A year later his company, Marc Rich & Co. AG, pleaded guilty to thirty-eight counts of tax evasion and paid a $150 million fine. The fine was small change to Rich, but Gray and Company made it into a celebration—into a media event. The deal was announced with great fanfare by then New York U.S. Attorney Rudolph Guliani who accepted a huge, oversized check as if he had just won the Publisher's Clearinghouse Sweepstakes. It was promoted as one of the largest fines paid in American history. In reality, it was pocket change for Rich, who was charged with gouging the American taxpayers for as much as Charles Keating had with his savings and loan boondoggles.[23]

Just what Gray and Company was supposed to do for Marc Rich was unclear, at least according to their Justice Department filing. ''They (Gray and Company) told us that the filing was vague because Marc Rich was vague about what it wanted Gray to do,'' explained department spokesman John Russell.[24] What is clear is that Gray and Company did more than just PR for Rich. It also lobbied governments on behalf of his businesses. ''At the time he [Rich] was seeking to make some kind of contribution and/or get some kind of recognition for a Caribbean group. Because of my relationship with some of the Caribbean [countries] . . . I was asked to at least at the preliminary level kind of check out the possibilities that might be of interest. I did a little bit of checking on the Hill, and a little bit of talking around the Caribbean community as to whether that would be palatable,'' said Adonis Hoffman, who had been the principle staff person for the chairman of the House Foreign Affairs Subcommittee which had oversight responsibility for of Caribbean countries before joining Gray and Company.

None of these efforts ever seemed to amount to much. ''I never knew if they did restore his reputation. As far as I know, he still lives in Switzerland and is a fugitive. I did see one cover story that was very negative . . . and was wondering if that was their idea of getting a great front page story. My impression of him was that he was a nice fellow [and] had no use for America, whatsoever, except for making money,'' Carter Clews said.

Gray and Company represented many controversial clients, and those who worked on the accounts offered many rationalizations to justify the ethics of lobbying for them. The rationalizations necessary to explain taking on the government of Haiti—during the reign of the murderous ''Baby Doc'' Duvalier—utilized an Orwellian logic that would be dazzling if it weren't so appalling. Adonis Hoffman, a self-described liberal, was one of the executives who worked on the account. "The real issue, as I saw it with respect to Haiti at that time, was that the Haitian people were suffering. The government, we now know, we have the benefit of hindsight, of knowing that the Duvalier government at that time was not a very legitimate regime in terms of providing for the Haitian people. Nevertheless, they were what we had to deal with. For me, as an African-American, Haiti is the first independent black republic in the Americas. It has historical significance far beyond its modern history. The revolution in the eighteenth century. The freeing of the slaves. . . . We were working for the people who in this hemisphere have the lowest standard of living, who are entrenched in the deepest poverty in this hemisphere."

Yet one of the reasons the Haitian people were so poor was the systematic pillaging of resources by the very government that Gray and Company represented. Baby Doc was using this devastatingly poor country's meager resources to pay, among other things, Washington's most expensive PR and lobbying firm to improve its justifiably horrible image in the United States. "What we said was that the Government of Haiti, rank it wherever you will on a continuum of one hundred fifty governments in the world, that the government of Haiti is entitled to make its position known in Washington to the U.S. government, and has the right to try to tell its side of whatever the story is to the media and to the American public. In order to do that, they are going to have to retain a firm that knows how to do those kinds of things and advice," explained a Gray and Company senior vice president. "By definition, people who hire lobbyists and PR people have problems, they have fears, and they have needs." It was as if one of the most brutal dictators of the twentieth century were a poor lost soul seeking his inner child and Gray and Company a benevolent, kindly therapist. (Ironically, Gray and Company's efforts on behalf of Haiti ended up being practically pro bono. "They never paid their bill," the Gray and Company executive said.)

Gray resented being questioned by the media about his "unsavory" international clients. "We don't represent any foreign government without first clearing it with the Secretary of State and the head of the CIA to ensure it is in the best interest of the United States for us to take the case," Gray said.[25] *Time* magazine wrote: "But how did he know, for instance, that more military aid for Turkey was in the national interest? 'I always check these situations out with Bill Casey,' says Gray, dropping like a brick the name of his friend the CIA director. For Bob Gray, friendships like that are not just to be made; they can be marketed."[26]

For all the *Sturm* und *Drang* brought out by Gray and Company's representation of controversial foreign accounts, it was often unclear exactly what the firm did for its clients. Barry Schochet, who was in the International Division, went through a list of clients which Gray and Company listed with the Justice Department on which the firm worked and could not remember any specific accomplishments. "Babak Farzeneh was like an immigration case. I never worked on the Cayman Islands, ever. Government of Haiti, I never worked on them. I had one meeting with them and the Republic of Turkey, I wrote a letter once. Again, this is an imagery kind of stuff. Not that much was going on. These are people who we represented, supposedly. Intelsat, Republic of Korea, Thai Embassy, Khashoggi, I think we were just paid retainers and didn't do anything. Or got them into parties. That's why to me, it just seemed crazy."

What seems hard to understand in retrospect is why, if Gray and Company was not as effective for its clients as its own public relations led them to believe, they kept coming in the doors. "Many of those companies and countries wanted to get the best and that was the best at that time," explained Hoffman. Gray and Company capitalized on the mystique that it was piped into how the inside works in Washington. "The farther away you get from Washington, the more mysterious it becomes," Hoffman said.

In less than three years, Gray and Company had become the largest PR and lobbying firm based in Washington. In a 1981 interview, Gray had said he wanted Gray and Company "to be the biggest and best PR firm in the United States."[27] By 1983 Gray knew he needed to raise money if his goal was to become a reality. He decided to take his company public. "Since you can only grow so much based on your own earnings you could have the most successful thing, but you can't grow geometrically on earnings just generated internally. It is a practical impossibility to be able to bill enough money to hire the extra staff to then bill enough money to hire more staff and grow like that. And the reason [is] because you have got a lag between the time that you are beginning to have to pay for a service and the time you collect from a company. And the bigger you get, the more monstrous this lag becomes," explained John Lawler, who supervised some of the business side to Gray and Company.[28] Many felt there was another reason for going public: "Ego," said another Gray and Company executive.

A stock offering was, by any standard, an audacious move. Most lobbying and PR firms have few assets besides the people working for them, and all of Gray and Company's assets walked out the door every afternoon.[29] More importantly, going public required Gray and Company to open its books to the public, which involves disclosures most lobbyists would rather avoid.[30] No large lobbying–PR firm sold public stock; it was a daring and complicated maneuver. "We were kind of pioneers in that regard. As it was, we had to come up with a system of valuing these assets," Moran said.

Gray said he expected to raise between $4.2 and $5.4 million by selling one-fourth of his company. According to the thirty-eight-page prospectus filed with the Securities and Exchange Commission, Gray planned to use the proceeds to fund corporate expansion and diversification into telecommunications technology and international markets. He formed an acquisition team to find other businesses he could buy with the money.

Gray and Company's access to the powerful was flaunted like a valuable product in the prospectus: "The company's competitive position is affected by public perception of the effectiveness of the company's contacts with persons in the federal government and in the business community who make or influence public policy." To increase the public's perception that Gray and Company had access beyond the Reagan administration, Gray hired two very high-profile new employees. From the international community, Gray hired the former Argentine Ambassador and then the current head of the Organization of American States, Alejandro Orfila, a well-known Washington figure, especially in the social and diplomatic community.

For the media and PR side, Gray hired Frank Mankiewicz, the former head of National Public Radio (NPR) to head the PR division. (John Jessar left to head Gray's largest competitor, Burson Marsteller.) Mankiewicz resigned from NPR, under pressure, because of financial irregularities by a subordinate discovered under his watch. One of Washington's most recognized liberals, Mankiewicz had worked as press secretary for Robert Kennedy, had headed George McGovern's 1972 presidential race, and was considered a friend of Fidel Castro's in Cuba. Gray signed all of his top executives to multi-year contracts to show prospective buyers that they would not be leaving, or worse, setting up competing firms. He tightened client contracts to show potential investors that these obligations were secure.

The media and competitors were skeptical. If the stock offering were successful, it would be the best PR job Gray had ever done. After all, investors did not have a building or equipment or other assets to fall back on. *Barron's* mentioned Gray's extensive self-dealing: that Gray leased his equipment to Gray and Company for $168,000 a year and paid himself $21,500 a month in rent, and that the advertising firm the company used was also owned by Gray. *Jack O'Dwyer's Newsletter*, read by most PR executives weekly, quoted a Wall Street analyst as saying "this stock is overpriced." The newsletter also accused Gray and Company of inflating its revenues by including "millions of dollars in reimbursed client costs (money that the company simply collected from clients and paid out to others, like advertisers.) PR industry practice is not to do this." It even criticized Johnston, Lemon & Co., the Washington broker that was handling the offering and was the sole underwriter. An unnamed source "wondered if the big, prestigious firms had turned it down."

Fortune said: "Another worry is that Bob Gray *is* Gray and Company. Asks a PR executive in another firm: 'How many people will invest in a one-man, one-location shop that has practically no assets?'"[31] Surprisingly, many did. On Wednesday, February 15, 1984, investors bought 500,000 shares of Gray and Company that yielded $2.9 million. At the time it was considered "less than hoped for" since the stock sale was at the low end of what had been reported as the ranges—down 100,000 shares from what Gray had expected to sell. The $7.50 price was also at the low end of the $7 to $9 range. Gray, personally, realized about $520,000, down from the $810,000 projected. "I think some people . . . feel that it was not successful in the sense that [the] stock didn't explode," Moran said.

The *Washington Post* said of the stock offering: "The belly flop by Gray and Company stock is his most conspicuous failure since Bob Gray started his own firm in 1981 and was instantly anointed 'First Flack' of the Reagan administration. Not that Gray did badly on the deal . . . but it was not a smash success, not what you expect from someone who calls his office The Power House. . . . Gray and Company not only overestimated its own worth and fell victim to its own hype, it was handicapped by playing under SEC rules (that do not allow firms to respond to criticism during public offering). There is probably a lesson in this. It is well understood that lawyers who litigate their own cases have foolish clients and the same might be said for public relations firms who try to sell themselves to the public."[32]

Some Gray and Company employees who worked on the stock sale, and others, thought the newspaper's criticism was unfair, and blamed the less than blockbuster sale on the drop in the stock market. "I guess is wasn't fabulously successful, but it may not have been as unsuccessful as the paper portrayed it," said Pate Felts, the Gray and Company accountant. Moran explained, "We went at a time in November 1983, when the market was really down. No public offerings were being done. . . . And we went out successfully. We had to lower the price somewhat because of the decline in the market. The reason the price was lowered was because there was a month and a half delay in the offering. In that month and a half, the market deteriorated rapidly. So people were looking at the price we had reported that we were seeking as the red herring and what we got, but, in reality, it was a decline in the market. . . . The offering sold, and certainly was successful for Bob, because his net worth went up four or five times in a single day. But that's why people take companies public. I don't know what people's definition of success is . . . but if it enables you to go out and double the size of your company in a year, and quadruple your net worth, I would say it's pretty successful."

Like John Hill had done with H&K, Gray offered stock to some of his employees. But unlike H&K, most did not buy any. "Those of us who didn't buy stock always thought it was really crazy. Why would anybody want stock in a PR firm whose one asset is one man and if he were run over by a truck the next day, Gray and Company would have been nothing as far as the public's concerned because it was Bob Gray. It's not like it was at Hill and Knowlton where Hill and Knowlton had been dead for years," said a Gray and Company vice president. Nonetheless those who did buy stock could have made some money. "The stock went up to, at one point, almost ten dollars. It dropped back down. . . . So people could have made a pretty good return had they sold out at the high point. Bob certainly made a lot of money,'' Moran said.

The following fall, Gray and Company bought Strayton Corporation of Wellesley, Massachusetts, Santa Clara, California, and Dallas, "a leader in the field of high-tech public relations."[33] The name of the company was changed to Gray Strayton International. "It always has been our intent to grow rapidly, and to position ourselves to take advantage of opportunities to become a model of the twenty-first century public communications company," Gray said. "In Strayton, we have found an entity as proficient in its market as we are in our."[34] Gray announced that this acquisition was only the beginning.

Moran felt the Strayton takeover was a sound decision. "Strayton had a tremendous respect in the high technology community, an area where we were not particularly strong, but wanted to be strong. Strayton did communication, corporate communication, for the high-tech industry, . . . films for corporations and commercials and things like that. I think [we] got Strayton for a very good price."

Gray's purchase received better reviews than his stock sale. "Going hi-tech was an unexpected move for Gray and Company. Their stock in trade has been peddling influence and political acumen rather than integrated circuits and biotechnology. . . . Market strategies, financial relations and corporate development will be more important to Gray's new clients than blue smoke and mirrors, and that is the direction the firm is headed. Gray is not going to be the flack who passes out press releases on new computers, but rather the mentor who advises merging techno-magnates on their best avenues for growth," wrote the *Washington Post*.[35]

Two years later, in 1986, Gray bought Tromson Monroe Advertising/Public Relations, a thirty-two-year-old firm that specialized in travel-related advertising which depleted the money raised in the stock offering, for the most part. "Bob was also able to merge with a couple of smaller companies here; part of the money was used, of course, to secure the new headquarters. We brought in small advertising companies. [These moves] provided capital for expanding the business, in general, you know, new equipment, particularly in the communications area. We moved from the Power House to Washington Harbour. The operation was expanded considerably," Moran said.

By 1984, Gray and Company was, by far, Washington's preeminent PR and lobbying firm. Gray was now called a "superlobbyist." The *Washington Post* wrote glowingly, "Suave and silver-haired, the sixty-two-year-old Gray is credited by many Washington insiders with raising what was once known as Washington influence peddling to respectability."[36] "Gray, who credits himself with bringing lobbying out of the closet, claims that he has yet to lose a legislative battle," *Fortune* said.[37] Gray and Company charged more than anyone else, if often, despite Gray's hype, the company was not very successful at meeting their clients' needs. But there was never a shortage of clients.

In 1984, Gray was featured in a two-part, front-page Style Section article in the *Washington Post*. *Time* magazine did an article entitled "Pitchman of the Power House," trumpeting Gray as "a new breed of lobbyist, preferring to enter by the front door and stay in the limelight."[38] The *Washington Post* captured the spirit of his driving ambition: "Bob Gray's goal is to turn Gray and Company into the biggest public communications agency in the world."[39]

11

MANIPULATING
THE MEDIA

I think he was the last of the great male hosts. He threw parties. I mean at the convention, there was at least ten parties that he organized.
Sheila Tate, Nancy Reagan's former spokesperson

For Robert Keith Gray, the apex of his public life came during the Republican National Convention in August 1984. The Republican Party had gathered in Dallas to renominate Ronald Reagan and George Bush. This was the height of the excess of the 1980s, and the rich and the middle class of the GOP congregated to pay homage to the man who had made it possible. There was no better spot for the celebration than this city devoted to wealth and consumption. The culture of Dallas revolves around money.

Downtown Dallas's sole public concession to human habitation is a handful of trees in the small park at Dealy Plaza hidden among its stark glass highrise office towers. That summer was brutally hot, the ceaseless heat and humidity magnified by the concrete of the city. But Gray was not about to let searing heat, a dull convention, or a host of personal and professional difficulties endanger his moment in the sun.

Others gathered for the convention complained about the unceasing heat and humidity, but Gray seemed at ease. His suit kept its crease and his custom-made shirts remained blindingly white even after a day full of meetings. At night he was in black tie, scurrying around the city from reception to reception, a CNN camera crew at his side. He was the perfect embodiment of his "superlobbyist" image.

The center of the political universe in Dallas was not the fortress-like Dallas Convention Center or the charming old Adolphus Hotel. This week the power was ten minutes farther down the freeway. The Anatole Hotel, Trammel Crow's monument to the 1980s, was where A-list Republicans registered. The Anatole had taken the cliche of open-atrium architecture

and turned it into a virus that replicated itself into one of the most impersonal, if well-lit, hotels in the world. If you were anyone in the GOP, you
stayed in the Anatole.

Power at the convention meant that you had to show identification to the
Secret Service to get to your room. It meant you counted enough to stay in
close proximity of the Reagans or the Bushes. Gray was in the same tower
as Ronald and Nancy Reagan, the Bush family, and most of the Reagan
Cabinet. Among the officials staying at the Anatole was the Attorney
General–designate Edwin Meese and his wife, Ursula. Mrs. Meese was
working for Gray as a volunteer at the convention. So were George Bush's
sons.

Gray had cultivated Ed and Ursula Meese to the point where he had
almost total access. Gray was their self-appointed emissary from the Old
Guard Republican party. He had successfully created the image of the
helpful insider, merely trying to provide "unbiased" information so an
official like Meese could help the President make the "right" decisions.
Gray had at least two major reasons for being nice to the Attorney General–
designate. One Gray client, Jackie Presser, was under federal investigation
for his organized crime ties and another, Marc Rich, was one of the richest
fugitives in the world.

Gray had learned in his almost three decades in Washington that his
proximity to power was only as good as the favors he could do for the
powerful. He looked at the favors as something friends do. Those who are
more cynical might say this is the commerce that Gray traded in to arrive in
Dallas in such an august position—Gray and Company was the convention's
official public relations channel. To hear Gray tell it, his access was good
because he made certain his information was good. "I have earned the
access," he said. Gray told Cable News Network: "I don't suppose there is
anything as perishable, potentially perishable, as access. If you misuse
access, you lose it. If you have access, it says that you are doing something
right, not something wrong."[1]

Gray had a way of making himself indispensable. He possessed a politician's talent for seeming concerned about everyone with whom he came in
contact. He was always there to write a speech, find a job, help with
publicity, or plan a party. No one examined his ideological credentials very
deeply. He was simply too valuable, too useful.

For Gray, the Republican National Convention in Dallas was his World
Series appearance, All-Star Game, and Super Bowl all wrapped in one. The
tone of the convention was set when Gray's company was hired to do the
convention's official public relations. Gray and Company put out the official
schedule. Gray was everywhere. Dallas was the place he could demonstrate,
once and for all, in full public view, that he had succeeded in Washington
on a scale unimagined by his competitors.

Gray presided over convention caucus groups, ran the Republican Eagles, a wealthy business club, and attended to the needs of the political super-stars. But these political activities were only sidelines to his real purpose in Dallas. For Gray, the GOP convention was really about business. Dallas was his chance for his clients to rub elbows with the politicians. It was an opportunity for Gray to exhibit just how much access he had, to showcase his company and his clout. Some clients wanted a chance to have their children's pictures taken with prominent politicians or time for a personal word themselves. Some clients wanted much more. In the high-powered social setting of Dallas, Gray could provide it all.

During the Dallas convention Gray and then Agriculture Secretary John Block made an appearance before the Nebraska delegation, at a hotel far from the center of action. The group cheered Gray; they applauded Block. The delegates did not seem to know much about the personal side of their home-state-boy-made-good. Even retired Senator Carl Curtis, who helped give Gray his start in Washington, spoke of him in impersonal, superficial ways on the car ride back to downtown Dallas. Gray seemed to have a steel curtain around his personal life, even with old allies.

Accompanying Gray in Dallas was a Cable News Network investigative correspondent and crew.[2] Gray allowed the crew unprecedented access. He had no reason not to. Although the reporter and crew did not know it, Gray had friends in high places at CNN, and Gray had reason to believe that whatever unpleasant material the reporter found would not be seen. As he did with politicians, Gray had arrangements with CNN that he felt would protect him. His manipulation of the news media is one of the key reasons he seemed so successful in the 1980s.

When Gray, with the reporter at his side, ran into the reporter's boss behind the two-story-high CNN booth on the convention floor, the reporter witnessed an unsettling scene. Ed Turner, CNN's vice president for news, and Gray started chatting like old friends. The reporter was being sent a very unsubtle message.

While Gray absorbed handshakes, congratulations, and media attention with joy, he also had an unexplained tenseness. He always seemed on guard against making a mistake that would make him look foolish or careless. He was poised as long as nothing unpleasant or unanticipated happened—nothing that was not in his carefully orchestrated plans. But when the unexpected occurred, Gray stumbled. When the reporter asked Gray about a spat of embarrassing incidents concerning Gray and Company officials, Gray became brittle and defensive. If he had a weakness, it was a habit of not dealing with direct challenges with the kind of grace one would expect from a high-powered public relations executive. It was the chink in Gray's well-tailored PR armor.

The Sunday before the convention officially started, Gray arranged a party at the luxurious Riverside Lodge in Hamilton, Texas. One of Gray's major clients, the financially troubled Diamond Shamrock Oil Company, based in Dallas, was picking up the tab although the party was being "hosted" by then Senator Paul Laxalt of Nevada and his wife.

The barbecue, which had an exclusive guest list, was held at the company's recreational ranch about a hundred miles south of Dallas. To save the drive, which might put off some important guests, Gray arranged for a government contractor, Bell Helicopters, to supply transportation for those coming to the Laxalt party. Attractive young Gray staffers made certain logistics went perfectly. The sprawling guest ranch soon turned into a bizarre receiving line as helicopters dropped off their important passengers. Diamond Shamrock executives waited with Gray as he made the introductions while the Washington luminaries were dropped off, one helicopter after another.

Diamond Shamrock seemed to get its money's worth that day. Guests, all dressed in Western attire, included former CBS newsman Roger Mudd, USIA Director Charles Wick, *Los Angeles Times* Washington Bureau Chief Jack Nelson, syndicated columnist Rowland Evans, and assorted other politicians and media figures, who waited in line for Texas-style barbecue served off of a chuck wagon. Men like Wick had their plates piled high with brisket and ribs. As they ate they listened to country music provided by Slim Chance and the Survivors in the 105-degree heat.

But William Bricker, the CEO of Diamond Shamrock, was not happy about one missing guest. Gray had led Bricker to believe that former CBS anchor Walter Cronkite would grace the party. When Gray informed Bricker that Cronkite could not make it, there was a cold stare from the white-haired Bricker. That afternoon, back at the Anatole in his suite, Gray, in shirtsleeves, played the telephone like a musical instrument. His personal assistant put through a phone call to Cronkite, the errant guest. It was vintage Gray: "Hello, Walter, how's everything going? . . . It was hotter than blazes. Jesus, it was hot. . . . Well, Walter, I am really calling to find out if you and Betsy are interested in going to a dinner party tomorrow night for Paul Laxalt?" Gray's charm paid off.

High above Dallas in the Diamond Shamrock Tower, a pianist played in air-conditioned splendor. Bricker, overstuffed in his tuxedo, beamed as he was introduced to Walter Cronkite, who arrived, on cue, with his wife Betsy. Diamond Shamrock executives and their spouses ogled Cronkite while Cabinet officials like Labor Secretary Ray Donovan and Ed Meese and assorted other administration officials were virtually ignored.

At the same time Gray was putting clients together with powerful political and media figures, he said he disapproved of lobbying at social occasions. Remarkably, he insisted, "I have never lobbied anyone at a social occasion. You will never find anyone in the thirty-four years I have been at it in Washington to say I have arm twisted them on any issue whether it was at my party or theirs."[3] It was an amazing reversal of all of his earlier pronouncements. Gray produced the Meeses and others, not only for the

Diamond Shamrock party but also for several other client-sponsored social occasions. To CNN, he was now claiming that these friendships were a handicap, not a help. "The closer you are to somebody, the more thoroughly you have to convince them of your case because he naturally has a resistance. He wants to be very sure that he is not giving you something you're not entitled [to] because of friendship," Gray said.[4] This contrasted with what the *New York Times* had written the previous January: "Although he has said he never 'abuses' a friendship for a client, he does concede that he uses his access to influential Washingtonians to 'influence public opinions on selected issues.' "[5] Gray and Company executive Joan Braden echoed this view of her boss: "Of all the men I have known and worked for in my life, I think Bob does work every minute of the day and every minute that he is awake."[6]

Gray's ability to put clients together with the powerful government officials they wanted to meet was showcased in Dallas. The culmination of this extravagant display was the appearance at the convention of one of Gray's most controversial clients, Jackie Presser, the President of the International Brotherhood of Teamsters, who at the time was avoiding prison by becoming an FBI informant. Although Gray had arranged for Presser to supply Ronald Reagan and George Bush the Teamsters' endorsement in 1984, Gray was careful to make certain Presser and the Teamsters entourage stayed far away from the Anatole.[7]

At the convention, Presser and his colleagues, who looked like characters right out of Damon Runyon, or an Ohio version of *The Godfather*, spent their afternoons in a hospitality suite at the Fairmont Hotel. Presser and his aides sat around a melting ice sculpture of the Teamsters' logo surrounded by hotel-supplied hors d'oeuvres. Occasionally a curious reporter or delegate would drop by. "Have some eats," one of Presser's aides would urge. The only member of Presser's staff who seemed to fit in with the Republican crowd was the slender, blond, and well-dressed Duke Zeller, Presser's number one publicity man and close friend of Gray's.

One afternoon at the Fairmont, Gray added his touch. This time the Teamsters officials had booked a large room. Tables were covered with bowls of shrimp, caviar, and the kind of finger foods not usually associated with Teamsters. The union leaders were on their best behavior. Amazingly, Gray and Company had come up with the idea of the union hosting a reception honoring Republican women officials.

The incongruity of violins playing as Teamsters, some carrying more than convention credentials, reached with their hands into the bowls of crab and shrimp and removed great quantities, did not faze Gray and Company staffers. The reception, which was by invitation only, was one of the most well-attended of the convention. Perhaps the most surprising guest was Senator Orrin Hatch, then chairman of the senate labor committee. How Gray got Hatch to the party may be more a reflection of Hatch's insensitivity than Gray's talent. Hatch's committee has the job of policing labor for ties to organized crime. Presser had been repeatedly questioned by the committee about his organized crime connections. When Hatch arrived, he put his arm around Presser and embraced him.

Presser was impressed by the turnout Gray had engineered for him. "I expect the impossible. These are the kinds of things he performs. Bob doesn't waste anytime with you. He asks you. He listens to what you have to say, and then he goes out and does it his way." Presser said that he was pleased with the personal attention he got from Gray, but he was not fooled like other, more naive clients and politicians, that Gray's friendship was anything more than a means to an end. He added, "But I pay him very well. . . . He's got credibility. It is really more than access. Bob Gray has credibility with almost all the people in Washington and other countries in the world as well."

Gray's notebook-sized convention schedule included speech writing for key speakers like Senator Laxalt and United Nations Ambassador Jeane Kirkpatrick. Gray closed out the convention with one black tie reception after another. He was Roy Cohn's guest at a private reception at the posh Mansion at Turtle Creek. Gray and client Bill Moss (Ursula Meese's boss) hosted a post-nomination champagne supper for Ronald Reagan for large Republican contributors called the Eagle Trustees. The scene at the Anatole ballroom was punctuated with leggy young women dressed as "Eagles" who welcomed the wealthy GOP donors.

Gray knocked them dead at the convention. He was truly at the apex of his career. His optimism about the future of Gray and Company seemed limitless. In the summer of 1984, everything seemed possible. "I would like to see my company become the twenty-first-century prototype of a communications firm. By the end of the century some firm is going to emerge as having all the muscle to do the best job in that field, and I want it to be this firm," he told CNN.

By the mid-1980s, image had truly triumphed over substance in Washington. With the advent of television as the public's main source of information, the scales seem to be forever tilted in favor of public relations. Whether it was the White House, the Congress, or Gray and Company, they based their decisions on the same criteria. Reagan was truly a PR product—his statements, his appearances, his appointments, his travel—everything was staged for a desired effect.

" 'PR equates to everything' was what the Reagan White House was about more than anything else. It was about photo opportunities, it was about managing the news. And so if somebody came along like a Gray and could make a case: 'There's going to be a bad spot on the evening news,' [they would listen to him]. . . . The influence of public relations firms is directly proportional to the integrity of the people in the office. . . . If what the *Washington Post* says about you is what you care about more than anything else, then the people who are the mavens of that world are going to have extraordinary influence," said a Reagan political appointee.

The White House press office acted like a PR firm representing a business—a product—not the leader of the free world. "You know, questions have been raised about did we try to control Reagan too much. . . . We did try to control our message, and I don't think we did anything more than any other President has done; maybe we did it more effectively. I hope we did. But any business would do that. Any business on a given issue tries to put their best foot forward and tries to explain the issue and get it aired in a form that gets their message out. And that's what we were trying to do. The first year on the economic program, we made a decision that everything we did was going to be judged on whether it helped passage of the economic program because that was our priority; and speeches, meetings, press conferences, trips—all that were basically judged on whether it helped the President pass the economic program. So we were able to focus the message. We did the old standard tactic of simplify your message and focus it and repeat it. I think the press, in a way, began to resent that because they knew that they were not able to deter us from that goal and that decision to stay the course, as Reagan says," explained Larry Speakes, who headed Reagan's press office.[8]

Besides Larry Speakes, who came from Hill and Knowlton under Gray, Mike Deaver, one of Reagan's top three aides, was a skilled PR professional. Speakes told how the White House operated: "Just as I had with Hill and Knowlton, much of my briefing room message was directed toward the legislative program on Capitol Hill. . . . One of the first assignments that we had was to prepare a communications plan for the President's economic program, the so-called 'Reaganomics' tax cuts and other things that went with it. . . . So I worked carefully . . . to develop a comprehensive press plan that would use television and magazines and other things to get the President's program out. . . . And it was many of the grass-roots things . . . particularly in . . . eighty-two, eighty-three, eighty-four—there was a lot of the grass-roots–type thing where the President would go out into the congressional districts, almost as we had done at Hill and Knowlton but we didn't go down to the district, we set up interviews and things like that at Hill and Knowlton, but in the Reagan administration it was sort of the similar type of, you know, 'Let's go to congressman so and so's district because he's undecided on this subject and let's go in there and make a speech and get him to go down with us,' " Speakes said.

There really was no big difference in working for the President of the United States at the White House or for Gray at Hill and Knowlton. "The similarities were so evident because when you get ready to do the economic program or a drug message or any economic summit or a meeting with Gorbachev, we essentially sat down and did a communications plan just like we did at Hill and Knowlton. They were plans that you would try to identify the target audiences, whether a geographic~audience or a demographic audience—whether it's young people or old people, minorities, or women or whatever you were trying to reach—and we would devise various means to do that. We would work with the networks to get people on there. It was a lot easier from the White House. I guess that's one difference . . . ," Speakes said. "With a PR firm you are often trying to sell a story that isn't a story."

Reagan's former Secretary of Health and Human Services, Richard Schweiker, offered an example of how major decisions at the White House were based on public relations rather than public policy. After Schweiker had obtained a final agreement with the Office of Management and Budget on cuts in the HHS budget, David Stockman came up, after they were all done, with "a Mickey Mouse list" of about seventy-five more programs that he wanted cut, "all of which were political dynamite," Schweiker said.[9] "So I was really mad so I decided I would appeal."

The White House appeal board was Ed Meese, Stockman, and James Baker. When Schweiker went to make his appeal, Baker was in Texas at a funeral, so he had to face the idealogues, Meese and Stockman. "I knew I wasn't going to win the argument that day. So I simply said, 'Look, I'll go through the numbers here, but I want to let you know that win, lose, or draw, I'm going to see the President about it because I want him to see who's putting him on CBS television every night about hurting the poor and cutting out the programs that are helping people.' Then I said, 'Let's just go down this list.' The first one was to cut back the measles vaccination program. I said, 'Okay, I can see CBS News comes. They're going to show closing the doors on the measles vaccine clinics, pushing the kids away cause there won't be any money for vaccines. The very first epidemic of measles that breaks out, which we're ninety-eight percent away of eliminating, will be called the Reagan Measles Epidemic because you guys are putting him there by that.' . . . The next one they were going to cut out, money for Indian health service . . . I said, 'Okay, the next one will show cameras on the Navajo reservation—all the original Americans—they're going to shut down the doctors. Move them out. And you have sixty percent unemployment, forty percent alcoholism. And you guys are going to shut the doors? Shove it to the Indians. Move them away. That will be the second night's CBS story.' And I started to go down the third one and show them what the third night was going to be with the cuts and at that point Stockman reaches in his pocket and he goes like this," Schweiker said, raising a white handkerchief in his hand. "He gave up because he knew that if I went to Reagan with those cuts, that Reagan would never agree to those cuts. See the trouble with a lot of the cuts that Reagan agreed to, nobody explained to Reagan. They didn't have the guts to go around Stockman and Stockman would bulldoze them. But I knew as much as Stockman from my own experience on the Hill, and I knew what to tell him. And I told him, 'I'm going up to Reagan and tell him that you, Dave Stockman, are putting him on television for batting the Indians over the head and cutting out the measle vaccine.' And I knew that Reagan would side with me. I just knew him well enough and so did Stockman.''

By the mid-1980s, attitudes about the excesses of the first half of the decade were just beginning to change. When the media began to question Gray about the unsavoriness of selling access, he began to deny it. "We don't sell access. I don't claim that that's something we have that others don't," Gray said.[10] But the protest was too late, and the previous boasts had been too public. "No matter how often Gray voices that caveat, many still view access as his main commodity," the *National Journal* wrote.[11] Gray and Company was no better, and in many ways, no worse than any other PR and lobbying firms in town. But it could get away with charging more than the others, because of the illusion of access that Gray had created.

Gray indicated to *Forbes* that he gave PR advice to Muffy Brandon, Nancy Reagan's social secretary, and, of course, to Ed Meese. "I meet with them from time to time to help them with image problems and ideas for presenting concepts to the public. . . . I don't expect a perpetual open door without reciprocating once in a while," Gray said.[12] He continued to make certain that the media and clients knew that members of the Reagan administration called him for advice. "Fortunately for my ego, I get called by members of the government, saying, 'Here's the situation, what would you do?' Many of these people I worked with in the [1980 presidential] campaign or the inaugural, and they get in the habit of thinking of you as a volunteer, outreach volunteer," Gray told the *National Journal*, in 1985, still emphasizing his now five-year-old roles even after another Reagan election cycle had passed.[13]

Gray reminded the media that several of his former employees—Larry Speakes, Sheila Tate, and Landon Parvin—were working at the White House. Often these former H&K executives did call people at Gray and Company for advice, but seldom, if ever, did they call Gray. "One of the things I missed most when I got there was working in that office environment where you could call people and say, 'Give me your advice on this . . . I'm thinking about doing this, what do you think?' You needed feedback, and I didn't have anyone over there who had any communications experience that I could do that with that would have the kind of judgment I needed. So I often called people like John [Jessar] and said, 'What do you think about this?' " Tate said. But neither Tate nor Speakes remember either calling Gray for advice or his calling them for a favor on behalf of a client.

For most clients, the services Gray and Company offered were routine. Although Gray and Company now called itself an international public communications firm, most of its public relations work was the same as other PR firms had been doing for a generation: ghostwriting newspaper articles or op-ed pieces, setting up press conferences with slick media kits touting their client's position, organizing real or fake coalitions, and training their clients how to handle the media.

William Bolger, the former Postmaster General and Gray friend, told the *National Journal* that an important part of his job was reading major newspapers "to see what's going on in the world."[14] From these sources he was supposed to identify issues and companies that might be affected by them. That was his way of identifying clients "who don't yet know that they need public relations."

"Broadcast Placement" was Gray and Company's term for trying to book clients onto television shows and, when successful, to help them prepare for the interview and to provide the host of the show with background information and suggested questions.[15] Like access to and friendships with government officials, Gray and Company's PR Division touted their relationships with the staffs of television shows: "Gray and Company maintains excellent relationships with producers and hosts of America's top news and talk shows on radio and television. For the client desiring exposure on these programs, Gray and Company calls upon its knowledge and familiarity with the individuals who make the placement decisions on a day-to-day basis," stated a Gray and Company brochure.

For an additional $5,500 to $8,500 a day, a client could take Gray and Company's media training program for client appearances on television and radio, as well as instruction on how to handle print interviews. "Through role-playing exercises using videotape and critiques," Gray and Company taught its clients how to feel "comfortable" with the media and how to underplay their intrinsic attitudes that most journalists "are inherently antagonistic or ill-informed."

Just like preparing a witness for testimony on Capitol Hill where Gray and Company executives pretended they were senators and asked the client questions, Gray and Company executives would pretend to be journalists or television talk show hosts and confront their clients. According to Gray and Company's brochure, these exercises included instruction on how to defuse "60 Minutes"–like "ambush journalism," how to respond to "ill-informed, apathetic, or outright antagonistic" talk show hosts or telephone callers in call-in shows, and how to keep messages focused, brief, and organized even when confronted with a "negative barrage of accusations" at a press conference.

Gray and Company's media training services included helping a client develop a fifteen-second sound bite called a "nugget." Clients were instructed how to introduce "nuggets" into interviews with phrases like "most important" so that busy radio or television editors, reviewing the videotape for the evening news, would recognize the most important point and even appreciate it being pointed out to them. Gray and Company advised clients to identify other points they wanted to make, to reduce them "aloud" to ten seconds each, and then to repeat them as often as possible in the interview. Like the Ten Commandments, Gray and Company had ten "Media Training Golden Rules," which advised clients not to argue with reporters, but to consider background lunches to keep them "abreast" of developments. Their stated goal was to assure "*control* of the media situation."

Many of the PR services that Gray and Company offered *were* new and innovative. It was a brave new world in terms of media coverage in the 1980s, and firms like Gray and Company were ready to take advantage of it. For the first time, the majority of Americans were getting their news from television. Gray recognized the importance of this. "In no area is change coming at a faster pace than communications. . . . We are developing electronic wizardry at incredible speed. And with every development we make future changes in communication's use and habits."[16]

In the past, the staple of the PR firm was the press release, written for print reporters. Rarely did a newspaper run a PR firm's press release in total. But radio and television—which seem so much more ephemeral—appeared much more promising to the PR industry. For the cost of a few minutes of satellite time, advertising packaged to look and sound like news stories could be fed to thousands of radio and television outlets. Called "electronic" or "video news releases," the idea was to get television networks and local radio and television stations to air these advertisements as their own news stories. Besides eliminating the built-in skepticism toward advertising, the impact of the message increased because it appeared to have the credibility of an unbiased news story.

In radio broadcasting, Gray and Company started with "Washington Spotlight," its own radio program for its clients that sounded like an independent news and features program. During these programs the radio stations did not disclose that they were produced by Gray and Company or that Gray had been paid by clients to do them. In the beginning, it was an experimental, seat-of-the-pants operation. One employee would write the scripts and another would come up with four clients each week to pay for the show. "For the radio show, we'd send it out over a couple of networks—Mutual and some other radio network. A surprising number picked them up. And then later they bought satellite time to send them out to TV," explained a Gray and Company PR executive.

By 1984, the radio show was a big success. *Advertising Age* wrote, "Gray's radio prototype has been building since August, when it bowed by offering stations a 15-minute monthly public affairs program featuring four three-minute news and feature stories. Each segment focuses on something important to a Gray client, who pays Gray $750. The latest count showed 656 'subscribers' in 'the Gray & Co. network.' Another 1,476 stations in the Mutual Broadcasting System and National Public Radio networks receive the program by satellite each month. Gray reportedly is planning to raise the participation charge to $1,000.'' Soon "Washington Spotlight" was being broadcast biweekly, within a ten-minute program featuring segments on three clients, "each two-and-a-half minutes long."[17] The charges were increased to $1,500 per program. Eventually, Gray and Company even had a daily radio feed called CapitoLink.

Besides the radio show, Gray and Company advertised to its clients that it could target their messages to smaller audiences as well. "Gray and Company has developed a network of radio stations across the country which frequently use our audio material. These stations can be broken down into geographic, demographic, or political areas for targeting. . . ." The PR firm charged $1,500 (not including billable staff hours) for radio actualities, or sixty-second "news" segments distributed to Mutual, Associated Press, and United Press International. It also offered clients for $75 to $125 per market, for telephone feeds to radio stations that news directors could call to obtain pre-recorded interviews for use on their news shows.

How did Gray and Company get the radio networks to carry their show? Amazingly, the Mutual Radio Network came to Gray and Company and asked to carry it. Radio stations receiving these advertisements unsolicited and using them as news stories seemed bad enough, but the stations actually soliciting the programs was incredible. The stations who subscribed were usually in small to mid-sized markets or independent stations in big markets that did not have network affiliation.

Many of these services had their roots, not in Gray and Company or other PR firms, but in Capitol Hill. Neil Livingstone hired Carter Clews, who had been Director of Communications for the Senate Republican Conference. While he was on Capitol Hill, the Senate broadcast its first ever television satellite transmissions from the Capitol. Clews wanted to do the same for Gray and Company. At first Gray was skeptical, but after some prodding, Clews got Gray to accept the idea.

Once Gray saw the potential profits, he authorized the spending of thousands of dollars to equip a full studio. "Bob was, and I assume he still is, just a very aggressive guy. So he would push the envelope of all of these things out as far as he reasonably could," Mark Moran remembered.[18]

Gray and Company hired many talented, creative people who tried to bring new, innovative concepts to the company. Frank Mankiewicz, Gray and Company's resident liberal, was the choice to head up the PR Division. He had the perfect soundbite mind and was also well-connected. "Frank was usually the person they put forward to be quoted on any issue [that] was controversial because he put the right spin on it. He was very good at that," said a Gray and Company vice president. "He's a great person to work for. . . . Great stories, great one-liners, very good at PR strategy. He and Gray had a very good relationship; still do. They play off each other well because one is a Republican and one is a Democrat. He's a good writer. Has unerring moves of what will sell: what's a story and what isn't a story,'' confirmed another Gray and Company PR executive.

CNN asked Mankiewicz, since he had been president of National Public Radio (NPR), whether he thought it was a conflict of interest that NPR was using Gray and Company's radio shows. ''I see no conflict of interest in saying, 'Gray and Company produced this material about a client. Listen to it. If you want to put it on a news show, feel free to do so.' . . . Why should there be any conflict of interest? . . . I had nothing to say about what they put on while I was president. They pay more attention to me now.''[19]

With the success of ''Washington Spotlight,'' Gray and Company decided to try to do the same for television. ''The stations are hungry for news,'' Mankiewicz said.[20] Gray's approach to both technically and psychologically controlling the airwaves was no different than his approach to lobbying— wherever he needed access, he bought it. The firm hired Jackson Bain to be their television talent. A former anchorman in Atlanta, Bain had recently been replaced by Maury Povich in a shakeup for the anchor slot for the ten o'clock news at Channel 5 in Washington. ''He was our talent. Make sure you have that in the book. I'd use that as our TV entertainment, not in a literal sense. Jackson would be the voice and the face, would do the interviews. He would also be on the feeds themselves. Meryl Comer would often be on the feeds,'' explained a Gray and Company senior vice president. Comer was another former Channel 5 anchor, who had gone to work for Gray in 1979. When he started Gray and Company, he shared Comer with the Chamber of Commerce, who reimbursed Gray for Comer's services.

Carter Clews had tried to push the firm in a ''high-tech media'' direction, but it was not until Jackson Bain came in that the operation really expanded. Gray and Company rented satellite time and hired freelance producers and camera people. It did not take long for its ''Broadcast Services'' to become a key part of its PR Division. In their brochure, Gray and Company bragged that they did more than simply distribute their ''news'' stories to television stations, as other PR firms did. To convince clients that they were not wasting money by reaching inconsequential audiences, Gray and Company claimed to ''narrowcast'' (or target television markets of importance to their client) with their materials. The PR firm promised to reach ''opinion leaders on specific issues and events, as well as the constituencies, which can ultimately effect attitudinal change.''

To meet these goals, Gray and Company said that they had surveyed the various television stations to determine what they wanted. The PR firm discovered that the stations, ''to turn the material into a localized news feature,'' wanted complete, two-minute reports with a reporter voiceover along with four minutes of isolated on-camera statements taken from interviews and four minutes of high quality scenes with natural sound track (B-role).

Once the video was produced, a Gray and Company PR executive would "work to presell the story and the satellite feed to station news directors and producers" by encouraging the stations "to use elements in this package to assemble their own localized stories." Gray and Company told clients that they carefully selected their satellite time "to insure station satellite dish availability, as well as the optimum time for producers to view and produce their stories." Then they made follow-up calls to determine whether or not stations used these materials and provided clients with "results reports." Gray and Company recommended "coordinating the television effort with similar or identical radio feeds, to achieve maximum market penetration." The firm said the costs for the satellite feeds varied, but a client might expect to pay $6,500 to $10,000 for each ten-minute feed.

By the mid-1980s, it was not unusual for large public relations firms to use electronic news releases and other forms of satellite communications to promote a client's interests. But Gray and Company broke new ground. As Gray had done in recruiting political figures for its lobbying division, he carefully hired former television journalists with familiar faces, who had credibility in the profession and with the viewers, for Broadcast Services. "Some of the idea was that Meryl was an on-camera personality and she was a recognizable commodity and we can produce some of these things together and take advantage of that," Moran explained. These broadcast professionals conducted interviews and voiced footage for the PR firm just as they had done for the television news. The final products were indistinguishable.

The controversy over re-creations in news stories seems frivolous compared to the airing of advertisements as news stories. But Ted Turner's pioneering news service, Cable News Network (CNN), did just that. As Gray and Company was coming of age in the early 1980s, so was CNN. Struggling to grow and gain respect, the network desperately needed inexpensive news programming to fill up its twenty-four hours of air time. Gray and Company was delighted to help.

Gray and Company–produced PR packages began appearing on CNN as news stories. In March 1985, Gray and Company sent by satellite "an exclusive interview" by Meryl Comer with King Hassan II, the ruthless ruler of Morocco. At the time the King was being criticized for signing a treaty with Libyan leader Muammar Qaddafi. In a standup outside the palace, Comer warned viewers that the West should not react harshly to the treaty and that any criticism of Morocco should be "tempered with the acknowledgement" of the country's strategic importance to the United States.

CNN and Channel 5 in Washington ran the story like their own. At no time did either the station or the network disclose that Meryl Comer was a

Gray and Company executive, or that Morocco was a Gray client that was paying the firm a minimum of $360,000 to improve its image in the United States, or that Morocco had paid Gray and Company to produce the piece.

Mark Moran explained how a network of associations led to the piece being aired. "Meryl Comer was working for Gray and Company, and at the same time she was doing a program for Biznet (the Chamber of Commerce) . . . So what happened was she was given an opportunity to go over to Morocco and interview the king, which was largely arranged because the king was a client of Gray and Company. And she did and she did a program on that. The program did not identify the fact that she was working for Gray and Company and Morocco was a client of Gray and Company. There was some question as to whether there should have been a Foreign Agent Registration Act acknowledgment before and after the program, which technically there probably should have been, but it was one of those close cases that nothing ever would have come out of it," Moran explained. "But it caused a lot of stir in the press because both Bob and Meryl were very identifiable figures."

One of the key purposes of the Foreign Agents Registration Act (FARA) is to protect "the public's right to identification of the sources of foreign political propaganda." A Gray and Company executive said, "They were doing an up-link and it wasn't labeled and it was broadcast as news, but it was paid for by Morocco. But I'm not sure even FARA had at that time . . . rules with regard to up-links. It was brand new. People were just beginning to do it."

When the *Washington Post* ran a critical, front-page story about this incident, the television outlets disavowed any involvement.[21] Channel 5 said it got the "news" feed from CNN. The late Betty Endicott, then Channel 5's news director, told the *Post* she felt "used." "I had no knowledge of the fact that Meryl Comer worked for Gray and Company. I knew Meryl as a newsperson in Washington. How would you know?" CNN executive vice president, Ed Turner (no relation to Ted), who made the decision to run the piece on CNN, and who allowed Comer to transmit it on CNN's satellite time, also denied knowing that it was a Gray piece. He said he thought she was doing it for the Chamber of Commerce, but the *Post* noted, "The U.S. Chamber of Commerce is a registered lobbyist for business causes. Why news directors at . . . CNN would deem a Chamber of Commerce report any more legitimate than a Gray and Company production is another question." Comer, who had worked for both Turner and Endicott at Channel 5 (Turner had hired her at the station), said that both of them knew about her affiliation with Gray and Company.

When asked about the incident, for this book, Gray said, "I believe CNN should have made known the origin of the video, but I do not believe that that omission hampered the clear communication of facts."

A Gray and Company PR executive who worked on the piece felt there was more than a little hypocrisy in the horrified media reaction. "I used to read in *Broadcasting* [magazine] the cache of letters from news directors after the story broke about electronic news releases saying, 'How despicable. Never in a thousand years!' And they were people I had talked to who had called me back so that they had the right coordinates on the satellite so that they could take the feed, including the late Betty Endicott and Channel Five. I made the call. I talked to her. I ran the feed. She knew it. I told her and I talked to her about it and after the storm broke, she [denied it.] You know why she denied it? Because she should have been fired."

The same was true with CNN. "Of course they knew, because that's how they get most of their feeds. They get ITN feeds, they get Burson (Marsteller), Hill and Knowlton. They know exactly where the stuff is coming from. And I added a disclaimer on it, front and back. And Betty then claims that it had no disclaimer. She didn't know where it was coming from. She thought it was news. Bullshit. I mean, she's dead now, so she can't respond, but I talked to Betty Endicott the night that we ran the feed and she knew exactly what she was getting. . . . She got it herself. She got it off our feed directly."

Gray and Company executives insisted that they labeled all of their material. "We were so scared that the Justice Department was going to come after us, that we made sure we labeled it front and back. We damn near labeled it in the middle," a senior vice president said. "We did label for domestic consumption and radio commercials, we made sure people knew where they came from," confirmed another Gray and Company executive. "I did that for Gray and Company [labeling the feeds]. . . . We fed that stuff all over the country via satellite and we labeled it and they knew it was coming from Gray and Company. I don't even know why anyone would want to attempt to [not label it]. . . . If the station needs the material, they use it. If they don't, they won't use it," Clews said. "It's very simple."

Despite the fact that many indignant television news director said they would never use PR "propaganda," a Gray and Company PR executive insisted that these very same people used to beg him for it. "But all I happen to know are the electronic news feeds—the ENRs [electronic news releases], because I was involved from the very beginning. Someone like myself, we never put anything out that wasn't labeled and we usually talked constantly to the news directors from around the country. They knew exactly who we were. They called us all the time. They asked us for stuff. They told us they couldn't get it. They forgot to turn their downlink on and could we send them a hard copy Fedex overnight because they'd use it tomorrow night." But when this practice was made public, the television stations acted like they did not know where the material was coming from. "Come on. So where's all this stuff coming [from]. 'Out of the blue,' 'The stuff is arriving in our newsroom from another side of Mars,' 'We have no idea where it's coming from,' " mocked the Gray and Company PR executive.

The Morocco story was not an isolated example of the cozy relationship between Gray and Company and CNN. The same thing had happened a few months earlier when another Gray and Company client, the Japan Center for Information and Cultural Affairs (JCIC), had hired Gray and Company to promote, among other things, the upcoming visit of then Japanese Prime Minister Nakasone to the United States. Like the Moroccan piece, CNN ran the clip as a news story. "It was a program we fed from Japan about the upcoming visit of the Prime Minister, giving background on him, on Japan–U.S. ties, B-role footage, interviews with the Foreign Minister. We sent it all over. Notified every station in the United States," recounted a Gray and Company PR executive.

The Moroccan incident triggered one of the two major federal investigations into Gray and Company. "I was told that the gist of the Justice Department investigation was for our failing to properly and adequately label and disclose what we were doing. Which is just a matter of sending a feed out and not saying, 'This isn't news; this is an advertisement,' " explained a Gray and Company executive. The Justice Department determined that Gray and Company had labeled the Moroccan story and took no action against either Gray and Company or CNN. It basically said, "Don't let it happen again," according to Moran. "Actually what that investigation did is it helped clarify the procedure because that issue had never arisen before. This was not so much a case of a lack of disclosure to Justice as it was a case of trying to determine what obligations a company had under similar circumstances, because the issue of satellites was not an issue when the law was written. . . . As I recall, the reason they [CNN] didn't use the leader was because it *did* mention the public relations firm and they didn't want to provide free advertising. Meryl Comer was well known to be a senior VP of Gray and Company. It was in all the papers. It was public knowledge, and she even had cards that she handed out," Moran said.

CNN, although its use of PR programs was more egregious than others, was not alone. Even the three major networks used Gray and Company footage. NBC, a Gray client, picked up Gray footage of the first Hyundais, another Gray client, coming off the docks into the United States. A Gray and Company employee went to the West Coast and filmed the first Korean cars landing in America and the footage ran on the evening news broadcasts. Like CNN, NBC did not disclose where it got the feed. "No. Why should the networks label it—that they got it from a PR firm? Where else are they going to get the tape?" said a Gray and Company executive.

"Most of what you see on TV is, in effect, a canned PR product. Most of what you read in the paper and see on television is not news," said a Gray and Company senior vice president. "The broader issue is where does television get its news, and who are they kidding. I was personally aggrieved at all this sort of self-righteousness of the media when that story broke because if you're talking to TV news directors out there in the United States of America, and you tell them what's coming, it's local to them, because it's their congressman or a local angle on the story. Of course it's labeled. It has our name all over it. They are free to use it. Not use it. Use it for B-role. Write their own scripts. Most of them take it straight off the air and broadcast it. Rip and read. Rip and read."[22]

The publicity and the controversy from the Moroccan/CNN controversy caused many PR firms to cut back on the use of electronic news releases, mainly because stations were a little more reluctant to use them; in addition they are expensive to produce. "The blush is off that rose. But it's still one of the arrows in your quill, that you can't forget about," said George Worden.

The relationship between Gray and Company and major news organizations had many sides. While NBC was a Gray and Company client, in 1982, NBC's news magazine show, "First Camera," did a glowing piece about Gray and The Power House. In case there were any doubters that Gray and Company had clout with the networks, CBS covered Gray's Super Bowl party in January 1984, the month before Gray and Company's stock was sold to the public. "Sorry. You know, the news isn't the news. The news is what somebody wants to be on the news and in the news. And it is either the White House and the spin doctors over there, or it is the couple million dollar Senate TV studio, or it is corporate America, or it's the embassy, or it's a PR firm. What's the difference?" said a Gray and Company senior vice president.

In 1984 Cable News Network's Special Assignment Unit, their first investigative team, decided to look at Washington lobbyists. The correspondent, Joseph Trento, decided to delve into the life of Gray, the most visible lobbyist in town.[23] Trento turned in a description of his planned story to CNN Executive Vice President Ted Kavanau; Kavanau, in turn, notified his boss, Ed Turner, in Atlanta.

What neither Trento nor Kavanau knew was that CNN had financial and other relationships with Gray. If, as everyone interviewed about the episode believed, Turner knew about the Gray and Company Connections, under the network's own rules of ethics, he should have recused himself from supervision of the piece, but he never did. The unit worked on the story, totally ignorant that its own company had been compromised by Gray.

The shooting on the three-part documentary began in the spring of 1984. After an initial interview with Gray, arrangements were made for a crew to photograph Gray and Company officials operating at the Democratic National Convention in San Francisco. To their surprise, Gray never made the promised arrangements. To make up for the miscommunication, Gray agreed to give the CNN crew access to him at the GOP convention in Dallas the following month.

As the investigative unit delved into Gray, it became clear that the piece was becoming very critical.[24] Gray tried to defuse the story by offering stories about two of his clients. He offered to fly the CNN crew to Morocco for an exclusive interview with King Hassan II. The CNN team turned the invitation down, as they had turned down an earlier invitation to fly to Switzerland to do a feature on Marc Rich, Gray's fugitive client.

In March 1985, while the Gray piece was still in production, the *Washington Post* broke its front page story describing how CNN was running videos made for clients of Gray and Company as news stories. At first Ed Turner denied that the Gray story ever ran on CNN, but Trento went to the CNN library and found the footage of the Moroccan piece narrated by Meryl Comer. Turner said he did not know Gray, but the reporter found the videotape from the Dallas convention of Gray running into Turner. From the videotape it was clear that Turner and Gray were more than passing acquaintances—they seemed to greet each other like longtime friends.

Kavanau and Trento fought openly over the implications. "In that piece there was some controversy related to CNN because . . . we included in the piece the fact that CNN had carried material that was linked through Gray. . . . That was a very controversial piece at CNN, because, essentially, we were attacking our own network," Kavanau said. "It was a thing that we felt was proper to do."

Trento's final interview with Gray was a tough one. He asked Gray about a series of unpleasant events. Gray, now fully aware Trento was off the CNN reservation, told him that the plans for the Gray Communications Center at Hastings College were going very well. Then Gray said, as if to say, 'Pay attention, boy,' that Ted Turner, himself, had agreed to serve on the Center's Board of Directors.

Ed Turner kept a close eye on the Gray story as it developed. He called Kavanau and asked for changes in the piece, including removal of all references to the electronic press release and the Justice Department investigation of CNN's role. Kavanau and Trento refused.

Kavanau was not aware that there were any deals between CNN and Gray and Company. "My opinion at the time was that Meryl Comer was an old friend and colleague of Ed's. They'd worked together at a station, and I thought, at the time, it was strictly a matter of Meryl Comer had something and Ed was helping out, essentially, an old friend. That's what I thought. I thought he had gotten into a little bit of a hole, because he was helping an old friend and the friend happened to have this deal with this guy [Gray] and Ed was just giving her some air time. That's what I thought had happened. I wasn't aware of who Gray was or anything else. Joe did, of course, his stories and CNN got a little bit of black eye from it, but we did it. We did the story and we took the lumps," Kavanau said. "I backed him up, and we did the story."

Though the piece ran, the inclusion of the Gray–CNN relationship had serious repercussions. CNN headquarters in Atlanta began cutting back the investigative unit. "Obviously there was tension between the unit and Atlanta because we did a piece that had the effect of criticizing the network's relationship with Gray," Kavanau said. Two years later, CNN closed down the entire Special Assignment unit. There were other problems between Atlanta and the unit, but Kavanau thought that the Gray piece hurt the chances for any positive relationship between the investigative unit and CNN headquarters in Atlanta. "That's what I thought. That's absolutely a fact," Kavanau said. "For any of us, it was, I think, a very tense time with Atlanta anyhow, and doing this story did not make the atmosphere any better. It permanently poisoned our relationship with Atlanta . . . because Ed Turner, of course, is sitting down there in Atlanta and I'm now way out in the boondocks of the empire, and I said to myself, 'This is going to really, if nothing else, this is going to finish the relationship if there ever was one left.' "

It was a network executive's worst nightmare. His own investigative team ends up investigating him. "One TV executive in New York was quoted as saying that it was unparalleled, essentially, our attack on our own network. But this was considered unparalleled in network history for a unit in a network to take this combative approach, which was true, and that's what we did," Kavanau said.

What Kavanau and the others did not know was that at the same time the investigative unit was looking into Gray and fighting with Atlanta about what should be included, CNN, Gray and Company, and the Japan Center for Information and Cultural Affairs (JCIC) had negotiated a contract that made Gray and Company the middle man between JCIC and CNN. In effect, CNN secretly had Gray and Company on its payroll at the same time CNN's investigative unit was looking into Gray.

"Japan Information Center came in, to the best of my knowledge, through Tongsun Park. Gray had a longtime relationship with Tongsun Park," said Neil Livingstone.[25] According to Livingstone, at the time Tongsun Park was trying to become a big player with the Japanese.

Remarkably, nothing had really changed since Koreagate, when Tongsun Park was given immunity from federal charges of conspiracy and bribery of government officials. He had made a triumphant return to Washington several years earlier, and many in Washington society, especially Gray, welcomed him back with open arms. He was a presence around Gray and Company, especially through The George Town Club, where Gray continued to conduct a great deal of his business.[26] Tongsun Park had established a business relationship with a prominent Washington attorney, Stanton Anderson, who had worked in the Nixon administration. Anderson had a consulting firm called Global USA, Inc. "Stan Anderson was on the same hall. Stan and I go back a long way. Stan brought me and Tongsun together for a deal with Alaska oil with the Japanese," Livingstone said.

Global USA, Inc. was also connected to prominent Washington lobbyist, Bill Timmons, also a former Nixon official, and Park friend. "He [Park] was a classmate of Bill Timmons [at Georgetown University], which is why Bill Timmons has a relationship with him," explained Richard Allen, Reagan's former National Security Advisor.[27] "Talk about conflict of interest, Bill Timmons . . . on one hand, Timmons and Company doesn't take any foreign clients, on the other hand, he had plenty in Global." Between Global and Anderson's law firm, Timmons and Anderson were representing dozens of Japanese accounts in the United States. "Stan Anderson shakes down more money from the Japanese in lobbying in this town than anybody," Allen said.

Susumu Nikaido, then the Secretary General of the Liberal Democratic Party (LDP), the ruling party in Japan, was one of the key contacts. "Tongsun Park was involved in some scandal in Japan. Some big scandal in Japan and they know him. The Japanese know him. . . . But they're pretty dirty—the Japanese—the underbelly," Allen said. Through Park and his Nixon associates, Gray got a contract not only with JCIC, but also many other Japanese clients. Gray and Company represented the LDP and was paid to handle Prime Minister Nakasone's visit to the United States. As previously noted, the other Gray-produced piece, besides Morocco, that CNN had carried as a news story was about Nakasone's visit.

"All I can tell you about that CNN thing was that . . . they had 'This Week in Japan' show," Livingstone said. "It was a half an hour show and it was really shitty. It was clear they were being paid to do this, and at that time, no one objected. This, apparently, put something on TV and you got all these Japanese companies underwriting us. The segments were filmed in Japan. We thought it was shitty. And they [JCIC] said, 'How can we better make this appeal to the American audience?' Well, CNN opened their network (bureau) here at that time. . . . So we did a report on issues and how it could make the show better and strengths and weaknesses every week. And they started doing it, and the show got a lot better."

Livingstone said he believed he signed a short letter of agreement between Gray and Company and JCIC to watch the CNN show and critique it for the Japanese government.[28] (He claimed to be unaware of the longer CNN–Gray and Company relationship until much later.) He assigned Adonis Hoffman to the account. "That CNN contract, as far as I know, what we did, I gave Adonis Hoffman the responsibility," Livingstone said. "But it was a very innocuous contract. They were putting on CNN this "Japan Today," which was kind of an iffy area for CNN, but my view was hell, if they would do it, that's great. But they were already doing it. They were putting on what was basically a paid advertisement, in effect, although they wanted it to have the appearance of not being such. It was great if you can get the networks to do stuff like that. Wonderful."

Another Gray and Company official confirmed Livingstone's account. "CNN had a feature for years, they may still have it, it's either "Japan Today" or "This Week in Japan," which was paid for by the government of Japan. And they've got a bogus CNN reporter. Their bureau chief over there does a weekly features program on interesting, fun stuff going on in Japan, and how close the Japanese people are to us. That program is paid for by the government of Japan. The government of Japan pays CNN to air that broadcast. Period. If you don't believe me, call CNN. That's not news." The Gray and Company official says he knew this from conversations with a variety of people: the CNN bureau in Tokyo, the CNN correspondent there, and Japanese government officials in Tokyo and the Japanese Embassy in Washington.

"The [Japanese] government didn't produce it. The people in the bureau produced it," said Jeanee von Essen, then head of CNN's foreign desk.[29] But the arrangements for "This Week in Japan" were not made by the foreign desk. "It came about as a *fait accompli*; it didn't come out by the foreign desk wanting to do a show out of Japan," von Essen remembered.

"I never felt good about that show," another CNN high-level executive said. "I just didn't think that it should be there, because it just stuck out like a sore thumb. There was no 'This Week in Europe,' although that had been the original plan. We were going to have different areas of the world and I remember thinking, 'Well, if you're going to do this, shouldn't it be 'This Week in the Pacific Rim?' But it never did grow into other parts of the world. It stayed 'This Week in Japan,' and then it became something else. It always struck me as peculiar that it stuck out like that. I mean it just didn't feel right to me."

According to Gray and Company executives, CNN was broadcasting pure propaganda, produced and paid for by a foreign country, to unsuspecting Americans and reporting it to no one. "You would think they would [have to report it]. If they got so hot and bothered about us labeling, you would think that they would probably ought to do that," said a Gray and Company senior vice president. Livingstone said that he brought in all the Japanese clients. "I got the Japanese clients . . . Nakasone, those were my clients . . . I mean I got the credit for these things on my raises and bonuses and everything. . . ." But the contract between JCIC and Gray was even kept secret from him. "Now, that was the only secretive contract . . . I never had the contract number," Livingstone said. "That came from Tongsun Park, I believe, and Gray personally." At CNN, von Essen said she knew nothing about such a contract. "I was never aware of, at any time, . . . CNN entering into any agreement like that."

Livingstone says he did not find out about it until he was questioned about the contract by a Gray and Company Board of Director committee, which was looking into other Gray and Company foreign contracts. "As far as I know, this came out as a possible suspect contract. Now all I can tell you is that the terms of the contract or the banking arrangements on the contract appeared to be funny. We only learned this after we asked the firm for information. Because they had initially said that as part of the [Board of Directors] internal investigation, they wanted to talk to me about Japan Information Center."

At first Livingstone was surprised that he was being asked about such a "mundane" account, but when he and his attorney received some of the documents in question, he remembered his attorney saying, "Geez, this is weird." The documents outlined what Livingstone termed "a strange financial arrangement" where JCIC made payments to Gray and Company and then part of these payments were passed on to another firm in New York State. "We were paid, but then we paid them a fee. And yet none of us ever knew who this firm was," Livingstone said. Livingstone explained that it was not unusual for Gray and Company to pay other consultants at the behest of foreign clients, but in most other incidences he at least was aware of who the other consultants were and what they were supposed to be doing. "What was weird was I never knew what this other firm was doing. Normally I did. This is Gray and Tongsun," Livingstone said.

As far as Livingstone knew there were three contracts that Gray handled personally and kept the details from others in the company. "There were certain things Gray handled personally. He owned seventy percent of the company, so he could be a eight hundred pound gorilla. Spain was one. . . . Those were the only two that I knew of in the firm (CNN and Spain). I heard later in the thing that there were like three contracts handled that way. The Teamsters—I always knew that one Gray pretty well handled personally."

Moran remembered that when he was trying to straighten out Gray and Company foreign contracts, he ran across the JCIC contract and demanded that the firm file a copy of it with the Justice Department. The contract was dated April 1984, but was filed in May 1985. "One of the things that I had to do was to go through and look at every contract that had been signed since the company had gone public. One of the reasons for that was, when I came on board, I changed the reviewing and filing procedures to make sure that all of this stuff that got signed did get filed [with the Justice Department]. But there was a lot of disorganization there, especially early on. Three guys would go out and they'd meet with some client and they'd get him to sign the agreement and then it would be lost in the process. There was, at that time, no central structure, this was before I came on, there was no central structure for ensuring that all of these things got done," Moran said.

To Gray, signing up the client was more important than worrying about details. "The way it worked at that time, they never were signed by a central person. Usually you'd have a group of three or four people go out and meet with a potential client and then, if they could, they'd get the client to sign

Candidate Dwight D. Eisenhower stopped in Hastings, Nebraska, Gray's hometown, on July 3, 1952 during a whistle-stop tour of the country. With Eisenhower were his wife Mamie and Fred Seaton, the local newspaper publisher and soon-to-be key staff aide in the White House. These three people would prove very important to Gray in Washington, but he did not attend the rally. His father was buried the same day. (*The Hastings Tribune*)

After receiving an MBA from Harvard in 1949 Gray returned to Hastings to teach a course in small business at Hastings College, where he was a popular professor. (*The Hastings Tribune*)

Gray was sworn in as Secretary to the Cabinet on May 16, 1958 as President Eisenhower and Gray's mother looked on. Despite the lofty title the position was mainly administrative. (Courtesy *Dwight D. Eisenhower Library*)

One of the few policy matters for which Gray was responsible was the resettlement of refugees from communist countries. Gray is pictured here with a young Latvian refugee in 1960. (*Omaha World-Herald*)

Gray posing with his White House memoir, *Eighteen Acres Under Glass*, in May, 1962. A year-and-a-half earlier, *McCall's* had published draft excerpts that offended many Eisenhower administration alumni. The finished book did not contain many of the controversial characterizations.
(*Omaha World-Herald*)

Immediately after leaving the White House, Gray joined Hill & Knowlton as vice president and director of its Washington office. Gray convinced Hill and Knowlton founder John Hill to let him set up a lobbying operation to act in concert with the firm's public relations staff, a move that would revolutionize the business of influencing the government.
(*AP/Wide World Photos*)

After leaving the White House Gray maintained his social ties to Washington hostesses and influential women with whom he had cultivated friendships, including Mamie Eisenhower. Gray is pictured here with Mrs. Eisenhower on his immediate left after receiving an award from the Italian ambassador.
(*AP/Wide World Photos*)

Gray was very adept at hiring both Democrats and Republicans to staff his companies. One prize Democratic catch was Frank Mankiewicz, who had been a key aide to Robert Kennedy and a president of National Public Radio. Mankiewicz, who had been a regional director of the Peace Corps in the 1960s, headed the "Citizens for a Free Kuwait" public relations blitzkrieg prior to the Gulf War. (*AP/Wide World Photos*)

Sheila Tate, who worked for Gray at Hill and Knowlton during the 1970s and for a brief period in the 1980s, was dismayed at the indiscriminate solicitation of clients at Gray and Company, calling the firm "a company without a moral rudder." (*Susan B. Trento*)

Ed Wilson, convicted of smuggling arms to Libya and attempting to murder federal prosecutors, is serving a life sentence in the Marion Federal Penitentiary. Gray says that the two were mere "elevator buddies" sharing the same office space, but documentary and eyewitness accounts indicate they had a significant business relationship. (*AP/Wide World Photos*)

Tongsun Park, the central figure in the Koreagate bribery scandal. Park received immunity from prosecution in exchange for his testimony and returned to do business in Washington in the 1980s. Gray's relationship with Park began in the 1960s when they were two of the founders of The George Town Club, which became notorious during the Koreagate investigations. (*AP/Wide World Photos*)

Gray was cochairman of the 1980 Reagan inaugural committee. It was the most expensive and elaborate inaugural ceremony in history, and set the tone for Washington in the 1980s. (*AP/Wide World Photos*)

Gray cashed in on his connections to the new administration by starting Gray and Company in 1981. Gray bought a former power plant in Georgetown to house his new firm. He called it "The Power House." (*Susan B. Trento*)

Gray in 1984, at the height of Gray and Company's perceived influence and power. Clients, lured by promises of Gray's access, poured through the doors. That summer Gray ran the show at the Republican National Convention. (*Omaha World-Herald*)

When the tax fraud conviction of the Reverend Sun Myung Moon was being appealed to the Supreme Court, supporters of Moon hired Gray and Company to try to influence the decision. Gray and Company invented a front organization called "The Religious Liberty Foundation" and put pressure on the U.S. solicitor general to file a brief on behalf of Moon.
(*AP/Wide World Photos*)

One of Gray and Company's most lucrative and controversial accounts was the International Brotherhood of Teamsters. Gray's cultivation of Teamster boss Jackie Presser paid off in other ways when the Teamsters endorsed Ronald Reagan in 1980 and 1984. Presser is pictured here being carried into the 1986 Teamsters convention in Las Vegas by union members dressed as Roman soldiers. Presser was under indictment for mob-related activities at the time.
(*AP/Wide World Photos*)

CIA Director William Casey after giving testimony to the House Foreign Affairs Committee on the Iran–Contra affair. Gray frequently invoked Casey's name in interviews, saying he always checked with the Director before taking on a foreign client. A number of Gray and Company employees had close ties to the intelligence community. (*AP/Wide World Photos*)

Gray; Dr. Gerald Hazelrigg, President of the Hastings College Foundation; actress Celeste Holm; and Robert Maxwell arrive in Hastings for the dedication of the Gray Center for the Communication Arts. Gray was personally registered as Maxwell's lobbyist and genuinely admired him; he expressed shock at the revelations that came out after Maxwell's death. (*The Hastings Tribune*)

Ronald Reagan fulfilled a long-held promise to Gray when he appeared at the dedication ceremonies for the Gray Center. When asked by a reporter if the visit—to dedicate a journalism center funded by a lobbyist and public relations executive—was Reagan's "most meaningless" stop, a White House official replied, "I'd have to say it's in the top five." (*The Hastings Tribune*)

right there and then one of them would sign it, so they'd lock the client in. Bob felt that if you have the client ready to sign, you sign them. You don't wait until it's reviewed by the lawyer. In a normally functioning organization, it might sound unusual to find different people signing different contracts, but, believe me, it was standard operating procedure at Gray and Company," Moran said.

The Gray and Company/JCIC contract was not the normal two or three page letter of agreement. It said:

1. . . . JCIC hereby appoints Gray as its agent in the United States in connection with an agreement for a project (the "Project") between CABLE NEWS NETWORK ("CNN") and JCIC (the "TV Agreement") dated February 24, 1984, and Gray hereby accepts such appointment in accordance with the terms and conditions of this Agreement.

2. . . . JCIC shall cause, pursuant to the TV Agreement (with CNN), CNN to pay to Gray as JCIC's agent a fee of Twelve Thousand Dollars (US $12,000) per month, except every third month the fee shall be Fifteen Thousand Dollars (US $15,000). Such fee shall be payable in arrears on the last business day of every month. Gray's obligations hereunder shall be contingent upon Gray's receiving such fee from CNN.

3. . . . (a) At the request of JCIC, but only at JCIC's request, Gray shall communicate and confer with CNN representatives (including Mr. Ted Turner, the Chairman of CNN, Mr. Burton Reinhart, the President of CNN, Mr. Gary Hogan, the Vice President of TV Sales for CNN, and other members of the CNN staff, including its production and PR staffs) in Atlanta, Georgia as necessary in order to maintain a strong working relationship between CNN and JCIC and to promote the Project goals.

(b) Gray shall research and send monthly reports to JCIC regarding developments affecting the Project or JCIC. Such reports shall include developments in broadcasting networks other than CNN (including, without limitation, by means of theatrical release, broadcast, or free television, direct broadcast satellite, multipoint distribution systems, cassettes, cartridges, tape or electronic visual recording system) and in the other major news media including radio, newspapers, journals, and magazines. . . .

5. . . . Except to the extent necessary (a) to enable Gray personnel to perform their duties pursuant to this Agreement or (b) required by law, Gray will not without the prior written consent of JCIC, either during the term of this Agreement or thereafter, disclose to any person, firm, corporation or other entity any information regarding the existence of this Agreement or regarding ideas, plans, programs, projects or other information relating to the Project or JCIC obtained by Gray or developed or prepared by Gray during the term of this Agreement. If Gray at any time believes it is required to disclose the existence of this Agreement or its relationship with JCIC, it will notify JCIC at least 30 days prior to any

such disclosure. JCIC may at any time thereafter terminate this Agreement effectively immediately upon notice to Gray. . . .

8. . . . this Agreement shall be effective from April 7, 1984, through March 31, 1985. . . .

Robert Keith Gray signed the contract for Gray and Company.

In the Justice Department registration forms signed by Gray and Company executive James Jennings, it said: "Registrant [Gray and Company] . . . reviewed information programs *produced by JCIC in conjunction with Cable News Network (CNN) and aired by CNN to cable recipients across the United States* [emphasis added]. . . . In addition, certain of the television segments produced by JCIC have related to subjects which might be considered political. For example, JCIC has produced video information pieces on the Japanese defense forces and U.S. military bases in Japan. The registrant's activities were confined primarily to reviews of the programs provided to Cable News Network by JCIC and advice on how to improve those programs."

When shown the contract Gray and Company filed with the Justice Department, Livingstone said he had never seen it before. "I thought I signed some rinky-dink contract. This is signed by Gray . . . which is so rare. The only other contract that I know of that has a Gray signature is Spain," Livingstone said. "They did something weird there. . . . As I told you, I thought I had signed a one-page little Mickey Mouse contract. Nothing like that. We didn't have contracts like that."

When a Gray and Company senior vice president who was familiar with the agreement looked at what was filed with the Justice Department, he said that part of the money remitted from CNN to Gray and Company was supposed to go somewhere else, but that part was not in the agreement that was filed. "Where is the netting the money out? This wasn't the whole transaction. Something is missing. But it is a lot of money to pay Gray and Company. CNN's paying Gray and Company to work for JCIC. It is odd. Well, there's an agreement out there between CNN and JCIC, the TV agreement, which we don't have. There was another agreement."

In amended Justice Department filings, Gray and Company reported: "The registrant, on behalf of the foreign principal, JCIC, . . . reviewed and critiqued the Cable News Network (CNN)–produced weekly segment, 'This Week in Japan,' and said that it received the $51,000 from JCIC, not CNN, and that it disbursed $31,000 of these monies to a subcontractor. In other filings Gray and Company reported receiving $96,000 from JCIC for the same services in subsequent periods. The LDP of Japan paid Gray and Company $246,000 for help with meetings with the Reagan administration and on Capitol Hill. Hakuhodo, Inc. paid Gray and Company $187,392.55 to promote Nakasone's meeting with Reagan in Los Angeles.

When told about the CNN–JCIC–Gray and Company contract, former CNN executive Kavanau was resigned. "I hope it's not true, but I tell you the truth, I'm not surprised at too much anymore. . . . If we would have known all of this, we would have reported it," Kavanau said. "I didn't know he [Ed Turner] had any relationships like this . . . I don't know what the pattern is of networks hiring public relations people and Washington lobbyists and all that stuff is really way over my head. I was never involved in that arena. That's something that would have been at a higher level."

Jeanee von Essen was equally unaware of the CNN–JCIC–Gray and Company contract, and although she confirmed the show was produced by CNN Tokyo, she also knew it was unusual fare for CNN. "The show kind of conducted itself. It was sort of a separate little deal. I didn't assign teasers for the show or anything like normally you would do for a bureau. It was a little entity that ran on its own." She believes that if there had been any pressure on the Tokyo bureau by the Japanese government, that the CNN reporter would have told her. "I feel like, at that moment, I would have known, unless he [the reporter] went above me and talked to Ed and Burt, both of whom he knew intimately from previous work and that may have been the case. The people that know the answers are at the very top." Jerry Hogen, a former CNN executive whose name appears on the contract, said that he remembered Burt Reinhardt, the president of CNN, negotiating the contract with JCIC and Gray and Company. Hogen was told that Gray and Company was receiving the standard fifteen percent commission for selling advertising for the network. Neither Ed Turner nor the CNN public relations office returned phone calls requesting comment on these matters.

The Justice Department never looked into the late filing of the JCIC agreement.

In 1984, the same year Gray signed the JCIC–CNN contract, Gray gave a speech before the Chicago Council on Foreign Relations on influencing American foreign policy and trade policies. Given his company's dealings with the media on behalf of foreign clients, his words seem ominous.

> Those who would change U.S. trade or foreign policies should take their cases directly to the people where in this country the real power on those issues resides. The public must be convinced. Without consensus the President and Congress cannot endorse great change.
>
> Americans as well as foreigners tend to lose sight of the fact that so much of our policy simply mirrors public opinion . . .
>
> What makes this process seem inscrutable to outsiders is that the catalyst to public opinion, the gatekeeper to the American consensus machine, is our free press . . .
>
> In short, our system of media-fired public opinion and policy making can be summarized: to move our government, get to our people. To get to

our people, get to our press. The media moves the message to the people. The people move the government. Then, and only then, our policy shifts. That's when America moves.

Gray continued to explain that the Midwest had some of the strongest protectionist sentiment in the country despite the fact that they profited tremendously from the export of their agricultural products. To him, it was "a tremendous contradiction." He said, "Who should communicate this contradiction? . . . This task must be left to foreign companies and governments."

Gray and Company's influence on the media was not limited to television and radio. For one client, Arent, Fox, Kintner, Plotkin & Kahn, a law firm, Gray and Company helped place an editorial in the *Wall Street Journal*. A lawyer with the firm represented the Swedish State Power Board and wrote an article in support of methane gas that mentioned his client favorably. "We have people who are friends on the *Journal* editorial board," William C. Bennett III, a Gray and Company account executive, told the *Washington Post*. When asked later, the *Journal* said the connection between the lawyer and his client should have been disclosed, but was not.[30]

Gray and Company also took credit for a favorable editorial in the *Journal* about another client, Marc Rich. The editorial said, "Had Mr. Rich been, say, a draft dodger, liberals would have been calling for his rights to hide out in a foreign land. Property rights don't seem to concern them." When the editorial ran, Gray and Company, of course, sent out announcements publicizing it.

Courting the press is just as important to the Washington lobbying-PR industry as courting politicans. Just as some politicians succumb to the allure of money and attention, so too do certain members of the media. James Lake, a prominent Washington communications executive, explained the importance of courting reporters. "In 1974 when I started my business I had to work at it. Finally you become somebody people get acquainted with and learn that they can trust you. Members of Congress have dozens of people after their ear. Reporters don't have so many people . . . they have more of an ability to listen. There is more time available to listen. Just like anything, human nature is such that if you know someone . . . even though they know that you are giving them your side of the story, reporters are going [to] deal more easily [with you] than a beginner or someone they've never known. We have a head start over the person who's starting from scratch because the person starting from scratch doesn't have access or can't get in. It just takes more work."[31]

Sheila Tate is one of the most savvy PR minds in Washington. Again, access is, for her, nine-tenths of the battle. "In terms of the media, the reporters that you know personally are invaluable. If you know [them], you get better responses from them. They really are a jaded press corps now, because they have so much to cover and so many things. We try to rely on creativity to sell a story, but I think it doesn't hurt to have people who at least know, for instance, me well enough to know that I won't mislead them on a story or that I can point them toward a really good story.''

A Gray and Company senior vice president agreed: ''One-on-one media relations, placing a story or the seed of a story, or getting interest or forming that story is not done very well. To one extent, the media aren't very responsive. They are a bunch of spoiled [children] in town. They are catered to so badly that they pick and choose. A top-flight media person in this town can have breakfast, lunch, dinner, and drinks, all with someone trying to place a story, if he wants. The pressures on them are so great. In media relations contact, a great deal depends on personal contacts.''

To get the media to cover a story for a client, PR firms spoon feed reporters. Carole Trimble, a Gray and Company public relations executive, sent a memo in 1982 to Barbara Newman, then a reporter with Jack Anderson, on behalf of the Asbestos Litigation Group, an organization fighting the Manville Corporation when it filed for bankruptcy, after its workers won large settlements for exposure to asbestos. The memo said that Gray and Company had located three asbestos victims willing to be interviewed by Anderson concerning their personal tragedies and how Manville's bankruptcy filing had affected them. The note then listed the victims' names, a brief biography, their addresses, their telephone numbers and their attorneys. The memo called Manville's bankruptcy ''an attempt to avoid its responsibility to the victims of its fifty-year policy of negligence'' and provided references to various published reports in *Time* and *Newsweek* supporting their client's position. The memo listed expert witnesses, including their addresses and phone numbers, on behalf of the client and a page full of lawyers. This is a fairly typical technique.

When Gray and Company hired a new employee, among the first things they wanted to know was who the person's friends and contacts were. ''When I came in, Chuck [Crawford] asked me, 'Do you know reporters you can call up by name?' and 'Who are they?' I gave them a few names, which I thought was strange, having worked at [another PR firm] for years. They never, when I started there, said what reporters do you know and can talk to,'' said a Gray and Company vice president. ''There was a list once that was sent around to see who had media contacts, and I think that the secretaries had about as many media contacts as anyone else,'' Clews said.

After former Secretary of Labor Ray Donovan was indicted and resigned from office, his former employer, Chivone, a construction firm in New Jersey, hired Gray and Company. Chivone was getting a great deal of bad publicity because of the Donovan indictment. ''I don't think they [Gray and Company] were very effective, parenthetically, but that was a decision made by the owners of Chivone Construction Company at that time to counter, I guess was in their minds, the negatives that were coming out as a result of [the Donovan indictment]," a Chivone employee explained.

Joe Volz, then a reporter for the *Daily News*, was invited to a luncheon at The Power House for Chivone. In Volz's opinion, Gray's efforts served more to impress his clients than help their cause. "Once the indictment comes down, there's not a hell of a lot you can do to add to the story until the trial. So the fact that Gray would take Chivone's case after the company was indicted and long before the trial, I mean to me was just a fraud. I mean there wasn't anything legitimate Gray could do for Chivone at that point. And there wasn't really anything legitimate that we could write about that would certainly be in Chivone's benefit. The guy had been indicted, you know, then you had to wait for the trial to see what happens. But it seemed to me that Gray just figured, I could make a couple of bucks. So what he did was round up the usual suspects to have lunch with [the Chivone] attorney. It seemed to me the whole purpose was just to show how Gray knew every reporter in town and to blow smoke at the client. If Gray had been honest, he would have said, 'Look, there is nothing we could do. We can't get you in the paper. We certainly can't get you in the paper in any kind of good light at this point."

Gray worked through many avenues to reach reporters. In Volz's case, he had his employee, John Berard, who knew Volz through the Washington chapter of Rutgers University Alumni, call Volz to invite him to lunch at the Power House. "We went over there, we were on the second level of The Power House. We had to walk in the hallway past all these pictures, dozens of them of Gray with Eisenhower, Gray with this pol, Gray with that pol, Gray with the next pol, and up on the second floor they had a sumptuous table laid out and there were about ten of us. There was a guy from the *Times*, Steve Engleberg. And Ann McDaniel from *Newsweek*. I don't know how they lured them there. They had been covering the Justice and covering the story, I guess. The whole thing, it seemed to me, was just to show [Chivone's attorney] that Gray was well connected. [The attorney] tried to piss and moan about Chivone's problems but there wasn't anything any of us could write about. There wasn't any news yet. None of us wrote anything. Gray came in for five minutes. Patted everybody on the back, made it look like he knew us. I'd never met the guy before. And then he went out. We listened to [the attorney] spread the bull about nothing of any substance for an hour and then left. And I thought later, 'Hey, I was a spear carrier. Like a spear carrier in an opera.'"

Donovan was later acquitted of all wrongdoing in the case. Despite the ineffectiveness of Gray and Company's PR efforts on Chivone's behalf, the PR firm took credit for another great victory. When told that Chivone did not feel that Gray and Company did much for them, a Gray and Company senior vice president said, "That's certainly contrary to what Gray and

Company thinks that they did for them. They think that they helped them win the case. That was one of their success stories, Chivone.''

Just as politicians make it possible for lobbyists to sell influence by permitting, if not encouraging the system of favors for access, the media acquiesce in the questionable symbiosis of public relations and journalism. PR firms would not send out packaged radio and television stories if no one was using them. Technology transformed PR firms in the 1980s. Many firms changed their names from public relations to communications. ''PR is flaky; selling access to the media and congressmen [is] nasty business. We try to change that perception. . . . We do it in an honorable way as we professionally can. We're not ashamed of our profession. We do it by the rules,'' Charles Crawford, one of Gray's top assistants, told the *Washington Post*. ''We have a profession that lives in the shadows.''[32]

Not only technology, but economics made things easier for PR firms in the 1980s. ''Here's the distinction I make and maybe it is a distinction without a difference. Even if we feed a fully produced piece, we also feed B-role [unedited video or audio tape] and with all the backup material so people can put their own pieces together. That's a fifteen thousand dollar proposition. Now there are two economics at work here on the television side. One, the big stations don't want prepackaged, pretaped. They have the money, the budget, and the manpower to put their own together. But the smaller stations across the country lap up stuff like this. But they won't use it unless it is done as a genuine news story. So you have to be careful that you don't editorialize,'' Sheila Tate explained. ''Radio, literally—and I take advantage, I grant you of the weaknesses of broadcast media in this regard—but radio has no manpower on weekends. You couldn't feed something because there is no one there to take it. So what we've learned over time is to feed something on a Thursday and, as a business feature, it will be used all weekend long. It will repeat Saturday, Sunday, all day long. But that's their decision. And they also know where it comes from. They'll know that it's being put out by a PR firm. It is not camouflaged in any way. So I think they make the decisions what they are going to use. And I think by and large that use is high because it is a well-done piece that is not distorted. If you wrote a piece that didn't fulfill the requirements of the media, they wouldn't use it,'' Tate said.

Like the written press release, the old, cumbersome market research apparatus that used to provide the information on which PR firms based their work gave way to the quicker, more-sophisticated polling techniques that until the 1980s were used mainly for political campaigns. Ronald Reagan's pollster, Richard Wirthlin, served on Gray and Company's Board of Directors. ''I remember that when we were at Hill and Knowlton, there was an internal research apparatus that was really ungainly. It was an old market research operation. You can't do opinion research the way they do market research, which takes six weeks for a report. We started using an outside political pollster because they do much better research and they do overnight," Tate said. "Again, that's driven by the changes in polling. The kinds of issues we work on, you really want a good, sensitive political pollster."

Political pollsters became essential to PR and lobbying research departments that needed instantaneous answers and overnight results. Polling is "part of the basic tool of any lobbying. It lets you track public opinion, lets you know where public opinion is going and whether your strategy is right. Whether it's having an impact. Whether you're moving the needle at all," explained a Gray and Company senior vice president.

Gray and Company had a research library headed by a professional who used to work at the Library of Congress. She maintained clips and files and directories and computer searches and polls, all expenses billed to various clients. (Research also kept a special file just on Gray himself.)

Like congressional staffers, government officials and others who tried to work as lobbyists, some journalists viewed the "revolving door" between PR and journalism as an opportunity for enrichment, and standards of objectivity suffered. Public relations executives found the media who wanted jobs more responsive to their efforts on behalf of clients. "A good number of the media harbor a desire at some point to work for a company like Gray and Company. We regularly had large numbers of resumes from fairly well-known print and broadcast journalists who were ready to give up the pursuit of truth to become flacks—who sought to double or triple their salaries and give them a company American Express card," said a Gray and Company senior vice president.

The extent of media manipulation by PR firms varied. "TV is easier to manipulate than print. Some print is easier than others," a Gray and Company senior vice president said. "[Television] is easier because it is really entertainment, and as long as you get past that initial set of realizations and realize that we're pitching 'Entertainment Tonight,' even if it calls itself the 'CBS Morning News,' then it becomes fairly easy. You have got to give them visuals. If it doesn't light up the evening news, then it won't be on. So you take a very, very important story and you put a guy in a room at a green-felt-covered table, and he can tell the most important story in the world, and you won't get on TV. But if you have a bear that can ride a unicycle and blow up a balloon, then you've got twenty-five to thirty seconds. So, especially if you write the copy for the person who is going to do the stand-up, [you will get picked up]."

"I feel like what we do is very professional, but I feel certain I could take advantage of the media in a lot of ways if I wanted to. I mean a real advantage in terms of things that perhaps weren't as factual. But our media isn't very discriminating, and it is driven by economics, and so they'll take stuff because they have no manpower. You know, it's an interesting little item; it is well-produced, the pictures are great, whatever," Tate agreed.

Of course some journalists, regardless of the medium, made better targets. Inexperienced reporters are more easy to manipulate. "They can be manipulated. Very easily. They don't know we are not going to help them with the bad questions. And they are too inexperienced to even know what they are, which is fine. So we get an interview. Great. 'Bye-bye,' " George Worden explained.

Today, foreign countries and companies not only hire American PR and lobbying firms, they own many of them. A former Gray and Company executive is not bothered by this; in Washington it is in line with the status quo. "It is no more serious a question than what are the implications of our automobile industry is going down the toilet and being run by the Japanese or Hollywood being run by the Japanese. Look at the war in the Persian Gulf. That has very quickly developed into official government propaganda. Ours and theirs. I mean Charles Jaco can stand there at night and look good on CNN and go out in the dark and narrate a piece. That's not the news. The news is all the file footage being fed, approved by U.S. military, approved by British military, approved by Israeli censors, approved by Iraqi censors. What you see on television is what somebody wants you to see, and it ain't the news. The most you can hope for is balance. Two balanced pieces of propaganda and then you can make up your mind which one to believe."

"The media's the fourth big element in the determination and development of public policy. The Congress, the Executive Branch, the representation industry, and the media. The media has a very significant role setting the agenda, very often determining the direction of debate. Media relations become a part of lobbying in this town in a broad sense. They compliment your public policy goals," explained a Gray and Company executive. Or as Gray often put it, "If we need the votes of certain congressmen, we go to their districts to fill [their] mailbags."[33]

In the Washington world that combines lobbying with public relations, other communication firms do not operate that much differently than Gray and Company. One competitor that specializes in "communications" consulting for lobbyists is headed by James Lake, who represented, among others, Michael Milken and Drexel Burnham Lambert. "All my people have been press secretaries to senior senators, committee chairmen, in the White House. They have all had the extensive campaign, political, press experience under pressure. They know how the press thinks and operates and how to deal with them effectively, and they also know how decisions are reached and how to affect decision making in this environment. I want people who have those skills, so that when we offer clients our services, we are offering them people who know how to deliver, who have been tested in the fire of campaigns."

Lake explained that his firm works "to help position the media to write a story or issue in such a way to get all the fact out so that the lobbyist has an easier job of selling his work when he goes up to the Hill. If newspapers report things in a way that is beneficial to the client, if op-ed pieces are written by knowledgeable, sound thinkers who give new insight and perspective, it helps sometimes for the lobbyists to get successful conclusion to his efforts when he is up on the Hill or at the White House. We get grass-roots media, media here, California, or whichever state the member of congress we're trying to communicate [with] is from. If we get the media in his state, his district to write things that help us, it helps us persuade him."

Lake spoke highly of Gray and his most effusive praise was for Gray's genius at self promotion. "I've gone against Bob Gray in competition for clients. Sometimes he wins, sometimes I win. I've gone with him on the issues and against on the issues, and I've won more than I've lost. It depends on what you are talking about as being effective as a firm. If you are talking about winning or losing for your clients, I will put my record against anyone's including Bob Gray's. But Bob Gray built a much bigger enterprise, a much bigger company, a much bigger reputation than I did. So what are you talking about in effectiveness? I think Bob Gray was very successful, very effective in building a firm. . . . Bob is absolutely brilliant and skillful in taking care of his self interest. He really is. Bob has a fine reputation and he deserves [it]. Oh sure, everyone has their naysayers, and Bob has his, but I'm a big fan of Bob's."[34]

12

THE INTERNATIONAL DIVISION

An angry Bob Gray to Rob Owen: "How many billable hours did you get today?"[1]

Foreign clients were one of the main reasons Gray and Company prospered during the early 1980s. But the decision to set up an International Division at Gray and Company also ended up destroying Robert Gray's dream of one day controlling the world's foremost public relations firm. His desire for an overseas presence would be overshadowed by a series of bizarre management decisions that would put him and his entire company in serious jeopardy.

Ed Wilson had gone to Libya in the late 1970s both to expand his far-flung business operations and to spy. By this time Wilson was conducting operations for the CIA, the National Security Agency, and the Department of Navy. As Wilson was pressing Gray to take on Libya as a client, the brazen arms dealer was caught in the cyclone of reform and rebellion hitting the CIA—a rebellion that later helped elect Ronald Reagan and George Bush and put Robert Gray in a position of power with the new Republican administration.

Ed Wilson's primary contact at the CIA was Theodore (Ted) G. Shackley, a legendary figure who had run stations in Miami, Laos, and Vietnam and had risen to be second in command of the CIA's Directorate of Operations—the covert action side of the CIA. Shackley had befriended George Bush when he served a single year as Director of Central Intelligence in 1976. In 1977 Jimmy Carter ordered his new CIA Director, Stansfield Turner, to reform the Agency. Turner fired or retired more than eight hundred of Shackley's most experienced operatives and then set his sites on Shackley himself.

In 1978, according to FBI documents, Shackley asked Ed Wilson to provide the seed money to start a private intelligence network. Wilson put up $500,000 for a company headed by Shackley's former CIA deputy, Thomas Clines.[2] Many of Shackley's fired spies formed the core of this private operation. Among its first assignments was to provide, in 1980, first the Bush campaign, and later the Reagan–Bush campaign with information and operations that contributed to the defeat of Jimmy Carter.

Gray worked with some ex–CIA clandestine operatives on the campaign. The significance of the personal letter, from Egyptian president Anwar Sadat to Jimmy Carter, in the package of material leaked to Gray's campaign office became clear when the actions of the private intelligence network later became known. Once Reagan was in power, these intelligence "professionals" were supposed to retake control of the CIA and their operations folded back into the Agency with Shackley as the new CIA director. But that never happened.

In 1979, Wilson was in no position to turn down a top CIA official. He said that the operation was only supposed to function until Reagan was elected and Turner's reforms could be reversed.[3] Wilson said that he went along with the scheme because his long relationship with U.S. intelligence depended on the good graces of Shackley and Clines. Clines and high-level Pentagon colleagues became secret partners in the company which was called EATSCO—Egyptian American Transport Company—that formed the basis for the privatized CIA. (Shackley insisted to the FBI that he was not a partner in EATSCO.) The company was supposed to handle all shipping for the $4.1 billion in military aid promised to Egypt under the Camp David Accords, ironically, all made possible by Jimmy Carter.

Ed Wilson also owned a security company, J.J. Cappucci and Associates, that trained Egyptian President Sadat's personal security force—the security guards who performed so miserably when Sadat was assassinated in October 1981. J.J. Cappucci was ostensibly managed by a former Air Force Brigadier General, Joseph Cappucci, who once held the top position in Air Force Intelligence.[4] At one point the federal government suspected the company of illegally shipping weapons to Egypt.[5]

Cappucci signed the contract to train Sadat's Presidential Guard in 1978. Ed Wilson was in Libya at the time and was furious when he learned about it. Sadat and Qaddafi were bitter enemies, and Wilson was understandably worried about angering the volatile Libyan strongman. Wilson quickly sold the security firm, two years before the Sadat murder, to several Americans affiliated with EATSCO.

One of the buyers was a self-proclaimed security expert named Neil C. Livingstone, who, according to Wilson, told Wilson he was financing the deal through inherited money. Livingstone, along with Douglas M. Schlachter, Jr. and Don Lowers (both Wilson associates) purchased J.J. Cappucci from Wilson for $40,000 cash.

Livingstone confirmed his involvement in J.J. Cappucci, but denied he ever bought an interest in the company.[6] Instead, he said, Thomas Clines took over J.J. Cappucci and folded it into the EATSCO operation. "We had Felix Rodriguez [a.k.a. Max Gomez, a former CIA agent and long time Shackley operative] over there and other people and we did the training of Sadat's Praetorian guard to protect Sadat. And then the contract was taken away from us and [given] back to the [Central Intelligence] Agency and he got killed. We never would have permitted the kind of security that was evident at the time Sadat was killed," Livingstone said.

Federal investigations later determined that EATSCO defrauded United States taxpayers out of $8 million.[7] Despite the scale of the fraud, no one at EATSCO went to jail. Company officials, like Thomas Clines, were slapped on the wrist with relatively light fines.[8] The main reason the cast of characters behind EATSCO went free was because by the time the fraud was uncovered, some of these men were key, behind-the-scenes players with Oliver North in the Iran–Contra operations.

Some U.S. government investigators who looked into the EATSCO case believed that the reason EATSCO operatives were not criminally prosecuted was that high officials in the U.S. intelligence community feared a public prosecution would reveal embarrassing information about Egyptian president Hosni Mubarak. The investigators uncovered evidence that Mubarak's brother-in-law, a top Egyptian military official assigned to Washington, was a secret partner in EATSCO. Sadat was assassinated by members of his bodyguard shortly after ordering an investigation into whether the Egyptians involved in EATSCO were defrauding the Egyptian government.

In addition, since many of those involved in EATSCO later played roles in the Iran–Contra Affair, some of the U.S. EATSCO investigators believed this was another reason why someone in the intelligence chain of command wanted to avoid a public prosecution.[9]

Livingstone had spent most of his adult years in graduate school or working for two U.S. Senators. In the months following Sadat's murder his old friend from Capitol Hill, Charles "Chuck" Crawford, set up a lunch between him and Gray to talk about a secret foreign client Gray wanted to represent. Livingstone said that at the time he was attempting to get a political appointment in the Reagan administration "which had been mired down in politics" when Crawford asked him to consult with Gray.[10] The secret country was Libya, according to Livingstone.

Ed Wilson had stayed in touch with Gray over the years after Wilson had left the K Street offices. In the late 1970s, Wilson was singing Libya's praises to Gray. Wilson had urged his old office mate to take on Libya as a client in Gray's last year at Hill and Knowlton. The drumbeat continued when Gray started his own company. Like his colleagues at Hill and Knowlton, Gray's subordinates at Gray and Company were aghast at the idea.

Livingstone said that he did not know that Gray knew Ed Wilson or that Wilson was the source of Gray's business interest in Libya. Livingstone maintains that Gray pursued the Libyan matter with him even after Livingstone had become a full-time employee at Gray and Company. "Gray had been interested in representing Libya; I told him that I would have to quit if he did it. But he would persist and he would call me in every so often. 'What amounts of business do you think we would lose if we took Libya on as a client?' Or, 'Is there a price I can represent Libya for?' " Later Gray told *Newsweek* and the *Washington Post* that he did not take Libya as a client because it was not in the best interest of the United States.

When the government no longer allowed EATSCO to ship arms to Egypt, Gray and Company helped Four Winds, a San Diego-based freight forwarder, get the contract. Gray wrote a letter on behalf of Four Winds to Defense Secretary Caspar Weinberger. The Pentagon official who had given the contract to EATSCO while he was, at the same time, a partner in EATSCO, was forced out of the Pentagon and became a consultant for Sears World Trade which also became a Gray and Company client.[11] Gray kept Livingstone on as a consultant for another assignment in 1981. It was only the beginning of Livingstone's association with Gray, but it was the beginning of the end of Gray and Company.

Under Ronald Reagan, the hidden government became the private government. Conservative foot soldiers were hidden away in the private sector to carry out the new agenda around the world. Covert action, once reserved for the professionals in the Central Intelligence Agency, became the province of conservative ideologues working for an Administration that did not play by constitutional rules and did not trust the entrenched professionals. Gray and Company employed people who were on the front line of the new, for-profit covert warfare.

William J. Casey did not waste any time making his intentions clear when he became Director of Central Intelligence (DCI) in 1981. When he summoned veteran intelligence official Robert T. Crowley to the CIA Director's seventh-floor office at Langley in early 1981, he wanted to rekindle the flame of cooperation between the CIA and big business overseas. For years, Crowley, a giant of a man, who is as crisply articulate as Casey was mumbling and uncommunicative, had been the CIA's ambassador to the corporate world. Crowley had made the special deals between ITT and scores of other companies and the CIA in the 1960s and early 1970s. Now the DCI wanted Crowley to do it again (as related in Chapter Seven). "He wanted me to arrange for corporations to front for his operations," Crowley said. But Casey's magic did not work on Crowley. Crowley told him that legal, security, and logistical problems made the idea outmoded and ludicrous. Casey was hearing more of the same from many of the CIA bureaucrats.

The Reagan years would be all but over when indications of Casey's covert operations gone private bubbled to the surface, in the Iran–Contra scandal in the fall of 1986. The tens of millions of dollars spent investigating the scandal, the successfully appealed convictions, the popularity of George Bush and Ronald Reagan, and the convenient death of Casey staved off the public's appetite for getting to the bottom of the mess. After Watergate, the public had grown weary of reading about scandal after scandal—Koreagate, Debategate, and the Congressional Sex and Drug Investigation—so that by the time the Iran–Contra affair broke, voters were strangely inured to the disturbing disclosures of extra-constitutional abuses in the administration.

When Bill Casey could not get Bob Crowley and the Agency to do his bidding officially, he began to improvise, to turn to old friends. Gray and Company was one of the places he turned.

Domingo Moreira is a mysterious figure who played a major behind-the-scenes role in the secret Contra resupply effort. Moreira is a Cuban-born businessman who left Castro's Cuba and made a fortune in the shrimp business in Guatemala. According to Michael Pilgrim and other intelligence sources, Moreira met Gray through the Cuban exile community in Miami that had supported George Bush due to the efforts of Ted Shackley. Pilgrim said Gray's connections to this community went back to 1960 when the CIA and the Eisenhower White House were preparing for the ill-fated Bay of Pigs invasion.

Gray asked his assistant, Charles Crawford, to arrange for Neil Livingstone to accompany them on a trip to Guatemala paid for by Moreira in late 1981. Livingstone said this trip amounted to his audition for a full-time job at Gray and Company as a Vice President. Livingstone claimed that Gray was attempting to get the Guatemalan government as a client. But others, including a former Secret Service official and the ex–U.S. Ambassador to Guatemala, are not so certain.

According to Livingstone, Moreira was "a client that was in Guatemala. He was a Cuban who had gone and made a lot of money in Guatemala and we wanted to represent the Guatemalan government." Livingstone claimed the trips to Guatemala were exploratory and never amounted to much. "You can't take a sow's ear and turn it into a silk purse every time. There were clearly human rights abuses in Guatemala and other problems. The question was what extent the government would try and get along with the new [Reagan] administration by meeting them halfway. But I didn't know anything more about it."

Livingstone was being modest. The work he did in Guatemala had little to do with public relations. William Casey was using ex-CIA operatives and others with ties to the intelligence community to perform services beyond the scrutiny of the congressional oversight committees, as the Iran–Contra investigations made clear. Neil Livingstone had ties to this network. The Guatemalan government was not "meeting the administration halfway," and

Livingstone's work for Moreira, a right-wing opponent for the regime, at least in part had a paramilitary component.

According to Livingstone, Gray asked him to join the firm in January 1982. Livingstone had been hoping for a mid-level job in the new Republican administration, but was tired of waiting for the administration to move; so accepted Gray's offer.[12] Livingstone was hired as one of several vice presidents. Within a month he was a registered foreign agent for Domingo Moreira, who had paid $10,000 to Gray and Company for "public relations/public affairs services for the purpose of improving Guatemala's image in the United States, and seeking support for changes in U.S. policies towards Guatemala."[13]

Livingstone made several more trips to Guatemala. On one of the trips he brought with him Jack McGeorge, a former Secret Service weapons expert who had gone into the security business with some colleagues from the presidential detail, including Charles Vance, former President Gerald Ford's former son-in-law.

What McGeorge witnessed was hardly evidence for the notion that Livingstone or Gray were interested in representing Guatemalan President Romeo Lucas Garcia's government. According to McGeorge, it was obvious to him that he was doing a security study for Domingo Moreira. Moreira, it turned out, was a key figure in Amigos del Piese—Friends of the Nation—the conservative opposition party. "The Amigos del Piese basically wanted to dump Garcia," McGeorge said.[14] The group, according to McGeorge, played a major role on March 23, 1982, in removing the very government Livingstone claimed Gray had been trying to secure as a client. The March coup was led by retired General Efrain Rios Montt. He, in turn, was replaced four months later by Bill Casey's candidate, General Oscar Humberto Mejia Victores.

McGeorge had no background in public relations; his expertise was in weapons and executive protection. To his surprise, one of the first people he met on the trip with Livingstone was Felix Rodriguez, the Cuban-born ex–CIA man who had served Ted Shackley around the globe, had played a role in ordering the execution of Che Guevara, and had trained Sadat's guards for Ed Wilson's former company, J.J. Cappucci. McGeorge found Moreira's operation amateurish and was not quite certain of Livingstone, either. "I was starting to become a little suspicious. I didn't much care for the death-head cufflinks and so forth that Neil sports, and I was beginning to take a jaundiced view of all of this . . . I did my job for his fish factory [Moriera's fish processing plant], looked at his house [for security], sat out in the dirt and talked to his troops. Looked at his armored car—that was total bullshit."

For the Guatemala account Gray and Company also brought in a consultant—John Carbaugh, an influential, but low profile, Washington power broker and conservative attorney. Carbaugh, a major player in North

Carolina Senator Jesse Helms's political career, was one of the private citizens Bill Casey called on to carry out assignments around the world. Carbaugh and Livingstone's role in Guatemala was to arrange for the leak of an embarrassing diplomatic letter in the Guatemalan press that eroded President Romeo Lucas Garcia's political support at home. According to McGeorge, the phoney letter had Garcia calling *for* American participation in Guatemalan elections. The letter was reportedly leaked by prearrangement from Secretary of State Al Haig to the Guatemalan press. "That is what triggered the downfall of Lucas Garcia," McGeorge said.[15]

Livingstone's comments on his role in the Guatemalan episode were much less expansive. "Carbaugh and I flew back on the same flight. . . . Everyone was saying that Carbaugh was overthrowing the government, and they accused me of overthrowing the government, being part of this." Livingstone protested that his involvement with the coup would have been foolish. "Look, we lost a client," he said.

Gray's written response when asked about the episode was similarly cryptic. "Gray and Company never had clients in Guatemala. However, we were hired by a Guatemalan patriot who was concerned the Government was unaware of modern techniques of public communications and insensitive and inexperienced in dealing with U.S. business and media communities. He hired us to develop an economic development plan for the Government of Guatemala but the Government leadership changed before our contract was signed." He further stated in writing that he did not recall any business relationship with a John Carbaugh.

Neither the Guatemalan operation nor the association with Domingo Moreira were financially profitable for Gray and Company, raising real questions about who Gray and Company considered to be the intended beneficiary of the effort—the government of Lucas Garcia or the political agenda of William Casey. Gray and Company also did work for another intelligence-related client on which the firm lost money. IRIS—International Reporting and Information Systems—was supposed to be the computerized clipping service like Nexis except it was of the moment; and the software was supposed to allow IRIS experts to instantly analyze trends and what events presaged.[16]

IRIS ended up in bankruptcy, owing Gray and Company over $70,000. To some Gray and Company officials, the scenario was "hauntingly familiar." IRIS was, in fact, a private intelligence service, run by former CIA operatives, for private businesses. IRIS had once approached Livingstone about a position.

In addition to these strange and murky accounts that tied Gray and Company to the new private intelligence world, both Gray and Livingstone claimed friendships with William Casey. Livingstone said he first got to know Casey when Casey headed the Import-Export Bank under Richard Nixon. Livingstone and Casey, who lived alone in Washington at the time (his wife Sophia remained on Long Island), occasionally had dinner together during those days.[17]

Neil Livingstone is a Washington enigma. There is nothing in his credentials to recommend him to the world of public relations. There are plenty of characteristics that indicate he wants badly to be an intelligence agent. Livingstone intentionally gives the impression that he is a member of the national security brotherhood. In reality, he is the intelligence "equivalent of a groupie," according to his business associate, Jack McGeorge.[18] Livingstone is the kind of man intelligence operatives befriend and use. But eventually his desires and proximity brought him into the secret world through the byzantine route of public relations. "I don't know shit about public relations," Livingstone said.

Very reluctant to talk about the details of his past, Livingstone conceded that his role in Ed Wilson's firm, J.J. Cappucci, included being vice president of operations and strategy. He claimed his activities were performed "in the national interest on a private sector basis" during the Carter administration. When pressed he said, "I came to Gray, but I had been in business in many parts of the world, primarily counterterrorism, security in Latin America and other places. Also my partners and I acquired an airline and our airline was nationalized in 1979. And it was a national airline in Panama."[19] The airline Livingstone was referring to was Air Panama. In fact, the late James Cunningham, a legendary CIA figure who was the force behind Air America, the CIA's secret airline during the Vietnam War, and a key figure in Ed Wilson's operations, brought Livingstone into both Air Panama and Ed Wilson's companies.

Livingstone's assertions of being a security expert are disputed by two of his associates. According to McGeorge and Pilgrim, both internationally recognized security experts, Livingstone exaggerated his almost nonexistent experience in security. Both men said that Livingstone's rather transparent ambitions made him useful to Israeli and American intelligence as a front man for business activities. Livingstone tried to pass himself off as the most well-educated of a handful of right-wing true believers who became the public part of the new for-profit intelligence netherworld. He confirmed that he was one of the administration's outside men "who went out front and put the spin on things" when activities of the private intelligence network emerged. When a handbook on murder authored at the CIA and distributed in Central America became public, Neil Livingstone (billed as a "terrorism expert"—not a Gray and Company PR man) would appear on CNN and discuss why U.S. taxpayers should not be concerned that their tax dollars paid for an instruction manual on how to kill and assassinate.

But many Reaganites were suspicious of Livingstone's loyalties, as were many liberals. "I got into a big brouhaha with the far right alleging I was a certified crypto communist and the far left asserting that I was a certified crypto fascist,'' Livingstone said. This is the reason he had trouble getting the political clearances for a job in the Reagan administration and ended up at Gray and Company. But after some books and articles he wrote and some of his work at Gray and Company, many in the intelligence game began to believe he was closer to Israeli intelligence (Mossad) than to the United States. "Obviously, writing as I do in the subject area, I have been called a Mossad agent a lot more than I have been called the opposite," Livingstone said.

Livingstone was one of many Capitol Hill aides that Israeli intelligence has cultivated over the years. The Israeli network in Washington made friends among staff members of the oversight committees that approved aid to Israel. Livingstone was a staff member on two Senate committees in which the Israelis had an exceptional interest. He had worked on the Senate Foreign Relations and the Joint Atomic Energy Committee staffs. Livingstone became involved with the Washington think tank—the Center For Strategic and International Studies (CSIS)—long suspected of housing a number of Israeli "agents of influence." After he left Capitol Hill, Livingstone began billing himself as an expert in terrorism and national security.

Considering the fact that Livingstone had absolutely no public relations qualifications, why was he brought into Gray and Company? Gray was vague about his decision to hire Livingstone. "I was introduced to Neil Livingstone by a colleague at Hill and Knowlton in the early 1980s. He had a good business background, and I was convinced his contacts would produce clients for the company."[20]

Robert Crowley, the former CIA official who used to arrange "cover" through American corporations, said flatly that after Stansfield Turner "reduced CIA cooperation with Israel in 1978, Ted Shackley took it upon himself to assure the Israelis that they could get what they needed through him."[21] In fact, Shackley's proximity to the Israelis at the time he was alleged to be in business with top Egyptian officials with EATSCO, caused Crowley and Federal investigators to wonder about Shackley's motivation for his alleged dealings with the Egyptians, given his close relationship with the Israelis.

Many, like Wilson, thought Shackley would become a high-ranking intelligence official in the new Reagan–Bush administration and fold his private operations back into the CIA. Unfortunately for Shackley, Ed Wilson's arrest made public Shackley's relationship with Wilson, both as his control officer and, allegedly, business partner, and Shackley's hopes of returning to the CIA were dashed. Instead, Shackley became an informal, private adviser to the Reagan–Bush administration. It was Shackley who the Iranians first approached on the hostage-for-arms deal. Neil Livingstone became one of Shackley's foot soldiers.

Livingstone acknowledged his association with Shackley, but refused to be specific. Livingstone became even more mysterious when it came to his role in "antiterrorism." "I really don't want to get into all the things that we did; but I've been involved for fifteen years basically providing extraordinary services, even while I was at Gray and Company. A lot of what we did publicly was not what I did much more discreetly. Clients that had crises, clients that had one-of-a-kind problems, corporations, individuals."

Gray had not only served as a loyal member of the Reagan–Bush election team, he also had a long history of cooperation with the intelligence community. Gray's possible motives for cooperating ranged from his self-professed patriotism to the more gritty possibility that he did it to improve business prospects or because his personal life put him in a vulnerable position.

Whatever the reasons, Gray and Company, particularly the International Division, became a center of foreign intrigue. Hill and Knowlton had cooperated with the CIA and Gray said in 1985 that he gladly did the same with his own firm.[22] Gray's prospectus said that he "would not accept clients whose interests would be inconsistent with the national interests of the United States." Gray has stated repeatedly that he avoided unacceptable clients by checking with the government. He told Cable News Network that he "always consulted with Director Casey" before he took any foreign account and *Time* magazine, "I always check these situations with Bill Casey."[23]

Again, in a written interview for this book, Gray asserted that at both Gray and Company and Hill and Knowlton one rule he always followed was to ask either the CIA, the NSC, or the State Department whether or not such represention would be antithetical to the interest of the United States. Interestingly, Libya was the example Gray cited as a potential client about which he sought the CIA's counsel, although this account differs from Gray's earlier claims that he summarily dismissed any overtures from Libya. "No agency of the U.S. government ever has told us we may not represent a foreign client. Nor have we ever asked for 'permission' to do so. We have asked if the stated goals of a potential foreign government client are consistent with the best interests of the United States. As example, once we were approached by intermediaries who wanted to introduce us to Libyan expatriates, exiles who felt the time was right to initiate 'back channel communications' to improve U.S.–Libyan relations gradually. As it happens, events overtook us—the U.S. government called for closure of Libya's missions in the U.S. However, before that I called William Casey—to find out if it would indeed be useful and timely and in the interest of the U.S. to serve in this role. Casey, then Director of the Central Intelligence Agency, said if Libya had changed its allegiances there was no evidence of it on his screen and 'I wouldn't touch them with a ten-foot pole.' While Casey did not tell us we could *not* represent Libya his comments were sufficient to wave us off. That decision was based on our own sense of patriotism as well as the conviction that we cannot communicate effectively if the audience is convinced the objective is immoral, illegal, or unpatriotic. In other cases where government officials were ambivalent, we simply had to make the judgement whether these were sufficient areas of identification with U.S. interests to make it appropriate to represent the client and possible to achieve the client's goals.''

But the cooperation with the CIA extended by Gray and Company employees went far beyond checking prospective clients or occasionally lending a helping hand. Unfortunately for Gray, those carrying out "intelligence" missions and operations at Gray and Company were amateurs.

Gray and Company's first major international forays should have raised serious questions. Charles Crawford, called "Gray's henchman" by many Gray and Company employees, headed the newly formed International Division. Livingstone said he was brought in to run the day-to-day operations of the International Division but Crawford was its titular head. Crawford had received some notoriety during the "Debategate" investigation into political espionage against Jimmy Carter. Crawford's conservative credentials hardly matched Gray's. Crawford had worked for former Nevada Democratic Senator Howard Cannon. Yet it was Crawford who brought in right-wing ideologues who used Gray and Company's International Division as their own branch office of Oliver North's "Enterprise."

Among the foreign accounts that Gray solicited were controversial clients from the Arab world. This put Livingstone, with his strong Israeli sympathies, in an awkward position. "Gray had a feeling the Arabs were a very lucrative marketplace. He talked regularly about the Jewish lobby in a derogatory way. He had made an active effort to solicit Arab clients. He felt they had deep pockets. It put me in an awkward position," Livingstone said.[24]

One of the clients Gray took during 1982 during the siege of Beirut was the Arab Women's Council, headed by the wife of the Saudi Arabian Ambassador. Gray and Company prepared a $300,000 media campaign to protest Israel's invasion of Lebanon. According to Livingstone, Gray also wanted to solicit the Palestinian Liberation Organization account. "He invited me to go to Tunis with him. It was paid for, to the best of my knowledge, by the Arab League. . . . He was to meet Yassir Arafat and talk about representing the PLO. I thought, 'This is madness. For Christ sake, Bob can't represent the PLO. Give me a break. It would be suicide aside from the fact it would be morally wrong.' But you couldn't talk to Bob about it being morally wrong. You have to talk to him about it being a bad business decision.''

Livingstone said that he refused to go with Gray on the trip, so Gray took Crawford instead. When Gray returned to Washington Livingstone said Gray told him that "Arafat's people had come for him at midnight or something but that he had chosen not to go. 'Oh, you go all the way to Tunis and then you don't meet with Arafat when he comes.' '' Nothing came of the PLO–Gray and Company talks.

With Livingstone and others sympathetic to Israel controlling Gray and Company's International Division, it did not take long for Gray's courting of Arab clients to leak into the media. The *New York Times* reported in 1983 that after Israel invaded Lebanon Gray and Company proposed to the National Association of Arab Americans that a $2 million telethon be held to raise funds "to benefit the survivors of the holocaust in Lebanon" and to change public opinion toward the Middle East. The proposal urged the group to avoid "obvious political references to transient political issues."[25]

At the same time, Steven Emerson, who like Livingstone had worked on the Senate Foreign Relations Committee, was writing a book about Saudi Arabia's increased political power in the United States. He also got a copy of part of Gray and Company's Arab proposal. In his book he highlighted the following excerpt "from a secret public relations document written by Robert Gray":

> It is the Israeli lobby's ability to politically reward or intimidate American politicians and the media that has led to such intractable support for Israel among U.S. foreign policymakers.[26]

Public exposure of Gray's courting of Arab clients and his criticisms of Israel caused quite a bit of turmoil in the firm. "We were being threatened by the Israeli lobby or somebody," a Gray and Company executive remembered. "They thought the phones were tapped." Gray has said he dropped this account because he was friends with Ronald Reagan, and what the Arab client wanted was contrary to American foreign policy. Charles Crawford, who was handling the account, told the *Times*, "We had some problems with their requests for advertising. What they wanted was too strident to be effective." According to Emerson, the Arab group placed billboards with Lebanon '82 on them dripping with blood and the caption: "Is this how we want our tax dollars spent by Israel?" Another one proposed linking unemployment with Israeli aid.

Some believe that things may not have been what they seemed at the International Division of Gray and Company. Robert Crowley believed that "Casey may have asked Gray to take on these controversial clients—for the very purpose of spying on them." If that were so it would explain why Gray considered countries like Libya, and took clients like Angola. Or why he met at the Israeli Embassy in December 1982 with then Israel Ambassador Moshe Arens to assure him that he was not anti-Israel and that he would not handle any anti-Israeli campaigns.[27] But others insist that Gray took clients for no other reason than the bottom line. Gray denies taking on any clients at the behest of the U.S. government.

Livingstone claimed to be "the rainmaker" while he was at Gray and

Company. He said that besides Gray, he brought in the most clients and, at one time, was the most heavily registered foreign agent at the Justice Department. "Ultimately, I was the second largest producer in the company at the time I left. After Gray, I brought in more clients and more business than anyone," Livingstone said. But many of his clients were not very lucrative for the firm, and, more often than not, others in the company did not know what the International Division was doing. Most of the International Division clients were right-wing governments tied closely to the intelligence community or businessmen with the same associations. For example, Gray and Company represented the government of Haiti under president-for-life "Baby Doc" Duvalier. Its job was "to improve the image" of this repressive regime in the United States.

Another client was Adnan Khashoggi, the "self-employed" Saudi Arabian businessman who played a role in Iran–Contra. "Khashoggi was notorious for using us and not paying us," a senior Gray and Company employee said. "Khashoggi wanted Bob to represent Imelda Marcos. [Too many senior Gray and Company executives objected, so he did not take the account] . . . Khashoggi was Gray's hero. [He] adored his lifestyle." But few in the firm recall what exactly Gray and Company did for Khashoggi.

When asked about some of the International Division accounts, Livingstone, Crawford, and Gray often had different stories. The levels of secrecy over accounts in Gray and Company seemed unusual for a public relations firm. For example, Livingstone and Crawford both confirmed that Gray and Company represented the Cuban–American Foundation, a tough anti-Castro organization with strong ties to George Bush, Ted Shackley, and Domingo Moreira. Although Livingstone personally serviced the account, in a 1985 taped television interview on Cable News Network, Gray claimed that the Cuban–American Foundation was not a client, even though Crawford acknowledged it was. When asked about rumors around Washington, Gray responded that his firm had nothing to do with Iran–Contra. Oddly, no one had mentioned Iran–Contra, and it was a year and a half before Attorney General Ed Meese's press conference where he announced the link between the arms-for-hostages and Contra supply operations.

Livingstone said he has no idea why Gray denied the Cuban-American Foundation as clients. "I thought they were clients. I worked for them. I acknowledged them as clients. We knew the Cubans through Domingo Moreira. I think we had something to do with Reagan going down and holding up Jorge Mas Canosa's [the head of the Cuban–American Foundation] hand and saying, 'To the first President of Free Cuba,' " Livingstone said.[28]

According to a senior Gray and Company official, much of the work done for such administration-backed organizations such as the "Coalition For A Free Cuba" and the "Cuban-American Foundation" was either not run through the Gray and Company accounts or was charged off by Gray and

Company to new business development at a fraction of its real cost. "I don't know that [Free] Cuba ever paid Gray and Company. We were just doing work for them. . . . But it didn't come through Gray and Company. In fact, Neil did the work for Free Cuba. I don't know what it was, though."

Livingstone described how he worked at Gray and Company on private projects. For example, Livingstone said that he was instrumental in anticommunist activities in Eastern Europe and had been "one of the three trustees of Solidarity" in Poland. "It was incestuous, but we were doing it on our time. I was not using my company's resources, but certainly everyone knew what everybody was doing. All of the people were carrying the administration's water in some way."

Among those that Livingstone brought into Gray and Company to "carry the administration's water" was Robert Owen, a conservative Republican true believer (Alejandro Orfila once described him as "having the temperament of a priest") who had especially close ties to Ted Shackley. Rob Owen's brother, Dewey, had been killed in Vietnam working for the CIA when Shackley was Chief of Station. Owen had been a member of then Senator Dan Quayle's staff, but by 1983, according to Michael Pilgrim, Livingstone brought him into Gray and Company because Owen was getting too visible on Quayle's staff and needed a lower profile. (Owen was hired by Carter Clews). Owen was deeply involved in the secret efforts to fund the contras run by Oliver North. "To the best of my knowledge, he never worked on anything except pretty much directly for Bob and Neil on their Central and Latin American problems, as they were defined. He was the cutout between them and Ollie North," Pilgrim said. When Eugene Hasenfus's plane was shot down by the Sandinistas (one of the first indications that contra supply efforts continued despite a congressional ban), one Gray and Company employee said he remembered laughing with several others when Owen kept popping up on news accounts of the incident. "Owen and Livingstone were doing all this spook stuff," he said.

According to Livingstone, Owen's first assignment involved Eisenhower College. The assignment was done as a favor by Gray for Susan Eisenhower, the granddaughter of Gray's old boss, on what Livingstone called a "semi-pro bono" basis. Owen's other assignments reflected his real purpose at Gray and Company. It was Rob Owen who was assigned to work with the right-wing Cubans in Miami involved in Contra fundraising. Livingstone said he used Owen to make certain that clients like the Cuban–American Foundation were involved in activities sanctioned by the Reagan–Bush administration.[29]

In the spring of 1984, when the Contras were beginning to run out of money, Owen later testified that they were told they should seek representation in Washington and the firm recommended was Gray and Company. When Oliver North began to look for new sources of funding for the Contras, one possibility was to build a public relations campaign around the Contras to elicit contributions. Neil Livingstone was told that the FDN in Nicaragua wanted to discuss the possibility of Gray and Company representing the Contras. According to Owen's testimony before the Congressional Committee investigating the Iran–Contra Affair, "in April of 1984, one of Gray and Company's vice presidents was approached by a representative of the FDN and, at that time, there was talk about the possibility, a possibility that Gray and Company doing representation."[30]

Livingstone instructed Owen to run the details of a contract between the Contras and Gray and Company by Oliver North. Owen confirmed that North "told me that the Contras knew their funds were running out, and that they had been told to look for representation in Washington." Livingstone confirmed this account. "I knew he had met North. I said, 'Go talk to North and see what he says,' and, of course, North said to take a contract."

Owen and Livingstone began preparing a "public relations proposal" for the Contras. Owen's testimony continued, "Initially after talking to Colonel North and another representative of Gray and Company [Livingstone] and I put together several different proposals. This was at a time when no one quite knew where the money for the Contras was going to come from.

"The first proposal was one on setting up proprietary companies that could be used to purchase goods overseas and provide assistance to the Contras. Another one was using a nonprofit organization to provide assistance through raising funds here in the United States to provide humanitarian and nonlethal assistance," Owen said.

After Owen and Livingstone met with North over the Gray and Company proposals, Owen said, "A decision was made that I would go down to Central America and visit both Costa Rica and Honduras, and come back with a report laying out what the probable needs would be for the next period of months."

At this point the story Owen told the Iran–Contra Congressional Committee omitted several salient facts. He said that in late May and early June of 1984 he twice used his own personal funds to finance trips to Central America on behalf of North. According to Owen's account, he left Gray's payroll in November of 1984, allegedly to go to work for North through a Department of State cover job at the Humanitarian Assistance Office.

After his first trip to Central America in June 1984, Owen returned convinced that the Contra leaders were running out of funds and would be in grave trouble because the congressional ceiling on aid was almost exhausted. According to Livingstone, Owen "was terribly disappointed" when Frank Mankiewicz, the head of the Public Relations Division, prevented Gray and Company from taking on the Contras as a client. "When we didn't take them on, Rob came to me and he said that he was going to take a job where he could be a direct help to the Contras, because this had reawakened so much and it was because of that relationship with Oliver North and all.

And I tried to talk him out of doing it because I really had bad feelings about it already . . . I was worried the White House was not doing things the way they should.''

Livingstone said he was worried about the then still secret Contra-supply policy because "there were some scumbags coming out of the woodwork on this one . . . I had known a lot of these people in the seventies, worked with some of them, and some of them I had great respect for. I had great respect for Felix Rodriguez." Rodriguez, who had been in Guatemala with Livingstone, was now a key player in the Contra resupply effort.

But Jack McGeorge, who had made the early trips with Livingstone to Guatemala, told a much different story when asked about Livingstone, Owen, Gray and Company, and Iran–Contra. Livingstone's behind-the-scenes activities at Gray and Company were in part shared with McGeorge. He later realized that he had witnessed the beginnings of the secret Reagan–Bush policy.

After Guatemala, McGeorge had continued his relationship with Livingstone, writing for an antiterrorist magazine in which Livingstone was involved, and briefly bringing the security firm he worked for into Gray and Company as a client. Two years later McGeorge found himself in Honduras on assignment for the United Brands corporation. "I was down there a couple of times having nothing to do with Neil Livingstone," McGeorge said. Ambassador Negropointe was running the preliminary Contra effort, and McGeorge was impressed with him and his staff. A former Secret Service colleague of McGeorge's was working on the Contra training effort and asked McGeorge to help. He agreed.[31]

In late 1983 McGeorge set up his own security firm and remained in close touch with Livingstone. McGeorge and several others with similar conservative political views set up a 501-3-C nonprofit corporation with the idea that if any of them came up with a project, "we would have a vehicle to do it through. I would never do it now. It's dumb. . . . Neil was the one actually trying to do something with the institute."[32] It was called the Institute on Terrorism and Sub-National Conflict. McGeorge, a member of the board of directors, said he had no idea that Livingstone was going to use it as part of the Contra supply operations. Indeed, Livingstone's and Owen's "public relations" plan for the Contras—the setting up of a nonprofit organization— was being carried out.

"Well along in this period of time I get invited to dinner at The Palm restaurant and there is Neil, Rob Owen, and myself. So we had dinner and they want me to do a job, and they were offering me a modest amount of money to go do this. There was a pile of RPG7s [an antitank weapon], some ten thousand. They told me that these were surplus to whatever the hell country it was. They never did tell me . . . I suspected South Africa. They wanted me to look at them, inspect them, see to their proper packaging. An airplane would arrive and I should turn them over to whoever is on the airplane," McGeorge said.

The only way McGeorge would agree to take on the assignment was if he had a contract with the National Security Council that his attorney could pick up at the Old Executive Office Building. McGeorge recalled, "They said no way we are going to put this in writing. . . . This thing stank to high heaven. I did not agree to do it. They were not happy."

Another year went by and, as far as McGeorge knew, nothing was going on with their institute when he got another call, this time an invitation to Rob Owen's house. Owen asked McGeorge to investigate the money and methods being used in Contra military training. McGeorge agreed, but, once again, said he wanted a contract in writing. Owen told McGeorge he would look into it, but McGeorge was never recontacted.

Jack McGeorge made a mistake. He never looked into the possibility that the Institute on Terrorism and Sub-National Conflict had become a major operation in the Reagan–Bush administration's secret operations while Owen and Livingstone were supposedly laboring full time at Gray and Company.

McGeorge recalled one incident which indicated that Gray was not at all happy about the amount of work Owen and Livingstone were producing for Gray and Company. "I do remember being there one day when Gray cut Owen off at the ankles." According to McGeorge, Gray came over to the Flour Mill building where the International Division was located. Gray went up to Owen, who towered over Gray, and said, "How many billable hours did you get today?" McGeorge said, "When Owen was mumbling, Gray just shot at him. He turns to Neil and does a similar thing in front of Neil. He sure as hell knew I was not an employee. He was clearly very angry with Neil and Owen. He felt their private agendas were causing him a lot of grief."

McGeorge soon found out that he, too, would share some of the grief. In October 1985, the phone rang at McGeorge's home. "It was a very cryptic phone call." The caller, who refused to identify himself, asked McGeorge, as a member of the Board of the Institute on Terrorism and Sub-National Conflict with a fiduciary responsibility, what he knew about two checks for $230,000 and $75,000 that went through the Institute's account. McGeorge responded to the caller that he had gotten his facts wrong because the Institute had no funds. The caller told McGeorge he was mistaken. Then the caller issued a polite but firm warning: "If you ever expect to do business with us again, sever your ties." McGeorge assumed it was someone from the CIA who called since he had done executive protection training for the Agency over the years.

Furious, McGeorge began to investigate. He learned that the Institute now had an office in downtown Washington. When he arrived at the office, he discovered that a secretary, Owen, and Livingstone shared the space.

Months after Owen had left Gray and Company, he and Livingstone were still operating in tandem. McGeorge announced himself as a Director to the secretary and demanded to see Livingstone. When she told him Livingstone was in conference, McGeorge barged into a meeting between Livingstone and Owen.

McGeorge explained what happened next: "He's kind of upset that I barged into his office. I said, 'I wanna know about money. I wanna know about checkbooks. I wanna know where all the money came from.' Neil asks, 'What money?' I said, 'The two hundred thirty thousand dollars and the seventy-five thousand dollars.' First he said, 'I don't know,' and I said, 'That's horse shit.'. . . Then he said it was CIA money. I said, 'That is also horse shit.' He said, 'Well, I have nothing further to say.' I then asked, 'Who authorized hiring Rob?' Neil said, 'We had a little meeting when you were not here.'"

McGeorge resigned from the Board of Directors on the spot. Two years later Joel Lisker, investigating Iran-Contra for Congress, called him. McGeorge told him about his experiences with Rob Owen, Neil Livingstone, and Gray and Company. To his surprise, the Institute or Gray and Company employees' real role never publicly emerged.

Senator John Tower of Texas shocked many associates in 1983 when he announced he was not going to run for reelection the following year. Tower thought that he had an agreement with the Reagan administration that he would be appointed Secretary of Defense in the second Reagan term to replace Caspar Weinberger. But after it was too late for Tower to seek reelection, Weinberger decided to stay on and Tower was left to fend for himself.

Tower, although not well-liked by his Senate colleagues, was one of the Washington establishment, and in his misfortune he found many friends, Gray among them. Gray had known Tower since the Texan's arrival in the Senate. In 1986, Gray asked Tower to join Gray and Company's Board of Directors.[33] "He wouldn't have been on the Board unless he was very, very, very, very close to Gray. [There's] not a person on there that wasn't very close to Gray other than Beverly Sills. I never quite figured that out," said a Gray and Company executive who worked with the Board.

In November 1986, Attorney General Edwin Meese called a press conference and announced what became known as the Iran–Contra scandal—that Oliver North and his associates in "the Enterprise" had skimmed money from overcharges on Iran weapons sales and diverted it to the Contras. A few weeks later, Reagan appointed John Tower to head a commission to investigate these matter, the so-called Tower Commission.

None of the senior members of the Commission knew much about computers, and, therefore, thought that most of the White House internal communication on the matters under investigation had been destroyed by

Oliver North and others. But a Harvard intern playing with one of the computers made the fortuitous discovery that the same password used at the library at Harvard opened the White House computer. Many of the messages that Oliver North and others thought they had destroyed or hidden away were revealed. It was a great coup and added credibility to the Commission, which prior to that had not really uncovered much substantive information.

No one at the Tower Commission ever questioned any Gray and Company involvement in the Iran–Contra affair. The congressional committee, despite the ongoing federal investigation into Gray and Company's Madrid office, despite people like Jack McGeorge coming forward with information, never targeted anyone from Gray and Company's International Division, except Rob Owen, in their investigation. In fact, the congressional committee seemed to clear the public relations firm. The only reference to Gray and Company in its report said: "After leaving Senator Quayle's staff in 1983, Owen joined Gray and Company, a public relations firm in Washington, D.C. Taking a leave of absence from his firm, Owen traveled to Central America in late May or early June 1984 and met with Contra leaders."[34]

Livingstone, by his own admission, was involved in Iran-Contra. "I had some limited involvement . . . I was helping out a lot of elements of the Administration," he said. Livingstone also said Gray knew about his involvement and approved of it. Ken Gray notes that Carter Clews, after he left Gray and Company, lived in a townhouse with Owen and they set up a consulting firm together. Clews called Owen "a very good friend" and asserted that he got Owen his first job in Washington. Clews also said he performed work on behalf of the Contras. Yet none of these connections were ever pursued by any of the investigating committees. Clews said that an FBI agent came once and interviewed him and his wife, but nothing ever came of it.

At best, the strange history of Gray and Company's International Division is indicative of some very peculiar notions of what constitutes "public relations." Whether or not Gray himself knew the specifics of what Livingstone and Owen were doing for the Contras, the firm clearly had a number of links to both the official and "private" intelligence community. Equally clear is that these links had an ideological component.

Unfortunately for Gray, there was a tremendous element of amateur cloak-and-dagger hijinks in the International Division's activities. And nowhere would that mix of amateurism and ideology have more disastrous consequences than in the comedy of errors that was Gray and Company, Spain.

13

THE BEST LITTLE WHOREHOUSE IN MADRID

My office was adjacent to Bob's. It was an area that interested Bob a lot. The foreign policy arena seemed to have more glamour, and Bob liked the embassy circuit.

Neil Livingstone

Gray and Company turned what Neil Livingstone called "carrying the administration's water" into a high art form. One largely overlooked endeavor involved the American conservative coalition's efforts to oppose what they considered liberal or communist governments around the world, by supporting ultra-conservative opposition political parties in those countries. William Casey was a key figure aiding these efforts. Fighting communism was their idealistic cover. The chance to make money was their reward. The conservative movement that helped elect Ronald Reagan and George Bush went worldwide in the 1980s.

The idea of the private intelligence network aligning itself with conservative political parties made perfect sense; it was true to the spirit of the Reagan doctrine of fighting communism, if not American and international law, and it relied on free enterprise. The plan was to export to unsuspecting electorates worldwide the same techniques that had put Ronald Reagan and George Bush in power in the United States.

After their efforts on behalf of conservative elements in Guatemala, the International Division launched an endeavor in a far bigger arena, this time not a small, Central American country, but a European nation—a member of NATO. This time their efforts would be to support the tiny, right-wing opposition party aligned against the unpalatable socialist government of Felipe Gonzalez in Spain.

In 1982 one of the key elements of Gonzalez's Socialist party's platform was a promise to hold a referendum on whether or not Spain should continue its membership in NATO. Spain's Communist party was the leading advocate of pulling out of NATO and having U.S. bases removed.[1] To conservative activists this was seen as a drastic development.

Gray and Company was brought into the project through the auspices of George Arnstein, an aide to United States Information Agency director Charles Wick, William Casey's good friend and Gray's cochair of the 1980 Inaugural. The USIA's ostensible function is to disseminate objective information throughout the world. USIA officials occasionally took foreign officials on tours of The Power House. Gray and Company, as a public relations firm, was, of course, not in the business of providing objective information but advocacy.

In August 1983 Arnstein called Livingstone and asked to bring by Gabriel Camunas Solis, a member of the Spanish national legislature—the Cortez. With Arnstein acting as translator, Livingstone explained the world of lobbying and public relations to Camunas, then the deputy party chairman of Spain's right-of-center Popular Alliance party (Alianza Popular), the leading conservative opposition party to Spanish President Felipe Gonzalez.

One reason the USIA official steered the Spanish politician to Gray and Company was because Prime Minister Gonzalez, the leader of Spain's Socialist party, had used American political consultants to help him win power in the last election. During the August visit to Gray and Company, Camunas expressed an interest in American public relations techniques to Livingstone. "I was intrigued, being more sympathetic to his party than to the current ruling party in Spain, that this was kind of an intriguing idea. So, Mr. Camunas and I started corresponding . . . I believe I sent a proposal on political representation," Livingstone said.

In fact, Livingstone sent a formal proposal in October 1983 describing how Gray and Company could assist the Popular Alliance party in winning power in Spain.

Camunas was essentially shopping around for political consultants, and, although the U.S. government could not directly aid an opposition party, placing Camunas with Gray and Company would allow the administration to further its goals without direct involvement. "Everybody is kind of going wink, wink a little bit. . . . Wouldn't Reagan sure like to see conservative parties in Europe, and particularly as we were very concerned about NATO at that time," Livingstone said, characterizing the discussions.

Kenneth DeForest Gray was a most unlikely person to be thrust into the center of a controversy that combined international public relations and murky undercover intrigue. Robert Gray brought his California-born nephew, who looks somewhat like the young W. C. Fields, to Washington to work for the Gray-owned company called National Leasing Consultants, which leased the office equipment and furnishings to Gray and Company. After a not very successful career as an insurance salesman, Ken Gray joined his father's brother hoping to prosper in a new profession. "Since he was the boss's nephew, we kind of took him and did stuff with him, found jobs for him. He was not considered to be very bright," a Gray and Company vice president said.

Ken Gray's adventure began in August 1983, when Neil Livingstone asked him to meet several Spanish legislators with the Popular Alliance party.[2] At the time Ken ran "Media Scan," a television monitoring service that made note of television programming of interest to Gray and Company clients and then billed the client for the hours of watching television. Livingstone told Ken that the Popular Alliance party was "right of center."

Camunas and the other politicians were interested in adapting American public opinion techniques to Spain. Ken remembered that the politicians were "fascinated about how we track public opinion and knowing where to target . . . our communications programs for clients."[3] Ken Gray stayed in the meeting long enough to hear his colleagues tell the Spanish legislators that they could not come to Spain and work for their political party. "We told them that we did not take on political parties to represent," he said. But Ken had left the room when the Spaniards went on to ask if there was any way that Gray and Company could advise them how to set up a modern political campaign.

First Livingstone had to come up with a justification for Gray and Company working for a political party in a foreign country. Although the Popular Alliance party had risen in a single election from a handful of seats to over a hundred, it had received little notice outside of Spain. "As a consequence, they felt that instead of immediately moving into the area of running their political campaign in Spain, that we would begin work in the United States . . . by taking care of certain external media relations and so on, which would build the stature of the party and the knowledge in other Western countries of who the party leaders were, what the party was, what it stood for and things of that nature," Livingstone said.[4]

In November 1983, Neil Livingstone took an around-the-world trip with Robert Gray that ended in Spain. Their host was Gabriel Camunas, who had visited Gray and Company in Washington. Camunas introduced Livingstone and his wife, Susan, to five other members of the Popular Alliance party, including Guillermo Kirkpatrick, who, in addition to being the "shadow" foreign minister of the party, was a distant cousin to then United Nations Ambassador Jeane Kirkpatrick; Jose Ramon Lasuen, the shadow finance minister and a behind-the-scenes power wielder in the party; and Miguel Herrero DeMinion, the number two man in the Party.

The Popular Alliance party was in essence the successor to the heritage of the late Spanish strongman Francisco Franco. While its fascist views were repackaged with a veneer of moderation, former Franco aides were well connected to the party. The Livingstones were entertained by Alejandro DeMuns, who was formerly on Franco's personal staff. The politicians asked Livingstone to advise them on how the party's stone cold image could be revitalized to compete with the popular Spanish Prime Minister Felipe Gonzalez.

As in many business deals, the question boiled down not to whether Gray and Company would do the work, but who would pay for it. At the end of the meeting the Spaniards told Livingstone that they themselves did not have the funds, but that they would deliver another Spanish client who would pay for the establishment of a Gray and Company office in Spain so the firm could get "acclimated."[5] Lasuen suggested the nuclear power industry of Spain as a likely client for Gray and Company's services.[6] The seeds of Gray and Company's first international office were planted.

Although Gonzalez was leaning toward the West, in June 1984 he faced mass demonstrations against his pro-Western views on NATO and the continuing presence of American bases in Spain.[7] Gonzalez's warm relations with the U.S. were nearly shattered when the Spanish government expelled two U.S. diplomats and charged them with espionage. Complicating relations further was the leak of a Reagan administration plan to stockpile nuclear weapons in Spain in the event of an emergency.[8]

Livingstone agreed with the idea of finding an alternate client to pay the bills. "We wrote and they said what could we do for the Spanish Nuclear Power Industry. It was under assault by the environmentalists and the Greens within the Gonzalez support group. And I felt strongly, because I had worked on nuclear power issues and as a convert to nuclear power, I was very strongly in favor of nuclear power. Secondly, Spain had not yet recognized Israel. . . . I had written some things that some might consider to be pro-Israeli, but it was in the sense that I felt that Spain's policies were overly pro-Arab and also Spain had not cooperated on combating terrorism the way they should and they had harbored Arabs as terrorists as a way of ingratiating themselves to the Arab world. And they were energy dependent, and I felt that this would make them less energy dependent on Middle East oil."[9]

Livingstone's interest in the Popular Alliance party was clearly more than just as a new client for Gray and Company. This party not only reflected the Reagan administration's strong conservative views, it also was the only party in Spain willing to recognize Israel. Livingstone, as he himself has noted, had long established ties to Israeli intelligence.

Madrid was the perfect place to set up an office. It was to Arabs and Israelis what Berlin was to the cold war East and West. It served as Checkpoint Charlie for transactions that needed neutral ground. The Israelis wanted the Spanish to be less dependent on Arab oil imports, so they viewed a campaign to void the Socialist government's moratorium on new nuclear power plants with great sympathy. As Livingstone later said, "The recognition of the State of Israel, which was a primary plank in the Alianza Popular, would have necessarily meant a diminishment of Spain's very cordial relations with the Arab states and, therefore, it was felt by Mr. Lasuen and others that it was in the Spanish national interest that they have alternative sources of power."[10]

This was the beginning of a relationship between Gray and Company and a phantom client in Spain that would serve as a cover for the firm's work on behalf of the Popular Alliance party. According to Michael Pilgrim, "In a large sense, we [the intelligence community] provided the vehicle to get the conservative Spanish parliamentarians to Gray and Company then backed away with the caveat that Gray and Company would keep certain elements of the U.S. government informed on the progress of this."

For more than eight months Ken Gray presumed that the Spanish deal was going nowhere. Gray and Company employees were not allowed to work for any political party unless they took a leave of absence. But in January 1984, Gray and Company completed and presented a public relations proposal for the secret Spanish utility client, that was, in reality, a way to fund support for the Popular Alliance party.[11] It was called the "Campaign in Defense of Nuclear Power In Spain."

Robert Gray later told the SEC that he took a personal interest in the proposal. The reason he found this secret deal so intriguing, Gray maintained, was that he had tried to obtain the account of the Committee for Energy Awareness, an umbrella group for the U.S. nuclear-power industry, and had been unsuccessful. "When I heard that here was a possibility of representing somebody who wanted to do the same thing, I was intrigued by it, and that got my involvement much more than otherwise I might have given at that particular time."[12]

Gray was "intrigued" from the start by Livingstone's efforts in Spain. Gray was impressed by the proposal from the conservative Spanish parliamentarians: "Not only did they want a finders fee, or part of the activity for bringing in an account, but they wanted to be serviceable to us, or of service to us, in dealing with our entry into Spain. It was intriguing to me. I must tell you, if I were a Spaniard coming to the States, I would be excited about the prospect of a couple of United States Senators legitimately helping me in the marketplace, opening doors, introducing me where I should be introduced, getting in the right clubs and introducing me to the right people. I liked the idea. The prospect sounded intriguing to me."[13]

Gray viewed the new venture as the "Committee for Energy Awareness Madrid. That's the way I like to think of it. It was the loss of a domestic client reincarnated abroad," he said. Whatever Gray said before the SEC or actually believed, it was clear from the record that the operation had a strong political component. Certainly Livingstone dealt with it that way.

The plan was to support a small opposition party in Spain that was willing to carry out the foreign policy goals of Israel and of the ultraconservative

American political coalition. In return, Gray and Company would work to change American foreign policy and public opinion toward the popular and Western-leaning Spanish Prime Minister Felipe Gonzalez. Livingstone said the link between the Popular Alliance party and the nuclear power industry in Spain was strong. The Popular Alliance party "had felt that particularly in the U.S., public opinion was critical to them as an ascendant conservative party and they needed support in the *New York Times, Washington Post,* etc. . . . We wanted to make the energy dependence of Spain a question in U.S. foreign policy; that this could jeopardize NATO."[14]

In early March 1984, Neil Livingstone stopped Ken Gray on the stairwell of the Power House and told him the Spanish deal was alive and well. Why Livingstone confided in young Gray is somewhat of a mystery. (He once said, "Ken needs directions to find the toilet paper.") But Pilgrim believed that from the start Livingstone had plans to involve Gray's nephew in the Spanish deal as part of a cover operation. And the Gray and Company employees in Spain were to be convinced that the office was used as a money laundering operation for the Reagan administration's private intelligence network.

The cover story progressed as follows: The two key legislators negotiating with Gray and Company, Lasuen and Herrero, proposed to Livingstone that they become partners. In return, they would help Gray and Company get clients in Spain.[15] The legislators wanted to control the proposed new Gray and Company office in Madrid. Finally, they reached a compromise. After the parliamentarians helped Gray and Company get started in Spain, eventually the office would be run completely by Spanish nationals. In the meantime, the Spanish politicians, Lasuen and Herrero, claimed that they would form their own consulting company. The agreement called for Gray and Company to make payments to the Spanish legislators through this firm, called Adicsa, for "consulting services."

But Livingstone's carefully laid plans were quickly sidetracked when Gray brought in the former Argentinean Ambassador, Alejandro Orfila, as the new vice chairman of Gray and Company. He would be the second in command, with control over the International Division. Not only did Livingstone have a new boss, but, to make matters worse, Orfila was a personal friend of Felipe Gonzalez.

Orfila was a major Washington figure. For years he had been the Secretary General of the Organization of American States (OAS). Many in the diplomatic community considered Orfila a lightweight, more interested in parties and beautiful women than major international business. In many ways, Orfila was an Argentine version of Robert Gray. Both men were charming, loved good tailoring, and enjoyed great parties.

Like so many others, Orfila's ties to Gray dated back to the Eisenhower administration. Orfila had first met Gray in 1959, when both men worked for their Presidents. He joined Gray and Company because he had been frustrated at the OAS, and Gray dangled huge amounts of money in front of him. Originally, Gray had proposed to Orfila that they form a separate company called Gray-Orfila. Instead, Orfila negotiated a $25,000-a-month contract and a percentage of all the business he brought in. Outside of Gray, no one was ever paid more.

Orfila was not all fluff. He had a long history of getting things done. He once defeated a move by the U.S. Senate to keep Ford Motor Company Argentina from being allowed to sell its products in Cuba. Orfila, with his Argentine accent and diplomatic connections, possessed the sort of allure and élan that appealed to a man like Gray.

Within a few weeks of his arrival, Orfila had come to the conclusion that the ambience and attitudes at Gray and Company were "very strange." He also realized, he said, that he had no future at Gray and Company after the first battles over Spain. He found that Gray did not accept his advice and that he was constantly facing back-stabbing and pettiness from many of his colleagues. "I was a very ineffective leader because I was not happy and because I was not performing. I was already thinking of how I could gracefully get out of there," Orfila said.[16]

Within a month Orfila realized he had made the professional mistake of his life by coming to Gray and Company. He was very uncomfortable with the practice of using "access" to his friends and associates in the Washington establishment for company business. "One of the things I cannot do is ask for anything. I cannot ask you for the time of day. It is not my nature," Orfila said. "I will never forget one day he [Gray] mentioned a very important figure. I said, 'I know him.' He said, 'I want you to ask him' this, that and the other. I don't even remember what it was. I knew that I wasn't capable of doing it, because I couldn't call the guy and ask him to do it for me. I just couldn't."

Orfila was frustrated with Gray, whom he could never get a fix on. He also had a low opinion of Gray's business acumen (a judgment shared by few others). "The guy was paying me a fortune and I didn't do a damn thing for nine months. I didn't do anything. I used to go, sit in this beautiful office, look around, and think, 'What the hell am I doing here?' " Worst of all, Orfila found Livingstone, Rob Owen, and most of the International Division, which he was brought in to run, completely out of control.[17]

The atmosphere in the International Division was unpleasant and alien to Orfila. One reason Orfila did not feel comfortable was he did not get along well with Charles Crawford, who was Livingstone's best friend in the company. Orfila believed another was that other senior company people resented Gray's enthusiatic courting of him and his high salary.

Orfila was appalled by the lack of foreign language ability in the International Division. "No one spoke Arabic or Japanese, yet they expected to do business in these places," he said. He found it strange that he was not introduced to other Latin clients, like the Cuban-American Foundation or Domingo Moreira. "I don't remember any other Latins except those I brought in," Orfila said.[18] "We [the International Division] were a complete fiasco." Because of that, Orfila believed that Livingstone and Rob Owen could have been running anything they wanted out of the division and Gray would not have known the difference.

What Orfila had no way of knowing was that his presence as the new head of the International Division was interfering with Livingstone's own agenda. Unfortunately for Orfila, he was quickly introduced into the kind of hardball that typified life at Gray and Company. The *Washington Post* learned that he had begun working for Gray and Company prior to his resignation from the Organization of American States. In effect, Orfila was collecting two paychecks, one from the OAS and one from Gray and Company. The newspaper stories caused a sensation in Washington.

Some at Gray and Company believed Neil Livingstone leaked the stories because he was angry that Gray had brought Orfila in over him. Livingstone denied the leak but made no secret of his displeasure at Orfila being brought in over him. Livingstone said he felt betrayed by Gray. "Alex came in on January 1 [1984]. He said that all the Spanish-speaking clients are mine and particularly Spain, because Felipe Gonzalez is a friend of mine, a personal friend. He was a little hesitant about the Alliance initially because his ties were to the other side. But he met Lasuen. He went over there. I was told to be a good soldier . . . I was pissed. . . . So anyway I dropped out . . . then Alex came back from a meeting in Spain and Bob went early in 1984. They come back, it was like February or March, probably, and everyone is all excited about the Spanish contract. . . . It was a done deal," Livingstone said.[19]

Orfila took control of the Spanish negotiations, Livingstone claimed, when Gray sent him to meet with legislators in Madrid not long after Orfila started working at Gray and Company. Orfila only told "me very scattered things about what had been negotiated and decided after he returned," Livingstone said. Orfila said that the Spanish deal was arranged before he ever arrived at Gray and Company. "The Spanish account was run mostly by Livingstone . . . I saw the basic thing that I was the only one who spoke the language of these people and most of them did not speak English so well." According to Orfila, the Spanish deal was "all set and arranged" by the time he arrived. Orfila said he never acted as more than a high-priced translator.

Gray had brought the company public during this period and "the stock had languished," Livingstone said. "Gray and Alex Orfila took this upon themselves, this [Spanish] project. Gray wanted to see the stock move and he felt a good way of showing that momentum was to show expansion of the firm." For Livingstone, who still had the responsibility of the day-to-day running of the International Division, his perceived lack of authority gnawed at him, but he said he understood why a deal that was his creation was taken away. "Bob and Alex were our two show pieces and Lasuen was an arrogant man . . . a very arrogant man who felt he was a king maker in Spain and that he did not want to work with underlings unless he absolutely had to."[20]

Orfila denied Livingstone's claim that he was in favor of the Spanish operation. To the contrary, he said he considered the whole approach to the Spanish deal insane. Orfila said that Gray and Livingstone had told him that they were going to use these Spanish parliamentarians to lobby Gonzalez. "This will be the first time in history you try to approach a government from the opposition," Orfila said.

Orfila did not like the deal. It made no sense to him. After all, he knew Gonzalez. Why didn't they just go to Gonzalez or his close associates directly? Why would Gray and Company want to work with the opposition party to influence the president? To him, it would be like hiring Ted Kennedy to lobby Dan Quayle. "I said, 'It made no sense,' ten times, a thousand times."[21]

Orfila said the trip he took to Spain with Gray only puzzled him more. But Gray explained that these Spanish parliamentarians, even though they were affiliated with the opposition political party, "were more located, you know, in circles in Spain that were not necessarily . . . in power at that particular time." Orfila said he favored setting up an independent Gray office, with its own staff.[22] Despite the high-profile visit with the Popular Alliance officials, no contract was signed in Spain. The final arrangements would be made by Gray, personally, in Washington.

Jose Ramon Lasuen and Miguel Domingo Herrero, the two key members of the Cortez and the right-wing Popular Alliance party, arrived in Washington the first week in April. On April 5, 1984, Gray and Orfila took the Popular Alliance legislators to dinner at The George Town Club. Gray told the SEC, "We wouldn't have been discussing business at the meeting. It's a fetish of mine, I suppose, but we don't discuss business things at social affairs."[23] Despite this assertion, Gray charged the dinner to Gray and Company as a business expense.[24]

Officially, the Spanish legislators proposed that Gray and Company represent a secret client for $500,000 a year, paying half of that fee to the two politicians for the introductions. Their $250,000 "fee" was to be paid $50,000 in cash and the rest in Gray and Company stock. If the stock deal was not approved by the Spanish government, Gray and Company would make the rest of the payment in cash. Supposedly the well-heeled "secret client" was UNESA—a Spanish utility consortium. Gray used his own metaphor to describe the contract: "If it were a steak, it would be medium-well. It was not average, it wasn't large, but it certainly was bigger than average."[25]

Mark Moran was like a thousand other Washington lawyers. He had worked for a top Wall Street firm's Washington office and had been involved in the public offering for Gray and Company. He had also worked on the Senate Foreign Relations Committee where he had helped draft amendments to the Foreign Corrupt Practices Act. That law was designed to prevent U.S. companies from bribing foreign officials to get contracts. He had gone to all the right schools and had been invited by Gray to work on the Reagan Inaugural Committee.[26]

Beginning in April 1984, Moran was the full time deputy corporate counsel to Gray and Company. Like Orfila, he was thrown into the middle of the Spanish deal almost immediately. Although he was friends with Charles Crawford, he made some early enemies at Gray and Company, including Neil Livingstone. Again, another new Gray and Company employee was interfering in Livingstone's plans. Livingstone described Moran as a "total asshole, dipshit. I can't say enough terrible things about this man."[27]

Like Orfila, Moran did not know when he went to work at Gray and Company that he was bothering Livingstone's plans in Spain. All Moran knew was that he found Livingstone very secretive and he was never at all certain whom to report to: "It depended on the day of the week and the week of the year."[28]

From the start, Moran found it strange Gray and Company had no written contract with its client. That same spring he, along with Carter Strong, an attorney with Arent, Fox, Kintner, Plotkin & Kahn, Gray's outside counsel, began using a Spanish lawyer to research the legality in Spain of hiring two members of the Popular Alliance party as consultants for Gray and Company.

Moran said he brought in outside counsel and organized a briefing for top Gray and Company executives because he found the Spanish deal legally "fraught with potential danger, and it was particularly critical, in this instance, that everybody be absolutely aware of where the lines needed to be drawn."

On April 26, 1984, at 11:00 A.M. in the conference room at the Power House, a key meeting took place that excluded both Ken Gray and Carter Clews. The top management, Robert Gray, Orfila, possibly Pate Felts (the comptroller), Charles Crawford, and Jim Jennings were joined by Mark Moran, the company lawyer, and Carter Strong, the outside counsel. Neil Livingstone, still resentful of being forced off the account, was also there. Livingstone said generally at such meetings the Gray lawyers would remind everyone that anything said at the meeting was confidential.

The subject of the meeting was whether Gray's deal—to pay Lasuen and Herrero half of the annual income from Gray and Company Spain—was legal under the Foreign Corrupt Practices Act. According to Livingstone, concerns were raised at the meeting about the effect publicity would have on Gray and Company if the details of these arrangements leaked out.

Moran distributed copies of articles and a briefing memo about the Foreign Corrupt Practices Act. He cautioned everyone present that the most important aspect of being in business with the Spanish parliamentarians was to make certain they did work and to document that work, otherwise it would look simply like payoffs to government officials.[29] As Moran understood it, the parliamentarians were supposed to help Gray and Company locate an office, introduce them to potential clients, and provide economic analysis.

To Moran's surprise, Gray spoke up at the meeting. According to Moran, "He said, 'Lawyers always have negative attitudes about everything. Let's find a way we can do this.' But, you know, he didn't see a reason why there should be a problem. . . . It clearly was, 'Let's get this done. There's got to be a way to do it legally and let's find the answer.' "[30]

Moran said Gray's attitude worried him. Afterwards, Orfila told Moran to collect all copies of the memo. Livingstone recalled that the memorandum on the Foreign Corrupt Practices Act was distributed to him, and then within a few hours retrieved.[31]

In response to a written interview for this book, Gray stated that at the time the decision was made to open the office in Madrid and engage the services of the Spanish legislators the firm asked their attorneys for an opinion, in writing, on the legality of the proposed office and its relationship with the Spanish legislators. Both the Gray and Company and the outside lawyer gave the firm a letter approving the transactions. Gray said he insisted that the contract contain a clause invalidating the agreement should any part of it violate either Spanish or U.S. law.

Livingstone's memory of the meeting discussing the legality of the partnership with the members of the Cortez differed somewhat from both Moran's and Gray's. "They are going to be our partners and we get this deal and we're going to open an office in Spain and Moran and Strong [outside counsel] bless this deal. We talked about it. Everyone said it was a secret meeting and the lawyers are sitting there telling us that it has the appearance of impropriety even if it is not improper. Well, you're damn right it has the appearance of impropriety," Livingstone said.

Federal law also required Gray and Company and all those connected to the Spanish account to register with the Justice Department under the Foreign Agents Registration Act. But according to Moran, Charles Crawford, and Justice Department records, that was never done.

On the first Sunday night in April 1984, Ken Gray got a telephone call at home from his Uncle Bob. The elder Gray asked his nephew if he was interested in going to Madrid to open the first international office of Gray and Company. Young Gray, who had been asking his uncle for more responsibility, was thrilled. Gray told Ken that the assignment was not solid yet, but might develop in the next few months. Gray also called Neil

Livingstone at home to tell him that he was thinking about his nephew and Carter Clews for the Madrid assignment.[32]

The next day, a Monday, Ken Gray went to his uncle's loft office inside The Power House to talk about the Madrid assignment. Gray told his nephew that the assignment in Spain would be for "a confidential client," and that it would be a great opportunity for him to gain experience. Ken learned from his uncle that the "confidential client" was some sort of utility company. Every few days Ken asked his uncle if anything were new on the Spanish office. Gray referred his nephew to Alejandro Orfila.

The decision to send Ken Gray and Carter Clews to Madrid was not based on their abilities or their language skills. It was a management decision to get two problems out of the way. Ken Gray's appointment to Spain had more to do with his last name than his competence. "Ken represented a difficult managerial problem for us because he bore the Gray name [and] always saw himself as a much more senior person in the company than, in fact, he was," said Jim Jennings, a top Gray and Company official.[33]

Charles Crawford said Carter Clews was selected to head Gray and Company's new Madrid office because he came from a conservative political background. "It was our understanding that our friends, meaning the businessmen who were willing to introduce us to the business community, would feel more comfortable with somebody that at least didn't think the conservative party of Spain was wrong, or anathema." In fact, according to Orfila and Livingstone, Clews was sent to Spain because he could not get along with his immediate supervisor, Frank Mankiewicz.[34]

Clews was considered a superior employee when it came to his ability as a public relations professional, but his management ability was a different story. "In terms of his management style, he was viewed by all of us to be out of the dark ages. Carter had a club. Carter was an extreme disciplinarian in an environment of creative professionals. He was extreme in the sense that if anybody was more than a minute late, they would be disciplined publicly, verbally abused. When he was annoyed at somebody, for whatever reason, he would castigate them severely, publicly. When he lost his temper, it would be outrageous. When he was annoyed, he would fire people repeatedly over offenses small and large," Jennings said.[35]

Livingstone protested sending Ken Gray and Clews to Spain. "We sent two people against my advice to Spain, who did not speak the language and neither had ever traveled abroad except one individual to Taiwan once. The personnel decisions were deplorable and, as a consequence, these were like two babes in the woods," he said. Livingstone was also worried about corporate security. "Ken Gray was known as someone who did not keep a secret in the company. . . . He talked too openly about all company business and every company has certain business or certain personalities, including his uncle, that one doesn't want to discuss."

Ken Gray was no fan of Neil Livingstone's either. "He [Livingstone] dressed like a cheap french pimp and I don't mean to insult the French pimps. I mean he has never been in the military. He has never been in any theater of action. [He] always [talked of his] great works and novels and books on terrorism [which] consisted of pamphlets. . . . I think he is a fraud.''

Robert Gray conceded to the SEC that the decision to send Ken and Carter was largely his. "I tried Ken Gray, my nephew, in many different places to try and find exactly the right fit for him. Failing to do that, it occurred to me that the name was likely a handicap for him here since his peers in the company would always discount what he did. . . . But his name might be an asset abroad since he would have the same name as the company. It might be a big help to him. It would be a clean slate. . . . But obviously he shouldn't go alone . . . Clews was suggested as his addition because we brought Frank Mankiewicz in to run the Public Relations Division of which Clews was a member, and there was considerable friction between the two. It seemed like a good way to solve both the problems of our staffing in Spain and alleviate two problems that we had in Washington.''[36]

Mark Moran said the assignment of Carter Clews and Ken Gray to Spain put both men in impossible positions. "I advised them both not to go because they were being set up for failure. . . . You just don't send people to an alien environment to sell public relations services,'' Moran said.

In early May, Ken Gray walked into Orfila's exposed-old-brick-walled and oak-furnished office which featured a series of oversized photographs of Orfila's glamorous wife Helga, a beautiful blonde former New York model. Orfila explained that the confidentiality of the client, a Spanish utilities consortium, was paramount to the deal. "He said there would be no formal contract . . . between Gray and Company and the utility. It would be a gentlemen's agreement. He stressed that confidentiality was very important. That I shouldn't talk about it with anyone, even the possibility of my going to Spain, or that we were going to open a Spanish office with anyone at Gray and Company,'' Ken Gray said.

Orfila asked Ken how he got along with Carter Clews. Clews had a personal history that included a stint as the Communications Director of the National Right to Work Committee and the Senate Republican Conference. Both of his feet were firmly planted in the ideological far right of the GOP. Ken Gray told Orfila he got along fine with Clews. Orfila told Ken, who was concerned about taking Spanish lessons before he left, not to worry about starting the lessons just yet.

To maintain secrecy, Ken Gray went down to see Carter Clews and both of them took a walk in Georgetown to talk about the pending assignment. Both men remembered being excited by the prospect of the assignment. Ken said that Clews had no more details about what their jobs actually entailed than he did. Later Clews said that he did not find it unusual that he was being sent to Spain and was not being told much about the client. To him, this sort of thing typified life at Gray and Company. "Because when somebody puts you in a room with the lights out, you figure out they want you to stay in the dark. There was no sense in questioning them about it," Clews said.[37]

After the key April meeting Orfila told Ken Gray to get started with his Spanish lessons. Orfila told both Clews and Ken that they could expect to be in Spain up to two years and that, in addition to working for the utilities firm, they were also to incorporate in Spain and to seek new business. Orfila told Ken that the $250,000 the utility firm had paid allowed Gray and Company Spain to open an office and be profitable from the start. In subsequent meetings with Orfila, Ken Gray learned that he would be Carter Clews's assistant. Both Clews and Ken were told they would report to Neil Livingstone in Washington. Clews objected to reporting to Livingstone. Orfila settled it by saying they could report to him, but were to work with Livingstone who remained in charge of the funding for the account.

Ken and Clews had a final series of meetings before they left for Spain. Gray met with them and gave the two men "a half-time speech." As Gray told the SEC, "I wanted them to know they would be flying the company's flag and we had a lot of confidence in them."[38] He wished them well and reminded them that the International Division was "Alex's show," but if they had any problems or questions to call him any time. Orfila called in Ken Gray and Clews just before they left for Madrid on May 10, 1984, and handed both of them a piece of paper entitled "Madrid Contacts" with four names on it—Herrero and Lasuen as well as Louis Magana and Pedro Rivero. Orfila went down the list and identified each person, which ones could be useful and what roles they were to play.[39]

Clews and Gray were told that they would be dealing regularly with Professor Jose Ramon Lasuen, an economics professor and member of the Cortez. Lasuen, whom they later nicknamed "JR," was to be their key contact in Spain. Ken Gray said, "The third person, Louis Magana, we were told, represented the investment of the utilities concern, that he was with the Banco de Pomento and that he would be our principal contact in helping introduce us to potential clients in business development and he would be our main contact point between us and the utilities and the fourth person, Pedro Rivero, we were told, was the Director of UNESA, which was the client."

Neither Ken nor Clews were told that Lasuen and Herrero were Gray and Company's business partners and were to be paid for bringing in the client. Gray said they decided not to tell them because "it was not germane to them. . . . It wouldn't have been appropriate to fold them into the details of the finances and so forth."[40]

Once again, before Ken and Clews left, Orfila stressed the importance of keeping a low profile in Spain concerning UNESA. For the first time Orfila explained to them that UNESA was an umbrella organization for the Spanish nuclear-power industry that was greatly concerned about a number of nuclear reactors at various stages of construction. "There had been a moratorium on nuclear power construction and UNESA needed to complete all their nuclear reactors and then put them in mothballs to comply with the moratorium. It was more cost effective than to stop a nuclear facility that was halfway constructed and then start it up in five or ten years again when they needed power. They were going to need some help on that, public opinion, influencing public opinion, to bring to bear on the attitudes and their legislative process over there. It was nothing unusual," Ken Gray said.[41]

Livingstone called Ken Gray to his office for yet another meeting before he left for Spain. Once again Livingstone stressed to Gray how important secrecy was. At the time Gray still believed that the reason for the secrecy was strictly business: "Public relations is not a well-practiced profession in Spain yet. It had a bad name in Spain because it's done in a different way than we do it over here. We were also dealing with a very large corporation and my understanding was they were nervous because it was something new at the time."[42]

According to Livingstone, the need to keep the client secret was because UNESA was publicly regulated and the Spanish government may have even had some ownership in the utility. Therefore, UNESA did not want anyone to know that they were opposing government policy on nuclear issues. In addition, when it was time for the next rate increase, they did not want anyone to be able to say that they had hired a high priced Washington public relations firm to lobby against the government and now they wanted the government to give them more money.[43]

Just before they left Mark Moran gave Clews and Ken Gray copies of the Foreign Corrupt Practices Act as well as a briefing and memorandum explaining that Americans could not pay foreign officials to obtain business. Moran did not mention that two members of the Cortez were, in reality, their bosses in Spain. After reading the material on the plane ride over, Ken Gray was nervous about both the secrecy of the agreement and fearful of the legal ramifications in Spain. This was the first time Gray ever saw his uncle's company work with a client without either a letter of agreement or a contract.[44]

In Madrid, Ken Gray spent nearly two hours a day on Spanish lessons, while Carter Clews got to know various journalists in Spain. Both men were working about twenty hours a month on the secret UNESA account. For Ken Gray, the adherence to secrecy soon became nervewracking. On May 23, two of the Spaniards on Orfila's contact list, Herrero and Lasuen, called and asked him to dinner at Madrid's Jockey Club. They also asked him not to mention the meeting to Carter Clews because they did not want his wife, Linda, along. Gray agreed.

At the dinner, the two men urged Gray to create a "front client." They told him that no one in Spain could learn that Gray and Company was really representing UNESA. Ken told them he was working on getting Quadrex, a nuclear decontamination company, as a client for Gray and Company in Spain. "I said then we would have an honest client; we wouldn't need any front. At that point Mr. Lasuen said, 'That's great. . . . You get them on board and I can guarantee you a contract out of the [Spanish] Department of Energy.' "[45] For the first time Ken Gray realized that there was some behind-the-scenes agreement between Lasuen and Herrero and Gray and Company.

The meeting then turned to the issue of how long Ken had known Neil Livingstone and just how close he was to his uncle. The two Spanish parliamentarians gave Ken a draft of the proposed contract between them and Gray and Company and left thinking they had found someone they could trust. But Ken Gray left the meeting decidedly uncomfortable.

Neil Livingstone's worst fears about Ken Gray's lack of discretion, and Jim Jennings's concern about Ken overly emphasizing his importance were well founded. Within two hours of the meeting, Ken called his uncle. "I told him I thought we had a problem . . . I just received a proposed agreement by the top two people on the contact list, and I said, 'Are you aware of this?' I told him it didn't make any sense. I didn't see what the purpose of it is and I wanted to know why weren't we told about this." Ken Gray told his uncle that he was going to send a telex with the proposed agreement because he believed Gray needed to check into it at once. Ken said his uncle then cautioned him about speaking on an open phone line, and said he would check into the matter. Ken told his uncle he would try to find a secure way to communicate, but, despite his uncle's warning, telexed the proposed agreement over unsecured lines anyway.

When Ken Gray did not hear from his uncle concerning their phone conversation and the telexed document, he became concerned. He called Gray again in Washington and this time was more adamant. He told his uncle that he feared the agreement might be in violation of the law. "It didn't look too good, in my opinion, to have any kind of arrangement with two members of Parliament. . . . I felt he needed to take a look at this because I felt it just wasn't right."[46]

Two days later Lasuen called Ken and asked him when he could expect payment. Ken told him that the lawyers in Washington were looking over the documents. That same day he received a call from Orfila, who admonished him in very strong terms not to use a telex or open phone line again. Orfila told him to use a pouch service and that they would have to establish security procedures for transmitting information.

Ken expressed to Orfila his fears that the terms of the deal with the politicians were not legal. He complained that neither he nor Clews knew about the contract beforehand. Orfila explained that it was simply an "oversight" and that arrangements like this one were made "all the time." After this conversation Livingstone established procedures for the transmittal of confidential information between Washington and Madrid.[47]

Ken Gray unilaterally fired the Spanish lawyer that Mark Moran had arranged for the office, Jose Arcila, because he did not like him and did not think he was prepared. To make matters worse, by the time the office was up and running in late May, Livingstone and Orfila had ordered Moran not to talk directly to anyone about Gray Spain. Moran was not told what was happening in Spain, and he was further prohibited from contacting Clews or Ken Gray without going through Livingstone or Orfila. The decision to cut the company lawyer out of the Spanish office came, according to Moran, from Clews and Ken Gray themselves, who felt Moran was out to "sabotage" their operation "because I was insisting on all sorts of precautions that needed to be taken about prior approval of contracts."[48]

Moran said he attempted to go through Orfila and Livingstone to make certain the Foreign Corrupt Practices Act was being complied with, but neither responded to his concerns. On three different occasions Moran asked to go to Spain to get information, but neither Orfila nor Robert Gray would permit it. Moran and Pate Felts, who shared some of Moran's concerns, found themselves in a running battle. The attorney and the comptroller were concerned that Ken Gray and Clews were not documenting their work and they were not providing any financial records on how much and on what they were spending.[49]

Ken Gray hired another Spanish lawyer in Madrid, and learned that the secret agreement between Gray and Company and UNESA had to be registered with the Spanish equivalent of the Department of Commerce. Although Livingstone was in charge of managing the Spanish operation, he claimed that he was never told what the Spanish parliamentarians were going to provide in return for their compensation. During the entire existence of the Spanish operation, Livingstone said he communicated with the senior man in Spain, Carter Clews, only twice, even though he was his immediate supervisor.

Livingstone said he became increasingly frustrated with the lack of performance out of the Madrid office. He claimed that he wanted to close down the office, but Orfila overruled him. He said that although he had line responsibility for the office, he had no real authority. Livingstone voiced the view that the office was failing so often that Charles Crawford actually warned him that his own position in the company would be in jeopardy if he continued to speak out.

In mid-June, Ken Gray contacted Jim Jennings in Washington and voiced his concerns again over the Spanish deal, but once again Gray and Company executives ignored his complaints. Finally, Ken filled Carter Clews in on what he knew. "We both were suspicious. Something wasn't right, and we couldn't figure out what it was, but our curiosity was aroused," Ken said.[50] "I told Carter and he concurred with me that I felt Lasuen was a very clever boy. I told Carter that I thought he was too slick for his own good and felt like I should count my fingers after I shook hands with him . . . Herrero seemed to be very bright and sharp, but he struck me as a weasel. I told him his eyes bugged out like a little weasel. That was the nickname we gave him, 'the weasel.' "

Forty-eight hours later Lasuen called Ken Gray again and asked for his money. This time the Spanish legislator was angry. Despite Ken Gray's efforts to calm him down, Lasuen demanded Alex Orfila's home number in Washington. Orfila told Ken Gray to string Lasuen along. It was during this period that Ken Gray learned that the legislators were to be paid $125,000 in cash and $125,000 in Gray and Company stock.

Ken Gray could not understand his uncle's continuing refusal to look into his concerns. He began to speak to his uncle in code about Lasuen, whom he referred to as "JR," and Herrero, "the weasel." He confided to Jim Jennings that he and Carter Clews were beginning to distrust Orfila and Livingstone. "We didn't believe that Bob Gray would mislead us, and we were concerned that Mr. Orfila or Mr. Livingstone might be running something that wasn't above board, trying to do something on their own that Mr. Gray wasn't aware. We kind of let Carter deal with Orfila straightforward, and Carter acted like he didn't know about the proposed agreement or the meeting. We were starting to become distrustful of a lot of people, and we don't know who was on what side or where, that things just weren't feeling right. So we decided we'd just kind of hang back and try and play ends against the middle and see where things shook out."

Ken met with Lasuen again in mid-June at a hotel bar across from the Cortez in Madrid. The Spaniard was now apoplectic about not being paid. "He was raising his voice and I was trying to calm him down because we were in this public bar in this big hotel with lots of people walking by and he's in a very loud voice going, 'Where's my money! Where's my money! Why haven't they sent it?' "

According to what Pate Felts told the SEC, although he was deeply involved in the planning of the Spanish operation, he had no idea that Jose Ramon Lasuen or Miguel Herrero Rodriguez de Minon had gone into business with Gray and Company, a remarkable lack of information on the part of the comptroller of the company.[51]

In late June, Ken Gray learned that the amount of money due Gray and Company through the UNESA connection was not $250,000, but $500,000. Once again when Ken Gray and Clews confronted Orfila by phone and complained about not being told of the arrangement, Orfila claimed it was another oversight. This time they hung up on him.

Ken Gray had become very agitated and was telling Clews that he feared Gray and Company had been turned into a "giant laundromat," where money was taken from the Spanish utilities and then funneled to the Spanish politicians. Ken Gray was adamant that his uncle would be "very upset" when he heard about what was occurring. Ken told Clews that he, himself, "would get to the bottom of this and find out what was going on." Clews replied that he "didn't care what Gray and Company is doing in Spain with politicians, rightly or wrongly, but my job here is to open an international office."

Finally Ken decided to confront Lasuen himself over his suspicions. "He wanted to impress his uncle so badly that he just tried too hard. . . . He was obsessed with his idea of laundering. He came to me one day and said, 'I went and confronted Lasuen directly, and I was right, it's a laundromat.' " Clews said he warned Ken that Lasuen "would not take this lightly."

It was during this period that Orfila asked Robert Gray to stop all business communications with his nephew in Spain. Gray said that he told both Clews and Ken that the office was Orfila's responsibility and he could not let them go over his head.[52] But later in June Ken Gray called his uncle again. This time he gave him an ultimatum: "I told him either you trust us or you don't." Once again, Gray told his nephew that he would have to "work it out with Orfila."[53] Orfila maintained he had so lost interest in his role at Gray and Company that he allowed Livingstone to handle most of the details on Gray Spain. "Livingstone was in charge of all the finances of the Division. . . . I was eight to five and was looking at the watch to see when five would come," Orfila said.

Gray and Company became incorporated as a wholly owned Spanish subsidiary on June 24, 1984. Washington's premier public relations and lobbying firm had officially gone international. But the Madrid office was, from the start, a joke. It was staffed by two men who had never lived abroad, could not speak the language, knew nothing about the culture, and did not know how to run a business. That seemed to be the point: It was never clear what Ken Gray and Clews were supposed to do. They were supposed to keep a low profile, but Ken Gray did not realize that. He thought he was supposed to attract new clients and build up the business. He also thought there were people taking advantage of his uncle and he was going to stop them. The Madrid office soon became nothing less than a comedy of errors.

"My concern [was] to try and open an international PR office. I really thought that was what we were there for. We weren't getting any clients, and they were saying, 'You're doing a great job.' I mean it was like saying to Stan and Laurel, 'You're so dumb. You're doing a super job,' " Clews said.

Matters were not made better by a growing friction between the two men. Clews felt that Ken Gray's judgment was not always politic—something that could prove disastrous for someone in public relations. At one meeting with seven middle-aged to elderly Spanish politicians and executives, Clews listened in horror as Ken Gray shared his cultural observations: "I've noticed something here in Spain and I wanted to know if the rest of you share this. I have noticed that Spanish women, when they are young, are very pretty, but when they turn forty, they turn into real dogs." "Everything instantly stopped," Clews said, "Everyone had a wife, of course, who was at least fifty years old. Everyday he'd do something else that you'd be shaking your head at."

Despite Ken's continuous problems, Clews thought of him as simply a man "trying too hard." But Ken thought he was his uncle's bloodhound, sniffing out possible problems. "Let me say this, I reported directly to my uncle. I did not take orders—directions—from Orfila, Livingstone, or Clews. My primary role and responsibility was to (a) ensure the integrity of the corporation, and (b) the integrity of Bob Gray, which are one in the same in my mind."[54] The respect was not mutual. Gray sometimes treated his nephew with open frustration. A senior Gray and Company executive remembered a bewildered Gray complaining that his nephew "renders me inarticulate." Gray told the SEC that he and his nephew had "a love-hate relationship."

If Clews was concerned about Ken Gray's mistakes, Ken was worried about Carter Clews. He believed that an individual has to be broadminded to be able to operate overseas, and that Clews's open admiration for the far right limited his ability to understand Spain. "He would go up to the Valley of Death outside Madrid and look at the castle where Franco was buried," Ken said. Another monument Clews admired was a cathedral Franco had forced Spanish Civil War prisoners to build; hundred of them were buried in a concrete wall that had collapsed. "Carter was fascinated by the raw power of that. Most of us would go, 'Geez, that is pretty barbaric.' If it had been me, dig Franco up and get him the hell out of there. That is pretty hard to do because you had the far right-wing political organizations everyday out there . . . doing their fascist salutes."

To add to his woes, Ken Gray broke his arm during a Fourth of July burro race. From his hospital bed Ken Gray called Jim Jennings and asked him where they stood legally and, according to Ken Gray, Jennings assured him that "they have outside counsel's opinion and that I shouldn't be concerned, but that he would continue to stay on top of it and make sure everything was fine."[55]

It was during the four days that Ken Gray was hospitalized that Carter Clews proposed to him that they set up their own version of Gray and Company. Clews was angry at the way the two had been treated by senior management, and felt they would be justified in striking out on their own. Ken Gray responded to Clews with a brief note firmly rejecting his proposal as "wrong."

Back at the Power House on July 10, Alex Orfila presented Mark Moran with a contract between Herrero, Lasuen, and Gray and Company to review. The contract called for payments totaling $200,000 in Gray and Company stock and $50,000 in cash in exchange for 500 hours of help in setting up the office and introductions to new clients. Orfila tried to pressure Moran into approving the contract immediately, saying Lasuen had to leave that day. Moran refused. "I said that it did not provide sufficient protection for the company. It didn't mention anything about the Foreign Corrupt Practices Act . . . I said there was a whole series of weaknesses and I refused to approve it unless it was substantially redrafted."[56]

To Orfila's and Lasuen's great frustration, Moran redrafted the contract to say that Gray and Company abides by Spanish law as well as the Foreign Corrupt Practices Act. (Robert Gray maintained in a written interview for this book that he insisted on this provision.) Moran also added a provision calling for Adicsa, the consulting firm the Spanish politicians said they had started, to limit their activities to the private sector.

Orfila objected to some of the changes. Moran said Orfila felt this was embarrassing to Lasuen because he was of high moral character. Lasuen and Orfila refused to okay clauses in the contract which required reports of their work, time sheets keeping track of their hours, and refunds if the legislators did not complete the work as agreed.[57]

In the end, Orfila ordered Moran to approve the contract without those provisions despite the lawyer's strenuous objection. Herrero and Lasuen were so important to Gray that he wrote them a letter assuring them that if Spanish authorities had a problem with transferring Gray and Company common stock, it would be replaced with $200,000 in cash.[58] In fact, almost everyone was led to believe that the legislators had already supplied Gray and Company with the UNESA consortium as a client, and that UNESA had paid Gray and Company $500,000 for its secret services. Half of that money was to go to the Spanish politicians; the remainder to fund the Spanish office.

Moran met with Gray and told him about his worries concerning the contract. Gray wanted to know if the agreement was legal. Moran said, "Well, if you're asking me my opinion as to whether the agreement is legal or not, if the facts are what we are being told, they are . . . and we have no evidence of that, there was no way I could determine that independently . . . then I think it is legal."

Despite this opinion Moran said he went on to communicate his deep misgivings about the contract to Gray, in large part because there was no way to independently confirm what the parliamentarians were telling them. Moran then added an additional warning: "I think that the dangers here of something going wrong and us finding ourselves in the situation of a possible

FCPA [Foreign Corrupt Practices Act] violation are so great that none of the rewards that we could possibly get from this are worth the risk.'' Moran also cautioned Gray that he felt the agreement violated the spirit of the Spanish law regarding the employment of legislators, if not the letter.

Despite his lawyer's warning, Gray signed the agreement to put the Spanish legislators on the company payroll.[59] What Gray really liked about the deal was that his company could have an international presence all paid for by a single client. "We wouldn't make money on just that client, but it looked like it could give us a floor from which we could begin to build and construct a new office,'' he told the SEC.[60]

By July, Livingstone knew he had lost control of the Madrid office. The operation was not going as planned. Ken Gray was running around making outrageous accusations and Carter Clews was spending thousands of dollars without providing any receipts. In meetings Livingstone continued to voice his objections to the Spanish office. He protested that Clews and Ken Gray had been billing the company for rent in Washington, for hotel space in Spain, and for a thirteen-room apartment in Madrid. "There were no vouchers from the parliamentarians. I had no timesheets,'' Livingstone complained.

Livingstone convinced Gray and Orfila to let him telex Spain demanding more accountability. But Livingstone said that Orfila ordered him to soften the tone of the telex. By this time, according to Livingstone's SEC testimony, he suspected that Clews was taking money from the company.[61]

Ken Gray returned to Washington in July 1984. His uncle was overwhelmed with activities for the Republican National Convention in Dallas. When Ken Gray finally saw his uncle, he told him how dangerous he thought the Spanish arrangement was. Gray acknowledged that his nephew warned him that the fees being paid to Lasuen and Herrero were out of all proportion to their work. He nonetheless referred his nephew to Ambassador Orfila once again. "Absent all the information, for some reason still inexplicable to me, Ken concluded that there must be something sinister if someone hasn't given him all the facts and shared with him every nuance of management's decision in coming to the conclusion . . . I said, 'Go talk to Orfila. It's his responsibility to satisfy you.' ''[62]

Neil Livingstone explained that because Ken Gray was not taken seriously, his concerns were ignored. "It was characterized to me by Chuck Crawford that Bob Gray was extremely angry—really angry at Ken Gray over this, and that Ken had shown a tremendous amount of disloyalty.''[63]

Ken Gray's allegations about the illegality and intelligence ramifications of Gray Spain caused a great deal of consternation at the Power House. He left within a month of his return to work on the Reagan–Bush campaign. Charles Crawford conceded that, prior to going over to the campaign, Ken expressed the need to get legal counsel because he feared the Spanish matter might reflect badly on him.

In September 1984, Gray and Company issued stock to the Spanish legislators as payment to their consulting firm—Adicsa.[64] Pate Felts entered payments to the legislators as services rendered on behalf of UNESA, the secret client.

On September 30, Gray took a side trip from what he described as a European vacation to visit the Madrid office.[65] (Others in the company testified before the SEC that Gray, in fact, was on a business trip to Geneva to meet with Mark Rich, an international fugitive whom he had solicited as a client. According to Charles Crawford, Gray had to meet with one of Rich's many attorneys in Madrid.[66]) According to Clews, Gray did not seem all that interested in the Spanish operation—he canceled his meetings with the Spanish principals and met with the exiled King of Bulgaria instead.

Gray told the SEC that it was on this visit that he discovered what a mess the company had on its hands. "I had gone into the office and was dumbfounded to see that he had enormous—by my standard—[an] enormous amount of space considering the people involved. Empty bookshelves with not a book on them. No signs of a going concern at all. . . . Then I discovered obviously that the bills weren't being paid. That was the final straw."[67] Gray found the lack of paying bills inexplicable since the funds were in Spain, and available.

Despite what Gray discovered on his trip to Spain, he took no real action when he returned, except to voice concerns to Orfila. The unpaid bills remained unpaid. The office remained open, and Clews remained in charge. In fact, Clews was not reprimanded but complimented on his operation. According to Clews, Orfila came over to Madrid shortly after the Gray visit. "He told me I was doing a great job. After that meeting, he [Orfila] said he knew what Livingstone did there. He said, 'It seems to me a one hundred thousand dollar finders fee is very expensive. Now I know what is going on.' "

After Ken Gray's stint in the Reagan–Bush campaign it became increasingly clear to him that things had gone terribly wrong in Madrid. Ken prepared a long memorandum about all the problems with the Spanish operation. Crawford said senior management again dismissed the young man's concerns. "When we got it, we said, 'This is right out of left field,' and it was just very characteristic of Ken to do something like this for shock effect."[68] Gray did not act on his nephew's charges; by this time he was sick of hearing them. He said he believed most of them had been dealt with by lawyers.

Ken Gray had explosive information in his memo. Beginning the day he turned it in, Jim Jennings and Charles Crawford should have implemented a massive damage-control plan. For example, in notes of one telephone conversation a phrase appeared noting that Orfila was startled that "principles" were aware of "kickback."[69] Mark Moran reacted differently from

Jennings, Crawford, Gray, Orfila, and Livingstone. He was so disturbed by these events that he insisted on bringing in outside counsel, Carter Strong, to begin an immediate examination of Ken Gray's charges. It was already too late.

When Carter Clews had first arrived in Madrid, he had called the American Embassy and had asked for a list of America media people in Spain. One of the women on the list, Marta Williams Diaz, had been successfully freelancing as a newspaper reporter. She had recently given birth to a child with a heart problem and was at home taking care of the baby when Clews called. She had no idea who Gray and Company was. "Clews called and he told me, 'I am with Gray and Company Spain and the U.S. Embassy recommended I get in touch with you.'" In fact, the Embassy had done no such thing and she would characterize it later as "a typical PR ploy."[70]

Clews hired Diaz to acclimate Ken Gray and him to Spanish society. She and her husband soon became friends with Clews, his wife, Linda, and Ken Gray. She tried to teach them about the culture of Spain, but it was not an easy job since neither man had brought any understanding of the country. "They could not understand why people did not eat enchiladas in Spain," she said.

In the end it was not Ken Gray or Mark Moran or anyone from Gray and Company who brought down the Spanish operation. It was Marta Williams Diaz. Months had gone by without Clews paying her or the other freelancers. Her letters to Gray and Company headquarters and Charles Crawford went unanswered. Clews claimed that funds had not come from Washington to pay the freelancers. He took a very aggressive attitude, threatening to take the freelancers to court. "He's crazy. . . . He took the attitude that I'll take you all on at once," Diaz said. She had a sick child at home, and Gray and Company owed her over six thousand dollars. She talked it over with the other freelancers and decided to take action. Diaz knew a woman who worked for the Popular Alliance party, who, Clews had let slip, were Gray and Company's "secret partners" in Spain.

Diaz went to see her friend who was highly placed in the Popular Alliance party and told her about Clews's abusiveness and indiscretions. "Not only have they not paid me," she said, "they have not paid five or six people that I introduced them to. . . . They are talking about the sex lives of these various people in your party and they are talking about it at cocktail parties. . . . Oh boy, did things move fast after that," Diaz recalled.

The next day Lasuen and Herrero announced to the press that they had advised Gray and Company as consultants on matters in South America. No one at Gray and Company in Washington knew, in advance, of the political announcement in Spain. Instead, Alejandro Orfila received a Thanksgiving-day call at his farm in Virginia from Jose Ramon Lasuen in Spain complaining that Clews had threatened to reveal the name of the Gray client, UNESA, and was not paying hotel and other bills in Spain. For those reasons, the two legislators wanted to terminate their agreement with Gray and Company.[71]

Lasuen demanded that Clews be recalled. Orfila talked to Clews, who denied Lasuen's allegations. Orfila tried to reach Gray, who was in Denver, Colorado, at the Browns Hotel visiting his sister for Thanksgiving. Next he called Neil Livingstone, who was hosting a Thanksgiving dinner at his Watergate apartment; one of the guests was Charles Crawford. Livingstone said that Orfila told him that a very agitated Lasuen said that because Carter Clews had failed to pay $6,500 owed to Marta Diaz Williams and other freelancers, she was threatening to reveal the relationship between Gray and Company and the politicians.

The parliamentarians and Gray and Company were fearful that exposure would lead to bad publicity as well as criminal investigations in both countries. Gray and Company had never registered as foreign agents with the Justice Department concerning their activities in Spain. To try to protect themselves, Lasuen sent Gray a letter on the letterhead of the consulting firm, Adicsa, rescinding the July 12 contract.[72] In reality, at the same time, behind the scenes, Orfila, Gray, and the parliamentarians were negotiating a new arrangement that still held out the possibility of a continued relationship, despite the fact that there was absolutely no evidence that the parliamentarians had succeeded in securing any new business for Gray and Company. Although Orfila would later contend that the two men had helped find an office and had provided introductions, he admitted that they had brought no clients to Gray's Spanish operation and had not provided the trade, technical, or economic data that they told Ken Gray they would supply. There was no documentary evidence beyond the contract that Lasuen or Herrero were anything besides politicians that Gray and Company had paid to do business in Spain or to funnel the money to the Popular Alliance party or both.

The next day, Gray dispatched Neil Livingstone and Charles Crawford to Madrid. Gray specifically selected Crawford over Jennings for the mission because, according to Jennings, "he thinks Chuck's a tougher, nastier guy than I am."[73] Livingstone said that Gray and his subordinates feared that publicity would reveal "the fact that the utilities industry had hired Gray and Company to oppose government policy and, in so doing, also connect the parliamentarians to it." Gray, according to Livingstone, also feared that UNESA would back out of the deal, because they feared that reprisals for their secret agreement with Gray and Company could negatively affect the Socialist government's decisions on electric utility rate increases.

Livingstone was not comforted by what he discovered when he got to Madrid. Lasuen suggested that UNESA be replaced by another Spanish industrial association called SERCOBE. Livingstone expressed surprise at this, since, he said, he tended to think of Lasuen as more of a client than a business partner. He believed the purpose of the Madrid office was to obtain the Popular Alliance party account. "I was only in a very foggy way aware of the business relationship that existed," Livingstone maintained. He also said he was surprised to learn from Lasuen that the Spanish parliamentarians had only met with Clews two to four times "I was concerned still that they were not performing any work, that I could see any evidence of . . . I think actually Lasuen volunteered it. He said, 'This guy Clews, I tried to be nice to him a couple of times when he first got here, but I've never seen him subsequently, except once in a while he calls me, and he doesn't seem to pick up on anything I do or tell him to do,' and Magana said the same thing. . . . I never made an assertion that they were laundering money because I had no evidence of it, but, in effect, this would be tantamount to that," Livingstone said.[74]

Next Livingstone and Crawford met with the head of their Madrid office. Livingstone was aghast. "Carter Clews walks in at the Ritz Hotel in Madrid. He's got on a couple-of-thousand-dollar Piaget watch. This is the guy that had Seiko. He's got on a six-hundred-dollar suit, or what looks like a six-hundred-dollar suit. He's got beautiful loafers. He's perfectly turned out. This is a guy who is not a well-dressed guy. He reeks of money. We talked to him and I'm getting more and more angry and he's beating around the bush giving us unclear answers about his relationship with this woman [Diaz]. I get furious about it." Crawford quickly realized that any communication between Livingstone and Clews was futile because of their mutual animosity. Crawford sent Livingstone on to London to deal with another client.

Charles Crawford called Mark Moran at 3:00 A.M. Washington time from Spain to tell him how serious the situation was. On November 26, Moran drafted a memo for Gray's signature calling for an internal investigation. Gray signed it but added a last paragraph shifting a great deal of responsibility for the matter to the attorneys. "What he was trying to do was dump it on the lawyers if anything went wrong," Moran said.[75]

Matters did not proceed smoothly for the Spanish parliamentarians, either. "Lasuen and Herrero had lost a lot of credibility with their party mates," Diaz said. But, fortunately for them, another scandal involving Gonzalez's Socialist party broke at the same time, which preoccupied the press. Lasuen and Herrero, now less threatened with exposure, attempted to get a few more dollars out of their relationship with Gray and Company. According to Livingstone, Crawford decided in Madrid that Clews would be given his computer and severance pay and quietly leave the firm. Gray and Company and the Spanish parliamentarians would then restructure their arrangements.

The events that followed were never revealed in Spain. In mid-December, both Lasuen and Herrero arrived in the United States to meet with Orfila and Livingstone. They dropped by the Power House and everything "seemed to be on an even keel," Livingstone said. The attorneys and Lasuen sat "cloistered" in Orfila's office restructuring their arrangements. According to Orfila, the Spanish politicians felt that they were entitled to the money from the original contract. Although they had returned the funds paid to them in Spain by Gray and Company, through the bank, Lasuen asked for a check to be issued directly to them in the name of Jean Pierre Blanc. No one at Gray and Company had heard of Blanc. Strangely, the Spaniards refused any payments directly to their business account, according to Orfila. The parliamentarians and Orfila settled on the sum of $81,000. "The problem came about how to pay the $81,000. For some reason they wanted this—Mr. Lasuen wanted to have a remittance directly to them. We were at all times consulting with counsel. . . . Then I asked Mr. Lasuen what name the check should be put at. He gave me the name of this gentleman [Mr. Blanc]," Orfila said.

Gray and Company lawyer Mark Moran told a different story. On December 18 he went to the Four Seasons Hotel, not far from the Power House in Georgetown. "As I arrived, Livingstone was coming out and I thought that was kind of odd. Lasuen shook hands with Livingstone and said, 'Thank you very much. It is a pleasure doing business with someone who understands how international business works.' That really caught my attention immediately," Moran said.

A few minutes after asking Herrero and Lasuen to sign a letter of recision, Moran learned that Orfila and Livingstone had given the parliamentarians a check for $81,000. Moran was furious. Most disturbing to him was the fact that Lasuen and Herrero told him that "they had discussed with Livingstone a method to pay the other $250,000."[76]

Moran learned that Gray had personally signed the check to Jean Pierre Blanc, who, as far as anyone knew, was a nonexistent person. "I could not understand how anybody could be so stupid as to do that," Moran said. Moran later told Orfila that the name on the check was not acceptable.[77] When Lasuen heard that, he exploded. Livingstone and Orfila went back to the Four Seasons Hotel to pick up the check. According to Orfila, Lasuen screamed: " 'We wanted to be your partners in Spain and create something that would be useful to you and to us. But we have a reputation. We have status. We don't want any sort of relation with people like yourself. Do not pay me. I don't want the money. Keep it. Forget about the whole thing.' And I never saw him again."[78]

Orfila later tried calling Lasuen. "He told me to go fly a kite. He said I never wanted to see you or anyone connected with Gray again."

Livingstone told a different story. He said that at the meeting at the hotel to retrieve the check he "apologized for the goddamn lawyers" and that he and Orfila got the Spanish legislators "working on new ways" to restructure their deal with Gray and Company. When Livingstone left for Christmas vacation, he thought the situation had been resolved.

In January Livingstone met with Orfila and was told to prepare a proposal for Gray and Company for promotion of high-tech industries for SERCOBE which he thought was the Spanish equivalent of the Chamber of Commerce. He hired Steven Saunders, a former deputy assistant U.S. trade representative, to write the proposal and delivered it to Lasuen in his room at the hotel. Lasuen was pleased with the proposal.

On January 4, 1985, Gray signed another check for $81,000. This one was made out to Luiz Magana. According to Orfila, it was an attempt to refund the fees Gray and Company was paid secretly by UNESA. Shortly after Gray wrote that check, he issued an order to Orfila and other company employees that no one was to have any further contact with UNESA or their representatives. Once again, Mark Moran stopped the check from being delivered. "I became convinced that the check was going to be passed to the politicians," Moran said.

Ken Gray, vindicated by the facts but hardly forgiven by his uncle, was dispatched with Moran to Spain to try and give the $81,000 check to UNESA directly and to close out the books on the Spanish disaster. Since Luiz Magana had negotiated the original deal with UNESA, Moran called him in Madrid to arrange repayment. Moran was shocked by what he learned. At first Magana treated Moran suspiciously when Moran proposed sending back the money to UNESA. According to Moran, Magana said: "'You really don't know, do you?' And I said, 'I have always understood it to be UNESA.' And he said, 'It's not UNESA. And they are not going to accept the check.'"[79]

Moran found out that UNESA "was not even aware we had an arrangement with these people, Herrero and Lasuen, that their introduction of UNESA to our people had been totally a social thing and [was not] in any way a concerted campaign on their part to get UNESA to come to Gray."[80] On February 5, Gray signed a third check, again, for $81,000, this time made out to Unidad Electrica, S.A., a utility company with close political ties to Lasuen and Herrero. Moran was at a loss when questioned as to the identity of Unidad Electrica or why a check was made out to such an entity.

Moran's visits to Madrid with Ken Gray confirmed his worst nightmares about the Spanish operation. In addition to allegations of money laundering and bribes to Spanish legislators, the office was hemorrhaging money and had not produced any new business. "When I got over there and started to see the way they were living, it was unbelievable! They were living like kings. They had servants. Carter had a penthouse overlooking a park in the center of Madrid. The penthouse was an entire block. The servants quarters had three or four bedrooms. I couldn't believe it. It was furnished with oriental rugs, enormous paintings . . . it was totally out of hand. We had an office that could accommodate fifteen people with only four [working there]. They were keeping the accounting in a shoe box. They had no books. Nothing. They were spending hundreds of thousands of dollars. They were so busy spending it, they didn't have time to keep track of it. To this day, God only knows what half this stuff was spent on.''[81]

Moran's worst fears about the operation were realized when Ken Gray took him to meet a potential client that Ken and Carter had been trying to develop. ''It sounded like a legitimate company, and they told us it was a nightclub chain. We were going to do PR for these guys. I went over there and I said, 'Okay I want to see this.' . . . It was a chain of houses of ill repute. When we walked into this place, I insisted on checking it out, we walked in it and all these scantily clad women came running up, 'Ken, Ken, we haven't seen you in months!' Everyone knew him by name. Oh God. Can you imagine if this got out? WASHINGTON'S PREMIER PUBLIC RELATIONS FIRM IS DOING PR FOR A SPANISH WHOREHOUSE.''

Moran said that Ken Gray defended the client by saying, '' 'This is the whorehouse that's frequented by members of the Spanish government. So we'll make lots of good contacts.' It was like a nightmare.''

Carter Clews was not curious why he was selected for the Spanish assignment. ''I think that they wanted to get someone who had no idea whatsoever about the financial end of it. Because I have no concept of finances. I'm the kind of person who adds two and two and gets five and is satisfied with the answer. In fact, [if] they were trying some sort of laundering operation, I can't think of a better person to have sent than me. One, because I wouldn't understand it and two, because I simply would not have cared.''

But Clews was being very modest. Although he grew to dislike Livingstone, Clews and Livingstone had known each other for years. In fact, he had come to work at Gray and Company in February 1983 at Livingstone's behest. It was Clews who recommended Rob Owen to Livingstone. According to Michael Pilgrim, Clews was also involved in intelligence operations and had been ''Rob Owen's control.'' But what Ken Gray and Carter Clews did not know was how they fit into the Madrid operation. What were their roles? How were they supposed to act?

''It [the Spanish Office] was originally intended as a smoke screen because these guys couldn't find their ass with both hands. Unfortunately, the smoke screen backfired because of their lack of understanding of their new role. They took it seriously. Being at such high-level exposure and using the wrong names in the right places screwed the deal,'' Pilgrim said.[82]

There are some indications that Clews knew more about what was happening in Madrid than Pilgrim suggests. In his notes of conversations with Lasuen, Clews wrote, ''JR will help est[ablish] a front group for energy PR.'' A week after arriving in Madrid, Clews and Gray went to a luncheon meeting with Pedro Rivero from UNESA, the utilities consortium, and Rivero's boss at UNESA, Indiges Oriole. At this meeting Clews passed a three-by-five note card to Rivero who, in turn, passed it to Oriole. Orfila had instructed Clews to present this card so UNESA could make the payment to Gray and Company. The card read: "The Equitable Trust Company, N.A., 100 South Charles Street." Under the address was the notation: "For credit to the escrow account of Gray and Company, Europe, account number 411-10-907."[83]

At that same luncheon Ken Gray discovered that the money that was supposed to be supplied to Gray and Company from UNESA was, in fact, *"coming from outside of Spain [and] going into the United States."*[84] Ken said that the money was coming "from what they referred to as an offshore well, an outside account, which is a Spanish expression, into Gray and Company's account." It was after that luncheon that "a warning light went off" in Ken Gray's mind. What was peculiar about the account was that there was no entity at that time called Gray and Company Europe.

According to Ken Gray, "There was a gentleman waiting in Baltimore for a phone call and the instructions to deposit the money."[85] That is when Ken Gray first began to get the idea that they were in Spain to operate a financial laundromat.

Livingstone later testified to the SEC that the money was transferred from a bank outside of Spain, he believed a Swiss bank account, because the Spanish parliamentarians were concerned about confidentiality and currency controls. In turn, Gray and Company was supposed to pay their Spanish associates through offshore accounts. "They wanted assets outside the country in the event that some cataclysmic event happened," Livingstone said. But when asked if he knew the source of the $250,000 transferred to Gray and Company, Livingstone said no.

Ken Gray learned that Clews had been involved with two other major transactions for Gray and Company. The first was an effort to land a major contract with McDonnell Douglas in Spain. The Spanish government had agreed to enter an "offset" program with the American aircraft company. McDonnell Douglas had sold the Spanish government $2 billion in aircraft, but it was on the condition that McDonnell find a comparable amount of markets for Spanish products. Gray and Company attempted to land a contract to help McDonnell find these markets to obtain the offset business, Ken Gray said.[86] Carter Clews noted that Lasuen wanted Gray and Company to tell the Pentagon that left-wing socialists were pushing hard to swap retention of NATO membership for dismantling of U.S. bases. "Perhaps we can help," he wrote. Neil Livingstone said that effort failed and the account was lost to a New York firm.

The Spanish/McDonnell deal was in conjunction with efforts Livingstone, Charles Crawford, and Robert Gray were making to become representatives of Defex—the giant Spanish arms consortium. Back at the Power House, Gray had asked the Ambassador from Spain to arrange an appointment with the visiting Spanish Defense Minister about representing Defex. Gray had Livingstone's assistant, Rob Owen, draft a proposal for Defex in which Gray and Company would assist them in getting Pentagon contracts. But

Owen, who was part of the secret Contra resupply operation while on Gray's payroll, wrote Gray a memorandum on June 11, 1984, saying, "I ran into some opposition from two sources. The sources were under the impression Gray and Company was chasing after the Defex account, and we were selling ourselves based on our friends at the Pentagon." Gray later said the charge made him livid.

According to Carter Clews, Lasuen and Herrero were assisting with the Defex account. On June 26, 1984, he referred to the two parliamentarians as "our established allies." In another memorandum Clews wrote "JR has promised to wield weight on our behalf."[87] The two legislators were also assisting Gray and Company in landing McDonnell Douglas Spain as an account. On that topic Clews telexed back to Washington: "JR is most interested in behind-the-scenes political help."[88] According to Pilgrim, Defex was being used to transship weapons in the arms-for-hostages, Iran–Contra deal. "Basically it goes Israel to Spain to Iran . . . and this is one of the things Neil is facilitating."

Marta Diaz said the Defex account was one that Clews talked about before his first week in Spain. Years later she discovered Defex was directly connected to the Iran-Contra scandal. Livingstone confirmed that the attempted deal was initiated through Spain's then Ambassador to the United States, who was a friend of Alex Orfila. Livingstone, to whom Owen reported, claimed he was out of town when Owen prepared his memorandum for Gray. According to Livingstone, "the Spanish defense industry was looking at that time for lobbying help, as is normal and customary for military sales offices of foreign governments, and there was a deep concern at the time there was not an adequate two-way street within the Spanish government, that we were not offsetting their purchases here—or their purchases from the United States with adequate procurement of defense material from Spain as per our NATO agreement. And so, that they were going to open an office in Washington to try to stimulate sales to the U.S. government." Once again Ken Gray found that Lasuen and Herrero were involved, insisting that they be the middlemen.

During this time, Lasuen was pressing Clews and Ken Gray to get Gray and Company Washington to lobby the Reagan administration to appoint the bank he worked with and two others to represent all 1,700 plus banks involved in the Latin debt crisis. The bank where Lasuen had connections, de Banco Central, along with two others, would negotiate the debt process by "leveling" the risk. Ken Gray said that Lasuen suggested that he "go and try and sell the bankers ways to offset the Latin American debt, and that there are two examples, that a banker, heavy in Argentina, but light in Colombia would trade with a bank light in Argentina and heavy in Colombia. He called that leveling. That was basically taking and leveling the debt and spreading the risk all over."[89]

The Spaniards wanted Gray and Company to intervene in getting the

United States to agree to limit the number of banks from over 1,700 to 3 Spanish banks involved in the Latin debt negotiations. "Lasuen also told us that Spanish bankers had tried to get the Spanish government to intervene, and he went on about how Felipe Gonzalez, the head of the Spanish government, . . . didn't want to and that was based because the United States and Great Britain don't do it. We thought there could be some lobbying done there to help him see the benefits of it."[90]

On September 15, 1984, Carter Clews telexed from Madrid that Lasuen was not releasing the second payment of $250,000 from UNESA because the consortium had become aware that the money was really being spent on right-wing political activity in Spain. Clews wrote, "Lasuen will not surrender funds. He says principal knows if kickback to be spent on right-wing PD, period."[91] Clews reported in the same memo on a phone call he had with Orfila, where Orfila expressed surprise that the clients knew of the "kickbacks" to Lasuen and Herrero.

Eventually Clews became so concerned over his own fate that he hired a lawyer in Spain, who advised him to get out of the country—there was a chance he would be arrested. Clews said he needed three weeks to straighten out his affairs but the lawyer said to leave immediately. "He said, 'You better have a suitcase and be at the airport in twenty-four hours or you're going to be here for the next fourteen years because you are the one they are going to put in jail.' So that is what I did. I went to the airport immediately and climbed on the plane and that was it, because of what Gray and Company had done."

Mark Moran wanted to try to keep the Spanish office open, but he soon learned how difficult it was to establish a public relations office in Spain. The cultural differences between the two countries' attitudes toward public relations and lobbying were almost insurmountable. Once he went to see the head of the Spanish Rail Company to try to get his business. The head of the company asked him, " 'What is public relations? Explain to me what this is.' And I explained, 'We'll help develop stories in the newspapers and improve the image.' And he said, 'Why would I want to pay you to do that because if I want a story in one of the papers, I'll just go and pay the reporter.' " Now Moran realized just what Gray and Company's first European office was really up against.

Moran asked Ken Gray to check out the business address of Adicsa, the parliamentarians' consulting firm. Ken Gray had one of his associates call Adicsa's telephone number scores of times at all times of day and night, but there was no answer. Gray sent him to the address listed by Lasuen and Herrero on the Adicsa letterhead. There were no offices at the address, only a run-down apartment building whose management and tenants had never heard of Gray's Spanish partners. This was the first real check anyone had done on the legislators.

Next Ken Gray went to the Ministry of Commerce to learn that Adicsa, or Analyses E Dictamenes S.A., had never been registered in Spain.

At the Power House, the mysterious Spanish deal caused suspicions to rise. "Internally, some people thought it was a front for the CIA. Other people thought it was a way to filter money illegally to the Spanish government," said one Gray employee. Michael Pilgrim speculates that one of the purposes of the funding route was to cover operations relating to the Iran-Contra scheme Oliver North had dreamed up.

Gray responded characteristically. He turned to the same company lawyers who had sat in on the meetings that had resulted in the contract with Spanish legislators to conduct a probe into the Spanish affair. Among those Gray chose to head the "investigation" were some of the least capable members of his rubber-stamp Board of Directors. Those investigating included a desperately ill Bryce Harlow, Robert Anderson—both of whom Gray had known since the Eisenhower administration—and William Bolger, who after leaving the Postal Service under a conflict-of-interest cloud eventually replaced Orfila as Vice Chairman. (Bolger, like Orfila, began his career at Gray and Company with a minor scandal. While still Reagan's Postmaster General, he negotiated for a job with the Direct Mail Marketing Association [now the Direct Marketing Association]. When the unions and others protested, he went to work for Gray and Company, instead, and brought the association to the firm as a client.)

In mid-January Charles Crawford went to Neil Livingstone's office and told him "that Alex may have been engaged in activities that would bring some disrepute upon the company." Crawford saw Livingstone's resumé on his desk and asked if Livingstone was planning on leaving the company. Crawford told Livingstone, "We're going to need you all the more if something happens to Orfila."

On February 11, Gray called Orfila to advise him to get a lawyer. Orfila insisted that he did not need a lawyer. Gray then told Orfila that there would be an internal investigation, and that after that day's Board of Directors' meeting he would probably be asked for his resignation. He again urged Orfila to get a lawyer. Orfila maintained that this was a tremendous shock to him.[92]

Jim Jennings, who sat in on the board meeting that resulted in Orfila's resignation, presented Gray's party-line statement to the SEC. "The Spanish matter had raised questions of Alex's ability to run his part of the ship as tightly as we want all aspects of the company to be run. This is kind of the straw that broke the camel's back. When Alex joined the firm, he joined under a cloud, because it was uncovered that he was taking two salaries. It was, while it was legal, it was considered an affront to the OAS. And so the rug was pulled out from under him from really the earliest days of his joining the firm. . . . The Spanish matter, being one of the first things he sank his teeth into, just left—it left a bad taste in everybody's mouth, because it wasn't as neat as our style. . . . There was just no way to put humpty dumpty back together again . . ."[93] Thus, Orfila became the first official scapegoat.

Livingstone met with the lawyers on the internal investigation and then left for a three-week trip to Turkey. He testified before the SEC that he was on company business to Turkey. Alejandro Orfila was uncertain what business Livingstone would have had in Turkey since the International Division had nothing to do with the Turkish account, because Gary Hymel, who ran the Turkey account, did not want the International Division involved.[94] Livingstone said that Michael Ledeen, who also played a key role in Iran–Contra and in the private intelligence network, was also on the trip.[95]

When Livingstone returned on February 11, 1985, he was told to go to Vice Chairman William Bolger's office. He was told that the Madrid office was under investigation and that he should take a leave of absence. Livingstone hit the roof. "You guys blessed the deal. I am the only guy in the whole firm that has been raising hell on it and it's cost me dearly within the firm."

Livingstone appealed to Gray and to his old friend Charles Crawford. Gray told him he had nothing to worry about, but Livingstone soon learned otherwise. He was told the company had concerns about his "management judgment" of the Spanish office. He was flabbergasted. "Questions had been raised of whether I'd exercised adequate prudence . . . had kept a close-enough eye on the Chairman and Vice Chairman [Gray and Orfila] of the company." Livingstone said. "I was so floored and I was on my way to my grandfather's funeral in Montana that day. I was in no mood to really respond. They said, 'Well, we just want you to take administrative leave, and, in the meantime, get counsel. I'm sure that we will resolve these various outstanding differences, but Orfila has been terminated.'"[96]

It soon became obvious to Livingstone that if he played ball and resigned he would be rewarded. "Comments that were made to the effect they were not at all interested in what I had to say, and that they expected me to terminate quietly by May thirty-first, and if I did that appropriately, that they would see that certain financial considerations were made and so on." Livingstone said he was outraged. "If there was a problem, . . . the problem would be in what I saw to be a cover-up, which would impact adversely on me, and I believed that if the company was not going to behave responsibly, that I would bring this matter to the SEC and the Department of Justice's attention and so inform[ed] the company in my resignation letter."

Livingstone's letters caused Gray and Company to rush to the Securities and Exchange Commission (SEC) and the Justice Department before him in hopes of mitigating federal investigations into the Spanish matter. The Department of Justice was supposed to investigate violations of the Foreign

Corrupt Practices Act and the Foreign Agents Registration Act. Since Gray and Company was a publicly traded business, the SEC also had jurisdiction.

Robert Crowley's warnings to Bill Casey years earlier about the problems that could arise if the intelligence community tried to use public companies had come true.

Carter Clews feared Gray would use his friendship with Attorney General Edwin Meese to make Clews the fall guy. "The Justice Department was supposed to be doing an investigation and what, it's been years, and I've never been talked to. Never. Gray was the one who told me that the investigation was dead . . ."

Clews went to the *Washington Post* to try to protect himself from retribution. When a story about the Spanish operation appeared on the front page in March, it included a statement from Gray's spokesman that said, "Robert Gray had no knowledge of the matter until questions were raised recently."[97] Livingstone's and Orfila's abrupt departures were now public for everyone to see. They both denied any wrongdoing.

Livingstone insisted that he was unfairly caught up in the scandal and that, in fact, he was the first to warn Gray about it. He felt that when he left the International Division would decline and that Gray and Company would not last much longer. If Gray and Company profited in part because of the perception that the firm had ties to the intelligence community, mostly through the International Division, the failures of that division contributed to its downfall. "That company was so profitable until early in eighty-five when it went downhill. Like that, the International Division collapsed. They brought in a succession of incompetent people . . . I can tell you truthfully that I am still not convinced a crime was committed. Whatever was committed bordered on impropriety, seemingly. But it looks like it may have violated Spanish law more than U.S. law," Livingstone said.

When asked about charges that he was part of a private intelligence operation run off-the-books by the Reagan–Bush administration, Livingstone was far less certain in his answer. "It was not the CIA manipulating the Spanish government, or anything. I admit I had an agenda that I wanted to see knock out Felipe Gonzalez." Livingstone said this was in line with his own ideology "and other things that we were doing for the administration, but it was not illegal or wrong or anything else. But it got changed, the deal got changed."

In the end Livingstone said the Spanish episode caused the fall of Gray and Company which "has never been as profitable again as it was prior to this time. . . . It killed the company. This was the watershed that killed the company."

For Carter Clews, the aftermath of Spain was not pleasant. "I just told them that I wanted a computer system and six months severance pay, that I was quitting and I have it in writing that I quit, that I resigned, not under any pressure. Then Mankiewicz told the *Washington Post* that I was fired, which was just a lie and he knew it.'' For Clews, the mystery of what went on in Spain got deeper at a dinner he had at conservative writer Victor Lasky's house one evening. Lasky asked Clews about what went on in Spain. Clews said a reporter called him and suggested it was an Agency operation. ''Victor said, 'Well, I've talked with Casey and why don't you just leave that alone. Pull back off that and leave it alone.' He was very close to Casey.''

When interviewed, Clews, the former head of Gray and Company's first and only international office, was working for a small publication in suburban Baltimore that answered its telephone by repeating the digits dialed. In retrospect, Clews said he believed the money funneled into Gray and Company was to influence the Spanish elections in favor of the Popular Alliance party.

Eventually Ken Gray married and returned to Nebraska where, like his uncle forty years earlier, he had little success in several small businesses. On the day he was interviewed, the former international public-relations executive was selling popcorn out of a basement storage room in a small town, not far from Hastings.

Michael Pilgrim said he saw his friend Neil Livingstone about four days after he was fired. ''Neil was a little bitter because he came over and was told that he was Gray's successor, his stepson, and was going to take over. Neil would have been excellent at that. He was embittered about that. . . . Even at that time he understood that Gray had to find a scapegoat and Neil was the logical scapegoat.''

Livingstone filed a law suit against Gray and Company seeking compensation. He claimed that he could not find work at comparable pay because Gray and Company had ruined his reputation. Instead, Livingstone left Gray and Company and followed Rob Owen to work at the Institute on Terrorism and Sub-National Conflict. Despite the discovery by Jack McGeorge that the Institute was a front for the private intelligence network, Livingstone has kept it going, running it out of his apartment at the Watergate. Publicly he continues to appear occasionally on television as a terrorism expert and to write books and magazine articles on the subject.

Alejandro Orfila left Gray and Company with a large cash settlement, plus retention of all of the clients he had brought to the company. He came to the realization years later that Gray and Company Spain was never supposed to be a successful public relations operation. ''This is the reason they didn't care if they were performing or not,'' Orfila said.

Mark Moran eventually reorganized the Spanish office, and, in doing so, cut its once uncontrollable budget by 75 percent. He recruited an American woman, who had been Ken Gray's girlfriend in Spain, to run the more modest office. According to Moran, ''after seven or eight months, it just wasn't making any headway. We made the decision that Spain was not the right place and we closed the operation down.''

After Moran had, as he put it, "gone through the ringer for a year or two and it really cost me my marriage," he decided to leave Gray and Company. Moran tired of being the inside investigator. "You constantly have to be the bearer of bad tidings and constantly have to tell the Chairman this person's got to go or that person's got to go; it's just a very tense position to be [in] because most businessmen look at lawyers as obstructionists anyway."

In Spain, the Popular Alliance party disappeared and Lasuen ran for Mayor of Madrid, finishing a distant third. Marta Williams Diaz became a reporter for ABC and distinguished herself with new information about Gray's alleged role in the "October Surprise." Diaz stayed in touch with Ken Gray. In January 1986—many months before Attorney General Ed Meese announced the diversion that became known as the Iran-Contra scandal—Diaz said Ken Gray detailed Iran-Contra over the telephone to her. Her notes reflect a "Larry North" (Lawrence Oliver North) as being a major figure in Ken Gray's scenario.[98]

14

POWER FAILURE

Gray is forever in controversy, as you may have noticed.

George Worden

By April 1985, Gray and Company, especially its International Division, was floundering. With Orfila and Livingstone abruptly gone, Gray needed to find someone quickly who could duplicate their key qualifications: Orfila's high-society and international contacts and Livingstone's ties to the intelligence community. Coincidentally, at the same time at the White House, there was a politician with a problem. It was perfect. Gray could help the politician and meet his personnel needs at the same time.

Admiral Daniel J. Murphy had a long, successful career in the Navy. He had gotten to know George Bush when Bush was CIA director in 1976 and Murphy had served as a deputy on his staff. According to Navy colleagues, Murphy was known for his organizational and administrative abilities. He was considered a good judge of character and good at getting work done on time.

Murphy became Vice President George Bush's Chief of Staff in the first term of the Reagan administration. Prior to taking that job, he had been the Deputy Undersecretary for Policy for the Department of Defense during the Carter administration. The Special Advisory Staff, a small organization that independently evaluated and reviewed all defense intelligence operations, reported to him. Like several others in 1979–80, it became clear to Murphy that he was not going to advance in a second Carter term, and he switched his allegiances to his old boss, George Bush.

After the 1984 election, Bush's closest advisors were not content to sit back and enjoy the landslide victory. Bush's performance during the campaign had been less than exceptional. The debate with vice-presidential candidate Geraldine Ferraro had not gone well. Bush's public statements often seemed awkward. The media ridiculed him. Comedians were making wimp jokes. The conservatives did not trust him. If Bush were going to become a viable presidential candidate in 1988 certain problems had to be addressed.

Two things, among others, had to be done. First, Bush's longtime companion and powerful member of his staff, Jennifer Fitzgerald, had to be removed from the White House; Bush's sexual indiscretions had to be covered up if he ever hoped to be president.[1] Fitzgerald left to head Bush's Senate office. For related reasons, Murphy had to go. The public story why Murphy left the White House was that he needed to earn more money to pay for treatment for his wife's illness. She was an invalid and needed a great deal of expensive medical care.[2] In reality, Murphy enjoyed the company of women besides his wife and had a worldwide address book worthy of any sailor.[3] His lifestyle and his close relationship with the Vice President greatly offended both Barbara Bush and Jennifer Fitzgerald. Murphy was not popular with either of these two, very powerful women.

At intergovernmental meetings, whenever the Vice President's office was represented by Murphy, "we'd wink at each other because we knew we could roll him," one high-level Reagan official said. "I mean that's an awful thing to say, but it's true. . . . It's my understanding that Mrs. Bush got him fired. When Bush was really being serious about the presidency, she said, 'Well, if you want it, I've got one condition and that is that he's got to go.' But she did put the law down, and it concerned Jennifer, and it concerned Murphy's black book. A friend of mine who traveled with him in the 1980s said it was absolutely unbelievable. It was Barbara giving an edict." "I understood he was not missed when he left the White House," said Sheila Tate.[4]

The arrangement that led Murphy to go to Gray and Company directly involved Bush. Murphy told the *Washington Post* that Bush telephoned Gray and said, " 'Dan is leaving and I'd appreciate it if you could talk to him.' I was offered vice president of the firm, an offer I couldn't refuse."[5] Gray told the *Post* a somewhat different story. "I was over talking with Bush about something else and he said Dan Murphy is leaving and I said that I'd like to talk to him." "The conversation was between the White House and Gray and Murphy because, I mean, he didn't put an ad in the paper or anything," joked a Gray and Company senior vice president.

In 1985 Gray did not need an administrator; he needed a "rainmaker" and a protector—someone who could bring in clients and shield him politically through his intelligence ties. Gray thought that Murphy could meet these needs, that he was a two-for-one bargain. The bonus was that Gray was also helping George Bush at the same time. "Gray was very active in working angles. His angle with Bush was Admiral Murphy," recalled a Gray and Company official.

Gray needed protecting. In May 1985 the SEC opened an official investigation into Gray and Company's Spanish operation. According to Livingstone, Gray ended up paying enormous legal fees because his attorneys had him convinced that he was going to prison. "Gray tried to get in Admiral Murphy quickly. . . . Again, Gray went to this agency-type connection. . . . He had to protect his ass here some way, particularly because I wasn't there and there was fear that I would go public," Livingstone said.[6] To try to keep Livingstone in line, Tongsun Park called and offered him an opportunity in his enterprises. Livingstone said he turned him down.

To Murphy, heading Gray and Company's International Division was a great job. He was making $200,000 a year (more than double his previous salary) and he had inherited Orfila's "air-force-carrier"–sized office. When Don Nielsen, who worked for Murphy at the Pentagon, went to visit him, Nielsen found him to be "a little bit dazzled" by the glitzy trappings of Gray and Company.[7] On the public relations side of the equation, the work at Gray and Company was a totally new environment for Murphy. "There's a difference when you have to be creative and think and when you 'follow orders.' In the Navy, it looked like he was a great guy because he did what he was told. At Gray and Company, you had to do a little thinking. Sometimes it wasn't very smart, but it was thinking," William Corson said. Nielsen had the impression that Murphy was out of his element. "I won't say he was a pushover, but I think he was a little bit naive. But he was an admiral, and he dealt with people like an admiral deals with them. He expected people to do what they were told when he told them to do something."

The atmosphere at Gray and Company changed dramatically with Murphy's arrival. Orfila had left under difficult circumstances, and the top officials of the firm were rethinking some fundamental operational procedures. Murphy was brought in to head the damaged International Division at a very difficult time.[8] "The focus of the division changed a bit, and the company was going through some different kinds of changes. There was some retrenchment going on, and there were merger talks going on. . . . It was very much a change. Not only was there a change in the style, I think there certainly was a change in direction and policy that was set by the management," said Adonis Hoffman.

At Gray and Company, Murphy's staff were mainly people whom Neil Livingstone and others had hired. The Spanish scandal had a demoralizing effect on what had been "the hottest shop in town," and there was a feeling that the glory years were over. Perhaps not surprisingly, Murphy, having stepped into this atmosphere, was not welcomed with open arms. "Nobody really cared for him very much when he took over and he wanted his own people there and at least, to me, it was not a happy place," recalled Barry Schochet.[9] Another top executive called Murphy "incredibly pompous, imperious, and obnoxious."

In addition to these problems, to many PR professionals, the whole idea of hiring former political figures, people who had no PR experience, seemed ridiculous. "Gray, with this star-quality thing, he's been wrong just about every time," George Worden said.[10] "He'd get carried away by these guys . . . I swear to God, he gets dazzled by Murphy's four stars and the fact that he was George Bush's Chief of Staff. Chief of Staff to the Vice President? What kind of job is that? Anybody can do that. The Vice President doesn't do anything."

Murphy was not at Gray and Company because of his knowledge of public relations or even military experience. "For those people who have served in high-level positions in Washington, it really is not necessarily a matter of the amount of substantive knowledge that they have about an issue. It's the position and relationships. Dan Murphy probably had interacted at some point with all the key members [of the Reagan–Bush administration]—just about anybody who was anybody in this town. So when he picked up the phone to call, he could get ahead and the door would be opened. And maybe somebody like me, or someone who had a background in substantive areas, would go in with him. We would be kind of the lieutenant or the worker and he would be the field marshal to open the door and get us in," explained Adonis Hoffman.

Murphy did not develop additional Pentagon business as Gray had hoped. "Murphy was supposed to take it commercial and do a lot of the [Department of Defense] work, and it just never came to fruition," said Mike Pilgrim. "I think Gray thought of Murphy as a disappointment," confirmed a Gray and Company executive, who then went on to say this was not Murphy's fault. "I think his uncertainty as to what he was doing was innocent because no one was telling him what to do. He spent a lot of time going to Korea and Taiwan looking for business, but for some reason, none of that business materialized. I don't know why."

But Murphy did have ties to the intelligence community. Gray and Company could continue to "carry water for the administration" whenever necessary. Gray advertised these connections by promoting Murphy in its brochures and SEC filings as a former deputy director of the CIA. Murphy happily played up to the media his connections. He told CNN, "When I left my White House job on a Friday, I reported to work here the following Monday. Four of the five problems I had worked on [at Gray and Company] . . . I had worked on the previous week [at the White House]. The relationship is that close. So you have to conclude that people who have gone to the Vice President for help have gone to other places for help, including Gray and Company."[11]

One problem area in which Bush's office was involved was Iran–Contra, as were individuals at Gray and Company. The *San Francisco Examiner* reported that Felix Rodriguez, the Cuban-American agent and friend of Neil Livingstone's, was involved in the secret airlift operation that carried guns to the Nicaraguan contras. The newspaper said that he had been placed in Central America by the Vice President's office.[12] The *Los Angeles Times* reported that Rodriguez had told associates that he reported to Bush on his activities.[13] Like Murphy and many of the others, Rodriguez had known Bush since his days at the CIA.

Another issue in which both offices were involved and that became controversial over the next few years was Bush's knowledge of drug-running by Panamanian leader Manuel Antonio Noriega. Murphy had been operations manager of a drug task force that Bush headed when Bush led the fight against drugs for the administration. Twice in 1987, Murphy flew to Panama to meet secretly with Noriega, ostensibly to try to develop business for the public relations firm, but in reality he was relaying information to Noriega for the administration.[14]

Arms dealer Sarkis Soghanalian confirms that he was asked to supply a jet and crew on an emergency basis for Murphy's trips to see Noriega. "I was told they did not want an official aircraft to be used, so they came to me."[15] (Soghanalian is currently in a federal prison serving a sentence for conspiring to sell embargoed arms to Iraq in the 1980s.) Murphy's traveling companion was Tongsun Park, who was representing Japanese interests as he had done with Gray, CNN, and the JCIC.

Another disturbing conjunction between the Reagan–Bush administration's agenda and a possible Gray and Company overture to a new client involved Iraq. During the Iran–Iraq War in the 1980s, the United States publicly led an arms embargo against these two countries while it secretly supplied both nations with weapons. In the early 1980s, representatives of Global Research, which was founded by Gray's old Nixon associate, former U.S. Attorney General John Mitchell, took a trip to Baghdad to facilitate a military supply deal with Saddam Hussein. Mitchell's daughter Marty, who was a registered foreign agent working for Gray and Company, went along on the trip to Iraq in an attempt to solicit Saddam Hussein's government as a client. (Ironically, several years later, Gray's company would be representing Iraq's mortal enemy, Kuwait.)

Gray flatly denies any effort on the part of Gray and Company to seek Iraq as a client in the 1980s.[16] Marty Mitchell was a research assistant at Gray and Company, and it is conceivable that Gray was unaware of her activities, including the trip to Iraq, though Neil Livingstone, Mitchell's boss, said Gray was aware of her efforts.

Soghanalian, who had supplied the plane for Murphy and Park to travel to Panama, also was a partner in arms dealing with Iraq. He agreed to bring Marty Mitchell and former Nixon Marine aide Jack Brennan to Baghdad (Brennan joined the Bush White House as director of administrative operations in October, 1991). Mitchell's purpose was to sell the Iraqi government on hiring Gray and Company to improve Iraq's image in the United States. According to Soghanalian and others on the trip, it was a public relations disaster.

At a gathering one weekend at the Iraqi Defense Minister's ranch outside of Baghdad, Marty Mitchell had her first encounter with the Arab practice of firing guns in the air as a way of celebrating. After an early barbecue, the men began to shoot at impromptu targets with machine guns. Soghanalian recalled that Marty Mitchell became very angry and later complained to her father. Soghanalian was so angry at Marty Mitchell's petulance that he refused to recommend Gray and Company to the Defense Minister.

In many of these areas Murphy could be as helpful to the administration on the outside at Gray and Company as he was in the White House. "He was doing some ambassador without portfolio . . . to make some contacts that the U.S. government doesn't want to do officially, but they all wink and nod and know that he's speaking for the big man," Corson said.

Publicly Gray and Company set about celebrating its fifth anniversary with all the hype one would expect from a prominent PR firm. The shareholder report was typically glowing: "Take off. Existence, survival, success, take-off, and resource maturity have been described as the five stages of small business growth in a study published by the *Harvard Business Review*. As we mark Gray and Company's fifth anniversary, we are both pleased and challenged to find ourselves poised at the 'take-off' stage that bridges our entrepreneurial success of the past five years with future longterm corporate diversification and growing earning power."[17] In reality, Gray and Company was heading for a crash landing instead of "resource maturity."

Although the Spanish office and the CNN/Moroccan controversy were beginning to blemish some of the once positive stories, the press still wrote of the firm in glowing terms. The *National Journal*, in a story on how the Washington PR industry is different from the rest of the country, that it peddles a product called access, and that this PR "mystique" was enhanced by the recent influx of well-known political figures who had left prominent government jobs to join public relation firms, wrote, "More than anything else, the access mystique has been built by one man, Robert Keith Gray."[18]

By 1985 Gray and Company was Washington's largest PR firm, with 127 employees divided not only into the three divisions (public relations, lobbying, international), but also into subgroup specialties, such as agriculture, trade, health, telecommunications, and other policy issues. In its public brochures and filings it flaunted the political backgrounds of its employees, which, along with Gray's continuing public socializing with top Reagan administration officials, left the impression that as much as anything else Gray and Company sold high-level access.

In its annual report to stockholders Gray and Company mentioned a joke told at The Gridiron Club dinner as evidence of its prestige and influence. The dinner, "an annual Washington rite where the city's most prominent politicians and journalists, along with the President and his Cabinet, meet for an evening of good-natured spoofing," featured a line from Treasury Secretary James Baker that Geraldine Ferraro (Walter Mondale's running mate in his unsuccessful bid for the White House) "seemed to be the only important Washington figure who has not gone to work for Gray and Company after leaving public office."[19]

But more than one can play the access game, and in 1985 Gray was joined by someone with undeniable Reagan access: Michael K. Deaver. Deaver had been President and Mrs. Reagan's advisor and friend for twenty years. He announced that he was leaving his White House job as deputy chief of staff because the pay was too low. There were discussions at Gray and Company about trying to hire Deaver, but he was not interested in working for someone else. Not far from the Power House, in elegant Georgetown offices, he started Michael K. Deaver and Associates. Instantly several top business clients hired him.

Like Deaver, Gray denied that he was selling access. Gray told the *National Journal* his PR mission in Washington was "prioritization. We all are so inundated with issues and so inundated with printed materials, electronic bombardment. It takes somebody to say, 'Ooooo, wait a minute, this is important. Pay attention to this right here.' Somebody has to ring the bell about the issues."[20] But there are only so many bells to ring in Washington and only so many clients willing to pay tens of thousands of dollars a month for PR Avon ladies. In the mid-1980s, Deaver had real access. He even kept his White House pass. The battle lines were drawn.

"Dual in the PR Corral," said the *New York Times* headline about Deaver's entry into the field. The move would obviously "pit him directly against the city's resident PR 'guru,' Robert K. Gray. . . . The experts say Mr. Deaver . . . is likely to cut a formidable figure in the image-shaping and influence-marketing field, possibly supplanting Mr. Gray as the man outside the Administration with the closest perceived ties to its leader."[21] To add to the thrill of the Beltway battle it was known that there was considerable animosity between the two men.

The last thing Gray needed was competition. His company was in serious financial and legal trouble and he was beginning to look for a buyer. To make matters worse, Deaver's "new brazenness" in leaving the White House and turning around and working on issues he had dealt with while in government (something Dan Murphy and countless others were doing) brought a wave of bad publicity that hurt the entire industry. *Washington Post* political reporter and columnist David Broder wrote: "What is striking now is the brazenness of the commercialization of contacts, the absolute unabashed exploitation of government service for private gain. It is this that is different [from the past] and disturbing to many of the old Washington hands—Republicans as well as Democrats."[22]

In February 1986, the *Post* ran a front-page story entitled "Foreigners Hiring Reagan's Ex-Aides." "Former officials of the Reagan administration and influential Reagan–Bush campaign aides are being paid millions of dollars by foreign governments and corporations, in many cases to help those clients block or counter administration initiatives.'' The article went on to say that U.S. business leaders complained that foreigners had greater access to the White House than they did, and quoted congressmen as linking influence peddling by lobbyists for foreigners to the record U.S. trade deficits.

The storm Deaver had started buffeted Gray as well. The *Post* article criticized Gray and Company for "collecting millions of dollars in fees from foreign clients, many of whom are involved in trade battles with American firms or the U.S. government. Gray and Company . . . was paid $1.9 million by foreign clients in a six-month period last year. . . . Among those fees was $246,000 for one month's work handling the American visit of Susumo Nikaido, vice president of Japan's ruling Liberal Democratic Party (LDP) and eight other party leaders. This visit, according to Japanese officials, was aimed at reducing trade tensions with the United States. Arrangements for the Nikaido visit were handled by retired admiral Daniel J. Murphy, former chief of staff for Vice President Bush."[23]

In March 1986, the cover of *Time* featured Deaver talking on the phone in his limousine with a headline reading "Influence Peddling in Washington." Inside was a similar picture of Gray. For the first time, the revolution Gray had helped initiate was getting national—and highly critical—attention. "There have been lobbyists in Washington for as long as there have been lobbies. But never before have they been so numerous or quite so brazen. What used to be . . . a somewhat shady and disreputable trade has burst into the open with a determined show of respectability. Tempted by the staggering fees lobbyists can command, lawmakers and their aides are quitting in droves to cash in on their connections. For many, public service has become a mere internship for a lucrative career as a hired gun for special interests."[24]

For a man like Gray who had spent decades carefully nurturing his public image, and who was used to glowing profiles in national media, the *Time* article must have made him wince. "A superlobbyist like Robert Gray, a former minor official in the Eisenhower Administration who parlayed his promotional genius and friendship with the Reagans into a $20 million PR and lobbying outfit, is in the papers more than most congressional committee chairmen. . . . As one of the most successful lobbyists in town, Bob Gray naturally has his detractors, and they accuse him of overselling businessmen on his ability to solve all their Washington problems with a few phone calls. 'Gray is so overrated it's unbelievable,' says one U.S. Senator. 'He makes a big splash at parties, but his clients aren't getting a lot for their money.' Gray insists that he never promises more than he can deliver. But his own clients sometimes grumble that, for a fat fee, they get little more than a handshake from a Cabinet member at a cocktail party.''

Gray had walked a fine line between self-aggrandizement and self-promotion, a distinction Deaver completely ignored. "His [Gray's] own hype never got to the point Deaver's did where everybody hated him for it," said Carter Clews, "Deaver's pose on the cover of *Time* magazine was so un-Washington that he should have known that he stepped over the line. Washington is a city where you don't flash it. You don't flaunt it and that was what he did. And that was just a step too far. Gray knew just how far to go in self aggrandizement."[25] But the bad publicity Deaver engendered hurt Gray at a time when he could least afford it. "That whole side of the business [foreign clients] just sort of flopped right when Mike Deaver had his problems. Both Gray and Deaver decided to be so highly visible representing countries— which is exactly what the countries did not want, that visibility. I know Gray and Company published a list of clients on which a lot of the countries appeared, which was instead of promoting the client, you're promoting yourself. In any event, it soon . . . turned to a liability. There was a period there in 1986 where that business just went away," explained a Gray and Company executive.

A month after the *Time* article, Gray wrote an editorial that appeared in the *New York Times* entitled, "In Defense of Lobbyists," which resembled the one he had written twenty years earlier:

> A glance at the press these days somehow makes it appear that . . . the major concern of Americans is an increase in advocacy here in the nation's capital. Reports speak darkly about the rapidly growing power of the lobbyist, about an "excess of access," about the "tidal wave" of Administration officials who have turned to private practice for profit.
>
> But access—the ability to reach decisionmakers on behalf of private clients—is Washington's most perishable commodity. Misuse it and you lose it . . .
>
> Access is an earned, essential raw material for the lobbying process but vastly overrated as a finished product all by itself . . .
>
> The successful lobbyist is a prism, refracting a client's need into a series of basic, attractive messages designed to get the attention of decisionmakers. Combining expertise with access over the years creates a credible voice . . .[26]

In the best PR tradition, Gray turned "influence peddling" into "advocacy"; trading on government service for personal profit to leaving for "private practice"; "access" to "raw material"; a lobbyist to "a prism." Gray promoted his published editorial to his stockholders "as part of a national debate concerned with the standards and responsibilities of public communications consultants in the nation's capital."[27] His defense was not compelling, and did little to help save his company or sway public opinion.

Nineteen eighty-six was a bad year for lobbyists, in general, and a terrible one for Gray and Company. In January, Gray and Company agreed to represent the Marxist government of Angola. Surprisingly, Admiral Dan Murphy recruited the new client. "I know that he [Murphy] was working very intimately there. He went to the country. It's a Marxist country. And the irony is: Here's a Marxist country that the United States does not recognize, has no formal or official relationships with, and the former Chief of Staff under the then current Vice President, former deputy director of the CIA, former Commander of the Sixth Fleet, [is] representing this Marxist government," recalled Adonis Hoffman.

There were many reasons why Gray and Company embraced such a controversial client. Barry Schochet said that some of the African-Americans in the firm were pressing to obtain some African accounts, but that when the Angolan government arose as a possible client some of the staffers, especially a woman named Lauri Fitz (now Fitz-Pegado, who still works for Gray), did not realize the complexity of the issues surrounding the Angolan Civil War. Once the Angolans and Murphy got together, events moved quickly. "Maybe [Murphy] already knew the U.N. people from Angola because Angola has not had an embassy here ever and no administration has ever recognized them since they seized power in 1975. Very quickly, all of a sudden, he [Murphy] was on the plane and was going to Luanda. He went to Luanda and gave a speech in a soccer stadium with a huge crowd of people, claiming the United States was going to start supporting the people of Angola and he was going to be there to help them. The thirty- to fifty thousand people went wild. People from within Gray were very, very upset about it, the more conservative people. This leaked to the *Washington Times* and the people in the White House found out about it and it was a very, very intense campaign to push Gray away from this," said Barry Schochet.

The United States had no diplomatic relations with Angola. The Reagan administration, both diplomatically and militarily, supported UNITA, a South-African–backed rebel movement headed by Joseph Savimbi fighting to overthrow the government of Angola, Gray's new client. To the American conservative movement, UNITA was the African equivalent of the Contras; their African "freedom fighters." Instantly, Gray and Company found itself in a tough, no-holds-barred lobbying and public relations battle with a competing, conservative, largely Republican firm, Black, Manafort, Stone, Kelly, Inc., which represented UNITA.

Washington conservatives were outraged. Before Gray and Company had a chance to hold its first National Press Club breakfast to showcase its new client, the conservatives swung into action. The conservative newspaper, the *Washington Times*, editorialized against Gray and Company. It pointed out that Morocco, one of Gray's other clients, was a UNITA ally. It indirectly blamed Frank Mankiewicz, "George McGovern's old campaign manager," not Murphy.[28] (Ironically, the newspaper is owned by the Reverend Sun Myung Moon, whom Gray had defended in his tax-fraud case.)

Conservatives, especially at Gray and Company, were not comfortable with the Gray/Mankiewicz alliance. "Gray said he was conservative, but conservative clients he didn't have much use for. Of course, Frank hated them. He tried to get us to take communist Nicaragua [and Cuba]," said Carter Clews. When the firm obtained Young Americans for Freedom, an ultraconservative political organization, as a client, Mankiewicz called in his staff and told them, "The Nazi Storm Troopers are coming over." The Angolan account brought these ideological tensions to the fore. Niels Holchs, as enthusiastic an employee as anyone at Gray and Company, refused to work on the Angolan account.[29]

Encouraged by conservative activists like Paul Weyrich and Charles Black, young "outraged" Savimbi backers picketed in front of Gray and Company's offices. First they tried to burn a hammer-and-sickle flag. Then they chained themselves to the railings outside of Gray's new headquarters inside the posh Washington Harbour complex on the Potomac River. This set up a showdown in which the best PR men got to battle it out. A Gray and Company senior vice president recalled a knockout blow with delight. "Frank Mankiewicz and I sent three junior Gray and Company employees down to the basement to get their car, and we gave them an empty video camera, and they drove around the corner and got out of the car. They were all three our employees, and one of them had done a bit of television work, and they walked up to the people who had chained themselves and said they were from Channel Five and they were doing a story. So we interviewed them—lights, camera, the whole thing—interviewed them for about ten minutes and then left. Frank said that as soon as we'd done the interview they'd leave, because all they were interested in was publicity. As soon as our people got in the car and drove around the corner, they all uncuffed themselves and left. So that's how we got rid of the demonstrators. We did a phony interview. I'm sure they're still turning on TV every night waiting for the six o'clock news."

Gray and Company instructed Angola's foreign trade minister to wear a conservative suit in his debate on the "MacNeil-Lehrer NewsHour" with Savimbi, who liked to wear Nehru jackets. But the firm's advocacy of Angola reached the absurd when Murphy bragged to the *Wall Street Journal* about the Marxist country's deep religious convictions. "I was surprised to learn that everybody goes to church on Sunday. At least one third of the Politburo members are practicing Presbyterians."[30]

Gray and Company had touched upon sacred conservative ground and the controvery was just beginning to heat up. An unsigned letter was circulated around the White House, allegedly from Pat Buchanan's communications office:

Dear White House Staffer,
    Bob Gray and Company, a Washington lobbying group, is now pimping

for the communist government in Angola. The communist government already has some 35,000 Cuban troops and thousands of Soviet, East German, Libyan, and PLO terrorists to defend it from the Angolan people. But now they are asking Bob Gray and Company to help them too.

Why?

Because Gray and Company told the Angolan dictatorship that they can make people like you do what they want.

While you work hard—at government pay—to promote the interests of the Reagan presidency, the American people and the freedom fighters of Angola, Gray and Company intends to make hundreds of thousands of dollars by asking you to betray your president, your nation, and your principles.

Let those who profit from tyranny know that you won't help them in their little get-rich-quick scheme.

For those who struggle for freedom in Angola, for those who have seen their churches burned, their land stolen, please do not answer the phone when the call says, "This is Bob Gray calling."

Please let the Angolan people and the American people know that the White House will not help Gray get rich by talking you into abandoning the brave people of Afghanistan, Angola, Cambodia, Nicaragua, and Ethiopia.

Remember, the phone call you take from Gray may be the one that justifies the hundreds of thousands of dollars he is getting from the communist government of Angola.

Don't help pay for the pink Cadillac Gray will buy with his contract money—a car that will match his morality.

BOB GRAY IS PIMPING FOR THE CUBANS AND COMMUNISTS IN ANGOLA.

DON'T LET HIM USE YOU.

Angola was reportedly offering more than a million dollars for representation in Washington at a time when Gray and Company desperately needed the money. One high-level Gray and Company executive said this was why Gray accepted such a controversial client. The company's high profile worked against him in this case, in part because the techniques of the early 1980s were beginning to backfire. "To take on something that controversial is all part of the 1980s. . . . The PR firm becomes too visible and the PR people are celebrities. You can't really do the job if you're the story. You're supposed to be the messenger, not the message. You get too high a profile," Sheila Tate said. "You become so controversial that you can't deliver for your client. Or the client is controversial as well and then you have a powder keg. When they took on the Angola account at Gray and the conservatives were picketing over there, I mean that was ludicrous." Tate said that Angola had approached Burson-Marsteller, a competing PR firm, but "Burson knew instinctively they weren't going to take that kind of business."

Once again *Time* magazine weighed in with a critical piece. "Two years ago, Gray told *Time* that he checks with his 'good friend,' CIA Director William Casey, before taking on clients who might be inimical to U.S. interests. It is unclear just what Casey could have said this time, since the CIA is currently funneling $15 million in covert aid to Savimbi to help his rebellion against the Angolan regime."[31] Some find it hard to believe that Murphy, with close ties to the intelligence community and the Reagan–Bush administration, would sign up a client like Angola just for money. "I would find it impossible to believe," said Mike Pilgrim, that Murphy would "carry out an operation like that without letting his buddies know about it." In fact, Gray and Company's Justice Department registration for Angola said, "Registrant also contacted officials at the Department of State and CIA concerning the U.S. role in finding a permanent solution." In a written interview for this book Gray confirmed that Murphy checked with the government.

Some believe that Gray and Company's representation of Angola was just another attempt by the intelligence community to have a PR firm take on a client to intentionally make it look bad and/or to spy on it. Livingstone remembered an earlier overture from Angola that came through intelligence-related sources, though he claims he begged off because his strong support of UNITA made the proposal untenable.[32]

John Lawler, a Gray and Company executive, said that Gray was always very careful about whether or not a client's interest was in the United States' national interest. If that was not the case, Lawler insisted, Gray would decline to take on the account. "He would have stuff checked out every which way. He was really a nut on that," Lawler said.[33]

But another Gray and Company executive said Gray assertions about clearing every client with William Casey were exaggerated. "Most of the big firms in this town, when they do overseas work, will check with the National Security Council, check with the CIA, check with DIA [Defense Intelligence Agency], and the intelligence committees on the Hill to make sure there is no real problem if our company represents these people and gets involved. Did Gray do that type of intelligence [checking] all the time when working for countries like Morocco, South Korea? Of course he did. Did he talk to Casey? He was a friend of Casey's. He'd see Casey around from time to time and sometimes Gray would ask. But did he have a hotline to Bill Casey and consult with Casey all the time? No."

This executive insisted that Gray played up his intelligence and White House ties to impress clients. "Gray was a very senior counselor and advisor and confidant to Reagan. And Gray had been in this town for twenty-five years before he even opened the doors of Gray and Company. Gray knew a lot of people. But that's what you trade on in this town is the contacts and the experience. Some clients like to hear that you can pick up the phone and talk to the White House or talk to the CIA. The fact is, you and I can do that, too—(202) 456-1414—or whatever the number is. I have got a woman who used to be my secretary at Gray and Company . . . [I] told her to get involved in the 1988 campaign. She did; she's now over doing presidential advance at the White House. I'm a liberal democrat, but I sit and run my lines [about checking] with my contact at the White House, and I can do that. So everybody in this town plays that game. The media play it. Lobbyists love to play it. So you have got to take a little of that with a grain of salt,'' he said.

Charles Black, the head of the lobbying firm representing Savimbi and UNITA, said that he checked with the highest levels of the Reagan administration during the controversy and no one had authorized Gray and Company's representation of Angola.[34] Barry Schochet agreed. "Gray had no sensitivity to it. He just basically was concerned about [money]. Going in, I don't think he had any knowledge of the situation. I have no idea whether Murphy did or not [but as a former] high-level CIA man, he should have known. It was the desire to have clients who brought money.'' Gray and Company was uncharacteristically low-key in their assessment of what services they provided Angola. The firm told the *New York Times* that its "limited role'' was "to aid the flow of information and facts to assist both Governments and those responsible for the U.S. foreign-policymaking process.''[35]

In Jim Jennings's testimony before the SEC, he said, "Actually, we did a three-page memo for an internal management committee discussion on why we were representing Angola. We pulled all of that because certain sentences, taken out of context of the whole memo, would be explosive.''

In mid-March, just six weeks after signing the account, Gray and Company dropped Angola because of the political pressure. Mankiewicz said that after delivering a policy message to the White House, the firm ended its ties with the Luanda government. When Gray finally gauged the intensity of the conservatives' ire, "he got very, very nervous, obviously, and responded to the pressures in the White House because the bigger chip that he had was his relations with the White House and Reagan,'' remembered Barry Schochet. "Murphy never really recovered. You know Murphy was not very successful there. Ultimately, he went out.'' Around the same time, Gray and Company lost another, very lucrative account, an enemy of the Angolan government: Morocco.

In February 1985 Gray and Company signed the Kingdom of Morocco as a client. In addition to the $10,000-a-month-retainer, this poor desert country agreed to spend at least $360,000 a year with the PR firm. Gray and Company ended up billing them much more. That summer, the Justice Department began its investigation into CNN and other broadcasters airing Gray and Company's video press release about Morocco's King Hassan II without identifying them as foreign propaganda for possible violations of the Foreign Agents Registration Act. The Justice Department took no action against

CNN or Gray and Company, but that was only the beginning of Gray and Company's problems with this account.

Morocco, a depressed country on the western tip of the Sahara Desert in northern Africa, had many problems, both domestic and foreign, that needed addressing. King Hassan II, Gray's client, has dictatorially ruled the country since his father's death in 1961. In Morocco, a Moslem country, Hassan is known to his subjects as the Finger of God, an appellation that has not prevented several attempts on his life. Morocco has high unemployment, huge foreign debts, drought, and depression. The contrasts between Hassan's life and the average Moroccan's are stark. Hassan has a half a dozen palaces, he sponsors his own international golf tournament, he entertains celebrities lavishly, and he has a fleet of jets (the Royal Air Force). The King's jet has an oval mink-covered bed, a throne room, and gold-plated bathroom fixtures.[36] By contrast, Morocco's cities are crowded, dirty, noisy, with beggars in rags pleading for money. The country is a police state with an abysmal human-rights record. Amnesty International reports that King Hassan tortures and executes his political opponents. He keeps political prisoners in detention without any means of communication, much less legal representation. Often opponents simply disappear. When Moroccans rioted in the streets for food, soldiers killed them. Families of demonstrators never report the dead, but bury them secretly at night for fear of reprisal.

Instead of addressing Morocco's problems head on, Gray and Company videotaped over them and tried to present a rose-colored picture to replace reality. For example, in 1984, King Hassan had signed a treaty with Ronald Reagan's leading international enemy, Libya's Muammar Qaddafi. The interview that CNN ran, which basically said that the treaty was meaningless, was an attempt to offset that problem.

By the mid-1980s, Jimmy Carter's foreign policy objectives of human rights and democracy had been largely abandoned. Pressure on right-wing allies to better their human rights records was nonexistent. To Gray and Company and to the United States government, Morocco deserved our friendship and aid because the King was one of our few Arab allies and the only Arab leader outside of Egypt who recognized Israel. Instead of showing the American people the poverty and problems of Morocco to help convince the American public that it needed our millions of dollars in foreign and military aid, Gray and Company threw a party. In March 1986, Gray and Company put together an entourage of movie stars, socialites, and reporters to help the King celebrate his twenty-fifth anniversary on the throne. The official U.S. delegation included: CIA director William Casey, USIA director Charles Wick, and U.N. ambassador Vernon Walters, among others. They were all invited to the annual *Fête du Trone and Ceremonie d'Allegeance.* For the attendees, it was an all-expenses-paid trip as guests of the royal government filled with cocktail parties, dinners, receptions, luncheons, and even a few state ceremonies.[37] The lavish dinners, one held for one thousand people with a buffet the size of a football field, a fountain filled with floating oranges, and Oriental carpets covering the ground, contrasted sharply to the Third World misery outside the hotel.

American foreign policy toward Morocco had changed dramatically with the advent of the Reagan administration. King Hassan was fighting a war in the Western Sahara against the rebel Polisario over a territorial dispute for control over the old Spanish territory. During the Carter administration, American policy remained neutral with regard to this territorial battle, taking the position that a military solution was neither possible nor desirable. But with Reagan in 1981, the United States's liaison with Hassan flourished. The U.S. began supplying Hassan with military weapons to escalate the war against what were now called his communist-supplied, Libyan-supported enemies. The CIA increased its base in Morocco for covert operations—targeted mainly against Libya and Angola. As with Spain and Turkey, arms could be legally transferred to Morocco and then covertly sent to the UNITA rebels in Angola.

The list of visiting American dignitaries to this area in the early 1980s could have filled a small phone book, including General Vernon Walters, a former deputy director of the CIA and then an Ambassador at large. The new U.S. ambassador was Joseph Verner Reed, a David Rockefeller protégé and Chase Manhattan Bank official.[38] Just prior to Walters's resumption of government service as a roving Ambassador, he had earned a $300,000 consultancy fee from Environmental Energy Systems Inc., which unsuccessfully tried to sell tanks to Morocco. Walters was also associated with DGA International, a Washington firm that lobbied the Carter administration and Congress to send more military weapons to Morocco.[39] The head of Environmental Energy Systems Inc. said it hired Walters because of his access to important Moroccan figures. (He was a longtime close friend of King Hassan.) Gray had known both Reed and Walters for years.[40]

Gray and Company and other lobbying firms attracted foreign clients many different ways. One way was to use friends, former colleagues, and even relatives on Capitol Hill and in the federal agencies to provide inside information about proposed changes in regulations or cuts in foreign aid. The lobbyists then contact the affected companies or countries and offer their assistance on these issues that have not yet been made public. This exchange is Washington's form of insider trading. It shows that firms have sources who can provide advance, sometimes secret information, and can also be of help.

Neil Livingstone maintained that he had tried to recruit Morocco as a client because he had heard the Senate Foreign Relations Committee was going to cut military aid to Hassan's regime, and he was convinced Gray and Company could prevent this from happening. Yet his overtures went nowhere, and when Gray and Company did get the Moroccan account it was due to other connections. According to Livingstone, Gray and Company got the account because the Moroccan Ambassador, Joseph Reed, was friends with Charles Frances, a Gray and Company employee. "My understanding was that this was very much a personal kind of deal," Livingstone said.[41]

However they obtained the account, the contract was short lived. After the incident with Angola, Morocco dropped Gray and Company. "I think one of the real *faux pas* that might have been made was that the firm did not check with their existing client base to see if that [representing Angola] would be a problem to them," Adonis Hoffman said.

But the Moroccan account caused Gray and Company more serious problems than merely losing another lucrative client. Morocco refused to pay Gray and Company for its services—and Gray and Company had provided many services. In its SEC filings, Gray and Company noted: "Included in accounts receivable of May 31, 1986, and February 28, 1986, is approximately $1.6 million and $1.4 million respectively relating to a 1985 contract with the Kingdom of Morocco which contract was not renewed. Discussions regarding collecting amounts due from the Kingdom of Morocco are currently in process."[42]

Having trouble collecting from foreign clients was not unique to Gray and Company. For one thing it is nearly impossible to successfully sue a government for refusing to honor a contract, especially a Third-World government. Other problems may arise if the government suddenly changes. Most PR firms took steps to avoid such problems. "With a foreign country, you would often get a big chunk of money up front and then request them to pay X thousands monthly in advance," George Worden explained. "Then you're never behind. Then as the government changes or something, you don't really lose anything."

But in the case of Morocco, Gray and Company did not get the money up front. Whether or not the Angola account was the reason, or whether, as one senior vice president asserted "the King never bonded with Bob," Morocco not only severed the account but refused payment as well, claiming that Gray and Company had not performed according to the agreement.[43]

What is a PR firm to do when it cannot collect millions of dollars from a foreign client? In the case of Gray and Company, the answer was to look to the United Nations, where Gray's friend Vernon Walters was U.S. Ambassador to the U.N. According to a high-level Gray and Company executive, Gray asked Walters to intercede with the Moroccan ambassador to the U.N. (Walter's sister ran a travel agency that had been part of Gray and Company's Morocco operation). Gray also paid former Attorney General William French Smith approximately $15,000 to help facilitate the payment, but Gray and Company never received full payment from the King.

Gray and Company was truly the PR firm of the 1980s. "They were kind of go, go, you know. Like the Wall Street business. There are a lot of people that appeals to. They just want to rub shoulders with the power. They think Bob Gray can deliver three Cabinet secretaries and get them invited to a State dinner. That's what they really want," Sheila Tate said. One Gray and Company senior vice president believed, on a whole, the clients who hired Gray and Company for the parties and the boat trips down the Potomac went away happy. "All I can tell you is that the clients loved it, the clients paid for it, and the clients, by and large, went away happy. I could show you the yellow pages so you can book the boat trip yourself. So much of what is available in Washington is available to the Ford dealer in Iowa if he wants to come here and make the phone call. He has a constitutional, God-given right to visit personally both his U.S. Senators and his member of Congress. He doesn't understand that. He thinks that he has got to hire somebody to get him access to the decisionmakers that he has by law, by birthright."

In the end, several Washington lobbyists feel that Gray and Company ultimately failed because it offered very little real substance. "It's all a perception. . . . You can go see Zilch who is the Acting Republican on this Subcommittee and Chairman. And we'll waltz you over to the Administration and see Y who is in charge of this. And you go around and do all of this stuff. Well, is that going to get you anything more than you had before? Probably not. They'll all be nice to you because if it's Tip O'Neill's former aide and he asked Tip to see him, he'll see him and he'll be nice to the guy. Will it get you anything in the end that you wouldn't get anyway? Probably not. But, you see, it looks . . . impressive . . . and you may pay for years just not to be worse off than you already are and count yourself fortunate," John Sears said.[44] Another prominent Washington lobbyist said, "I've watched Gray and Company over the years, and I think they did a lot of stuff with smoke and mirrors."

Regardless of all the problems, several employees enjoyed working at Gray and Company and miss it, especially its heydays in the early 1980s. "We got all the interesting clients, and all the interesting accounts, we had. It really was the place to work. Everybody knew about it," remembered Betsey Weltner.[45] "That was sort of a once-in-a-lifetime thing and we'll never get it back again," another Gray and Company executive said wistfully.

Like so many other seemingly rich and powerful men in the 1980s, privately, Gray was anxious to sell the company before it had to publicly post substantial losses. Gray and Company was on the road to financial ruin; if Gray could not find a buyer quickly, he stood the chance of losing almost everything. The investigations into the Madrid office alone were costing Gray and Company hundreds of thousands of dollars and sapping the morale of the employees.[46] Even worse, the firm had stopped growing. No longer were big clients flooding through the door, and lucrative foreign accounts were terminated without being replaced.

On top of all this, the acquisition of Strayton had turned out badly. Gray bought Strayton just before the first of many slumps in the computer industry. He had paid top dollar. The projected profits for Gray and Company's first and most expensive acquisition never materialized. To make matters worse, the two firms never interacted well. Gray and Company treated Gray Strayton more like a stepchild. When Gray Strayton started losing money, Gray responded by instituting severe cost-cutting measures (25 percent for fixed costs) and consolidating Strayton's administrative operations with the Washington headquarters.[47]

As early as 1985, Gray began discussions with Ogilvy & Mather, a large advertising and PR firm, about the possibility of buying Gray and Company. Ogilvy & Mather turned him down because they were concerned about the trouble surrounding Gray's Madrid office, Gray and Company's high client turnover, and some of Gray's "politically unsavory clients such as the repressive regimes of Haiti and Turkey."[48] Saatchi and Saatchi, the large international advertising firm, also walked away from Gray and Company, for similar reasons.

Finally, in June 1986, in what to outsiders seemed like an unlikely miracle, JWT Group, Inc. agreed to buy Gray and Company and make it a part of its subsidiary: Hill and Knowlton. "I think Bob Gray's big coup is that—think about this: How many people do you know could leave a company, set up a competitive company, sue the previous company, win, and then sell that company back to the same company? How does this work? I want in on this. . . . Only Bob Gray, I guess," said Sheila Tate.

For Gray, it was a sweetheart deal, and it came about just in time. "His luckiest day was when he was able to get bought out by Hill and Knowlton. . . . Had that not happened, who knows. He certainly wouldn't have grown any more. He might have had trouble sustaining himself," Barry Schochet said.

Originally, JWT agreed to pay about $21 million for Gray and Company. Gray and Company would be merged into Hill and Knowlton's Washington operation, with Gray in charge. Part of the merger agreement created an entirely new division of H&K called Hill and Knowlton Public Affairs Worldwide that placed Gray in charge as its chairman. H&K returned Gray to its Board of Directors and made him chairman of its policy committee.[49]

To Gray and Company stockholders, the deal was not as beneficial (although without the sale it could have been much worse). They received $8.75 a share, having paid $7.50 two years earlier. Financial analysts called it "a good deal" for JWT and "disappointing" for Gray and Company stockholders. "Clearly, the largest shareholder [Gray] believed he struck the best deal. But it remains to be seen whether the best deal for him is necessarily the best for the outside shareholders," George F. Shipp, an analyst with Investment Corp. of Virginia told the *Washington Post*.[50] Gray himself was reported to receive $14 million worth of JWT stock. Gray said the terms represented "a very good price in today's market and an honest evaluation of the company."[51]

For the quarter just prior to completion of the merger, Gray and Company had to set aside an additional $1.3 million beyond the $672,200 reserve from the previous quarter, creating a pool of almost $2 million to cover bad debts.[52] The company posted "a significant net loss" in the second quarter. In its SEC filings, it specifically mentioned the investigations into the Spanish office and the legal expenses associated with them as a cause of uncertainty.

> The Company is unable to predict what, if any, specific actions may be instituted by the SEC or the Justice Department against the Company or any of its current or former directors and officers.
>
> During the years ended February 28, 1986, and February 25, 1985, the Company expended approximately $300,000 and $650,000 respectively in legal fees and other expenses relating to these matters . . .

Gray and Company attributed its financial problems primarily to three factors: "the downturn in the high technology sector of the nation's economy, which adversely affected the business of the Company's Gray Strayton subsidiary; an increase in the Company's allowance for uncollectible receivables; and legal expenses as discussed in Note K [referenced above]."[53] In addition, it noted that there was an increase in costs connected with the Company's merger.

By the time the merger with Hill and Knowlton was complete, the deal was not as profitable to Gray as had been reported. Hill and Knowlton put $4,560,000 worth of JWT Group Common Stock that would have otherwise gone to Gray in escrow to protect it from Gray and Company's liabilities.[54] Nonetheless, Gray profited handsomely from the deal. Instead of facing bankruptcy he was now six to seven million dollars richer.

Just as had happened with his businesses in Nebraska thirty-five years earlier, in the end Gray and Company failed. Although in terms of money, the merger with H&K was profitable, Gray's dream of owning the largest public communications firm in the world—the prototype for the twenty-first century—was shattered in 1986. But once again Gray avoided catastrophe. "You can bet if the ship is sinking, Gray will be the first to jump on the admiral's barge. He won't get a pinky wet," said Bob John Robison, who headed H&K's Washington office before the merger.[55] Now Gray was back in charge of Hill and Knowlton's Washington office. This time he had no intention of leaving.

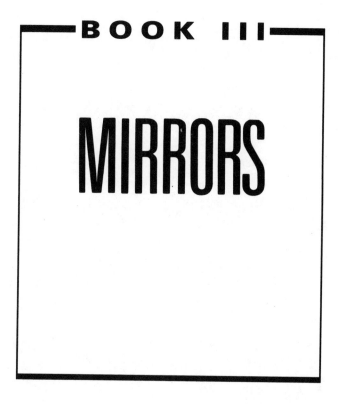

BOOK III

MIRRORS

15

BACK IN THE WOMB

Gray tended to blur with the admirers. If you wanted a lobbyist, you hired him. If you wanted a PR guy, you hired him. If you wanted an advertiser, you hired him. He was a promoter par excellence. . . . The imagery was taken to excess. So the goal of the firm became less client service. It became profiteering.

Marty Gold

Gray abruptly quit Hill and Knowlton in 1981 at a time when the company fully expected him to bring to H&K the rewards of Ronald Reagan's election. He had left H&K's Washington office with large losses, set up a competing company, took away key staff, took away important clients and then sued them. The lawsuit between Gray and Hill and Knowlton in the early 1980s was bitter and bruising. Now, just three years after the lawsuit was settled, H&K not only was buying Gray back, but they were buying him at a generous price at a time when others had looked at the books and walked away. To many in Washington it was incomprehensible, but within the PR community, the answer was simple: Robert L. Dilenschneider.

Dilenschneider had headed H&K's Chicago office since 1978. He had made his reputation recruiting utility companies using the same PR plan, but personalizing it for various locations. He had known Gray for years. H&K had been under pressure for several years from its parent company, JWT Group, to increase revenue. To Loet Velmans, then the head of H&K, and other disciples of John Hill, that was a difficult demand. There is only so much anyone can make from a PR firm, and Velmans felt strongly that H&K's profit margins had been squeezed to the the limit. But Dilenschneider was much more in the Gray tradition of limousines and flamboyance, of profits and bottom line performance, than Velmans and others at H&K. In 1986 Dilenschneider replaced Velmans as head of H&K.

H&K had been the largest PR firm for many years, but Burson-Marsteller, H&K's longtime competitor, had overtaken it in size in 1983. The following year, H&K slipped further behind in size and revenue. That did not seem to overly concern Velmans, who said at the time, "A lot of people were shocked [when H&K slipped to number two], but we don't pay too much attention. That's not the measurement of how well you do the job."[1] A 1985 *Regardie's* article about H&K's Washington office laid the blame on the firm's "staid image." "It's as old-line and white-shoe as PR firms get, using the word *counseling* so often it sounds like a law firm. . . . Not every client who walks in the door waving a fat wad of cash gets represented, and the firm has dropped clients that want to push a point of view the firm disagrees with. Unlike Gray's firm for instance, which apparently will take almost any regime, Velmans's won't represent countries, except occasionally for tourism. 'If the politics of a country is unpopular by American standards and they say, 'What can you do for me?' I say, well, maybe you should change,' Velmans said."[2] An example of H&K dropping a client who would not take their advice was the Tobacco Institute, one of H&K's most lucrative accounts. When the Tobacco Institute rejected H&K's advice to follow the Surgeon General's report, wanting instead to fight the report, H&K dropped the account. It went to Gray and others instead.

But when Dilenschneider took over in 1986, he wanted to be in charge of the largest PR firm in the world, to restore H&K to its earlier prominence. "Macho, money, power," said Sheila Tate.[3] "Dilenschneider is obsessive about it. He has to be the biggest. He has to be. He doesn't care about being the best. Hill and Knowlton used to be the best, used to be the Tiffany. When I went to college, every case history was Hill and Knowlton's case."

To become the biggest, Dilenschneider needed to create an event. It is the way PR people think. One of Dilenschneider's first events was buying Gray and Company. The purchase instantly increased H&K's size and presence in Washington. Gray was regarded as the quintessential lobbyist with the contacts, the White House entrée, and the recognition. Dilenschneider was right. The merger was an event that caught Washington's attention. In the main the press, unaware of Gray and Company's severe financial distress, saw it as a "buyout" rather than a "bail out," as George Worden characterized it.[4]

When Gray folded his firm into Hill and Knowlton, there was an obvious culture clash which needed to be resolved, whether Gray would return to the white-shoe, old-line world of H&K or continue his colorful and controversial style. Penney P. Burnett, JWT's vice president of investor relations, told the *Washington Post* that H&K would honor all of Gray's client contracts, but may not renew some of them. "There are certain types of business which Hill and Knowlton does not take."[5]

But Gray had no intention of changing his ways to fit back into H&K's conservative corporate culture. He told the *Post* that "he would be surprised if Hill and Knowlton tried to tone down his operations. 'We've taken the toughest assignments, and I'm proud of that,' he said. 'We have color and flair and hopefully will inject that into Hill and Knowlton.' "[6]

"Well, when he came back, when Dilenschneider bought Gray and

Company, Gray kept running the Washington office just the way he had Gray and Company. And that's where he's gotten into all of his fights with Dilenschneider, but, indeed, he had a pretty good five-year iron-clad contract, and also the threat that if I walk out of here, it will hurt you, and it would have," Worden explained. It did not take long for the competition between H&K's Washington office and its New York headquarters to return.

Gray convinced Dilenschneider to let him set up a separate division of H&K called Hill and Knowlton Public Affairs Worldwide. Dilenschneider was the titular head, since he headed up all of Hill and Knowlton, but Gray was in charge. Dilenschneider made Thomas Eidson, in New York, the number three man. Technically Eidson reported to Gray, but it was understood that Eidson's real purpose was to represent Dilenschneider's interests. As a consequence, Gray was noticeably reticent about keeping Eidson informed.[7]

Gray and his subordinates in Washington technically did not work for Hill and Knowlton, Inc., but for Hill and Knowlton Worldwide. Gray operated from his H&K Worldwide division independently, using H&K's international offices as if they were his own. "Damn near . . . he'd just show up. Gray would turn up in Rome or somewhere or let them know he was coming and here's what I'm going to do, and here's what I want you to do, and they did it," Worden said. All of the accounting went through New York, "but he could go wherever he wanted in the world and do things independently of any other international structure that might exist in the organization. . . . The other way [without H&K Worldwide], Gray would only have had Washington. . . . This way he's got Washington as his operating base and he's got the world as his little oyster . . . he's the pearl."

Dilenschneider's purchase of Gray and Company began a trend that would forever change the face of public relations around the world. To ensure H&K's status as the largest PR firm in the world, Dilenschneider purchased Carl Byoir & Associates, a competing firm. As with Gray and Company, Byoir was folded into H&K. Once again Hill and Knowlton became the nation's largest public relations firm. The Gray and Company, Carl Byoir & Associates mergers were only the beginning. Increasingly, largely as a result of Gray's efforts at Gray and Company, public relations firms felt the need to offer lobbying as a service to their clients. To increase their lobbying capabilities, Ogilvy & Mather, then the third largest PR firm, bought a third of Charls E. Walker & Associates, Washington's oldest independent, non-lawfirm lobbying firm, and Bozell bought Robinson, Lake, Lerer, Montgomery, headed by Washington lobbyist James Lake.

But the nature of these mergers—and the nature of the public relations industry—changed dramatically when the acquisitions began coming about through hostile takeovers. More importantly, some of the corporate raiders were from overseas.

Martin S. Sorrell was a boyish-looking forty-two-year-old health-conscious Londoner with a high-pitched laugh, who was considered a "financial whiz

330 SUSAN B. TRENTO

kid.'' He had learned the merger game as the financial officer for Saatchi and Saatchi, the world's largest advertising agency, when he had helped engineer its American buying binge in the early 1980s. In 1985, Sorrell, Cambridge and Harvard Business School trained, thought he could do for himself what he had done for Saatchi and Saatchi. He started out on his own, first buying a company called Wire and Plastic Products in Kent, England, that made supermarket carts, wire baskets, and teapots. Sorrell changed the name to WPP Group P.L.C. He turned it into a $130 million marketing services organization, through fifteen acquisitions in less than two years, including graphic design, sales promotion, and video communication companies. At the same time Sorrell was gobbling up British companies, his acquisitive eyes turned to this side of the Atlantic. He wanted to include advertising and public relations to round out his "marketing services." His eyes focused on JWT, then the world's fourth largest advertising group, and the owner of Hill and Knowlton, the nation's largest PR firm.[8]

In 1987, only a year after Gray's return, H&K was besieged by Sorrell's hostile takeover offer for the JWT Group. In the past, the experts believed it could not be done. If foreigners bought these firms, the clients and executives would go somewhere else, they thought. After all, the executives were the firms' assets. But that did not dissuade Sorrell. He was mainly interested in the much larger J. Walter Thompson advertising company. Hill and Knowlton and the other companies involved in the takeover were simply a bonus.

JWT Group, like other companies targeted for takeover, had troubles: weak earnings and management unrest. On June 10, 1987 Sorrell made an unsolicited bid for JWT Group. Sorrell's initial bid was so high, $450 million or $45.50 a share for stock then selling for around $29 to $31, that other interested buyers quickly dropped out. In the end Sorrell ended up paying $566 million, or $55.50 a share, almost double the stock price.

Wall Street and Madison Avenue saw this hostile takeover as a minnow swallowing a whale—a young man who two years earlier had not owned any business was now buying a huge advertising firm four times WPP's size. "The deal was the most remarkable that Madison Avenue has ever seen, a daring and audacious move by WPP," the *New York Times* wrote.[9] With Margaret Thatcher's "Big Bang" deregulation approach in London, Sorrell was just displaying the new risk-taking financial attitudes in Great Britain, which were not much different from those of American corporate raiders.[10] Sorrell financed the deal by issuing new stock (24 million new WPP shares) and borrowing heavily. Like Rockefeller Center, Universal Studios, and other American institutions, one of the United States' premier advertising and its largest and most distinguished public relations firm were lost to foreign ownership. Now the companies competing for control of America's minds and politicians would not even be American owned.

Although there was little public outcry over the wave of foreign takeovers of American lobbying/PR firms, some within the industry were greatly troubled.

Sheila Tate was one who expressed dismay. "I don't like the foreign ownership by companies that aren't even in the communications business and don't have an appreciation for some of the ethics and sensitivities and needs for confidentiality with the clients and just some of the special business considerations you have in this business. I mean all they care about is the bottom line. . . . The idea of something like WPP buying Hill and Knowlton as part of that. That's what I find offensive. It makes me very uncomfortable."

Both advertising and public relations attract competitive, creative executives who are often difficult to manage. If they become disgruntled, they leave, usually taking clients with them. The question with Sorrell was whether his management ability matched his ability to attract financing. Could he increase the profitability of his new companies without harming their reputations for quality and integrity—something others with much more experience in these businesses had failed to do?

Sorrell indicated to the *New York Times* that the financial and creative sides of the businesses would be kept separate. "The financial side will always come second, but a close second to the professional and creative side of the business," he said.[11] An H&K executive said that Sorrell was a "very, very smart business guy. A little under-canny initially of how Washington worked. But the deal was as long as the Washington office [of H&K] met his numbers, he would leave the Washington office alone."

Sorrell eliminated JWT Group, the holding company for J. Walter Thompson (the advertising agency), Hill and Knowlton and the others. Now Gray's real bosses were in London, not New York. The relationship as outlined seemed perfect. Gray's attention to the bottom line would please London, and, in turn, his "creative" accounts would not come into question.

The old days of Hill and Knowlton were truly gone. Eventually the ethical standards and much of the respect the firm once commanded were also lost. John Hill wrote in the 1960s, "We have tried over a period of three and one-half decades to build a reputation for high standards of service. My ambition never was to be the largest firm, but the best."[12] Now it seemed like H&K would take almost any client and do whatever the client wanted even if it was counter to their advice, thus ending the importance of PR counseling.

The old practice of not soliciting business from clients who were represented by other agencies ended. H&K began aggressive marketing campaigns. "Raidings come and cold solicitations come. That means you don't know and you don't care whether the organization you're raiding has an agency or not. We're going to say, 'Hey, we're the best. You really ought to have us.' Somebody says, 'Well, I'm represented by so and so.' 'So what,' " George Worden said. He believes that these changes happened because of "greed" and it started in the 1980s. To him, H&K and others were reflecting what was happening in the rest of the country. "We were becoming products of the time. Everybody else was doing it. Wall Street. All the stuff I said, 'Gentlemanly ethics,' all that stuff applied to Wall Street, too. Not in the eighties it didn't."

The pressure on the bottom line replaced the emphasis on client service. Sheila Tate agrees with George Worden that the unethical in the PR business are the ones who focus on the bottom line "and are so driven by profit that anything is fair game." At H&K, practically any prospective client was fair game, and almost everyone was pressured to find clients. "We always made money. John [Hill] had us all working our butt off, but we never—one thing we absolutely didn't do that these guys do all the time, they go down to the lowest junior troop and say, 'Find new business.' How can a kid find [business]?" Worden said.

H&K's Washington office inherited the Gray and Company appearance that it never met a prospective client it did not like. Gray's philosophy that everyone deserves representation, that PR firms do not shy away from difficult clients, that if they did not represent them then someone else would, not only prevailed, but flourished in the new generation filling the ranks. Gray expanded the concept of client service from doing a good job for a client, to doing a good job for a client regardless of how controversial the client might be, regardless of your personal beliefs. To Gray's protégés, refusing a client for personal reasons was *itself* unethical and unprofessional. John Lawler, a Gray and Company senior vice president who now works for another Washington PR firm, offered a rather strange analogy to justify the principle. "That is back to the principle of client service. That is the lawyer that believes the client deserves representation. There is every bit as high a principle in the governmental relations lobbyists. In fact, I have less respect today for somebody that holds out to be a major governmental relations lobbyist or a public relations person that would say, 'I am not going to work on that account because I personally don't believe in it.' I think when people hold out to be general practitioners and will discriminate because their personal belief is different is no different than a builder that says, 'I won't sell a house to a black.' "

Betsey Weltner, who left after the H&K and Gray and Company merger, agrees that everyone deserves representation, but not that every professional is obliged to work on the account. "I don't feel that. I mean I think there will always be somebody around to do it, but I think everyone, just like lawyers, that everyone deserves to be represented, but you do have to have your own sense of ethics. You have to have some kind of moral guidepost. And for some people, maybe they don't want to work for nuclear power plants or for fur companies, but for me it's tobacco companies. I think that unless you have some kind of strong ethical principles, you don't serve your clients well, because you can't be amoral and be able to make good judgments on behalf of your clients, especially if your clients are moral people."

The young executives entering the field are now baptized into a PR and lobbying culture that makes justifications for every client. "Where's the line? You keep pushing it. And you push the line farther over. You don't cross it. You move it. . . . God, the things that many of us do *routinely* were worth your job if you ever tried to do it. In the olden days, you'd get fired. No discussion. If you lied, you were through. Just through," Worden said. Today Worden, who enjoyed his work and was proud of his years at Hill and Knowlton, feels that the business has changed so much that when people come to him for advice, he recommends that they do not work in public relations. "I really don't think a person ought to enter this business. I honestly don't . . . especially a young person."

About the same time WPP's purchase of JWT was complete, the stock market crashed in 1987. H&K lost $4 million that year. The financial strains on the company increased as Martin Sorrell and WPP went further into debt. WPP kept buying firms while both the advertising and public relations industries continued to decline. The pressure on the bottom line of the individual companies increased. By 1988 Sorrell had made thirty-two acquisitions in just over two years. WPP's gross revenues had risen from $6.6 million to $477.258 million. The number of employees had grown from 204 to 10,821.[13]

In 1988, WPP reinstituted Carl Byoir & Associates which, like Gray and Company, had been dissolved into H&K in 1986, to be its second public relations firm (in addition to H&K).[14] In 1989, Sorrell bought Ogilvy & Mather, another large advertising agency, which like J. Walter Thompson came with a public relations subsidiary. Sorrell said his goal was to create the number one multinational marketing services company in the world.[15] With this $864 million acquisition he created a $13.5 billion supergroup that made him a real rival with his old employer, Saatchi and Saatchi.

In Washington, the purchases and mergers were seen in more personal terms. Jody Powell, President Jimmy Carter's press secretary, headed Ogilvy's Washington public relations office. Employees feared that their office might be merged with Hill and Knowlton. Powell did not want to work for Gray, a Republican, and he had no use for Frank Mankiewicz. "We were all laughing because Jody Powell and Frank Mankiewicz hate each other's guts. They wouldn't be in the same room with each [other]. . . . Mankiewicz was quoted once when Powell first moved into the business . . . 'Oh yeah, he ought to be head of an office, he's been in the business for forty-five minutes,' mocking him in print and so there was really bad blood and I'm sure it still exists," Sheila Tate said. "Amid rumors Powell might quit, Ogilvy says no PR merger is planned," the *Wall Street Journal* reported.[16]

Charls Walker, a third of whose firm was owned by Ogilvy & Mather and now WPP, said in 1990 that he had no relationship with WPP. "We're independent," he said. He explained that his firm might occasionally have clients who formed coalitions with H&K clients to work on an issue, but they normally do not work together, and WPP has never insisted that his firm represent any client.

To many PR old timers, WPP buying another large advertising and public relations firm like Ogilvy & Mather and resurrecting Carl Byoir made no sense. They would all be operating in competition with H&K and other

WPP companies. To them, it was the equivalent of Coca Cola bringing out New Coke which took market share away from Coca Cola Classic and not Pepsi. Since Sorrell could not afford to buy up all the PR and advertising firms, why did he want to own companies that compete with one another?

In 1989, WPP bought the Washington lobbying firm of Timmons & Company.[17] The firm was suppose to report to H&K's Washington office, but Tom Korologos, one of the partners, said that before they sold to WPP, they had an agreement that they would be able to continue to operate independently.[18] "In our deal with WPP, who bought us out, was we have our complete independence. We have our own board. That was the deal we struck when we came together. They do not dictate to us what clients to take. We inform them, of course. And we tell them how much we are charging and what the profits are. But they cannot tell us who to lobby for or against. We are an independent entity," Korologos said.[19]

WPP was not alone in its acquisitions. Others, including H&K's rival Burson-Marsteller, were doing the same. It started to make many in Washington uncomfortable. "You've got huge firms like Hill and Knowlton and Burson-Marsteller and they're gobbling up the smaller firms. . . . Really the power in the big firms is getting very, very consolidated," former Senator Paul Laxalt said.[20]

A Gray and Company and H&K executive explained that WPP and the others were basically buying individuals who had political access and influence. "What happens is that when they buy smaller companies, they lock in the principals of those companies. Generally, it's three, four, five years. . . . You are buying the principals in those firms and the equity in their names and their rolodexes and you want to have them. . . . It's much more complicated than a manufacturing company buying another manufacturing company. It doesn't matter, within reason, who the workers are or even who the management is, because you'll keep producing ball bearings. But it's critically important in our business, because that's all we have— brains by the pound. And the cliché about the assets go down the elevator every night—truth," he said. Senator Laxalt agreed, "If you buy Timmons and Company, you're buying Bill Timmons and Tom Korologus . . . and if someone bought my shop, they're buying me."

Senator Laxalt does not believe that foreigners or others buy these lobbying and public relations firms to make money. "I think it's a prestige kick . . . I don't think it's economic. I don't think they make any money out of these things. But I don't think that they lose any since they enslave these people for at least—an employment contract usually up to five years, where they actually work the money out of them. . . . I guess, and I don't know, I haven't asked, but imagine that Timmons and Korologos probably got eight million dollars each up front. That's not bad. And then over a period of time they'll maybe pick up another two or three million. So they retire in five years. Everybody's won. Except somebody maybe got prostituted along the way. Who knows," Laxalt said. (Korologos declined to discuss how much WPP paid for his firm or his salary.)

The revolution Gray had foreseen in the 1970s was exceeding even his predictions. An executive who has worked at several large PR firms put it in perspective. "The interesting phenomenon of the eighties is the redefinition of public affairs in Washington representation. I think the earlier significant development in Washington was the addition by law firms of public affairs, and ultimately public relations capabilities, because they saw that they were leaving money on the table and that part of their business was starting to be taken away by firms like Gray and Company. . . . Then everybody else is going to get worried and they're going to have to catch up. I think what we're evolving toward is an industry—if you take a step back from Washington and just think of an international management consulting business—I think we will all become indistinguishable from each other in the sense that we'll be one-stop shopping (lobbying, public relations, legal work, regulatory work, special events, advertising). . . . What a company like this does is if we get business from a major corporation in a particular area, we do that business, we do it effectively, and then we start to sell in the other things that we do."

Besides foreign ownership, a big concern about these huge international firms are clients with conflicting interests. It is not unusual for the companies owned by the same international holding company to be representing clients with opposing positions. "You wonder where accountability is, to begin with. And I don't know how these big shops keep track with conflicts. I've got a very small shop and John Connally called me about a matter and we've got just a handful of clients. We check it out, and damn if in our small shop we didn't have a conflict. I couldn't take on that account and we were sick. Now just imagine—now I've got a handful of people—just imagine what kind of problem you have in these big shops . . . They've got to have some damn computer to determine whether there's a conflict or not and they're not working against themselves," Senator Laxalt explained.

But many of the large firms do not really care who their clients are and whether or not there is a conflict with another client. "Yeah, it's a job. There's not a hell of a lot of loyalty involved, that's for sure. It's a very mercenary business," Laxalt said. "Do you know none of us at H&K, or even in the top ten firms, I'll bet you there are officers at the company who don't know all the clients. I don't mean they can't find out, but they just don't know," Worden said.

After the mergers among Gray and Company, H&K, and WPP were complete, Gray continued to operate much the same way as he had at Gray and Company, but the atmosphere changed. Many longtime Gray staffers left over the next couple of years. They felt the office had lost its entrepreneurial spirit and excitement. It was no longer the "hot" place, except in terms of bottom line pressure. One H&K and Gray and Company executive said he left after all the mergers for two reasons. "The fun went out of it, and a lot of the craziness went out of it when Hill and Knowlton bought Gray. . . . Most of us didn't like the idea of taking orders from New York, and then taking orders from London and New York."

The pain that often accompanies mergers was magnified: first by the fact that three companies—Hill and Knowlton, Carl Byoir, and Gray and Company—had to be integrated, and then by the WPP takeover. "Everyone was worried about their positions. I just realized that it wasn't much fun anymore. It was very competitive. A lot of office politics. I just began to find that very tiresome . . . I just sort of reached my threshold," Betsey Weltner said.

Gray's two top deputies, James Jennings and Charles Crawford, remained after the merger, as did Frank Mankiewicz in public relations and Gary Hymel in lobbying, both of whom, like Gray, had longterm contracts. Most of those who left ended up doing well, in part because of the aura that had been created around Gray and Company.

On a personal level, WPP's purchase of JWT was a windfall for Gray. By almost doubling the value of his JWT stock, it almost doubled his net worth. It allowed him to purchase more real estate, something he had been doing since his early days in Washington. In 1987 he paid $1.1 million for a house in Maryland on the Severn River near Annapolis.[21] He ended up with "five houses, four [swimming] pools—three outdoor, one indoor. . . . That's expensive, keeping all that up. The company pays for that," said an H&K executive.

Even Gray's dogs were treated to luxury accommodations. In 1988, the *Washington Post* ran an article entitled "Fanciful Homes for Pampered Pets" that featured a large doghouse that Gray's companion Bill Austin had designed for Gray's two dogs, to match Gray's large brown-and-white Tudor home in Arlington (which he had purchased after the 1980 fire). "The doghouse has dark-brown tongue-and-groove plywood siding and [a] cedar-shake shingle roof; white trim and a large white window from a razed Georgian mansion; and a porch light matching the ones of the large house. Inside, Bruin and his friend Pate [Gray's dogs] . . . are kept comfortable by a window air conditioner in the summer and baseboard heating in the winter. The decor includes wall-to-wall carpeting, an original oil painting of a reclining nude woman [perhaps the same painting that Gray's White House staff had had the Navy fly from Europe as a Christmas gift for Gray when he was Cabinet Secretary] and a poster of two puppies. . . . The fully insulated house was so sturdily constructed—with a two-by-four wall frame and two-by-six rafters—that it was too heavy to move from the back porch, where it was built, to the spot reserved for it by the pool."[22]

Throughout the mergers with H&K and WPP, the SEC continued to call Gray and Company officials, one by one, to give depositions on the Spanish operation. Sitting at a conference table in a small room, surrounded by lawyers, these executives answered questions, sometimes for hours, sometimes for days. The Justice Department never really investigated, and dropped the matter long before the SEC did, according to Mark Moran. In 1987, the SEC was still calling witnesses. The last hold out was Carter Clews, who had demanded immunity from prosecution before testifying.

Gray and Company attorneys asserted attorney/client and work-product privilege over most of its documents and information. Thus the SEC was prohibited from exploring many of the areas in which it was interested. In the end, the SEC took no action against either Gray or Gray and Company. Livingstone said that eventually they gave up. "My attorneys told me that they [the SEC] could never find out what happened because it happened offshore. They could never prove that there was an illegality. That's why the case has always languished," Livingstone said.

When Alejandro Orfila left Gray and Company in 1985 after the Spanish operation became public, he had gotten a large cash settlement. Gray had basically bought out the rest of Orfila's employment contract and let him take all of his clients with him. Gray had done the same with Carter Clews, but a lesser amount of money was involved. But Neil Livingstone, who, like several others, thought that he was being groomed to take Gray's job when he retired, ended up with no severance package. In 1987, he sued Gray and Company, in part because he felt he had been led to believe he would one day replace Gray. The suit was eventually settled out of court. Livingstone said he could not discuss the terms of the settlement except to say that they put on the record his lack of any role in the Spanish operation. He told his friend, Mike Pilgrim, that he received a generous settlement.

Livingstone's protégé Adonis Hoffman also sued Gray based on racial discrimination. Again Gray settled out of court. Hoffman subsequently said that he was "not sure" whether racial discrimination was a factor at Gray and Company. "My sense was that here we had a high-powered, Republican organization interacting in a very high-profiled, high-powered context. I think the general perception was that white males, and to a certain extent white females, were the people that were connected in that regard." Some who were at Gray and Company thought Hoffman was taking advantage of Gray by suing. As one said, "It's cheaper to settle."

Livingstone and Adonis Hoffman were not the only ones to sue. Over the years more than a dozen lawsuits have been filed by or against Gray or his companies. In 1990, Burton Hoffman (no relation to Adonis), a sixty-one-year-old H&K senior vice president, filed a $10-million lawsuit against H&K for age discrimination. He maintained that when he returned from an assignment in Indonesia, one of H&K's largest accounts, James Jennings, who managed the Washington office, told him they did not want him and had no work for him. He was encouraged to resign. Hoffman, a former editor with the *Washington Star* and *National Journal*, was not given an office, a secretary, a computer, or any support services provided others even with a lesser rank. Instead, he was given a desk vacated by an intern in the bullpen with the secretaries and office equipment. He was not included in any meetings or listed on the staff rosters. Throughout this time, the Washington office was hiring younger executives to fill jobs he had previously held. When he finally complained that he thought he was being pushed out because of his age and that H&K was violating the law, he was fired.

"A lot of this defies common sense. . . . How could anybody, how could management reach these decisions? How could they have antagonized [employees] so badly and handle it so poorly that they wind up under a lawsuit?" George Worden said.

Unfortunately, with the $100,000-a-month rent at Harbour Place, its glamorous offices overlooking the Potomac River on the Georgetown waterfront, and the high salaries committed to the top personnel to keep them with the company, the Washington H&K office was still not profitable. Furthermore, the high-profile high-ticket accounts that had led to the explosive growth of Gray and Company were no longer coming through the door in droves. "Those gravy clients weren't there. They'd gone away," a H&K executive explained. But Gray's friend, Attorney General Edwin Meese, helped out. In 1987, the Justice Department awarded a $10.7 million contract to Hill and Knowlton and two small Hispanic businesses to publicize the new immigration law among employers and aliens.[23]

Gray, personally, was no longer as visible as he had been in the past. His name was no longer on the company, and the explosion of bad publicity about lobbyists did not provide incentive to promote himself as aggressively as in the past. Although the limousines still lined up outside Harbour Place for client parties, outside exposure was kept to a minimum. "The big party type of PR and lobbying is gone. That's died with the Reagan era. And it was a liability," a Gray and Company executive said. "Today, the lobbying is done in a much less visible way, returning to the law-firm approach that has always been more low key and less evident," agreed another Gray and Company and H&K official.

Some thought that the reason H&K was buying other lobbying firms was because Gray's party-oriented approach no longer attracted or satisfied clients, especially foreign clients who composed many of their largest accounts. "The stuff that they do isn't substantive anyway. There are no substantive lobbyists for Hill and Knowlton, really," Barry Schochet said.[24] Schochet went on to amend this assertion when the name Gary Hymel was brought up, but he still maintained that H&K had not adjusted to the new, subtler methods of public advocacy. "You'll go over to the Washington Harbour in the late afternoon and you'll see a bunch of limousines out [front] and a bunch of young kids out of college with placards saying 'Hill and Knowlton' and throwing some party.'' Schochet thinks the end of the cold war means foreign countries are looking for lobbyists with strong policy backgrounds, particularly in international economics, not access-oriented firms. ''I think that was more the phenomena of the late seventies and eighties than [it] is becoming now. This [business] is not a party. It went through the party phase and now it's serious.''

Nineteen eighty-eight was an election year and Gray, the PR executive, bravely wrote an editorial for *U.S. News & World Report* entitled ''A presidential field to take pride in.'' Gray praised all the candidates running for president, both Republican and Democrat, and chastised the public and the press for not holding them to the right standards. He said that by the time someone won in November, ''his motives will have been challenged, his integrity questioned, his human shortcomings revealed, but he will have . . . passed all the moral litmus tests by which we now measure candidates. But if we truly seek to measure their abilities to lead the nation and solve its pressing problems, we should give that moral yardstick a rest.''[25]

When Admiral Daniel Murphy left Gray and Company in 1987, Gray lost his closest ties to George Bush. But in 1988, Gray was more interested in wringing out the last vestiges of prestige and favoritism from the Reagan administration than he was in shoring up his Bush connections. In January, he helped with Reagan's State of the Union Address. Despite his lower profile, Gray could not resist showing off his influence and access. *The Washington Post Magazine* wrote: ''Suddenly Gray reaches into his desk drawer and pulls out a draft copy of President Reagan's upcoming 1988 State of the Union Address. Gray is working on a section of the speech, which is about as close to the heartbeat of Washington as any PR man could ever hope to get. 'We're working on this thing on line-item veto,' Gray says. He's searching for sexy instances of pork-barrel projects in the federal budget that Reagan can cite to prove that Congress should give the president line-item veto authority to reduce the deficit.''[26] (This is a longstanding PR ploy to dramatize potential federal budget cuts that sound good, but in reality, if made, would only have a minuscule effect on the federal budget deficit. George Bush did the same thing in his 1992 State of the Union Address, pointing out the proposed Lawrence Welk Museum.)

By 1988, Gray's friend, Attorney General Edwin Meese, who had remained controversial throughout his White House and Justice Department tenure, was in need of PR counseling. He discussed with Gray the possibility of Hill and Knowlton handling a public relations campaign to promote the Reagan administration's successes in the war on drugs. Charles Crawford, who was manager of H&K's Washington office, told the Knight-Ridder news service that the Justice Department was negotiating with Hill and Knowlton for a ''short term'' and ''personal'' contract to ''help in the drug program.''[27]

The proposed contract might seem at least eyebrow-raising to the layman but inside the Beltway it was Washington connections coming full circle. Gray, who had been investigated for drug use by the Drug Enforcement Administration (a branch of the Justice Department), was now being considered for a contract to offer "advice on how to communicate drug programs and policies to the public," by his friend, Ed Meese, who was being investigated by a Special Prosecutor for "actions affecting telephone companies in which he held stock, helping his close friend win military contracts for the Wedtech Corp. and support for a proposed pipeline project in Iraq."[28]

Gray had one more favor to ask of the administration that had been so instrumental in his success, an event that seemed to encapsulate so much of where Gray had come from and what he had become. On September 6, 1988, Ronald Reagan came to Hastings.

The State of Nebraska often seems trapped in a time warp of post–World War II America. The parking meters still accept pennies. Clerks respond to your thank you with an enthusiastic "you bet." The radio news is centered around agricultural commodity reports or tornado warnings. It is a state where the President is revered and the flag is something very special.

If the word ordinary could be defined as a place, then Hastings, Nebraska, would be the perfect definition. Hastings looks like 1950s America, but like the rest of the country, the 1950s sense of confidence and visible prosperity is gone. Hastings is a town that gets by on less than its share of the American dream.

Even though Hastings is mentioned on the Interstate 80 exit sign eighteen miles away, there is really not much for an outsider to exit to or for. There are no tourist attractions. There are no historical sights. The town of 23,050 has lost population in the last twenty years.

In Hastings there are hardly any African-American, Hispanic, or Asian faces. Almost everyone from the maid at the motel to the librarian is white. The First Presbyterian Church, the largest in town, has but one African-American family in the congregation. The citizens worship at thirty-four protestant and two Catholic churches. There are no synagogues.

Downtown Hastings, like many other small towns in America, looks forgotten. The boarded up businesses were abandoned to the shopping mall on the outskirts of town. The old movie theater sits empty, replaced by a multiscreen complex next to the mall. Hastings was never a rich town. It is a town of working-class people. There are no tree-lined streets with old mansions on either side. Even in the days of great farm prices, when the railroad and manufacturers thrived along with agriculture, Hastings never really saw much of the wealth.

Despite its name, the Imperial Mall outside of Hastings does not look very regal. The floors are concrete, not marble. There is no brass or crystal or full-grown trees or two-story fountains. The mall is not anchored by

Neiman Marcus—but by Sears and Walgreen's. Fashion and wealth seem as alien to Hastings as people of color. Dining venues in Hastings consist of either fast-food outlets or restaurants with laminated menus.

But on Tuesday, September 6, 1988, Hastings was overrun with Secret Service agents, federal, state, and local law enforcement officers, the media, and the curious. The local newspaper ran banner headlines and issued a special souvenir edition. The schools closed for the day. Ronald Reagan, the most popular president in history, came to Hastings. It was among his last official stops as President, and it could not have been more appropriate. Middle class, largely white, working Americans had twice elected him. His rhetoric had reflected their Midwestern heritage and values. But the prosperity that Reagan had promised bypassed Hastings, just as the Interstate Highway had thirty years earlier.

The President of the United States flew half way across the United States, at taxpayer's expense, to visit this small town that no other president had visited since William Howard Taft on October 2, 1911, to dedicate a communications facility—The Gray Center for the Communication Arts— as a favor to a friend.[29] After a year of promises, Gray had delivered the President to his hometown.

Nothing had been left to chance. Joyce Ore, the head of public relations for Hastings College, was overwhelmed the last week with outsiders— professional public relations executives from Gray's firm in Washington, White House advance teams, and the Secret Service. The Sunday before Reagan's visit they had had a trial run. The helicopters flew from the airport and landed on the golf course behind the communications building. That alone was enough excitement to attract three hundred observers.

Gib Neal, the chairman of the college's art department, and some of his students finished painting signs, and hung paintings from Gray's private collection in the Center to help decorate it. (The art works were returned to Gray once the ceremonies were over.) That night Gray hosted an ice cream social for Congresswoman Virginia Smith, who was seeking reelection. He held it at the Kensington, formerly the old Clarke Hotel and now a home for the elderly, although the facility still rents out some of the rooms. During his youth, Gray's mother had worked for years as a bookkeeper at the hotel. Some of Gray's staff, including the First Lady's press secretary, Elaine Crispen's daughter Cheryl, stayed there over the weekend making final preparations. They had hosted a party the night before with a cake decorated like the Gray Center and a banner reading "Hastings—Communications Center of the World."[30]

The morning of the ceremony Gray went to the Hastings Airport, across from the Imperial Mall, to greet some of his honored guests who arrived on a private jet. It was a distinguished group of friends. Celeste Holm, the actress who had had a small part in the recent movie *Three Men and a Baby*, Gray's boss, Martin Sorrell, the Chairman of the Board of WPP, the parent company to Hill and Knowlton, and Robert Maxwell, the British publishing mogul.

Maxwell, who became a Hill and Knowlton client after this trip, said he was in Hastings because of his friendship with Gray. "One of the reasons I am here is to honor Bob . . . I've known him and value his humanity. He's a great man," Maxwell said. Maxwell told the local newspaper that he admired Gray's way of dealing with people, a quality Maxwell said he shared. "To me, people are more important than things. But he has more of it than I have. He's a very sensitive person," he said.[31] Maxwell returned to Hastings College in the spring of 1990 to be their commencement speaker. Martin Sorrell added to the encomiums for the small-town boy made good. "I've only known Robert [Gray] for a year, when my company bought out Hill and Knowlton and several other communications companies, but in that time he's become a friend."[32]

The crowd began to gather that morning at the college, but no one was admitted through the three gates until noon. The U.S. Marine Logistics Bass Drum and Bugle Corps, along with other, local talent, entertained with "Hail to the Chief" and other patriotic songs, including "The Presidential Dedication March," commissioned by Gray especially for the ceremony, until the President arrived two and a half hours later.

The weather was perfect: clear, mild, and sunny. The crowd, which grew to ten thousand people, could hear the noise before it saw the U.S. Marine helicopter, carrying the President, disappear behind the Gray Center as it lowered onto the nine-hole Elks Country Club. Security was tight. SWAT team members stood on top of the building with binoculars and guns. Secret Service agents, looking bigger and better dressed than the locals, could be spotted with their tell-tale lapel pins.

In keeping with the Reagan tradition of patriotic imagery at every stop, the dais was draped in red-white-and-blue festooned fabric. Small American flags were handed to the crowd as they passed through the metal detectors.[33] A perfectly lettered banner, carrying out the red-white-and-blue theme, was flawlessly hung so when the President assumed the podium, with a presidential seal on a royal-blue background on front and several microphones on top, the banner, which read, "Hastings College Welcomes President Reagan," would be ideally positioned in the center just above his head. It was a perfect picture. It was designed to be.

At the ceremonies, on cue, Gray began to address the crowd as the President made his way to the wooden platform that had been built in front of the new communications building. Turning to the college president, Gray joked, "Now, Tom . . . now, do you believe he's really going to come?"[34]

At the ceremony, Gray spoke movingly of his past and present, of his rural childhood during the Depression, of his hopes for the future fulfilled through an institution dedicated to his mother and father.[35] Looking at his friend, Ronald Reagan, Gray quoted from a 1940s script from a movie in which Reagan played Grover Cleveland Alexander, the great baseball player: "It is one of the best lines ever written for an actor. 'God must like us a lot to have given us friends like this.' "[36] Hastings mayor Bob Allen summed up the import of the visit, apparently without irony, when he said later in an interview with the local newspaper, "This just shows what can happen when somebody like Robert Gray can do what he does. . . . His friendship [with President Reagan] was such that he could get the President of the United States to our city during a busy time for him. . . . It was evident what having friends in high places can be worth."[37]

The President was returning from California to Washington after a three-week vacation in California, and stopped off in Nebraska on his way back to the White House. After receiving an honorary degree, the President addressed the crowd. The lead story the next day in the *Hastings Tribune* surrounded a five-column color picture of President Ronald Reagan dedicating the Gray Center for the Communications Arts at Hastings College.[38] In a two-column, black-and-white picture below the fold was a picture of Gray. "Gray's challenge a dream come true," the headline read.

Like a successful public relations person, Joyce Ore filled several large, burgundy-with-gold-inlaid scrapbooks with newspaper articles and other memorabilia from the time the President's visit was first announced until the actual ceremonies. She presented one to the president of the college, one to Gray, and kept one for her office.

Gray had been planning and dreaming about that day for years. On Friday, December 16, 1983, Gray, who had taught business administration at Hastings College before embarking on his Washington career, had given a $1 million challenge donation on behalf of his brother and sisters to the college for the communications facility, which would bear the names of his parents, the late C. J. Gray, and the then ninety-one-year-old Marie Burchess Gray. He said in a press release his parents "taught us the contributions to success made by the solid foundation of a Midwest background and the blessings of a good education."[39]

"It began with Bob Gray's gift. He was interested in the concept of 'Window on the World.' . . . The campus has always been a liberal arts campus and he saw that as the perfect location, as well as geographically a good location, for his idea of what communications for the future should be in terms of education. Liberal arts is a concept that he has built on. In fact, he told us when we visited with him in Washington and here on visits that he's made home, that if he would recommend anything to a communications student at this point, it would be a law degree," said Sharon Brooks, a professor at Hastings College.[40]

During the three-year campaign to finish raising the funds to build the center, the college began to discuss the concept of the building and what it would accomplish. Though the college was certainly grateful, the notion of what the center was supposed to accomplish was a bit fuzzy. "I guess at the time the announcement was made, we knew it would be communication arts, but we were really unsure about how the building would evolve,'' Joyce Ore said. To a liberal arts college, the idea of training students to use radio and television equipment seemed more the role of a vocational school.

It was decided that the new building would focus on television, radio, and print. Also, the speech department and the forensic team would be transferred into communication arts. There would be no journalism major, just communications arts with an emphasis in different areas: television, radio, print reporting, photojournalism, advertising, and public relations.

In 1984, Gray and Hastings College announced the Advisory Board for the Gray Center for the Communications Arts. It was a very impressive list: Walter Cronkite, the former CBS anchorman and the late William S. Paley, the then Chairman of CBS, both of whom had been friends with Eisenhower; Grant Tinker, then NBC chairman and a Gray client; and stage, movie, and television actresses Dina Merrill and Celeste Holm, society friends of Gray's since his Eisenhower years. John Denver, the singer and composer, Walter Annenberg, the former Ambassador to the Court of St. James and founder of *TV Guide*, and Beverly Sills, the then General Director of the New York City Opera, were added to the board. Gray also asked Ted Turner to serve on the board, at the same time CNN's investigative unit was investigating Gray and Company.

"The Gray Communications Center Board of Advisors will offer the center an exciting opportunity to draw upon the collective wisdom and expertise of many of the nation's leading innovators in communications and performance arts," said Dr. Gerald Hazelrigg, the president of the Hastings College Foundation. But much like Gray and Company's rubber-stamp Board of Directors, the Gray Center Advisory Board was impressive, but did very little. Celeste Holm was the only member of the Advisory Committee to attend the dedication. In fact, she is the only member to visit the center at all. "We hoped, you know, that we would get some of them on campus. Mr. Gray, I think, has tried to get some on campus, but it's not happened," Ore said.

The local newspaper wrote appreciatively of Holm's enthusiasm at the dedication. "Holm already has made her contribution to the newest building at Hastings College in the form of technological help. 'I can tell you if a theater will work or not so as not to close off anything from the audience unless you want it closed off,' " she said.[41] Holm obviously did not realize that there is no theater in the new building, and the dramatic arts are not part of the communication arts department.

On May 18, 1986, Gray used his father's gardening shovel to turn the first shovel of dirt to break ground for the new center. He said at the ceremonies that the Gray Center was the fulfillment of a dream inspired by his father, who, when walking through Hastings almost fifty years before, had pointed out where an experimental Westinghouse broadcasting station used to stand, one whose signals reached the whole world. Gray said that the new center would renew his father's vision.[42]

The commencement speaker that year was then head of the United States Information Agency (USIA) and Gray friend, Charles Wick, who had cochaired the 1981 Reagan Inaugural with Gray. Wick gave a speech filled with the cold war rhetoric so popular with Reagan administration officials. He cautioned that while the Gray Center might be a window on the world, the United States was fighting a "war of ideas" with the Soviet Union. He warned that the Soviet Union and its client states, through the United Nations, wanted to control the mass media of all countries. That if left unchecked, "the Soviet Union sees this moment in history as a great opportunity to extend its sphere of totalitarian influence."[43]

A year later, in the fall of 1987, the red-brick building was ready for classes. The center is located on an attractive, isolated corner of the campus on the edge of the college-owned golf course with a stream running nearby and a park across the street. Across the front is a long, arched window-lined gallery, with a two-story rotunda in the center that features oil portraits of Gray's parents. On either end are towers with satellite dishes on top.

Just before commencement in May 1988, the President's visit was announced for the following September. "It is especially appropriate that Reagan, 'the world's premier communicator,' should dedicate the new communications center," Gray said when he made the official announcement.[44] Gray said that when he asked the President, "Reagan said from the very start, 'I want to do this.'" The President even helped with some of the arrangements, such as having one of the U.S. Marine Corps bands perform. "He said, 'Let's really do it right,'" Gray explained.[45]

Thirty-three years after leaving Hastings for Washington, Gray returned home with not only the President of the United States, but also his boss from England and his movie-star and media friends. For one afternoon every element that had made him successful surrounded him: powerful politicians, media executives, academia, lobbyists, public relation executives, international businessmen, entertainers, his boss, his friends, his family, and ordinary people, the "grass roots" on which Washington thrives. It was a microcosm of the nation's power structure. It was perfectly staged, perfectly carried off, and largely forgotten, except by those who were there.

The national media hardly covered the event. None of the network news broadcasts that evening mentioned it. The only national television coverage was on CNN. Lou Cannon, then covering Reagan for the *Washington Post*, wrote:

> Reagan's trip back to Washington on Tuesday will be a long one. It includes stops in Hastings, Neb., to dedicate a journalism center named after Washington lobbyist Robert K. Gray. . . . The Hastings stop, aides say, is a months-long commitment to Gray by former White House Chief of Staff

Howard H. Baker, Jr. When a reporter asked a White House official if this
was Reagan's 'most meaningless' stop, the official thought a moment and
replied, 'I'd have to say it was in the top five.' "

The Gray Center for the Communications Arts has met some of its
promise. It has brought a new facility to the campus, with some good
equipment where students can learn about radio and television. But it is not
state-of-the-art and the campus has not become a media center, the promised "window on the world." As former Nebraska Senator Carl Curtis said,
"You cannot move a media center to a place just because you've got a good
building."[46]

"It [the Gray Center] was sort of Bob's legacy to himself," Mark Moran
said.[47] In 1990, students taking a class in the Gray Center were asked which
ones wanted to be journalists, or writers, or television correspondents or
any other communications professional. Out of a class of thirty, only one
student raised his hand.

George Bush won the 1988 presidential election. In time, Gray would hire
another top Bush aide, as he had done with Daniel Murphy, to shore up his
White House ties. But by now in Washington, it really did not matter to
lobbying and PR firms like H&K who won or lost presidential elections. A
PR man who worked for Gray at Gray and Company and Hill and Knowlton
calmly summed up just how little the great partisan debates of the nation
matter in Washington. "It's sort of an outside Washington assumption—that
there are Democrats in Washington, Republicans in Washington, and when
your administration leaves, your senator gets beat, your party is out of
power, that your influence is reduced by that exact amount. That's not the
case. Now the perception is Gray could get to Reagan, so that's why we got
all that business . . . But the fact is we're all very, very well connected and
because it's all a big revolving door in Washington, the people who come
here and become hitters and decide to stay in Washington, it really doesn't
matter, within reason, who's in power because your influence doesn't go
away. There are very few people who have to pack up and leave town or get
a real job if their party is out of power because the really good, solid hitters
who know how to play this game and love playing it are going to be
successful and are going to stay. You don't go through every election and
throw people's rolodex cards out because their party has just gotten beat.
There is a permanent, unelected government here or unelected political
power structure that stays and is constantly added to as time goes on and
does not—Democrats don't lose business because the Democrats don't win
the White House. We've also settled into a rather permanent split between
Republican control of the White House and Democratic control of the Hill,
and that's fabulous for consultants."

16

WALTZING WITH WASHINGTON

Our job is not to make white black or to cover the truth, but to tell the positive side regardless of who the client is.

Robert Gray[1]

By the 1990s, the influence-peddling abuses of the 1980s had started to surface, and Americans literally began to pay for them.[2] The cozy relationships among the lobbyists and the Congress and the Executive Branch became publicly evident in one scandal after another. Members of Congress worked in tandem with lobbyists to generate "grass-roots" support for pet issues. Lobbyists formed coalitions to support the White House's favorite issues. The White House recruited lobbyists to help with controversial appointees needing Senate confirmation. The Congressional committees or the White House Commissions who were supposed to be looking out for the people's interest, who were supposed to do oversight of the agencies, who were supposed to clean up the messes when discovered, worked with *and were often comprised of* lobbyists and publicists. The very organizations designed to protect America from an abusive system had become part of the system.

The next major Washington scandal to come to light after Iran–Contra involved the Department of Housing and Urban Development (HUD) and the letting of housing contracts for political favors. The person who had originally drawn the attention of HUD's inspector general's office was Thomas T. Demery, the assistant secretary for housing. Specifically, in 1989 the HUD investigators were looking into contributions made to a charity called Food For Africa by consultants and housing developers with whom Demery routinely worked. During the first twenty months after Demery assumed his HUD position, Food For Africa raised $546,000, more than half of which came from companies and individuals who had interests in HUD housing programs. The first nine months prior to that, Food For Africa had raised only $34,000.[3]

Congressman Tom Lantos (D-CA), whose Government Operations subcommittee had oversight of HUD programs, began hearings into influence-peddling at HUD in the spring of 1990. Just before Demery was scheduled to testify, he hired H&K to advise him on how best to make his case to the news media and Congress. Remarkably, Lantos announced at the hearings that the subcommittee was not going to investigate the relationship between Food For Africa and HUD contractors, a key portion of the inspector general's report that had started the HUD investigations in the first place.

In 1985, Lantos and Congressman John Porter (R-IL) had founded the Congressional Human Rights Foundation. In 1988 Lantos had asked Gray to donate office space at Washington Harbour, one of the most expensive addresses in town, for the foundation. The H&K switchboard forwarded calls to the foundation. A private, nonprofit organization, the foundation was supposed to publicize human rights abuses around the world. Ironically, they did not have to look much farther than their landlord to find governments with poor human rights records. Many of H&K's international clients over the years (Haiti, Turkey, Indonesia, South Korea, Morocco, China) have, according to Amnesty International and other human rights groups, some of the world's worst human rights records. But often the foundation overlooked H&K's clients.

The *San José Mercury News* first reported the connections between Lantos and H&K. Demery, Lantos, and H&K's Frank Mankiewicz denied that Lantos's relationship with H&K had any influence in his decision not to investigate Demery. "The fact is, I've known Tom Lantos, as I've known a . . . lot of people in this town, for forty years," Mankiewicz told the *Washington Post*.[4] It was not the last time that H&K and Lantos would be linked in controversy.

Perhaps what shocked Washington the most about the HUD scandal was not the corruption, about which many had known for years, but a statement made by a prominent Washington lobbyist and political consultant at one of the congressional hearings. When Paul Manafort said during the hearings that his work for clients seeking HUD contracts could be termed "influence peddling," it was clear that Manafort saw nothing wrong with what he had done or how he operated. The new generation of Washington lobbyists, unencumbered by ethical concerns, had truly arrived.

Along with the HUD influence-peddling scandal, the enormous cost of the saving-and-loan crisis was beginning to be realized by the American people. Perhaps more than any other controversy this best reflected the triumph of special interests over the common good. Both the Congress and the Reagan–Bush administrations contributed to the crisis. Both Republicans and Democrats actively participated in it. And lobbyists not only helped create the crisis, but profited handsomely from it.

By 1990, the Congress and the media needed someone to blame. Charles Keating became the prime example of a savings-and-loan executive run amok. Five United States Senators, dubbed "The Keating Five" because of their dealings with Keating, became the congressional representatives most clearly identified with the controversy.[5]

Robert Thompson became the lobbyist who was held out as the embodiment of the evil influence peddler. In the mid-1980s, several executives had left Gray and Company and had started their own lobbying firms, one of whom was Robert Thompson. Many of these smaller, sons-of-Gray-and-Company firms were very successful—both in terms of profitability and of substantive accomplishments for their clients. They reflected the new attitudes toward lobbying, and, in several cases, their fuzzy ethics.

As a young man, Thompson had first worked for George Bush during the 1980 presidential campaign as a glorified baggage carrier. He then worked as the Vice President's Executive Assistant for Congressional Relations during the first Reagan–Bush term. Thompson had never worked in Washington, knew little about congressional procedure, or even where anything was located. But he learned quickly. Since Bush was also President of the Senate, Thompson got to know the congressional leaders and their staff personally and had almost instant access to most members of Congress. He was the type of person Gray wanted for his firm, because he had connections both in Congress and the White House. Towards the end of the term Gray hired Thompson.

Thompson did not like working at Gray and Company. He said he wanted more independence and could make more money on his own. At Gray and Company, since he was not a salaried employee, he received only a percentage of his billable hours. Nor did Thompson like working on accounts for people he had never met, accounts that had been turned over to him after Gray had successfully pitched the client, but whose promises and plans he had never been a part of. In 1985, only a few years after arriving in Washington, Thompson opened Thompson and Company.

Thompson operated his firm in a manner almost diametrically opposed to the way Gray ran Gray and Company. He did not want hundreds of clients, but a few well-paying ones to whom he could give his complete attention. He was young, ambitious, energetic, and eager to put what he had learned at the White House and on Capitol Hill to use. "My business basically is personal relationships and understanding the process and being able to learn what the client's problems are and then sense the political [and personal] needs of the people on the Hill," Thompson said of his modus operandi.[6]

Thompson's career path would fit most Americans' definition of Washington-revolving-door-influence-peddling politics: someone who leaves his government job and turns around and uses his knowledge and friendships for personal profit. But Thompson does not see it that way. To him, he is simply doing what thousands of others have done, only he is doing it more successfully. To him, what he does is ethical because he is honest with his clients and honest with the politicians. "Ethics are intuitive and visceral anyway. I don't think they can write an ethics law that is stronger than the way I feel about the way I should do things. . . . What I really have to sell is an understanding of the process and relationships with people that they— members of Congress or Executive Branch officials—that trust me and that feel like my client's issues are good ones. It is a personal relationship business. I really can't get my mind around peddling influence. I'm not sure even what that means," he said. Thompson worked quietly, one on one, and kept a low profile until the summer of 1990.

In 1990 Thompson became one of the targets of the Senate Antitrust Subcommittee, chaired by Senator Howard Metzenbaum (D-OH), which was investigating the savings-and-loan scandal. Thompson was the lobbyist for James M. Fail, an Arizona businessman whose purchase in 1988 of Bluebonnet Savings (the consolidation of fifteen Texas savings and loan associations) in Dallas had cost the U.S. Treasury over a billion dollars in subsidies. The subcommittee criticized federal officials for approving the sale, because Fail had put only one thousand dollars of his own money toward the sale.

Thompson readily admitted that he had helped Fail win approval of these purchases by helping him understand the Washington process and introducing him to the right government officials. One official was M. Danny Wall, who at the time was head of the Federal Home Loan Bank Board which had approved the sale. Thompson had gotten to know Wall when Wall worked as a Senate aide and Thompson worked for Bush. In return, Fail had not only paid Thompson, but had arranged a $150,000 loan for him, and agreed to give him a share of any future profits from Bluebonnet. Metzenbaum characterized Thompson's efforts on behalf of Fail as an exercise in high-level influence-peddling. He said that the sale of the Texas S&Ls was an "outrageous" government giveaway.[7]

Thompson believed that he had done nothing wrong, that, in fact, he had done a great job for his client. He characterized Metzenbaum's inquiry as a partisan witch hunt. After all, there were many other Washington lobbyists doing the same thing as he had who were never questioned. His defense, like the Keating-Five Senators, was that he was doing nothing different from what everyone else was doing. The Keating-Five Senators said they were simply trying to protect a contributor against the mean federal regulators. Thompson was simply trying to help a client understand the system. But no one seemed to be trying to help the American taxpayers and the thousands of S&L depositors who lost all of their savings.

In a complaint reminiscent of Judith Reisman's disastrous antipornography battle with the Congress, the media, and the special interests, Thompson felt like he was used and discredited because he was an easy target. "Metzenbaum was laughing with some of the lawyers involved about how much money he was making from me and Jim Fail, and the *New York Times* reporter was laughing saying, 'Look, it is just summer theater; no one takes this seriously.' . . . So they can take someone's life and destroy it at least temporarily and not even care. . . . 'Don't take this personally; that is the way Washington works.' . . . I think that it is worse now because you have the media and people understand how to manipulate it and get media working in concert with the staffs and hype interest in hearings," Thompson said. In the end the "summer theater" resulted in little substantive change to correct the problems the congressional hearings had exposed. Thompson and other lobbyists continued to operate just as they had before the hearings. The savings-and-loan costs continued to grow exorbitantly.

Gray's involvement in the S&L crisis was not limited to spawning a lobbyist who was implicated. He and H&K became involved in the S&L bailout. By 1990, the Resolution Trust Corporation (RTC), which had been created to handle the S&L crisis, faced disposing of $16 billion worth of properties once owned by failed S&Ls. The more property the RTC could sell and the higher the prices the RTC could obtain, the less the American taxpayer would have to pay for the bailout, not to mention the cost of maintaining the properties. James Gall, Jr., a flamboyant Miami-based auctioneer, won the RTC contract in May 1990 to auction off the first $300 million worth of property. Although Gall had little experience in handling real estate auctions on this scale (hardly anyone did), he did have a key backer: Robert Gray.

To win the contract as the lowest bidder, Gall had asked for only 2.48 percent commission on the properties that sold, far lower than the normal 4 to 10 percent. Gall had also agreed to put up $2 million to cover the costs of the auction. Usually the seller is required to pay the marketing costs and other expenses.

Gall knew the RTC wanted to have a great deal of favorable publicity for the auction since it was constantly being badgered by the media for misman-agement of the properties. He knew he needed a firm that could handle the publicity "on a big scale." Gall was aware of H&K's reputation, and he reasoned that hiring the largest PR firm in the world made sense since "we were going to conduct the largest auction in the history of the world."[8] He also knew Gray was powerful politically.

Gray saw this as a good opportunity to make money. After H&K declined to go into partnership with Gall, Gray personally pledged half of the $2 million—$1 million of his own money—for the marketing fund. In addition, Gall gave H&K a $450,000 subcontract to publicize the auction.

The deal worked out between Gray and Gall was not the first time Gray had tried to do personal business on the side with a client. In this case, it seemed like a good arrangement, placing Gray at no risk, except if the auction were a complete failure. For his $1 million, Gray was to receive the first $1 million in Gall's commissions. Gall's company, The Auction Company of America, would get the second $1 million and then Gray alone would get the next $500,000. After that they would split the remaining commissions. Gall's company would have to sell more than $100 million in properties just to pay Gray, his key investor, before his company stood a chance of breaking even, much less making a profit.

The promotion for the auction was almost instantaneous. It was touted to be "the biggest real-estate auction in the history of the world," possibly the biggest auction ever. The auction, scheduled for the following fall, was supposed to be "a high-tech, high-rollers-only, international event."[9] Only $1-million-plus properties would be sold at an auction broadcast live via satellite to several U.S. cities, Tokyo, and London.

The big kickoff for the auction was scheduled for July. H&K had arranged a large press conference, inviting one thousand members of the press. But the day before the event, the RTC canceled it without warning. It said that Gall was not prepared and the information packages that the buyers needed for the auction were incomplete. Gall and H&K insisted that the problems were with the RTC, not them. Roger Lindberg, a H&K vice president who worked on the project, told the *South Florida Business Journal*, "We have five volumes of memos that are seven inches thick. For example, we did seventeen different drafts of the press kit. This is a world record, I am sure. It was easier to plan the Iceland summit on ten days notice. We had the best minds in the business working on this. Our company and Jim's felt sort of patriotic about this thing, doing something good for the taxpayers. We brought in Bob Gray and Frank Mankiewicz. We had the best satellite communication vendors. We lined up "60 Minutes," the BBC, Tokyo Broadcasting, CNN, but we could never get an approval from RTC. We finally got the press kit. But we never got the marketing approvals."[10]

The same month of the canceled press conference, Gray pulled out of the deal with Gall. He told the *Legal Times* that Gall had lowered the commission from 4 to 2.48 without consulting him and he had serious reservations. "Auction Company costs mounted, and it did not look like they would be covered by the 2.48 percent. . . . It was more risky than I had thought to get a fair return on my investment. . . . I had an option to walk without penalty and decided to walk," Gray said.[11] Not only were Gall's costs mounting, so were H&K's. "Hill and Knowlton spent a fortune photographing, filming, and making brochures for properties that had already been quietly removed from the auction by the RTC. They hired 200 vendors . . . only to have the bid specifications changed by the RTC," the *South Florida Business Journal* reported.[12]

There was more trouble. The RTC sold $39-million worth of property that was supposed to be in the auction, thus undermining buyer and broker confidence. In addition, H&K could not communicate directly with the RTC because it would not provide them with the correct forms. "We could not send anything directly to the RTC because they required what they called an acceptance form. This was some form for tracking through the layers of authority. We could not get an acceptance form because you have to have an acceptance form to get an acceptance form," Lindberg said.[13]

Gray's withdrawal jeopardized the auction. "It could have . . . I never want anyone to fail, but I must keep my own business reputation here," Gray said.[14] But H&K continued to do work for Gall. By September, the RTC canceled the auction entirely. Most blamed either RTC mismanagement or Gall and his company for the failure. But others said that the failure rests with Gray. At the time L. William Seidman was the embattled chairman of the Federal Deposit Insurance Corporation (FDIC), which also made him in charge of the RTC. White House Chief of Staff John Sununu and others in the Bush administration were pressing for Seidman's resignation. Seidman did not like Gray either personally or politically. A high-level FDIC official told the Auction Company that they were having problems because they simply had gone into business with the wrong people.

The RTC inspector general began an investigation into, among other things, whether Gall had hired subcontractors like H&K without competitive bids as the contract required. Gall said that they were never serious. No one from the RTC inspector general's office ever contacted him. Gall faced severe financial hardship after the RTC canceled the auction. H&K did not get most of its $450,000 or the $125,000 for advertising, including a full-page ad in the *Wall Street Journal*. The American taxpayers had the additional cost of maintaining these properties for another year. One expert estimated that carrying $300 million worth of property for a year cost the government $50 million. But once again Gray walked away unscathed.

Marty Gold was another Gray and Company veteran who, like Robert Thompson, had left and had started his own son-of-Gray-and-Company firm. In the early 1980s Gold had been the Senate Republican equivalent of Gary Hymel in the House of Representatives. Gold was Tennessee Senator Howard Baker's top aide when Baker was Senate Minority and later Majority Leader. Like Thompson, Gold was convinced that he could do far better on his own than he could at Gray and Company.[15] Gold had known Thompson when he had worked at the White House and had recruited him for Gray and Company. In the mid-1980s, Gold and Thompson left Gray and Company and joined Howard Liebengood, who then was the Sergeant-at-Arms of the Senate, to start their own lobbying firm. Within a couple of months, Thompson went out on his own, leaving the new firm called Gold and Liebengood. Like Thompson and Company, Gold and Liebengood operated differently from Gray and Company. It only lobbied and concentrated on Capitol Hill. "We emphasize the fact that most of us here are former staff people. We have a sense of what the staff does. . . . For a firm to be successful, it has to be one that has a philosophy of dealing with the staff,'' Gold explained.

The number and power of congressional staffers had exploded since the mid-1970s. Gray said that he recognized very early the increasing power of congressional staffers and began hiring younger lobbyists and women.[16] "I can remember when I first started with [Senator] Mark Hatfield,'' Marty Gold said, "He was just completing his first term. He basically still saw and signed his mail. That went out about the middle of the 1970s. . . . More and more he just got insulated and depended upon his staff.'' The congressional staffer became the filters through which everything—visitors, phone calls, faxes, letters—had to flow before reaching an elected official. Soon the majority of work was handled by the staff, leaving members of Congress isolated and often ignorant. It was a great breeding ground for lobbyists. "Most young people particularly who come into the government now, stay for less than eighteen months and it's purely on the basis of establishing credentials. They go into the private sector and make more money and that's what's happening," former Senator Paul Laxalt said.[17]

Most young people years ago thought that coming to Washington and working for their senator or congressman or the President was an end in itself. Many still do. But more and more, government service is seen as an item to enhance a resumé. "A lot of people work on the Hill to get their ticket punched or they want it on their resumé that they worked for Senator so and so for two years and they're ready to get out of there and do something else. . . . A lot get congressional experience and they leave and try to market that in some fashion where they don't have any sense of putting anything back into the institution. All they want to do is take away an item on their resumé. It's a line-item for them," Gold said.

In the end, lobbying and public relation executives have more ability to hold onto power for longer periods of time and make more money than any of the media or the politicians. "They might be more of an institution now," said Senator Laxalt. "There are very few sort of final endings to stories in Washington. It is a revolving door where people keep changing positions. . . . The people who have been with us for the last ten or fifteen years will stay with us. You don't make permanent friends or permanent enemies in town, [just] shifting alliances. It is just a dance. And it is a dance that a couple thousand people in Washington do for the benefit or entertainment of two hundred and fifty million Americans and countless others around the world, and everybody understands that it is a dance," said a former H&K executive.

Like Thompson, Gold believes the key to lobbying is developing personal relationships with members of Congress and their staff. "When you get to be very compressed in time, they're getting near a mark up [a congressional committee session where legislation is refined], fifty calls are coming in, ten can be returned. What makes your call get returned? It might be who your client is; it might be who you are or how much you know the person. Something has to distinguish them. They're not throwing up these messages in the air and just picking whatever lands on the floor. I think it's very important to develop those relationships,'' Gold said.[18]

Buying a lobbyist in Washington is like buying into the system. As the Keating Five showed, a contributor, regardless of whether or not the person is a constituent, has influence. Most lobbyists work hard and spend money developing relationships with key individuals on Capitol Hill. Hiring a lobbyist means, in effect, renting their relationships. So what happens to people who cannot afford lobbyists? "They do the best they can with what they have. It's like saying, 'What about the person who can't afford the best lawyer? What about the person who can't afford the best doctor?' Not all doctors are equal. Not all lawyers are equal. . . . There's all sorts of inequalities that are built in the system. Obviously, not everybody can afford it [a lobbyist], which does not mean that the ones who can't shouldn't have it. What is the solution? I don't think there is a solution. What I'm really saying to you is the system is replete with inequalities. . . . If there were no lobbyists, there would be inequalities in that system. . . . The presence or absence of lobbyists is just one more inequality in the system,'' Gold said.

What Dilenschneider had started with Gray and Company, paying a high price for a politically prominent firm, continued in Washington. By the end of the decade, Gold's firm had been swallowed in the merger mania. Burson-Marsteller, H&K's competitor, bought it in late 1989. Gold said that when Dilenschneider bought Gray in 1986, the purchase created the perception that H&K had increased its strength in Washington. Other companies wanted to do the same. Gold did not feel his company would have been purchased by Burson-Marsteller if it were not for the H&K move. The wave of mergers, in his view, had less to do with any real needs on the part of the giant PR and lobbying firms than with a peculiarly Washington brand of one-upmanship. "I think it has a lot less to do with real capability . . . and [is] more a matter of perception. What does the market think about our presence in Washington? How effective does the market believe that we can be vis-à-vis our competitors? Why should they do business with us when they can do business with somebody else? It's because we have 'X' in our stable or 'Y' in our stable. The acquisition of one firm can lead to the acquisition of other firms. The market, in that sense, drives itself,'' Gold explained.

In Washington, the market was the rich. Big corporations, successful executives, bankers, real-estate developers, whoever could afford a stake were the people the lobbyists solicited. People without resources were often ignored. Issues in which the beneficiaries of change did not have financial muscle were put on the back burner. A prominent Washington lobbyist described how it works today. "You have to be up there [on Capitol Hill] and see the problem coming as early on as possible. The further down the road it gets in a negative direction from your interest, the more difficult it is to turn it around because it takes on a life of its own. Early warning systems are important. That's why there are a lot of tax lobbyists or lawyers who charge all these outrageous fees. *Success fees* are sort of a rage these days. They'll announce a tax bill and say we want to wrap this up in one month's time and the world starts calling. 'Oh my God. I've got to get a change in this effective date from June first to June fifteenth, otherwise my bond deal won't close.' And some people say, 'Well, send me fifty thousand dollars for making the effort and if it works, I want a half million.'

"The more compressed the time frame, the more relationship-driven it is. You can't get in to see Rob Leonard, who's chief counsel for Rostenkowski, or the top Ways and Means staff people when you've got that much time. They get four hundred or five hundred calls per day. The question is how does a staff member or member decide how to spend your time. Well, it's the three or four years prior to that getting to know someone, getting comfortable with them, trusting them, liking their clients, knowing they are honest; all of that gels at that one period of time. That's why it is worth so much money to people. So it is an access. Therefore, a lot of people that don't have that are disadvantaged in the process."

This lobbyist described the government—Congress and the Executive Branch—as a large casino. There will always be nickel slots, but the real attention goes to the high rollers. "Someone who makes forty thousand dollars per year doesn't have much at stake anyway, I don't think," he said.

Sometimes the richest and the biggest do not win in Washington. H&K being the biggest and representing the richer clients meant very little when the national media and Hollywood decided to team up on behalf of a public interest group. Fenton Communications is a small PR firm that was located upstairs in a townhouse in a marginal neighborhood in Washington. But it managed to get the American public to quit buying apples or drinking apple juice practically overnight, despite the fact that H&K represented the apple industry. First "60 Minutes" ran a story in 1989 that said that apples sprayed with Alar, a chemical often used to keep apples on trees longer, could cause a health risk for children. A wave of publicity followed, culminating in a personal campaign by actress Meryl Streep on talk shows and in congressional testimony. "We got rolled," Frank Mankiewicz told *The Washington Post Magazine*. "It was a very good example of what the hell can go wrong."[19]

Despite H&K's best efforts—press releases, video press releases, advertisements, dozens of experts, government officials—all declaring apples were safe, the apple industry lost millions of dollars in sales. Eventually the EPA banned Alar. The PR campaign, in effect, killed the chemical. It also hurt many small apple growers who never used Alar and whose apples were perfectly safe. Most of these farmers suffered financial hardship; some lost their farms.

But the Alar controversy gave a great boost to the PR industry. Food and health-related issues became a cash cow for many PR firms, including H&K. Industry could see how bad PR could devastate it in just a couple of weeks. Even worse, the new, activist head of the Food and Drug Administration, David Kessler, was making new demands for honest food labeling and consumer safety. Gray brought Nancy Glick, who had left in 1989, back to head consumer and nutrition affairs. She said, "What we are all realizing is that food can no longer be a side dish in the industry. . . . Food PR is a coming field."[20]

The Health Division operated almost like a separate entity within H&K's Washington office. It became its most successful area. (Even Gray was not immune from food-related controversy. When there was speculation that it might be the White House water that was causing the President's and the First Lady's thyroid problems, Gray brought his own bottle of Perrier to a White House luncheon.[21])

Where would a "church" that was "a hugely profitable global racket that survives by intimidating members and critics in a Mafia-like manner," as *Time* magazine described it, go to change its public image and enhance its credibility?[22] Where else but to Gray. Not long after Gray had tried to help the Unification Church's Reverend Moon with his tax and legal problems, he took on another religious cult: the Church of Scientology. The Scientologists had been having trouble with the federal government, particularly the IRS, since 1967 when the IRS denied Scientology tax-exempt status.

By 1985, the IRS was seeking to indict Scientology founder L. Ron Hubbard for tax fraud. Like the Reverend Moon, Hubbard tried to take protection under the First Amendment freedom of religion clause. He died in 1986 before the case was prosecuted. Not long after Hubbard's death, the Scientologists hired Gray to handle their public relations. (Another firm that had been approached by the Scientologists to improve its public image told them to "clean up their act" and "stop being a church," but the Scientologists did not like that advice and turned to Gray instead.)[23]

Over the next several years, the Scientologists became one of Gray's and H&K's most lucrative accounts. The "church" spent millions trying to improve its image as a fringe group. Jackson Bain handled the media coaching and the television. "H&K was involved with every aspect of Scientology. I mean the writing of stuff. Organizing things. They worked on this IRS [problem] . . . That was a *broad* program," said one former executive who worked on the account. The H&K program for the Scientologists was inches thick and pounds heavy. Its aim was to convince the American public that the Scientologists were really good people who were simply misunderstood. "Everybody had L. Ron Hubbard sayings and Scientology books and everything [in their offices]. You know the leader is supposed to be sort of god. I mean he's dead, but he's not really dead. . . . I think they created National Religious Day or something where congressmen signed on and really the Scientologists were behind it and it looked great, like celebrate your religion day," an H&K executive remembered.

H&K provided almost every service imaginable to the Scientologists. When two Scientologists were jailed, two H&K people were sent to bail them out. Gray lobbied on Freedom of Information Act issues on behalf of the church to help it get government documents at a time when it was under investigation by the IRS and the FBI. The Scientologists became one of the main sponsors of Ted Turner's Goodwill Games. H&K worked with their clients on media and congressional presentations. H&K wrote and handled the radio broadcasts, the magazines, the advertisements. It lobbied on Capitol Hill.

Gray personally registered as a lobbyist on behalf of Scientology. "He liked the whole idea of that account—it was big bucks and it was his baby and they wanted to always see him," one former executive remembered. Often five or more H&K Washington employees would fly out to Scientology headquarters in Los Angeles for meetings. "Can you imagine paying for five days, full time, five or ten H&K people who are going to see their clients? First class. Hotels. Great big pockets, so, of course Gray loved that," she said.

When obvious conflicts of interest arose, H&K publicly dropped clients, such as dropping Coke when H&K, which handled Pepsi, merged with a lobbying firm that represented their competitor. But in other less obvious situations, it did not. The very size of WPP and all of its related companies made conflict-of-interest possibilities a continuing quagmire. The Scientologists opposed many prescription drugs. At the same time Gary Hymel, Gray's chief lobbyist, was organizing efforts on Capitol Hill for the Scientologists to call for a congressional investigation into the anti-depressant Prozac, Eli Lilly & Co., the pharmaceutical manufacturer and maker of Prozac, had a huge advertising account with WPP-owned J. Walter Thompson. Eli Lilly and the Scientologists became bitter enemies. When Eli Lilly questioned WPP, the parent company, about H&K representing the Scientologists, Martin Sorrell, himself, flew from London to Indianapolis to assure Eli Lilly that Gray and others were not helping the Scientologists' efforts against Prozac. But he was wrong.

In the midst of this controversy, *Time* magazine ran a very critical cover story entitled, "Scientology—The Cult of Greed." For a client paying handsomely for good PR, it was a disaster. Rudy Maxa wrote in *Washingtonian* magazine's gossip column, "After one of the largest clients at Hill and Knowlton's Washington office, the Scientologists, took a hard hit in a *Time* cover story last month, I ran into H&K chief Robert Gray. 'I promised them the cover of *Time*,' joked Gray, 'and there it is!' "[24] Others at H&K were not laughing.

At the time H&K was negotiating with SmithKline Beecham Corp. to handle the PR for the introduction of the pharmaceutical company's new anti-depressant drug. SmithKline Beecham executives were sitting around a conference table during a meeting with the H&K executive when in walked a SmithKline official with a copy of *Time*. The executive threw it on the table and said to the H&K executive, "You lied to us. You told us you had dropped this account over a year ago." The SmithKline executives caucused, returned, and asked the H&K representative to leave. They actually ushered him off the premises. H&K lost a million-dollar account.

Eventually, Gray was forced to drop the Scientology account after several drug manufacturers joined in the complaints.[25] In addition, Jackson Bain, the longtime talent in Gray's television media operation, left, like so many others, to start his own firm. The Scientology account, on which he had worked over the years, went with him.

On February 14, 1992, David Miscavige, the thirty-two-year-old head of Scientology, appeared on "Nightline." When Ted Koppel asked him what Scientology had to offer a person who was happy with a nice family and a good job, Miscavige replied that one of their services were lessons on communicating effectively. It appears that to learn H&K's communication techniques one can either hire H&K or simply join Scientology. It is probably a toss up, however, on which would be cheaper.

In the spring of 1990, H&K's Washington office's agreement to represent a new client started another controversy, only this time its impact publicly spread to the whole company, especially the New York headquarters. To many in the H&K Washington office, which had been representing the Church of Scientology, this new client did not seem controversial at all. To the Washington office, the new client was respectable, even prestigious. But at the other H&K offices around the country which were not used to handling political, often divisive, issues for clients, this client was not only controversial, it was explosive. The Catholic Church hired H&K to change public attitudes toward abortion.

When John Cardinal O'Connor, the Catholic Archbishop of New York, assumed the leadership of The National Conference of Catholic Bishop's Committee for Pro-Life Activities, the Committee decided to hire a major public relations firm to help them devise a PR counteroffensive that would offset the increasingly successful abortion-rights campaign, spearheaded by the National Abortion Rights Action League (NARAL). The Catholic Bishops wanted help in altering the debate and creating a more conducive political climate for their antiabortion position. It was the first time the Catholic Bishops had ever turned to an outside firm to wage a campaign on a public-policy issue.

The Catholic Bishops gave their administrative arm in Washington, the U.S. Catholic Conference (U.S.C.C.), the assignment to find the right PR firm. Although H&K and Gray had historic ties to the Catholic Church, that was not the reason it got the account.[26] The U.S.C.C. representative simply opened the yellow pages and began calling various PR firms to ask what they could do to increase public support against abortion. Some PR firms declined to participate from the start, but H&K did not. Based on the responses, the U.S.C.C. narrowed down the competition to two firms. The Washington H&K office prepared a presentation to solicit the account. On March 19, 1990, it made its presentation and won.

Gray called Dilenschneider in New York, who, at first, was hesitant about taking on the account. But when Gray told him the Catholic Bishops were willing to spend $5 million, Dilenschneider's hesitancy quickly evaporated. WPP, struggling to restructure $800 million in debt from its mergers, continued to apply enormous pressure on its subsidiaries to reduce costs and increase profits. Martin Sorrell in London had been pressuring Dilenschneider to increase profits. The U.S.C.C. became one of H&K's largest accounts.

To most at H&K, the first time they heard about their new client was when they read about it in Rowland Evans and Robert Novak's syndicated newspaper column in the end of March. The response was immediate and vocal. But the greatest consternation among H&K employees came not from Washington, which over the years had grown accustomed to clients of this nature, but New York. Many New York employees were outraged. Some said they would work for free for NARAL and other opposition groups. They even provided NARAL with H&K's super-secret client lists so that NARAL could pressure these clients.

More than a hundred in the New York office signed a petition protesting H&K's actions. The New York office's petition said in part: "We should not be representing any group in its advocacy of a position which would restrict the fundamental rights of all of us as Americans. It would be the equivalent of supporting a group in its effort to repeal the Votings Rights Act." One H&K employee told the *New York Times*, "There has never been anything so divisive here before. . . . You know it's bad when you have people talking about how they're going to subvert the campaign."[27]

H&K's problems were not just internal. In New York, hundreds of protesters picketed outside H&K's offices carrying signs and distributing leaflets saying, "HILL AND KNOWLTON = HIRED LIARS," and "H&K wants to force women to back-alley abortionists!" H&K had to lock the door to their building. Although the Washington office was used to picketers, to New York, it was upsetting and embarrassing.

Obviously H&K had ignored its own advice to clients, that companies should first discuss controversial or divisive policies with their workers and smooth out internal wrinkles before going public. H&K's job, after all, is to counsel clients on how to avoid public controversy. Now, suddenly, it happened to them. *The New York Times Magazine* said, "Had managers followed the advice they often give to others about how to manage a corporate crisis—'Tell it all and tell it fast'—much of the trouble and embarrassment Hill and Knowlton would face in the next months might have been avoided. Or at least minimized.'"[28]

Gray's Washington office managed the abortion account. Several in the Washington office protested in writing to Gray about not being consulted prior to taking the account. Some even refused to work on the account, a privilege given to all H&K employees. But in Washington, religious, moral, and civil-rights concerns did not matter as much as political ones. Several H&K Democrats thought the account would hurt them politically—with clients and with politicians—since Bush and the conservative movement were so widely identified with this issue. (Not all staffers took this attitude. One H&K executive said working for the Catholic Bishops one day and the Scientologists the next made him laugh out loud. Others joked that H&K, which represented evangelist Larry Jones and the Ba'hai as well as the Bishops and the Scientologists, should set up a "Religious Division.")

John Berard, the H&K Washington office's deputy general manager, said Gray, himself, was assembling the team to work on the account. Later, although a reporter had trouble finding anyone to admit he or she was working on the account, Berard said, "I've had no problem staffing this account. I think what the media has neglected to mention is the *professionalism* of the employees at Hill and Knowlton."[29] Berard, like John Lawler and other Gray devotees, felt that PR professionals should work on accounts regardless of their beliefs—that is, if they have beliefs. Berard told the same reporter that "maybe everyone might ought to do some 'blue-sky thinking' on the issue, and then they'll be able to foresee, as he does, an America where the issue of abortion can be discussed without strong, passionate feelings on either side."[30] Gray's position was in sync with this peculiar morally neutral ethic: "We would have taken whatever side came to us first."[31]

In late April, H&K sent its office managers a confidential memorandum with a Q&A section on how to deal with reporters. "If asked, 'Has H&K lost any people? Any accounts?' they were to reply, 'One person. One client.'"[32] When asked by the *New York Times* if H&K had lost any staff or clients, Berard replied, without hesitation, that they had lost one account and one junior staffer. Others in H&K admitted that there was "a significant loss of business" and several staffers had left.

Berard told the *Times*, "I don't think there's anybody who feels we've shot ourselves in the foot. This is a firm that has always taken on controversial issues. . . . No one is thinking about giving up the client. . . . Part of what the conference asked us to do is move the debate from being a polarizing, neverending political battle into a reasonable debate and maybe the spirited discussions we are now having are part of that.''[33] Gray said to *Manhattan, Inc.*, "Hill and Knowlton's roots are so deep, we've been in business so long now, that the controversy over this account will be no more than a momentary blip. Internal dissent is often very attractive."[34]

Berard and Gray were wrong. Many publications wrote that H&K had, in fact, shot itself in the foot. "Hill and Knowlton, the nation's largest public relations firm, has created a public relations problem on its own turf by taking on an anti-abortion campaign for the nation's Roman Catholic bishops," the *New York Times* wrote.[35] "In the future, maybe even PR firms will hire PR firms. Hill and Knowlton needs one now, thanks to poor handling of its new client, the United States Catholic Conference," *Legal Times* said.[36] By accepting this account, the Washington office began what turned out to be a seemingly neverending stream of bad publicity, something that hurts any company, but is devastating to a PR firm. Many blue-chip clients started to feel uncomfortable with H&K. It was not so much who the patient was, but the fact that the doctor had botched the operation.

With the Catholic Bishops account, much of the criticism that had plagued Gray and Company and had followed Gray to H&K was now all being lumped, practically all at once, publicly onto his company. Remarkably, although Gray and his office had won the account and were taking the lead in handling it, the condemnation fell not on Gray, but on Dilenschneider in New York. When the media called for comment, Gray often refused to speak. Dilenschneider not only spoke, but was featured very prominently in *Manhattan, Inc.*, *The New York Times Magazine*, and other high-profile publications. His ego refused to allow him to either admit he had made a mistake in letting Gray take the account or to place the responsibility for the account with Gray.

Although the old Hill and Knowlton had died quietly and unceremoniously years before, this account publicly ended H&K's long-held, affectionate reputation as "the gray lady of PR," as the "quiet, highly professional company whose client list was limited to the cream of corporate America."[37] It also marked the beginning of the end for Dilenschneider.

An H&K employee said, "The best PR advice Hill and Knowlton could have given the church was 'Don't hire a PR firm.'"[38] But James Lake, an H&K competitor and close Bush advisor, felt that H&K should be commended for taking on the abortion issue, not criticized. The Catholic Bishops, Lake said, "have a right to be heard. They have a legitimate viewpoint. If Bob or Hill and Knowlton says we want to work for the Catholic Bishops, that's their business. . . . I respect firms and people who are willing to take on controversy."

George Worden felt that John Hill would have never taken the Catholic Bishops or any of the other religious accounts. "First of all, it made no sense. . . . There are some guys in that [H&K] Washington office that would take that kind of account and couldn't spend fifteen minutes with a Catholic bishop and survive intellectually. They just couldn't. The other guy [the bishop] would be so much smarter than they are. And I would hate to advise all these people [what to] do. All ministers are the same, whatever their denomination. They do the same thing. They're persuaders. That is what we [in PR] do. That's what they do. How can we help them? How in the world can we help them? . . . You guys are the original persuaders and in the Catholics' case, they've been doing it for two thousand years in an organized way. Now if they can't tell their story, we can't help them."

There was another, more basic problem with the account. As Worden explained, abortion is an almost impossible issue to "promote" or "lobby" in the usual sense. "What you have to have in any proposition is the gray area. They'll be a whole bunch of folks who absolutely do not agree with you. They're all in the black areas. Now there are the guys who hire you. The white hats, let's say, and they have a position and you have to agree with them. They have their supporters and they're one hundred percent on that white side. Now, who is in the middle. It's all in the gray, in the middle, and they don't care all that much about the issue. You have to tell them about the issue and then persuade them to your white side or the black guys persuade them over to their side. But the gray area has to exist. On the abortion issue, in the United States, there is no gray area. It is black or it is white."

Like the pornography issue, Dilenschneider cited First Amendment rights of free speech as a reason for taking the account. H&K wanted to refocus the abortion debate from NARAL's successful efforts at framing it to be a freedom of choice issue, to the Catholic Church's position that it is taking a human life. The H&K campaign for the Catholic Conference was all-inclusive. A bishop told the *New York Times* that H&K's approach was educational and informational.[39] The PR firm said it would try to address both the concerns of public officials and to change the attitudes of the American public. It said such an effort would take three to five years. The Knights of Columbus, a Catholic fraternal group, agreed to provide the majority of the funds.[40]

For the bishops, like most other PR campaigns, first a poll was conducted (by the Wirthlin Group) to set a benchmark from which they would work. Then it test marketed different ideas to see which ones worked to change public attitudes. In the meantime, H&K's Washington office analyzed the Catholic Bishops's current approach—its messages and literature. The initial surveys by Wirthlin indicated that most Americans do not know how many abortions were being performed a year and how some women were using abortions (as a means of birth control). H&K believed that it could change public opinion once some of these facts were skillfully presented to the public.

For the approximately two years it serviced the account, H&K had about thirty people working on the Catholic Conference campaign. It never mounted a large, national media campaign, but concentrated, instead, on internal communication within the organization. In the end, after spending $3 million, the Catholic Bishops, like so many other accounts, dropped H&K. When some of the account's biggest supporters inside H&K left the firm, the Washington office had trouble servicing the account. Mankiewicz refused to work on it. When a Catholic representative wanted to go on one of the talk shows in opposition to abortion, H&K had difficulty finding someone willing to call the television stations and networks, despite the fact that the U.S.C.C. was paying H&K $100,000 a month. One executive who worked on the account said that if it were ever audited, one would find incredible expenditures from Gray and every other high-level official for strategic advice. "It's garbage," he said.

A prominent Washington lobbyist said, "I have no reason to dislike Bob Gray for anything that he's ever done to me. I just don't think that he runs his business the right way. If you take on any and all clients. I don't like that." By taking almost anyone who walked in the door who could pay, H&K began to lose its prestige. It was no longer considered the Tiffany of PR firms. "They've become a K Mart," Senator Laxalt said. "There's big dollars around and everybody has to be represented in Washington, and Hill and Knowlton is going out there doing their best to get these clients, and I'm not sure what they get in return," said former NSC director and Washington lobbyist Richard Allen.[41] Former Gray and Company executive John Lawler said about Gray, "He wasn't afraid of a controversial client. He wanted to make sure that the issue was right. He always believed that it would be like a lawyer. Your client deserves to be represented in the best way that they can. . . . You have to be able to pay for it. That is the only difference."

In 1989 the Vatican asked Gray to address the International Conference on AIDS in Rome. He did not want to do it, but it was an invitation that was impossible to refuse. The Vatican invited Gray to speak not because of his sexual preference and firsthand experiences with this dreaded disease. (At the time Gray's longtime companion as well as other friends were dying of AIDS.) Gray was there because of his expertise in public relations. "I have studied this subject from my professional perspective and perhaps my views may be helpful."

Gray explained that a private White House survey showed how ignorant Americans were about AIDS. He cited numerous statistics and said, "Statistically the most discouraging public opinion information reveals we may be losing ground. In 1986, the percentage of those who believed they could catch AIDS from shaking hands with an AIDS patient was seven percent— today nine percent hold that view." Gray failed to say that it was the same White House that he had actively supported that refused to ask for or spend the money necessary to adequately educate the public. In Gray's opinion, it would take massive efforts from three major groups to properly communicate AIDS information. The first was big business. Gray said, "Major corporations, major advertisers, and the captains of major communications systems need to receive individual attention. They must know the importance of the role they can play in conveying the message. They must hear the urgency of the need for their doing so." Gray was Chairman and Chief Executive Officer of one of the largest PR firms in the world which represented some of the largest corporations. But there is no indication that he had urged his clients to "convey the message" in any significant way.

The second group was world governments. He criticized one by one American government policies toward AIDS as if he had not worked hard to put in place the very officials who had designed and were implementing these policies.

The third group was the Catholic Church. The Catholic Church teaches that homosexuality is a mortal sin. At first, it sounded as if Gray was going to take a strong stand when he said, "The Church has the moral authority to combat the mythology that AIDS is a direct punishment from God. As the disease spreads, so spreads fear and bigotry and the pulpit of the Catholic Church is the mightiest of weapons against these dark forces." But then he concluded, "The Church can offer a message of hope to those already suffering from AIDS and of moral discipline to help prevent its spread."

Gray said, "In the case of AIDS, there are added communications barriers in the powerful stigma attached by both society and religion to the behaviors most prominently associated with HIV infections." It was a stigma he had fought his entire adult life. In the best Gray tradition, he billed part of his trip to Italy to the Scientology account.

Bill Austin, Gray's longtime companion, died of AIDS at age thirty-eight. In December 1991 Barbara Bush dedicated the Bill Austin Day Treatment and Care Center for the Nation's Capital. Within the press material for the dedication ceremony was a touching biography of Bill Austin that mentioned an "eighteen-year partnership." Nowhere in any of the press materials or articles was Gray's name mentioned.

By 1990, Ronald Reagan, Gray's political gravy train, was in need of a public relations boost himself. Reagan had retired to a very expensive home in Los Angeles, financed by his friends, and had traveled to Japan to earn millions in "speaking fees." Meanwhile, the country was trying to sustain an enormous debt he had helped create and was in the middle of a savings and loan, Wall Street, and banking crisis for which generations to come would have to pay. In a courtroom testifying on Iran–Contra, Reagan appeared as if he had been the Alzheimer president, remembering hardly anything about one of the most important foreign policy initiatives in his administration.

But Gray, like a good lobbyist and PR man, rose to Reagan's defense. In a *Newsweek* column he wrote, "It is time somebody said it: 'Let's hear it for Ronald Reagan!' "[42] Gray went on to cite what he felt were Reagan's greatest accomplishments in military preparedness and foreign policy. But the American public had grown tired of Reagan-era PR rhetoric. In the letters to the magazine the following week, the responses said: "Robert Keith Gray's essay 'In Defense of Reagan' appalled me. Ronald Reagan spent us into the largest deficit ever because of his penchant for weaponry. It's easy to buy things if one doesn't have to pay for them. And during the Reagan years, we were treated to his private war in Nicaragua, the Iran–Contra scandal and the HUD scandal. His insistence on getting government off our backs resulted in the deregulation that helped create the savings and loan debacle" or "Gray seems to suffer from the same disease that plagued Reagan in the face of bothersome facts: he forgets."[43] Only one letter from a military man, out of five, supported Gray's views, not too convincing a showing for a PR guru.

Gray and Company lasted six years. Six years after Gray returned to head H&K's Washington office, similar signs of stress and trouble were evident. The high rate of turnover that had plagued Gray and Company continued at H&K. The decisions on what to do on behalf of a client were driven by what the client would pay, not what needed to be done. For the small clients, staffers were told, "Go do it, but don't spend much time." There were ceilings on the hours. If a professional needed to work five hours beyond the ceiling to accomplish something for the client, too bad. The client was only willing to spend so much and therefore the company would not get paid for the work. Staff bonuses and raises were based on the number of hours the staffer billed.

It did not take long for the continuing trickle of professionals leaving H&K's Washington office to turn into a flood. For example, in 1989 H&K bought The Government Research Corporation for $1.8 million. Three years later, all but one of the firm's two dozen employees had left H&K. Government Research Corporation was essentially a for-profit think-tank, staffed with Ph.D.s who researched and analyzed issues for clients. The firm was essentially academic in function, so staffers left in droves after being subsumed into the high-pressure, "bucket shop" atmosphere of H&K.

By 1990, Gray once again needed "more reach" into the White House. With his H&K office hemorrhaging employees, he needed to increase the perception of political power. He needed access. So he did what he has always done: he hired it. H&K bought Wexler, Reynolds, Fuller, Harrison & Schule, a lobbying firm headed by Craig Fuller, Bush's vice presidential chief of staff who had lost out to John Sununu for White House Chief of Staff in 1989. And just as he had promised Neil Livingstone, Alejandro Orfila, Dan Murphy, and others, Gray indicated to Fuller, then thirty-nine, that he was the heir apparent to succeed Gray, who was then sixty-nine years old. Fuller was named president and chief operating officer of H&K, reporting to Gray. He moved into the Washington Harbour offices. "The job was, what's new, misrepresented to him. He comes in as president. 'Now you run the store. You're in charge of the whole thing,' says Gray, with Jennings sitting there who had been in charge of the whole thing. And as Fuller would learn, [Jennings] continued to be in charge of the whole thing," Worden said.

Fuller remained an advisor to George Bush, often speaking on behalf of the Bush administration on television shows and in other forums and attending campaign planning sessions and White House State dinners. He continued to handle his own accounts, but he was by no means in charge. "Fuller was left adrift. . . . They hired people without him even knowing it, and he's supposed to be running the place. He couldn't even get a look at somebody. I don't mean a clerk; I mean a professional," Worden said.

Others in Fuller's former firm were unhappy about the merger. Many refused to move to Washington Harbour. They stayed in their old offices and tried to operate as a separate entity renamed the Wexler Group. Anne Wexler, the former Carter White House official (whose confidential memos had been found in Gray's trash after the 1980 campaign), quickly became disillusioned and began to look for ways to get out of the deal. She told a friend who had warned her not to merge, "Oh what a horrible mistake. I should have listened to you." Sheila Tate said that there was "great consternation among" the Wexler Group after the merger.[44]

In response to H&K's Wexler purchase, Burson-Marsteller bought another Washington lobbying firm, Black, Manafort, Stone & Kelly (the same Paul Manafort who admitted "influence-peddling" in helping clients obtain HUD grants). By 1991, practically all of the major international public relations firms had purchased all or a portion of Washington's most politically connected lobbying outfits. Tom Bell, Gray's counterpart at Burson-Marsteller, told the *Washington Post* that these PR firms wanted to "practice governmental relations on a global basis for clients with global needs." Now the nation's top lobbyists were working equally hard for foreign interests as they would for any American client. Global concerns replaced national interest. More and more the lines were not so clearly drawn.

The Foreign Agents Registration Act, enacted after U.S. agents learned that German Nazis had hired public relations firms to secretly lobby Congress, was supposed to throw "the spotlight of pitiless publicity" on foreign agents by making them report their activities to the criminal division of the Justice Department for the media to scrutinize. But the law has proven to be largely ineffective in terms of filings by lobbyists, of enforcement by the Justice Department, and of coverage by the Washington press corps. Few bothered to question what these lobbyists were supposed to accomplish which could or should not be done through normal diplomatic channels.

Washingtonian magazine casually wrote in 1992 about Craig Fuller, "With his White House access, Fuller soon was being sought by clients with interests in Europe and Japan."[45]

By the 1990s Gray's idea of "one-stop shopping"—of combining lobbying with PR—had become truly international. The American public would not only be bombarded with information and advertisements designed to influence their opinions on domestic issues, but also barraged with "information" designed to shape their opinions of world events, much as Gray and Company had done with "This Week in Japan" and CNN. By the 1990s practically all of Washington's most prominent firms were doing the same. Overseas, companies and governments were sending over satellites their own video press releases. Clients flooded in from abroad—from Europe, Asia, and even former communist-bloc nations. H&K, just like Gray and Company, became reliant on foreign clients. The story of two of those accounts—the Bank of Credit and Commerce International and the "Citizens for a Free Kuwait"—seem to symbolize both the power of Robert Keith Gray, lobbyist and the ethics of Robert Keith Gray, influence peddler.

17

A GRAY
NETWORK

It's Washington at its worst.
Washington Post columnist Mary
McGrory describing H&K's work on
behalf of Citizens for a Free Kuwait[1]

After the mysterious demise of the Australian-based Nugan Hand Bank in 1980, the CIA needed another international banking network to handle many of its accounts. The agency turned to the Bank of Credit and Commerce International (BCCI), a mammoth enterprise run by a Pakistani named Agha Hasan Abedi. The bank quickly developed into an important asset for the Agency. As former Carter OMB Director Bert Lance told NBC News, "BCCI became an off-the-books operation of the CIA all around the world." It also became the bank of choice for the private intelligence organization put in motion during the early Reagan years. In 1981, not long after William Casey took control of the CIA and started to reinvigorate its off-the-books operations, he also began secretly meeting with Agha Hasan Abedi, the founder of BCCI, at the Madison Hotel in Washington. The private intelligence network used BCCI, among other things, for Iran–Contra arms shipments. For example, BCCI funded eight secret shipments of American arms to Iran with the money moving through then Gray and Company client Adnan Khashoggi's BCCI accounts in Paris and Monte Carlo. It was reported that Khashoggi needed the BCCI money to make the Iran–Contra deal work.[2] Some of the same men using BCCI were behind Iran–Contra and other Reagan–Bush private intelligence operations. It is not surprising then that Gray was once again linked to an international financial and intelligence scandal.

BCCI had been trying to gain a foothold in the United States since the 1970s. The bank hired Democratic luminary and Washington lawyer Clark Clifford, who had been an advisor to presidents since Harry Truman. In

1981 the Federal Reserve finally approved the purchase of First American Bankshares, Washington's largest bank holding company, by wealthy Middle Eastern investors. The Federal Reserve based its decision on Clifford's assurances that there was no relationship between these investors and BCCI. Clifford became the chairman of First American Bankshares and named his young protégé and law partner Robert Altman president. Gray was named a member of the Board of Directors of First American Bank, N.A. in Washington that same year.

According to his memoirs Gray first encountered Clark Clifford during the transition between the Eisenhower and Kennedy administrations.[3] (Though when asked for this book, Gray said he first came in close contact with Clifford in the 1970s when they did work on behalf of the same client and that the two had met no more than four times total.[4]) Gray had often said he admired Clark Clifford and had patterned his company after Clifford's law firm. Gray wrote in his 1986 defense of lobbyists that Clark Clifford had been the "distinguished example for decades" of Washington's best. Gray and Company used First American for its employee payroll and pension plan accounts.

Both Clifford and Altman profited handsomely from their association with BCCI and First American Bank. BCCI arranged a series of transactions in First American stock that produced a $9.8 million trading profit for the two attorneys.[5] It enabled Altman to buy a mansion in one of the most expensive neighborhoods in the Washington suburbs, which was cared for by a staff of white-gloved servants. In 1984 he married "Wonder Woman" actress Lynda Carter.

In February 1988, a few months after former Admiral Daniel Murphy flew to see Panamanian strongman Manuel Noriega on behalf of George Bush, the federal government indicted Noriega on drug trafficking charges. Investigators called BCCI "Noriega's bank," since it laundered so much of his drug money through the bank. In the fall of 1988, the Senate Subcommittee on Terrorism, Narcotics and International Operations, chaired by Senator John Kerry (D-Mass), held hearings on Noriega's involvement in cocaine trafficking. The subcommittee also began looking into links between BCCI and Noriega. Amjad Awan, BCCI's Latin American chief, was also Noriega's personal banker. When the subcommittee subpoenaed Awan, he told an undercover agent that Robert Altman had told him he should leave the country to avoid being served with the subcommittee's subpoena.[6] Altman told the House Banking Committee he advised Awan to leave the country out of concern for Awan's safety.

Former National Security Council economist Norman Bailey said he remembered seeing information about BCCI, illegal technology transfers, and the financing of guerilla groups as early as 1981. The State Department said that it had linked Middle Eastern terrorist Abu Nidal's organization— called by the State Department "the most dangerous terrorist organization in existence"—to a European BCCI branch as early as 1986. In 1988 then Customs Commissioner William von Raab had asked Robert Gates, the then deputy CIA director, for information on BCCI. Von Raab said Gates replied that the bank was known as "the Bank of Crooks and Criminals International." Gates said the CIA in 1986 had prepared a paper on the bank. The CIA memo said that BCCI had secretly gained control of the Washington-based First American Bank in 1982 without permission from the Federal Reserve. For a fee, prominent Middle Easterners had served as fronts for BCCI to gain control of First American.

In 1987, the Customs Service Tampa office started investigating BCCI drug money-laundering operations for the Colombian cocaine cartel in an operation code named "Operation Sea Chase." On October 8, 1988, federal agents arrested several BCCI officials in a sting operation. The bankers thought they were going to a bachelor party, but the groom was an undercover federal agent. On October 11, a federal grand jury indicted BCCI for conspiring with Colombia's Medellin cocaine cartel to launder $32 million in illicit drug profits. Also indicted were Awan and nine other BCCI officials. Von Raab hoped this would be only the beginning, that the Justice Department would go after more and higher BCCI officials, but that did not happen.

After the indictments, Altman and Clifford assembled a team of Florida and Washington lawyers to defend the bank. Among them was E. Lawrence Barcella, Jr., a close friend of both Clifford's and Altman's. Barcella, a former Assistant U.S. Attorney, had considerable knowledge of the private intelligence network, since he had worked extensively on the Edwin Wilson case. But BCCI did not only hire lawyers. On October 14, 1988, three days after the indictment, H&K signed a contract to represent BCCI.

The contract was between H&K's London office and BCCI's London headquarters, but it did not take long for the news to reach Washington. Larry Brady, then a senior executive at H&K, first heard of the contract from Charles Frances, who worked for Frank Mankiewicz.[7] Frances, whose background was in banking, knew about BCCI's bad reputation and the Noriega allegations and was very upset about H&K accepting the bank as a client. "He was very exorcised over it. He was bouncing off the walls," Brady said. "I remember Mankiewicz saying, 'Well, there was just a couple of individuals, a couple of the individual offices involved in the trouble.' " It was this comment and the concern of some H&K executives that caused Larry Brady to approach his friend, Customs Commissioner William von Raab, for help.

Many at H&K knew that Brady and von Raab were friends, but they did not know at the time that it was von Raab's agency that was leading the investigation of BCCI. Brady was equally unaware of von Raab's role in the BCCI probe; he approached von Raab with a general query about the bank and the wisdom of the contract at the request of his superiors at H&K. Von Raab said, " 'Larry, it's not in your interest to become associated with that.

Stay away.' I went back and I told Mankiewicz . . . I did the errand. I asked Willie. And Willie was emphatic,'' Brady said. Von Raab referred to BCCI as "a sleaze operation" and "Noriega's bank."

Brady said he told Mankiewicz flat out that von Raab had said to stay away from that account. He also said that H&K did not deny that the information from von Raab was true. But H&K did not act on von Raab's warning. Instead, the firm preferred to ignore it. Gray denied that any government official ever alerted the firm that there were serious difficulties with BCCI.[8] Mankiewicz told the *Legal Times* that no one made a big deal about the client.[9]

Don Deaton was a crisis management expert for H&K. In Deaton's recollections H&K was, essentially, conned by its client. "Individuals were indicted in '88. We were told by BCCI people in London in their headquarters that this was all news to them. They heard it literally on CNN. And they professed their innocence. They professed as an organization their innocence. I can't get into what counsel was given to them, and I can tell you that I have firsthand knowledge that they were told to do the things that you would expect organizations to do under such circumstances and on the basis of cultural disclaimers and that sort of thing, they elected not to do those things. But they were professing their innocence as an organization. . . . In hindsight we can say, 'Boy were we stupid.' Had we had known there is no question we would not have touched them with ten foot pole. We would not get in bed with a rogue organization. I can tell you that right now."[10]

But Brady and others insist that H&K was warned in the strongest possible terms that BCCI was indeed a rogue organization, and worse. Von Raab told Brady that the bank was involved in massive money laundering operations, and Brady passed this information on to his superiors. Although it was kept quiet, there was dissent among some of the top executives in the Washington office. "There was a group of us that wouldn't work on it. Charles [Frances] wouldn't. I wouldn't. Chuck [Pucie] wouldn't."

When pressed, Deaton remembered the warning, but he discounted the vehemence of the internal dissent. "When this thing first came up, voices were raised in management in Washington that we shouldn't get involved because of all of these innuendos and so forth. We said, 'Well, let's don't convict them before we listen to them.' On that basis, we met with them. They professed their innocence . . . so Washington was assuaged." The bank's contention that ongoing criminal investigations involved only "rogues" and not the institution itself was made easier because of the sheer size of BCCI—H&K viewed the bank as if it were Citicorp. "The role of BCCI as a Third World institution was very important. They were involved, we didn't realize it was money laundering, but they were involved in a major portion of the foreign exchange movement around the world. They were a fairly important enterprise in the cause of international commerce," Deaton said. Of course, BCCI was also, potentially, a hugely lucrative account. Whatever the reasons, von Raab's warnings were ignored. "I don't think anyone went into it not aware that it was a controversial client. But I think we went into it wholeheartedly believing that the organization itself was legitimate," Deaton said.

Brady, Pucie, and Frances were not "assuaged." They held further conversations and became convinced that the American business and banking communities had a very low opinion of BCCI's legitimacy. They continued to "put up a fuss," but, despite the warnings, Mankiewicz registered Hill and Knowlton with the Justice Department as the foreign agent for BCCI on December 8, 1988. "All we know is it just kept going forward. Who was responsible for it to keep going forward? In an organization where nobody is responsible for anything, we'll never really know," Charles Pucie said.[11] Whether the final decision was made by Mankiewicz, New York, or London was never made clear to the three dissenters.

In the Justice Department filing H&K announced that it intended to "provide services to advise and counsel the foreign principal," and planned to "contact by telephone, written correspondence or personal visits appropriate representatives of the media and representatives of the business community in representing the public relations/public affairs interests of the foreign principal." Two H&K executives who asked not to be identified offered similarly blunt explanations why H&K proceeded. "I would assume it was because they were paying money," one said. "I suspect because the company was over-leveraged; they had bottom lines to meet," the other stated.

Several former H&K executives do not remember H&K doing much for BCCI, beyond the Tampa office monitoring events pertaining to the drug money laundering investigations and New York issuing a press release. (After the indictment, H&K's New York's press release said that BCCI's "detailed and professional banking procedures observe the law and the spirit of the law in all of the seventy-three countries in which it operates."[12]) Gray categorically denies that either he or Mankiewicz billed even one minute to the BCCI account.[13]

Von Raab left the Customs Service in 1989 amid controversy. He was accused of constantly criticizing top Reagan and Bush officials for not being aggressive enough in pursuing the antidrug effort. "Not a team player" is a deadly tag for an administration official to obtain, but subsequent events seemed to bear out von Raab's complaints. On January 16, 1990, BCCI reached a plea bargain agreement with the Justice Department on the Tampa case, that, in effect, prevented the investigation from reaching high-level BCCI officials and hindered federal investigative efforts on the case. Former Assistant U.S. Attorney Barcella was instrumental in drafting the plea agreement on behalf of the bank. (At the time of this writing, Barcella is head of a congressional task force investigating the "October Surprise.")

Von Raab said that he became "annoyed" when the 1988 indictments did not reach high-level bank officials, and was appalled by the 1990 plea bargain agreement between the Justice Department and BCCI. "I think it was a shameless agreement," von Raab told a Senate subcommittee.

The agreement forced BCCI to plead guilty to money-laundering and to pay a $15 million fine. In a PR move reminiscent of Justice Department boasting about the fine paid by Marc Rich's company, the BCCI fine was touted to be largest ever assessed against a bank for money laundering. In reality, as von Raab said, it was "less than the bank had made from its money-laundering activities." Senator Kerry called it a slap on the wrist. The fine and the plea agreement were so lenient that a Senate report concluded later that it would undermine efforts to deter others from laundering money.

H&K reported to the Justice Department that its BCCI account ended in March 1990, two months after the plea bargain agreement. But that did not end Gray's and Mankiewicz's involvement. H&K continued to represent First American Bank. In May 1990 *Regardie's* magazine ran an article about the connections between BCCI and First American Bank. It was part of H&K's job to discredit the article. First American prepared an eight-page fact sheet disputing the accuracy of the story. Mankiewicz sent the fact sheet to Senator Kerry, personally urging him to read it.[14]

In 1991 the links between First American Bank and BCCI became front-page news, publicly contradicting H&K's indignant denials. Gray and Mankiewicz handled PR for the bank. Personally, Altman and Clifford coordinated their public relations strategies through Hill and Knowlton.[15] (Gray himself said he personally was not a consultant for Clifford or Altman.[16]) As the stories unfolded about BCCI's ownership of First American, Mankiewicz was out front fielding questions and providing his trademark quick, clever responses. "It's often not enough to win [in court]. You need to seem to have won it. Sometimes that is not that easy," Mankiewicz told the *Washington Post*.[17] But as the facts came out "winning" would become impossible.

In July 1991, BCCI's branches around the world were shut down by banking regulators for alleged criminal activities. That same month a New York grand jury indicted BCCI on bribery and fraud charges. *Time* magazine ran a cover story saying BCCI had a "black network" of 1500 thugs who smuggled currency, arms, and drugs and sometimes committed murder and collaborated with the CIA. (The CIA called these assertions "absurd," but later admitted that the Agency had maintained accounts at the bank and had used BCCI to move money around the world. The *New York Times* reported that the CIA had used the bank to help finance covert operations.)

In August 1991, the growing scandal hit home at H&K when von Raab stunned a Senate hearing by blaming Washington lobbyists, among others, for preventing the vigorous pursuit of the case against BCCI. He asserted publicly what many knew to be true, but what few had the courage to say: Government investigators and law enforcement officials are often stymied in their investigations by lobbyists, lawyers and PR firms that use their own reputations and connections to lend respectability to some of the worst criminals in the world. In sworn testimony, von Raab criticized high-level "influence-peddling," and named the Washington office of Hill and Knowlton and Gray and Mankiewicz specifically for the "general softening of resolve on the part of U.S. officials" made possible by the "incredible pounding they were taking by the influence peddlers in Washington." Von Raab described the "lackadaisical and sort of worked-over" attitude of high-level officials "tired" from fending off the public relations assault. "Whatever the Washington brokers got for their involvement in protecting BCCI from the federal government, they earned every million dollars they received," he said.[18]

Von Raab called the lawyers, lobbyists, and PR professionals a "gray network." "There wasn't a single influence peddler who wasn't being used to work this case. The result is that senior U.S. policy-level officials were constantly under the impression that BCCI was probably not that bad, because all these good guys that they play golf with all the time were representing them."

These scathing and angry comments were met with blustery denials from Mankiewicz and Gray. Gray wrote to von Raab accusing him of making "libelous statements" and asking him to refrain from "further defamatory comments." On August 29, von Raab wrote to Mankiewicz and said in part, "I do not have any information that Mr. Gray or you spoke to or contacted any official in either our Federal Government's executive or legislative branch on behalf of BCCI . . ." Before that letter arrived Mankiewicz had issued a statement discounting von Raab's assertions, saying, "neither I, nor Robert Gray, nor anyone else from Hill and Knowlton ever contacted, on behalf of BCCI, anyone in the Department of Justice or anywhere else in the Executive Branch or, for that matter, on Capitol Hill."[19] But Mankiewicz was splitting hairs. He did make contact on Capitol Hill for First American, which was owned by BCCI.

H&K never filed with the Justice Department about how much money BCCI paid the PR firm. The contract between BCCI and H&K called for the bank to pay them 25,000 pounds, or roughly $50,000, a month, paid monthly in advance. H&K often said what it did not do on behalf of the bank, but not what it did, besides its Tampa office monitoring the situation and that the firm "reviewed news accounts and forwarded selected reports to principal."[20] If the contract was adhered to BCCI must have paid H&K a minimum of $750,000 over a fifteen-month period. As a former H&K executive said, "A client has to be pretty stupid if he's paying that kind of money and those kind of hours for a monitoring service that Burells or somebody else can do a hell of a lot better."

Clifford and Altman continually maintained that they did not know that they were dealing with front men for BCCI, a stand echoed by Don Deaton. "BCCI was an instance of massive fraud and I don't think there's any question about it. We were misled. We were duped. We would not have taken on the BCCI that you know today under any circumstances. We would not take on a money launderer. . . . We would not willfully take on a client like that. So there's a case—call it human error. They said, 'We're innocent.' We believed them."

In mid-August 1991, Clifford and Altman, under pressure, resigned as top executives of First American. First American then dropped H&K as its public relations representative. The scandal kept growing. In October 1991, the former head of BCCI's U.S. operations told a congressional hearing that BCCI routinely paid off foreign leaders around the world in exchange for influence. "There was a pattern to buy relationships and to buy influence," Abdur R. Sakhia told the committee.[21] Bribery of government officials was BCCI's way of doing business. One of the *Time* reporters said that the head of BCCI's Washington office, Sani Ahmad, spent millions on cultivating relationships. Congressional investigators said that Ahmad and a dozen other employees' main job was to make contact with and entertain government officials, embassy personnel, and the executives of financial institutions such as the World Bank and the International Monetary Fund.[22]

Several members of the First American Board of Directors, the very men who, like Gray, were supposed to be protecting the bank's shareholders, testified before Congress that they did not know who owned the company because of its complicated corporate structure. Gray, who had been a board members of First American Bank N.A. for ten years, said in an interview for this book that he had no knowledge of any links between First American and BCCI until 1991. BCCI has admitted that it illegally owned First American. Its liquidator pleaded guilty in January 1992 to racketeering charges that included fraud and money laundering. In California, depositors of a BCCI-owned bank filed a class action law suit against BCCI and named H&K as one of the fifty-five defendants.[23] A Federal judge later dismissed the suit.

Perhaps BCCI is the most egregious example of how a lobbying and PR firm can represent foreign clients to the detriment not only of American citizens, but of people around the world. Gray's old defense for handling controversial foreign clients—that he cleared them with Bill Casey and the State Department—was not echoed by H&K chief Tom Eidson. To the contrary, Eidson said that turning down BCCI would have been "like passing on [the] Bank of America." Like Deaton, Eidson said that BCCI was considered one of the world's greatest financial institutions, and the firm accepted the bank's denial of criminality, despite the fact that H&K was hired to represent it after the indictment for drug money laundering.

"[In qualifying such an account], we do not have the resources to penetrate the veil of [an international criminal network] like BCCI—we really have no way."[24]

Larry Brady responded angrily to Eidson's assertion that BCCI had the same reputation as a Bank of America. "That's an absolute outright lie. I went to highest-level enforcement officer in the U.S. government who was looking at the damn company and it's an insult to me for them to make a comment like this and I frankly resent them . . . I'm fed up with it." Pucie agreed. "The general problems that BCCI's reputation had as BCCI back when they went to work for BCCI—it did not have a Bank of America reputation." Both men said that the indictments on drug money laundering should have been enough to prevent H&K from taking the account.

In February 1992, Gray told the Washington Times newspaper that his greatest feat was "getting President Reagan and Robert Maxwell to Nebraska at the same time to inaugurate the Gray Center for the Communication Arts."[25] It was after this trip to Hastings that Robert Maxwell signed on with Gray to handle some of his public relations. According to Justice Department filings, Gray served as an intermediary between Reagan and Maxwell whenever Maxwell wanted a favor from the former President. H&K handled the PR when Maxwell started his USA Today–style newspaper, called The European, in Europe. The firm drafted his speeches and issued press releases when Maxwell spoke in the United States, coordinated his speaking engagements and conducted research for potential support for charitable organizations. H&K even drafted and distributed a press release in 1990 on Maxwell's end-of-year earnings. "They had to assign their best fiction writer to that one," joked one former H&K staffer.

One executive who worked on the Maxwell account believed Gray placed the most value on the social cachet he got from dealing with Maxwell. "Well, he was Gray's personal friend. Robert Maxwell would call from his jet, and Gray would go and do these different things. And people would plan parties on his yacht when it came through Washington . . . He was very much like Gray, the same kind of charge. They got along fabulously."

But the entire Maxwell story took a bizarre turn just before the publishing tycoon's death in the fall of 1991. Investigative reporter Seymour Hersh accused Maxwell of spying for Israel. Hersh also said that one of Maxwell's top newspaper editors had been a Mossad agent who had brokered arms sales to Iran in 1983. Maxwell sued Hersh for libel. In November 1991, Maxwell died under mysterious circumstances after he had fallen off his yacht as it sailed off the Canary Islands. In another twist, after Maxwell's death a former Soviet spy alleged that Maxwell had had close ties to the KGB. As the Maxwell story unfolded over the next couple of months, it was revealed that Maxwell had enormous debt, in the billions of dollars, and had been, in effect, running a giant Ponzi scheme for years—borrowing money to pay off previous debts—even taking money from his companies's pension funds. H&K was not spared similar treatment, despite the Gray–Maxwell friendship. "When I left there, Maxwell's bills were close to a million that he owed H&K," a former H&K executive said.

The string of bad luck and controversial clients continued. Despite what happened to H&K as a result of the Scientology account, possible conflicts of interest did not seem to bother Gray. "I don't recall a client opportunity ever that Bob was inclined not to take for any reason at any time no matter what," a former H&K senior official said. At the same time H&K was representing Communist China, they were pitching their client's enemy: Taiwan. Gray earlier had attempted to pitch Taiwan in the 1970s, when another president had an abiding interest in China.

The People's Republic of China hired H&K for its fight to retain Most Favored Nation trading status after the Tienanmen Square massacre. There was little public outrage over H&K representing a communist country with an abysmal human-rights record. There was no army of conservative protestors handcuffing themselves in front of H&K as had happened when Gray and Company signed up Angola. This time the Bush administration supported H&K's efforts. "Hill and Knowlton has daily contacts at the highest echelons in the White House, which will help us guide . . . an overall image campaign for [China]," the firm wrote in its proposal to the Chinese government.[26]

H&K took on a very different sort of client when, in the fall of 1991, Oliver Stone hired H&K's Washington office to help him with media relations for his controversial film *JFK*. Stone thought Frank Mankiewicz, who had been Robert Kennedy's press secretary, and whose father had been a Hollywood screenwriter, would be the perfect PR representative. The film was being criticized for popularizing conspiracy theories that blamed the CIA and other government agencies for President Kennedy's death. H&K was successful in arranging media coverage for Stone in almost every major newspaper and on top television shows as well as appointments on Capitol Hill. Unfortunately, the vast majority of the coverage was critical of Stone's history. Ironically, the man who had brought conspiracy theorists back into vogue should have looked more closely at whom he was hiring: Stone, who sought PR refuge at H&K, was, in reality, hiring a firm with long ties to the CIA, one of the very organizations Stone felt was responsible for JFK's murder.

On a different level, Stone's hiring of H&K was ironic. He was being criticized for making a film that many would believe was historically accurate. He was being represented by a PR firm that distributed video news releases and other information that journalists reproduced as truth. Many of the news organizations that criticized Stone were the same ones that accepted stories generated for other H&K clients without question.

"PR can be put to very insidious uses," the head of marketing for an investment bank told *Manhattan, Inc.* "Persuasion, by its definition is subtle. The best PR ends up looking like news. You never know when a PR agency is being effective; you'll just find your views slowly shifting."[27] In the past, H&K's job was to make Americans feel good about their clients (AT&T, Exxon after the oil spill, Ford, Gerber, Proctor & Gamble, the New York Stock Exchange). Now they wanted to make Americans feel good about going to war.

At the same time H&K was receiving bad publicity on the Catholic Bishop account, and was working away on the Gall-RTC Auction, Scientology, and First American Bank, the firm received one of the most lucrative and controversial accounts in PR history: Citizens for a Free Kuwait. The timing on the account was interesting. On August 1, 1990, Craig Fuller, Bush's friend and advisor, assumed his duties as President and Chief Operating Officer of H&K Worldwide. The next day, Saddam Hussein invaded Kuwait. On August 6 Bush committed American troops to the Persian Gulf. On August 10, a little over a week after the invasion of Kuwait, H&K had a contract prepared to handle PR for Free Kuwait. On August 20, H&K registered as a foreign agent on their behalf. Gray's signature was on the contract.

A few days after the invasion Don Deaton received a call from a prominent Kuwaiti who had been a past client, asking for H&K's help.[28] Although technically Citizens for a Free Kuwait was supposed to be composed of people described by its name—citizens worried over Kuwait's travails—in reality the overwhelming majority of the funding came from the exiled government of Kuwait. "Citizens for a Free Kuwait," was, like "Americans for Constitutional Freedom," a propaganda front. "We were not told where they were getting their money and that wasn't really our concern. Our concern was that we got paid up front because that's the way we work with them. So when they filed their reports with FARA, for the most part the money came from the government," Deaton said.

If the savings-and-loan scandal was the epitome of coziness among executives, lobbyists, and the government, then "Free Kuwait" was the quintessence of the corresponding intimacy among foreign interests, lobbyists, and the American government.

At first blush, improving the image of Kuwait and pushing for active American military intervention on the emirate's behalf, seemed like a challenging task. Kuwait was not a democracy, but a feudal system with an emir (king) whose family had ruled for generations. H&K's Frank Mankiewicz told the *Washington Post*, "I think that too much weight is given to the fact that Kuwait is not as democratic as we are. What country is?"[29] Some at the White House used to joke about keeping the world safe for feudalism.[30] The emirate did not tolerate religious freedom. Women were treated like second-class citizens. Workers and their families who immigrated to Kuwait, regardless of how long they lived there, even for generations, were never entitled to citizenship. The emir had dozens of wives. Just a month before the Iraqi invasion, Amnesty International issued a report that stated that Kuwaiti authorities arrested dissidents and tortured them without trial. Political opponents of the emir were jailed.[31] The richest Kuwaitis were not staying in their country to fight, but were fleeing to Europe. Many in the royal family were noted for their flamboyant lifestyles, such as frequenting casinos, living in expensive hotel suites, surrounding themselves with beautiful women, and drinking too much.

Painting Saddam Hussein as evil incarnate was also a formidable job, not because Hussein was not a vile dictator, but because the U.S. had long courted him as a bulwark against Iran. The United States had been supporting Hussein with weapons and intelligence for the past decade during the Iran–Iraq war. The State Department, even after it knew he was developing nuclear weapons, and had used some of his large chemical weapon arsenal against his own people, prevented the Congress from invoking economic sanctions against him. When Hussein signaled the American Ambassador, April Glaspie, that he was going to invade Kuwait, she did not object.

In reality H&K's job was not difficult. Once the President committed a half a million American troops to foreign soil, the overwhelming majority of the country supported him. In addition, the PR apparatus put into place beyond H&K to win the minds and hearts of America was enormous. The White House, Pentagon, and State Departments all barraged the media and the public with carefully controlled information. Whether or not H&K's effort on behalf of Kuwait was technically necessary or effective remains a question. But beyond a doubt, it served a purpose.

With money as no object, the H&K Washington office assigned over seventy people almost instantaneously to the account. For over a million dollars Wirthlin immediately produced polls that determined what PR buttons should be pushed to stimulate America's predilections against Saddam Hussein and for Kuwait. The polls indicated that Iraqi atrocities against Kuwait were among the issues that upset Americans the most. To show that the United States was not alone in the world against Iraq, the pollster produced an international poll that confirmed H&K's assertions.

The H&K Washington office spent as much as it could as quickly as possible. Everything was free game. There was no need to fight over who got the billable hours for this account. There was plenty of money to go around. Lauri Fitz-Pegado, whom Neil Livingstone had hired at Gray and Company years ago, was the account supervisor. Over the years she had worked for Haiti under Duvalier, for government contracts for Univox, for Angola and other African governments. She was friends with top Democratic leaders such as Democratic chairman Ron Brown and Jesse Jackson. Fitz-Pegado served as the traffic manager for the huge account.

On the lobbying side, Gary Hymel began working the Congress. Just as he had done with the Scientologists and Turkey and countless other clients, he and his staff set up meetings, sent out information, and coordinated efforts—only this time, they were lobbying for war. On October 10, H&K staged a hearing with Tom Lantos's Human Rights Caucus. Hymel and his staff provided witnesses, wrote testimony, and coached the witnesses for effectiveness. The PR staff produced videotapes detailing alleged atrocities and ensured that the room was filled with reporters and television cameras. Perhaps the most emotional witnesses with the most explosive testimony was a young, teary-eyed fifteen-year-old girl named Nayirah, who told about Iraqi soldiers removing babies from their incubators and leaving them to die on the hospital floor. Her full identity was kept secret, ostensibly to protect her family from reprisals. Amnesty International believed her assertions. President Bush and several senators repeated the incubator story.[32] Nayirah was to become the most controversial component of H&K's propaganda machine.

The Kuwaiti ambassador to the United Nations made arrangements for a repeat performance before the United Nations in New York. On November 27, 1990, just before the U.N. Security Council vote on whether or not to authorize military force should Saddam Hussein not leave Kuwait, out came the giant photographs of Iraqi atrocities, the videotape program, and the Kuwait spokesman—insisting that Kuwait was "an oasis of peaceful harmony" before the invasion—providing unusual and spectacular theater. Again, the media covered the proceedings extensively.[33]

The H&K dog-and-pony show gave a final performance to the House Foreign Affairs Committee on January 8, just before the congressional vote on President Bush's request for a resolution supporting the use of force to remove Saddam Hussein from Kuwait. H&K's efforts succeeded in the United Nations, the Congress, and the media because, in each case, there was a receptive audience. The diplomats and congressmen and senators wanted something to point to to support their positions. The media wanted interesting, visual stories.

H&K used every form of media to thrust Kuwait's viewpoint onto the American public. To offset the view that Kuwaitis were fleeing their country, H&K arranged for a press conference with a Kuwaiti "freedom fighter" in early September to outline the activities of the Kuwaiti resistance. H&K spent over $600,000 to produce and distribute video news releases that were sent to outlets reaching millions of people. (The cassettes fill a cardboard box at the Justice Department.) Like the seemingly forgotten CNN/Morocco controversy, many television stations aired them with their evening news. The networks, when they used the videotape, identified them as H&K products, but did not question their accuracy. Often an unsuspecting public absorbed this information as authentic, unbiased reporting.

H&K's "religious division" pushed a different button. Staffers organized

September 23 "National Prayer Day" in which pastors were asked to encourage their congregation to pray for Kuwait (a country that would not let many of the congregants practice their own religion if they lived there). Like the Scientologists, who published books and then bought enough of them back to put them on the best seller list, Free Kuwait paid for quickie paperback books. H&K arranged a "National Free Kuwait Day" and a "National Student Information Day." In September, H&K sent a press release to ninety-five newspapers entitled "KUWAITI STUDENTS ORGANIZE 'FREE KUWAIT' RALLIES AT 21 U.S. COLLEGE CAMPUSES." The public rallies were arranged with perfectly lettered signs, color-coordinated balloons and T-shirts.

Women for a Free Kuwait promoted an Islamic Art tour. H&K produced and distributed a constant flow of radio shows. It prepared advertisements for major newspapers and arranged luncheons with journalists, providing them with letters from Kuwaitis with descriptive details of torture and abuse by Iraqis in their homeland. The Kuwaiti finance minister told the National Press Club about the rape of Kuwaiti women and the mass killings of Kuwaitis. Twenty or more speakers were arranged daily.

By the time of H&K's next Foreign Agents filing in December 1990, which covered the period through November 10, Free Kuwait had paid the PR firm $5.6 million in just two and a half months. It was only the beginning. Over the next ten weeks, H&K received an additional $5.1 million. More than half the $2.3 million H&K said it spent on behalf of Free Kuwait during this time frame went to research, polling, and consulting.

On January 8, 1991, Free Kuwait abruptly terminated its contract with H&K, which was supposed to run through April. The client may have ended the contract because by this time the war Kuwait so desired was imminent. A week later Marlin Fitzwater, the White House press secretary, would announce, "The liberation of Kuwait has begun." But like many other clients, Free Kuwait was displeased with not only the costs of the H&K PR campaign, but also with some of the publicity it had generated. (H&K spent hundreds of thousands of dollars "monitoring" stories, which meant watching television, reading newspapers and magazines to keep track of stories about Kuwait and what they said. Although the Kuwaitis fired H&K, they kept the other PR and lobbying firms they had hired.) Not long after the Persian Gulf war ended, one former H&K executive said the Kuwaiti Ambassador went into a rage every time he heard H&K's name. Another former H&K official said the services Free Kuwait received were no different than the ones Gray and Company had offered. "If you went back to Gray and Company and you looked at the big hit clients like the ones that were in intense programs like that [Free Kuwait], probably they wouldn't tell it publicly, but if you pulled them aside and said, 'Did you get your money's worth?' they'd say no. What happens when they turn that spigot on, everybody just starts [drinking]. And there's no supervision."

Despite the rancor at the end H&K's client had obtained its goal—a war fought with American troops on a foreign country's behalf—and H&K had pulled in millions of dollars. But much later, after the war itself had faded in the public consciousness, some of H&K's activities on behalf of Kuwait would be brought to light and bring the firm unfavorable publicity at a time when it could little afford it.

In 1991, WPP, H&K's parent company, announced lower than expected profits and suspended stock dividends for two years. "They are in very big financial straits," Jack O'Dwyer, the author of a New York–based PR newsletter, told the *Washington Post*.[34] The pressure from London to cut budgets and increase profits was enormous. Employees began to feel distrusted, and the tension and stress began to take its toll. Responding to these pressures, Gray and his assistant, James Jennings, began downsizing the Washington office, cutting mainly junior staff jobs. The company did not do it in a straightforward manner, denying that layoffs were imminent when in fact they were. "Lying is the environment there," said a former H&K vice president. "I remember Jennings at some operations committee meeting saying, 'My guillotine is not being polished. Whoever is spreading that [is wrong].' And whoops, that next pay period, fifteen more people got summarily dismissed."

In addition and exclusive of the downsizing, in the first four months of 1991, thirteen or more top executives quit H&K's Washington office, many to start their own competitive consulting and lobbying firms. Many more followed. They cited the bottom line pressure as one of the key reasons for leaving. George Worden stressed, once again, the importance of human capital to H&K and the disastrous consequences of WPP's profitability demands. "It's very bad management because they aren't interchangeable parts. They've lost skilled people by the tons, all of whom are gainfully employed. Everybody wanted to get out of here . . . when they're out of there, they're all immediately happy."

Mankiewicz, hoping to obscure the reasons for the departures in PR fog, insisted that the departures were not unusual in such a large firm, and regardless would have little effect. He even claimed that H&K would refer business to the other firms. "We wish them well," he told the *Washington Post*.[35] But even Mankiewicz admitted the increased pressure on the bottom line. He told the *National Journal*, "We have formal financial plans and targets and goals . . . I would be dissembling if I said there was less rather than more attention to the bottom line."[36]

The WPP bean-counters installed a huge bureaucratic system to account for every expenditure. But the climate had changed in advertising as well as PR, and Sorrell's company was $800 million in debt. Lucrative, longterm clients were becoming more and more difficult to find. "Many embassies won't talk to them because they got raped and pillaged," one former H&K vice president said.

H&K executives were constantly pressured to increase their billable hours. Gray's combining of public relations and lobbying, in this environment, was waylaid by institutional pressure. There was so much pressure on the bottom line that the PR people did not want to refer clients to the lobbyists, and vice versa, because they would lose billing credits. The high rate of turnover that had plagued Gray and Company continued at H&K. One H&K executive cleaning out his desk came across his old H&K telephone directory. He counted the names. From October 1989 to April 1991, there was a 78 percent turnover in the office.

The biggest blow came in April 1991, when four top H&K executives very publicly and rather abruptly left together to start a competing firm, called Capitoline. Three others followed closely behind. "Even with all this hoo-cha-cha, the Washington [H&K] office made money. It did not make enough money to satisfy New York; it did not make enough money to satisfy London, and there was no way in the world they could have made any more money than they did. And they are driving themselves crazy and losing people in the process. That loss [Capitoline] was the biggest one yet because that's a lot of senior manpower. People power," Worden said.

Frank Mankiewicz told the media that the break up was amicable and that he did not believe that members of the Capitoline group were dissatisfied with H&K.[37] In reality, the parting was not only hostile, in one instance, it was even violent. Just before this group left H&K, Charles Pucie, one of Capitoline's founders, was in Gary Hymel's office discussing a client, when James Jennings came in in a great fury. Jennings started yelling and screaming at Pucie, who screamed back at him. It got so bad that Hymel excused himself, left his own office and walked down the hall. Hymel had a brick in his office as a memento or door stop. Jennings picked up the brick and threw it at Pucie. Pucie dodged the brick, but it slammed into the wall with such force that it knocked paintings off the wall of Roger Lindberg's office next door. After the Capitoline group left, the H&K switchboard had all of their phone lines ring busy instead of answering and forwarding the calls.

Craig Fuller, still waiting in the wings for Gray to relinquish control of the office, thought that sooner or later New York and London would have to realize what was going on in Washington and put him in charge. His hopes grew with the Capitoline mass exodus. A former executive quoted him as saying, "Maybe this will help. There may be just too many bodies littered along the road now." But Gray remained in control and Fuller remained on the sidelines.

The Capitoline group threw a party the night they left H&K. The H&K alumni association in Washington grew larger by the day. "The alumni society is getting almost too big for a convention center. You never lose your interest [in Gray and H&K] because you were part of such a wild, abusive environment," one alumni member said. Gray and Jennings thought these employees should have stayed out of a sense of loyalty. Gray felt betrayed. Even his personal assistant, Paul Locigno, left. He did not seem to understand the effects of what he was doing had on the staff. Within a few weeks of opening their office, Capitoline received a threatening letter from Gray's attorney. (Gray never took any legal action against them, even though some former H&K clients eventually went to the new firm.)

The stream of bad publicity also continued. The *Legal Times* wrote, "Buffeted by defections, layoffs, and the loss of some major clients in recent months, lobbying and public-relations giant Hill and Knowlton Public Affairs Worldwide, is facing uncertain times."[38] In May 1991, the *National Journal* featured Gray and Fuller on its cover with the headline: "Out of Steam—Is their public relations shop losing its edge?" Inside the title was "Dead in the Water?"[39] Besides executives leaving en masse, the office had lost some of its biggest accounts, like Free Kuwait and Scientology. The Catholic Bishops were cutting back.

Since Gray and H&K had set the pace in Washington in terms of expansion, acquisitions, mergers, and services offered, many looked to what was happening to H&K as a possible sign of the future. Could an international communications firm get too big? Had the concept of marrying lobbying with public relations, in the end, failed?

The *National Journal* blamed WPP and its enormous debt for many of the problems. In reality, Gray was not operating much differently than he had in the past, only this time instead of having executives in New York monitor and sometimes overrule his actions, he had bosses who encouraged him to do more. Prior to 1980, Gray's bosses had prevented him from going too far off the reservation; now the reservation had few boundaries.

At a time when by all accounts Gray should have been falling from favor with his New York and WPP bosses, remarkably, his powers increased instead of decreased. In June 1991, H&K named him chairman of the board. The chairmanship once had been a largely ceremonial post, but Gray said he intended "to make it a very active role. What it has been in the past is not what it will be in the future."[40] The animosity between Dilenschneider and Gray, which had been growing for years, bubbled into the press. Dilenschneider replied to the *Wall Street Journal*, "With all due respect, I'm the CEO. Gray really is a nonexecutive chairman."[41] In addition to Gray's chairmanship, WPP set up a new executive committee, chaired by David Wynne-Morgan, a close associate of Sorrell's. As an organization, H&K had lost much of its independence in terms of finances. Now clients would also have to be approved by the committee.

Many, including Craig Fuller, expected Gray to retire when his five-year contract ended in the fall of 1991. After all, Gray would be seventy years old. In addition, Fuller, left on the sidelines for a year, was eager to take over, as he believed he had been promised. What several H&K executives later said was that if Fuller ever wanted to gain control of the Washington office, he should have taken over from the first day he started, and not waited for Gray to leave.

But others at H&K knew that Gray had no intention of retiring. Mark Robertson, one of Gray's closest associates, told one former H&K official that Gray had no intention of retiring in the fall of 1991, saying, "If Fuller thinks that he can win this one, he has no idea what he is in for."

Besides his workaholic temperament and love of his stature and position, Gray had other pressing reasons to stay at H&K. He could not afford retirement. The prices of the stock and real estate he owned were depressed. His overhead on his four houses was enormous. Gray tried to sell The Power House, but it was a difficult real estate property to sell. The unique cachet it gave Gray and Company did not translate to other businesses. Gray had bought it mainly because of its name. As an office building, it was impractical, so it sat with a For Sale sign in the window for years. Some of Gray's other properties were also difficult to sell, such as a former bank building that had asbestos problems.

It was not Gray who retired from H&K in the fall of 1991, but Dilenschneider. In September, Dilenschneider was abruptly forced out and replaced by Thomas Eidson, whom he had promoted from the Los Angeles office. A number of factors contributed to Dilenschneider's ouster. Relations between him and Sorrell had deteriorated rapidly. The perception that H&K was seriously off-course had grown over the course of the year. When the Executive Committee took over control of the company earlier that summer, Dilenschneider's days were numbered. "That move followed more than a year of controversy and bad publicity for the firm," the *Wall Street Journal* wrote.[42] "When they formed that management committee chaired by the Brits, that was the kiss of death," Worden said.

Gray not only emerged unscathed in the purge but signed a new three-year contract. And while H&K was getting hammered in the press, Gray himself got favorable notice. The January 1992 issue of *Washingtonian* magazine ran a flattering profile of Gray, saying, among other things, "He has influence beyond all but a few in this city. . . . Almost single-handedly, Gray is manning the dike against corporate chaos. . . . Gray is poised once again to emerge a winner."[43] "Everybody was sick," said a former H&K vice president. "People said, 'Aren't you nauseous?' . . . 'How about that piece of Cool Whip?' . . . 'Am I on another planet?' "

Removing Dilenschneider and making Eidson, Dilenschneider's protégé, the new head of H&K was not the answer to H&K's problems. Although Eidson was well-liked and considered to have a good grasp of details, many at H&K did not believe that Eidson had either the skills or the experience to pull H&K out of its financial and public relations difficulties. "Now this might not be entirely fair to him. I have a dim view of Los Angeles and the way business is done there and the executives that come out of Los Angeles.

I think La-La Land is a perfect description of that place, and that's his whole background. He's part of that world," Worden said, summing up the attitude of several others.

Eidson announced that H&K, in the future, would be more selective about its clients. Although Eidson insisted H&K would not shy away from controversial clients, he said it would be more careful about who they would solicit.[44] But in a circumstance reminiscent of the H&K buyout of Gray and Company, Gray was saying just the opposite. "We're proud of the fact that we get the tough ones. If someone is in trouble, they come to us. We like that. We're not ashamed of it."[45]

To appease Fuller, he was promoted in October 1991 to head of U.S. operations for H&K, but despite the new title, his authority stayed the same. He remained in Washington, still the bridesmaid to Gray. In November 1991, Jennings was promoted to chief of staff to Eidson. His job was to coordinate activities between Eidson and Gray, traveling between the two offices.

The question of whether the administrative shuffling would restore H&K to preeminence was soon overshadowed by a forgotten figure from the Persian Gulf War—the teary-eyed Kuwaiti girl named Nayirah.

After the Persian Gulf war ended, many journalists began to realize that they had been manhandled by flacks. Thomas Friedman of the *New York Times*, appearing on "Washington Week in Review," complained that, during the war, State Department correspondents covering Secretary James Baker during his Saudi Arabia trip were freely ushered to the Penthouse suite at the Sheraton, courtesy of H&K, to meet with the emir. After the war, when travelling in Kuwait, a country the United States had just liberated, the emir would not see them.

New York Times and ABC News reporters working in Kuwait after the war could not verify through hospital sources that babies were taken from incubators and left to die, as "Nayirah" had so movingly testified (although many other atrocities were confirmed). On January 6, 1992, in a *New York Times* op-ed piece, John MacArthur, the publisher of *Harper's Magazine*, revealed Nayirah's true identity. The brave young witness whose name had to be withheld for the sake of her family in Kuwait was, in reality, the daughter of the Kuwaiti Ambassador to the United States. That information, coupled with the fact that there was no independent verification of her story, led many to question Nayirah's credibility, and H&K's honesty. Many questioned whether Nayirah was even in Kuwait at the time. Soon it was disclosed that along with H&K, Congressman Lantos also knew her identity, but did not tell his colleagues. The connection between Lantos, the Congressional Human Rights Foundation, and H&K's donated office space once again surfaced. In addition, Free Kuwait had donated fifty thousand dollars to the foundation after the Iraqi invasion. In October 1991, Frank

Mankiewicz had been named to its board. The *New York Times* ran an editorial critical of H&K and calling for an Ethics Committee investigation into Congressman Lantos. The publicity was soon to get worse for H&K.

With very unusual back-to-back coverage, both "20/20" and "60 Minutes" aired programs January 17 and 19 respectively on H&K's use of Nayirah as an "anonymous" witness before the Congressional Human Rights Caucus. The H&K spokesman was not Gray or Eidson or Mankiewicz or Hymel, but Lauri Fitz-Pegado, who had managed the account. The day before the first show aired, staffers threw Fitz-Pegado a party to celebrate their new media star. But the celebration quickly turned to embarrassment.

Both "60 Minutes" and "20/20" accused H&K of manipulating public opinion in order to push the United States into war. The shows criticized H&K for showing that "war can be marketed, just like soft drinks and toothpaste." Craig Fuller told "60 Minutes" that "almost spontaneously, as the Kuwaitis were talking to us, we were talking to people in the administration to find out how we could be supportive with respect to the President's program." Fuller apparently saw nothing wrong with this linkage.

The media coverage of H&K's "Citizens for a Free Kuwait" was extensive. The only problem was that the coverage happened a year too late. With the exception of a few articles in the *Washington Post*, few in the media at the time gave the situation much attention. So much for throwing the pitiless light of publicity on foreign agents. "In terms of working with the media, we worked with the media every day and throughout a long and intense relationship. There was very little back biting in the media about Hill and Knowlton. . . . With all that we were doing to make information available, there was nobody in the press crying foul. Now why do you suppose it is? I mean, we're working with sophisticated people here. We're working with people that one could say have more than an average bit of skepticism," Deaton said.

The basic concerns about H&K's running of media and lobbying campaigns—whether they are antidemocratic—have existed for years. But these concerns were magnified during a time when the country was debating war and H&K's client was a foreign country with a direct interest in the debate's outcome. Is there a limit to what this country should allow foreign agents to spend on propaganda efforts and government manipulation, especially during war time? Since H&K is not even American owned, what effect did British concerns—such as the possible collapse of its financial institutions if the Kuwaiti currency, the dinar, became worthless—have on H&K's efforts? With the longstanding ties between H&K and the intelligence community, was this effort simply another part of an attempt by our government to cynically shape world views? (CIA Director Robert Gates, then deputy national security adviser, headed an interagency government group to counter Saddam Hussein's propaganda efforts and "manipulate world public opinion."[46])

In the end, the question was not whether H&K effectively altered public opinion, but whether the combined efforts of America's own government, foreign interests, and private PR and lobbying campaigns drowned out decent and rational, unemotional debate.

The Free Kuwait controversy was not the only bad publicity for H&K. The January 13, 1992 issue of *Newsweek*, which appeared the same day as MacArthur's op-ed piece, ran an article entitled "The Real Price of Buying Influence." The piece detailed how Washington lobbyists "regularly milk clients." Daniel Murphy's billing on the Hyundai account at Gray and Company was given as an example. Gray came in for special opprobrium. "A typical lunch by Hill and Knowlton chairman Robert Gray could cost a client $1,000, including his $450-an-hour fee, the cost of the staffer who briefed him beforehand, the secretary who made the reservations, and the chauffeur who drove him to the restaurant." It quoted Joan Worden, one of the executives who left H&K to work for Capitoline as saying, "Billability, billability, billability—you'd hear that word until you screamed." One former H&K employee said a client was charged $1,000 for the time he spent looking for a gift for a client. Gray denied charging clients for gifts. It all sounded familiar—the same complaints that Orfila and others had made about Gray and Company. The article concluded: "Robert Gray rose to the top of his profession in part because clients heard he was friends with the Reagans. Yet asked to name the most common mistake businesses or foreign governments make when selecting a lobbyist, Gray says, 'They're too impressed with who you know rather than what you know.' Free advice— worth a lot of money."[47]

A poster on Frank Mankiewicz's office wall read, "When your clients are being tried in the press . . . talk to us. We're Hill and Knowlton."[48] Once again the PR firm had to ask itself how to handle a barrage of bad press, but in doing so the firm did not follow the advice it gave clients.

Instead of admitting mistakes, H&K tried to defend itself. Hill and Knowlton released a letter from the United States Ambassador to Kuwait, defending the "killing-babies-in-incubators" story. On January 27, the Ambassador sent a cable to Lantos defending the contents of Nayirah's testimony. He stated that she was in Kuwait at the time of the alleged atrocities and asserted that "there is no question that a number of premature babies died in Kuwait due directly to actions taken by Iraqi authorities." An unusually emotional cable was leaked from the State Department attacking human rights groups for "cursory and biased" investigations and "cynically casting doubt on accounts of atrocities."[49] Eidson wrote a letter to the editor of the *New York Times* defending H&K, but MacArthur quickly replied, pointing out the inaccuracies in Eidson's letter.

Eidson had flown down to the Washington office the Tuesday after the *Newsweek* article and the MacArthur op-ed piece in the *New York Times* appeared. Eidson told staffers H&K had a "strategic plan" for answering all of the bad publicity. Eidson's strategy did not involve improving H&K so it would not be in a position to get bad publicity. Instead, Eidson wrote letters to the editor and did not let any negative publicity go unanswered, which of course generated more stories and interest. "Tom doesn't get it. The best way to get on with this is the same thing you'd advise a client. Sweep clean. Come clean. And start conducting your business very differently. . . . There's been a neglect of the old-fashion business virtues for too long," a former senior H&K executive said.

At the same time H&K was being lambasted in the press the internal turmoil continued. After Gray renewed his H&K contract, Fuller decided to flex his presumed new authority. He fired several H&K employees, including Gray's friend, Mark Robertson. Gray immediately rehired them. Furious, Fuller got on the Concorde and flew to London to see Sorrell. He wanted complete control, he said, or he was leaving. Sorrell backed up Gray. Among other things, Sorrell pointed to the flattering profile of Gray that had just appeared in *Washingtonian* magazine.

In January 1992, when Fuller returned from London, he quit. He finally realized that there was no chance that he was going to take over H&K's Washington office from Gray. "All of the people who are hired as the deputies [to Gray] are slated for the guillotine before they are even hired," said one former H&K executive. In addition, the White House was becoming embarrassed by the H&K media controversy. When Washington lobbyist James Lake was under consideration to head the White House communications operation, commentator and presidential candidate Patrick Buchanan made an issue out of Lake representing Japanese and other foreign clients. If Fuller wanted to remain active in Republican politics and continue to be in charge of the Republican National Convention in Houston, he needed to sever his H&K ties. He left to head PR for Philip Morris, Inc.

"The Gray people were applauding when Fuller [left]. And they were thrilled when the announcement was made of Fuller leaving. They had this meeting and Gray said, 'We can do anything he can do. He served his purpose,'" one H&K executive recalled. Some at H&K even criticized Fuller for not giving more notice. When asked by the *Legal Times* what Fuller's departure meant, Mankiewicz said, "Not a whole hell of a lot. It's not like one of the pillars has been pulled out."[50]

With Fuller gone, many of the remaining high-level, longtime executives such as Charles Frances also left. A friend remembered Frances saying, "I don't want to be on the elephant when it falls down."[51] Many in the Washington H&K office had liked Fuller. He had also brought in new business. Several executives had stayed on because they had hoped things would change when Fuller finally took over. They thought that only Fuller had the power to take on Gray, that Fuller was "their great white hope." But they were wrong.

In the Washington office morale was at an all time low. From a staff of 250 a year earlier during the Persian Gulf war, the office now had ninety people, including drivers and clerical positions. It began to look like a ghost town. Empty offices. Moving boxes. Piles of papers and files all over the place. The office manager decided to move the only successful division, the Health Division, to the front of the office so it did not look abandoned when a visitor reached the top of the staircase. H&K alumni laughed when they remember the fights over who got the offices along the Potomac River. It all seemed so silly now. They remembered the big investment made for Jackson Bain and the media operation—space H&K was now looking to sublet.

Several clients also left, especially ones Fuller had recruited. One client fired H&K after the president of the organization saw the "60 Minutes" piece. A former H&K executive said that for the first time he started to run into people saying, "Oh, you were with Hill and Knowlton," as if it were a black mark against him. George Worden said, "It used to be the other way around, 'Oh my, you are with Hill and Knowlton.' " One New York H&K executive said his father was too embarrassed to tell his golfing buddies where his son worked.

Had Gray finally miscalculated? Had he finally taken one too many controversial clients, been implicated in one too many scandals? Some say the Washington office is barely hanging on. "I think it's [the Washington office] going to really implode. Even people who are still there are saying 'I'm keeping my head down and sending out my resumé,' say the place is going to implode shortly." Another former H&K executive agreed, "I don't see how they're going to salvage it."

But others believe that Gray remains the Teflon superlobbyist. Despite the high client and staff turnover and the controversial clients, Gray, personally, seemed to remain above the fray. "Bob Gray still remains the renowned number one governmental relations lobbyist type of figurehead in Washington, D.C., so there is no question that the premier stature of the man carried through not only through the decade of Gray and Company, but into his current position with Hill and Knowlton. . . . Gray was probably the real visionary to change the concept of governmental relations and lobbying in Washington and to really professionalize much more a way of trying to change congressional/public perception or administration perception on issues. You did it through contacts, but it is no longer done just through contacts alone. There is coalition building, grass roots, and how you affect the press. It's done through testimony on the Hill, which witnesses you are going to bring up. How they are approached and trained. It's an incredible process now to think about lobbying. . . . The name Bob

Gray became synonymous with governmental relations in Washington,"
said John Lawler. Another H&K official put it more succinctly: "Well, he
still has his car, his driver, his two secretaries, everything else. A full
expense account. Fuller's gone. Big salary."

VITAE
Chairman, Hill and Knowlton, Inc.

BIRTHDAY
Every other year

HOMETOWN
Hastings, Nebraska

MARITAL STATUS
Available

SELF-PORTRAIT
Hyperactive, workaholic, loyal

MOTTO
Promise no more than you can deliver; deliver more than you promise

WALTER MITTY FANTASY
The president asks me to fill ALL Cabinet positions: "Only you can do
it, Bob."

INSPIRATION
Eisenhower chief of staff and New Hampshire Governor Sherman Adams

GREATEST FEAT
Getting President Reagan and Robert Maxwell to Nebraska at the same
time to inaugurate the Gray Center for Communication Arts at Hastings
College.

BAD HABITS
Starting phone calls with "How can I help?" and occasionally voting for
Democrats.

PET PEEVES
Inactive road crews and unsynchronized stop lights

HOBBIES
Indoors: Nintendo; outdoors: skiing, tennis, rafting, rollerblading

LUXURY DEFINED
25-hour days; seeing a movie other than on an airplane

DRINK OR WINE
San Pelligrino water, Diet Pepsi, Stoli vodka, Budweiser beer

FAVORITE RESTAURANT
Allegro at Sheraton Carlton, Aux Beaux Champs at Four Seasons

VACATION SPOT
Istanbul, Turkey

CLOTHING STORE
Hecht's men's store, Hugo Boss

TV PROGRAMS
McNeil Lehrer, C-Span, "Nightline"

CAR IN GARAGE
1992 Mazda 929

BOOK AT BEDSIDE
Galley proofs of *The Candidate's Wife; Nine Nations of North America*
and *Three Blind Mice*

LAST WORDS
"I am ready."

Almost every answer was calculated for an effect, either dropping a name
or promoting a client. The response that caused the most mirth among H&K
veterans was his favorite vacation spot, Istanbul. "They had to drag him,
kicking and screaming, to go to Istanbul at all to see the Turkish client,"
said one, "He went out of his way to see how many clients he could get in
that little profile . . . I mean people broke up. It was faxed all over town
because everybody knew, you know, and circling clients. Clients. Clients. I
mean, what a portrait of a person. Unreal."
In 1992, Gray finally sold The Power House.

The linkage between public relations, lobbying, and advertising became
stronger and stronger throughout Gray's career. The clear lines that used to
exist among them eventually faded. Today, firms offer polling, research,
political analysis, political gossip, economic analysis, speechwriting, advertising, graphic artists, publicists, media and congressional coaches, PAC or
campaign contribution management, broadcast studios; the list seems endless. Gray's personal pitch on the subject over the years has changed little.
"We fill the congressional mailbags by taking the story to the public and
getting them to react back to the members [of Congress]. And then we can
go to the members to lobby. If you accept the premise that in this country
the power is with the people and the free press moves the people, this is a
logical conclusion."[52] But, in reality, the people have little control, influ-

ence, or voice. As individuals, people without money cannot compete in the media or governmental processes. At best, they can be used by interest groups who convince them that their self-interest would be enhanced by mailing in a post card, writing a letter or calling their congressman, going to Washington to see their congressman, joining the organization, or contributing to the organization. But somewhere along the way, the greater good often seems to get lost.

NOTES

CHAPTER 1

1. Darius Holscher, "Reagan, Gray longtime friends," *The Hastings Tribune*, September 2, 1988.
2. Charles C. Osborne and Dorothy W. Creigh, "A Brief History of Adams County and Hastings."
3. Hastings is named after Thomas Hastings, a construction engineer with the railroad.
4. Catherine Renschler, an untitled article, *The Adams County Historical Society*.
5. From Robert Keith Gray's birth certificate.
6. Interview with Harry A. Borley.
7. "Nebraska's State Mother of The Year Is Mrs. Marie Gray," *Hastings Daily Tribune*, March 18, 1961, p.1.
8. "A New Career as a Mother," *Sunday World-Herald Magazine*, May 11, 1961, p.6.
9. Kathy Stokebrand, "Gray Sees News Center As Window to World," *Hastings Tribune*, December 27, 1983, p.2.
10. *Ibid.*
11. Interview with Vern Anderson.
12. Charles M. Anderson, *The Western Land Roller Story*, 1958.
13. Vern Charles Anderson, *The Western Land Roller Story, Part Two*, p.48.

Interview with Vern Anderson.

14. Written interview with Robert Gray.
15. Julie Clopton Kiiker, "Gray Proud to Put Spotlight on City," *Hastings Tribune*, September 5, 1988, p.1.
16. "Gray children honor their parents," *Hastings College Today*, Fall, 1988, p.8.

Interviews with Tom Jorgenson, Vern Anderson, and Harry Borley.

17. Catherine Renschler, untitled article.
18. Vern Anderson, pp. 48, 49.
19. Interview with Bob Hardin.
20. Interview with Richard Hoffman and several other Gray friends from Carleton College and Harvard.
21. Interview with Wesley Jones.
22. Interview with Gratia Coultas.
23. Interview with Wesley Jones.
24. Interview with Alice Heley.
25. *Hastings Tribune*, December, 1942.
26. Interview with Grace and Bob Bauske. Interview with Wesley Jones.
27. Interview with Bob Cowgar.
28. Based on research by André Colaiace and Carleton College Archivist Eric Hillemann.
29. Written interview with Robert Gray.
30. Gray played the string bass in the Carleton Orchestra. He also played in the Carleton Field Band and cymbals in the Pep Band.
31. Interview with Richard Hoffman.
32. *Ibid.*
33. Interview with Elton Hailey.
34. Lt. A.J. Hunter, U.S.N.R., "The History of our Ship—The U.S.S. *Collingsworth* (APA-146), The Navy Department Library.

35. Robert Keith Gray, *Eighteen Acres Under Glass* (New York: Doubleday & Co., Inc. 1961), p.181.

36. His sister, Jean, was a student at the college.

37. "Small Business Course Appeals to HC Students," *The Hastings Collegian*, February 11, 1950.

38. Interview with Tom Jorgenson.

39. Interview with Tom Jorgenson.

40. "Robert Gray To Deliver Lecture Series at USC," *The Hastings Collegian*, May 19, 1950.

According to the article, Gray lectured one hour a day on various phases of industry management and was available three hours a day for consultation. The course was mainly for graduate students. It required no text book and there was no final examination.

"College Board of Trustees Promotes Faculty Members," *Hastings Tribune*, February 28, 1950.

"HC Prof Named 'Man of Year' By Hastings C of C," *The Hastings Collegian*, 1951.

41. Interview with Ken Gray and with Ruth Devaney.

42. "Just Between Us," *The Hastings Collegian*, May 11, 1951.

43. Interview with Bob Hardin.

44. "Ike Is Given Big Welcome," *Hastings Daily Tribune*, July 5, 1952, p.13.

Fred Seaton was appointed to the Senate by Governor Val Peterson when Senator Kenneth Wherry died. After Eisenhower won the election, Seaton went to Washington to work for Eisenhower at the White House and, later, became his Secretary of Interior.

45. Interview with Jerrold Scoutt.

CHAPTER 2

1. From Assistant for Executive Appointments collection, Robert Keith Gray's speeches, Dwight D. Eisenhower Library, Abilene, Kansas.

2. Interview with Carl T. Curtis.

3. Fred A. Seaton Chronological Series, White House Chronology April/May 1955, Dwight D. Eisenhower Library.

4. Interview with Robert Gray.

5. Megan Rosenfeld, "Inaugural Insider," *Washington Post*, December 15, 1980, p.B1.

6. Interview with Carl Curtis.

7. "Bob Gray Joins Navy Department," *Hastings Tribune*, January 3, 1956, p.3.

Interview with Albert Pratt.

8. "Navy Official to Take Over Federal Personnel Affairs," (AP), *New York Times*, Sunday, May 13, 1956, p.48.

9. Op.Cit. Assistant for Assistant for Executive Appointments collection.

10. Megan Rosenfeld, "Inaugural Insider," *Washington Post*, December 15, 1980, p.B1.

11. Fred A. Seaton Appointment Book Series, 1956, Dwight D. Eisenhower Library.

12. At the Dwight D. Eisenhower Library in Abilene, Kansas, all of the correspondence referenced on Gray's white index card about his job search are missing from the general files. The only records found were in Fred Seaton's personal files which he later donated to the library.

13. Robert Keith Gray, *Eighteen Acres Under Glass* (New York: Doubleday & Company, Inc., 1961), p.259.

14. Gray, *Eighteen Acres*, p.96.

15. Marquis Childs, *Eisenhower: Captive Hero* (New York: Harcourt, Brace and Company, 1958), p. 213.

16. Dwight D. Eisenhower, *Waging Peace* (New York: Doubleday & Company, 1965), p.311.

"The Adams Legend," *New York Times*, September 23, 1958, p.18.

17. James Reston, "A Two-Fold Problem," *New York Times*, 23 September, 1958, p.18.

18. Drew Pearson, *Diaries 1949–1959* (New York: Holt, Rinehart and Winston, 1974), p.324.

19. Interview with Elton Hailey.

20. Gray, *Eighteen Acres*, p.78.

21. Gray, *Eighteen Acres*, p.79.
22. *Ibid.*
23. Office of the Special Assistant for Executive Records 1952–61, Confidential Files, 1955–57, Memorandum for Governor Adams, June 18, 1956, the Dwight D. Eisenhower Library.
24. Office of the Special Assistant for Executive Records, 1952–61, Confidential Files 1955–57, Memorandum for Governor Adams, June 18, 1956, Dwight D. Eisenhower Library.

In July 1956 Gray wrote in a memorandum to the file stating that Governor Adams had given him the authority to work out with Mr. Floete the situation regarding the appointee. "I suggested that Floete give [him] his notice and toss him in our lap with assurances that we would find him something," Gray wrote. Floete asked for and got a delay in firing [him] until he could line up a replacement. By the fall of 1956, Gray was trying to find [him] a job at the Securities and Exchange Commission. He writes: ". . . and his rating is substantiated by a large file of recommendations which we have received from his home state, Oklahoma."

25. Office of the Special Assistant for Executive Records 1952–61, Confidential Files 1955–57, Dwight D. Eisenhower Library.
26. Office of the Special Assistant for Executive Records 1952–61, Confidential Files 1955–57, Memorandum for Governor Adams, Dwight D. Eisenhower Library.

Jack Martin worked in Eisenhower's Congressional relations operation. Gray wrote the following Memorandum for the File on July 27, 1956:

Re: Railroad Retirement Board

On a strictly confidential (underlined by hand) basis, Robert C. Jones, Assistant to the Administrator, Small Business Administration, called in behalf of Wendell Barnes, Administrator, to say that they understood [the candidate] (underlined by hand) was under consideration for Chairman of the Railroad Retirement Board. In their opinion, [the candidate], in his work on the Senate Small Business Committee, had seemed to side with the Democrats against the Administration far more frequently than not. They emphasized the importance of keeping this confidential for if [the candidate] were to remain on the Committee, it would be most harmful to SBA if it were known that they had passed this information along to us.

27. Gray, *Eighteen Acres*, p.63.
28. Interview with Eddie Jordan.
29. "Gray's White House Office Gets Most Mail and Calls," *The World Herald*, October 6, 1957.
30. Gray, *Eighteen Acres*, pg. 64.
31. Gray, *Eighteen Acres*, pp.289–290.
32. Gray, *Eighteen Acres*, p.48.
33. In September 1956, his secretary, Carolyn G. Wilhide, sent his expenses to the Republication National Committee for reimbursement. He had travelled to Columbus, Ohio, Rochester, New York, and New York City. The total cost: $55.14. The round-trip airfare to New York was $30.14.
34. "Nebraskan Calls Ike Hard Worker," *Omaha World-Herald*, May 11, 1958.
35. "Ike Working Hardest Ever, Nebraskan Gray Declares," *Omaha World Herald*, January 29, 1960.
36. Robert Keith Gray collection, 1954–1960, A-67-59, Dwight D. Eisenhower Library.
37. Gray, *Eighteen Acres*, p.80–81.
38. Eisenhower's Second Inaugural Address, January 21, 1957.
39. On December 28, Gray sent a memorandum to Tom Stephens, Eisenhower's Appointment Secretary, passing on a complaint that Arthur Vandenberg, Jr. and Harold Talbott were on the "gold list." (Talbott was Secretary of the Air Force. Arthur Vandenberg's father was a senator from Michigan who died in 1951.)
40. Gray, *Eighteen Acres*, p.85.
41. Gray, *Eighteen Acres*, p.75.
42. Office of the Special Assistant for Executive Records 1952–61, Confidential Files 1955–57, Dwight D. Eisenhower Library. The name was deleted by the library.
43. Office of the Special Assistant for Executive Records, 1952–61, Confidential Files 1955–57, Dwight D. Eisenhower Library.

In the files was a letter from Malcolm Forbes to Sherman Adams asking for an ambassadorship to Turkey and enclosing an article he had written about Turkey for his magazine.

44. Official Files 72-A-2, Dwight D. Eisenhower Library.

In a memorandum to Gerald Morgan, President Eisenhower's assistant, he wrote "I am having my mail prepared for your signature, carefully proofed and grouped as to subject. If it handicaps you too much, in addition to your many other chores, perhaps you will want to have Arthur Minnich take over this job.

45. Official Files 72-A, Dwight D. Eisenhower Library.

When the appointment for a new Governor of the Virgin Islands came due, Gray got involved when a senator sent over his recommendation. Interior Secretary Seaton recommended replacing the current, black Governor with a white man. Gray wrote a memo to the file in early April: "Seaton advises that the top man be white and that the 2nd spot could be colored." Later Seaton had second thoughts. In a memo to Sherman Adams, Gray said, "Secretary Seaton has changed his thinking on the Virgin Islands. He reasons that Governor Gordon is one of the top Negro appointments in this Administration and should not be moved to less than a judgeship."

46. Office of the Special Assistant for Executive Appointments 1952–61, Confidential 1958, Box 46, Dwight D. Eisenhower Library.

47. Office of the Special Assistant for Executive Records 1952–61, Confidential Files 1955–57, Dwight D. Eisenhower Library.

48. "Ike's Dog Buzzed for Nebraskan," *Omaha World-Herald*, May 2, 1958.

49. "Gray 'Safe Bet' for Appointment," *Hastings Tribune*, December 13, 1957, p.13.

New York Times story's wording was different, but the information was the same.

50. "A Day in the Life of the President," *U.S. News and World Report*, March 14, 1958, pp. 35–42.

51. Gray, *Eighteen Acres*, p.216.

52. Gray, *Eighteen Acres*, p.165.

53. George Dixon, Washington Scene . . . "The 'Third Man' at the White House," *Washington Post*, March 26, 1958.

54. Jack Scott, "The Life of a Bachelor in Washington," *Cosmopolitan*, May, 1958, p.45.

55. Gray, *Eighteen Acres*, p.97.

56. Sue Seay, "Washington Party Crasher—To meet the elite . . . all you need is gall," *Look*, April 26, 1960, p.46.

57. "Will You Marry Me, Kind Sir?—137,000 Washington Men 'Eligible,' " *Omaha World-Herald*, March 13, 1960.

58. Gray, *Eighteen Acres*, p.249.

59. Gray, *Eighteen Acres*, p.248.

60. Stevens had held the Appointments Secretary job before Bernard Shanley.

61. Gray, *Eighteen Acres*, p.166.

62. Gray, *Eighteen Acres*, p.135.

63. The President responded:

Thank you for your note and, more particularly and much more importantly, for serving as Acting Appointment Secretary these last months. Your willingness to undertake cheerfully that chore, in addition to your own regular duties, delighted me. And for the splendid and efficient manner in which you carried the dual and difficult assignment I can only say that I am profoundly grateful.

I have just read the talk you made at the Harvard Club in Boston in January (and of course I shall write Lev Salstonstall the little note you suggest). Sometimes I too wonder how all of us have survived this worst of all possible Washington winters.

With warm regards,

CHAPTER 3

1. Robert Keith Gray, *Eighteen Acres Under Glass* (New York: Doubleday & Company, Inc. 1962), p.156.

2. Interview with Bryce Harlow, by Joe Trento, at 1984 Republican National Convention in Dallas, Texas.

Drew Pearson, *Diaries 1949–59* (New York: Holt, Rinehart and Winston, 1974), pp. 437,447,457,485.

Gray, *Eighteen Acres.*

Robert Keith Gray collection, 1954–60, A67-59, Dwight D. Eisenhower Library. Copies of drafts of his speeches.

3. "Meteor," *Omaha World-Herald,* April 30, 1958.
4. "A Key White House Post Goes to Robert K. Gray," *U.S. News and World Report,* May 9, 1958, p.22.
5. Gray, *Eighteen Acres,* p.209.

Interview with Bradley Patterson in May 1991.

6. "Robert Gray Gives Farewell for Rabbs," *The Evening Star,* May 17, 1958, p. A-14.
7. Gray, *Eighteen Acres,* p.293.
8. Interview with Bradley Patterson, May, 1991.
9. Lester Tanzer, "Behind the Cabinet Meeting Today: Drills, Coaching for Speakers," *Wall Street Journal,* June 13, 1958, p.1.
10. *Ibid.*
11. Interview with Charls Walker in October 1990.
12. Tanzer, *Wall Street Journal,* p.1.
13. Prior to Eisenhower, there was no set written agenda sent out in advance of the meetings.
14. Sidney Hyman, "The Cabinet's Job as Eisenhower Sees It," *The New York Times Magazine,* June 20, 1958, p.37–41.
15. Gray, *Eighteen Acres,* p.103.
16. Gray, *Eighteen Acres,* p.267.
17. "Cabinet Secretary Bob Gray Finds His Work Interesting," *Hastings Tribune,* December 23, 1958, p.11.
18. Gray, *Eighteen Acres,* p.109.
Within Gray's immigration responsibilities were international travel issues. He worked with other members of the intelligence community—J. Edgar Hoover, Allen Dulles, and Justice and State Department officials—on concerns about pre-flight inspections and waivers for nonimmigrant visas for Cuba, Mexico, the Bahamas, and Japan.
19. Years later, Gordon Gray's son, Boyden, would follow his father, an heir to a tobacco fortune, to the White House, working for George Bush as White House counsel.
20. Interview with Jerrold Scoutt.
21. William M. Blair, "Adams Bills Paid by Industrialist," *New York Times,* June 11, 1958, p.1.
22. Russell Baker, "Sherman Adams Resigns: Sees 'Vilification' Drive; President Voices Sadness," *New York Times,* September 23, 1958, p.1, 18.

One of the books used as "props" on the set used by Sherman Adams to resign was *The Happiest Man in the World.* James Hagerty, the White House press secretary, removed the book just before the broadcast.
23. Gray, *Eighteen Acres,* pp.94–95.
24. Gray, *Eighteen Acres,* p.97.
25. Gray, *Eighteen Acres,* p.91.
26. "How Cow Ate the Cabbage," *Omaha World-Herald,* May 9, 1960.
27. " 'Scare' Not Even A Close Shave," *Omaha World-Herald,* February, 1960.
28. Robert Keith Gray collection, 1954–60, A67-59, Dwight D. Eisenhower Library.
29. After interviewing thousands of Yugoslav refugees, the Catholic Welfare Conference was "convinced they are unanimously fleeing from religious persecution in the hands of the Communists." Archbishop Keough wrote to President Eisenhower "that Yugoslav refugees were bewildered at the realization that the United States is selective about the kind of communism and oppression from which a person must flee in order to benefit from the help of the American people."
30. Memorandum for General Persons, March 3, 1959, from Robert Gray, Dwight D. Eisenhower Library.
Copy of letter to Mr. W.G. Middelmann, October 1, 1958, from Robert Gray, Dwight D. Eisenhower Library.
31. Letter to the Honorable David K.E. Bruce from Robert Gray, October 11, 1958, Dwight D. Eisenhower Library.
32. Robert Keith Gray collection, 1954–1960, A-67-59, Refugee Misc., Dwight D. Eisenhower Library.

33. Robert Keith Gray collection, 1954–60, Dwight D. Eisenhower Library. Memorandum dated September 14, 1960 to Douglas Dillon at the State Department.

As the White House expert, Gray was instrumental in promoting administration support for a White House Conference on Refugees, as part of the United Nations' World Refugee Year. Once the President had agreed, Gray was the point man in setting up the conference. He wrote to Gerald Morgan, Eisenhower's Deputy Assistant, on May 6, 1959, just a couple of weeks before the conference:

> . . . Because we are asking the invitees to pick up their personal tabs State Department is anxious that we make at least a gesture of hospitality . . . The Department . . . wonders if it would be possible to have a White House buffet luncheon or possibly a picnic on the White House lawn . . . The picnic would be preferred since it would be a relatively cheap inexpensive way to entertain. Either would give an opportunity for the President to make an informal appearance before the group.

> Although this is being titled 'White House' Conference, the above will be the only demand made on the President's time or budget.

Gerald Morgan wrote in long-hand across the bottom of the memorandum:

> The Pres made it clear when he agreed to a 'White House Conference' that he was not to be asked to participate. . . . So the answer to the lunch or the picnic is no.

The *Washington Post* on July 11 ran an article and editorial calling the World Refugee Year a failure.

34. Robert Keith Gray collection, 1954–60, A67-59, Dwight D. Eisenhower Library.

35. Gray met with important representatives in the field of world relief organizations, and faithfully reported his contacts to the State Department. "While I never would want a visitor of Dr. Lindt's calibre [the Swiss Ambassador] to think that I would not welcome him unescorted, I always make it clear that I intend to discuss our conversations with the Department," Gray wrote in a memorandum to John Hanes at State.

Robert Keith Gray collection, 1954–60, A67-59, Dwight D. Eisenhower Library, memorandum from Gray to John Hanes, March 1, 1960.

36. Robert Keith Gray collection, 1954–60, A67-59, Memorandum for Mr. Morgan, July 29, 1959, Dwight D. Eisenhower Library.

37. Robert Keith Gray collection, 1954–60, A67-59, Dwight D. Eisenhower Library, personal letter to Robert Gray from John Hanes on September 14, 1959.

38. Gray, *Eighteen Acres*, p.268–269.

39. James Reston, "A Two-Fold Problem," *New York Times*, September 23, 1958, p.18.

40. Gray also worked closely with Charles McWhorter, Vice President Nixon's top aide.

41. "Gray Says Russians Spy on U.S. Embassy," *Washington Post*, May 24, 1960.

42. "Nixon Called Best Trained," The Omaha *World-Herald*, May 8, 1960.

43. Gray, *Eighteen Acres*, p.279.

44. Gray, *Eighteen Acres*, p.280.

45. Gray, *Eighteen Acres*, p.309.

46. "Bobby-Soxer 'Not Needed'—Kennedy Backed—for 1976, Says Speaker," *Omaha World-Herald*, May 22, 1960.

47. "Ike Working Hardest Ever, Nebraskan Gray Declares," *Omaha World-Herald*, January 28, 1960.

48. "Gray Quotes Nixon Ideas," *Omaha World Herald*, June 22, 1960.

49. "Reds Spy on Embassy, Eisenhower Aide Says," *New York Times*, May 24, 1960, p.16.

50. Gray revealed in his speech: "Tonight in Moscow, in front of the same American Embassy sits an $8,000 jet propelled motorboat—intended as the personal gift to Nikita Khrushchev from the President whose friendship he called fishy." Eisenhower was going to present Khrushchev with the boat when he met with him in their scheduled meeting in the Soviet Union until Khrushchev withdrew the invitation.

51. Gray, *Eighteen Acres*, p.284.

52. Gray, *Eighteen Acres*, pp.106–107.

53. Gray, *Eighteen Acres*, pp.105–107.

54. "Plan of Long Standing—Aide Clarifies Eisenhower's Entry Into Campaign," *New York Times*, November 7, 1960, p.16.

55. Gray, *Eighteen Acres*, p.311.

56. Gray, *Eighteen Acres*, p.323.
57. Gray, *Eighteen Acres*, pp.320–321.
58. Gray, *Eighteen Acres*, p.328.
59. Interview with Bradley Patterson.
60. Meg Greenfield, "Buy—And Read With Care," *Newsweek*, June 10, 1991, p.68.
61. Interview with Elton Hailey.

CHAPTER 4

1. *Hastings Tribune*, December 23, 1958, p.11.
2. The following paragraphs about Washington, lobbying and public relations are based on the following:

Robert Keith Gray, *Eighteen Acres Under Glass* (New York: Doubleday and Co., 1962), p.351.

Interview with Carl Curtis, December 1990.

Tim Taylor and Frederick Christian, "Rumors, Gossip and Lobbies," *Cosmopolitan*, May 1958.

CQ Lobbying book

Interview with Sheila Tate.

3. Megan Rosenfeld, "Inaugural Insider," *Washington Post*, December 15, 1980, p.B1.
4. Gray, *Eighteen Acres*, p.326.
5. Interview with Clifford Guest in August 1991. Guest started working for Hill and Knowlton in 1949 and worked in the Washington office for 29 years. He retired in 1978.
6. "It [lobbying] was natural for me because I didn't have a press background. At the White House my primary activities had been political and I liked that side . . . ," Gray told *Washingtonian* magazine.
7. Interview with George Worden.
8. John Hill, *The Making of a Public Relations Man* (New York: David McKay Company, Inc., 1963), p.16.
9. Hill, *Public Relations*, p.36.
10. Interview with George Worden.
11. Hill, *Public Relations*, p.259.
12. Hill, *Public Relations*, p.100.
13. Hill, *Public Relations*, p.105.
14. *Ibid.*
15. Joseph C. Goulden, "I Am Robert Keith Gray. I Have Social Connections. I Have Political Connections. I Represent Powerful Companies. I Work Very Quietly. I Get Things Done Expensively and Well," *Washingtonian*, 1974, p.139.
16. Public relations firms did lobby, but they applied pressure on legislatures more indirectly, through a grass roots approach—placing editorials, briefing the local press, organizing letter writing campaigns, advertising. In the early 1930s, the electric power companies trying to prevent enactment of the Public Utility Holding Company bill sent hundreds of fake telegrams and letters from names they picked out of a telephone book. By the 1950s, the public relations firms were organizing public opinions on behalf of an issue so that the lobbyists in Washington could more honestly say, "This is how your constituents feel, so this is how you should vote."
18. Robert Alden, "Advertising: Campaign to Quiet the Critics," *New York Times*, April 21, 1961, p.46L.
19. *Ibid.*
20. Taylor et al., *Cosmopolitan*.
21. Interview with Marvin Liebman.
22. It is ironic that the same amendment to the U.S. Constitution that protects freedom of the press also protects lobbyists. The First Amendment protects ". . . the right of the people peaceably to assemble, and to petition the Government for a redress of grievances." Throughout the years, the courts have been the lobbyists' best protector; the media their worst critic. Influencing public opinion and lobbying were rights for which the founding fathers sought protection. But had they been able to foresee the results, one wonders if their wording might have been a bit more precise.
23. Robert Keith Gray, "Sherman Adams: The Inside Story," *McCalls*, February, 1961.

"Adams Overprotected Ike at Times, Says Nebraskan," Omaha *World-Herald*, January 24, 1961.

24. Belair, "Adams Bills."
25. "Recall?" *Omaha World-Herald*, January 30, 1961.
26. For example, the passage about Sherman Adams keeping people and information from Eisenhower was changed to: "Every employee at the White House . . . shares in the responsibility of keeping petty people and petty problems from the Chief Executive. With the best of intentions, and with excellent results, Adams spared the President from mediocrity whether of people or of paper." (Gray, *Eighteen Acres*, p.40.)
27. "Nebraska's State Mother of The Year Is Mrs. Marie Gray," *Hastings Daily Tribune*, March 18, 1961, p.1.
28. Robert Keith Gray, "How Washington Society Goes To A Party," *McCalls*, January 1962.
29. Joy Miller, "Interview with Robert Gray Reveals Life of Bachelor in Washington, D.C.," Associated Press, *Hastings Tribune*, June 14, 1962, p.3.
30. "Nixon Lost Election for President Because of GOP Me-Too Tactics," *Omaha World-Herald*, May 25, 1962.
31. *Ibid.*
32. "Also Plans to Stay Active in Politics," *Omaha World-Herald*, February 13, 1961.
33. "Gray to Give Barry a Party, Guests will Include 4 of Ike's Cabinet," *Omaha World-Herald*, November 14, 1963.
34. "Firm Cancels Gray's Book," *Omaha World-Herald*, December 17, 1963.
35. Goulden, "I Am Robert Keith Gray."
36. Robert K. Gray, "Lobby Links You, 'Uncle'—'Congress Could Not Operate Without It,' " *Omaha World-Herald*, December 18, 1966.
37. Interview with Clifford Guest.
38. Goulden, "I Am Robert Keith Gray."
39. "Arabs?" *Omaha World-Herald*, May 16, 1966.
40. "Former Nebraskan On Nixon Committee," *Omaha World-Herald*, December 3, 1967.

CHAPTER 5

1. Rudy Maxa, "Six Persuaders—Have They Got PR for You," *Washington Post/Potomac*, March 10, 1974, p.14.
2. Joseph C. Goulden, "I Am Robert Keith Gray. I Have Social Connections. I Have Political Connections. I Represent Powerful Companies. I Work Very Quietly. I Get Things Done. Expensively and Well.," *Washingtonian*, 1974.
3. Goulden, "I Am Robert Keith Gray."

The resolutions began: "Whereas, the ___is dedicated to maintaining a competitive business development position and to preserving the reliability of supply and comparative low cost of natural gas in this area and . . ." According to *Washingtonian* magazine, 37 Washington States chambers of commerce passed these identical resolutions.

4. *Ibid.*, p.81.
5. Maxa, *Washington Post/Potomac*.
6. *Ibid.*
7. Goulden, "I Am Robert Keith Gray."
8. Interview with Liz Carpenter. She said she recommended Shirley Hofstedler for Hewlit-Packard and Delores Cogan for the company that makes Alka-Seltzer.
9. Rudy Maxa, "Influence and Image: D.C. Public Relations," *Washington Post/Potomac*, March 10, 1974, p.12 & 14.
10. Goulden, "I Am Robert Keith Gray."
11. *Ibid.*
12. Interview with George Worden.
13. Goulden, "I Am Robert Keith Gray," p.80.
14. Other clients were Warner Lambert, The Tobacco Institute, Campbell Soups, Sterling Drug Company, Puerto Rico Tourists Development Corporation, Pennsylvania Electric Association (and many other utility companies around the country), Richards and Merrill (pharmaceutical company), Mellon Bank, Union Pacific Railroad, the Licensed Beverage Industries.
15. Goulden, "I Am Robert Keith Gray."
16. Maxa, *Washington Post/Potomac*.

17. Interview with Larry Speakes.
18. Goulden, "I Am Robert Keith Gray."
19. *Ibid.*
20. *Ibid.*
21. *Ibid.*
22. *Ibid.*
23. *Ibid.*
24. *Ibid.*
25. *Ibid.*
26. *Ibid.*
27. *Ibid.*
28. *Ibid.*
29. *Ibid.*
30. *Ibid.*
31. Robert Keith Gray, "Washington Public Relations: The Next Twenty-Five Years," *Vital Speeches*, January 1, 1975, pp. 172–175.
32. Interview with Paul Laxalt in 1990.
33. Post-Presidential papers. Eisenhower Library. On Sunday April 9, 1967, the Eisenhowers and the Reagans lunched together at Walter Annenberg's home.
34. Interview with Carl Curtis.
35. Interview with James Lake.
36. Interview with James Lake.

Nancy Reagan, *My Turn* (New York: Random House, 1990) pp.114–115.

CHAPTER 6

1. My husband, Joseph Trento, was the CNN correspondent. The interview was in August 1984.
2. Interview with Sheila Tate.
3. Interview with Robert Crowley.
4. In *The Making of a Public Relations Man* (David McKay Inc., 1963), Hill writes of his decision to take Hill and Knowlton overseas in Chapter 15, page 185.
5. Goulden, "I Am Robert Keith Gray," p.145.
6. Joseph Trento and David Roman, "The Spies Who Came In From The Newsroom," *Penthouse*, March 1977.
7. Peter Maas, *Manhunt* (New York: Random House, 1986), p.32.
8. Interview with Howard Wickham.
9. General Erskine was Defense Department liaison to the CIA.
10. Phil McCombs, "Tongsun Park's Club," *Washington Post*, October 16, 1977, p.C1.

Interviews with club members, the club manager, and club founders.

11. Interview with William R. Corson.
12. See chapter two (page 29) of *The Power Peddlers* (Garden City, New York: Doubleday, 1977) by Russell Warren Howe and Sarah Hays Trott for a detailed look at the China Lobby. Another excellent history is Stanley D. Bachrack's *The Committee of One Million* (New York: Columbia University Press, 1976).
13. From a World Airways annual report, an interview with Jerrald Scoutt, a boyhood friend of Gray's and a Washington attorney, and from Gray's Who's Who listing.
14. Interview with Anna Chennault.
15. Written interview with Robert Gray.
16. Steven Ambrose, *Nixon: The Triumph Of A Politician 1962–1972* (New York: Simon and Schuster, 1989), pp.206–222.
17. Anna Chennault had violated the Logan Act. The so-called neutrality law says it is illegal for any citizen to "intercourse with any foreign government . . . with intent to influence [its] conduct . . . in relation to any disputes or controversies with the United States or to defeat any measures of the United States."
18. See pages 48–49 of *The Power Peddlers*.
19. Interview with Tullius Accompura.
20. Interview with Henry Preston Pitts.
21. Interview with Milton G. Nottingham. According to Wilson, Nottingham introduced Gray and Park.

22. The first club manager was a former U.S. Foreign Service officer.

23. Interview with William Corson.

24. Interview with Richard Hanna.

25. Interview with Tullius Accompura.

26. Wilson worked for Task Force 157 from 1971 until 1977.

27. Written interview with Robert Gray.

28. This trip was confirmed by government investigators. Neil Livingstone also said that Gray told him about the trip.

29. Goulden, "I Am Robert Keith Gray," p.145.

30. See Chapter Two of *The Power Peddlers*, "Fighting A Hill War in Asia."

31. Richard Boetcher and Gordon L. Freedman, *Gifts of Deceit* (New York: Holt, Rinehart & Winston, 1980) pp.238–240.

32. Maxine Cheshire and Scott Armstrong, "Rep. Robert Leggett: Life of Immense Complications," *Washington Post*, July 18, 1976, p.1.

33. Today he is George Bush's Veterans Administrator after serving as a high-ranking State Department official during the Reagan administration.

34. Beth Brophy, "The Gray Eminence," *Forbes*, January 18, 1982, p.102.

A year later, Gray again bragged that he had turned Libya down as a client. "The government of Libya has asked us a number of times to represents them and we flatly refused each time. It would be ridiculous. America does not have a more clear-cut enemy than Libya," Gray told *The Carletonian*, his alma mater's newspaper in 1983. (John F. Harris, "The Wizards of Washington," *The Carletonian*, September 30, 1983, p.2.)

CHAPTER 7

1. Megan Rosenfeld, "Inaugural Insider," *Washington Post*, December 15, 1980, p.B1.

2. Interview with James Lake.

3. Interview with Richard Allen.

4. Elizabeth Drew, *Politics and Money—The New Road To Corruption* (New York: Macmillan Publishing Company), 1983, p.111.

5. Interview with Marvin Liebman.

6. Interview with Lyn Nofziger.

7. Interview with Richard Allen.

8. Letter from Williams and Connolly dated June 29, 1990.

9. Joseph E. Persico, *Casey* (New York: Viking, 1990). Interviews with James Lake, John Sears, Paul Laxalt, Lyn Nofziger, and Richard Allen.

10. Interview with Lyn Nofziger.

11. Margaret B. Carlson, "Rescue Mission," *Regardie's* magazine, December, 1985, p.55.

12. Harris, John F., "The Wizard of Washington," *The Carletonian*, September 30, 1983.

13. Interview with Dan Jones.

14. Interview with Larry Speakes.

15. Howell Raines, "Lyn Nofziger: Barometer in Reagan Strategy Shift," *New York Times*, September 28, 1980, p.36.

16. *Ibid.*

17. Michael Pilgrim, a security expert who said he had personal knowledge, agreed that if Crowley was correct, "It would certainly explain why George Bush would put his ass on the line to renominate such a person," he said.

Gates' meteoric career in the CIA culminated in his being confirmed Director of Central Intelligence in November 1991.

18. Interview with Robert Crowley.

19. Interview with William Corson.

20. Interviews with Neil Livingstone and Michael Pilgrim. They had both worked for J.J. Cappucci, an international security firm, that was once owned by Ed Wilson.

21. Debategate report and interview with Dan Jones.

22. Interview with Dan Jones.

23. The significance of the Sadat letter may come from the fact that, at the time, Livingstone was working for a former Ed Wilson company that had the contract to train Sadat's personal body guards. He was also working closely with former contacts with the Egyptian Embassy and who were also playing major, behind-the-scenes roles in the 1980 Reagan–Bush campaign.

According to Neil Livingstone and J.J. Cappucci, the former Ed Wilson Company was taken over by Tom Clines, a former Ed Wilson control for the CIA.

24. Interview with Dan Jones. Debategate report.

25. Debategate, pp. 68, 1189.

26. Ibid., p.1190, and interview with Dan Jones.

27. Debategate report, p.162. Martin Schram, "Reagan Volunteer Got Memos From A Carter 'Mole,' " *Washington Post*, July 7, 1983.

28. Debategate document on p.77 and interview with Dan Jones.

29. *Ibid.*

30. Schram, "Reagan Volunteer Got Memos . . ."

31. Ibid. The materials from the souvenir hunter were turned over to the *Washington Post* in 1983 when the Debategate controversy arose.

32. According to Gary Sick, who was the Iran expert on the National Security Council under Carter, who wrote about it in an op-ed piece in the *New York Times* in April 1991, and a "Frontline" documentary.

Larry Martz with Jane Whitemore, "A Reagan Bargain with Iran?" *Newsweek*, April 29, 1991, p.33.

Frank Snepp, Curtis Lang and Dan Bischoff, "Chronology of the United States/Israeli Arms-for-Hostages Deals with Iran, 1980–1982," *The Village Voice*, June 25, 1991, p.35.

33. Interview with Marta Diaz Williams.

34. ABC "Nightline" interview with Gray on May 5, 1991.

35. Debategate report, p.49.

36. Debategate, p.51.

37. "Hasting Native to Be Honored," *Lincoln Star*, October 20, 1980, p.4.

38. Nancy Reagan, *My Turn* (New York: Random House, 1990), pp.114–115.

39. Megan Rosenfeld, "Inaugural Insider," *Washington Post*, December 15, 1980, p.B1.

40. *Ibid.*

41. *Ibid*, p.B12.

42. Persico, "I Am Robert Keith Gray," p.204.

43. Drew, *Politics and Money*, p.114.

44. Lynn Rosellini, "A Preview of the Reagan Inauguration," *New York Times*, December 10, 1980, p.D22.

45. *Ibid.*

46. *Ibid.*

47. *Ibid.*

48. *Ibid.*

49. Dave Neilson, "Gray's job ends when Reagan regime's begins," *Hastings Tribune*, December 27, 1980, p.2.

50. Dave Nielson, "Gray promotes inaugural rites," *Hastings Tribune*, December 24, 1980.

51. Rosellini, *New York Times*.

52. Rosenfeld, *Washington Post*.

53. Enid Nemy, "The Bushes Come to Town for a Private Party," *New York Times*, January 9, 1981, p.B5.

54. Ward Sinclair and Bill Peterson, "Faithful Flock to Town," *Washington Post*, January 21, 1981, p.A-29.

55. Pete Earley and Thomas Morgan, "Reagan Sworn in as the 40th President," *Washington Post*, January 21, 1981, p.A30.

56. Tom Shales, "Stunning & TV's Day," *Washington Post*, January 21, 1981, p.E1.

57. Pete Earley, "Inaugural Panel Owes $450,000 in Refunds," *Washington Post*, January 31, 1981, p.A2.

58. *Ibid.*

59. *Ibid.*

60. Beth Brophy, "The Gray Eminence," *Forbes*, January 18, 1982, p.103.

61. Interview with Sheila Tate.

62. Carlson, *Regardie's*, p.55. He also gave a similar quote to *Forbes* and other media.

63. Carlson, *Regardie's*, p.57.

64. Carlson, *Regardie's*, p.65.

65. According to Robert Crowley.

CHAPTER 8

1. Megan Rosenfeld, "Inaugural Insider," *Washington Post*, December 15, 1980, p.B12.
2. Interview with George Worden.
3. Interview with James Lake.
4. Gray had long maintained a close relationship with the various postmaster generals. He had to pull several strings to get the Postal Service to approve his new address.
5. Interview with Pate Felts.
6. Interview with Mark Moran.
7. Interview with Adonis Hoffman.
8. Interview with Betsey Weltner.
9. Interview with Sheila Tate.
10. Lynn Rosellini, "Bob Gray: Public Relations Man to the Powerful," *New York Times*, February 26, 1982, p.A18.
11. Gray and Company's SEC filing.
12. Joan Braden, *Just Enough Rope* (New York: Villard Books, 1989), p.220.
13. Rosellini, *New York Times*.
14. Rudy Maxa, "Wired," *Washingtonian*, July, 1983, p.90.
15. Barbara Gamarekian, "Bob Gray Has a Party," *New York Times*, July 10, 1981.
16. Braden, *Just Enough Rope*.
17. Gamarekian, *New York Times*.
18. *Ibid.*
19. Interview with Larry Speakes.
20. Interview with Bette Anderson.
21. Ann M. Reilly, "Washington's Super Lobbyists," *Dun's Business Month*, August, 1983, p.30.
22. Amy Nathan, "Party Lines," *Washington Post*, March 11, 1981, p.B3.
23. Maxine Chessire, "VIP," *Washington Post*, March 13, 1981, p.C4.

Interviews with Alejandro Orfila and Richard Schweiker.

24. Gamarekian, *New York Times*.
25. *Ibid.*
26. Interview with Mark Moran.
27. Interview with Barry Schochet.
28. Interview with Richard Schweiker.
29. Rudy Maxa, *Washingtonian*, p.129.
30. Lois Romano, "Ursula Meese Speaks Out," *Washington Post*, April 17, 1982, p.B1.
31. *Ibid.*
32. *Ibid.*, p.B11.
"I'm looking forward to getting out of the job," Ursula Meese said.
33. Interview with Richard Berendzen.
34. Mary Thornton, "Wife Works for GOP-Linked Group," *Washington Post*, April 15, 1984.
35. Interview with Richard Berendzen.
36. Interview with Neil Livingstone.
37. "Zorthian Claims No PR Conflict," *California Courier*, January 19, 1984, p.1.
38. Press release, excerpt from "Haratch," February 24, 1984.
39. Phil McCombs, "Fired Gray and Company Officer Claims Bias," *Washington Post*, April 13, 1991, p.A11.
40. Written interview with Robert Gray.

D.C. Human Rights Commission, docket # 84-P-275.

41. Francis X. Clines and Lynn Rosellini, "You Are What You Charge," *New York Times*, May 4, 1982, p.A28.
42. Interview with Lyn Nofziger.
43. TRB, "At the Power House," *The New Republic*, December 31, 1983.
44. Rosellini, *New York Times*.
45. *Ibid.*

CHAPTER 9

1. Tolbert, Kathryn, "Home of Reagan Official Damaged by Kitchen Fire," *Washington Post*, December 22, 1981, p.B3.

Arlington County, Virginia Fire Department Fire Investigation Report.

2. *Ibid.*
3. Interview with Carl Curtis.
4. Dave Neilson, "Gray's Job Ends When Reagan Regime's Begins," *Hastings Tribune*, December 27, 1980, p.2.
5. "Former Executive of Hill & Knowlton Takes JWT to Court," *Broadcasting*, August 23, 1982, p.37.

Gray vs. JWT Group Inc. et al. U.S. District Court for the District of Columbia. Civil Case No. 1:82-CV-02295.

"Reagan Confidant Is Suing JWT," *New York Times*, August 18, 1982, p.D-17.

Gray and Company's filings with the Securities and Exchange Commission.

6. Interview with George Worden.
7. Interview with Mark Moran.
8. On December 15, 1983, Gray and JWT Group, Inc. settled their lawsuits. In the settlement Gray received $315,000 from the defendants and claimed a great victory. H&K said that the money was only the amount Gray's stock lost in value and it was cheaper to settle than to pay the legal fees.
9. Interview with Neil Livingstone.
10. Walter Pincus and Joe Pichirallo, "House Unit to Probe Page Sex Charges," *Washington Post*, July 2, 1982, p.1.
11. Metropolitan Police Department, Investigative Services Division, Confidential Memorandum, September 9, 1982.
12. Jack Moriarity told his partner Richard Powers about his conversation with Shoffler and Powers passed the information on to Tom Fortuin, not Jack Moriarity.
13. The information on the Capitol Hill sex and drug investigation is based on federal law enforcement, police department, and House Ethics Committee records and interviews with several of the investigators.
14. Leslie Maitland, "Califano Suspends 2 Investigators In Congress Sex and Drug Inquiry, *New York Times*, September 26, 1982.
15. Maxine Chessire, "VIP," *Washington Post*, March 13, 1981, p.C4.
16. Interview with Betsey Weltner and other Gray and Company executives.
17. Interview with Richard Allen.
18. Interview with Paul Weyrich.
19. Maxa, *Washingtonian*, p.91.
20. Interview with Mark Moran.
21. Interview with Carter Clews and several other Gray and Company executives.

CHAPTER 10

1. Interview with Mark Moran.
2. Lynn Rosellini, "Bob Gray: Public Relations Man to the Powerful," *New York Times*, February 26, 1982, p.A18.
3. Kathy Stokebrand, "Gray Says Landing Job is Serious Task," *Hastings Tribune*, May 17, 1982.
4. Interview with James Wootton.
5. Former AU President Richard Berendzen remembered what happened. ". . . The man who used to be the chief of protocol for President Carter back in the Democratic administration was from Texas and he introduced me to a friend of his who was the publisher of something called *Texas Business* magazine. . . . And one day he calls me in my office in Washington, and he said, 'I'm also involved in some other publishing . . .' and he said he was aware of some woman that was doing research and would we be interested in meeting her and that she had, apparently, grants and she had a manuscript and she was doing all kinds of research . . . and that various people thought very highly of her. . . . So I took the materials I had about this woman whom I had never met to . . . the Vice Provost who dealt with research and special projects."
6. Interview with Richard Berendzen.
7. Gray and Company's client was the Media Coalition. Besides *Playboy* and *Penthouse*, the coalition also included The American Booksellers, Association of American Publishers, Freedom to Read Foundation, American Civil Liberties, Association of University Presses.

8. Interview with Carter Clews.

9. Interview with Paul Weyrich.

10. With this and other clients, Gray and Company abandoned another Hill principle, Hill's abhorrence to the use of fake fronts to hide real clients. Hill wrote in his book: "One (unethical) practice which I believe should be eliminated is that of the so-called 'paper front.' A client is advised to finance an 'organization' to promote or fight for its cause under the guise of an independent and spontaneous movement. This is a plain public deceit and fraud and of course is a technique developed with the consummate skill and in great profusion by the Communists. In a free country any interest with a cause has a right to present its case to the public, to inform and, if possible, to persuade to its heart's content. But that right of free speech also carries the obligation that the source of it will be in the open for all to see. Attempts to fool the public by making it believe an 'organization' existing only on paper is really a vociferous group favoring this or that cause have helped cast a shadow upon the business of public relations counselling." (Hill, p.40.)

11. Evan Thomas, "Pitchman of the Power House," *Time*, April 30, 1984, p.19.

12. Obviously, if Gray did check with Casey about taking Libya, Casey must not have objected since Gray continued to pursue it with his company.

13. Interview with Neil Livingstone.

14. Jeff Gerth, "Reagan Advisers Received Stock in Laser Concern," *New York Times*, April 28, 1983, p.1.

According to the *Times* article, in 1977, the SEC accused Bernard Katz, Helionetics's largest stock holder, and others of violating securities laws by playing undisclosed consulting fees and stock options and stimulating artificial demand for stock in Xonics, a company founded by Katz. Katz entered a consent decree with the SEC, neither admitting nor denying the charges, but agreeing to an order enjoining him from future similar activities.

15. Capaccio, Tony, "Aspin Aided California Firm Said to Mismanage Funds," *Defense Week*, January 20, 1987.

Michael Isikoff, "Defense Contractor's Spending Under Fire," *Washington Post*, December 2, 1987, p.1.

16. Department of Justice pamphlet explaining The Foreign Agents Registration Act of 1938 as amended.

17. Robert Keith Gray, "Getting the Story and Getting It Right," *Vital Speeches*, October 1, 1984, p.763.

18. Interview with Niels Holchs.

19. McCombs, *Washington Post*.

20. Interview with Carl Curtis.

21. Critics of Korologus's firm, Timmons and Company, say that they hide their foreign clients in a sister firm called Global Consultants, so that they can take the high ground.

22. Interview with Paul Laxalt.

23. A Craig Copetas, "The Sovereign Republic of Marc Rich," *Regardie's*, February, 1990.

A. Craig Copetas, *Metal Men*, G.P. Putnam's Sons, 1985.

24. Jack Anderson and Joseph Spear, "Lucrative Lobbying," Washington Merry-Go-Round, February 8, 1986.

25. Op.Cit. (Harris)

26. Evan Thomas, "Pitchman of The Power House," *Time*, April 30, 1984, p.19.

27. Mark Potts, "Gray & Co. Plans Public Stock Sale," *Washington Post*, December 30, 1983.

28. Interview with John Lawler.

29. Interview with Betsey Weltner.

30. McComb, *Washington Post*.

31. "The Selling of Bob Gray," *Fortune*, February 6, 1984.

32. Jerry Knight, "Gray and Co. Believed Its Own Hype, Priced Its Stock Too High," *Washington Post*, February 20, 1984, pp.19, 21.

33. "Gray & Company Is Acquiring Strayton," *New York Times*, September 6, 1984, p.D17.

34. Sari Horwitz, "Gray & Co. to Acquire Mass. PR Firm," *Washington Post*.

35. Jerry Knight, "Gray, Brown Driving to Top of Ads, PR Set," *Washington Post*, September 10, 1984.

36. Mark Potts, "Gray & Co. Plans Public Stock Sale," *Washington Post*, December 12, 1983.

37. "The Selling of Bob Gray," *Fortune*, February 6, 1984.

38. Evan Thomas, "Pitchman of the Power House," *Time* April 30, 1984, p.19.

39. Jerry Knight, "Gray, Brown Driving to Top of Ads, PR Set," *Washington Post*, September 10, 1984.

CHAPTER 11

1. From the Cable News Network Special Assignment documentary "Pipeline To Power" which aired in 1985 and was reported, written, and produced by Joseph J. Trento. Joseph Trento is my husband.

2. Correspondent Joseph Trento, cameraman Mike Wimberly, technician Jon Moore, and producer Sandy Myers.

3. From Cable News Network's "Pipeline To Power."

4. From "Pipeline to Power" which aired on CNN in 1985.

5. "Capital Practitioner of Public Relations," *New York Times*, January 23, 1984, p.D2.

Gray had told *Forbes*, "Social functions give people in power a chance to be with each other in a relaxed setting . . . Washington business was always conducted that way." (Brophy, "The Gray Eminence.")

6. Interview with Joan Braden.

"Pipeline to Power," 1985.

7. Sheila Tate remembered, "Well, that the entrée, I think, into the Reagan administration, [was] getting the Teamsters support. Bob was instrumental in getting the Teamsters to endorse Ronald Reagan."

8. Interview with Larry Speakes.

9. Interview with Richard Schweiker.

10. Cooper, *The National Journal*.

11. Cooper, *The National Journal*.

12. Beth Brophy, "The Gray Eminence," *Forbes*, January 18, 1982, p.102.

13. Ann Cooper, "Image Builders," *The National Journal*, September 14, 1985, p.2060.

14. Cooper, *The National Journal*.

15. Gray and Company's brochure said: "Gray and Company provides thorough background material to the producers and hosts prior to the interview, *and suggests story angles for them to pursue.*" Emphasis added.

16. From the fundraising brochure for the Gray Center for the Communications Arts.

17. Gray and Company's brochure.

18. Interview with Mark Moran.

19. CNN's "Pipeline to Power."

20. "Gray takes spotlight," *Advertising Age*, 1984.

21. Mary Battiata, "Public Relations or 'News': Gray and Company Blurs the Boundaries," *Washington Post*, March 27, 1985, p.1.

22. Today PR-produced radio and television are commonplace. "We do a lot of radio actualities," said Tate, "They are already prerecorded news stories with that announcer's voice." When asked why these radio spots were considered news and not advertisements she replied, "because it is factual" and radio stations do not have to broadcast them, like paid advertisements. "They're free if they want to just take a soundbite and put their own announcer's voice on it. They don't have to use it. Most of them will use it because it is broadcast quality."

23. As previously noted, Joseph Trento is my husband.

24. Interview with Ted Kavanau.

In 1984, Kavanau was one of the top three executives at CNN. He came to Special Assignments after successfully starting CNN Headline News. Threatened by ABC's effort to put CNN out of business with a headline service called Satellite News Network, Kavanau is credited with saving CNN by creating a competitive headline service and getting it on the air in just six weeks. The creation of the second CNN channel marked the end of the other networks' attempts to stop CNN.

25. Interview with Neil Livingstone.

26. According to *Mobbed Up*, by James Neff, Gray held a party for Jackie Presser and the

Teamsters with prominent administration officials and members of Congress at The George Town Club.

27. Interview with Richard Allen.

28. According to Gray and Company, "While JCIC is a private, nonprofit foundation, the Japanese Ministry of Transportation and the Ministry of Foreign Affairs have sponsored the foundation and have had a role in supervising the foundation's activities."

29. Interview with Jeanee von Essen.

30. McCombs, *Washington Post*.

31. Interview with James Lake.

32. Phil McCombs, "Inside The Power House," *Washington Post*, June 28, 1984, p.D9.

33. *Ibid.*

34. Like Gray's speech in defense of lobbyists, Lake's pitch on why a client needs PR is standard:

> The pressures on . . . the media and by the media are such, unless you do everything that you can to protect yourself and defend yourself, to pursue your interest, other people will pursue their interest at your expense. If you don't make every effort to try and tell people what you are, who you are, how you operate, other people will define you. If you leave it up to others, good luck, because most of the time others have an agenda or point of view that is very different from yours. A story about you, without hearing from you, will be filled by those who don't necessarily have your interest at heart. If you don't defend your interest, you don't stand much of a chance at having your story told in a manner that is going to be fair to you.

> The media today, like congressmen today, react to short term stimulus; to television and newspapers. They don't have time to do research and analysis on what's going on on a given issue in a given company to do a thorough, complete, and fair job and often they don't. Not because they intend to be unfair or harmful, but they do it as they see it and the way they see it is not necessarily right.

> If they have the other side presented to them, they have a chance to see the whole story and read pros and cons and evaluate and make choices. . . . So you try to make sure that they see the whole story and report the whole story so that the public who reads their stories or watches it on television can get the benefit of a less bias, more complete view and then make his choices, a decision of public opinion rather than getting a one-sided view.

CHAPTER 12

1. Interview with Jack McGeorge.

2. These events are based on interviews with Ed Wilson and confirmed by Justice Department, Maritime Administration and court documents.

3. Interview with Edwin P. Wilson.

4. Cappucci headed The Office of Special Investigations.

5. According to Bureau of Alcohol, Tobacco and Firearms Briefing Paper 3210 0578 3004.

6. Interview with Neil Livingstone.

7. From court papers filed in the *United States v. EATSCO.*

8. The fine was assessed against Clines's wholly owned corporation, not Clines personally.

9. From White House and Justice Department memoranda and a confidential interview with a Justice Department official present at the White House meetings and interview with J.J. Cappucci.

10. Page 16, Neil Livingstone's deposition, taken by the Securities and Exchange Commission on October 16, 1985.

11. Maas, *Manhunt*, p.32 and McComb, *"Inside the Power House,"* *Washington Post*, June 28, 1984 p.D1.

12. Neil Livingstone's deposition to the SEC regarding the Gray and Company Spanish office.

13. Neil Livingstone's U.S. Department of Justice registration form. Moreira paid Gray and Company an additional $60,000 between July and October 1982.

14. Interview with Jack McGeorge.

15. After Carbaugh had successfully established himself as a behind-the-scenes power with the Guatemalan operation, with the subsequent successful overthrow of the Guatemalan government, he would play a major role in getting a right-wing Cuban emigre named Alberto Martinez Pedro named as an Ambassador to the Organization of American States, and,

subsequently, to the more friendly new regime in Guatemala, according to Carbaugh's former law partner, William Joyce.

Joyce got a first-hand look at the CIA's involvement in the overthrow several years later while dining with the Guatemalan Ambassador at the men's grill at Chevy Chase Country Club. Ambassador Martinez Pedro was there to seek Joyce's help in getting his son a membership in the exclusive club. In the middle of their meeting, a balding man walked into the grill and Joyce said the Ambassador suddenly excused himself, with no explanation, and went off in a corner with the stranger. "The man, I subsequently learned was Alan Friers [the head of CIA operations for Latin America]. The discussion had been about a secret supply line to the Contras." (From an interview with William Joyce.)

16. Gray and Company Justice Department registration for IRIS and interviews with Gray and Company officials.

17. Livingstone said he and Casey worked together on a joint presidential and congressional commission called The Murphy Commission during this time.

18. Interview with Jack McGeorge.

19. Interview with Neil Livingstone.

20. Written interview with Robert Gray.

21. Interview with Robert T. Crowley.

22. A CNN documentary, "Pipeline to Power," which aired in early 1985.

23. *Time*, April 30, 1984.

24. Interview with Neil Livingstone.

25. Phil Gailey and Warren Weaver, Jr., "Washington Talk," *New York Times*, January 4, 1983, p.B10.

26. Steven Emerson, *The American House of Saud* (New York: Franklin Watts, 1985), p.336.

27. Emerson, *House of Saud*, pp.344, 345.

28. Interview with Neil Livingstone.

29. Interview with Neil Livingstone.

30. From Page 325 of Owen's testimony before the Iran Contra Select Committee.

31. McGeorge's Secret Service colleague was a resident security officer in Honduras.

32. The original organizers were Livingstone, McGeorge, an attorney named Robert Blair, and Cary Arnold, a former official in the federal government's anti-terrorism office.

33. Gray and Company merged with Hill and Knowlton before Tower had a chance to attend a Board meeting. Written interview with Robert Gray.

34. "Report of the Congressional Committees Investigating the Iran-Contra Affair," Times Books, 1988.

CHAPTER 13

1. Tom Burns, "100,000 Spaniards Protest U.S. Bases, Membership in NATO," *Washington Post*, June 4, 1984, p.A8.

2. From the deposition of Kenneth Gray taken on August 7, 1985 as part of an investigation by the Securities and Exchange Commission into the activities of Gray and Company.

3. From page 21 of the Kenneth Gray deposition before the SEC.

4. From Page 37 of Neil Livingstone's deposition before the SEC.

5. Interview with Neil Livingstone.

6. From page 52 of the SEC deposition of Neil C. Livingstone.

7. Tom Burns, "100,000 Spaniards Protest U.S. Bases, Membership in NATO," *Washington Post*, June 4, 1984, p.A6.

8. Tom Burns, "Gromyko, U.S. Envoy Meet With Spanish Leader," *Washington Post*, March 1, 1985, p.A10.

9. Interview with Neil Livingstone.

10. From Page 61 of Neil Livingstone's deposition before the SEC.

11. From Page 33 of the SEC deposition of James Jennings taken on February 24, 1986.

12. From Page 20–21 of the SEC deposition of Robert Keith Gray taken on February 27, 1986.

13. From page 36 of Robert Keith Gray's SEC deposition.

14. Interview with Neil Livingstone.

15. From page 38 of Alejandro Orfila's SEC deposition.

16. Interview with Alejandro Orfila.

17. Interview with Alejandro Orfila.

18. *Ibid.*

19. Interview with Neil Livingstone.

20. From page 86 of Neil C. Livingstone's deposition before the SEC. In a later deposition, Livingstone claimed that Lasuen admired him because he was an academic.

21. Interview with Alejandro Orfila.

22. From page 56 of Alejandro Orfila's SEC deposition.

23. From page 29 of Robert Keith Gray's SEC deposition.

24. From page 40 of Jim Jennings's SEC deposition; the expense receipt was SEC Exhibit No. 56.

25. From page 27 of the SEC deposition of Robert Keith Gray.

26. Interview with Mark Moran.

27. Interview with Neil Livingstone.

28. From page 13 of Mark Moran's SEC Deposition taken on June 26, 1986.

29. Neil C. Livingstone's SEC deposition, June 27, 1986, p.26.

30. From page 41 of Mark E. Moran's SEC deposition.

31. From Page 36 of Mark Moran's deposition before the SEC.

32. From Neil Livingstone's SEC deposition.

33. From page 57 of James Jennings's SEC deposition.

34. From page 75 of Alejandro Orfila's SEC deposition.

35. From pages 58-59 of James Jennings's deposition before the SEC.

36. From page 88 of Robert Keith Gray's deposition before the SEC.

37. From page 53 of the Carter Clews's deposition before the SEC taken on February 26, 1987.

38. From page 90 of Robert Keith Gray's deposition before the SEC.

39. From Kenneth Gray's deposition before the Securities and Exchange Commission on August 7, 1985.

40. From page 91 of Robert Keith Gray's deposition before the SEC.

41. From Kenneth Gray's deposition before the Securities and Exchange Commission on August 7, 1985.

42. From page 101 of Kenneth Gray's Security and Exchange Deposition.

43. Neil C. Livingstone's deposition to SEC on June 27, 1986, pp.20–22.

44. From page 73 of Kenneth Gray's SEC deposition.

45. From page 99 of Kenneth Gray's Securities and Exchange Commission deposition.

46. From page 120 of Kenneth Gray's Securities and Exchange Commission deposition.

47. From Neil Livingstone v. Gray and Company.

48. From pages 58–59 of Mark E. Moran's deposition before the SEC.

49. From page 40 of Mark Moran's SEC deposition.

50. From page 127 of Kenneth Gray's deposition before the Securities and Exchange Commission.

51. From page 20 of John Pate Felts SEC deposition taken on February 20, 1986.

52. From page 79 of the SEC deposition of Robert Keith Gray.

53. From page 159 of Kenneth Gray's deposition before the Securities and Exchange Commission.

54. Interview with Ken Gray.

55. Carter Strong of the Washington law firm of Arent, Fox was the lawyer Jennings told Ken Gray he had consulted.

56. From page 247 of Mark Moran's deposition before the SEC.

57. From page 152 of Mark Moran's deposition before the SEC.

58. SEC exhibit #70.

59. From pages 162–163 of Mark Moran's deposition before the SEC.

60. From pages 38–39 of Robert Keith Gray's SEC deposition.

61. From page 120 of Neil Livingstone's deposition before the Securities and Exchange Commission.

62. From pages 82–83 of Robert Keith Gray's SEC deposition.

63. From page 188 of Neil Livingstone's deposition before the SEC.

64. John Pate Felts's SEC deposition, p.39.

65. From SEC Exhibit No. 89, Robert Keith Gray's travel schedule.

66. From page 235 of Charles S. Crawford III's deposition before the SEC.

67. From page 160–161 of Robert Keith Gray's deposition before the SEC.

68. From page 219 of Charles Crawford III's deposition before the SEC.

69. Page 227 of Charles H. Crawford III's deposition before the SEC.

70. Interview with Marta Williams Diaz.

71. From page 217 of Alejandro Orfila's deposition before the Securities and Exchange Commission on January 31, 1986.
72. SEC exhibit #125.
73. From page 145 of James C. Jennings's SEC deposition.
74. Livingstone's June 27, 1986 SEC deposition, p.34–36.
75. From page 210 of Mark Moran's SEC deposition and Exhibit 93 of the SEC.
76. From page 219 of Mark Moran's deposition before the SEC.
77. See SEC Exhibit #95.
78. Page 249 from the deposition before the SEC of Alejandro Orfila.
79. From Page 235 of Mark Moran's deposition before the SEC.
80. From page 86 of Mark Moran's SEC deposition.
81. Interview with Mark Moran.
82. Interview with Michael Pilgrim.
83. Securities and Exchange Commission Exhibit #6.
84. From page 141 of Kenneth Gray's SEC deposition.
85. From page 94 of Kenneth Gray's SEC deposition.
86. From page 187 of Kenneth Gray's deposition before the SEC.
87. From exhibit 13 of the SEC investigation into Gray and Company.
88. From page 115 of Robert Keith Gray's deposition before the SEC.
89. From page 231 of Kenneth Gray's deposition before the SEC.
90. From page 229 of Kenneth Gray's SEC deposition.
91. From page 140 of Robert Keith Gray's SEC deposition.
92. Page 264 of Alejandro Orfila's deposition before the SEC.
93. From page 164 of James C. Jennings's SEC deposition.
94. Interview with Alejandro Orfila.
95. Interview with Neil Livingstone.
96. From pages 276–277 of Neil C. Livingstone's SEC deposition.
97. Lois Romano, "Orfila Departure at Gray Followed Internal Inquiry," *Washington Post*, March 9, 1985, p.1.
98. Interview with Marta Williams Diaz.

CHAPTER 14

1. In a 1986 interview with the late Ambassador to the disarmament talks in Geneva, Louis Fields said that when Barbara Bush was out promoting her book about the family dog (J. Fred, not Millie), he made arrangements for George Bush and Jennifer Fitzgerald to use a guest house in Geneva while they visited.

"It became clear to me that the Vice President and Ms. Fitzgerald were romantically involved and this was not a business visit . . . It made me very uncomfortable . . . after I left the government I realized how serious all this was. . . . I am not a prude . . . but I know Barbara [Bush] and I like her; it was just so heavy-handed." Fields said the couple was "staying in adjoining bedrooms and there was no household staff for the visit. That's why I had to help make certain arrangements for the laundry, that kind of thing."

Jay Gourley, Editor of *Justice Department Alert*, and William Joyce, formerly an attorney at Vance, Joyce and Carbaugh, also heard Fields's account.

The Bush-Fitzgerald relationship has been written about before.

Richard Ryan wrote in the October 14–20, 1988 *L.A. Weekly*:

"In 1985, the source relates, a member of George Bush's office staff, distraught over what the staffer said was Bush's long-running affair with his appointments secretary, Jennifer Fitzgerald, visited the source—an extremely close friend for years—to complain about the effect the liaison was having on the vice president's circle of aides and associates . . .

The staffer said that she and other office workers knew about the affair not only from the behavior of Bush and Fitzgerald at the office, but because Fitzgerald had referred openly, even boastfully on occasion, to it . . .

This distressed woman was not the only Bush staff member ever to have been alienated by Fitzgerald. In 1982, *The New York Times* reported, two aides resigned in the midst of a turf battle with Fitzgerald. Given her sway over her boss, it's not surprising that when Craig Fuller took over as Bush's chief of staff in 1985 one of his first acts was to exile the imperial secretary to Capitol Hill, where she remained as Bush's aide on legislative affairs . . .

Throughout those years (when Bush was seeing Fitzgerald), other sources have said, Bush's marriage was frequently on the rocks . . ."

More recently Fitzgerald has held the number two position in the State Department's Protocol Office. She became embroiled in a controversy with U.S. Customs when she and others apparently returned with purchases from a Latin American trip that were not declared.

2. Murphy and his wife separated and divorced after he started working for Gray and Company.
3. Interviews with several former employees of Murphy at Gray and Company, former White House and Reagan administration officials, and William Corson.
4. In the 1988 campaign between Bush and Dukakis, the Bush mistress story did, in fact, cause concern in the Bush camp. During the campaign the rumor was floated that Dukakis had mental health problems. At a live CNN press conference, a reporter questioned Dukakis about it. Whether or not it was true, a national audience now knew about it.

In turn the Bush mistress story was floated. "Well the Bush [mistress] story, I wish someone could trace it. Remember, the rumor circulated on the stock market with the market dropping? *The Post* was about to publish a story about his personal life and the market dropped. That creates news. That allows others to speculate on [the story]. I truly believe that it was the other campaign that placed that story, as they believe we placed the mental health thing," Sheila Tate remembered.

5. David Hoffman, "A Politician Who Puts Personal Ties First," *Washington Post*, Friday, August 12, 1988, p.A10.
6. Interview with Neil Livingstone.
7. Interview with Don Nielson.
8. Interview with Adonis Hoffman.
9. Interview with Barry Schochet.
10. Interview with George Worden.
11. CNN documentary, "Pipeline to Power," 1985.
12. The article said that he had been sent to Central America by Don Gregg, then Bush's national security adviser.
13. Hoffman, *Washington Post*.
14. Kevin Buckley, *Panama, The Whole Story* (New York: Simon & Schuster, 1991), see Chapter 5, "Admiral Murphy Pays a Call."
15. Interview with Sarkis Soghanalian.
16. Written interview with Robert Gray.
17. Gray's report "To Our Shareholders," filed with the SEC.
18. Ann Cooper, "Image Builders," *The National Journal*, September 14, 1985, pp.2057–2058.
19. The SEC report went on to say:

We are proud to count among our professional staff men and women who have held such positions as chief of staff to Vice President George Bush, postmaster general of the United States, assistant secretary of Commerce, chief aide to Speaker of the House Thomas P. O'Neill, Jr., director of a presidential campaign and president of National Public Radio, deputy Washington bureau chief of *Newsweek*, press secretaries to senators and governors and 29 who were prominent staff professionals in Congress or with the Reagan and previous Administrations. In addition, we number among our Board members and senior consultants two former ambassadors, a former senator, three former generals, a former secretary of the Treasury, a presidential pollster, a deputy assistant to a President, and a counselor to three Presidents.

20. Cooper, *The National Journal*, p.2060.
21. James F. Clarity and Warren Weaver, Jr., "Duel in the P.R. Corral," *New York Times*, January 7, 1985, p.B6.
22. David S. Broder, "Deaver: A New Brazenness," *Washington Post*, April 30, 1986.
23. Stuart Auerbach, "Foreigners Hiring Reagan's Ex-Aides," *Washington Post*, February 16, 1986, p.A1, A14.
24. Evan Thomas, "Peddling Influence," *Time*, March 3, 1986, p.26.

25. Interview with Carter Clews.

The General Accounting Office and congressional committees began investigating whether Deaver broke Government Ethic laws that prohibit high-level government officials from contacting their former colleagues for one year. Eventually a special prosecutor was appointed and Deaver was convicted of perjury.

26. Robert K. Gray, "In Defense of Lobbyists," *New York Times*, April 24, 1986, p.23A.
27. Gray and Company's 1986 SEC filing. Gray's editorial opinion was offset and included as one of the pages.
28. "Gray's unsavory company," *Washington Times*, February 11, 1986, p.7A.
29. Interview with Niels Holchs.
30. Peter Carlson, "The Image Makers," *The Washington Post Magazine*, February 11, 1990.
31. Thomas, *Time*, p.28.
32. Livingstone said, "I had some relationship with the Knights of Malta during this period of time and Paul Dietrich, who was the Secretary to the Knights of Malta was introduced to me through Gray and Paul started turning business my way. That's how I got John Denver and all these people. I knew a whole bunch of the Knights of Malta because they were all with the intelligence community from one place or another. [William] Casey was a Knight of Malta. [William] Colby was a Knight of Malta. I can't even remember now, but they were very active in the early Reagan administration. Ambassador [William] Wilson [Reagan's ambassador to the Vatican] was a Knight of Malta and Wilson was conducting some weird diplomacy both in Angola and Libya. A lot of that [business] went through me. Wilson would call and I would go check with mission control and say, 'What is this all about?' We did an overture from the Angolan government for undercuts of them at one point which I have always been a supporter [of UNITA] so I didn't agree with that, so I went to mission control and I backed off of it."
33. Interview with John Lawler.
34. Interview with Charles Black.
35. "U.S. Publicity Concern Ends Its Angola Links," *New York Times*, March 19, 1986, p.8A.
36. Mark Frankel, "Bob Gray and the Finger of God," *Regardie's*, July 1986.
37. For an often humorous account of the Gray and Company-sponsored events in Morocco, see Mark Frankel's article in *Regardie's*.
38. Claudia Wright, "Reagan's new sweetheart," *New Statesman*, January 1, 1981.
39. Jeff Gerth, "Former Intelligence Aides Profiting From Old Ties," *New York Times*, December 6, 1981, p.1.

Wright, *New Statesman*

40. Walters, a linguist and a former Army lieutenant general, had been a translator for Eisenhower.
41. George Bush's friend, Jennifer Fitzgerald, ended up working for Joseph Reed, as his top deputy in the State Department Protocol Office.
42. "Notes To Consolidated Financial Statements (Unaudited), Gray and Company Public Communications International, Inc., Note B—Other Matters.
43. One Gray and Company executive believes that the real reason Morocco dropped Gray and Company was purely economic. He believes that when efforts were made to start an import-export business, the Gray and Company officials involved did not arrange payment with the right people at the Embassy.
44. Interview with John Sears.
45. Interview with Betsey Weltner.
46. Interview with Mark Moran.
47. Gray and Company's February 1986 SEC filing. In a written interview for this book, Gray outlined his reasons for selling Gray and Company. [insert 765-A]
48. Margaret B. Carlson, "Rescue Mission," *Regardie's*, December 1985.
49. Philip H. Dougherty, "Hill & Knowlton to Buy Gray, the Lobbyist," *New York Times*, June 4, 1986, p.D1.

"Robert Gray sells company to JWT," *Chicago Tribune*, June 4, 1986, Sec.3, p.6.

50. Nell Henderson, "JWT to Buy Gray for $21 Million," *Washington Post*, June 4, 1986, p.G1.
51. *Ibid.*

52. Nell Henderson, "Gray & Co. to Increase Its Reserve for Bad Debts," *Washington Post*, September 27, 1986.

53. Gray and Company's February 1986 SEC filing.

54. According to the Escrow Agreement, the shares were held by the Escrow agent as follows:

$1,000,000 for satisfaction of claims regarding Spain

$1,641,000 for satisfaction of claims for Morocco

$600,000 for employee bonuses that Gray had promised

$1,319,000 for "general liabilities"

55. Carlson, *Regardie's*.

From a written interview with Robert Gray, Gray offered different reasons for the sale to H & K: "From its first day, my goal was to make Gray and Company the largest public relations company in the world. It would have been better to concentrate on making it the most profitable firm in the world but I was very competitive with Hill and Knowlton and determined to topple it from the number-one spot.

Gray and Company was the first—and I believe still the only—public relations/public affairs firm to go public. Once we were listed on the exchange, selling became a constant option.

One day accounting informed me our payroll had passed the $50,000-a-day mark and I decided it was time to sell. We were doing well and the payroll was not a burden, but it was a burden thinking how those dollars translated into college tuitions, home payments, etc. I became very aware of the number of professionals who with their families were depending on me for their futures. While many of them could match or top my qualifications, and certainly collectively they could have done so, the Company bore my name. It could have survived very well without me but the perception was otherwise.

There also was the desire to have the reach of a Hill and Knowlton without wait. In its five years, Gray and Company had grown to nearly one-third the size of sixty-year-old H&K. Eventually it, too, could have had offices around the globe and all across the States. Merging with Hill and Knowlton gave us that delivery system without wait while providing expanded professional opportunities for our people under an evergreen cover. H&K offered a larger canvas to paint on, continuous opportunities for employees, more resources, and obvious 'fit.' "

CHAPTER 15

1. Margaret B. Carlson, "Rescue Mission," *Regardie's*, December, 1985, p.65.

2. *Ibid.*

3. Interview with Sheila Tate.

4. Interview with George Worden.

5. Nell Henderson, "JWT to Buy Gray For $21 Million," *Washington Post*, June 4, 1986.

6. *Ibid.*

7. Interview with George Worden.

8. Eileen Prescott, "How Don Johnston Lost JWT," *New York Times*, August 9, 1987, p.B10.

9. Steve Lohr, "Tiny WPP's Dramatic Coup," *New York Times*, July 9, 1987, p.D2.

10. *Ibid.*

11. Steve Lohr, "JWT's Acquisitive Buyer," *New York Times*, June 30, 1987.

12. *Ibid*, p.148.

13. Valerie Free, "Beyond Advertising—Part Two: Martin Sorrell's WPP: A New Global Force," *Marketing Communications*, September 9, 1988, pp.25–40.

14. "WPP Group Begins Revival of Byoir Agency," *The Wall Street Journal*, July 19, 1988.

15. Richard I. Kirkland, Jr., "Confessions of an Advertising Man," *Fortune*, June 5, 1989.

16. "Impolitic Takeover," *The Wall Street Journal*, May 19, 1989.

17. Bill Timmons, like Gray an associate of Tongsun Park, had a relationship with Global, which handled foreign clients so Timmons & Company could tell their American corporate clients that they do not handle any foreign firms. See earlier chapter.

18. "Addenda," *New York Times*, January 27, 1989.

19. Interview with Tom Korologus.

20. Interview with Paul Laxalt.

21. *Washingtonian* magazine's annual "Houses of the Stars," article in 1990.

22. Terri Shaw, "Fanciful Homes for Pampered Pets," *Washington Post*, October 20, 1988, p.22.

23. "Group to Explain Alien Law," *New York Times*, April 9, 1987, p.A18.

24. Interview with Barry Schochet.

25. Robert Keith Gray, "A presidential field to take pride in," *U.S. News & World Report*, February 22, 1988.

26. *The Washington Post Magazine*, February 28, 1988.

27. Aaron Epstein, "Meese seeks positive PR on drug war," *Atlanta Journal*, May 14, 1988.

28. *Ibid.*

29. Eisenhower and others had visited Hastings as presidential candidates, but not after they had won the election.

30. Kiiker, "Gray proud to put spotlight on city."

31. Joel Lau, "Gray's friends answer his call," *Hastings Tribune*, September 7, 1988, p.11A.

32. *Ibid.*

33. Julie Clopton Kiiker, "Reagan at HC, 10,000 cheer speech," *Hastings Tribune*, September 7, 1988, pp.1, 3.

34. Dianna Johnson, "Gray's challenge a dream come true," *Hastings Tribune*, September 7, 1988, p.1.

35. *Ibid.*

36. *Ibid.*

37. *The Hastings Tribune*, Presidential souvenir edition, September 7, 1988, p.6A.

38. Hastings College was founded in 1882, not long after the town. It is a Presbyterian-affiliated liberal arts college, one of thirteen liberal arts colleges in Nebraska. It has about one thousand students, up from 800 just a few years ago. The majority of the students are from Nebraska with the rest mainly from Colorado. It is overwhelmingly white.

39. Kathy Stokebrand, "Gray gives college new building," *Hastings Tribune*, December 21, 1983, p.1.

40. Interview with Sharon Brooks.

41. Denise Anderson, "Actress has personal interest," *Hastings Tribune*, September 7, 1988, p.11A.

42. Tami Humphreys, "Gray Center fulfills a dream," *Hastings Tribune*, May 19, 1986, p.1 and "Ground Broken for Gray Center," *Hastings College Today*, Summer, 1986.

Gray was two years old when the Westinghouse station opened in Hastings.

43. Tami Humphreys, "Wick sees challenge in 'war of ideas,' " *Hastings Tribune*, May 19, 1986, p.1.

44. "President coming to Hastings," *Hastings Tribune*, May 12, 1988, p.1.

45. Julie Clopton Kiiker, "Gray proud to put spotlight on city," *Hastings Tribune*, September 5, 1988, p.1.

46. Interview with Carl Curtis.

47. Interview with Mark Moran.

CHAPTER 16

1. Kim Eisler, "Gray Eminence," *Washingtonian*, January, 1992, p.62.

2. Some estimates of the taxpayer liability for the massive savings and loans failure run to $500 billion.

3. Gwen Ifill, "HUD Was 'Byzantine,' " *Washington Post*, Thursday, May 24, 1990, p.A10.

4. Gwen Ifill, "HUD Prober's Rights Group Received Free Office Space," *Washington Post*, April 18, 1990.

5. Senators John Glenn (D-OH), Dennis DeConcini (D-AZ), John McCain (R-AZ), Donald Riegle (D-MI) and Alan Cranston (D-CA). Of the five, only Cranston, who was ill with prostate cancer and planning to retire, was severely rebuked by the Senate.

6. Interview with Robert Thompson.

7. Tom Kenworthy, "S&L Buyer Defends '88 Transactions," *Washington Post*, 1990.

Sharon LaFraniere, "FBI Probes Sale of S&Ls to James Fail," *Washington Post*, August 3, 1990.

Jerry Knight, "D.C. Lobbyist Defends Role in S&L Deal," *Washington Post*, 31 July 1990.

8. Interview with James Gall.

9. Jerry Knight, "S&L Assets: Going, Going . . . ," *Washington Post*, May 13, 1990, p.H1.

10. Rick Eyerdam, "Gall: RTC's disarray killed auction," *South Florida Business Journal*, September 24, 1990.

11. Robert Sherefkin, "RTC Fire Sale Goes Up in Smoke," *Legal Times*, December 17, 1990, p.18.

12. Eyerdam, *South Florida Business Journal*.

13. *Ibid.*

14. *Ibid.*

15. Interview with Marty Gold.

16. Written interview with Robert Gray.

17. Interview with former Senator Paul Laxalt.

18. There are various criteria that determine who gets attention on Capitol Hill besides friendship. Whether someone is a constituent—better yet worked in the campaign—better yet contributed to the campaign. Gold said that when he worked on Capitol Hill, "If I knew that somebody was a significant contributor and thus important to the member . . . I would have done what I could to ensure that that person got due process; made sure he was listened to; made sure he was heard . . . I think that's appropriate . . . I think it is clear there are only so many hours in a day. You probably have more on your plate than you can possibly deal with . . . To say that you're not going to pay any attention to these people by comparison to everybody else, that you're going to walk with complete blinders on, is completely unrealistic."

19. Carlson, *Regardie's*.

20. Gary Lee, "Food Spices New Menu at P.R. Firms," *Washington Post*, 1991.

21. Chuck DeConconi, *Washington Post*, May 31, 1991.

22. Richard Behar, "The Thriving Cult of Greed and Power," *Time*, May 6, 1991.

23. *Ibid.*

24. Rudy Maxa, "Rudy Maxa's Diary," *Washingtonian*, June 1991, p.15.

25. Op.Cit. Matlack (5/18/91)

26. Besides Gray's ties to the Catholic Church going back to his Eisenhower years and including client referrals from the Knights of Malta and being asked to speak at the Vatican, H&K had handled Pope John Paul II's visit to the U.S. in 1987. The Chicago office had handled the PR in Chicago when the archdiocese had to close several schools.

27. Tamar Lewin, "Abortion Divides Firm Hired to Help Fight It," *New York Times*, April, 1990.

William Gifford and Anne Kornhauser, "Hill and Knowlton, In the Abortion Storm," *Legal Times*, April 16, 1990, p.1.

28. Goodell, *The New York Times Magazine*.

29. Stevenson, *Manhattan Inc.*

30. *Ibid.*

31. Eisler, *Washingtonian*.

32. Peter M. Stevenson, "Hill and Knowlton's BIG PR Problem," *Manhattan, Inc.*, July, 1990, p.62.

33. Lewin, *New York Times*.

34. Stevenson, *Manhattan, Inc.*

35. Lewin, *New York Times*.

36. Gifford et al., *Legal Times*.

37. Jeffrey Goodell, "What Hill & Knowlton Can Do for You," *New York Times Magazine*, September 9, 1990, p.44.

38. Stevenson, *Manhattan, Inc.*

39. Peter Steinfels, "Knights Aiding Anti-Abortion Effort," *New York Times*, 1990.

40. Dan Balz, "Bishops Retain PR firm to Assist Abortion Fight," *Washington Post*, April 6, 1990, p.A10.

41. Interview with Richard Allen.

42. Robert Keith Gray, "In Defense of Reagan," *Newsweek*, June 4, 1990.

43. Nan Lewis, Santa Monica, California and Steven R. Sachoff, Chagrin Falls, Ohio, *Newsweek*, letters to the editor, June, 1990.

44. Interview with Sheila Tate.

Eventually, former Carter press secretary Jody Powell quit his WPP-owned PR firm and he and Sheila Tate started their own company. "There is something wonderful about being part of a self-contained group where you are in control of your own destiny. We're certainly motivated by the bottom line, too, but we make a lot of concessions to a lot of valued clients. We make business decisions differently than we would if we were part of some huge conglomerate," Tate said.

45. Kim Eisler, "Gray Eminence," *Washingtonian*, January, 1992, p.115.

CHAPTER 17

1. Mary McGrory, "Capitol Hill & Knowlton," *Washington Post*, January 12, 1992, C1.
2. Brian Ross and Ira Silverman, "Sunday Today," February 23, 1991.
3. Gray, *Eighteen Acres*.
4. Interview with Robert Gray.
5. Mark Potts and Robert J. McCarthy, "BCCI Is Indicted on Fraud Charges," *Washington Post*, July 30, 1991.

The American Banker estimates that Clifford and Altman may have made as much as $33 million in profits by buying and selling First American stock.

6. Murray Waas, "Clifford's Partner Warned BCCI," *The Village Voice*, July 31, 1991.
7. Interview with Larry Brady.
8. Written interview with Robert Gray.
9. Judy Sarasohn, "Suit Accuses Hill and Knowlton of Flacking Too Well for BCCI," *Legal Times*, January 6, 1992.
10. Interview with Don Deaton.
11. Interview with Charles Pucie.
12. Paul Starobin, "BCCI's Washington Web," *The National Journal*, September 7, 1991.

Starobin also reports that Frank Mankiewicz contributed a thousand dollars to Senator Kerry's reelection campaign. It was the only direct political contribution Mankiewicz made that year to any federal candidate.

13. Written interview with Robert Gray.
14. Starobin, *The National Journal*.
15. Jim McGee, "Fed Rejects Foreign Bank's Slow Stock Sell-off Plan," *Washington Post*, June 10, 1991.
16. Written interview with Robert Gray.
17. Saundra Torry, "Public Relations Seen as Another Weapon in the Legal Arsenal," *Washington Post*, June 24, 1991, p.5.
18. Guy Guliotta and Michael Isikoff, "U.S. Let BCCI Probe Languish, Hill Told," *Washington Post*, August 2, 1991.
19. Starobin, *The National Journal*.
20. H&K FARA filings on BCCI at the Justice Department.
21. Mark Potts, "Witness: First American Seen as Part of BCCI," *Washington Post*, October 23, 1991.
22. Sharon Walsh, "Ex-Head of BCCI's D.C. Office Arrested," *Washington Post*, January 15, 1992. Ahmad was arrested as a material witness and was not charged with any crime.
23. Sarasohn, *Legal Times*.
24. *Bulldog Reporter*, Volume 3, Issue 4, February 19, 1992.
25. "Doers Profile," *The Washington Times*, p.E2.
26. Marcy Gordon, "Powerful Hill and Knowlton Has Finger in Every Washington Pie," The Associated Press, January 27, 1992.
27. Stevenson.
28. Interview with Don Deaton.
29. Gary Lee, "Kuwait's Campaign on the PR Front," *Washington Post*, November 29, 1990, p.1.
30. Tom Post, "With Friends Like These," *Newsweek*, May 6, 1991, p.42.
31. Lee, *Washington Post*, March 17, 1991.
32. On January 2, President Bush in a television interview pointed to an Amnesty International eighty-eight page special report on human rights abuses in occupied Kuwait. The White House then passed out reprints and mentioned it in letters to campus newspapers. It was a good example of how the administration distributed information to support its PR war, while ignoring other relevant facts and information. At first Amnesty International objected to the way the President was using their information. Later, it backed away from the incubator story entirely.
33. Arthur E. Rowse, "Flacking for the Emir," *The Progressive*, May 1991.

34. Maria Koklanaris, "Five Hill and Knowlton Alumni Team Up on PR, Policy Analysis," *Washington Post*, April, 1991.

35. Koklanaris, *Washington Post*.

36. Carol Matlack, "Dead in the Water?," *National Journal*, May 18, 1991, p.1158.

37. Carol Matlack, "Opting Out At Hill and Knowlton," *The National Journal*, April 4, 1991.

In addition to the Capitoline defections, Henry Hubbard, a former deputy bureau chief at *Newsweek*, and others left for Fleishman Hillard, a competing PR firm. Harold Furman II, Richard Spees, and Edwin C. Graves left to either join law firms or set up their own operation. Elaine Crispen, Nancy Reagan's former press secretary who joined H&K at the end of Reagan's term, started her own firm. Ira P. Kaminow, Michael A. Samuels, and Andrew G. Durrant did the same. They had all been top H&K executives.

38. Peter H. Stone, "Executives Flee Pressures at Hill and Knowlton," *Legal Times*, April 15, 1991, p.5.

39. Matlack, *National Journal*.

40. John B. Hinge, "Hill & Knowlton Names Chairman, Executive Panel," *Wall Street Journal*, June, 1991.

41. *Ibid.*

42. Joanne Lipman, "Hill & Knowlton Drops Dilenschneider," *Wall Street Journal*, September 27, 1991.

43. Eisler, *Washingtonian*.

44. Lipman, *Wall Street Journal*.

45. Eisler, *Washingtonian*.

46. "Playing Good Cop, Bad Cop," *Newsweek*, October 15, 1990, p.38.

47. Steven Waldman, "The Real Price of Buying Influence," *Newsweek*, January 13, 1992, p.46.

48. Art Levine, "Publicists of the Damned," *Spy*, February 1992.

49. Alan Elsner, "Row Over Kuwaiti Babies Flares Again," *Reuters*, February 6, 1992.

50. Judy Sarasohn and Greg Rushford, "Hill and Knowlton Downplays Craig Fuller's Sudden Departure," *Legal Times*, January 20, 1992.

51. Of the long time employees, Mankiewicz and Hymel continue to stay on. Many of their former colleagues say that they stay because they both need the money and they really have nowhere else to go. They retain the titles of Vice Chairman of H&K Worldwide. "But it's a paper organization . . . It has this phony facade on it [H&K Worldwide. It's like being Vice Chairman] of nothing. You have no responsibilities whatever . . . None. Just a fancy title," Worden explained.

52. Randall Rothenberg, "P.R. Firms Head for Capitol Hill," *Wall Street Journal*, January 4, 1991.

INDEX

421